PRESIDENT CASTELLO BRANCO

PRESIDENT CASTELLO BRANCO

Brazilian Reformer

By

JOHN W. F. DULLES

Texas A&M University Press
COLLEGE STATION

Library of Congress Cataloging in Publication Data

Dulles, John W. F.
President Castello Branco, Brazilian reformer.

Bibliography: p.
Includes index.
1. Castello Branco, Humberto de Alencar.
2. Brazil—Presidents—Biography. 3. Brazil—History
—1954— I. Title.
F2538.22.C37D85 981'.062'0924 [B] 79-5281
ISBN 0-89096-092-5

Manufactured in the United States of America
FIRST EDITION

Contents

Illustrations

I

Defining Directions and Imposing Punishments

(April–June, 1964)

Let us move ahead with assurance that the remedy for evil deeds by the extreme Left will not be the birth of a reactionary Right, but of the reforms that have become necessary.

1. "Virtually Unknown to the General Public"

ON April 6, 1964, the *New York Times* published an article calling attention to General Humberto de Alencar Castello Branco, chief of staff of the Brazilian army. Noting that he was being considered for the Brazilian presidency, the *Times* pointed out that he had "remained virtually unknown to the general public." It described him as a "short, stocky, bull-necked general" who had spent forty-five years in the army without following the examples of colleagues attracted to the limelight and public posts. Readers learned that if this "general's general" became president he would probably "show unspectacular seriousness" and regard his new new position "as just another assignment to be carried out on a no-nonsense basis."

Castello Branco could not have been expected to win a large vote in an ordinary presidential election, one of those popularity contests in which millions of citizens made the selection from among candidates who covered the country promising the impossible and often displaying xenophobic nationalism. But there was nothing ordinary about the manner in which a new president was chosen in April, 1964, after the army, supported by the worried middle and upper classes, overthrew João Goulart when his administration appeared to have become chaotic and strongly influenced by well-known Communist labor leaders.

Officially the selection of the new president was made in Brasília on April 11 by a Congress that on the previous day was purged of forty members considered subversive by the victors of the military coup. The decision of Congress, however, was merely the ratification of an informal, unplanned electoral process that developed in Rio de Janeiro. Military officers and civilian leaders who had helped bring about the fall of Goulart's regime gathered during several days at meetings to recommend a choice to complete the twenty-two months that remained of the presidential term. Although the meetings were scattered, taking place in residences, offices, barracks, ministries, military clubs, and the palace of the governor of Guanabara state, those who attended them might be said to have formed an electoral college committed to finding the man most qualified to deal with the difficult situation.

Leaders of business associations and women's groups, state governors (some coming from afar), and military officers reflected on the corruption, subversion, inflation, and maladministration that had brought on the country's economic and political crises, and they agreed on the need for a military figure able to instill discipline. Ademar de Barros, the populist governor of São Paulo, was forced to concede that the prevailing opinion favored a military officer "because Goulart left such a devil of a mess."[1]

Like Ademar de Barros and Carlos Lacerda, the governor of Guanabara, many who helped to choose the new president had not met General Castello Branco. But from his associates they learned some things about him that seemed attractive to them at the time. The general had earned a solid reputation in the army for his thoroughness, even severity, in training officers. Prominent civilians reported that at the Escola Superior de Guerra (Brazil's National War College) Castello Branco had been an effective debater with a broad interest in national problems. And all of his acquaintances, military and civilian, vouched for his hatred of dictatorship and his lifelong dedication to legality and democracy. The most ambitious politicians were convinced that he had the will and ability to preside impartially over what they expected to be the main event of his fairly short term: the popular presidential election of 1965.

It also appeared that Castello Branco would be an excellent choice to lead the campaign, launched by Goulart's enemies, against corruption and subversion. Stories of how the general had maintained his personal probity by paying for minor gifts that he considered improper might seem a bit ludicrous to some, but at least they were reassuring. As for

[1] Ademar de Barros, interview, São Paulo, December 1, 1965.

subversion, who could forget the figure of the bespectacled Castello Branco at the lecterns of the advanced military schools, solemnly urging a strong stand against the growing influence of Communism in Brazil? His concern had been repeated in his confidential circular of March 20, 1964, addressed to his subordinates—a circular that had convinced many a legalist in the army that the only patriotic step was to oppose the Goulart administration.

On April 7, 1964, *Jornal do Brasil* assured the public that Castello Branco had another much sought attribute: he would "restore" authority to the office of president. This was a safe assumption in the case of a general reputed to be tough. Colonel Vernon Walters, U.S. military attaché in Rio, reported to Washington on April 11 that Castello Branco, "when provoked, . . . can administer a tongue-lashing not readily forgotten by the recipient."[2]

But this trait was hardly responsible for the authority with which he had clothed his many army posts. The key can be found in the admiration expressed by the Military Academy cadets for Major Castello Branco in 1942. They were amazed at his knowledge, unexpected in a major, of every detail that should have been in the minds of sergeants as well as commissioned officers. He did his homework, and if he was demanding of others, he was at least as demanding of himself. "Authority," Castello Branco sometimes remarked, "cannot be imposed; it is earned by our example of fulfilling our duty."[3]

This is not to say that he had ever disregarded the outward manifestations, such as etiquette, dress, and posture. He had been dismayed at the informality with which President Goulart had received him in Laranjeiras Palace in Rio after calling him there in April, 1963. Goulart, without jacket or necktie, had spoken with the general while sitting on an unmade bed, explaining that hangers-on in the palace made the bedroom the only place for a confidential talk.

By April 12, 1964, Goulart was in exile in Uruguay, and Castello Branco had been chosen, by an overwhelming congressional vote, to replace him in the presidency on April 15. The sixty-six–year-old

[2] Telegram, signed Gordon, April 11, 1964, copy in Lyndon Baines Johnson Library, Austin, Texas (hereafter cited as LBJ Library).

[3] Theódulo de Albuquerque, speech in Congress (typewritten manuscript, n.d., probably 1967), p. 3.

president-elect took a few moments off from his pressing task of forming a cabinet in order to make an unsolicited declaration of his possessions so that it could be compared with another statement which he promised to make at the end of his term. He listed an apartment in Rio, some shares of stock, an automobile, and a grave site in Rio next to that of his wife, who had died in 1963.

Jornal do Brasil on April 12 tried to give a new dimension to the conventional picture of the disciplinary general by supplying an account of his habits, which it described as "simple." Readers learned that he did not smoke or drink hard liquor and that he spoke no more than necessary. He was reported to act "only after much thought."

The article revealed that the president-elect enjoyed reading history and the fiction of the great Brazilian writers. It mentioned his fondness for classical music and his devotion to his native state of Ceará, in the far north. He was said to have a good collection of books about the Brazilian north and to find it hard to resist the fruits, melons, and dried meat that came from Ceará. In conclusion, *Jornal do Brasil* pointed out that the widower was a good family man. Quoting his daughter, Antonietta Diniz, it spoke of his affection for his seven grandchildren: the four children of Antonietta and the three children of his son, Paulo (who was taking an advanced naval training course in the United States).

Much still remained to be learned about Castello Branco, not only because he had so suddenly come on the national scene but also because, as one of his associates wrote later, he was "not a person with whom it was easy to become familiar." This observer explains that Castello was "modest, affable, and very polite," kind to his friends and helpers, "but he maintained the distance that was indispensable for shielding authority."[4] Another associate recalls that the sentimental general was filled with tenderness but was like a night flower, appearing closed, with a severe look, much of the time.[5] Although he was certainly not famous for laughing or for following the example of Franklin D. Roosevelt and Getúlio Vargas in frequently flashing an engaging smile in public, he had a keen sense of humor, often described as ironic. It

[4] Osvaldo Trigueiro, "Humberto Castelo Branco" (typewritten manuscript), p. 17.
[5] Mem de Sá, interview, Rio de Janeiro, October 31, 1975.

was best appreciated by those who were intelligent and knew him well, for he used it with a serious tone, making no play for comic effect.[6]

More important characteristics of Castello, not generally appreciated in April, 1964, would give a clear tone to his presidential administration. He was a reformer. As a young army captain in 1935, he had completely revamped procedures at the regiment in Curitiba in the process of revitalizing the unit. He always seemed to be revising educational methods and programs at the Army Staff and Command School, although only after much consultation and study. In his last army post, that of chief of staff, he and his subordinates were drawing up a plan for reorganizing the entire Brazilian army when they were interrupted by the political events of March, 1964. His habit of finding things that he felt should be changed, combined with his distaste for inactivity, made it more likely than most people realized that his presidential regime would inundate Brazil with reforms and be of little comfort to conservatives fond of laissez-faire.

Although many army officers were familiar with Castello's tendency to revise army procedures, not many of them appreciated fully his zeal for reforms. And fewer still had had the opportunity to learn of his eagerness to witness reforms devised to improve the lot of the underprivileged. Only close friends knew that on past occasions, when he had felt that it might be necessary to use troops to preserve order, he had contemplated with reluctance the protection of the privileges of the rich—the privileges of "individualistic capitalism" that he associated with sugar plant ownership in the Brazilian northeast.[7]

As far back as 1945, when Castello Branco wrote from Italy to his wife about the participation of Brazilian troops in the postwar occupation, he had expressed his repugnance of having to preserve properties for rich and prominent Italians. Writing again from Italy a few days later, Castello had told his wife: "It is impossible that a hecatomb such as we have seen will not bring a great revolution of ideas, from which will spring a more humane, more Christian, social evolution, less hard on the poor and limiting as much as possible the exploitation of man

[6] Raimundo Padilha, letter to Luís Viana Filho, Niterói, December 11, 1971, p. 2.
[7] Vernon Walters, interview, Arlington, Virginia, July 15, 1976.

by man."[8] Even as he attacked Communism in the early 1960's, he argued that the anti-Communist movement should not "lose itself in the interests of capitalism" when those interests were disassociated from "the interests of the national community and the well-being of the people."[9]

Besides being dedicated to reforms, the president-elect had, to a greater extent than was realized, the ability and experience necessary to deal with the political infighting that reform proposals would generate. He would surprise those congressmen who felt that generals, accustomed to having their orders blindly obeyed, were likely to be rather poor judges of men and at a disadvantage when required to engage in dialogue with politicians.

The ability of Castello to judge men had been noted by the prominent engineer Glycon de Paiva, who came to know him when the two were lecturing at the Escola Superior de Guerra in the mid-1950's. The engineer found the general steeped in virtues and principles that he attributed to an upbringing in the home of God-fearing and unprosperous parents: Castello had been hard working, truthful, frank, and a good listener. "He had," Glycon de Paiva adds, "an ability to evaluate people after a few minutes, and to select staff members. He was an unusual man in that."[10]

In one of his letters written from Italy to his wife in 1945, Castello had said: "War is a very difficult and brutal undertaking. For this reason, we see men as they are and not as they want to be. We appear as in X-ray pictures. Men, then, reveal matchless sentiments, including unselfishness and the sacrifice of their lives. But others are truly in less attractive garb: they lower themselves, they become weak, they rush to ruin or become useless. Ah! men. How I know them."[11]

For dealing with men in a civilian setting, Castello had the advantage of several experiences. One occurred in 1947 and 1948, after he agreed, reluctantly, to serve as the president of the Federal District sec-

[8] Humberto de Alencar Castello Branco (hereafter cited as HACB), letters to Argentina Castello Branco, May 23, 26, 27, 1945, File H2, Castello Branco papers in the possession of Paulo V. Castello Branco (hereafter cited as PVCB).

[9] HACB, "O Dever Militar em Face da Luta Ideológica," speech given at the ECEME on December 15, 1961 (typewritten copy).

[10] Glycon de Paiva, interview, Rio de Janeiro, December 9, 1975.

[11] HACB, letter to Argentina, February 16, 1945, File H1 (p. 107), PVCB.

tion of the Associação dos Ex-Combatentes do Brasil, a World War II veterans' group whose board consisted of Communists and non-Communists. Before his term ended he gained considerable ability in handling the debates with people who were essentially civilians or below him in military rank but who, in Associação affairs, never hesitated to tell him, "You are wrong." Later, when he was engaged in a more important experience, the examination of national problems with civilians at the Escola Superior de Guerra, he confessed to having a greater facility thanks to his term as president of the lively veterans' association.

Above all, President Castello Branco's task of dealing with civilians would be helped by an experience that might be said to have taken place throughout his life, starting when he was a fourteen-year-old student at the Colégio Militar de Pôrto Alegre, in the southern state of Rio Grande do Sul. Such had been the boy's interest in following political affairs and quoting the liberal orators of the day that he had invested his few available milreis in a subscription to the *Diário do Congresso*. He had continued to be a constant reader of serious nonfiction, acquiring a culture unusual for an army officer. Some of the culture had been absorbed in Europe while attending the French Ecole Supérieure de Guerre from 1936 to 1938. Thus he never felt at a disadvantage during the discussions he so much enjoyed having with well-educated civilians, such as those he came to know at the Rio home of his intellectual brother-in-law, Hélio Vianna.

Most of the men who constituted Brazil's informal electoral college in April, 1964, were looking for a disciplinarian who respected legality and opposed subversion and corruption. They found more than they were seeking. The new president-elect, an uncommonly well educated general, was far better equipped than they realized to work with members of Congress in order to usher in reforms.

2. The Inauguration (April 15, 1964)

On the morning of April 15, 1964, Humberto Castello Branco left his house in the Ipanema district of Rio to be driven to the military airport of Santos Dumont. He was accompanied by his daughter, Nieta (Antonietta); her husband, Salvador Diniz; and two of their children.

The car stopped for fifteen minutes at the São João Batista cemetery, where Castello, filled with emotion, left red roses at the grave of his wife, Argentina.[1]

At the airport, military contingents and well-wishers greeted the president-elect. Having retired from the army two days earlier, he now bore the rank of marshal of the army. But he preferred to be known as general and had already revealed his desire to see an end to the military regulation that was giving Brazil scores of retired marshals.

Castello made the two-hour flight north in the presidential Viscount with Nieta and her family and with assistants who had been at his side during the previous turbulent months. Among them was General Ernesto Geisel, who was to become chief of the presidential Gabinete Militar (Military Office). Castello traveled also with Luís Viana Filho, the author and congressman from Bahia whom he had come to know only recently after choosing him to head the presidential Gabinete Civil (Civilian Office).

During the flight Castello retired to the presidential cabin in the rear of the plane to revise his inauguration speech, which was designed to provide clues for turning a military coup into a revolution. The recent victors had been in agreement about the need to depose Goulart, but their unexpectedly rapid success left a need for defining a positive program and rallying support for it.

At the time of the military outbreak on March 31, Castello had sent a note to army officers in the south to explain the purposes of the movement. Under one overall heading, "To restore legality," he had written: "The reestablishment of the Federation; Eliminate development of plan for communists to take over power; Defend the military institutions that are beginning to be destroyed; Establish order for the advent of legal reforms."[2] Upon becoming president-elect, Castello had given further attention to the goals, not forgetting the need to attend to the poor in neglected areas, when he had jotted down some inauguration speech ideas for Luís Viana Filho. Viana, asked by Cas-

[1] Antonietta Diniz, interview, Rio de Janeiro, December 13, 1975.

[2] HACB, handwritten note sent to General Adalberto Pereira dos Santos, March 31, 1964, copy in File L2, Castello Branco Collection, Centro de Pesquisa de Documentação de História Contemporânea do Brasil, Instituto de Direito Público e Ciência Política, Fundação Getúlio Vargas, Rio de Janeiro (hereafter cited as CPDOC).

tello to set the ideas "to music" in a brief form, had turned for literary help to erudite Congressman Aliomar Baleeiro.[3]

Castello's original notes, and consequently the speech prepared for him, spoke of his allegiance to the constitution and to the Institutional Act, which had been issued by military leaders on April 9 to foster congressional action on executive proposals and to allow the suspension of political rights of those felt to have made the recent coup necessary. Reviewing his inauguration speech in the airplane, Castello struck out any reference to the Institutional Act.[4]

Among the large group that met the Viscount in Brasília were Lieutenant Colonel Gustavo Morais Rego, who had been helping prepare for the inauguration, and Congressman José Maria Alkmin, the vice-president-elect. Nieta, watching her father review troops after landing, was thrilled. "Now, for the first time, he looks like the president," she thought.[5]

Brasília was in the most festive mood of its four-year official life. By noon, when the Castello Branco party was being driven for a lunch at Alvorada Palace, the presidential residence, crowds were making their way under a warm sun through the spacious Esplanade of the Ministries to the Square of the Three Powers for ceremonies scheduled to commence three hours later.

The Chamber of Deputies, decorated with flowers, was packed with legislators and distinguished visitors by the time Castello and Alkmin took their oaths of office. Castello read his speech, and although he appeared nervous to those who knew him well, he made a good impression that was reflected in the comments in the press the next day. The speech lasted only fourteen minutes and would have taken less time but for twenty-two interruptions of applause. Supporters of former President Juscelino Kubitschek, who hoped to be reelected in 1965, applauded heartily when Castello said that he would turn over his office to his elected successor on January 31, 1966.

Castello promised a government based on law and a government with its eyes on the future. "I do not exaggerate when I say that, in

[3] Aliomar Baleeiro, "Recordações do Presidente H. Castelo Branco" (typewritten), p. 24; Luís Viana Filho, *O Governo Castelo Branco*, p. 67.

[4] Viana Filho, *O Governo Castelo Branco*, p. 67.

[5] Diniz, interview, December 13, 1975.

this journey to the future, we must exert ourselves with the passion of a crusade, for which it is necessary to summon all Brazilians." Touching on foreign affairs, the new president declared that Brazil's allies would be the "democratic and free nations" and that the historic alliances with the free countries of the Americas would be preserved and strengthened. Turning to domestic matters, he stated that raising the moral, educational, material, and political level of the nation would be the central concern of the government, and he added that the state would not impede private initiative or neglect "the imperative of social justice owed to the worker." "Let us move ahead," he said, "with assurance that the remedy for evil deeds by the extreme Left will not be the birth of a reactionary Right, but of the reforms that have become necessary."[6] In conclusion, Castello spoke of the humility he felt. Never, he said, had one single man so much needed the understanding, backing and help of all of his fellow citizens.

More ceremonies followed at nearby Planalto Palace, the presidential office building. There Castello received the chief executive's sash from Chamber of Deputies President Ranieri Mazzilli, who had been interim head of state for two weeks. Then he took his place on the terrace to receive the applause of the crowd in the square and to watch a parade by thirty-five hundred members of the armed forces.

Later, in the third-floor office of the president, Castello signed cabinet appointments. Many of the names had been chosen by Castello in the days following his election, but in a few cases the final decisions had not been reached and the appointees of the Mazzilli interim regime were asked to remain, perhaps for a few days but perhaps indefinitely. War Minister Costa e Silva, who had headed the "Revolutionary Command" following the fall of Goulart, appeared to be in this category, and he asked the new president about his future. Making a historic decision, Castello told him: "You will stay on."

After the cabinet list had been revealed to the press by Luís Viana Filho at 6:30 P.M., the American Embassy cabled Washington to comment on its "strong democratic and pro-Western orientation," its average age (about 60), and its "high level of competence." Congressman Daniel Faraco, the new minister of industry and commerce, was

[6] HACB, *Discursos, 1964*, pp. 12–15.

described as an opponent of the Goulart administration's stringent profit remittance bill and an advocate of free enterprise, who had declared, in words critical of Kubitschek, that "to finance progress through inflation is to try to promote it at the expense of the hunger of the workers and the ruin of the middle class."[7]

With the cabinet appointments signed, Castello shook hands with dignitaries at a formal Planalto Palace reception that lasted until 7:30 P.M. Then he returned to his new residence, Alvorada Palace, to spend a few hours with relatives and close friends. He was tired but appeared happy.[8]

Before retiring to bed at 10:30, Castello asked a palace attendant to buy him some pills for his liver. When he gave the attendant five cruzeiros to pay for them, the attendant tried to return the money, with the explanation that the pills would be paid for by the palace. "Buy the pills with my money," the president said firmly. "They are for my personal use."[9]

3. Lunch with Walters (April 16, 1964)

In the presidency Castello Branco gained a reputation for unexpectedly phoning people. His custom of making early morning calls, which he enjoyed dialing himself, began in Alvorada Palace at 6:00 A.M. on April 16, 1964, when he phoned the Hotel Nacional and asked to speak with Colonel Vernon Walters, the linguistically proficient U.S. military attaché who had come from Rio to Brasília with Ambassador Lincoln Gordon for the inauguration ceremonies. Walters had been a close friend of Castello since the Italian campaign of 1944–1945 and was a man with whom Castello could relax, engaging in light and serious conversation and exchanging jokes. It would be pleasant for the new president to lunch with Walters, who had always been discreet and had never used his friendship to try to pry information from the general.

[7] National Security Files, Country File, Brazil (hereafter cited as NSFB), Vol. IV, cables, 4/64–8/64, LBJ Library.

[8] Diniz, interview, December 13, 1975.

[9] Frederico Mendes de Morais, interview, Rio de Janeiro, December 20, 1975.

And it would allow Castello to speak quickly to a high-ranking American about the democratic principles of the new Brazilian government.

"Walters, were you asleep?" Castello asked.

"No, sir," Walters replied.

Castello, who knew Walters well, told the military attaché that he probably had been asleep and went on to invite him to lunch that day in Alvorada Palace. Walters accepted even though it meant canceling another lunch date.[1]

When Castello arrived for work at Planalto Palace at 9:20 A.M. he surprised reporters and others by instituting a ritual that he decided to observe in the future to add dignity to the presidential office. Unlike his predecessors, he did not enter the building from the downstairs garage. In full sight of the curious, he walked up the Planalto ramp while members of the Presidential Guard stood at attention and while the presidential bugle call was played. At the top of the ramp he was received by General Ernesto Geisel, head of the Gabinete Militar, and by the chief of protocol.[2]

During Castello's first morning in Planalto Palace he held a fifteen-minute session at which, with the help of Luís Viana Filho, he swore in some of his cabinet members: Justice Minister Milton Campos, War Minister Costa e Silva, Education Minister Suplici de Lacerda, Industry and Commerce Minister Daniel Faraco, Agriculture Minister Oscar Thompson, and Transport and Public Works Minister Juarez Távora. The ceremony began at the moment scheduled by Castello, which was embarrassing for Faraco, who arrived late.[3] When Faraco had an opportunity to speak with Castello, the new minister said that he expected to be able to work well with Otávio Gouveia de Bulhões, who had been appointed finance minister while Mazzilli was acting president. But Faraco learned that Castello was still uncertain about the Bulhões appointment. "I am studying the matter and shall not go to sleep tomorrow without settling it," Castello said.[4]

Castello, who had a few words for each of the men being sworn

[1] Vernon Walters, "Humberto de Alencar Castello Branco: The Years of the Presidency" (typewritten), p. 1.

[2] Mendes de Morais, interview, December 20, 1975; *O Estado de S. Paulo*, April 17, 1964.

[3] *O Estado de S. Paulo*, April 17, 1964.

[4] Viana Filho, *O Governo Castelo Branco*, p. 69.

in, told Justice Minister Milton Campos that his task was the restoration of juridical order. So deeply was Milton Campos committed to constitutional liberties that he had hesitated to accept a portfolio in a "revolutionary government," but Castello had insisted, knowing that Campos' inclusion would emphasize the legalistic intentions of the administration.[5]

Castello sought at once to give prestige to the judicial and legislative branches of the government. Getting in touch with Chief Justice Álvaro Moutinho Ribeiro da Costa, the president made arrangements to pay an official visit the next day, April 17, to the Federal Supreme Court, which was being attacked by radical devotees of the March 31 revolution. At the same time, the president surprised leaders of Congress by speaking to them personally on the phone to find out if it would be convenient for them to come to Planalto Palace that afternoon, April 16, to talk with him about legislation. He invited the acting president of the Chamber of Deputies as well as Congressman Paulo Sarasate, his old friend from Ceará, and Congressmen Ernani do Amaral Peixoto and Olavo Bilac Pinto.[6] Amaral Peixoto headed the PSD (Partido Social Democrático, which had recently nominated Kubitschek for president) and was considered by the radical supporters of the March 31 revolution as having been too closely associated with past regimes now held responsible for disorder in Brazil. Bilac Pinto headed the UDN (União Democrática Nacional), which was the most satisfied with the March 31 revolution; as the largest of the "opposition" parties, the UDN had long combatted the alliance that had dominated politics—that between the PSD and Goulart's PTB (Partido Trabalhista Brasileiro).

When Castello left Planalto Palace at 12:20 for his two-hour midday break, the ceremonial was repeated at the ramp and he was driven to Alvorada Palace. The lunch there with Walters, a modest meal served in Castello's upstairs "studio room," was the start of a custom that would bring, as lunch guests of the president, from one to three individuals with whom he usually had business to discuss. It was quickly made clear that Alvorada Palace was no longer a place where innumer-

[5] Carlos Castello Branco, *Os Militares no Poder: 1. Castelo Branco*, p. 21; Luís Gonzaga do Nascimento Silva, interview, Brasília, October 25, 1975; Roberto Marinho, interview, Rio de Janeiro, August 11, 1977.

[6] *O Estado de S. Paulo*, April 17, 1964.

able people connected with the presidency could expect to have meals.[7]

Castello motioned Walters to have a chair and said: "Here I am where I never expected to be, and sitting in a seat I have not sought." Walters quoted Harry Truman: "When you are President, the only future you have is in the memory of the people." After Castello agreed thoughtfully, Walters told him about the sign on Truman's desk: "The Buck Stops Here." To convey the sense of the word "buck," Walters said *abacaxi* (pineapple), a word frequently used in Brazil to denote a messy or difficult situation. Then he handed the president a life-sized wooden pineapple, realistically painted. Castello smiled and asked why Walters was giving it to him. It would, Walters said, symbolize that Castello now had the largest and prickliest pineapple in Brazil. Castello laughed and acknowledged the truth of this observation.[8]

Speaking of his wife, who had been a friend of Walters' mother, Castello said: "She was a beautiful, gracious woman of family and birth. All this together with good humor and wit she brought to our marriage, and all that I could bring as a poor second lieutenant was whatever I could achieve in a material way. Now that I have come to this place where the only thing I can hope for is to save my immortal soul and be remembered as a good President, is it not ironic that she is no longer at my side?"[9]

Walters heard Castello express his determination to serve his country as best he could during an appallingly difficult economic and political situation. Castello also spoke of his intention to maintain constitutional government and democracy in Brazil. He explained that his assumption of the presidency had brought an end to the all-powerful "Revolutionary Command," which had been made up of the three military ministers who had come to office with the fall of Goulart and which had dictated to interim President Mazzilli (picking his cabinet for him).[10]

Castello's reaffirmation of his democratic intentions was made at a time when the press and the reports from the Brazilian Embassy in

[7] Diniz, interview, December 13, 1975.

[8] Walters, "Humberto de Alencar Castello Branco," p. 2.

[9] Ibid., p. 4.

[10] Walters, "Humberto de Alencar Castello Branco," p. 2; cable, American Embassy, Rio de Janeiro, to Washington, April 17, 1964, NSFB, Vol. IV, LBJ Library.

Washington were bringing to the Brazilian administration the concern in American public opinion about the Institutional Act of April 9 and about some of the suspensions of political rights, notably those of economist Celso Furtado, who was widely respected in American university circles. Ambassador Gordon had been dismayed with the Institutional Act and particularly its prologue, which proclaimed the right of a victorious revolution to make its own rules. His first impulse had been to withdraw to Washington as a gesture of disapproval and he had only overcome that impulse because of the prospect that the legalistic Castello would be elected president and would use his arbitrary powers with restraint and guide the nation back to legitimacy within a few months.[11]

4. A Chat with the American Ambassador (April 18, 1964)

Ambassador Lincoln Gordon, no doubt pleased with Castello Branco's words to Walters, was received on Saturday morning, April 18, at Planalto Palace. There he told Castello, whom he had not previously met, that the United States looked on the recent Brazilian revolution as a possible turning point in the affairs of Latin America and the world, as well as Brazil, provided that proper use were made of the opportunity. Expressing United States interest in a strong and progressive Brazil, Gordon referred to the "convergence" of the interests of the two countries on major issues and the desire of the United States that possible divergences on minor issues be approached with good will on both sides.[1]

Castello concurred with the ambassador's ideas. He noted that although the American press reaction to his inauguration speech had been favorable, concern clearly existed in the United States as to possible "revolutionary excesses." Gordon replied that such concern indeed existed, not because of disagreement with the basic purposes of the revolution but because repressive measures could be arbitrary or exces-

[11] Lincoln Gordon, "Recollections of President Castello Branco" (typewritten notes prepared at the request of Luís Viana Filho), p. 16.

[1] Lincoln Gordon, letter published in *Brazil Herald*, November 30, 1977; idem, cable from Rio de Janeiro to Washington, April 20, 1964, NSFB, LBJ Library.

sive, and he said that acts of the São Paulo state police seemed "very extreme." Some judicial or other review procedure, Gordon said, would have a good effect on the opinion of the free world. Gordon received the impression that Castello appreciated the desirability of such a review procedure, but he noted that Castello avoided making any commitment.[2]

The president, mentioning the past interest that Gordon, an economist, had shown in Brazilian economic development, spoke about Brazil's economic and social problems, and he touched on the financial situation when he remarked: "Every time I open a drawer I find unpaid bills."[3] The ambassador stated that Brazil, with a good administration that adopted the proper policies, had excellent medium and long-term prospects, but he emphasized the difficult immediate task of coping with inflation, which he calculated had reached an annual rate of 150 percent in January–February 1964. Gordon suggested that the burdens of austerity be spread as equitably as possible and that their shock be cushioned by a well-planned investment program.[4]

Gordon indicated that the United States was ready to support Brazil's short and long-term efforts, within the framework of the Alliance for Progress and in accordance with the availability of resources. Gordon answered the president's questions about the status of debt rescheduling negotiations and the prospects for additional foodstuffs under Public Law 480, and, at Castello's request, he discussed recent Alliance for Progress coordinating efforts and gave a brief history of Brazilian government planning. Castello said that he placed the highest importance on an effective public investment planning and coordinating mechanism. Adding that the matter was under active study, he advised that he hoped to arrive at a decision by Wednesday, April 22.[5]

To Gordon, the new president appeared to be a man of unusual reserve, whose sense of humor, marked by irony, he especially appreciated.[6] In his cable to Washington, Gordon said: "Castello Branco was alert, attentive, intelligent, and responsive. He made no incautious predictions on future line of action, and I did not seek any. He obviously

[2] Gordon, cable to Washington, April 20, 1964; idem, "Recollections of President Castello Branco," p. 16.

[3] Lincoln Gordon, interview, Washington, D.C., June 11, 1975.

[4] Gordon, cable to Washington, April 20, 1964.

[5] Ibid.

[6] Gordon, "Recollections of President Castello Branco," p. 9.

is still feeling his way on many matters of organization, administration, and policy, but appeared to be doing it thoughtfully and conscientiously."[7]

After leaving Planalto Palace the ambassador called on Justice Minister Milton Campos to express concern about possible extremism in the "revolutionary purges" and its unfavorable repercussions overseas. The minister said that during the "first phase" some excesses had been inevitable but that with the inauguration of Castello Branco, constitutional liberties were being reasserted, including the issuance of habeas corpus writs by the courts. Milton Campos admitted to having had disturbing news about police excesses in São Paulo and to a lesser extent elsewhere and said that these matters were receiving his prompt attention.

Conceding that some aspects of the Institutional Act were undesirable, Milton Campos sought to explain them as a reaction to "the first maneuvers by Kubitschek and the PTB" and as a manifestation of the "intense desire by the revolutionary military leaders" not to repeat a failure in 1954 to use an opportunity "to deal effectively with Communism and corruption."[8]

5. Completing the Cabinet (April 20, 1964)

When Castello Branco invited Roberto Campos to be minister of planning and economic coordination, the economist told the president: "You will dismiss me in forty-eight hours. You won't accept my ideas. An objective of mine will be to fight the inflation."[1]

Roberto Campos, ironic, witty, and intellectually resourceful, appeared to be the man Castello was seeking, not only to fight the inflation but also to contribute ideas about reforms. His files, full of past government plans that he had helped to prepare, included anti-inflation programs that previous administrations had abandoned. He had built up an international reputation as a brilliant economist in the course of a somewhat frustrating career as planner and National Economic Bank

[7] Gordon, cable to Washington, April 20, 1964.

[8] Ibid.

[1] Raimundo Padilha, interview, Niterói, August 3, 1977 (recalling the account of the incident given to him by HACB). For comments about Roberto Campos, see Max Lerner, "Brazil's Paradoxical Regime," *Evening Star*, April 30, 1966.

head under Kubitschek, as foreign debt negotiator during the seven-month administration of Jânio Quadros, and as Goulart's ambassador to Washington.

When President Castello Branco spoke with Otávio Bulhões, who had been serving as finance minister since Goulart's fall, he told the quiet financier he had decided that Planning and Economic Coordination should have the status of a ministry, instead of becoming, as some had suggested, a bureau within the office of the presidency.[2] Castello added that he was considering appointing Roberto Campos to head Planning and Economic Coordination. Although Bulhões and Roberto Campos had not worked together in the past, they were old friends who respected each other, and Bulhões told the president that it would be a pleasure for him to work with Roberto Campos in the new government.[3]

A ministry of planning (without portfolio) was not new to Brazil, but the importance that it assumed for Castello, a great believer in making and adhering to plans, was an innovation. Other significant changes from the past resulted from Castello's decisions to create (1) the Ministry for Coordination of Regional Agencies to supervise organs set up by previous administrations for the development of regional areas, and (2) the National Information Service (SNI), an expansion of the secretaryship of the National Security Council, to analyze intelligence matters and report to the president. With these two new organizations needing congressional approval, the new administration set about eliminating the fears of legislators who thought that the SNI might become concerned with censorship or propaganda for the executive (both of which Castello detested).[4]

To head the future Ministry for Coordination of Regional Agencies, Castello had no difficulty in persuading General Osvaldo Cordeiro de Farias, an artillery officer who had come to know Castello professionally during the Italian campaign in World War II. Cordeiro, a long-time

[2] José Maria Arantes, interview, Rio de Janeiro, November 22, 1974.

[3] Otávio Gouveia de Bulhões, interview, Rio de Janeiro, December 30, 1974. (When an author's name appears next to one of his works, as in the case of Octávio Gouvea de Bulhões in the Sources of Material, it is spelled as it appears in that work and thus may differ from the reformed spelling more frequently used in this book.)

[4] Viana Filho, *O Governo Castelo Branco*, p. 72.

anti-Goulart conspirator, had been in touch with Castello during recent months. He was a politically oriented general whose good relations with many congressmen would be useful to an administration with a cabinet more notable for technical competence than political acumen.

Castello felt that no one was better suited to run the forthcoming SNI than the intellectual General Golberi do Couto e Silva. Known as the "pope of the Sorbonne" as the result of his teaching at the Escola Superior de Guerra, General Golberi had headed the intelligence work of the National Security Council under President Quadros and then had been in charge of intelligence for an anti-Goulart businessmen's organization. Early in 1964 Golberi had formed, together with Castello, Ademar de Queiroz, and Ernesto Geisel, the foursome of army officers (*estado maior informal*) set up by Castello to coordinate the work of preventing a coup or any subversive act by Goulart. As president-elect, Castello had consulted Geisel, Ademar de Queiroz, and Golberi while selecting his administrative team, but he had not agreed with them that War Minister Costa e Silva should be dropped.[5] Once in the presidency, Castello frequently reviewed problems with Golberi and Geisel, whose offices were close to his own, and he kept in touch with the other member of the foursome, retired Marshal Ademar de Queiroz, who now headed Petrobrás, the government's petroleum extracting monopoly.

Within two days of becoming president, Castello officially added three new members to a cabinet that he had been given little time to select: Finance Minister Otávio Bulhões, Health Minister Raimundo de Brito, and Mines and Energy Minister Mauro Thibau. Raimundo de Brito, a medical doctor and energetic administrator, had been secretary of health in the Guanabara state cabinet of Carlos Lacerda; engineer Mauro Thibau had been director of the state electrical power company of Minas Gerais.

To replace Navy Minister Augusto Rademaker Grünewald, a radical who was warning the public against work being done by "the enemies of the Democratic Revolution,"[6] Castello appointed Admiral Ernesto de Melo Batista, who had worked in harmony with Castello in the north of Brazil in 1959. As for the air force, Castello transferred the minis-

[5] João Carlos Palhares dos Santos, interview, Rio de Janeiro, November 22, 1975.
[6] *O Estado de S. Paulo*, April 21, 1964.

ter, a famous stunt pilot, to the Superior Military Tribunal and put Brigadeiro Nelson Freire Lavanère-Wanderley in his place. Lavanère-Wanderley had received training as a cadet from Castello in 1927 and had worked with him at the Escola Superior de Guerra in 1957.

At Planalto Palace on Monday morning, April 20, Castello attended a ceremony at which his cabinet was completed with the swearing in of Roberto Campos, Melo Batista, and Lavanère-Wanderley, together with Labor Minister Arnaldo Sussekind and Foreign Minister Vasco Leitão da Cunha. Sussekind and Leitão da Cunha, veteran professionals in their fields, had been in the cabinet during the two weeks before Castello became president.

In his brief remarks, Castello explained that the political parties and governors had renounced any claims to naming cabinet ministers, thus permitting the realization of the "eminently national composition of the government, formed as a consequence of the events that brought a restoration of legality."[7]

After the ceremony, Roberto Campos told the press that "the role of state planning is not to asphyxiate private initiative, but, on the contrary, is to discipline public investments, rationalize government action, and thus construct a framework within which private enterprise should operate." He declared that "one of the most urgent tasks of planning is the planning of democratic reforms," which should bring concrete solutions and "not personal messages." He observed that "all men of good will and good sense in Brazil recognize that our rate of economic efficiency is below what we can reach and that our rate of social injustice is much above what we can tolerate." In conclusion he emphasized that "without economic development there is no wealth to distribute; but without social justice neither stability nor continuity will exist and the institutions will be permanently threatened."[8]

Foreign Minister Leitão da Cunha also issued a press statement on April 20. Expressing regret that Venezuela, critical of the coup against Goulart, had decided to break diplomatic relations with Brazil, he attributed the step to Venezuela's "lack of understanding about our present government."[9]

[7] HACB, *Discursos, 1964*, p. 17.
[8] *O Estado de S. Paulo*, April 21, 1964.
[9] Ibid.

6. Getting into the Routine

Castello, writing to his son, Paulo, and his family, said that "I am truly the caretaker of a bankruptcy, of a collapsed body that is in incredible disorder. The work is Herculean. I count on many individuals, the patience of the people, and the hopes of an enormous number of Brazilians. I do not fool myself with popularity that deceives. I try to see everything with simplicity and at times with humility. It seems that the military regards me with confidence. But militaristic politics does not exist." Castello also mentioned his suffering caused by the loss of his wife, Argentina, and compared the memory of her to a religion dominating his thoughts and feelings. As for his daughter, Nieta, Castello wrote that she was "more enthusiastic about the presidency than I am."[1]

For almost three months Nieta resided at Alvorada Palace with three of her four children and her husband, an economist working as a presidential assistant, and then they moved to their own home in Brasília. Nieta tried to brighten the cold downstairs rooms of the presidential residence by filling them with flowers, a step that her father, intent on austerity, did not encourage.[2] Of the less formal second-floor rooms, Castello particularly enjoyed using the studio that adjoined his bedroom; he furnished it with his books and a record player for his music. Later a painting of Argentina, done in refreshing colors by Maria R. Campos, was added.

Castello ate most of his meals in his studio. There, following a breakfast of fruit, bread, and coffee with milk, he began work at 7:00 A.M., often humming a tune as he turned to his paper-covered desk; and there he occasionally received assistants and early callers who were not on the official agenda.[3] After his lunch at Alvorada Palace he dismissed his guest or guests and put on his pajamas for a one-hour nap, without which he was apt to fall into a poor humor late in the afternoon, marked by circles under his eyes.

[1] HACB, letter in longhand to Paulo, Nena, Heloiza, Helena, and Cristina Castello Branco, Rio de Janeiro, July 30, 1964, File P1 (p. 6), CPDOC.

[2] Júlio Sérgio Vidal Pessoa, interview, Rio de Janeiro, November 21, 1975.

[3] Artur Aymoré, "A Devoção de uma Vida" (based on interview with Wilson Leal), *Jornal do Brasil,* July 13, 1972 (Caderno B, p. 1); Luiz Fernando Mercadante, "Este É o Humberto," *Realidade*, June 1966.

Supper, which began at 7:30 P.M., was usually with a member or members of his family; like lunch, it was a simple meal, served without wine. Castello liked to spend his evenings writing speeches, reading reports and books, and listening to classical music until he went to bed at 10:30 or 11:00. Before going to sleep, he would carefully peruse the leading newspapers, which did not reach Brasília early in the day, and he would jot down notes about things to do (and phone calls to make) the next day. Nieta, who occupied a bedroom next to her father's during her stay at Alvorada Palace, could hear her father talking by phone with Ademar de Queiroz nearly every night. It was said that only Ademar de Queiroz, Castello's best friend, addressed the president as *você*.

In Planalto Palace, Castello ordered that the oil painting of former President Getúlio Vargas, which hung in the waiting room of the presidential office, be replaced by one of the Duke of Caxias, hero of the Brazilian army. In other ways, too, he began to implant his own thinking. More than Vargas, Kubitschek, or Goulart, he believed in the usefulness of cabinet meetings to "create the ties of common work,"[4] and he instructed his cabinet members to be at Planalto Palace at 3:00 P.M. on April 24 for their first meeting.

The cost of building Brasília, during the Kubitschek administration, led Castello to remark that "the calamity started here."[5] But he planned to govern in Brasília, at least while Congress was in session, despite the fact that most of the work of the ministries was done in Rio. Wits remarked that Castello held cabinet meetings in Brasília to require that visits to the capital be made by Otávio Bulhões, who detested going there.[6]

Iris Coelho, a former Chamber of Deputies stenographer who became the new president's secretary, observed that Castello was invariably dressed formally, using black or dark suits and black ties. He was, she soon decided, a man of unusual simplicity and humanity who had great strength and knew how to deal with subordinates. No one, she discovered, asked a favor of him because no one had the nerve. She learned also that the president was fond of joking. An example of the presidential humor followed the permission she received from Castello to save

[4] Viana Filho, *O Governo Castelo Branco*, p. 95.

[5] Rui Mesquita, interview, São Paulo, November 6, 1975.

[6] Severo Gomes, interview, Rio de Janeiro, July 25, 1977.

for posterity the longhand notes he gave her for typing. His secretary, Castello told an aide, was saving his papers in order to sell them.[7]

From the start, Iris Coelho recalls, Castello spent much of his time in Planalto Palace in discussions with congressmen, seeking to persuade them to resolve problems out of a sense of responsibility for Brazil and uninfluenced by personal interests. In his office he would see that congressmen were seated in comfortable armchairs, and then he would draw up for himself a small straight-backed chair, appropriate for his troublesome spinal column.[8] Soon after his inauguration he held talks with legislative leaders, and government technicians about giving Brazil an agrarian reform,[9] to the surprise of those who identified agrarian reform with the mass demonstrations in its favor that had been organized by the Goulart administration.

Besides flying constantly between Brasília and Rio, Castello traveled all over the country, taking with him on each trip a politician and a relative or friend interested in the state being visited. The trips allowed him to crusade for the revolution, observe conditions, and confer with local leaders. Frequently the trips were made over weekends, when Brasília was considered "a sad and deserted place."[10] But the first trip, somewhat disorganized and with more emphasis on security than Castello wished, took place on Tuesday, April 21. With Costa e Silva, Milton Campos, Ernesto Geisel, and Luís Viana Filho, the president flew from Brasília to Belo Horizonte, Minas Gerais, in order to accompany Governor José de Magalhães Pinto and a vast throng of Mineiros on the drive to colonial Ouro Preto for the traditional ceremonies to remember Tiradentes, the martyr of the nation's independence movement. In his speech in Ouro Preto, Castello explained that it would be impossible to offer detailed plans at the outset of his administration. He said that "in the place of flippant improvisation, frequently destined to furnish only deceptive appearances, we prefer the reliability of study."[11]

From Belo Horizonte, Castello flew to Rio to spend his first night at Laranjeiras Palace, presidential residence and place of work. His bed-

[7] Iris Coelho, interview, Rio de Janeiro, December 15, 1977.

[8] Baleeiro, "Recordações do Presidente H. Castelo Branco," p. 14.

[9] Daniel Krieger, *Desde as Missões*, p. 19.

[10] Vidal Pessoa, interview, November 21, 1975.

[11] HACB, *Discursos, 1964*, p. 21. Mineiro: pertaining to, our native of, the state of Minas Gerais.

room and adjoining office, on the second floor of a wing of that rambling edifice, were directly above the offices that had been set up for the Gabinetes Civil and Militar and Golberi's SNI. For his meals Castello selected a tiny dining room on the second floor of a parallel wing, with space for few guests. He would use but infrequently the formal dining room, one of the large, ornate rooms in the main part of the palace.

At Laranjeiras Palace on the morning of April 22 the president held a series of audiences, seeing his older brother Cândido, his military ministers, Congressman Sarasate, and Mines Minister Thibau. To deal with some of the mines minister's problems, such as those arising from Goulart's expropriation of private petroleum refineries and Goulart's failure to implement arrangements made for the nationalization of properties of the American and Foreign Power Company, Castello advocated studies by competent commissions.

7. Early Cabinet Meetings

Executive decisions were usually reached during small meetings at which Castello, doing much listening, presided over groups of three or four cabinet ministers, or their representatives, and sometimes others who specialized in the matters under consideration. The formal meetings of the entire cabinet, of which eleven were held by Castello in 1964, contributed to the spirit of teamwork that the president prized. As the ministers gathered for a cabinet meeting, they usually found Castello in an affable mood, but as soon as the session began, the president, a short figure at the head of a long table, with Geisel on his right and Viana on his left, became deadly serious, and his appearance throughout remained that of a man with a mission.

At the first full-scale meeting, held in the cabinet room on the third floor of Planalto Palace, Castello called on the foreign minister to give the opening report. Leitão da Cunha pointed out that the new Brazilian regime was considered by some governments to be the result of an armed coup, and therefore it remained unrecognized by Venezuela, Cuba, Mexico, and Uruguay.[1]

Following this brief report, the finance and planning ministers pre-

[1] Viana Filho, *O Governo Castelo Branco*, p. 86.

sented their discouraging accounts. Bulhões said that, without even considering the wage increases for the public sector being studied by Congress, a federal budget deficit of 800 billion cruzeiros (about 570 million dollars) seemed to be in store for 1964. It was a deficit that nearly equaled the total federal revenues of 1963. In view of its size, Bulhões suggested that the ministries trim their budgets by 30 percent; that the import subsidies for petroleum, wheat, and paper be ended; and that taxes be increased as soon as legislation made that possible.[2]

Planning Minister Roberto Campos, who had distributed documents about the economic situation when the ministers arrived, held the floor during most of the meeting. Speaking rapidly and undramatically, he painted a dismal state of affairs: inflation well above 100 percent annually, a per capita decrease in the gross national product, and a lack of foreign exchange, making it impossible to pay foreign debts that were due. He said that Brazil, following the demagoguery of the Goulart years, found itself "between a capitalism without incentives and a socialism without conviction." He proposed that the government announce clearly its support of private initiative and revise the Goulart administration's profit remittance bill in order to attract foreign capital and technology.

Roberto Campos also touched on housing, agrarian, fiscal, banking, and administrative reform. The housing reform was to provide jobs that would be badly needed during anti-inflationary austerity and was to help correct a housing shortage that Campos blamed in part on the Goulart administration's "demagogic rent freeze." Agrarian reform, at this stage envisaging a fund for financing machinery, fertilizers, and seeds, was to help revive production that had fallen off because of fears that Goulart had built up in landowners. To prod large landowners into producing, Roberto Campos proposed that their unproductive properties be taxed at rates that would increase yearly.[3]

Following the cabinet meeting, the president presided over a brief meeting of the National Security Council, thus revealing that he proposed to make regular use of that body and establishing clearly its membership: the chief of staff of the armed forces, the chief of staff of each branch of the military, and the cabinet, including the head of the

[2] *O Estado de S. Paulo*, April 25, 1964.

[3] Ibid., April 25, 26, 1964; Viana Filho, *O Governo Castelo Branco*, pp. 86, 89.

Gabinete Militar (who was secretary of the National Security Council) and the head of the Gabinete Civil.

Upon the conclusion of these meetings, Castello's office made it known that austerity was being practiced in the presidency. The press reported that the Planalto Palace payroll was being shorn of "800 wage earners," mostly *fantasmas* (payroll recipients who did not work), and it described the frugality at Alvorada Palace. Newspaper readers learned that Castello, who enjoyed eating apples, especially before sleeping at night, would limit himself to two apples a day![4]

The president asked Congress not to enact too generous a pay increase for the military. But it proved impossible to keep the overdue increase below 100 percent, especially because the minimum wage had been increased by that amount in February and because Costa e Silva declared that the military leaders were in close touch with Congress to assure a response that would alleviate the "anxieties of the military family."[5]

At the second cabinet meeting, held in Brasília on April 30, the economy again had top priority. In a press release issued after the meeting, the Planning Ministry advised that, at the request of Castello, "a man who gives the maximum importance to planning," Roberto Campos had presented "a veritable calendar of concrete measures" to be tackled by the government. The measures dealt with reducing the deficits of the government-run companies, stimulating exports, and setting up a Five-Year Plan to help the next administration. Projects for housing, banking, and emergency fiscal reforms, said to be nearly ready for presentation to Congress, were to be followed by a proposed agrarian reform and, finally, a proposed administrative reform.[6]

In discussing these and other reforms, Castello saw a good deal of Senator Filinto Müller (PSD, Mato Grosso) and Congressman Pedro Aleixo (UDN, Minas). They had been given leadership posts by a combination of three parties (PSD, UDN, and the smaller PSP) that had

[4] *O Estado de S. Paulo*, April 26, 1964.

[5] Cable, American Embassy, Rio de Janeiro, to Washington, April 17, 1964, NSFB, LBJ Library; see also Donald E. Syvrud, *Foundations of Brazilian Economic Growth*, p. 162.

[6] *O Estado de S. Paulo*, May 1, 1964.

decided to band together to give legislative support to Castello.[7] The climate was good for enacting the administration's program.

When Castello met with his cabinet for a third time in Brasília on May 7, Justice Minister Milton Campos presented a long exposition about the proposed constitutional amendments he was elaborating in order to modify the electoral laws. Roberto Campos then discussed a report that he and Labor Minister Sussekind had drawn up recommending the creation of a National Housing Bank. According to the report, the Fundação da Casa Popular had constructed only 17,174 units in seventeen years, leaving Brazil with a deficit of 6.7 million units.[8]

8. Operação Limpeza

While studying reform projects, Castello devoted time to his painful duty of decreeing punishments of individuals found to have been subversive or corrupt. The duty, defined in two articles of the Institutional Act of April 9, had been transferred by the terms of that act from the Revolutionary Command to the president on April 15, making him responsible for Operação Limpeza, the work of "cleaning up" Brazil. Article 7, which was to expire on October 9, required investigations and allowed the dismissal of civilian and military personnel, regardless of tenure or constitutional guarantees. Article 10, which was to expire on June 15, called for the president to cancel mandates and suspend the political rights of individuals for ten years, upon the recommendation of the National Security Council.

Before Castello became president, the Revolutionary Command had issued three lists in accordance with Article 10, punishing 172 individuals (including former presidents Quadros and Goulart), and two lists in accordance with Article 7, dismissing 146 military officers.[1] The Revolutionary Command had also made arrangements for military police

[7] Ibid., April 29, 1964. PSP: Partido Social Progressista, in which Ademar de Barros, governor of São Paulo, was influential.

[8] *O Estado de S. Paulo*, May 8, 1964.

[1] Edmar Morel, *O Golpe Começou em Washington*, pp. 248–255; Gordon Chase, memorandum to McGeorge Bundy, May 6, 1964, NSFB, LBJ Library.

investigations (IPM's) of organizations considered to have been responsible for subversion. The Castello administration set up a supervisory General Investigations Commission, headed by retired Marshal Estevão Taurino de Rezende Neto, who had been a classmate of Castello and Costa e Silva at school in Porto Alegre and at the military academy in Realengo.

While Castello studied hundreds of cases submitted to him by the General Investigations Commission and the secretaryship of the National Security Council,[2] civilian and military hard-liners demanded a large-scale purge. Taking a different position, the State Department in Washington objected to the fact that those who were punished were not allowed to defend themselves or even learn what accusations were made against them.[3] To add to the State Department's concern, the *Washington Post* published an article, "Brazil Caught in Grip of Army Dictatorship," which estimated that ten thousand Brazilians had been arrested or deprived of their political rights. São Paulo Governor Ademar de Barros was quoted as boasting that he had "arrested over 3,000 in his state, including every labor leader he could lay his hands on, Communist or not."[4]

Early in July, Lincoln Gordon cabled Washington to say he estimated that the number arrested was "substantially less" than his earlier guess of two thousand. But Castello disappointed Washington because he carried out *cassações* (suspensions of political rights), as stipulated in the Institutional Act, and he assumed full responsibility for them. He acted on all the recommendations coming from the military ministers, with the exception of the case of oppositionist journalist Carlos Heitor Coni, whom he refused to punish.[5] The total on Castello's eight lists, issued between May 1 and the June 15 deadline, came to about two hundred, which was a bitter disappointment to hard-liners, who complained of Castello's "failure adequately to punish those involved in

[2] HACB, letter to Hélio Ibiapina, Brasília, June 25, 1964, File P1 (p. 5), CPDOC.

[3] Cable, Secretary of State to American Embassy, Rio, June 9, 1964, NSFB, LBJ Library.

[4] Dan Kurzman, "Arrests Estimated at 10,000: Brazil Caught in Grip of Army Dictatorship," *Washington Post*, May 3, 1964.

[5] Lincoln Gordon, cable to Washington, July 6, 1964, NSFB, LBJ Library; HACB, letter to Hélio Ibiapina, June 25, 1964, File P1 (p. 5), CPDOC.

the 'Goulart conspiracy.' "[6] Despite pressure, Castello refused to touch members of the Supreme Court. Nor would he agree with federal legislators who demanded cancellation of the mandates of Senator Afonso Arinos de Melo Franco and Congressman Francisco San Tiago Dantas, foreign ministers of Quadros and Goulart who had strengthened Brazil's relations with Communist nations.[7] Writing later about his problem to hard-line Colonel Hélio Ibiapina, Castello described himself as having encountered "opposing forces in the case of *cassações*, some complaining that the revolution knew only how to carry out a purge and others wanting the revolution to devote itself only to a purge. If we immerse ourselves exclusively in Operação Limpeza, Brazil will end up in Communist hands."[8]

Rio de Janeiro state Governor Badger da Silveira, the first to be *cassado* by Castello, was impeached at about the same time by his state assembly, which soon chose General Paulo Torres to replace him. When hard-liners early in May called also for the removals of the governors of Pará, Amazonas, and Goiás, Castello explained to interested congressmen that many investigations still had to be completed and studied by the National Security Council.[9] In June, however, Castello canceled the mandates of the governors of Pará and Amazonas, both considered corrupt; the state assemblies, somewhat "cleansed" by *cassações*, chose in their places Lieutenant Colonel Jarbas Passarinho (Pará) and Professor Artur César Ferreira Reis (Amazonas), both long-time acquaintances of Castello.

Politicians and the press devoted much more attention to the case of Goiás Governor Mauro Borges Teixeira, whose father, Senator Pedro Ludovico Teixeira, was an important figure in the PSD, the largest political party. Borges' past associations with the far Left were well known, and some of his state cabinet members were felt to have participated in subversion. A retired general, investigating the Borges administration, suggested that the governor dismiss his state cabinet, but

[6] Robert W. Dean, memorandum, São Paulo, August 13, 1964, NSFB, LBJ Library.

[7] Viana Filho, *O Governo Castelo Branco*, p. 97; for attacks in Congress on these former foreign ministers, see *O Estado de S. Paulo*, April 26, June 16, 1964.

[8] HACB, letter to Hélio Ibiapina, June 25, 1964.

[9] *O Estado de S. Paulo*, May 6, 1964.

Borges refused, and on May 13 he took his case to Castello in Brasília. After hearing Castello describe Ludovico's Senate speech of May 12 as "insulting," Borges defended himself and his cabinet against the charge of being Communist. All belonged to the "democratic Left," Borges said. Asking whether the members of the British Labour Party were Communists, he added that if that were felt to be the case he should be overthrown, because he had never been a conservative. "I, too, am not a conservative," the president said.[10]

The Castello Branco administration felt that the best solution lay in a revision of most of the Goiás state cabinet, but on May 15, after the state cabinet resigned, Borges refused to accept the resignations. By this time a list of thirty-four *cassações* affecting Rio Grande do Sul politicians had been signed by Castello, and *cassações* of Goiás politicians were known to be in preparation. PSD President Amaral Peixoto told Castello that the cancellation of the mandate of the PSD governor would have a profound repercussion in the party, forcing it to reconsider its political position.[11]

9. Kubitschek Loses His Political Rights (June 8, 1964)

In mid-May, Juscelino Kubitschek decided that, as a PSD senator from Goiás, he should speak in the Senate in defense of Mauro Borges. He was more than ready to express himself. For a man of his temperament it had been difficult to adhere to his month-old policy of maintaining a low profile; besides, that policy seemed to do nothing to deter the appearance of press reports about his so-called past corruption and subversion. But Kubitschek's advisers, such as Francisco Negrão de Lima, argued that a defense of Mauro Borges would only irritate the military and increase the chances of Kubitschek joining Goulart and Quadros as a former president without political rights. With regret Kubitschek canceled his Senate speech at the last moment.[1]

However, the campaign by Kubitchek's opponents became even

[10] Mauro Borges, *O Golpe em Goiás: História de uma Grande Traição*, pp. 121–128; *O Estado de S. Paulo*, May 9, 13, 14, 16, 1964.

[11] *O Estado de S. Paulo*, May 14, 15, 16, 20, 1964.

[1] *O Estado de S. Paulo*, April 19, May 14, 15, 1964.

more pronounced. His very failure to use his Senate seat brought him the title of "Brazil's most expensive senator," and he was accused of having secured the seat only because he wanted the immunities that went with it. Old stories were repeated about how he had made "a fortune" in real estate as a mayor of Belo Horizonte. Groups that had supported his reelection to the presidency in 1965 withdrew their backing. And countless military officers, directing anti-Kubitschek appeals to Costa e Silva, expressed surprise that Kubitschek's candidacy still existed—in view of his "well-known unpatriotic activities."[2]

Unable to remain quiet any longer, Kubitschek issued a statement on May 25 to explain that "the terrorist process chosen by my political adversaries will not result in my withdrawal." He pointed out that as president he had respected his opponents, been loyal to the institutions, and presided impartially over the election of his successor. Mentioning the struggle he had undertaken "without respite" for Brazil's economic independence, he argued that the resulting development had prevented the advance of Communist subversion, and he added that "when extremist infiltration threatened our continent, I stimulated pan-Americanism, launching Operação PanAmerica, and I cultivated all the traditional friendships of our country abroad." In conclusion he said that "the people have already made their judgment of me and I am sure that they want to do so again at the first opportunity. Only for this reason my detractors move against me. They seek to strike down not only a candidate but also the democratic regime itself."[3]

Costa e Silva, in São Paulo with Castello on May 26, gave the press his personal view: "The pronouncement of Sr. Kubitschek—due to its violent language and also, in a certain sense, its defiance—appears to me much like the speech of Sr. Jango Goulart on March 30." Heartily applauded, the war minister said that he had nothing to add.[4] But during his plane ride from São Paulo to Brasília, with a group that included Castello and Geisel, he had more to say. Obviously moved by the anti-Kubitschek sentiment he had found in São Paulo army circles, Costa e Silva exclaimed that the president "must decide *now* about the *cassação*

[2] Ibid., May 17, 22, 24, 1964.
[3] Ibid., May 26, 1964.
[4] Ibid., May 27, 28, 1964.

of Kubitschek." Geisel closed the subject by observing that the matter should be handled in Brasília, not in public.[5]

Kubitschek, stunned by Costa e Silva's remarks to the press, told friends that his own statement had been directed against political adversaries and not the military. He told the press that he could see no similarity between his recent "manifesto" and Goulart's inciting speech of March 30 to sergeants. "The violent language of my manifesto," he said, "is much softer than the violent and slanderous language with which I am being assailed daily."[6]

In Brasília on May 28, Castello conferred with Costa e Silva. Then on the twenty-ninth, just before making a weekend trip to Rio, he had another of his meetings with the increasingly alarmed Amaral Peixoto. He told the PSD president that the war minister's remarks in São Paulo did not mean that Kubitschek's political rights were to be suspended.[7]

Kubitschek's relief was short-lived, for on Saturday, May 30, the press reported that "a high officer," working on "the Kubitschek case," had found "more than enough to justify the suspension of the former President's political rights." Investigators claimed that between 1942 and 1950 Kubitschek had obtained loans of 950 million cruzeiros from the Caixa Econômica, "in violation of the rules," and that during Kubitschek's presidency all sorts of financial irregularities, contrary to the constitution, had been practiced by the president, the Superintendency of the Plan for the Economic Improvement of Amazônia (SPVEA), and government financial institutions, in part as the result of President Kubitschek's interest in a construction project on Bananal Island in the interior.

Furthermore, the investigators asserted that Kubitschek, in order to be elected president in 1955, had signed an agreement under which twenty million cruzeiros had been paid to the Communist Party and that a similar agreement, this one for two hundred thousand dollars, had been reached in 1963 to secure Communist support in 1965, with Kubitschek paying the first installment of fifty thousand dollars in November, 1963.[8] The 1955 deal, according to the investigators, had

[5] Ernani do Amaral Peixoto, interview, Rio de Janeiro, December 20, 1975.

[6] *O Estado de S. Paulo*, May 27, 1964.

[7] Ibid., May 29, 30, 31, 1964.

[8] Mário Victor, *Cinco Anos que Abalaram o Brasil (de Jânio Quadros ao Marechal Castelo Branco)*, pp. 587–588.

been with both Goulart and the Communists, many of whom had joined the PTB, and had resulted in President Kubitschek turning over to Goulart and the PTB the Ministries of Labor and Agriculture, the worker pension funds, and a department of the Bank of Brazil. Investigators argued that these steps had contributed decisively to the atmosphere of corruption and subversion that had made the 1964 revolution necessary, and they added that they had strong indications that Kubitschek had enriched himself from the corruption "implanted" during his administration, becoming in this way "one of the wealthiest" men in Brazil.[9]

Castello was studying the Kubitschek dossier at Laranjeiras Palace in Rio on May 30 when he received a visit from Rafael de Almeida Magalhães, who was acting governor of Guanabara in the absence of Carlos Lacerda. Showing the young acting governor hundreds of dossiers, the president pointed out that the work was very time-consuming, limiting the attention he could give to the nation's real problems, and was difficult, "for all I have are the versions of the foes of these men." He said that the Kubitschek case worried him, and he listed reasons why he felt that it would be best not to punish the former president: punishment would appear to be simply a political matter and would bring harm to the revolution in view of Kubitschek's world-wide renown. An impassioned plea by Augusto Frederico Schmidt had led Castello to feel that Kubitschek might even commit suicide in case of an adverse decision. Castello told Rafael de Almeida Magalhães that he would do his best not to punish Kubitschek, provided Kubitschek would not create an impossible situation for him by remaining a candidate.[10]

The idea of having Kubitschek withdraw as a candidate, which was not new, was transmitted at about this time by Ernesto Geisel to PSD President Amaral Peixoto through a congressman who had military connections.[11] With the pressure for Kubitschek's punishment mounting daily, the suggestion interested Amaral Peixoto. When he discussed it with Kubitschek, the senator decided to accept it, for the PSD leaders felt that the *cassação* idea was a political one and that the party could

[9] Arnaldo Sussekind, notes for JWFD, Rio de Janeiro, December 1974.

[10] Rafael de Almeida Magalhães, interview, Rio de Janeiro, November 19, 1975.

[11] Amaral Peixoto, interview, December 20, 1975.

reconsider Kubitschek's candidacy at a later date, should "normal conditions" return.

Amaral Peixoto asked Kubitschek not to complicate matters by issuing more public pronouncements, and then flew to Brasília with PSD Congressman Joaquim Ramos to sound out the situation. Although Amaral Peixoto had no way of knowing how overwhelmingly Costa e Silva was supported by members of the National Security Council, he sensed that developments unfavorable to Kubitschek were occuring "at a precipitous rate" and that it had become unlikely that the suggestion received from Geisel could be made effective.[12]

On June 2, while "well-informed military areas" described Kubitschek's *cassação* as "absolutely certain," Chief Investigator Taurino de Rezende sought an extension of the Institutional Act's June 15 deadline for suspending political rights. He pointed out to Geisel that the studies of the General Investigations Commission would take a long time and asked him to consult Castello. In reply Castello phoned Taurino de Rezende to explain that for "material and political" reasons an extension would be impossible and that he was certain the members of the National Security Council would confirm this decision when they were consulted on June 4.[13]

With the approach of that date, Costa e Silva drew up a petition calling for a ten-year suspension of Kubitschek's political rights. The war minister declared that the destiny of the revolution was at stake and called on its leaders "to prevent future political maneuvers, already quite well planned, for interrupting the process of restoring moral and political principles." Citing the revolution's "exemplary acts" that had already affected many secondary figures, he found no justification for ignoring "important political figures who were notoriously responsible for the deterioration of our government system and of the high standards of morality observed during decades of the monarchical and republican regimes." Documents accompanying the war minister's request included a study about real estate purchased by Kubitschek when he was mayor of Belo Horizonte.[14]

From Planalto Palace on June 3, Castello phoned Amaral Peixoto

[12] Ibid.

[13] *O Estado de S. Paulo*, June 3, 4, 1964.

[14] Viana Filho, *O Governo Castelo Branco*, p. 95.

at his Brasília apartment and invited him for supper that evening at Alvorada Palace. The PSD president, preferring not to be alone in case party matters were discussed, asked if he might bring his friend Joaquim Ramos. "Bring him," Castello said.[15]

In the upstairs studio room the president, very friendly to Amaral Peixoto, inquired about the working habits of President Vargas, Amaral Peixoto's father-in-law. The conversation did not touch on the Kubitschek matter, and after two hours Amaral Peixoto suggested that it was probably time for him to leave the president, who, it was clear from messages, was being sought by several ministers. As Amaral Peixoto prepared to leave, Castello said: "We have a matter to take up. I want to inform you—it is an attention that I owe you—that in the next forty-eight hours a decision will be made that is very important for Brazil. You know that it will not be made due to any pressure. I shall resolve it only in the country's interest. I am certain that you see the necessity for the country." The president accompanied Amaral Peixoto all the way to his car, a VW, and even joked with him, saying that, "for a man of your importance, you use an unusually small car."[16]

After leaving the palace, Amaral Peixoto remarked to Joaquim Ramos: "Juscelino is already *cassado*." He phoned Kubitschek, who was in Rio, to say that the evening with the president had left him with a very unfavorable impression about the outlook. Kubitschek decided to come to Brasília the next day.

By the time of Kubitschek's arrival on June 4, almost every politician in Brasília knew that a majority of the National Security Council members, consulted individually by Castello or Geisel, considered the *cassação* of Kubitschek a step that had been made logical by the revolution.[17] The PSD therefore arranged a special night session of the Senate so that the former president could deliver what would clearly be his final speech there. In it Kubitschek said:

> The workings of the Institutional Act are such that those who are threatened are not given access to the accusatory dossiers. Thus the revolutionaries of Brazil turn against the most sacred conquest of the law. . . .

[15] Amaral Peixoto, interview, December 20, 1975.
[16] Ibid.
[17] Vasco Leitão da Cunha, interview, Rio de Janeiro, November 23, 1974.

I know that in the Brazilian land tyrannies do not last. . . . I repeat, the blow which they wish to deal to my person, as a former Head of State, will strike the democratic life, the free will of the people. . . . This act is an act of usurpation and not an act of punishment. They cancel much more than my political rights; they cancel the political rights of Brazil.[18]

With one exception, every member of the National Security Council signed the decision that suspended Kubitschek's political rights. Roberto Campos offered his resignation instead of his signature, but his resignation was not accepted.[19]

Before Castello signed the official decree, he spoke with a long-time acquaintance, Senator Daniel Krieger (UDN, Rio Grande do Sul), and told him that his responsibilities to the revolution did not allow him to spare Kubitschek. He asked Krieger to try to minimize the problems that Kubitschek's *cassação* might create in the Senate, and, at Krieger's request, he promised to reexamine the cases against other senators.[20] Then, with the decree still unsigned, the president flew to Recife for two days of attention to the problems of the northeast.

In a speech in Recife, Castello attacked members of past governments who had used their posts to enrich themselves. He asserted that Brazilian communism had become "a factor of national corruption. Under the form of agreements, the most debasing conspiracies were worked out, ones that corrupted programs and vitiated democratic expressions at elections." Referring to the postulate placed on the revolution by the Institutional Act for the defense of "peace and national honor," he declared that the government would fulfill that mandate, serenely and without compromise; justice would be imposed with impartiality on the powerful as well as the humble.[21]

In Brasília on June 8, Castello signed and issued decrees suspending the political rights of forty, including Kubitschek. In Rio, Kubitschek asked Brazilians "not for one moment to be impressed with the calumnies and lies which sworn enemies of democracy will certainly con-

[18] Victor, *Cinco Anos que Abalaram o Brasil*, pp 585–586.

[19] Amaral Peixoto, interview, December 20, 1975; PVCB, interview, Rio de Janeiro, December 21, 1975.

[20] Krieger, *Desde as Missões*, p. 176

[21] HACB, *Discursos, 1964*, pp. 25–29 (the date shown for this speech is incorrect).

tinue to heap upon me." "I am paying," he added, "for the crime of having fought resolutely for the economic independence of my country, for the crime of having governed without hate."[22]

While supporters of the presidential aspirations of the UDN's Carlos Lacerda demonstrated gleefully in Rio against the fallen Kubitschek, Castello phoned the acting governor of Guanabara to ask that Kubitschek be given full protection. Kubitschek, expressing fear for his life, sought asylum in the Spanish Embassy, located in the apartment building that he owned. He also made arrangements for an early departure to Spain.[23]

10. Reactions to the Cassações

Luís Viana Filho, asked by the press to comment on the *cassação* of Kubitschek, said that the step was "a political act, which finds its explanation in the revolution itself." It was not, however, a political act that promised to help the administration's relations with Congress. PSD lawmakers issued a note expressing their solidarity with Kubitschek and announcing their separation from the majority bloc in Congress.[1]

Castello, while preparing to exchange impressions in Brasília with PSD leaders, received Lincoln Gordon. The ambassador, who had been sending cables to the State Department urging the "maximum possible" economic support for the Brazilian government,[2] was scheduled to leave for Washington on June 10 and had therefore already arranged to meet with Castello on the ninth.

The president told the ambassador that the *cassação* of Kubitschek had been a political necessity and an act fully justified by the record, and he added that it would "embarrass the nation" to publish that record in full. Gordon noted that, although the decision about Kubit-

[22] *O Estado de S. Paulo*, June 9, 1964.

[23] Victor, *Cinco Anos que Abalaram o Brasil*, p. 586; Almeida Magalhães, interview, November 19, 1975; cable, American Embassy, Rio de Janeiro, to Washington, June 11, 1964, NSFB, LBJ Library.

[1] *O Estado de S. Paulo*, June 9, 10, 1964.

[2] Lincoln Gordon, cable from Rio de Janeiro for Bell, Mann, Rogers, and Solomon, June 8, 1964, NSFB, LBJ Library.

schek had been difficult, Castello showed not the slightest "nervousness or anxiety" but revealed, on the contrary, a "calm resolve to get on with the problems of clean-up, administrative rebuilding, and positive program." The president, Gordon decided, was looking forward with eagerness and relief to the early expiration of his arbitrary powers and the reestablishment of constitutional norms.[3]

Aided by a staff report on "areas of friction abroad," Castello discussed each subject that interested the ambassador, and he showed him the government's proposed new legislation on profit remittances. Castello also expressed satisfaction with the progress being made about reforms, especially considering that he and his ministers had come to office unexpectedly, without time for preparation. He said that the threefold goals of inflation containment, development, and reform were no mere slogans, and he emphasized that systematic staff work was the basis of his administration. Gordon noted that Castello had gained confidence about economic subjects and was fully backing the policy lines recommended by Roberto Campos. In his cable to Washington, Gordon reported receiving a "very favorable" general impression.[4]

Gordon, on the eve of his departure to the United States, received a cable from Washington that expressed the State Department's grave concern about the *cassações* and pointed out that the Brazilian government's failure "to follow due process of law and proceed in a democratic manner will increase our difficulties in responding to Brazil's requests for economic assistance." The reply from the American Embassy, sent after Gordon left, suggested that, in the case of Kubitschek, Castello had felt it necessary to prevent the formation of a destructive opposition coalition capable of frustrating economic recovery and reform and had acted to prevent a devastating split in the armed forces, where anti-Kubitschek sentiment was strong.[5]

In Washington, Gordon argued successfully for an immediate fifty-million-dollar "program," or balance of payments, loan (in addition to

[3] Gordon, "Recollections of President Castello Branco," p. 16; idem, cable from Rio for Secretary of State, June 10, 1964, NSFB, LBJ Library.

[4] Gordon cable to Secretary of State, June 10, 1964.

[5] Secretary Rusk (T. C. Mann), cable to American Embassy, Rio de Janeiro, June 9, 1964, and American Embassy, Rio de Janeiro (Mein), cable to Washington, June 11, 1964, NSFB, LBJ Library.

USAID project loans to be approved in June and July).[6] Meanwhile, in Brasília, Castello spoke with PSD leaders about the Kubitschek case. Filinto Müller, government leader in the Senate, was particularly disturbed because he considered himself a personal friend of Castello and regarded the party's association with the president as a means of carrying out reforms that he had dreamed of since rebelling in the 1920's.[7]

Castello explained to the PSD leaders that the *cassação* of Kubitschek was not an act of hostility to their party. The decision, he said, had been taken after careful investigation and after a majority of the Security Council members had recommended it, and it was not due to pressure or to favoritism of any party or presidential candidate. He told of his appreciation of past support from the PSD and expressed the hope that the party would continue to cooperate on the same plane of national interest. But he said that he recognized the trauma suffered by the party, at least in the sector closest to Kubitschek, and could understand why the party leaders might want to break with the administration.[8] Müller decided to continue to help the revolution, but no longer as Senate leader of the government. Following the suggestion of many senators, including Müller, Castello offered the post to Daniel Krieger of the UDN.[9]

While the halls of Congress rang with speeches in defense of Kubitschek, seventy federal legislators signed a declaration of "independence." Castello told Amaral Peixoto that he respected the decision of the PSD to assume this independent position. For the government it hardly seemed to rule out cooperation in legislative matters and was to be preferred to a hostile PSD. Many members of the PSD also preferred to dispense with hostility. Among them was Congressman Antônio Silva Cunha Bueno, head of the PSD of São Paulo, who announced that the *cassação* of Kubitschek constituted "a legitimate act of the revolution."[10]

[6] Department of State, cable to American Embassy, Rio de Janeiro, June 19, 1964, NSFB, LBJ Library.

[7] *O Estado de S. Paulo*, June 11, 1964.

[8] Ibid.

[9] Krieger, *Desde as Missões*, p. 176.

[10] *O Estado de S. Paulo*, June 10, 1964.

"There are," the American Embassy cabled Washington, "some indications that the PSD's historic predilection for the fruits of power may in the long run be the controlling factor." In the White House an analyst concluded that "the action against Kubitschek has caused only a small ripple in Brazil. The government apparently has the goods on him, but his offenses probably are no greater than those of most Brazilian and Latin American politicians. Kubitschek's party has not supported him."[11]

Krieger, after becoming Senate leader of the government, was apprehensive at the prospect of a vast purge, recommended by Military Club President Augusto César Moniz de Aragão and others in the armed forces. Marshal Taurino de Rezende, unable to get an extension of the June 15 deadline for *cassações*, submitted five-hundred recommended *cassações* to the National Security Council on June 8.[12] Krieger and Justice Minister Milton Campos expressed their concern to Castello.

Castello, in Rio for the June 13–14 weekend, made a final review of recommended *cassações* and handled another unpleasant matter, the dismissal of Agriculture Minister Thompson for inefficiency and for prematurely revealing the government's sugar policy to friends.[13] Still in Rio on the fifteenth, he decreed seventy-one *cassações* and then phoned his new Senate leader to inform him that "happily" it had been possible to take care of the requests that he and Milton Campos had made. Castello's statement that "not one senator was *cassado*" brought Krieger one of the greatest joys of his long political career.[14]

Disgruntled hard-liners complained that the Castello government had been "too soft on Goulartist and Kubitschek elements." A Fourth Infantry Division major expressed surprise that only 10 Mineiros had lost their political rights, whereas the list of possibilities had included the names of 238 Mineiros. Hard-liners in São Paulo were convinced

[11] American Embassy, Rio de Janeiro, cable to Washington, June 11, 1964, and Robert M. Sayre, memorandum to McGeorge Bundy, June 15, 1964, NSFB, LBJ Library.

[12] *O Estado de S. Paulo*, June 9, 1964.

[13] Roberto de Abreu Sodré, interview, São Paulo, July 28, 1977; Trajano Pupo Neto, interview, São Paulo, July 27, 1977; Gonzaga do Nascimento Silva, interview, October 25, 1975.

[14] Krieger, *Desde as Missões*, pp. 176–177.

that "at least a part of the blame for the shortness of the various lists of *cassações*" could be attributed to Ambassador Gordon.[15]

In Recife, Hélio Ibiapina was shocked to find no Pernambucanos on Castello's lists. The president, replying to the colonel's complaint, said that the fault was not his because, despite numerous investigations carried out in Pernambuco, neither the General Investigations Commission nor the secretary of the National Security Council had furnished him any denouncement originating in Pernambuco. As for the "case" against wealthy José Ermírio de Morais, PTB senator from Pernambuco, Castello told Ibiapina that it had been so poorly drawn up he could not possibly have acted on it.[16]

Thus, during its first two months the administration planted seeds that would produce serious problems: it alienated hard-liners, including many military officers, who liked to proclaim that "revolution is revolution." After one of them, a general, took it upon himself to remove the head of the University of Minas Gerais without consulting the education minister, Castello reinstated the university head. As a result of such incidents, the new president was criticized for confining himself to "bureaucratic channels" and wanting to normalize things too soon.[17] Although War Minister Costa e Silva did not agree with this criticism, the hard-liners began to consider him their leader because of his role in the *cassação* of Kubitschek. They also liked Governor Carlos Lacerda and shared his view that Justice Minister Milton Campos, the nation's most renown legalist, was an unwise choice for the moment because he was so dominated by "juridical scruples" that he would have been "an excellent minister after a revolution or to avoid a revolution."[18]

While the early alienation of hard-liners indicated one facet of the future, another was begun in Castello's work with congressmen and the cabinet to turn the uprising of March, 1964, into a positive force. The cabinet itself gave promise of a notable administration. Chosen

[15] Robert W. Dean, report, São Paulo, August 13, 1964, NSFB, LBJ Library; *O Estado de S. Paulo,* June 20, 1964.

[16] HACB, letter to Hélio Ibiapina, June 25, 1964, File P1 (p. 5), CPDOC.

[17] Carlos Luís Guedes, *Tinha que Ser Minas*, pp. 248–262.

[18] Carlos Lacerda, *Depoimento*, p. 300.

without the usual need to hand out rewards or pacify political groups, it included two heroic military figures of the distant past (Juarez Távora and Osvaldo Cordeiro de Farias) but consisted for the most part of trained technicians. The first sixty days had not elapsed before Castello, interested primarily in "inflation containment, development, and reform," viewed with considerable optimism the key roles that he believed would be played by two of the technicians: Otávio Bulhões and Roberto Campos.[19]

[19] PVCB, memorandum, June 1979, p. 5.

II

Early Political and Economic Reforms

(June–October, 1964)

I am not simply a president of purges and imprisonments.

1. Lacerda Explains the Revolution (April–July, 1964)

FOR years Castello Branco had admired UDN politician Carlos Lacerda, combative foe of Vargas, Kubitschek, and Goulart. Described by Ademar de Queiroz in 1963 as "really a great pillar of democracy," Lacerda emerged from the 1964 revolution as its civilian leader, with good connections in the military. After Lacerda helped to organize civilian support for placing Castello in the presidency, the president-elect met with him at the home of General Juraci Magalhães, who was to become Castello's ambassador to Washington. At that meeting Castello listened in silence while Lacerda said that he would welcome a temporary mission abroad because of his physical and emotional exhaustion, his poor financial condition, and his wife's need of an ear operation by specialists.[1]

In the succeeding days Lacerda became upset at not being able to see more of Castello, and he declared to São Paulo UDN leader Roberto de Abreu Sodré that he would not attend the inauguration of a government whose ministry was made up of "conservatives and *entreguistas*." Castello, told that the illness of Lacerda's wife prevented the governor's attendance, phoned Lacerda, just after taking office, to inquire about her health.[2] The gesture was beneficial to a relationship that the new president valued. Castello hoped to be succeeded by a civilian, and he

[1] Ademar de Queiroz, letter to HACB, May 27, 1963, File L2, CPDOC; Armando Falcão, quoted in Viana Filho, *O Governo Castelo Branco*, pp. 63–64.

[2] Roberto de Abreu Sodré, letter to Luís Viana Filho, São Paulo, September 28, 1971, p. 6. *Entreguista*: term used to describe a Brazilian said to be working to turn Brazil's assets over to foreigners.

regarded the Guanabara governor, who had revealed administrative ability, as a logical choice.[3]

From Armando Falcão, a Ceará federal congressman being considered as a possible running mate for Lacerda, the president learned of Lacerda's interest in a mission to explain abroad what the Brazilian revolution was about.[4] Lacerda's experience, eloquence, and knowledge of languages made him an admirable choice. And little doubt existed about the need of the mission, for in much of the world the revolution was being attacked, especially by the press. French newspapers denounced the "coup" viciously.

Lacerda, invited to lunch with Castello at Alvorada Palace on April 20, confirmed to journalists in Brasília that he was a presidential candidate. "Without false modesty," he said, "I expect to be living here in 1966."[5] At the palace Castello asked Lacerda to undertake the mission abroad. Suggesting that the governor select the countries to visit, the president lamented that the revolution was being described as a fascist or United States coup in much of the world press.[6]

Back in Rio, Lacerda overcame difficulties with his usual forcefulness when he arranged that state cabinet secretary Rafael de Almeida Magalhães become acting governor of Guanabara. And then, on the evening of April 22, he left by plane for Europe accompanied by his wife, daughter, and niece, the Abreu Sodrés, and the president of the Guanabara State Bank. At the Galeão Airport, outside Rio, three thousand admirers saw him off on the flight to Milan with brief stopovers in Madrid and Paris.

Early the next morning a swarm of journalists greeted Lacerda in Madrid with questions so "indiscreet" that Lacerda, tense and tired, agreed with Abreu Sodré to remain quiet during the ninety-minute stopover at Orly Airport in Paris.[7]

But Lacerda, in the company of Brazilian residents of Paris at an

[3] Leitão da Cunha, interview, November 23, 1974; Arthur S. Moura, interview, Rio de Janeiro, December 11, 1974; Raimundo de Moura Brito, interview, Rio de Janeiro, December 22, 1974; José Jerônimo Moscardo de Sousa, interview, Brasília, October 23, 1975; Rui Mesquita interview, November 6, 1975.

[4] Abreu Sodré, letter to Viana, September 28, 1971, pp. 6–7.

[5] *O Estado de S. Paulo*, April 21, 1964.

[6] Lacerda, *Depoimento*, p. 310.

[7] Abreu Sodré, letter to Viana, September 28, 1971, p. 9.

Orly Airport restaurant at 7:30 A.M., was provoked by the "insults" to Brazil expressed by about thirty pro-Goulart reporters who had brought radio and television broadcasting equipment with them. Shocked to hear talk of torture in Brazil, he denied it emphatically.[8] Asked how many had been jailed by the Brazilian "revolution," he replied that of 860 originally held, only 200 remained in jail, including 9 Red Chinese agents. When a reporter described Lacerda as the "overthrower of presidents," the governor declared: "I do not overthrow presidents. They fall like ripe fruit. Anyway, I have overthrown fewer presidents than General de Gaulle."[9]

Lacerda said that Castello Branco was the foremost intellectual among the generals and the foremost general among the intellectuals, and he argued that if France did not understand what had occurred in Brazil it was because her newspaper correspondents in Brazil, with two exceptions, were Communists.[10] In particular Lacerda accused the Brazilian correspondent of *Le Monde* of being a Communist, and he described that daily's director as a witch doctor. To a reporter who defended *Le Monde's* objectivity, Lacerda said: "When it is claimed that the Brazilian revolution received assistance from abroad, I say that this is not objectivity. Before the war, the French press presented Hitler as a pacifist because Hilter spoke of peace. Today it commits the same error when it believes that Goulart was a reformer."

What, reporters inquired, could be expected from de Gaulle's proposed visit to Latin America? "Banquets and speeches," Lacerda replied. Expressing doubts about the possibility of France assisting Latin America, Lacerda went on to say that "Brigitte Bardot is the best ambassador that France has sent to Brazil for a long time." Asked for his opinion of de Gaulle, Lacerda described him as "a great writer, a politician, a statesman," but he noted that he had revealed a "royal tone." "France," Lacerda observed, "is not yet a monarchy."[11]

Abreu Sodré found Lacerda's performance brilliant. But the Paris press was loudly critical. "General de Gaulle," *Le Monde* wrote, "will be enchanted to know that his visit to Brazil is going to be reduced

[8] Lacerda, *Depoimento*, p. 311.

[9] *O Estado de S. Paulo*, April 24, 1964.

[10] Protásio D. Vargas, letter to Ivan Lins, Porto Alegre, December 13, 1965, File N1, Part I, CPDOC; *O Estado de S. Paulo*, April 24, 1964.

[11] *O Estado de S. Paulo*, April 24, 25, 1964.

to banquets and speeches, that he should not behave like a king, and that Brigitte Bardot is the best ambassador from our country." *Le Monde* made the point that Lacerda, "who today approves of military dictatorship," had once belonged to Communist organizations, a charge that was repeated in other Paris newspapers.[12]

While shopping and sightseeing with his family in Milan, Venice, and Florence, Lacerda sent cables to Brazil to express his extreme annoyance with Itamarati (the Brazilian Foreign Ministry) for the delay in the receipt of his official credentials. During Lacerda's subsequent visit to Athens, Itamarati asked Abreu Sodré to try to avoid his returning to Paris before delivery of the credentials, but Lacerda, imagining that his troubles with Itamarati were somehow related to a conspiracy against his presidential ambitions rather than to Itamarati's difficulty in persuading France to accept his mission, resolved to visit Paris with or without credentials.[13]

Lacerda's arrival in Paris coincided with an announcement in which Itamarati confirmed his mission but explained that it had become official only after his Orly interview of April 23. He was avoided by representatives of the French government, and he avoided the French press. In the course of explaining the revolution to an Associated Press correspondent, Lacerda asserted that the visit of de Gaulle to Brazil had been arranged before April, 1964, "by a Brazil that no longer exists."[14]

While Lacerda's enemies in Brazil argued that he had revealed intemperance unsuited to the presidency,[15] Castello decided to discuss Lacerda's situation with Guanabara Social Services Secretary Sandra Cavalcanti. Sandra, devoted to Lacerda and an old friend of Argentina and Humberto Castello Branco, had given the new president a popular housing bank study in April, 1964, before the administration, with the help of lawyer José Luís Bulhões Pedreira, sent a message on the subject to Congress. Now the president arranged for her to be flown to Brasília, and, when she arrived, he even insisted that she spend the night at Alvorada Palace.

Castello told Sandra that he wanted her to fly to Paris to get first-

[12] Ibid., April 25, 1964.

[13] Abreu Sodré, letter to Viana, September 28, 1971, pp. 11–12.

[14] *O Estado de S. Paulo*, May 23, 1964.

[15] Abreu Sodré, letter to Viana, September 28, 1971, p. 13.

hand information about a rumor that Lacerda was interested in leaving the governorship if he could become a roving ambassador, and he told Sandra to tell Lacerda of his opposition to any extension of his own presidential term, a possibility being mentioned by some congressmen. Sandra attributed to acting Governor Rafael de Almeida Magalhães, whom she disliked, the report about Lacerda's interest in leaving the governorship. "All people have their weaknesses," Sandra told Castello. "Yours was to name Roberto Campos minister. The weakness of Carlos Lacerda is Rafael."[16]

Sandra's trip to Paris, described by the press as one to study popular housing in Europe, was a peace mission.[17] Lacerda was happy about the consideration shown by Castello and to learn of his opposition to the extension of his term in the presidency, and he told Sandra, as they strolled in the springtime by the Seine, that he planned to return soon to the governorship and could not imagine how a rumor had developed about his lack of interest in doing so.[18]

De Gaulle refused to receive Lacerda. But the remainder of his European tour, which lasted until June 16, was more successful than the stay in Paris. From West Germany, where he was received by President Heinrich Luebke, Lacerda went to London to speak with the prime minister and other high officials and to explain to the *Financial Times* that the Brazilian profit remittance bill would be revised "spectacularly." After a six-day stay in Portgual, where Lacerda was received by Salazar, the Lacerdas flew to the United States.

The Guanabara governor, speaking in excellent English to the hundreds of reporters who greeted him in New York, said that the Brazilian revolution was already understood in Europe. But not much of what he said at Kennedy Airport was carried by the press, leading Lacerda to feel that the United States had little interest in Brazil. Nevertheless, he made the best of his opportunities to present his message to influential lunch and dinner groups, and at one of them he described the suspension of Kubitschek's political rights as a "courageous step by Castello Branco." "How can a revolution punish under-

[16] Sandra Cavalcanti, interview, Rio de Janeiro, November 18, 1975.

[17] *O Estado de S. Paulo*, May 21, 1964; Abreu Sodré, letter to Viana, September 28, 1971, p. 13.

[18] Cavalcanti, interview, November 18, 1975.

lings and not the chief?" he asked.[19] When he spoke on the "Meet the Press" television program, he addressed an audience of millions.

Late in June, Lacerda told the Overseas Press Club in New York of his objections to a recent proposal made to the Brazilian Congress by Castello to require an absolute majority of the popular vote for election to the presidency. Soon the questions of American reporters and the cables from Rafael de Almeida Magalhães made it clear that Congress was seriously considering extending Castello's mandate.[20] Suddenly Lacerda announced that he would return to Brazil on July 2 and therefore was canceling a meeting scheduled with Assistant Secretary of State Thomas C. Mann.

2. Proposals for Electoral Reform (June–July, 1964)

Castello, while working on the electoral reform package that worried Lacerda, pointed out that the Institutional Act was a call for legislative decisions that would prevent demagogues and subversives from claiming exclusive possession of the flag of reforms.[1] During the life of the Institutional Act, scheduled to expire when Castello left office, projects submitted by the executive were to become laws if Congress reached no decisions within a time limit (thirty days were given to each house), and constitutional amendments proposed by the executive were to be made effective by absolute majority votes (instead of two-thirds votes) of the Senate and Chamber, each house voting on two occasions.

The fact that these rules would have a short life simply meant to Castello that he should keep the lawmakers busy. And he wanted to do this early, he said, so that the "sovereign" decisions of Congress would be reached in an atmosphere unaffected by the "carnival of pressures" and passions of the coming presidential election. In his letter to Colonel Ibiapina, Castello wrote: "I think the government of the Revolution should ask Congress to study all the political ideas that have been agitating Brazil for ten years."[2]

[19] *O Estado de S. Paulo*, June 18, 25, 30, 1964.

[20] Ibid., June 26, 1964; Lacerda, *Depoimento*, p. 319.

[1] HACB, *Discursos, 1964*, p. 62.

[2] *O Estado de S. Paulo*, July 1, 1964; HACB, letter to Hélio Ibiapina, June 25, 1964, File P1 (p. 5), CPDOC.

Some of the new administration's suggestions for electoral reform, such as the one giving political rights to noncommissioned military officers and another stipulating that the president and vice-president be elected on the same ticket, appeared likely to be approved. But doubt existed about the outcome of the proposal requiring an absolute majority in presidential elections and the proposal to give illiterates the right to vote (even if that franchise were limited to municipal elections, which was as far as the most liberal PSD congressmen would go).[3]

Congressman Oscar Correia, vice-leader of the UDN and a Lacerda supporter, felt that Castello was deserting the revolution and the UDN by proposing such things as votes for illiterates ("an absurdity") and agrarian reform. When he brought his list of complaints to Castello, the president merely said that he would introduce his reforms and that Correia was free to try to defeat them.[4]

On June 18, Castello discussed reforms at Alvorada Palace during lunch with UDN Congressmen Bilac Pinto (UDN president), Paulo Sarasate, and Pedro Aleixo (government leader), and in the afternoon he spoke with PSD leaders. To both groups he said that the administration's prosposals were the best that it could come up with and that no administration pressure would be exerted on their behalf. In the evening Castello's dinner guest was Senator Krieger, who agreed with the president about agrarian reform and disagreed about votes for illiterates.[5]

Castello, speaking to Krieger about the absolute majority proposal, said: "We must transform this proposition of our party into a constitutional precept." The UDN, which Castello was calling his party, had been demanding the absolute majority rule ever since its opponents had won the top national offices in 1950 and 1955 without gaining such a majority. But now the Lacerdistas, their eyes on the 1965 election, opposed the proposed requirement or argued that it should not become effective until 1970.[6]

Members of all parties, discussing what should be done under the

[3] American Embassy, Rio, cable to Secretary of State, June 24, 1964, NSFB, LBJ Library; *O Estado de S. Paulo*, June 20, 1964.

[4] Oscar Dias Correia, interview, Rio de Janeiro, September 24, 1975.

[5] *O Estado de S. Paulo*, June 19, 1964; Krieger, *Desde as Missões*, p. 180.

[6] *O Estado de S. Paulo*, July 4, 1964.

proposal if no presidential candidate received an absolute majority, appeared to accept the idea of a second election by Congress, with Castello recommending that the candidate most voted for in the popular election should be considered along with others who had not run, but that those who had been defeated at the polls should be ruled out.[7] Another complication resulted from the feeling that the Congress should be a Congress chosen at the time of the presidential election rather than a Congress reflecting bygone sentiments. Krieger, when dining with Castello, said that "the purpose of the absolute majority is to give Presidents a majority in Congress" and that a coincidence of congressional and presidential elections could be achieved in 1965 by abbreviating the term of Congress for one year, or in 1966 by extending Castello's mandate for one year. He added that the congressmen would not accept the first alternative and that the second would reflect "the highest interests of the Revolution."[8]

Castello told Krieger that in principle he opposed a one-year extension of his term because he had always fought against *continuismo*. But he said that he would submit to it because the change was designed to perfect the regime and would not give him a mandate that was longer than usual. At the beginning of July, when Castello discussed the political reforms with Krieger and Pedro Aleixo, he acquiesced again, saying that military leaders insisted on the extension.[9]

Those who saw the extension as an opportunity for stabilization before a disrupting presidential election included rivals of Lacerda. Governor Magalhães Pinto, who had been hoping to be the UDN standard bearer, spoke in favor of the extension for Castello. Amaral Peixoto, no friend of Lacerda, proposed a "stopgap mandate," with Congress voting that Castello or someone else serve for the additional year.[10]

But Castello soon had a change of heart about his own availability.

[7] Ibid., July 3, 1964.

[8] Krieger, *Desde as Missões*, p. 180. The words *revolution* and *revolutionary* were often used during this period in references to (1) the overthrow of Goulart, (2) "revolutionary war" by "subversives," and (3) the overall change from the past undertaken by the victors of the movement of March 31, 1964. For the sake of clarification (and following the practice of Castello Branco, Krieger, and others), a capital *R* will be used in the text when the words reflect the sense of (3). In the case of quotations, however, the words will be reproduced as they originally appeared.

[9] Ibid.

[10] *O Estado de S. Paulo*, May 27, July 4, 1964. Stopgap mandate: *mandato-tampão*.

After calling Senate and Chamber leaders to the formal, downstairs library of Alvorada Palace, he told them, in a tone of annoyance, that he would not accept an extension. Pedro Aleixo agreed with his position. Krieger, however, said that he would continue to work for the extension, which was now a matter for Congress to decide, and that Castello could accept or reject the decision of Congress.[11]

Krieger worked with success in the Senate. There Filinto Müller said that an extension of Castello's term was simpler than Amaral Peixoto's "stopgap mandate." The simpler version was drafted, as a subamendment, by Senator Afonso Arinos de Melo Franco, but due to the disfavor in which the former foreign minister was held by the "revolutionaries," it was signed by Senator João Agripino (UDN, Paraíba) and was recommended by him to the joint legislative commission that was studying the administration's proposals.[12]

In the meantime Castello let everyone know that he opposed an extension of his mandate. "The cemeteries," he was fond of remarking, "are full of the bones of irreplaceable persons."

3. Extension of Castello's Mandate (July, 1964)

Carlos Lacerda reached Rio on July 3 and lunched the next day at Laranjeiras Palace with the president. Castello praised the clarifications Lacerda had made abroad and impressed the governor so well, when discussing the administration's plans, that Lacerda, leaving the palace, took the Brazilian press to task for pessimistic reporting. "The Revolution," he told reporters, "has not yet reached the press, which is full of little old women."[1]

A few days later Lacerda announced that the absolute majority requirement in presidential elections was acceptable "neither now nor in 1970" and had been advocated by him in 1955 simply as a tactic to try to prevent Kubitschek's inauguration. Lacerda also opposed votes for illiterates ("humiliating to those who can read and write") and a post-

[11] Krieger, *Desde as Missões*, p. 181.

[12] *O Estado de S. Paulo*, July 9, 1964. Ernani Sátiro, interview, Rio de Janeiro, December 17, 1975. (Afonso Arinos de Melo Franco was much opposed to Lacerda's reaching the presidency.)

[1] *O Estado de S. Paulo*, July 5, 1964.

ponement of the presidential election (allowing time for opponents of the Revolution to reorganize).[2]

In Brasília, Lacerda presented his arguments during a heated debate with the UDN leadership at the residence of UDN President Bilac Pinto, a supporter of the extension of Castello's mandate. But despite Lacerda's efforts there and in the halls of Congress, the joint legislative commission recommended the proposed amendments on July 8. In Rio on July 9 an irritated Lacerda telegraphed Bilac Pinto to ask that a UDN convention be held soon to reaffirm his candidacy and to judge the conduct of UDN congressmen in the case of "the plot to extend mandates." The plot, Lacerda told the UDN president, was an act of cowardice for assisting opportunists and sinister adventurers who connived to rob the people of the Revolution. Attacking "Amaral Peixoto and his kind," Lacerda described the decision of the congressional commission as the beginning of "the counter-revolution in Congress."[3]

Bilac wrote to Lacerda to say that the governor's request for a UDN convention would be submitted to the party's national directorship. In his letter Bilac also defended the honor of the men of the UDN and declared that they would not be intimidated by "a type of charismatic leadership" that made "unjust attacks against their political conduct."[4]

In the meantime, advisers of Castello, including Ademar de Queiroz, tried to persuade him to withdraw his opposition to an extension of his mandate.[5] But Castello remained unmoved, and when he was accused of being stubborn, he denied the charge, explaining good-humoredly that the stubborn people were the people who opposed his view.

Castello asked Krieger to cease working for the extension, but the result was Krieger's resignation as government leader in the Senate, a resignation that Castello refused to accept.[6] Then, on July 13, three days before the first plenary votes on the amendments, Castello addressed a letter to Krieger stating that Krieger's work for the extension was the "legitimate and exclusive" work of a legislator, not the work of the government's leader. Repeating his own opposition, Castello said that an extension would be a disturbing factor that would not help perfect

[2] Ibid., July 9, 1964.

[3] Ibid., July 10, 11, 1964.

[4] Krieger, *Desde as Missões*, pp. 183–185.

[5] Ibid., p. 181.

[6] Ibid.

Brazilian political institutions and that could have unfavorable international repercussions.[7]

In Belo Horizonte on July 14, Governor Magalhães Pinto declared that he found no voice in military circles opposing extension. Costa e Silva, visiting Belo Horizonte, spoke publicly in favor of extension three times in one day. Lacerda followed the war minister to Belo Horizonte, and there he delivered a violent speech in which he warned that it was time "to think a little less about amending the constitution and a little more about amending the amenders." In a television program, Lacerda surprised listeners (especially those familiar with his statement in New York) by describing the suspension of Kubitschek's political rights as "an injustice" because Kubitschek had been refused the right of defense. Lacerda added that Bilac Pinto's recent letter was "incoherent." "I do not have to contest with anyone the leadership of the UDN, because I have it," he said.[8]

In Brasília the first roll calls on the electoral reform proposals began on the evening of July 16 and lasted until 5:00 A.M. the next morning. Ample majorities in both houses favored extending the franchise to the lower ranks of the military and adopting the absolute majority rule for presidential elections. Extension of the franchise to illiterates in municipal elections passed easily in the Senate and only just achieved the 205 necessary votes (absolute majority) in the Chamber of Deputies.[9]

At 3:30 A.M. senators began to vote on the João Agripino subamendment to extend Castello's term to March 15, 1967, and to assure future coincidence of presidential and congressional elections by reducing the presidential term from five to four years. The upper house adopted the proposal overwhelmingly, with all the UDN senators present (two were absent) voting in its favor.

In the Chamber, however, the succeeding roll call was dramatic. At 4:40 A.M., when the last *deputado*'s name had been called, the proposal had 203 votes, two short of the absolute majority, and opponents were shouting "close the voting." Although the president of Congress, Senator Auro de Moura Andrade, opposed the subamendment, he called

[7] Ibid., p. 182.

[8] *O Estado de S. Paulo*, July 15, 16, 17, 1964.

[9] Ibid., July 17, 1964.

for time to allow missing congressmen to appear and vote. Bedlam broke loose when a UDN congressman changed his vote from "no" to "yes." Then Krieger argued that 204 was a majority because two seats, formerly occupied by *cassados*, had not been filled. The issue was settled when a PSD congressman announced that an absent UDN colleague was coming to the Chamber to cast a favorable vote. Moura Andrade declared that the proposal had passed, 205–94, and that the second roll calls would take place during the following week.[10]

Lacerda described the vote as "incredible," "illegal," and "immoral" and said that Congress had transformed Castello into a "dictator, usurper, and king" against the president's own wishes. Accompanied by Falcão and Rafael de Almeida Magalhães, he lunched again at Laranjeiras Palace with Castello, who showed him a copy of his letter of July 13 to Krieger. Speaking to reporters after the meal, Lacerda criticized Krieger for not having been influenced by the letter and for not having made it public. In a new letter to Bilac Pinto, the governor described Castello as relying on the worst political advice and said that history would hold Bilac Pinto responsible for a tragic error.[11]

During the following week, sentiment for the extension of Castello's mandate increased so that on July 22 it carried easily (294–38 in the Chamber). On the other hand, the lower house this time rejected the partial enfranchisement of illiterates by a close vote.[12]

Castello, whose letter to Krieger was at last made public, spoke on the radio to say that his personal and political preference was to retire on January 31, 1966, but that, as he was faced with a "situation of fact" and did not want to desert the destiny of the Revolution, he would respect the decision of Congress. "In spite of my repeated objections," he said, "many politicians worked for the idea, with the resultant formation of a large favorable current of opinion."[13]

The American Embassy cabled Washington to say that the extension postponed a "probably disruptive presidential election campaign." The embassy admitted that one election postponement could "theoretically

[10] Ibid., July 18, 1964.

[11] Ibid., July 18, 19, 1964; American Embassy, Rio de Janeiro, cable to Washington, July 20, 1964, NSFB, LBJ Library.

[12] *O Estado de S. Paulo*, July 23, 1964.

[13] Ibid., July 25, 1964.

at least," lead to another, but it observed that "the United States should be reassured in this regard by Castello Branco's obvious determination to help . . . Brazilian democracy." Suggesting that Lacerda might have suffered a setback, the embassy added that "the question of whether Lacerda would be the best successor to Castello Branco is impossible to answer for the time being."[14]

About a week later, Gordon advised Washington of a "tantrum" of Lacerda, because at the end of July the governor released to the press letters containing his attacks on the federal government. In one of the letters Lacerda praised *Tribuna da Imprensa* publisher Hélio Fernandes for criticizing Castello's cabinet. In another letter, addressed to a Guanabara assemblyman, Lacerda wrote that the Revolution was negating itself with "the stupidity of 'reforms' that reform nothing" and had achieved only one objective: the defeat of his candidacy and the postponement of the election. He congratulated PSD President Amaral Peixoto and others for having "transformed the revolution into a wilted coup" that had become old and withered, "gnawed away by those who are ashamed of it."

Castello was asked by reporters whether he would confer any more with Lacerda. Replying stiffly, he said: "If it is necessary and in the interest of the government."[15]

4. Economic Measures (April–August, 1964)

Attacks against cabinet ministers, such as those made by Lacerda and Hélio Fernandes, were regarded by Castello Branco as attacks against the president. Loyal to the team he had chosen, Castello gave full authority to its members and assumed the responsibility for their handling of government matters.

In particular the president had to put up with denouncements of the architects of the economic and financial policies, Roberto Campos and Otávio Bulhões, and frequently these denouncements came from São Paulo. When Oscar Thompson was still agriculture minister, he per-

[14] American Embassy, Rio de Janeiro, cable to Washington, July 23, 1964, NSFB, LBJ Library.

[15] Ibid., July 31, 1964.

suaded Castello to receive a group of unhappy Paulista coffee growers. The president told the growers that he would call in Bulhões, who was in charge of the matter, but the growers irritated the president by telling him that Bulhões knew nothing about coffee. Castello, agreeable to having a logical discussion about specific points, insisted that Bulhões join them. Some of the Paulistas were so upset at this propect that they retaliated by speaking among themselves, in audible voices, about having no alternative but to return to their plantations and set fire to their coffee trees. Then the president, also in an audible voice, told an aide to jot down the names of his visitors so that he would know who were responsible in case the fires broke out. The visitors left.[1]

In May, 1964, the new administration made the annual crop prediction for the coffee year that begins on July 1. Forecasting a production of only nine million bags, it set a minimum price, the basis for Bank of Brazil loans to growers, at a level that was attractive enough to bring to market much coffee that had been stored in the past.[2]

Neither this step nor the first decisions about wages were anti-inflationary. With the wage pattern already established by the 100 percent minimum wage increase decreed in February, the Castello Branco administration granted a 110 percent increase for civil servants in July, and the private sector followed with increases of 80 to 90 percent.[3]

To try to prevent future wage increases from aggravating the inflation, the president revived the National Council on Wage Policy, appointing as its members the ministers of labor, finance, transport, industry, mines, and planning.[4] On July 14, Castello and the justice minister, together with this council, issued Decree 54,018 to regulate future wage increases within the government, government-controlled companies, and private companies having government concessions or subsidies. The increases, never to be given less than one year after any revision, were to be calculated on the basis of a formula established by Roberto Campos in accordance with the suggestion of economist Mário Henrique Simonsen.[5] It included three factors: (1) the average cost of living increase

[1] *O Globo*, March 26, 1978; Severo Gomes, interview, July 25, 1977.

[2] Dênio Nogueira, interview, Rio de Janeiro, December 20, 1977.

[3] Syvrud, *Foundations of Brazilian Economic Growth*, pp. 155, 157.

[4] *O Estado de S. Paulo*, August 27, 1964; see also Decree 54,018 (July 14, 1964), Article 1.

[5] Sebastião de Sant'Anna e Silva, memorandum, July 1979.

for the preceding twenty-four months, (2) the estimated productivity increase in the previous year, and (3) the "inflationary residual" (one-half the inflation rate projected by the government for the following twelve months). State and municipal governments were asked to cooperate with the new system.

The general disgust with the many strikes during the Goulart years encouraged legislators to pass, late in May, a new law restricting the legality of strikes. Illegal strikes were defined as those called for political purposes (not a new concept) and those called by workers of the federal or local governments or of government-controlled companies; strikes called to alter working conditions already established in contracts or by the Labor Justice system were also invalidated.[6] At Laranjeiras Palace, Castello signed the new law in the company of the labor minister and scores of labor leaders, many of whom had come to the fore thanks to the government's steps against leaders considered pro-Communist.

Like housing for workers, schooling for the workers' children was on Castello's mind. At the University of Ceará on June 23, he said that Brazil could not continue with over thirty million illiterates and needed 100,000 classrooms for the primary education of six million children. The government, he said, lacked funds and would propose a *salário-educação* law requiring payments by companies that did not already provide primary education for their workers' children.[7] The legislation, approved by Congress in August, became one of the chief stimulants to primary education.[8]

Many of the early reforms reflected Castello's vow to turn over to his successor a nation whose finances were in order.[9] Bulhões, seeking to balance the budget, concluded that the low rate of government receipts was not attributable merely to inadequate taxation. Because of the currency devaluation, firms had found it worthwhile to postpone making income tax and social security payments. In an effective reform to counteract this practice, the Finance Ministry introduced its first mone-

[6] *O Estado de S. Paulo*, June 1, 1964.

[7] HACB, *Discursos, 1964*, pp. 133–139; *O Estado de S. Paulo*, July 27, August 26, 1964.

[8] Raimundo Moniz de Aragão, interview, Rio de Janeiro, December 16, 1975.

[9] *O Estado de S. Paulo*, April 30, 1964.

tary correction factor, increasing the amounts due on a scale corresponding to the currency depreciation.[10]

Quickly monetary correction was used to reestablish use of the public debt. The administration's law project of May 11, authorizing the issuance of 700 billion cruzeiros in 6 percent treasury bonds, stipulated that the face value would be subject to monetary correction, and it required that the bonds be bought with the 3 percent of payrolls that firms had to set aside, according to legislation of 1958, for possible dismissal payments to workers. The law project also required firms to revalue their assets and pay a tax of 5 percent (reduced from past legislation) on the value increase, but it waived this tax for firms that would invest twice the amount of the tax in the new treasury bonds.[11] The adminisration's proposals became law on July 16, 1964.

At about the time the electoral reforms were adopted, Congress overwhelmingly approved the administration's proposal that the incomes of journalists and professors, along with royalties received by authors, no longer be tax-exempt.[12] The proposal to increase the already heavy consumption tax by 30 percent was regarded less favorably by the lawmakers. The vote took place on the night of August 14, just before the expiration of the thirty-day period in which the Chamber could act. After Amaral Peixoto declared that the PSD would support the bill, Ademar de Barros and Congressman Arnaldo Cerdeira brought the PSP in line and the bill escaped defeat.[13]

Other economic measures were aimed at distortions that had resulted from the fondness of earlier administrations to deal artificially with inflation. These measures, such as the authorization of a badly needed 85 percent telephone rate increase, sent living costs higher. When the government eliminated the subsidies for petroleum, wheat, and paper in order to conserve 260 billion cruzeiros annually in foreign exchange, Bulhões tried to calm those who feared that the end of the petroleum subsidies would increase living costs by 50 percent. His calculations, he said, showed that the increase would be 9 percent.[14]

[10] Gouveia de Bulhões, interview, December 30, 1974.

[11] Ibid.; Ministério do Planejameto, Documentos EPEA (No. 3), *O Programa de Ação e as Reformas de Base*, I, 45–55 (Law 4,357, of July 16, 1964); *O Estado de S. Paulo*, May 12, 13, 27, 1964.

[12] *O Estado de S. Paulo*, May 31, July 15, 1964.

[13] Ibid., August 14, 15, 1964. Consumption tax: *imposto de consumo*.

[14] Ibid., May 12, 29, 1964.

The finance minister took a dim view of price controls.[15] But, in accordance with the government's program of applying gradualism to corrections, he agreed that the prices of some products should continue to be controlled by SUNAB, the price control organ. Gradualism was also adopted in relaxing rent controls, held responsible for "the practically complete paralyzation of housing construction."[16]

The new administration's hopes of remedying this situation through its low-cost housing plans were shared by Congress. Together with numerous amendments, it passed the administration's bill late in July. The bill, which featured monetary correction in its financial provisions, looked to savings associations, federal and local government organs, government-controlled companies, and, especially, the National Housing Bank to increase construction. The new bank, subordinated to the Planning Ministry, was to have an initial capital of one billion cruzeiros and was to receive company contributions amounting to 1 percent of their payrolls.[17] Furthermore, the bank was authorized to borrow up to one trillion cruzeiros in Brazil and up to $300 million abroad.

Sandra Cavalcanti confirmed her appointment to head the new bank and said that "the approval of this plan is the first great social reform produced by the Revolution."[18]

5. Economic Measures Affecting Foreigners (June–October, 1964)

On June 30, Lincoln Gordon, just back from financial discussions in Washington, was invited to Laranjeiras Palace. For fifteen minutes the ambassador replied to Castello's questions about civil rights legislation and political developments in the United States, and then the president called in Bulhões, Roberto Campos, and Leitão da Cunha for a further discussion about the ambassador's recent trip. Gordon reported concern in Washington that the Brazilian inflation was not being attacked with sufficient vigor, notably in the area of wages, and he stressed

[15] Ibid., May 12, 1964.

[16] Ibid., May 12, August 14 (editorial), 1964. SUNAB: Superintendência Nacional do Abastecimento.

[17] Ibid., June 20, 1964; Ministério de Planejamento, Documentos EPEA (No. 3), *O Programa de Ação e as Reformas de Base*, II, 31.

[18] *O Estado de S. Paulo*, July 24, 1964.

the interest of the United States business community in "improved profit remittance legislation."[1]

In Brasília, Roberto Campos discussed with congressmen the need to liberalize the profit remittance law promulgated by Goulart. Armed with figures, he argued that the current legislation had cost Brazilian workers one hundred thousand jobs and that the liberal legislation in effect from 1954 to 1961 had not only stimulated capital inflow but also resulted in an average annual exodus of profits lower than that during the preceding period of restrictive legislation. He declared that "to err is human but to remain in error is diabolic."[2]

Despite Campos' reasoning, the administration's proposal was defeated by an 8–7 vote in the Chamber's Economic Commission. But it fared better in the Finance and Justice commissions. By a 152–146 vote in the full Chamber on July 15, a slightly modified bill won a victory made possible by the *cassações* of "nationalist" congressmen early in April. The Senate then added twelve amendments, eight of which were subsequently approved by the Chamber. The final product, which substituted a graduated remittance tax for the limitation on profit remittances, was pronounced generally satisfactory by Castello. He employed only one partial veto when promulgating the new legislation late in August.[3]

Like the profit remittance question, the negotiations between the American and Foreign Power Company (AMFORP) and Brazil had been hotly debated for some time. Following Goulart's proposal to President Kennedy for the "peaceful nationalization" of foreign utilities "with just payments," studies by commissions had persuaded Goulart's finance minister in 1963 to authorize Ambassador Roberto Campos to sign a memorandum calling for Brazil to buy the AMFORP utilities for $135 million. But the down payment of $10 million, due on July 1, 1963, had not been made in the face of attacks on the "deal," particularly by Lacerda (who argued that "scrap iron" was being purchased) and by Congressman Leonel Brizola of the "radical Left." After Cas-

[1] American Embassy, Rio de Janeiro, cable to Washington, July 6, 1964, NSFB, LBJ Library.

[2] Ministério de Planejamento e Coordenação Econômica, *Programa de Ação Econômica do Governo, 1964–1966*, p. 145; *O Estado de S. Paulo*, June 17, 1964 .

[3] *O Estado de S. Paulo*, July 4, 16, August 13, September 1, 1964. A presidential partial veto to legislation had been permitted since 1926; a two-thirds congressional vote was needed to defeat a partial veto.

tello became president, the United States said that its $50 million program loan, arranged during Gordon's visit to Washington in June, depended on a Brazilian settlement with AMFORP.[4]

Late in June, Castello called for an investigation by an interministerial commission made up of the ministers of finance, planning, foreign affairs, and mines. A subcommission, headed by Eletrobrás President Otávio Marcondes Ferraz, then carried out a study and recommended execution of the 1963 agreement subject to the approval of Congress and a new independent verification of the value of the assets. A previous requirement that 75 percent of the purchase price be invested in Brazil was to be replaced by the requirement that AMFORP, using installment payments from Brazil, loan $100.25 million to Eletrobrás. The subcommission mentioned the acute energy supply problems that would arise from a prolonged impasse. And the interministerial commission, transmitting the findings to Castello, spoke of the "need to reestablish Brazil's credit in international financial circles."[5]

After the National Security Council approved the findings unanimously, Castello sent them to Congress. There Roberto Campos, Marcondes Ferraz, and Mines and Energy Minister Thibau found a determined opponent in Senator João Agripino, a former mines and energy minister. When Agripino spoke about "scrap iron," Campos said that the term might be applicable to 25 percent of the properties, and Thibau pointed out that the fifteen-year average age of the properties was about the same as that of the government's Paulo Afonso hydroelectric works in the northeast.[6]

Outside Brasília, Agripino was supported by Governors Magalhães Pinto and Lacerda. The governor of Guanabara, on a speaking tour to condemn the government's economic policy and Golberi's "misinformation service," said that the "high price" for the AMFORP properties was to be paid to keep the position of Roberto Campos "coherent" in the eyes of his "bosses" in the American companies. Eletrobrás President Marcondes Ferraz, upset at the failure of UDN congressmen to defend him against Lacerda's "personal attacks," wrote a dramatic note

[4] Department of State, Washington, cables to American Embassy, Rio de Janeiro, June 19, August 7, 1964, NSFB, LBJ Library.

[5] *Revista Brasileira de Política Internacional* (of the Instituto Brasileiro de Relações Internacionais), June 1965 (Ano VIII, No. 30), pp. 216, 220, 226, 287.

[6] *O Estado de S. Paulo*, August 22, September 5, 13, 15, 1964.

disassociating himself from the party to which he had belonged since its beginning.[7]

In Congress the legislative joint commission for studying the AMFORP matter rejected substitute projects submitted by Senators Agripino and Ermírio de Morais. Just before the commission approved the administration's proposal, the PTB withdrew its members, and it used the same tactic in the plenary of the Chamber. When, after several days, the attendance reached a quorum on October 7, the AMFORP purchase was approved by a vote of 187 to 91. Following a rapid confirmation in the Senate, the PTB announced that, despite its defeat, it had shown by its obstruction that the government could count on an active opposition.[8]

Mines and Energy Minister Thibau, although busy with the AMFORP case, found time in June to take up mining policy with the president and Congress. The administration was eager to stimulate the expansion of exports from Brazil's immense iron ore reserves, but presently it found that it had inherited a thorny problem because of the iron ore export intentions of the Cleveland-based Hanna Mining Company. Hanna, with properties in Minas Gerais, was under heavy attack in Brazil by "nationalists," leftists, and the government-controlled iron export company, Companhia Vale do Rio Doce (CVRD).

For a while everything went smoothly. On June 26 the president issued a policy decree that emphasized the importance of increasing mining production and encouraged private enterprise to bring this about.[9] The Senate confirmed that the constitutition allowed foreigners to engage in mining, and the administration took steps to straighten out the mining tax situation, complicated by Magalhães Pinto's recently imposed state tax. In September, Congress ruled in favor of a single federally imposed tax to be distributed between the federal and local governments.[10]

[7] Ibid., September 2, 17, 1964; American Embassy, Rio de Janeiro, cable to Washington, August 19, 1964, NSFB, LBJ Library.

[8] *O Estado de S. Paulo*, September 22, 24, 26, October 1, 6, 7, 8, 1964.

[9] *Diário Oficial* (Section 1, Part 1), July 2, 1964, p. 5766: E.M. 391–64 of June 26, 1964.

[10] Resolution 16 of 1964, dated June 26, 1964, in *Diário do Congresso Nacional*, June 27, 1964; see also Castello Branco Decree 54,042, of June 23, 1964, canceling Goulart Decree 53,115, of December 10, 1963, that had given the government broad authority to close down mining activities; Minas Gerais, *Diário do Executivo*, June 27, 1964 (Decree 7,696); *O Estado de S. Paulo*, June 1, September 30, 1964.

A storm broke out when two port authorities disagreed about whether Hanna should be allowed to construct a private ocean ore embarcation terminal in Sepetiba Bay west of Rio. Those who objected were now joined by Companhia Siderúrgica da Guanabara (COSIGUA), which Lacerda hoped would construct a state steel plant and iron ore export terminal, also in Sepetiba Bay. While Lacerda and *Tribuna da Imprensa* launched a particularly bitter campaign against Hanna, Roberto Campos, and Thibau, the president appointed an interministerial commission to define in detail the norms that all large-scale iron ore export projects, foreign and domestic, should obey and thus settle a question that had aroused emotion since 1919—generating, as Roberto Campos observed, "more heat than light." Castello, keenly interested in the subject, participated in the work of the commission and contributed ideas.[11] The commission, made up of Thibau, Távora, Bulhões, Faraco, Roberto Campos, and Geisel, did not complete its work until December, 1964.

6. Foreign Loans (June, 1964–early 1965)

When the Castello Branco administration took office, Brazil's indebtedness abroad amounted to $3.3 billion. More serious than the total amount were the large payments due in 1964 and 1965 ($1,038 million and $436 million, respectively) and the lack of foreign exchange with which to make any payments. By March 31, 1964, Brazil's foreign creditors, poorly impressed with Goulart's negotiators and financial program, were ready to deny a rescheduling of the debts, and Goulart appeared to be on the verge of declaring a unilateral moratorium on payments, which would have made new credits impossible.[1]

Measures taken by Bulhões to balance the budget, establish a realistic rate for the cruzeiro (fostering exports), and end the subsidies on imported petroleum, wheat, and paper helped Trajano Pupo Neto, who was chosen by Bulhões to negotiate in June with private creditors in New York. There Pupo Neto, president of Anderson Clayton of Brazil, explained the economic meaning of the Brazilian Revolution to bankers and to General Electric, Westinghouse, and other suppliers.[2]

[11] Mauro Thibau, interview, Rio de Janeiro, June 6, 1972.

[1] Ministério do Planejamento e Coordenação Econômica, *Programa de Ação Econômica do Govêrno, 1964–1966*, p. 128; Viana Filho, *O Governo Castelo Branco*, p. 132.

[2] Pupo Neto, interview, November 15, 1975.

Meanwhile, in Paris, diplomat José Sette Câmara met with creditor nations of the "Hague Club" (the United States, Japan, and Western European countries). In the presence of observers from the World Bank and the International Monetary Fund (IMF), Sette Câmara on June 30 and July 1 negotiated the first important breakthrough: a rescheduling that reduced the debts due in 1964 and 1965 by $149.9 million.[3] Later in the year the private creditors in the United States extended the due dates on $56 million, and the IMF rescheduled $106 million in fund "repurchases" that were to be made by Brazil.[4]

The government's 1964–1966 economic program, issued by the Planning Ministry, was to be useful as a guide to Brazil and a basis for negotiating new loans abroad. On August 6, Castello presented a draft of the plan (Economic Action Plan of the Government, abbreviated PAEG) to the cabinet and asked for suggestions. In the following week the planning and finance ministers explained to congressmen how the plan would reduce the inflation rate to 10 percent in 1966 while giving Brazil that year an increase in the gross national product of approximately 6 percent (compared with 1.5 percent in 1963).[5]

As Gordon was preparing to visit Washington for more financial discussions, he made an appointment to see Castello at Planalto Palace on October 14. The president reacted "with vigor" to Gordon's negative references to the heavy government subsidies for the railroads, merchant marine, and postal service. He had, Castello said, made it clear to Juarez Távora and others that he was determined to hold the line on wages in the government-run companies. When the ambassador emphasized the importance of the IMF as a possible provider of resources and also as a "green light" for the international financial world, Castello said that he appreciated this and had instructed Roberto Campos to do his best to secure a new IMF standby credit.[6]

[3] Ministério do Planejamento e Coordenação Econômica, *Programa de Ação Econômica do Govêrno, 1964–1966*, pp. 129–130. The "Hague Club" was named after the group of creditor nations that had first met in 1961 to reschedule Brazil's debts.

[4] Ibid., p. 130; Brazilian Embassy, Washington, D.C., *Survey of the Brazilian Economy, 1966*, p. 281.

[5] *O Estado de S. Paulo*, August 7, 1964; Ministério do Planejamento e Coordenação Econômica, *Programa de Ação Econômica do Govêrno, 1964–1966*, pp. 18–35.

[6] Lincoln Gordon, cable to Secretary of State, Washington, October 15, 1964, NSFB, LBJ Library.

In Washington, Gordon argued that the program (balance of payments) loan to Brazil for the 1965 fiscal year (ending June 30) should be $150 million, compared with the $50 million authorized at the last minute for the previous fiscal year, and that Brazil should receive also from USAID another $100 million in specific project loans. When Roberto Campos reached Washington in the same month to present Brazil's case to the Alliance for Progress, Gordon told reporters that Campos would be well received because United States fears about "revolutionary excesses" had practically disappeared.[7]

The World Bank, which had refused to grant a loan to Brazil since 1959, sent a twenty-two-man team to Brazil in October. After the IMF and USAID decided to send missions to join the World Bank mission, Campos said that "November will be a busy month."[8]

A part of the task of Campos and Bulhões was to deal with visiting economists who maintained that Brazil's anti-inflation program should be a drastic "shock treatment." IMF technicians, in particular, argued that a "gradualistic treatment" in Brazil would have to extend beyond an endurable period.[9] Campos and Bulhões insisted that a "shock treatment" would have lamentable consequences: the paralysis of development along with widespread unemployeml and bankruptcies. As the IMF technicians remained unmoved, Bulhões lost his habitual composure and called for a break in the negotiations with them.[10]

A break would have given the Brazilian administration some badly needed popular support, but Castello Branco felt that the national interests would best be served if the break could be avoided. In the hope that the United States, the IMF's most influential member, might gain a better understanding of the Brazilian position, he decided on a review of the situation with Lincoln Gordon.[11] Thus, the ambassador was invited to join Castello, Bulhões, and Campos at a dinner meeting at Alvorada Palace on November 14. About the evening Gordon has written:

[7] Robert M. Sayre, memorandum to McGeorge Bundy, The White House, October 23, 1964, NSFB, LBJ Library; *O Estado de S. Paulo*, October 20, 1964.

[8] *O Estado de S. Paulo*, October 20, 1964.

[9] Gordon, interview, June 11, 1975; Viana Filho, *O Governo Castelo Branco*, p. 137.

[10] Sant'Anna e Silva, memorandum, June 1979.

[11] Ibid.; idem, interview, Rio de Janeiro, June 30, 1979.

Castello Branco set forth the alternatives in his own words, and then developed a chain of logical reasoning from each one, weighing the possible moves and countermoves at each branch in the chain like a master chess player. He invited comments from each of us at various points, and welcomed pertinent factual information as he went along. The decision was not an easy one. He held the entire pattern of arguments on the subordinate issues firmly in his mind throughout several hours of deliberation. When he came to his conclusion, he knew the risks involved but he also had a full grasp of the reasoning in support of his decision. The contrast with Goulart, who had also discussed major policy issues with me from time to time, was as night and day.[12]

The IMF accepted Brazil's "gradualistic treatment" of inflation, and in January, 1965, it granted a new one-year $125 million standby credit to Brazil. The World Bank again became a lender to Brazil, putting up $79.5 million for two power projects.[13] As for the U.S. government, it accepted Gordon's recommendation of $150 million for the new program loan and set capital project loans at $70 million. Comparison for fiscal years (ending June 30) are shown below:

United States Resources Made Available to Brazil[14]
(Millions of dollars and dollar equivalents)

	1963	1964	1965
AID program loans	26	50	150
AID project loans	36	115	70
AID development grants	24	14	15
Food for Peace (Public Law 480)	73	81	97
U.S. Treasury loans	25	—	53
Export-Import Bank loans	34	—	6
Social Progress Trust Fund	6	3	7
	224	263	398

[12] Gordon, "Recollections of President Castello Branco," p. 12.

[13] Brazilian Embassy, Washington, D.C., *Survey of the Brazilian Economy, 1966*, p. 281; Department of State, Briefing Book for Fulbright Mission to Brazil, August 1965, NSFB, LBJ Library.

[14] Background paper, January 18, 1967, for Washington visit of Costa e Silva, January 26–27, 1967, NSFB, LBJ Library.

AID Director David E. Bell, after visiting Brazil in December, 1964, expressed his view in a memorandum to President Johnson:

I was very favorably impressed with the seriousness of purpose of President Castello Branco and his principal associates. They face real problems of political support over the next several months, as their anti-inflationary program squeezes businessmen and workers. Castello Branco looked to me, however, like a man who would hold to his chosen course against severe opposition, and if he can last out for a few more months, his program—plus the major help he is getting from us, the IMF and others—can begin to yield visible gains for everyone in the country.[15]

7. International Relations: The Tonkin Gulf Incident (April–August, 1964)

After Fidel Castro said, "We are not going to plead for relations with gorillas of any species," Castello authorized Leitão da Cunha to break relations with Cuba. Itamarati's note to the press, dated May 13, declared that the Cuban exportation of subversive doctrines to free nations of the continent, and the activities of Cuban agents in Brazil, violated the nonintervention doctrine of the charter of the Organization of American States (OAS).[1] In Washington in July, at the Ninth Consultive Meeting of the Foreign Ministers of the OAS, the Brazilian delegation listened sympathetically while the Venezuelan delegation told of subversion stimulated in their nation by Castro's government. Then Brazil supported a resolution, which was passed by a 15–3 vote, calling for sanctions against Cuba.[2]

Castello, in a confidential memorandum to guide Itamarati, wrote that the OAS, unfortunately, came to life only during crises, and the crises were "almost always characterized by the direct or indirect in-

[15] David E. Bell, memorandum to President Lyndon B. Johnson (hereafter cited LBJ), Washington, December 22, 1964, Papers of LBJ, EX CO 32, Bechuanaland, Box 16, LBJ Library.

[1] *O Estado de S. Paulo*, April 21, 1964; Brazilian Foreign Ministry, press release, Brasília, May 13, 1964, in *Revista Brasileira de Política Internacional*, June 1964 (Ano VII, No. 26), pp. 338–339.

[2] *O Estado de S. Paulo*, July 24, 26, 1964. While Bolivia abstained, Mexico, Chile, and Uruguay voted against the motion.

terest of the United States." Citing criticisms heaped on the OAS, he noted that the foreign ministers of Argentina and Uruguay, recently in Brazil, were so disgusted with the stagnation of the OAS that they were considering setting up a new organization.[3] In his foreign policy speech of June 31, Castello expressed the determination of Brazil to strengthen the OAS.

In this speech, delivered to future diplomats who were graduating at the Rio Branco Institute, the president described "independence" as an objective of foreign policy but not "a method of operation" and pointed out that "in the existing bipolar power struggle," the preservation of independence presupposed acceptance of a certain degree of interdependence, be it military, economic, or political. "We have," he said, "made a fundamental choice": cultural and political adherence to the Western democratic system. "Subject to that general condition, our independence will be expressed in the careful scrutiny of each specific problem strictly in terms of our national interest."

The president told the future diplomats that an objective of foreign policy should be the channeling of resources to Brazil's economic and social development, and he praised the Alliance for Progress. Pointing to foreign policy inconsistencies stemming from recent "explosions of nationalism," Castello pictured Brazil as having protested internationally against the inadequacy of foreign aid and capital investment while accepting domestic attitudes that were hostile to foreign capital. Nationalism, he added, had become deformed to the point of opting in favor of socialist systems, "whose possibilities of commerce with us and capacity to invest in Latin America were overestimated."[4]

A few days after delivering this address, Castello received an urgent telex message from President Johnson about attacks by the North Vietnamese on American vessels in the Gulf of Tonkin. The message was confirmed in Johnson's confidential letter of August 4 to Castello describing the "deliberate attacks which have been made by communist Vietnamese torpedo boats on American vessels operating on the high seas." "As I am sure you will agree," Johnson wrote, "these attacks could not go unanswered. The response we are making is, however, limited and fitting." Johnson expressed his conviction that Castello

[3] HACB, "Política Internacional," document sent to Itamarati in mid-1964.
[4] HACB, *Discursos, 1964*, pp. 107–117.

shared fully "our deep concern over these deliberate acts of aggression" and that Castello's government would "give appropriate expression to this concern in the Security Council."[5]

"Your Excellency," Castello wrote in reply, "is right in believing that I share your deep concern in view of this attack. I consider this resort to force contrary to the provisions of the Charter of the United Nations and I deem it to justify fully the exercise of the right of self-defense, as was carried out by the United States of America." Castello added that he had given instructions to Brazil's representative on the Security Council to act in accordance with these views and to express "our hope that the authorities of North Vietnam will modify their attitude" and that all governments would work to prevent the increase of tensions in Southeast Asia.[6]

This letter brought a reply from Johnson that was suggested by Assistant Secretary of State Thomas C. Mann and prepared by the State Department and the White House staff. McGeorge Bundy, presenting the letter to Johnson for his signature, admitted that it was "a little bit fancy in style," and longer than Johnson liked, but he explained to the president of the United States that Brazilians "are a people who measure interest by length."[7]

Signed by Johnson on August 25, the letter conveyed his thanks for Castello's "message of solidarity" and pointed out that "we found in the Cuban missile crisis in 1962, and again in the Foreign Ministers' meeting at Washington in July 1964, that our adversaries take heed when the free world stands solidly together and refuses to be intimidated by wanton aggression or threats of aggression. I especially welcome the renewed strength which Brazil brings to the cause of peace and allied unity."

Johnson's letter referred to the efforts of Castello's government to reverse the serious economic deterioration that had confronted Castello

[5] LBJ, letter to HACB, The White House, August 4, 1964, File O1, Part II (p. 23), PVCB.

[6] HACB, letter to LBJ, August 11, 1964, Papers of LBJ, President's Staff File, Head of State Correspondence, Brazil, Vol. 1, Presidential Correspondence, LBJ Library; *O Estado de S. Paulo*, September 6, 1964.

[7] McGeorge Bundy, memorandum to LBJ, The White House, August 24, 1964, Papers of LBJ, President's Staff File, Head of State Correspondence, Brazil, Vol. 1, Presidential Correspondence, LBJ Library.

when he took office and went on to assure him that, as he pressed forward on constructive programs for the welfare of Brazil, the United States stood ready "to give its sincere support through the Alliance for Progress."[8]

8. The de Gaulle Visit (October, 1964)

In Paris on September 11 the seventy-four–year–old Charles de Gaulle, who had recently undergone a difficult prostate operation, discussed his forthcoming Brazilian visit with the new Brazilian ambassador, Antônio Mendes Vianna. The visit, the first to Brazil by a French head of state, was to be the final stop on de Gaulle's "grand tour" of South America—a faintly disguised anti-United States ploy about which Castello was rather skeptical.[1]

The French president told the ambassador, a rotund bon vivant, that France hoped to extend credits and set up a joint nuclear energy study group, and then he expressed his wish to have as little contact as possible with Lacerda. Mendes Vianna wrote Castello to say that their problem about Lacerda was magnified by de Gaulle's "very uncommon notion of grandeur."[2]

In Colombia, early on his one-month tour, de Gaulle developed the theme of *latinité* as a bond between the French and the South Americans.[3] While he continued down the west coast of the continent, part of the time on the cruiser *Colbert,* arrangements were made to receive him in Brazil. Six thousand men were assigned to protect him in Rio, and sixty rooms in the Glória Hotel were set aside for foreign journalists. Castello made plans to reside at quarters of the Bank of Brazil while in Brasília so that de Gaulle could occupy Alvorada Palace.[4] And in Rio, Castello moved to the presidential suite of the Copacabana Palace Hotel ten days before de Gaulle's arrival to allow Laranjeiras Palace

[8] LBJ, letter to HACB, The White House, August 25, 1964, File O1, Part II (pp. 24v and 25), PVCB.

[1] Gordon, interview, June 11, 1975.

[2] Antônio Mendes Vianna, letter to HACB, Rome, September 14, 1964, File O2 (p. 48), PVCB.

[3] Gordon, interview, June 11, 1975.

[4] *Jornal do Brasil,* October 10, 1964; PVCB, interview, November 9, 1974.

to be refurbished in time for the visitor to spend the last night of his visit there.[5]

Ademar de Barros, speaking to the press after a conference with Castello at the Copacabana Palace Hotel, said that Lacerda ought to receive de Gaulle. But Lacerda issued a note saying that the plans did not require his presence because de Gaulle was not scheduled to visit Rio—which, Lacerda added, was equivalent to going to France without visiting Paris. Governor Magalhães Pinto complained of not having been informed by the Foreign Ministry of the de Gaulle visit.[6]

In Argentina, de Gaulle's appearance delighted the Peronistas, who filled the air with balloons acclaiming "de Gaulle, Perón, and a Third Position."[7] From Uruguay, where de Gaulle's presence evoked less passion, the *Colbert* brought the French statesman to the Rio docks on the morning of October 13. There Castello Branco, surrounded by dignitaries and troops, welcomed President and Madame de Gaulle while amused spectators commented on the striking difference between the physical stature of the two presidents.

During the drive of the presidents in an open Rolls Royce down throng-lined Rio Branco Avenue, French journalists scuffled with Brazilian marines. Placed in a bus, the journalists screamed, "Brézil naziste, Brésil naziste!"[8]

De Gaulle laid a wreath at the Monument to the Unknown Soldier (in a simple and solemn ceremony planned by Castello), and then he and his wife flew to Brasília with Castello and Nieta in the presidential Viscount. During the lunch on the plane the French president asked why Vargas had committed suicide. Castello replied that "Vargas loved power too much and was not agreeable to turning it over to his successor."[9]

That evening at a magnificent banquet at Planalto Palace, de Gaulle declared Brazil to be prepared, politically, economically, and socially, for a new and exemplary era, and he invited Brazil "to act truly in con-

[5] Paulo Henrique de Paranaguá, "Visita do Presidente de Gaulle," File O1 (p. 17), PVCB.

[6] *Jornal do Brasil*, October 4, 13, 1964.

[7] Ibid., October 4, 7, 1964.

[8] Ibid., October 14, 1964.

[9] Viana Filho, *O Governo Castelo Branco*, p. 175.

cert with France" to help the world find equilibrium and peace.[10] On the next day de Gaulle spoke to students at the University of Brasília. Like most of his speeches, this one was memorized, and Luís Viana Filho observed that the French president, speaking for over an hour, did not miss a single word from the prepared written version.[11]

By this time the front pages of the Brazilian press told of the "insults" hurled at Brazil in Paris newspaper accounts of de Gaulle's visit. *Paris Presse, Le Figaro,* and *L'Aurore,* commenting on Lacerda's absence, likened him to a prima donna in a provincial theater who would allow no one else on the stage. *Paris Presse* reported that Lacerda, in defense of United States' interests, had incited the army to throw out Quadros and Goulart, but that now a new *putsch* could be expected, this time by military men "unhappy with Castello Branco's ultraconservative policy." *Paris Presse* also stated that de Gaulle, on reaching Rio, had found "a continent in corruption," and it concluded that "Brazil, more than ever, is a sick giant."[12]

De Gaulle, chatting with Castello about "South American dictatorships," learned from the Brazilian president that the problem arose because it was easy to start dictatorships and difficult to end them.[13] Roberto Campos noted the aggressiveness "that was almost impertinent" with which de Gaulle asked: "Senhor Marechal, I have always wanted to know what a South American dictator is and why history is so full of them." Castello replied: "Mr. President, a South American dictator is a man, not necessarily a military man like you and me, who finds it extremely agreeable to hold on to power and extremely disagreeable to let it go. I shall let go of power on March 15, 1967. And you, what plans do you have?"[14]

When the conversation turned to foreign policy, de Gaulle argued that the world could not remain at the mercy of two dueling powers and that a "third force," made up of many countries, would command the respect of the United States and the Soviet Union and thus avoid

[10] *Jornal do Brasil*, October 14, 1964.

[11] Viana Filho, *O Governo Castelo Branco*, p. 177.

[12] *Jornal do Brasil*, October 13, 1964; *O Estado de S. Paulo*, October 14, 1964.

[13] Paranaguá, "Visita do Presidente de Gaulle," File O1 (p. 17), PVCB.

[14] Roberto Campos, "O Caso do Carisma," *O Globo*, November 18, 1970, reproduced in Viana Filho, *O Governo Castelo Branco*, p. 176.

a general catastrophe.[15] Castello said that Brazil, while also condemning bellicosity, was firmly a part of the Pan American system and was not interested in "third force" or non-aligned positions.[16] Although Castello's lengthy defense of this position left de Gaulle unconvinced, the visitor concluded that among all the presidents he had met on his tour, Castello alone was a statesman.[17]

After de Gaulle left Brasília for São Paulo, Castello received Gordon. Castello agreed with the ambassador that the popular response to de Gaulle was more to a great historical figure than to someone offering new ideas and prospects. But the president admitted that the "third force" idea found some responsiveness in Brazilian quarters that disliked the United States and his own government, and he added that while he expected few substantive results from de Gaulle's visit, it nevertheless provided an opportunity for France to learn something of Brazilian realities.[18]

From São Paulo, de Gaulle flew to Rio on the evening of October 15 to give his farewell banquet on the *Colbert*. There Castello stressed the importance of Brazil and France joining forces to help stabilize the coffee market, and he praised his visitor for having conquered everyone by his cordiality.[19] After a night at Laranjeiras Palace, de Gaulle and his party took an Air France flight to Paris.

Castello, as famous for having no neck as de Gaulle was for his stature, would sometimes remark, in a tone serious enough to have some believe him, that he had made a gift of a Volkswagen to de Gaulle. Then Castello would add that in return de Gaulle had presented him with a scarf.[20]

Although Castello received an invitation to visit France, he declined, as he had in the case of similar invitations, with the explanation that his duties in Brazil were too demanding to permit foreign visits. What

[15] Lincoln Gordon, cable to Secretary of State, October 15, 1964, NSFB, LBJ Library.

[16] Ibid; idem, cable to Secretary of State, October 10, 1964.

[17] Paulo Guerra, interview, Brasília, November 11, 1975.

[18] Gordon, cable to Secretary of State, October 15, 1964.

[19] *O Estado de S. Paulo*, October 16, 1964; Viana Filho, *O Governo Castelo Branco*, p. 178.

[20] Osvaldo G. Aranha, interview, Rio de Janeiro, September 25, 1975.

he hoped, as he advised Gordon and Walters, was that President Johnson would visit Brazil.[21]

9. End of the General Commission of Investigations (October, 1964)

As the end of his first six months in office approached, Castello looked forward to the expiration of Article 7 of the Institutional Act, which required him to dismiss those who were shown, in "summary investigations," to be guilty of subversion or corruption.[1] The president was not opposed to the punishment of the guilty, but he welcomed a return to the use of the regular justice system.

Colonel Ibiapina, addressing a new letter of complaint to the president in September, accused him of living with corrupt politicians and abandoning the military. In reply, Castello wrote: "I am not simply a president of purges and imprisonments."[2]

Marshal Estevão Taurino de Rezende Neto, head of the General Commission of Investigations (CGI), felt that the Revolution was being frustrated by the Castello Branco government because some of the most corrupt politicians remained at liberty and were even considered "men of the Revolution."[3] Late in July, when the marshal's son, a professor at the Catholic University of Pernambuco, was jailed for distributing an antigovernment manifesto to his economics students, Taurino defended his son, calling him "an idealist, like his father." Castello called for the marshal, and as he did not come at once from Recife, the president let it be known that he had dismissed him. When the marshal reported to Castello on August 7, he was accused of having spoken to the press against the government and of failure to attend the presidential summons.[4]

To replace Taurino, Castello turned to retired Admiral Paulo Bosísio. Bosísio, admired by Cordeiro de Farias, was prodded from his pleasant retirement in São Paulo by telephone calls from Cordeiro and

[21] Gordon, cables to Secretary of State, October 12 and 15, 1964.

[1] Ferdinando de Carvalho, interview, Rio de Janeiro, October 30, 1975.

[2] HACB, letter to Hélio Ibiapina, September 10, 1964, File P1 (p. 7), CPDOC.

[3] *O Estado de S. Paulo*, August 12, 1964.

[4] Ibid.; Ronald M. Schneider, *The Political System of Brazil*, p. 138.

Geisel. While Bosísio began to study thousands of investigations that had already been carried out, Castello named General Hugo Panasco Alvim, an FEB artillery veteran, to take charge of military-police inquiries (IPM's) that were still under way.[5]

Castello made it clear to Bosísio that he had to complete his work in time to allow the last presidential punishment decrees to be signed by October 9. Helped by two auditors, the admiral worked day and night on a pile of papers that grew because he decided to receive written defense statements from the accused. He considered his work that of a "moderator" and was determined not to recommend punishments unless he had concrete evidence. Nevertheless, he forwarded many lists, usually bearing hundreds of names, and on the afternoon of October 9 he went to Laranjeiras Palace with a final list of 730 that included the names of Professor Darci Ribeiro, who had headed Goulart's Gabinete Civil, and Gilberto Crockett de Sá, labor affairs adviser of Goulart. Bosísio suggested that although the CGI had come to an end, the IPM's should continue.[6]

The president, well impressed with Bosísio, followed all his recommendations. As a result of the work of the admiral and his predecessor, retirements were forced on a total of 4,454 individuals (1,697 civilians and 2,757 members of the military) during the six-month life of Article 7 of the Institutional Act.[7]

The lists did not include the names of Chamber of Deputies President Ranieri Mazzilli and some other prominent legislators who were the victims of leaks to the press by investigators who accused them of having made improper use of fiscal agents for electoral campaigns and, "to the disgrace and shame of the nation, for economic advantage."[8] Shortly before Bosísio submitted his last list, a lieutenant colonel, at work on an IPM, leaked a report that Moura Andrade, president of the Senate and Congress, had been involved in corruption.[9] While Castello cautioned the lieutenant colonel to stick to concrete facts and calmed the PSD by saying he understood that Moura Andrade was not "directly

[5] Paulo Bosísio, interview, São Paulo, November 8, 1975; *O Estado de S. Paulo*, August 7, 1964.

[6] Bosísio, interview, November 8, 1975; *Jornal do Brasil*, October 11, 1964.

[7] *Jornal do Brasil* and *O Estado de S. Paulo*, October 11, 1964.

[8] *O Estado de S. Paulo*, October 9, 1964.

[9] Ibid., October 20, 1964.

involved" in the irregularities, Moura Andrade, who had been abroad, rushed back to Brazil to defend his name. Justice Minister Milton Campos told the press that the remaining papers of the CGI would be delivered to the regular courts of justice, which, he said, would handle the cases involving Mazzilli, Moura Andrade, and other well-known politicians.[10]

Castello, chatting with Vernon Walters on the evening of October 11, said that he was "amazed at the depth of corruption, graft, and tax evasion" that had come to light in the inquiries and that he intended to eradicate, or make as dangerous as possible, such practices in Brazilian public life.[11]

Although Paulo Bosísio, like Taurino de Rezende before him, observed that corruption had been more widespread than subversion, the IPM's that were continued focused on subversion by looking into the PCB (Brazilian Communist Party), the ISEB (Institute of Advanced Brazilian Studies), and the UNE (National Union of Students). With General Panasco Alvim's retirement from heading the IPM's late in October, direction of the remaining inquiries was transferred to the military ministers.[12]

During the first six months of the Castello Branco administration, the step that affected the nation's future most profoundly was the extension by Congress of the president's term. The extension added 13½ months to the 21½-month life of an inflation-fighting team that was still in the process of gaining experience, much of it discouraging. And the extension postponed a presidential election campaign that might well have promoted demagoguery and culminated in October, 1965, with the election of a candidate pledged to oppose the hard steps that the inflation fighters were finding necessary.

The amount of suffering that lay ahead for the Brazilian people, if the work of past inflation makers was to be undone, seems not to have been appreciated by David E. Bell. Nor had it been appreciated by the Brazilian government. A year after enacting the limited decree of July, 1964, to restrain wage increases, the administration would have

[10] Ibid., October 28, 1964.

[11] Gordon, cable to Washington, October 12, 1964, NSFB, LBJ Library.

[12] *O Estado de S. Paulo*, November 4, 1964.

to ask Congress to extend its scope so that the most painful program of all could be undertaken.

From a political point of view, Carlos Lacerda was right when he attacked the government's financial and economic policies. It was a position he would have taken even if his ambitions had not been so rudely shattered by the extension of Castello's mandate. The hard-liners may have been the first to show signs of giving future trouble to the administration, but the popular governor of Guanabara was not far behind them.

Agrarian Reform, Iron Ore, and Naval Aviation

(October, 1964–March, 1965)

Through well-directed propaganda, a climate of real "nationalistic" terror has been built up [in Brazil]. . . . Now, freed from delusions . . . , it behooves us to reach decisions considering only and exclusively the supreme interests of Brazil. And that is what the government is going to do.

1. Relaxed and Confident

AFTER six months in office, Castello Branco was relaxed, in good health and spirits. He was helped by his ability to go to sleep quickly at any time, which allowed him to nap during airplane flights, and by his adherence to a frugal diet imposed by doctors who felt that he had shown a tendency to overeat.[1]

Even when the president spoke to Walters about the depth of corruption being unearthed, he revealed himself full of confidence and optimism. He expressed particular pleasure with the work being done in Washington by Juraci Magalhães, whom he described as "a great Brazilian," and with the conduct of Costa e Silva, whose command changes, he said, had greatly strengthened the ability of the armed forces to maintain order and stability.[2]

Far from showing worry during critical moments, Castello exhibited coolness. Navy Captain Euclides Quandt de Oliveira, who worked in the Gabinete Militar early in Castello's administration, noted that "a peculiarity about Castello Branco was that the bigger the problem the calmer he was." He found pleasure in careful decision making and welcomed challenges that had vast implications. During moments that were critical for the government, anxious associates were amazed to find the president almost exuberant. Some of them likened him to a bird of prey that enjoyed the tempest.[3]

[1] Américo Soverchi Mourão, report (typewritten, 3 pages, no title), Brasília, April 2, 1975.

[2] Gordon, cable to Washington, October 12, 1964, NSFB, LBJ Library.

[3] Euclides Quandt de Oliveira, interview, Brasília, October 21, 1975; Moscardo de Sousa, interview, October 27, 1975.

Castello's confidence, stubbornness in sticking to chosen courses, and aloofness (no embrace for soccer star Pelé, just a handshake) were not the result of personal vanity. Early in his regime he scoffed when office assistants sought to have him imitate de Gaulle, for while he admired the French president, he rejected the idea of the indispensable man and thought that de Gaulle was too proud.[4] When Castello gathered with a few congressional leaders, or three or four members of his team, for a debate, he did not seek to impose arguments and showed no sign of believing that his own opinions should be considered meritorious because they were those of the head of state. He was usually less interested in speaking than in hearing the opinions of the others. He would often prod ("going down a person's throat," Manuel Pio Corrêa has said) in an effort to get full and frank ideas, disliking anything to remain under the carpet. And he would make an apparently weaker member of the group feel that he had a worthwhile contribution to offer.[5] Castello particularly enjoyed his discussions with intellectuals in government, such as the so-called *bacharéis* among UDN congressmen, had little esteem for "yes-men," and was considerably influenced by the arguments he heard. Assistants did not hesitate to show him that part of his correspondence which was faultfinding.[6]

Insisting on frankness from his assistants, the president was frank with them. With a report on his desk that needed his attention, and an assistant at his side who asked him if there was anything further he needed, the president replied: "What I need now is to have you favor me with your absence."[7]

Castello is said to have "conquered Congress less by military intimidation than by persuasion, moral authority, and public spirit."[8] One day after congressmen had overridden one of his vetoes, he surprised those who had led the opposition by inviting them to lunch at Alvorada Palace and then added to their surprise by discussing everything except the veto.[9]

[4] Moscardo de Sousa, interview, October 23, 1975.

[5] Ibid.; Manuel Pio Corrêa, interview, Rio de Janeiro, December 19, 1977.

[6] Moscardo de Sousa, interviews, October 23, 27, 1975. *Bacharéis*: degree holders.

[7] "A fórmula de Castello," *Jornal do Brasil*, February 3, 1976.

[8] Trigueiro, "Humberto Castelo Branco," p. 9; see also Mem de Sá, "Castelo e os Parlamentares."

[9] Raimundo de Brito, paper prepared for Luís Viana Filho, p. 7.

The president dined frequently at the homes of congressmen, making the best possible impression on their wives,[10] and he included many congressmen and their wives on the invitation lists of approximately thirty names that were issued about twice weekly for the movies shown in the basement theater of Alvorada Palace. Although UDN Congressman Aliomar Baleeiro wondered aloud why no French wine was served, the guests at the movies were offered only fruit juices and other soft drinks before and after the showings. The films, chosen by Castello, were apt to be musicals of a past era. Occasionally Castello left early, but in the case of *Dr. Zhivago*, he stayed to see part of a second showing.[11]

Although Castello did not smoke or care for whiskey, he did not force others to adhere to his habits in his presence, and occasionally he made gifts of whiskey to those who enjoyed it. After he served fruit juice (*maracujá*) at a ceremony on October 28, the Day of Public Servants, Roberto Campos remarked jokingly that "we public servants deserve Scotch; why not observe the day by employing international standards?" Scotch was brought in. And when, during the late stages of a particularly long meeting, mineral water was made available, the president saw to it that whiskey was served to Roberto Campos and Daniel Krieger.[12]

In the mornings in Brasília, Castello was apt to leave Alvorada Palace for Planalto Palace shortly after 8:00 A.M. Sometimes, before being driven to his official place of work, he made a stop at the residence of his daughter and son-in-law in order to spend time with their children. His devotion to the six-year-old João Paulo Diniz, said to be his favorite, was reported extensively in the press.[13]

By the time Castello had been in office for six months, it was well known that he attended most of the good theatrical performances in

[10] Theódulo de Albuquerque, interview, Brasília, October 24, 1975.

[11] Osvaldo Trigueiro, interview, Brasília, October 23, 1975; Moscardo de Sousa, interview, October 23, 1975; Vidal Pessoa, interview, December 16, 1975; Sátiro interview, December 17, 1975; Mendes de Morais, interview, December 20, 1975; Severo Gomes, interview, July 25, 1977; Baleeiro, "Recordações do Presidente H. Castelo Branco," p. 35.

[12] Moscardo de Sousa, interview, October 23, 1975; Daniel Krieger, interview, Brasília, October 21, 1975.

[13] Mercadante, "Este É o Humberto."

Rio. Occasionally he was accompanied by friends, such as Health Minister and Sra. Raimundo de Brito (at whose elegant Rio home he sometimes attended lunches), but more frequently he went alone after giving an aide the money to buy two adjoining seats, one of which went unoccupied so that the president, using an aisle seat, could avoid unwanted conversation. He liked to surprise performers by dropping in backstage to offer them his congratulations. Interested in the welfare of actors, he persuaded Raimundo de Brito to have a small hospital built for them.[14]

The president enjoyed discussing literature with José Olympio, Rachel de Queiroz, and others and was happy when his Laranjeiras schedule allowed him to invite authors for lunch. If he found himself unexpectedly free to have a lunch guest in Rio, he might phone Austregésilo de Ataíde, president of the Brazilian Academy of Letters; Austregésilo lived in the nearby Cosme Velho district and could reach the palace quickly.

Austregésilo discussed literature and answered the president's inquiries about public opinion. A subject that Austregésilo tactfully avoided during these lunches was one that he had brought up early in the administration: a request that the government give the Academy of Letters a piece of government property that adjoined the old Academy building (Petit Trianon) in downtown Rio. "Do you think I am a crazy man?" Castello had asked, adding that the precedent set by such a donation would give him trouble with all sorts of organizations and and that Austregésilo was the one who was out of his mind. It had become the president's custom to wave a finger in a circular motion near his head when he met Austregésilo at public ceremonies and to repeat: "Do you think I am crazy?"[15]

2. Lacerda, Presidential Candidate (July–November, 1964)

Carlos Lacerda, tired of the governorship, let it be known in July,

[14] Brito, interview, December 22, 1974; idem, paper prepared for Viana Filho, pp. 3–4; Trigueiro, "Humberto Castelo Branco," p. 17; Diniz, interview, December 13, 1975; Mendes de Morais, interview, December 20, 1975; Bosísio, interview, November 8, 1975; "Castello, uma vida em revisão há 10 anos," *Jornal do Brasil*, July 18, 1977.

[15] Austregésilo de Ataíde, interview, Rio de Janeiro, August 5, 1977.

1964, that he would be happy to serve in Castello's cabinet as minister of finance, justice, or education. Arguing that a cabinet reform was necessary, he belittled those in office. Speaking of Otávio Bulhões, he asked: "Do you think that a man who for sixty years was always a clerk can be a cabinet minister?" He declared that Roberto Campos had served every government and had "sunk them all."[1]

Armando Falcão and Abreu Sodré felt that it might be useful to have a man of Lacerda's popularity replace Education Minister Flávio Suplici de Lacerda, whose conviction that students should stick to their studies was irritating political-minded student leaders.[2] "Brazilian youth," Abreu Sodré writes, was so "intoxicated by the ideas of the Left" that only a man of Lacerda's ability to communicate "could win that area." Lacerda, pleased with the idea, agreed with advisers who recommended that he should behave discreetly as education minister and not compete for popularity at Castello's side in public.[3] He told the press that he had not broken with the government.[4]

Early in August, after Castello said that Lacerda "is not a factor of intranquility," Lacerda declared that "all of us, even those who disagree with the president, recognize" the value of having the government in the hands of "a man who is honest and who, besides, is a worker."[5] Following this exchange of compliments, Castello told Falcão that he would be happy to receive the governor, but he added that he had no desire to discuss his cabinet with him.[6]

Lacerda, overwhelmingly supported in his presidential ambition by the less prominent members of the UDN, continued to push for an early nominating convention despite the arguments of UDN leaders that the extension of Castello's mandate gave no urgency to a convention. Lacerda feared some unfavorable maneuver. When Magalhães Pinto asserted that all existing parties should be abolished so that the regime could be "remodeled," General Olímpio Mourão Filho, a La-

[1] Viana Filho, *O Governo Castelo Branco*, p. 115.

[2] Ibid., pp. 114, 122.

[3] Abreu Sodré, letter to Viana Filho, September 28, 1971, pp. 15, 16.

[4] *O Estado de S. Paulo*, August 1, 1964.

[5] Ibid., August 9, 11, 1964.

[6] Diary of Paulo Sarasate, entry for August 12, 1964, cited in Viana Filho, *O Governo Castelo Branco*, p. 115.

cerda admirer and Military Tribunal member, dismissed the suggestion of the Minas governor as "nothing more than a maneuver."[7]

Castello decided that the government of the Revolution should show its appreciation of Lacerda by appointing him to head the Brazilian delegation to the OAS. Vice-governor Rafael de Almeida Magalhães, consulted by Castello, said that Lacerda would consider the idea a maneuver and an attempt to get him out of Brazil, and he added that if the president insisted on paying tribute in this way, the United Nations would be more fitting than the OAS. Early in October, when Lacerda learned from Falcão that Castello wanted him to head the delegation to the United Nations, his reaction was as the vice-governor had expected.[8]

Lacerda traveled much, working successfully for the early UDN convention. The state directorships, replying to telegrams from Bilac Pinto, supported the idea, and so the convention was scheduled for November 7 and 8. Magalhães Pinto said he would not attend. Mourão Filho, more enthusiastic, proclaimed that "a Carlos Lacerda is born once a century."[9]

Castello, unhappy with the precipitation of the presidential campaign, called Lacerda to his second-floor office in Laranjeiras Palace and told him that his vigorous voice was needed to defend Brazil in the United Nations but that it should be the voice of all Brazil, not that of a candidate. Lacerda observed that the United Nations was filled with presidential candidates, including his "dear friend, Adlai Stevenson."[10]

The question of the UN mission was left pending until after the UDN convention reached its decision, and in the meantime Lacerda campaigned in the north. Back in Rio, he wrote Castello to say that "our revolution is placing excessive hope in laws" and to advise against "the simple formation of new parties" out of the old ones. When he called on Castello at Planalto Palace early in November, Castello expressed the hope that the UDN would demonstrate understanding for the government's economic-financial policy. The candidate replied that the party

[7] Cláudio Lacerda Paiva, interview, Rio de Janeiro, December 16, 1977; Abreu Sodré, letter to Viana Filho, September 28, 1971, p. 14; *O Estado de S. Paulo*, August 1, September 20, October 1, 1964.

[8] Almeida Magalhães, interview, December 21, 1977.

[9] *O Estado de S. Paulo*, October 11, 20, 25, November 6, 1964.

[10] Baleeiro, "Recordações do Presidente H. Castelo Branco," p. 17; Carlos Lacerda, interview, Rio de Janeiro, September 23, 1975; Lacerda, *Depoimento*, pp. 323–324.

could not present that policy in a convincing way to the public unless it had a role in developing it.[11]

"When people speak badly of me," Lacerda confessed to Castello during one of their talks, "I can't eat, or drink, or sleep." The president said that his own reaction was different: "When they speak badly of me, I eat and drink, and I sleep very well—especially when that speaking is done by you."[12]

The UDN delegates, meeting in a spacious São Paulo auditorium on November 7, chose pro-Lacerda Congressman Ernani Sátiro as chairman, and on the eighth they enthusiastically acclaimed Lacerda the UDN candidate for president. Then the Guanabara governor entered the delirious convention hall and, after an embrace by Bilac Pinto, delivered his acceptance speech. The habitual attacker of General Golberi warned against members of the presidential "entourage" who sought to separate the president from personalities who could link the president with the "revolutionary masses," and Lacerda insisted that the government could get popular backing if it would "free itself from the notion that to repair the nation is an unpopular idea." He spoke against excessive taxation, lest it cause a deflationary crisis, and called for "a policy of fair wages." "The people," he declared, "must not be starved in order to save the currency."[13]

Victoriously Lacerda rode in the Trem da Esperança (Train of Hope) to Rio, speaking to crowds at stations along the way. At Laranjeiras Palace he called on Castello and left a letter to advise that, as his candidacy had just been confirmed, the president should feel free to withdraw the UN appointment.[14]

Castello said that he would think about the matter, and Lacerda sped to New York to be the guest of the *Reader's Digest* at a lunch to mark the publication of Clarence W. Hall's article, "The Country That Saved Itself." After his return to Brazil he received Castello's decision about the UN appointment in a letter dated November 22. Noting Lacerda's nomination by the UDN and the resulting "impropriety" of confirming

[11] Carlos Lacerda, letters to HACB, Rio de Janeiro, October 26, 28, 1964, File N4 (pp. 2, 3), CPDOC; *O Estado de S. Paulo*, November 5, 1964.

[12] Mercadante, "Este É o Humberto."

[13] *O Estado de S. Paulo*, November 10, 1964.

[14] Ibid., November 11, 1964; Lacerda, letter to HACB, Rio de Janeiro, November 9, 1964, File N4 (p. 5), CPDOC.

his UN assignment, Castello expressed his profound regret at being unable to name Lacerda, "one of the greatest revolutionary leaders."[15] Instead, Castello named Foreign Minister Leitão da Cunha.

3. Agrarian Reform (November, 1964)

The administration's ideas for agrarian reform grew out of Castello Branco's early conversations with Roberto Campos, during which the president called for a gradual, flexible solution that would show respect for property ownership, avoid *minifúndio* (excessively small properties), and combat unproductive *latifúndio* (large properties).[1] While Campos, assisted by engineer Paulo de Assis Ribeiro, economist Mário Henrique Simonsen, and lawyers Bulhões Pedreira and Luís Gonzaga do Nascimento Silva, worked on agrarian reform, the administration sought to remedy the existing agricultural underproduction by other measures, such as the elimination of price controls on foods, the use of minimum prices, and the establishment of exchange rates favorable for exports.[2]

These measures and agrarian reform were studied in July at a meeting of state agriculture secretaries organized by Magalhães Pinto and the new minister of agriculture, Professor Hugo de Almeida Leme. The meeting, held in Viçosa, Minas Gerais, produced a Declaration of Principles in which the participants called expropriation an "indispensable instrument" for dealing with insufficiently utilized properties.[3]

Opponents of agrarian reform, particularly numerous in the UDN of Minas and São Paulo, expressed fear lest expropriations create *minifúndio*, and they had reservations about Campos' proposal for progressive taxation of large unused holdings. In contrast to Campos, who argued that urban industry could not, and need not, absorb rural workers, Congressman Antônio Godinho (UDN, São Paulo), said that social tension was the result of excessive rural manpower and that it should

[15] HACB, letter to Carlos Lacerda, Brasília, November 22, 1964, File N4 (p. 5), CPDOC.

[1] Viana Filho, *O Governo Castelo Branco*, p. 278.

[2] Ibid.; Syvrud, *Foundations of Brazilian Economic Growth*, p. 229; Hugo Leme, quoted in *O Estado de S. Paulo*, April 24, 1964.

[3] *O Estado de S. Paulo*, August 1, 7, 15, 1964.

be reduced. Congressman Herbert Levy of São Paulo, a former president of the UDN, pointed out that rural property owners had decisively backed the anti-Goulart movement, and he warned against provoking them.[4]

Less upset than the UDN were the PTB, which had supported agrarian reform in the Goulart days, and the PSD, which wished to avoid a reactionary image.[5] PSD legislators, led by Amaral Peixoto, submitted suggestions that were considered in August, along with those from the Viçosa meeting, by an interministerial commission headed by engineer Paulo de Assis Ribeiro, a Planning Ministry expert on agrarian reform.[6] Castello himself presided at meetings of technicians that resulted in a preliminary draft of a pair of legislative proposals: (1) a constitutional amendment to allow that expropriations be paid for by bonds subject to full monetary correction and (2) a land statute that would be complementary to the amendment and deal also, as Campos had suggested, with colonization, assistance to farmers, and "model municipalities."[7]

Castello, who had originally hoped to submit the administration's agrarian reform proposals to Congress in June, now planned to do so on October 1. But his meetings with legislative leaders on September 30 led him to revise his timetable again. Bilac Pinto, assisted in his studies by economist Antônio Delfim Neto and Bank of Brazil executive Severo Gomes, both Paulistas, seemed ready to combat the government on the floor of Congress. Castello therefore spent about six hours in a continuous exchange of arguments with the UDN president. Although Bilac withdrew most of his objections to the constitutional amendent, he continued strongly opposed to a tax whose purpose was nonfiscal, being designed to bring about a "forced redistribution of property."[8]

[4] Ibid., June 28, September 29, October 4, 1964; Ministério do Planejamento e Coordenação Econômica, *Programa de Ação Econômica do Govêrno, 1964–1966*, p. 105; Viana Filho, *O Governo Castelo Branco*, p. 279.

[5] Viana Filho, *O Governo Castelo Branco*, p. 279; HACB, *Entrevistas, 1964–1965*, p. 25 (interview of October 30, 1964).

[6] *O Estado de S. Paulo*, September 3, 1964.

[7] Krieger, *Desde as Missões*, p. 189; Eudes de Souza Leão Pinto, interview, Rio de Janeiro, December 2, 1966; Vera Jaccoud and Antônio Encarnação, interview, Rio de Janeiro, December 14, 1966.

[8] *Jornal do Brasil*, October 1, 2, 1964; *O Estado de S. Paulo*, October 2, 1964.

During October, Herbert Levy said it was inconceivable that the land tax should be applied unless the government first carried out a complete census of all properties, and he warned against technocrats who lacked practical experience and "identification with the objectives of the Revolution." Lacerda assailed the "utopians" in the cabinet who wanted to use agrarian reform to carry out their "more or less vague dreams."[9] Roberto Campos, accustomed to such attacks, had already said on television that he could not understand why the possession of theoretical knowledge ("the crystallization of practice") should be considered "an illness" and had explained that the economies of Germany and Italy had been restored by Professors Erhard and Bernardi, both accused of being theoreticians.[10]

While Castello continued to meet with legislative leaders, Magalhães Pinto told the press that the administration's land statute would succeed only if the executive functions were carried out by the states. In a long letter to Castello, the Minas governor argued that the taxes should be collected by the states, and he maintained that the suggested coefficients of tax progression were difficult to understand and that the projected Instituto Brasileiro de Reforma Agrária (IBRA) would be too powerful.[11]

Finally, on October 19, the president called Daniel Krieger, Pedro Aleixo, and Peracchi Barcelos (PSD, Rio Grande do Sul) to advise that the administration's proposal was about to be sent to Congress.[12] The proposal established progressive land taxes that were much lower than those originally contemplated, thus allowing Bilac Pinto to support it, "the objectionable nails having been removed."[13] The proposal stipulated that the collection of these taxes would be made by the states, which were to keep 20 percent and distribute 80 percent to the municipalities. Furthermore, the proposal included the thorough census of landholdings that Levy insisted was necessary, and it called for the use

[9] *O Estado de S. Paulo*, October 4, 20, 1964.

[10] Ibid., August 11, 1964.

[11] Ibid., October 11, 1964; *Jornal do Brasil*, October 11, 1964; José de Magalhães Pinto, letter to HACB, October 17, 1964, File N3, CPDOC.

[12] *O Estado de S. Paulo*, October 20, 1964.

[13] Olavo Bilac Pinto, interview, Brasília, October 21, 1975.

of government bonds, instead of cash, only in the case of expropriations of large properties.[14]

Although Levy said that he saw no need for a constitutional amendment, the administration's proposed amendment was warmly received by most of the legislators during the two roll calls. In the meantime the land statute was presented to Congress with a presidential message that mentioned Brazil's commitment to be guided by an Alliance for Progress clause calling for the "modification of the structures and unfair systems of landownership and use."[15] UDN Congressman Raimundo Padilha worked effectively for the administration, and on November 26, just within the thirty-day deadline imposed by Castello, Congress voted the Aurélio Viana Land Statute, which followed the main lines of the administration's proposal. To carry out the census and execute most of the law's provisions, it set up IBRA, directly subordinate to the presidency, and it also set up the Instituto Nacional de Desenvolvimento Agrário (INDA), a new organ of the Agriculture Ministry, to improve living conditions in the rural areas.[16]

IBRA, headed by Paulo de Assis Ribeiro, was soon criticized for getting off to a slow start.[17] But the problems were enormous, not the least being the census and evaluations of about four million private landholdings. The lengthy census forms were to provide, for each region and major activity, four coefficients for establishing the taxes, which were to increase from 25 percent of the total tax in the second year to 100 percent in the fifth year. The coefficients were land utilization, economic efficiency, social conditions, and agricultural yields.[18]

[14] Ministério de Planejamento e Coordenação Econômica, *O Programa de Ação e as Reformas de Base*, II, 123–130.

[15] *O Estado de S. Paulo*, October 27, 30, November 7, 1964.

[16] Ibid., November 13, 19, 1964; Law 4,503 of November 30, 1964; see also Eudes de Souza Leão Pinto, *Brazilian Statement at FAO's World Conference on Agrarian Reform, Rome, June 20–July 2, 1966*, and INDA, *INDA's Invitation to the Church for a New Role.* Instituto Nacional de Desenvolvimento Agrário: National Institute of Agrarian Development.

[17] Viana Filho, *O Governo Castelo Branco*, p. 284.

[18] Souza Leão Pinto, interview, December 2, 1966; Jaccoud and Encarnação, interview, December 14, 1966; the coefficients mentioned here are those given in William R. Cline, *Economic Consequences of a Land Reform in Brazil*, p. 6; for further discussion, see Armin K. Ludwig and Harry W. Taylor, *Brazil's New Agrarian Reform.*

IBRA, responsible also for supervising contracts between landowners and about 1.5 million leaseholders, set up four areas in Brazil where it hoped to demonstrate that it could better conditions. In one of the areas, in the northeast, it expropriated a twenty-thousand-hectare sugar property, paying bonds for the land and cash for the sugar mill and other improvements, leaving the former owner well pleased.[19]

4. The Iron Ore Decision (December 22, 1964)

Castello received long letters from Governors Lacerda and Magalhães Pinto expressing opposition to private ore-loading ocean terminals, which Hanna and ICOMINAS (a Brazilian private company) were seeking permission to construct in Sepetiba Bay. Magalhães Pinto, in his letters of October 16 and 29, advocated a single port under government control and asked the president to prevent Hanna from obtaining any new mining concessions. "The people and government of Minas," he wrote, "watch, with melancholy and an increasing sensation of frustration, the gratuitous transfer of their riches to groups that are entirely alien to their interest."[1] He annoyed Castello by writing that "certainly" the president had no "direct or proper understanding" of the matter.[2]

On November 15 the press published a long letter to Castello in which the president of the government-controlled iron ore export company, CVRD, reiterated Magalhães Pinto's fear that a private terminal for Hanna would affect iron ore prices adversely.[3] *Tribuna da Imprensa*, which had described Roberto Campos as trying to perpetuate the "scandal of the century" because he had belonged in 1960 to Consultec, a firm advising "sordid Hanna," wrote in November that "in any civilized nation" Roberto Campos "would by this time have been fired."[4]

[19] Jaccoud and Encarnação, interview, December 14, 1966; Cline, *Economic Consequences of a Land Reform in Brazil*, p. 7.

[1] Magalhães Pinto, letters to HACB, October 16, 29, 1964, File N3 (pp. 1, 3), CPDOC; the letter of October 16, 1964, was published in *Correio da Manhã*, November 15, 1964; see also Lacerda, letter to HACB, September 29, 1964, File N4 (p. 1), CPDOC.

[2] Magalhães Pinto, letter to HACB, October 16, 1964; Viana Filho, *O Governo Castelo Branco*, p. 165.

[3] "Vale do Rio Doce É contra a Concessão," *Correio da Manhã*, November 15, 1964.

[4] *Tribuna da Imprensa,* August 24, 25, 27, November 4, 1964.

The president replied in a major speech delivered on November 17 in Vitória, Espírito Santo, where CVRD loaded its vessels. He said that the government's investigations showed that a monopoly for CVRD would reduce the flexibility needed to compete for iron ore markets. Declaring that the government would not stand in the way of private ocean loading terminals, he sought to calm those who feared that some exporter might hurt CVRD; exporters using Sepetiba Bay, he said, would have their shipments limited to the volume contracted with the Central do Brasil Railroad and their sales supervised by government agencies so that price cutting would not prevail.

Castello spoke harshly about those who, he said, sought to impede Brazil's development by "beating the drums" about *nacionalismo* and *entreguismo*. His language was strong: "Through well-directed propaganda, a climate of real 'nationalistic' terror has been built up. People who do not follow the primer of the barkers of this propaganda are immediately crushed with the debasing label of treason. . . . Now, freed from delusions maliciously placed in the way of thoughts and actions of Brazilians, it behooves us to reach decisions considering only and exclusively the supreme interests of Brazil. And that is what this government is going to do."[5]

Following the president's speech, most of the leading newspapers took positions in opposition to a loading terminal for Hanna. *O Estado de S. Paulo*, was an exception. *Tribuna da Imprensa* directed some of its fire against the mines minister because in 1960 Thibau had been subcontracted by Consultec to evaluate hydroelectric plants being sold by Hanna to Brazilians. Thibau and Campos, their patriotism under attack, sued *Tribuna* for libel.

Lacerda, writing to Castello on November 28, said that the "protection of Hanna's interests" by two cabinet ministers "is a crime against the national interest," and he added that the government's economic policy was "leading to a national and international disaster."[6] Speaking to the press on November 30, he said that "we did not make the Revolution so that Sr. Roberto Campos could hand the national industry over to foreign groups." When he spoke that evening on a radio-televi-

[5] HACB, *Discursos, 1964*, pp. 189–193.

[6] Lacerda, letter to HACB, November 28, 1964, File N4 (p. 7), CPDOC.

sion program, he said that he would resume his journalistic collaboration with *Tribuna da Imprensa*.[7]

Castello wrote Lacerda on December 3. In a reference to credit policy, said to be promoting denationalization, Castello pointed out that the government was reducing its expenses to release funds for productive activities and that it had successfully negotiated to have a part of international loans used for the purchase of equipment from Brazilian industry.

Over a month ago, the president wrote, he had investigated the charges brought against Roberto Campos and Mauro Thibau, learning that Thibau, "like any professional," simply made an appraisal, while Campos, out of government in 1960, had participated in a study about iron ore, "having previously ascertained the government's intentions in that respect and having informed it of Hanna's intentions." After explaining the makeup of the Interministerial Commission, "presided over by me," Castello wrote that "the governor's accusation goes beyond the two ministers and squarely hits other ministers and the president of the Republic. I believe, Sr. Governador, that we too have the fiber and public spirit for attending the national interests."

Castello added that he deeply regretted Lacerda's decision to join the campaign of *Tribuna da Imprensa.* "I express," he said, "my profound sorrow at losing the help of one of the most authentic and historic revolutionaries, and, at the same time, at gaining an opponent."[8]

Júlio de Mesquita Filho, director of *O Estado de S. Paulo*, and Roberto de Abreu Sodré rushed to Rio in a special plane on December 4 to speak with Lacerda about his relations with the president.[9] The governor, after conferring with them for three hours, signed a letter to Castello that was taken to Laranjeiras Palace by Mesquita Filho on the morning of the fifth. In it Lacerda said that he had never wanted the "divergence" to be anything personal or something that might endanger the Revolution. His divergence, Lacerda wrote, was motivated by no interest other than Castello's success, "which is the success of us all." After assuring Castello that the decisions about everything to which

[7] *Correio da Manhã*, December 1, 1964; *Brazil Herald*, December 2, 1964; Lacerda's articles in *Tribuna da Imprensa*, December 2 and 3 have the titles "Em Defesa da Revolução" and "A Revolução ou a Hanna."

[8] HACB, letter to Lacerda, December 3, 1964, File N4 (p. 8), CPDOC.

[9] *O Estado de S. Paulo*, December 6, 1964.

Lacerda had alluded remained in the president's hands, Lacerda asked Castello to receive his words "as a sign of my friendship and my confidence in your integrity."[10]

Castello read the letter and told Mesquita that he had never doubted the disinterestedness of Lacerda. Therefore Mesquita, speaking to journalists, expressed pleasure at the success of his conciliatory effort.[11]

In faraway Belém, Pará, Costa e Silva praised the government for displaying courage in reaching an "entirely correct" iron ore export decision.[12] Juarez Távora, a member of the Interministerial Commission on Iron Ore, likewise followed Castello's wish that cabinet members defend the government. In a radio-television program on December 8, Távora announced that private terminals built in Sepetiba Bay would become government property after thirty years and that companies using such terminals would have to finance the Central do Brasil Railroad for the purchase of locomotives and cars and for the construction and rehabilitation of rail line. Pointing out that exporters who stole markets from CVRD or failed to comply with other conditions would not be allowed to transport, he said that Brazil did not fear Hanna because Hanna was not greater than Brazil.[13]

Jornal do Brasil, which in the past had been financed by CVRD for a campaign against Hanna,[14] published an editorial accusing Távora of committing "a crime against Brazil." *Correio da Manhã*, which had been financed to favor Magalhães Pinto over Lacerda for the presidency, expressed concern lest Lacerda provoke Castello into supporting the planning minister and the mines minister (the "pupil" of Roberto Campos). It argued that Lacerda, frequently a traitor to Brazilian interests, was inspired by ambition, not by patriotism ("a sentiment he does not know").[15]

Magalhães Pinto addressed a nine-page letter to Castello on Decem-

[10] Ibid.; Carlos Lacerda's recollection of this incident is given in Lacerda, *Depoimento*, pp. 328–329.

[11] *O Estado de S. Paulo*, December 6, 1964.

[12] Ibid.; December 9, 1964.

[13] Ibid.

[14] The role of CVRD in the newspaper publicity against Hanna is mentioned by Lucas Lopes, quoting Gabriel Passos, in the testimony of Lopes at the Parliamentary Investigating Commission examining Hanna in Brazil, March 17, 1965.

[15] *Correio de Manhã*, December 5, 1964.

ber 15 and he sent copies to the press.[16] *O Estado de S. Paulo*, denouncing Magalhães Pinto's statements, said that it would be absurd to be guided by the governor's assertion that public opinion polls opposed Hanna. Asking whether banking reform and other complex technical matters should be decided by public opinion polls, it accused Magalhães Pinto of emulating Brizola and Darci Ribeiro in "a conscious and methodical exploitation of ultranationalistic prejudices and grudges." It concluded that Castello, having rejected a specific solution of the Hanna case, was producing a general solution for advancing the national interests.[17]

At Laranjeiras Palace on December 15, Castello listened to Armed Forces Chief of Staff Peri Constant Beviláqua describe Hanna as a threat to Brazil,[18] and two days later he received João Agripino, who objected to exclusiveness for private loading terminals and argued that all profits from private iron ore exports should be invested in Brazilian metallurgical works.[19] The whole matter was settled on December 18, when the National Security Council met at Laranjeiras Palace for five hours to examine the recommendations of the Interministerial Commission. After the meeting the education minister told reporters that the views of the commission had been "totally victorious."[20]

Four days later the government issued Decree 55,282, signed by Castello and the cabinet, and lengthy Complementary Instructions, signed by the Interministerial Commission. They confirmed what Távora had told the public on December 8, but they contained points not mentioned by him. One of them stipulated that Brazilian-controlled firms of ore exporters were to reinvest in Brazil at least 50 percent of the profits

[16] Magalhães Pinto, letter to HACB, Belo Horizonte, December 15, 1964 (with markings by Castello Branco), File N3, CPDOC; HACB wrote "neo-nacionalismo" next to the governor's argument on behalf of "economic independence"; Magalhães Pinto's letter appeared in *Jornal do Brasil*, December 17, 1964.

[17] "Demagogia em Tôrno da Exportação de Minérios," *O Estado de S. Paulo*, December 18, 1964.

[18] *Tribuna da Imprensa*, December 16, 1964; see also Peri Beviláqua, "Hanna É Altamento Lesiva ao Legítimo Interêsse Nacional," *Tribuna da Imprensa*, November 22, 1967.

[19] *O Estado de S. Paulo*, December 18, 1964; see also João Agripino Filho, testimony at Parliamentary Investigating Commission examining Hanna, Brasília, February 12, 1965.

[20] *O Estado de S. Paulo*, December 19, 1964.

in excess of a return of 12 percent on capital, whereas foreign-controlled firms were to reinvest all profits in excess of 12 percent. These reinvestments were to be made in the state from which the ore had been mined and were to go into mining or metallurgical works or some other industry approved by the states. In addition, foreign-controlled firms were to reinvest in Brazil the 12 percent return for at least five years. Another ruling affected foreign iron ore exporters with railroad contracts and port authorizations: they had to offer at least 40 percent of their capital shares to Brazilian investors.[21]

Lacerda issued a statement promising that if he were elected president he would revoke "the unconstitutional and illegal decree." The president of CVRD wrote a letter of resignation to Castello in which he said that the new decree was harmful to the state of Minas and filled all of CVRD with "sadness and worry." Castello accepted the resignation.[22]

5. Intervention in Goiás (November, 1964)

In addition to settling long-pending issues, the government inevitably had to resolve problems caused by immediate developments. Such problems arose from the unexpected arrival of former Argentine strongman Juan Domingos Perón in Brazil and from the increasing controversy surrounding Governor Mauro Borges Teixeira of Goiás.

Castello was flying from Brasília to Rio on the morning of December 2 when a radio message advised him that Perón and his retinue of ten, having left Spain on an Iberia Airlines flight bound for Buenos Aires, were being held at Rio's Galeão Air Base for violation of the Brazilian law prohibiting airline passengers from carrying firearms. Castello was further advised that the Argentine government had requested Brazil to prevent the continuation of the exile's journey.[1] While some

[21] C'auses 5 and 6 of Complementary Instructions of Decree 55,282 of December 22, 1964.

[22] *O Estado de S. Paulo*, December 25, 1964; Paulo José de Lima Vieira, letter of resignation to HACB, December 28, 1964, File M (p. 3), CPDOC; HACB, letter to Lima Vieira, Rio de Janeiro, January 7, 1965, File M, CPDOC.

[1] *O Estado de S. Paulo*, December 3, 1964.

observers felt that Perón, expecting to be turned back by Brazil, was executing a "mere maneuver" to show his supporters that he was trying to fulfill promises to return to Argentina, others saw a sinister Peronista plot involving Communists and Brizola, who was in Uruguay.[2]

Castello, met by officials at Santos Dumont Military Airport, said the best solution was to get Perón back to Spain but that he wanted full information about Perón's legal rights. Learning that no problem existed for Brazil on that score, he gave his instructions, and at 10:00 P.M. the Iberia plane started back to Spain with Perón and his party.[3]

Castello was told that his decision resulted in demonstrations in Buenos Aires by Peronistas, who burned a picture of the Brazilian president as a sign of protest. "I would hope," Castello said, "that it is one of those horrible pictures of me that are circulating."[4]

The case of the Goiás state government, being investigated by an IPM, aroused emotion among military foes of Governor Mauro Borges and among PSD politicians who defended him. Robert W. Dean, head of the American Embassy's Brasília office, cabled Washington that Borges had included in his government "conservative landholding elements as well as leftists and known Communists." "This," Dean said, "has been partly due to opportunism and climate of 'ideological tolerance' which reigned in Brazil under Quadros and Goulart governments, but also the leftists have worked hard for Governor Borges, furthering his development programs while attempting to influence them along socialistic lines."[5]

For a while the IPM was directed by the hard-line colonel who headed the Tenth Infantry Battalion, stationed in the state capital, Goiânia. The colonel filled the local press with accounts of the governor's "subversion" and provoked Borges into handing Castello a letter complaining of the IPM's "techniques of terror, insults, curses, mental coercion, isolating people in unsanitary cubicles" and threatening transfers to out-of-state penitentiaries. When Castello asked if the colonel had done all this, the governor replied, "He did much more."[6]

[2] Ibid.; Viana Filho, *O Governo Castelo Branco*, p. 498.

[3] *O Estado de S. Paulo*, December 3, 1964.

[4] Viana Filho, *O Governo Castelo Branco*, p. 498.

[5] Robert W. Dean, telegram from Brasília to Secretary of State, November 16, 1964, NSFB, LBJ Library.

[6] Borges, *O Golpe em Goiás*, pp. 146–147.

After *O Globo* published an article criticizing methods used by army officers investigating Goiás, hard-line Lieutenant Colonel Francisco Boaventura Cavalcanti Júnior, a member of Geisel's staff and brother of Congressman Costa Cavalcanti, sent a harsh telegram to *O Globo* publisher Roberto Marinho. This unauthorized message from the presidential office displeased Castello, and Boaventura Cavalcanti was dismissed.[7]

In October the IPM was placed under the supervision of retired General Riograndino Kruel, who headed the Federal Department of Public Safety (DFSP) and who, like his brother, Second Army Commander Amauri Kruel, had been a classmate of Castello at school. Mauro Borges believed that Riograndino disliked him because the state had not cooperated with the general's personal real estate schemes. Therefore Borges was not surprised at a national press campaign painting him as a subversive. Borges' father, the seventy-four–year–old senator who had been strongman of Goiás since 1930, infuriated the DFSP with a speech that ridiculed the charges and mentioned torture by the Tenth Infantry Battalion.[8]

Riograndino went to Goiânia to question Borges about old charges such as the use, by the government organ *Diário de Goiás*, of the word *gorilas* to describe army officers.[9] Then, after consulting Geisel and Golberi, he told the press that the military court at Juiz de Fora, with jurisdiction over Goiás, might quickly decree imprisonments for Borges and two hundred codefendants. Therefore lawyers Heráclito Fontoura Sobral Pinto and José Crispim Borges appealed to the Supreme Court for a habeas corpus decree in favor of the governor. When the governor was asked to name the aggressor from whom he needed protection, he named the president of Brazil.[10]

The crisis came to a head with the theft of rifles and munitions from an army depot in Anápolis, Goiás, before dawn on November 14. At a Planalto Palace meeting, Castello and key cabinet ministers decided

[7] Francisco Boaventura Cavalcanti Júnior, interview, Rio de Janeiro, November 20, 1974.

[8] *O Estado de S. Paulo*, October 27, November 17, 18, 1964; Borges, *O Golpe em Goiás*, pp. 153–155.

[9] Borges, *O Golpe em Goiás*, pp. 156–157, 164, 190–215; *O Estado de S. Paulo*, November 6, 1964. *Gorilas* (gorillas) was a term that Brizola had used in 1963 and early 1964 to describe military officers opposed to his ideas.

[10] *O Estado de S. Paulo*, November 14, 1964; Carlos de Meira Mattos, interview, Washington, D.C., August 2, 1976.

to send troops from Brasília to help local army troops act "rapidly and decisively" to maintain order and prevent "resistance by the governor." Borges called on his state police to defend the governor's palace.[11]

On November 23 the Supreme Court, in a unanimous decision, ruled in favor of Mauro Borges' petition and affirmed that as a state governor he could be judged only by the state assembly for crimes connected with his handling of his office. Despite the *cassações* of three Goiás assemblymen in May, the governor had the backing of twenty-three of the thirty-nine members of the legislature.[12]

Shocked military officers declared that the consequences of the Supreme Court decision could not be foreseen because the armed forces would not permit the subversion to continue. Costa Cavalcanti, spokesman for the hard line, said that the ministers of the court did not understand what had happened in Brazil since March, and Mourão Filho promised to "resist until death" the forces of corruption and subversion.[13]

A message from Castello said that investigations demonstrated the ties of the Goiás government to strong subversive groups, including foreign ones, and its determination to shelter and make use of *cassados* and others eager to destroy democracy by violence. The president promised to fulfill his duty by eradicating this "threat."[14] Messages of support from governors and women's groups poured into Planalto Palace.

While PSD congressmen praised the Supreme Court, the military court in Juiz de Fora decreed "preventative imprisonments" of six Goiás administrators, including the secretary of government. An army commander went to Goiânia to make sure the jailings were carried out. Amaral Peixoto also went to Goiânia, where he found Borges furious at Castello's "pamphleteering" message and unwilling to offer concessions.[15]

[11] Dean, telegram from Brasília to Secretary of State, November 16, 1964; *O Estado de S. Paulo*, November 15, 1964; Borges, *O Golpe em Goiás*, pp. 151, 161, 163, 165.

[12] For details see Osvaldo Trigueiro do Vale, *O Supremo Tribunal Federal*, pp. 68–92; *O Estado de S. Paulo*, November 24, 25, 1964; Dean, telegram from Brasília to Secretary of State, November 16, 1964; Borges, *O Golpe em Goiás*, p. 172.

[13] *O Estado de S. Paulo*, November 24, 25, 1964.

[14] Ibid., November 24, 1964.

[15] Borges, *O Golpe em Goiás*, pp. 168–170; Viana Filho, *O Governo Castelo Branco*, p. 190.

Castello, agreeing at last with advisers who recommended federal intervention in Goiás, explained its need to Daniel Krieger and Pedro Aleixo, for congressional approval was required. After he instructed Milton Campos to draft a decree for fifteen days of intervention, "specifically to preserve the national unity," Colonel Carlos de Meira Mattos, assistant head of the Gabinete Militar, argued that at least six months were necessary "to clean things up." Golberi, who spent the night at Alvorada Palace because of the crisis, felt that fifteen days were not enough, and so did Geisel and Cordeiro de Farias. Castello consulted Ademar de Queiroz and then agreed on sixty days, but when Milton Campos wrote "60 days" in the decree, the president changed the wording to say "up to 60 days."[16]

Members of the Gabinete Militar, observing a birthday at an office party, were surprised to be joined by the president at what they regarded as the most critical moment of the Goiás crisis, the moment when intervention was decreed. It also surprised them to find Castello the only calm member of their group.[17]

Castello named Meira Mattos interventor to take over the Goiás government, and he sent a message to Congress that cited clandestine radio messages sent from Goiás to Montevideo and elsewhere and that called the Goiás executive branch a center of forces that sought to break up Brazil's political unity. Castello also wrote to Amaral Peixoto to praise him for having sought to intercede despite the president's reluctance to negotiate with Borges. His duty, he wrote, was to "eliminate a focal point against the national integrity and the peaceful achievements of the Revolution."[18]

Castello took command of the work to get Congress to back the intervention. He cabled Maranhão political leader Vitorino Freire, who was in Paris, to urge him to send an appropriate message to the *bancada Maranhão*.[19] After Cordeiro de Farias spoke with many congress-

[16] Meira Mattos, interviews, January 5, August 2, 1976; Viana Filho, *O Governo Castelo Branco*, p. 190.

[17] Quandt de Oliveira, interview, October 21, 1975.

[18] HACB quoted in Viana Filho, *O Governo Castelo Branco*, pp. 190–191; *O Estado de S. Paulo*, November 28, 1964.

[19] Viana Filho, *O Governo Castelo Branco*, pp. 191–192; Borges, *O Golpe em Goiás*, p. 172; Osvaldo Cordeiro de Farias, interview, Rio de Janeiro, December 26, 1974; HACB, cable to Vitorino Freire, File N1, Part 1, CPDOC; Vitorino Freire, interview, Rio de Janeiro, December 10, 1975. *Bancada Maranhão*: Maranhão congressional bloc.

men, the president conferred in the evening at Alvorada Palace with Congressman Rui Santos (UDN, Bahia), famous for predicting the outcome of congressional votes. Using the phone later that night, Castello followed suggestions of Rui Santos about whom to call and, in some cases, about what to say.[20]

The voting in the Chamber on the evening of November 29, a victory for the Castello Branco administration, demonstrated the accuracy of Rui Santos. Although a majority of the PSD and PTB opposed intervention, the PSD supplied so many votes in its favor that Amaral Peixoto regarded the occasion as the start of a serious division in his party.[21] The outcome was as follows:[22]

	For Intervention	*Against Intervention*
UDN	86	4
PSD	37	59
PTB	21	63
PDC	10	6
PSP	18	1
Small parties	20	7
	192	140

On December 1, after the PTB's nine senators decided to vote for intervention in order to end a serious crisis, the upper house backed the administration by a 42–8 vote.[23]

The end of the crisis, however, required more than federal intervention. For weeks Castello, Golberi, and Meira Mattos negotiated with the PSD to find a formula that would place a nonpolitical figure in the governorship before intervention expired. In the meantime, hardliners and PSD state assemblymen argued about where the IPM records implicating Borges were to end up.

[20] Santos, interview, October 27, 1975.

[21] Amaral Peixoto, interview, December 20, 1975; Dean, in his cable of November 27, 1964, from Brasília to Secretary of State, mentions an "air of resignation among congressmen who by and large appear relieved that extreme tension of past two weeks has been broken by decisive federal action."

[22] *O Estado de S. Paulo*, December 1, 1964.

[23] Ibid., December 2, 1964.

Early in January the gubernatorial candidacy of sixty-seven–year–old Marshal Emílio Rodrigues Ribas Júnior, an FEB veteran, was launched at the suggestion of Castello.[24] The idea was well received and was followed by arrangements that put the IPM's in the hands of the state assembly and the vice-governorship in the hands of the PSD. The formalities were completed on January 7 when the Goiás assembly voted to file away the IPM's and place the marshal in the governorship, which it declared had become vacant due to "a state of necessity."[25] On January 19 Castello signed a decree ending federal intervention in Goiás.

6. The End of an Economically Difficult Year

With the approach of the new year, journalists who covered Laranjeiras Palace voted Costa e Silva the cabinet minister most accessible to reporters in 1964, and they unanimously gave last place to Roberto Campos. Listing the most important Brazilian events of 1964, they voted for the following (in the order shown): (1) the movement of March 31, (2) the intervention in Goiás, (3) the government's decision about Perón's trip, (4) the agrarian reform law, (5) the suspension of Kubitschek's political rights, and (6) the iron ore debate.[1]

O Estado de S. Paulo, impressed with the amount of work done by Congress, attributed it to the many projects proposed by Castello and to Article 4 of the Institutional Act, giving deadlines to Congress. Congress, which had begun meeting in mid-March, actually received only 26 projects under Article 4; 188 came from the executive in the ordinary way, and 582 were presented by congressmen.[2]

Late December was a time for optimistic forecasts. Castello, speaking about the gross national product at the graduation exercises of the National War College, said that, "with stagnation overcome," the increase should be 6 percent "and later we shall create conditions for a stable 7 percent rate without the inflation and the exaggerated foreign

[24] Ibid., January 5, 1965; Schneider, *The Political System of Brazil*, p. 148.

[25] Schneider, *The Political System of Brazil*, p. 148; *O Estado de S. Paulo*, January, 1965.

[1] *O Estado de S. Paulo*, December 22, 1964.

[2] Ibid., January 3, 1965.

indebtedness that characterized the previous period of increase." Finance Minister Bulhões predicted that the inflation rate in 1965 would not exceed 25 percent.[3]

Castello spent Christmas with his family at Alvorada Palace and then flew to Fortaleza, Ceará, for a few days with friends. He was back in Rio on December 30, speaking with Golberi about Goiás and consulting cabinet ministers about information needed for his year-end message to the nation.[4]

The year-end message, delivered by Castello by radio and television on the evening of December 31, mentioned "the enormous sacrifices" that had been demanded of the people. Castello explained that "at times it was sorrowful for us to call for them" but that "the conscience of duty and the certainty that we would be understood gave us the strength necessary for the task." He referred to the steps taken to unfreeze prices and utility rates; lift rent controls; eliminate the subsidies on gasoline, wheat, and paper; and devalue the cruzeiro, some of which had contributed to a fourth-quarter cost-of-living increase that exceeded the third-quarter increase.[5] But he maintained that without those steps, currency issuances "in a regime of subsidies" would have inflated prices 100 percent between April and December instead of the 50 percent actually experienced. And he added that those steps, together with an end of hostility to private enterprise, gave promise of a period of abundant production in place of "a panorama of scarcity."

"If," Castello said, "it is difficult to explain today the steps that contributed to the increase of prices . . . , they will be easily understood next year, when the flow of merchandise and services will contribute to the progressive relief of the consumer." The president pictured the times as putting the national conscience to the test, and he predicted that the result would be "the construction of a great nation, for which 1965 will be an unforgettable landmark in history."

After delivering his message, Castello was driven to Vernon Walters' apartment. The two friends, who had enjoyed eating ice cream

[3] Ibid., December 22, 1964; HACB, *Discursos, 1964*, pp. 90–95.

[4] *O Estado de S. Paulo*, December 31, 1964.

[5] HACB, *Discursos, 1964*, pp. 44–48; *Conjuntura Econômica*, February 1969; Law 4,494 of November 25, 1964, which ended rent controls, was considered partially responsible for a fourth-quarter cost of living increase of 18 percent (compared with 13 percent in the third quarter).

together from time to time, sometimes at Laranjeiras Palace and sometimes at Walters' apartment, saw the new year in with the customary champagne drink to the future.[6]

Early in January, Castello received Juraci Magalhães, who had come to Brazil for the holidays after having advised the State Department of Castello's desire to invite President Johnson to visit Brazil in 1965.[7] At Laranjeiras Palace the ambassador spoke with the president and some of his ministers about coffee, the price of which had declined since May, 1964.[8]

It was agreed that Leônidas Bório, head of the Brazilian Coffee Institute, would accompany Juraci to Washington and that Castello would give Juraci a letter for President Johnson announcing a Brazilian "special plan" to have the export quotas of the coffee-producing nations vary with the coffee quotation, thus assuring a plentiful supply if prices increased. As the success of such an arrangement depended on the passage by the United States of legislation for implementing the International Coffee Agreement, the letter would mention the great interest of the coffee-producing nations in the enactment of that legislation.[9]

Juraci was surrounded by reporters when he left Castello's office. He told them that in his thirty-four years of public life he had never witnessed before, in any government, "the seriousness with which the present one studies the solution of all the problems that concern the life of the nation."[10]

7. Naval Aviation

The most difficult problem faced by the president early in 1965 concerned naval aviation. Contributing to the difficulty was the passage of time since the Kubitschek administration had purchased the aircraft

[6] Walters, interview, June 12, 1975.

[7] Memorandum, Robert M. Sayre to McGeorge Bundy, The White House, December 16, 1964, NSFB, Memorandums, Vol. V, LBJ Library.

[8] *O Estado de S. Paulo*, January 7, 1964.

[9] HACB, letter to LBJ, January 8, 1965, Papers of LBJ, President's Staff File, Brazil, Vol. 1, Presidential Correspondence, LBJ Library.

[10] *O Estado de S. Paulo,* January 7, 1964.

carrier *Minas Gerais*. The navy had sought to develop its own air arm and had operated a naval airbase, São Pedro d'Aldeia, near Rio. Air force officers had adopted the slogan "everything that flies is ours" and disrespectfully referred to naval planes and helicopters as "unidentified flying objects."[1]

In August 1964, air force officers screamed in protest when the *Minas Gerais* set forth from Rio with naval training planes aboard to participate with the U.S., Argentine, and Uruguayan navies in the fifth annual UNITAS antisubmarine maneuvers. Castello wrote to Navy Minister Melo Batista that the carrier should participate without the training planes. He said that those planes were inappropriate and that while the Brazilian air force had suitable planes, the maneuvers called for the use of U.S. planes. Pointing out that legally no navy aircraft carrier aviation existed, he expressed regret that a solution had not yet been reached and said that the decision he expected to render would not include a naval air branch and might establish an aircraft carrier aviation in which both the air force and navy would participate.[2]

This step by Castello brought him a violent letter of resignation from José Santos de Saldanha da Gama, general director of naval aviation. The admiral wrote that Castello, disarming Brazil at sea at a moment when a world war might break out, would be "held responsible before the nation, by the future, and by history." Saldanha da Gama's remark about "the disgrace of an imperfect participation in an international operation" prompted Castello to write Melo Batista to ask how Brazil would look using training planes instead of combat planes. Castello added that "history, which Saldanha da Gama thinks is on his side, is going to judge the two of us. I shall not desert my duty." In another letter, written a week later, Castello praised Melo Batista and navy officers for patriotically withdrawing the training planes under tense circumstances.[3]

[1] José Santos de Saldanha da Gama, letter to HACB, Rio de Janeiro, August 19, 1964, File R2 (p. 3), CPDOC; Moura, interview, December 11, 1974. General Moura quoted Kubitschek as having told him that the strife between the airforce and navy had served a useful purpose, reducing the amount of time that officers of those branches spent planning conspiracies against him.

[2] HACB, letter to Ernesto de Melo Batista, August 13, 1964, File R2 (p. 2), CPDOC.

[3] Santos de Saldanha da Gama, letter to HACB, August 19, 1964; HACB, letters to Ernesto de Melo Batista, August 19, 26, 1964, File R2 (pp. 4, 5), CPDOC.

Generals Geisel and Golberi were closeted in a room in Laranjeiras Palace, working on a proposed solution, when the president unexpectedly presented his own suggestions, and they were forwarded to the two interested ministries.[4] The navy staff, asked for its observations, submitted a report that Castello considered sarcastic, disrespectful, and unsound.

"Recent administrations," Castello wrote Melo Batista in September, 1964, "never gave importance to the general staffs. I hold the firm intention of having them contribute. But now, when I seek an opinion from the navy staff, I receive a document by an organ apparently not trained to assist superiors in reaching decisions." The president, noting that the naval document dismissed his proposals as an amplification of the ideas of Armed Forces Chief of Staff Peri Bevilápua, compared this view with *Última Hora's* statement that Castello's papers were written by Roberto Campos. "Outside of the fact that the EMFA [Armed Forces Staff] is my principal adviser," he wrote, "any document signed by me becomes mine, and my subordinates should have the intellectual discipline to respect it as such. I might not be original, but I have always been responsible and I am well educated militarily." Castello dismissed as "disrespectful and provocative" the statement by the navy staff that his suggestions might prove to be a "disturbing element."[5]

On the morning of December 5 a navy helicopter landed at the field of the Brazilian air force in Tramandaí, Rio Grande do Sul, to receive fuel. When three armed air force captains said that they were taking the helicopter into custody, the pilot tried to fly it away, whereupon the air force officers fired on it, damaging a rotor and preventing its departure.[6] While the admiral commanding the Fifth Naval District con-

[4] João Carlos Palhares dos Santos, "Depoimento sôbre a Minha Convivência com o Presidente Humberto Castello Branco," File R2 (p. 21), PVCB.

[5] HACB, letter to Ernesto de Melo Batista, Rio de Janeiro, September 9, 1964, File R2 (p. 6), CPDOC.

[6] Nelson Freire Lavanère-Wanderley, interview, Rio de Janeiro, December 10, 1974; Levy Pena Aarão Reis, interview, Rio de Janeiro, December 15, 1977; Levy Penna Aarão Reis, Ernesto de Mello Baptista, Waldeck Lisboa Vampré, Mário Cavalcanti de Albuquerque, and Armando Zenha de Figueiredo, "O Segundo Revez Político da Aviação Naval (1964)," pp. 18–19. According to this document, Lavanère-Wanderley reported to Castello Branco on December 4, 1964, that an incident of this nature had occurred on the fourth, when no incident occurred, and then an incident did occur on the fifth.

sidered sending a marine battalion to rescue the helicopter,[7] newspapers carried sensational headlines.

In Brasília on December 9, Castello called in the navy and air ministers separately and, after hearing conflicting accusations from each, drew up and signed a memorandum, in the presence of both, that was designed to avoid new clashes between the two services.[8] He also named a general to investigate.

Following the Tramandaí affair, Air Minister Lavanère-Wanderley submitted his resignation because the air force officers refused to support positions taken by the president. The *brigadeiros* and the minister wanted the São Pedro d'Aldeia base to be transferred to the air force and the navy to be excluded from having any aircraft, including helicopters. They maintained that the legislation in effect supported their view and that any concession to the navy required an act of Congress, scheduled to reconvene in March, 1965.[9] Castello accepted Lavanère-Wanderley's resignation on December 14 in a letter advising that the post would be filled by Brigadeiro Márcio de Sousa e Melo, commander of the São Paulo Air Zone. Speaking with Viana, the president described the outgoing minister as "the thoughtful type" and the hearty new minister as a "man of action."[10]

On January 6, Geisel handed Sousa e Melo a copy of the president's proposed settlement, and, as it displeased the air force officers, Sousa e Melo submitted his resignation at once.[11] At Laranjeiras Palace, Castello asked him to remain until a successor could be found, adding that this might take twenty hours or twenty days. The minister then met with thirteen *brigadeiros,* members of the Conselho Superior da Aeronáutica, and found that all of them backed his decision to resign, making it appear that the president would not easily find a successor within the air force.[12] But Castello was successful when he turned to

[7] Palhares dos Santos, "Depoimento sôbre a Minha Convivência com o Presidente Humberto Castello Branco."

[8] Penna Aarão Reis et al., "O Segundo Revez Político da Aviação Naval (1964)," p. 20.

[9] Written statement of Nelson Lavanère-Wanderley, prepared for Luís Viana Filho; Conselho Superior da Aeronáutica, "Uma Sugestão," File R2 (p. 8), CPDOC.

[10] HACB, letter to Nelson Freire Lavanère-Wanderley, Rio de Janeiro, December 14, 1964, File R2 (p. 7), CPDOC; Viana Filho, *O Governo Castelo Branco*, p. 200.

[11] Márcio de Sousa e Melo, letters to HACB (one typed, the other handwritten), Rio de Janeiro, January 6, 1965, File R2 (pp. 10, 11), CPDOC.

[12] *O Estado de S. Paulo*, January 9, 1965.

Eduardo Gomes, twice the UDN standard-bearer for the presidency. This historic figure, the most eminent of the *brigadeiros,* was in Araxá, Minas Gerais, recovering from an operation.[13]

On January 11, at the ceremony installing Eduardo Gomes, Castello said that "the intrigue to divide the military, the insane imputation about a desire to harm one force in order to benefit another, the unfortunate and absurd insinuation that the president changes doctrine on account of political pressure—none of this is going to weaken our effort." Outgoing Minister Sousa de Melo was asked by reporters about the creation of an overall Defense Ministry, an idea favored by Castello. He replied that such a ministry would inevitably be formed and would not benefit or harm any branch of the armed forces.[14]

Two days later Castello issued his decision about naval aviation. It stipulated that all planes controlled by the navy were to be turned over to the air force, but that the navy was to retain anti-submarine helicopters, and it further provided that "the navy installations at São Pedro d'Aldeia will be used for training personnel of both forces." The public was advised that the president had considered not only areas in conflict and Brazil's international commitments, "but also, and principally, the financial situation of the nation."[15]

Whereas Lavanère-Wanderley had prepared the *brigadeiros* for disappointment, Melo Batista had unrealistically kept the admirals hopeful of a "total victory."[16] Now the navy minister expressed his immense surprise and rushed to Laranjeiras Palace to try to persuade the president to change his mind. When Melo Batista said that no naval chief would get the navy to comply with the decision, Castello observed: "I understand that last year there was a soviet of sailors in the navy; this year the soviet is made up of admirals and you are the Cabo Anselmo of this group." As Melo Batista simply repeated that the decision could not be imposed on the navy, Castello told him: "Then you cannot continue as my minister." So great was Castello's disappointment in the

[13] Ibid.; according to *Jornal do Brasil*, January 8, 1965, Castello Branco threatened to appoint an army officer to head the Air Ministry if Eduardo Gomes would not accept (see Schneider, *The Political System of Brazil*, p. 152, n. 71).

[14] HACB, *Discursos, 1964*, pp. 259–269; *O Estado de S. Paulo*, January 12, 1965.

[15] *O Estado de S. Paulo*, January 14, 1965.

[16] Palhares dos Santos, interview, November 22, 1975; idem, "Depoimento sôbre a Minha Convivência com o Presidente Humberto Castello Branco." Palhares mentions, among other things, a speech given by Melo Batista at the end of 1964.

admiral, whom he had regarded as a sincere friend, that he considered that evening with him "the worst moment" he had so far spent in the presidency.[17]

Melo Batista met with top-ranking admirals and then, on January 14, sent the president a letter of resignation that made a legal case for the navy's position. The letter of resignation of Navy Chief of Staff Levy Pena Aarão Reis told the president: "Your decision is based on the theory that led to the defeat at sea of the only two countries to adopt it."[18]

The choice of a new minister narrowed down to retired Admiral Paulo Bosísio, who had headed the General Commission of Investigations, and Commander of the Fleet Zilmar Araripe Macedo, who felt that Brazil could not afford separate air forces and understood that the president's decision, once made, had to be carried out.[19] After Castello told aides that he admired Admiral Araripe but considered him "the Milton Campos of the navy," a plane was sent to bring Bosísio to Rio from his small country place in São Paulo state.[20] Although Bosísio felt that Castello had made the correct decision about a matter that had been viewed with too much emotion, he proved very reluctant to become navy minister. At Laranjeiras Palace he finally agreed, with the understanding that he would leave once the navy had been calmed down and no later than the end of the year.[21]

Bosísio took office at a ceremony notable for an aggressive speech of Melo Batista that was loudly applauded by Admiral Rademaker. The outgoing minister declared that the president's decision violated Brazilian law and "the universally adopted doctrines and concepts of naval warfare" and had been taken "in order to leave the navy totally incapacitated, presently and in the future." Later in the day, when reports reached Laranjeiras Palace that Saldanha da Gama was organizing a

[17] Palhares dos Santos, "Depoimento sôbre a Minha Convivência com o Presidente Humberto Castello Branco." Cabo (Corporal) Anselmo had headed a sailors' mutiny in March 1964.

[18] *O Estado de S. Paulo*, January 14, 1965; Ernesto de Melo Batista, letter to HACB, Rio de Janeiro, January 14, 1965, File R2 (p. 12); CPDOC; Levy Pena Aarão Reis, letter to HACB, January 15, 1965, File R2 (p. 13), CPDOC.

[19] Zilmar Campos de Araripe Macedo, interview, Rio de Janeiro, August 9, 1977.

[20] Palhares dos Santos, "Depoimento sôbre a Minha Convivência com o Presidente Humberto Castello Branco."

[21] Ibid.; Bosísio, interview, November 8, 1975.

Navy Club meeting to issue a proclamation to repudiate Castello's decision, Castello informed the club that he would close it down if it carried out any act disrespectful of the president.[22]

On January 28 the president used a navy helicopter to board the *Minas Gerais,* which had returned to Rio from the north with Fleet Commander Araripe aboard. In the company of his three military ministers, Castello praised Araripe and his men for having accepted the decision with no interruption of normal service. Explaining that "a decision that comes from above can be fulfilled only when it is inspired by legality and legitimacy," he added that he was absolutely opposed to the defense of authority simply for the sake of authority.[23]

Late in 1965, following UNITAS-6, the U.S. commander of the South Atlantic Force wrote Castello that "the cooperation and performance of the aircraft embarked in the *Minas Gerais* was excellent and proved the workability of your solution." Congressmen, in dismissing a denouncement of Castello made by retired Admiral Carlos Pena Boto, also noted the "harmony" demonstrated in the UNITAS-6 maneuvers by the *Minas Gerais,* operating at full capacity for the first time. More recently, General Arthur S. Moura, long-time U.S. military attaché in Brazil, commented: "the statesmanlike decision worked out beautifully in purely professional terms. There have been no accidents. Each service is determined to maintain the best. A professional contest on a high order has now developed into rapport."[24]

8. Closing Panair (February–March, 1965)

The decision to close down the thirty-three–year–old Panair do Brasil Airline stirred up so much emotion, Roberto Campos recalls, that it would have been difficult to carry it out without the "revered" Eduardo Gomes in the Air Ministry and impossible without the presi-

[22] *O Estado de S. Paulo,* January 19, 1965; Palhares dos Santos, "Depoimento sôbre a Minha Convivência com o Presidente Humberto Castello Branco."

[23] *O Estado de S. Paulo,* January 29, 1965.

[24] A. R. Gralla, letter to HACB, "at sea enroute to Salvador, Brazil," November 18, 1965, File R2 (p. 18), CPDOC; "Denúncia Apresentada contra o Sr. Presidente da República, Marechal Humberto de Alencar Castello Branco, pelo Almirante Penna Boto," Relator: Deputado Carlos Werneck, File R2 (p. 19), CPDOC; Moura, interview, December 11, 1974.

dency in the hands of "a military man who could face the music." Panair do Brasil, the first Brazilian airline to fly abroad, had acquired the status of a "sacred cow." Its twenty-six hundred employees included many placed in the company by politicians who had been under pressure to find jobs for supporters.[1]

The government's decision grew out of a discussion by Castello and Roberto Campos about the heavy subsidies going to airlines, particularly the two engaged in overseas flights, Panair and VARIG. The president and his planning minister concluded that Brazil could not afford two competing international carriers, with the accompanying "inflation of training facilities" and excessive diversification of equipment (Panair used Douglas planes and VARIG used Boeing), and they felt that the absorption of Panair by the stronger VARIG might improve Brazil's bargaining power for securing international routes.[2] Panair had gone downhill financially, especially after control of the stock had been acquired in 1961 by a group headed by Mário Wallace Simonsen and Celso da Rocha Miranda, and was 101 billion cruzeiros in debt early in 1965.[3]

A report to Castello from Eduardo Gomes pointed out that the flights of Panair were being made despite the refusal of the Directorship of Civil Aviation to authorize them and despite the danger caused by the company's financial inability to acquire spare parts. As the Air Ministry's investigations showed that Panair could not be saved even if it were to receive the combined subsidies going to all the Brazilian airlines, Eduardo Gomes recommended that its domestic and international flights be suspended.[4]

After the president approved the recommendation, the Air Ministry canceled the company's flight concessions and instructed VARIG to carry passengers booked by Panair on flights between Europe and Brazil. A court in Rio then declared Panair in bankruptcy, and Panair prepared to contest the ruling. A former Panair president telegraphed Cas-

[1] Roberto de Oliveira Campos, interview, Rio de Janeiro, December 23, 1974; Moura, interview, December 11, 1974.

[2] Roberto Campos, interview, December 23, 1974.

[3] *O Estado de S. Paulo*, February 24, 1965.

[4] Ibid., February 13, 1965.

tello that "Panair is a national heritage and therefore must be preserved."[5]

At this point Carlos Lacerda set out to save Panair do Brasil. After pledging the support of the Guanabara State Bank for the Rio-based Central Commission of Panair Employees, he helped draw up a rescue plan: the stock held by directors and others would be transferred to a new foundation which would operate the company and be in the hands of the employees, the state government, and the federal government. Panair offices displayed photographs of the governor bearing inscriptions "PANAIRIANOS HAVE FAITH IN HIM" and "ONE HOPE STILL REMAINS." São Paulo Governor Ademar de Barros, less interested in saving Panair, sought to gain Panair's international routes for VASP, a São Paulo–based domestic airline.[6]

Panair supporters filled the press with statements about the "assininity of the federal government," and the airline's employees put on headline-catching demonstrations such as a one-day hunger strike. A march of employees to Laranjeiras Palace, planned for mid-February, was postponed when it was discovered that Castello was in Brasília.[7]

Employees of the company, meeting daily in a Panair hangar, received encouraging messages from Lacerda. They announced that they would accept any decision that did not give the Panair routes to VARIG, and when it appeared doubtful that the president would accept Lacerda's scheme, they sent other suggestions in a letter to Castello: intervention by the federal government or the purchase of Panair by VASP. They begged him to reconsider his "unilateral step," bearing in mind the fate of "5,000 families with more than 20,000 dependents" who were living "in agony."[8]

On March 17, ten uniformed Panair stewardesses encamped in front of Laranjeiras Palace. Asked by the Gabinete Civil to leave and await advice of an appointment with the president, they refused to budge. During the afternoon, after they had waited for six hours, one of the stewardesses was chosen by a Gabinete Militar colonel to meet with the

[5] Ibid., February 13, 16, 20, 1965.
[6] Ibid., February 13, 16, 17, 18, March 7, 1965.
[7] Ibid., February 16, 17, 21, 1965.
[8] Ibid., February 21, 24, 1965.

president. Castello told her that he was deeply interested in resolving the problem of the Panair workers and would speak with Eduardo Gomes. As for the proposals to save Panair, he said that none of them would relieve the government of Panair's debts and therefore they could not be accepted.[9]

On the next day Eduardo Gomes announced that the administration would ask Congress for credits with which to pay back wages and dismissal indemnifications to the employees. Asked about stewardesses still encamped at the palace, Gomes said that they would be employed by VARIG and other companies or by government companies. When a reporter said that this answer implied the end of Panair, the *brigadeiro* declared: "We have absolutely no thought of reestablishing the company."

In the meantime, at the *brigadeiro's* request, João Agripino discussed the Panair case in the Senate. He said that control of the company by the Rocha Miranda–Simonsen group had been acquired in order to benefit firms associated with the group, such as Rocha Miranda's Ajax Insurance Company. The senator accused the group of draining Panair in the expectation that the government would intervene, taking over Panair's management and debts. But, Agripino said, federal intervention would be "a wretched business" for the national Treasury, loading it with huge debts, and therefore the government preferred to send Panair into bankruptcy. While Agripino insisted that the government was not "obligated to employ the workers of companies that have gone bankrupt," he pictured it as not indifferent to the situation of Panair's employees.[10]

Panair President Paulo Sampaio took exception to some of Agripino's remarks. He also explained that the mechanical shops had been in excellent condition and the flights had been "absolutely safe." "Sixty million dollars in planes," he said, "are rotting in the four corners of the country, while 5,000 employees are being treated as though they were cattle."[11]

In Rio the camping Panair stewardesses were furnished tents, blankets, food, and kerosene lamps by residents of the Laranjeiras district.

[9] Ibid., March 18, 1965.
[10] Ibid., March 19, 1965.
[11] Ibid., March 20, 26, 1965.

After spending five days and nights in front of Laranjeiras Palace, they learned that Castello planned to leave for Brasília. They said they would continue their encampment in front of Planalto Palace and call it off only when they were in possession of a concrete solution.[12]

Two days later they had their solution in the form of an announcement that VARIG was taking on all the employees of Panair and assuming all the indemnification rights they had built up while working for Panair. VARIG denied that it planned to dismiss the workers after adding them to its payroll and pointed out that it would not have assumed a labor indemnification of between eight billion and ten billion cruzeiros unless it meant to retain them. Workers at the mechanical shops sent a telegram to thank Eduardo Gomes for authorizing the payment of their back wages.[13]

Castello Branco, well into his second half-year as president, was in a strong political position. This was principally evident from the vote of Congress on the Goiás intervention, but it was evident also in the support the president gained in Congress for agrarian reform legislation. If the legislation differed from the administration's early views, at least it was the result of careful study, and, above all, it was a decision finally taken about an issue that had long stirred the nation.

The failure of past administrations to reach clear decisions, as in the case of naval aviation and iron ore export policy, had resulted in an unhealthy situation. Thus, when the decisions were reached by the new administration, which wished to leave no such problems for its successor, they were greeted with violent attacks that were in part the result of emotions that had long been growing.

As the value of the decisions has been enhanced rather than diminished by the passage of time, it is more difficult to explain the continuation of some of the violent attacks. Those who still describe the iron ore decision as unpatriotic ignore the terms of the decision itself, favorable to the national companies, and give little attention to the subsequent events. After the decision was reached, Hanna entered into an agreement that transferred the control of its Brazilian iron ore project to

[12] Ibid., March 21, 1965.
[13] Ibid., March 23, 1965.

Brazilian interests; and the United States Steel Corporation, upon discovering the enormous Serra dos Carajás deposit, set up a joint company controlled by CVRD. The spectacular growth of CVRD itself hardly indicates that there was much reason for the "sadness and worry" said to have afflicted CVRD on account of the decrees signed by the Castello Branco administration in December, 1964.

IV

Persevering Legalistically Prior to Ato 2

(February–September, 1965)

The elections will take place on the dates established by the law.

1. Mazzilli's Defeat (February, 1965)

WITH Congress in recess in January, Castello spent most of the month in Rio. On January 18 he lunched at the Military Club with War Minister Costa e Silva, First Army Commander Otacílio Terra Ururaí, Second Army Commander Amauri Kruel, and eighty-one others who had graduated from the Military Academy in 1921. In a short speech to his classmates he made a promise: "I shall not permit my reelection, nor another extension of my mandate."[1]

While the president studied proposals to present to Congress in March, among them a reform to reduce the number of political parties, the lawmakers prepared to meet in a special session in February to select their officers. Ranieri Mazzilli, a pleasant Paulista who had been elected to the Chamber presidency annually for seven years, was being challenged in his own party, the PSD, by Walter Peracchi Barcelos of Rio Grande do Sul. Peracchi, whose candidacy had been quietly launched by Cordeiro de Farias, rejected the thesis that the party and Chamber should reelect Mazzilli to give him moral support while fiscal investigators in São Paulo charged him with improper conduct.[2]

When the special session began on February 3, the race between Mazzilli and Peracchi looked like a contest between "anti-Revolutionaries" and "Revolutionaries" because the PTB supported Mazzilli while

[1] Baleeiro, "Recordações do Presidente H. Castelo Branco," p. 13; *O Estado de S. Paulo*, January 19, 1965. Of the 219 members of the class, 74 had died.

[2] Castello Branco, *Os Militares no Poder: 1. Castelo Branco*, p. 200; "Peracchi Fala de Mazzilli," *O Estado de S. Paulo*, January 8, 1965.

hard-liners in the military demanded a change. Castello, during a plane trip to Rio from the northeast on February 2, spoke to Ceará Congressmen Martins Rodrigues (PSD) and Paulo Sarasate (UDN) about the evils of *continuismo* and said he opposed Mazzilli's reelection. He hoped that Mazzilli and Peracchi would both withdraw in favor of PSD veteran Gustavo Capanema, but the announced candidates would not step aside, preferring that the PSD congressmen decide which of the two should be the party's candidate.[3]

Although Castello wanted new leadership in both houses, he avoided a war "on two fronts" and declared in Brasília on February 12 that he saw "no inconvenience" in Moura Andrade's reelection in the Senate. At the same time, he announced that the candidacy of Mazzilli was "incompatible with the Revolutionary government" and warned that his reelection would upset the harmony between the governmental powers. But when the PSD congressmen met on February 17, they gave fifty-eight votes to Mazzilli and thirty-two to Peracchi, whereupon Peracchi stepped aside. Pedro Aleixo, government leader in the Chamber, observed with irritation that "the battle is on, because that is what the PSD leadership wants."[4]

That evening at Alvorada Palace, Castello had supper with Generals Golberi and Cordeiro de Farias and Congressmen Adauto Lúcio Cardoso (UDN, Guanabara) and Nilo Coelho (PSD, Pernambuco).[5] Agreement was reached on the need to organize a new congressional bloc not only to try to defeat Mazzilli in the election by the full Chamber but also to give the administration and its reform program permanent support. Therefore, early the next morning Castello and Cordeiro met at Alvorada Palace with twenty congressional leaders favorable to the idea. The organizers, who included two PTB members (Teódulo de Albuquerque and Manoel Novais), then collected signatures on a manifesto which declared that the bloc's purpose was to enact the reforms initiated by Castello "for achieving the most legitimate popular aspirations." They limited their work to the lower house because Krieger saw no need to share his leadership with that of the new bloc in the Senate.[6]

[3] *O Estado de S. Paulo*, February 3, 5, 1965; Viana Filho, *O Governo Castelo Branco*, pp. 285–286.

[4] *O Estado de S. Paulo*, February 18, 1965.

[5] Viana Filho, *O Governo Castelo Branco*, p. 287.

[6] Albuquerque, interview, October 24, 1975; *O Estado de S. Paulo*, February 19,

Castello canceled a trip to Rio Grande do Sul and helped the bloc choose a candidate to oppose Mazzilli. After Cordeiro and others almost convinced him that the most viable selection would be a PSD member, Castello learned from Ernani Sátiro, UDN leader in the Chamber, that the UDN adamantly opposed this idea. Adauto Cardoso, who would have liked to become Chamber president, stepped aside and recommended UDN President Bilac Pinto in order to be in a better moral position to argue with Castello in favor of the UDN. When Castello settled on Bilac, a man he admired, the military was more pleased than Carlos Lacerda.[7]

Bilac returned from a trip to the United States to head the multiparty slate of the bloc, which became known in the press as the Bloco Parlamentar Revolucionário and which called itself the Bloco Parlamentar Renovador. Mazzilli's reaction was to issue a manifesto denouncing "intolerable" outside interference in the Chamber's affairs.[8]

Castello remarked: "I shall not carry out a cadet operation, but a general staff operation." He was fed information by Golberi, Cordeiro, and Ernani Sátiro, who became president of the Bloco. Rui Santos, whom Castello consulted, felt that the reserved and intellectual Bilac was not the easiest candidate to elect, but a study which he carried out gave Bilac a 210–170 edge over Mazzilli. Costa e Silva, on the other hand, saw the likelihood of a Mazzilli victory, and this led to speculation about the possibility of a Second Institutional Act to be signed by Castello and the military ministers in case of a victory by "anti-Revolutionaries."[9]

During the voting on February 24, Mazzilli's lead reached 20 votes midway through the opening of the envelopes, but in the end it gave way to a 200–167 victory for Bilac Pinto.[10] Magalhães Pinto's comment

1965; "Declaração de Congressistas: Formação do Bloco Parlamentar," File N1, Part 1 (p. 4), CPDOC; Sátiro, interview, December 17, 1975.

[7] Sátiro, interview, December 17, 1975; Baleeiro, "Recordações do Presidente H. Castelo Branco," p. 19; Castello Branco, *Os Militares no Poder*, p. 203.

[8] Albuquerque, interview, October 24, 1975; *O Estado de S. Paulo*, February 20, 1965.

[9] Viana Filho, *O Governo Castelo Branco*, p. 289; *O Estado de S. Paulo*, February 20, 23, 24, 1965; Albuquerque, interview, October 24, 1975; Sátiro, interview, December 17, 1975; Santos, interview, October 27, 1975.

[10] Santos, explaining Mazzilli's early lead (interview, October 27, 1975), said that groups that were friendly to each other deposited their envelopes together: "Minas and

was contained in a letter to Castello that was given wide publicity. The victory of the Bloco, he said, revealed the "evident collapse of the parties," which should be extinguished so that the nation's political life could be restructured.[11]

The success of the Bloco in carrying the Câmara presidency and other posts was an impressive victory for Castello, and it paved the way for the administration to put its supporters on important congressional commissions.[12] Another result was a call by Armando Falcão, of the PSD, for Amaral Peixoto to resign his party's presidency. Amaral Peixoto retorted that "what concerns Armando Falcão is the fate of the UDN, which he seems to serve with extraordinary dedication."[13]

2. Decision about the 1965 Gubernatorial Elections (March, 1965)

Of the fifty-two messages that the president was said to be preparing for Congress,[1] the most important dealt with having all gubernatorial elections coincide with presidential and congressional elections. Popular elections for governors were scheduled to be held in eleven states in October, 1965, but if coincidence was to be achieved in 1966, the solution seemed to lie in their postponement for a year, in which case the mandates of the incumbents could be extended or else the eleven states could be governed for the additional year by individuals selected in the state assemblies or imposed by federal intervention.

Senator Krieger agreed with those who felt that popular elections for one-year terms would be impractical, and he argued for selections by the assemblies. Military leaders favored this solution, for they objected to extending the terms of governors they disliked, such as Aluísio Alves in Rio Grande do Norte,[2] and they felt that October was too

São Paulo supported Mazzilli and these envelopes were all deposited in a batch together. The north was for Bilac." See also *O Estado de S. Paulo*, February 23, 24, 25, 26, 1965; Baleeiro writes ("Recordações do Presidente H. Castelo Branco," p. 20) that Lacerda was "furious" at the election of Bilac Pinto to the Chamber presidency.

[11] *O Estado de S. Paulo*, March 12, 1965; Viana Filho, *O Governo Castelo Branco*, p. 289.

[12] Ibid.

[13] *O Estado de S. Paulo*, March 13, 1965.

[1] *O Estado de S. Paulo*, March 4, 1965.

[2] Krieger, *Desde as Missões*, pp. 191–192; Almeida Magalhães, interview, November 19, 1975.

early to hold popular elections that would be interpreted as rendering a verdict about a Revolutionary regime whose economic measures had not yet had a chance to provide beneficial results.

In Minas Gerais, one of the eleven states with an election coming up, Magalhães Pinto persuaded the state legislature to extend his term for a year. But this step irritated the president because it was taken before the administration and Congress had settled the problem.[3]

From Guanabara, another state due to elect a new governor in October, Castello received advice in the form of long letters written by Lacerda. The first, dated February 6, was not cordially received because it contained accusations that had led Lacerda to declare publicly that Luís Viana Filho "spared all the thieves of Bahia" to further his own political interests and was working for the return of Kubitschek, "the biggest thief of all." As for the 1965 direct gubernatorial elections, Lacerda told Castello that they should be held if they were "an indispensable condition for the presidential election of 1966," but the governor also wrote that Castello had given his word to hold the 1966 election—a word that surely would prevail over the views of "flatterers and experts."[4]

Milton Campos, after conferring with Castello at Laranjeiras Palace, told the press that on March 22 he would deliver a message to Congress about the coincidence of gubernatorial mandates. Guanabara Vice-Governor Rafael de Almeida Magalhães then called on the democratic justice minister and found him unhappily preparing arguments in favor of elections by the eleven state assemblies to decide who would govern for an additional year.[5]

"I hear it said," Lacerda put in a new letter to Castello, "that in a matter of hours a message will be released about this year's state elections, suppressing them in order to adopt another formula—the selection by indirect election of the assemblies." Lacerda fulfilled what he called his "imperative duty to the president and nation" by telling Castello that the intrusion of Congress into the lives of the states was an attack on the federation. He said that the cancellation of the October

[3] *O Estado de S. Paulo*, March 9, 1965.

[4] Ibid., February 5, 1965; Lacerda, letter to HACB, Rio de Janeiro, February 6, 1965, File N4 (p. 11), CPDOC; see also Lacerda, letter to HACB, February 9, 1965 (heavily underlined by HACB), File N4 (p. 12), CPDOC.

[5] *O Estado de S. Paulo*, March 19, 1965; Almeida Magalhães, interviews, November 15, 1975, August 8, 1977.

direct elections would maim "the perfecting of democracy," and that "what is best, correct, courageous, and democratic is to hold the elections." If they were not held, he added, it would be better to extend mandates than to allow the state assemblymen, such as the immodest spenders in the Guanabara legislature, to choose governors.[6]

The president was upset by the letter, which he considered hypocritical.[7] After receiving it at Laranjeiras Palace on Saturday, March 20, and marking it well in red pencil, he phoned Krieger, who was also in Rio, to invite him for lunch at Alvorada Palace on Monday. Krieger took advantage of the phone call to ask that the message to Congress recommend that incumbents, such as Magalhães Pinto, be eligible in the indirect elections. "I'll bear that in mind," Castello replied.[8]

Castello flew to Brasília on Sunday. It was the day on which voters in the city of São Paulo went to the polls to choose a mayor, because Castello, despite the warnings of Costa e Silva and hard-liners, had insisted that the Revolution respect the democratic institutions.[9] After Brigadeiro José Vicente Faria Lima (supported by Jânio Quadros and favored by Eduardo Gomes) won the mayorship by a large margin, the outcome was interpreted as indicating that the voters had not been much concerned by the pro- and anti-Revolution issue. Young nonpolitical engineer-businessman Paulo Egídio Martins, picked to run almost at the last minute by *O Estado de S. Paulo* and the UDN to give the Revolution a candidate, came out in fifth place in the field of eight. But Castello felt that Paulo Egídio did so well in delivering the message of the Revolution that he phoned to congratulate him after the results were known.[10]

When Krieger lunched with the president in Brasília, Castello showed him Lacerda's letter and said: "Concerned about his reputation, Lacerda prefers direct elections. Let's do what he wants. Will the change give you trouble?" The senator replied that the step, unwise "in

[6] Lacerda, letter to HACB, March 19, 1965 (heavily underlined by HACB), File N4, CPDOC.

[7] Viana Filho, *O Governo Castelo Branco*, p. 294.

[8] Krieger, *Desde as Missões*, p. 191.

[9] Schneider, *The Political System of Brazil*, p. 154.

[10] Ibid.; Paulo Egídio Martins, interview, São Paulo, November 10, 1975; *O Estado de S. Paulo*, March 23, 1965.

the present emergency," would give him no difficulty because direct elections were "an aspiration" of most of the lawmakers.[11]

Castello sent for Lacerda, Magalhães Pinto, and Paraná Governor Nei Braga (whose mandate could have been expected to be extended by a friendly state assembly). Therefore, on Monday afternoon, while Milton Campos happily advised Congress of the administration's decision, Nei Braga and Lacerda were flown to Brasília to hear of the development directly from Castello. Magalhães Pinto, regarded as the chief loser, was delayed in reaching Brasília.

Lacerda told reporters that Castello's decision was the one he had always defended. "Only the people," he said, "have the right to choose." "Today," he added, "I won the election of 1966."[12]

Within the next two weeks Congress passed a constitutional amendment that made the coincidence of gubernatorial elections effective in 1970 by providing that the eleven governors elected in October, 1965, would serve for five years instead of four.[13] The new amendment also made absolute majority a requirement in gubernatorial elections.

Castello Branco, addressing the nation from Brasília on the eve of the anniversary of his inauguration, said that the government was not afraid of the vote by the people. "It is the people," he added, "who should be afraid of making a mistake, because, whenever this happened, they had to pay a sorrowful and irretrievable tribute."[14]

3. The UDN Convention of April, 1965

Castello made his only presidential visit to foreign soil late in March, 1965, when he helped the president of Paraguay inaugurate a bridge near Iguaçu Falls, Paraná. Returning to Rio, he observed the first anniversary of the 1964 revolution by holding a press conference in which he referred to a recent unsuccessful rebellion against his regime by fifteen men coming from Uruguay. "The elections," he said, "will take place on the dates established by the law, despite the

[11] Krieger, *Desde as Missões*, p. 192.
[12] *O Estado de S. Paulo*, March 19, 1965.
[13] Ibid., April 9, 1965.
[14] Ibid., April 15, 1965.

wretched demonstration of bandits scheming in Montevideo and Paris."[1]

While Costa e Silva tried to assure hard-liners that the October elections would not be conducted in a way to allow the return of anti-Revolutionary persons or habits, Magalhães Pinto argued that it was a mistake to hold elections under the old political party system. The Minas governor also prepared to use the courts to defend the extension of his mandate by the state assembly. But as he was not expected to win his case, he set to work to arrange the nomination of a successor, preferably a state cabinet secretary who would "maintain the unity of the bloc of parties" that had supported him: the UDN, PTB, and PR.[2]

Lacerda likewise prepared for the October elections. To the name of Rafael de Almeida Magalhães, a popular and able administrator, he found opposition, some of it from Sandra Cavalcanti and some from Church authorities who maintained that the vice-governor had violated the indissolubility of marriage. At a meeting of the Guanabara UDN on April 19, Lacerda backed the state secretary of transport and public works, Enaldo Cravo Peixoto. But UDN federal congressmen from Guanabara favored Adauto Cardoso, and state legislators worked for their own colleague, Health Minister Raimundo de Brito.[3]

Lacerda traveled to Belo Horizonte to discuss politics with Magalhães Pinto, who was complaining of "intriguers" in the federal government.[4] After the two governors lunched together on April 26, Magalhães Pinto used radio and television to demand "better conditions for the people" and to lament the "bankruptcies, inflation, and unemployment" brought about by the "erroneous" policy of Castello Branco. Lacerda told the press that he agreed with the analysis made by Magalhães Pinto and had come to speak with him just as he had done before Goulart's downfall. After explaining that the governors of Guanabara and Minas were being stabbed in the back, Lacerda proposed a meeting of the revolutionaries to discuss the course of the federal government and a revision of its cabinet, which, he said, was "no more revolutionary than that of Maria Theresa of Austria."[5]

[1] HACB, *Entrevistas, 1964–1965*, pp. 64–65.

[2] Costa e Silva speech, in *O Estado de S. Paulo*, April 4, 1965; *O Estado de S. Paulo*, March 23, 27, April 10, 1965. PR: Partido Republicano, a small party.

[3] Lacerda, interviews, February 17, 18, 1976; *O Estado de S. Paulo*, April 20, 22, 25, 27, 30, 1965.

[4] *O Estado de S. Paulo*, April 16, 1965.

[5] Ibid., April 28, 29, 1965.

Lacerda spoke with Magalhães Pinto about the UDN national convention to be held in Niterói on April 29 and 30 to choose a party president to succeed Bilac Pinto. The governor of Minas agreed not to veto the name of Ernani Sátiro, Lacerda's choice for the UDN presidency. He also declined to attend the convention, a decision that commentators attributed to a movement in the UDN to adopt a "motion of congratulations" to the president of the Republic.[6]

Arrangements to hold the convention had been made by Sátiro despite Castello's advice that such conventions might better be held after the enactment of new legislation about parties. "Let's wait for the weather to clear," Castello had said to Sátiro, who was in the uncomfortable position of supporting both the president and Lacerda.[7]

To oppose Sátiro for the UDN presidency, Congressman Antônio Carlos Magalhães of Bahia launched the candidacy of Aliomar Baleeiro, a proponent of the parliamentary system of government who was annoyed at Sátiro for excluding him from the congressional commission studying an amendment for adopting that system. Lacerda praised Baleeiro in a talk he had with him before the Niterói convention and told Baleeiro that Sátiro was "a simpleton from the intellectual point of view." But Lacerda said he would stick with Sátiro because Baleeiro considered politics from a national perspective and not a Carioca perspective.[8] Baleeiro had the support of his long-time friend Bilac Pinto, but that seemed insufficient to overcome the strength enjoyed by Lacerda in the rank and file of the UDN.

During the Niterói convention the most evident opposition to Lacerda was demonstrated by popular Carioca federal Congressman Fidelis Amaral Neto, who had broken with Lacerda. While Lacerda addressed the convention, Amaral Neto, using television cameras and microphones that he had brought with him, gave his own speech, which was carried to listeners and television viewers outside the meeting hall. Although Lacerda's microphone was connected to the sound system in the hall, the hissing of Lacerda by Amaral Neto's backers, and the simultaneous speech by Amaral Neto, made it difficult to hear Lacerda's appeal for unity in the UDN.

[6] Ibid., April 28, May 1, 1965; Sátiro, interview, December 17, 1975.

[7] Sátiro, interview, December 17, 1975.

[8] Antônio Carlos Magalhães, interview, Rio de Janeiro, August 11, 1977; Baleeiro, "Recordações do Presidente H. Castelo Branco," p. 20.

"I did not come here," Lacerda said, "to give a speech against the president of the Republic, because I desire that he stay in our favor. I maintain loyal and objective opinions about certain aspects of his government's policy, but I do this with the loyalty of a companion; I do this with the severity of a companion."[9]

During the voting that followed, Sátiro received 221 votes against 60 for Baleeiro. Upon assuming the presidency of the UDN, Sátiro resigned from the leadership of the Bloco Parlamentar Renovador and was succeeded by Adauto Cardoso.

4. A Habeas Corpus for Arraes (April–June, 1965)

Hard-liners, unhappy about the forthcoming October elections, were furious on April 19 when the Supreme Court ruled favorably on a habeas corpus petition that would free former Pernambuco Governor Miguel Arraes. In a unanimous verdict the justices agreed with lawyer Sobral Pinto that the year of imprisonment of Arraes had been "flagrantly excessive," and they ruled that the Military Justice system was not competent to judge a former governor.[1]

The verdict had been expected by Colonel Ferdinando de Carvalho, head of the IPM investigating the Communist party, and he had obtained the approval of First Army Commander Ururaí for a scheme that would deprive Arraes of his freedom by having him transferred from the northeast to Rio's Fort Santa Cruz and held there, under an arrest order, for questioning by the IPM colonels.[2]

When the Supreme Court issued its verdict, Arraes was being held at Fort Santa Cruz, and the First Army, in the absence of Ururaí, was under the command of General Edson de Figueiredo, the chief of staff. Edson de Figueirdo telegraphed Chief Justice Ribeiro da Costa to say that Arraes would continue under arrest because he had to testify at an IPM. Sobral Pinto then sent two telegrams to Brasília, one to ask Ribeiro da Costa to imprison the general and the other to advise Castello

[9] *O Estado de S. Paulo*, May 1, 1965.

[1] *O Estado de S. Paulo*, April 20, 1965.

[2] Carvalho, interview, October 30, 1975. Ferdinando de Carvalho was advised by the secretary of security of Pernambuco to expect that the habeas corpus petition would result in the freedom of Arraes.

Branco of the situation. Ribeiro da Costa responded by telegraphing Edson de Figueiredo that he was in rebellion against the sovereignty of the judicial power and had to respect the Court's decision. Later the chief justice consulted Castello, who said that he would handle the matter in Rio.[3]

At Laranjeiras Palace on April 21, Castello called in Edson de Figueiredo and Décio Escobar, who was acting war minister while Costa e Silva visited the United States and Canada. The president ordered compliance with the Supreme Court decision. Therefore, Arraes, much to his surprise, was released on the twenty-second. He joined his wife at the Rio residence of his uncle.[4]

The eight officers heading IPM's in Guanabara reacted by threatening to leave their assignments, and Costa Cavalcanti declared in Congress that "the Revolution is dead." The chief of the São Paulo Naval Commission flew to Rio to discuss with superiors "the sneer to the armed forces" and the "contempt for the Revolution" contained in the telegram of the chief justice to Edson de Figueiredo. Lacerda, long critical of the Supreme Court, called the liberation of Arraes a demagogic act by criminals "who have turned themselves into judges."[5]

Pernambuco Governor Paulo Guerra, reaching Recife from Rio, found the local military units furious at Castello, and the Cruzada Democrática Feminina protesting the Supreme Court ruling. Rushing back to Rio on the same day, he surprised Castello, who asked, "What goes on that you're here again?" Guerra replied, "In my area, nothing goes on, but in your area things go badly."[6]

Castello told the governor that if Brazil failed to respect the Supreme Court, it would fall to "the level of some of those Central American countries." Observing that "what these young officers want is for me to be a dictator," he pointed out that he had fought in Europe for democracy and lacked "the moral condition" for becoming a dictator. "To establish a dictatorship is easy, governor, but what is difficult is to emerge from it."

The president persuaded the IPM heads to continue with their work,

[3] Heráclito Fontoura Sobral Pinto, interview, Rio de Janeiro, December 8, 1975; *O Estado de S. Paulo*, April 22, 1965.

[4] *O Estado de S. Paulo*, April 23, 1965.

[5] Ibid., April 22, 23, 24, 1965.

[6] Ibid., April 22, 1965; Guerra, interview, November 11, 1975.

and he alleviated the military discontent by writing Décio Escobar to ask that Edson de Figueiredo's army record not be affected by the reprimand in the telegram of the Chief Justice. "I consider," Castello wrote, "that the general committed no disciplinary transgression nor intended to take a position of rebellion against the sovereignty of the Judicial Power."[7] The chief justice then wrote Castello that the justices knew all too well that no judge could "impose a disciplinary penalty" on a soldier and that he had not been so "presumptuous" as to consider punishing the general. Castello, he said, had made a "lamentable mistake."[8]

Costa e Silva, back in the War Ministry, defended the "worthy officers" directing the IPM's and took issue with the Supreme Court's decision, for he declared that the military justice system was competent to judge cases of subversion. Constitutional lawyer Francisco Campos, author of the preface of the Institutional Act, supported the war minister's opinion about the competency of military justice, and he added that the agitation aroused by the decision to have elections in October was proof that they would be "premature and inopportune."[9]

On May 7, Arraes was forced to take a long automobile ride with hard-liners who were organizing the Radical Democratic League (LIDER). After the ride, Colonel Gérson de Pina, investigating the defunct Institute of Advanced Brazilian Studies (ISEB), told the press that Arraes was virtually a prisoner in the apartment where he was staying. The military, Gérson de Pina said, feared that Arraes would seek asylum in an embassy before concluding testimonies about the ISEB and Brizola's Groups of Eleven Companions.[10] Colonel Osnelli Martinelli, investigating the Groups of Eleven, spoke at this time to *Jornal do Brasil* about his fame for being "the toughest of the hard-liners." His toughness, he explained was the fruit of idealism. "Daily," he said, "I suffer threats of death, and the more I am threatened, the tougher I become."[11]

On May 10, after hard-liners conducted Arraes to the army police barracks, an army captain told the press that "Arraes is a prisoner held at the disposition of Colonel Martinelli, and the continuation of his im-

[7] *O Estado de S. Paulo*, April 23, 25, 1965.

[8] Ibid., April 27, 1965.

[9] Ibid., April 27, 29, 1965.

[10] *Jornal do Brasil*, May 8, 1965.

[11] Ibid., May 9, 1965.

prisonment will be determined by the First Army command." Sobral Pinto sent more telegrams to Brasília, and Arraes was released on the evening of the tenth on orders issued by Castello Branco.[12]

A few days later, the president's office announced that Castello was considering proposing a constitutional amendment for canceling special immunities of governors who no longer exercised their mandates. The proposal, the president's office said, represented a view that Castello had long held and did not constitute a capitulation before the pressure of the radical sectors of the armed forces.[13]

The Guanabara IPM colonels received helpful legal opinions from Francisco Campos, Vicente Ráo, Prudente de Morais Neto, Justo de Morais, Prado Kelly, Alcino Salazar, and Carlos Medeiros Silva. Using a legal study prepared for the First Army, they concluded that anyone indicted in an IPM could be imprisoned. When they insisted that Arraes testify about the ISEB as an indicted person, the former governor, arguing that he had had nothing to do with the ISEB, refused to consider himself indicted.[14]

In a dramatic manifesto issued on May 20, Arraes declared that he would not turn himself over to "arbitrary imprisonments" or testify further at IPM's whose purpose, he said, was not to find out the truth. He accused Castello Branco of favoring his imprisonment in order to placate "military groups of a radical tendency," and he accused the men of the IPM's of wanting to "create conditions indispensable for a new wave of repression, the postponement of the elections, and the installation of an arbitrary regime even more formidable than the present one." Explaining that he would be able to find safety when conditions made it impossible for him to remain in Brazil, he predicted that a "democratic regime—in all its fullness" would be reimplanted "much sooner than the present rulers imagine."[15]

While military authorities said that the manifesto might be a call for a counterrevolutionary movement, hard-liners blamed it on the anti-Revolutionary attitude of the Supreme Court. With the Justice Ministry now ruling that a new imprisonment of Arraes would be legal, the military searched for the former governor, and the SNI and the Guanabara

[12] Ibid., May 11, 12, 1965.

[13] Ibid., May 15, 16, 1965.

[14] *O Estado de S. Paulo*, April 27, 1965; *Jornal do Brasil*, May 12, 13, 1965.

[15] *Jornal do Brasil*, May 21, 1965.

Department of Political and Social Order (DOPS) watched embassies to which they felt Arraes might turn for asylum.[16]

Castello Branco ordered the armed forces to be on the alert "to avoid any subversion of order." Speaking with Magalhães Pinto, the president said that he would do nothing to cancel the 1965 elections although he recognized that in certain military circles and in "considerable political areas" it was argued that they were "not convenient."[17]

On the night of May 23, Arraes reached the Algerian Embassy, where he was received personally by the ambassador. Castello, consulted by Leitão da Cunha, decided that although Brazil had no argreement about asylum with Algeria, the government would issue a safe-conduct for Arraes, allowing him to leave Brazil, as soon as the Algerian Embassy requested the document. This news, released by Itamarati on May 25, disappointed members of the military who wanted Arraes to be treated like ex-Admiral Cândido Aragão, who was confined to the Uruguayan Embassy because he could not get a safe-conduct.[18]

The safe-conduct for Arraes was issued early in June, and on the sixteenth the former governor and his wife departed for Algeria at the Galeão Airport. The crowd of about one hundred that saw them off included members of the air force police, the navy intelligence, and the SNI[19]

5. The Decision to Send Troops to the Dominican Republic (May, 1965)

"The simultaneous presence of three Brazilian cabinet ministers in Washington," Juraci Magalhães wrote Castello in April, 1965, "caused jealousy on the part of other Latin American countries but was evidence of the immense prestige of your government in this country. All three were completely successful in their contacts. The United States administration applauds your constructive work." The ambassador, putting in long hours, told of his exhaustion in a letter to Antônio Carlos Ma-

[16] Ibid.

[17] Ibid., May 25, 26, 1965.

[18] Ibid.

[19] Ibid., June 5, 17, 1965.

galhães: "Today, old and long-suffering, I feel that I lack the necessary vigor and have reached the point of a nervous breakdown."[1]

Castello took an active interest in all important matters that affected Brazil's relationship with the United States, such as pending U.S. legislation about the International Coffee Agreement and the sale or loan of destroyers to friendly nations, the plans of the OAS to revise its charter, and the hoped-for visit of President Johnson to Brazil. Early in 1965, Castello was pleased with White House plans for a meeting, to be held in Rio in April or May, at which Johnson would confer informally with the heads of the ten South American countries—including Venezuela, the only one that continued to refuse to recognize the Brazilian government. The choice of Rio, a diplomatic triumph for Brazil, would be explained to Argentines, Chileans, and others in communications from the United States that referred to Rio's "central location" and four hundredth anniversary.[2]

Late in March, Ambassador Gordon brought Castello a letter from Johnson which explained that "recent developments in Viet Nam" made the visit to "Brazil next month" impossible; Johnson added that he nevertheless hoped "to have the opportunity for a personal exchange of views" with the Brazilian president "at a mutually convenient time." Castello, aware that Johnson had planned to come to Brazil before visiting any European nation, told Gordon he hoped that when Johnson felt he could travel, he would still make Latin America his first point of call.[3]

Rio had also been chosen as the site of a Second Special Inter-American Conference to be held in May, 1965, to revitalize the OAS by reforming its charter. As the date approached, Itamarati indicated to U.S. diplomats that a charter revision would take six to twelve months, whereas Roberto Campos advocated that the basic outline of charter changes be completed at the Rio conference itself. The American Em-

[1] Juraci Magalhães, letter to HACB, Washington, D.C., April 13, 1965, File O2 (pp. 9–11), PVCB; idem, letter to Antônio Carlos Magalhães, Washington, D.C., July 16, 1965, File O2 (p. 13), PVCB.

[2] Gordon, cable from Rio de Janeiro to Secretary of State, February 8, 1965, NSFB, LBJ Library.

[3] LBJ, letter to HACB, The White House, March 13, 1965, in Papers of LBJ, EX CO 32, Box 16, LBJ Library; Gordon, cable from Rio de Janeiro to Washington, March 29, 1965, NSFB, LBJ Library.

bassy decided that Campos, playing an active role in the Brazilian preparatory work, was "more alert" than Itamarati to Castello's "desire for accomplishment," and this led the Americans to conclude that they were faced with "more homework" than they had originally thought would be necessary.[4]

Juraci saw grave prospects for the conference. Writing to Castello on April 13, he said that many delegations, inspired by anti–United States sentiment, planned to propose the formation of a new economic bloc that would exclude the United States but exert pressure on it for economic concessions. The ambassador wrote that Chile, whose Christian Democratic government was considered leftist but not extreme, was taking the lead in the new scheme and that Argentina's participation was believed to be definite. "What concerns me the most," Juraci said, "is the establishment of some connection between the proponents of this anti-American position . . . and the Brazilians interested in creating difficulties for your government." The conference, Juraci feared, could become a forum for attacks against Brazil's foreign policy and the United States.[5]

Early in May the plans for the OAS to rewrite its charter were overshadowed by its concern with a civil war in the Dominican Republic, and the subsequent developments there made it necessary to postpone the Rio conference. The United States, having sent a military contingent to the Dominican Republic on April 28, asked the OAS to deal with the situation. The OAS foreign ministers, meeting in Washington on May 1, formed a peace-seeking commission and considered the creation of an inter-American military force to bring about peace and democracy.[6]

Ambassador W. Averell Harriman, President Johnson's personal envoy to the American republics, set forth to consult with governments about the creation of the inter-American force. Arriving in Rio with Leitão da Cunha on May 3, Harriman declared that the Dominican fac-

[4] United States Embassy, Rio de Janeiro, cable to Washington, May 4, 1965, NSFB, LBJ Library.

[5] Magalhães, letter to HACB, April 13, 1965.

[6] Center for Strategic Studies, Georgetown University, *Dominican Action—1965: Intervention or Cooperation?*, pp. 35–50; Jerome Slater, *Intervention and Negotiation: The United States and the Dominican Revolution*, pp. 79–80.

tion associated with Colonel Francisco Caamano Deno was dominated by Communists trained by Russians, Cubans, and Chinese.[7]

At Alvorada Palace that evening Leitão da Cunha joined Castello in a meeting with congressional leaders. The president, apparently uninterested in seeking the opinions of the congressmen and senators, advised that he had authorized the Brazilian ambassador to the OAS to support the United States' proposal to send an inter-American "police force" to the Dominican Republic. Leitão da Cunha, leaving the meeting, told reporters that "Communist activity is far advanced in the Dominican Republic, with the danger of the formation there of another Cuba."[8]

At Alvorada Palace on May 4, Castello and Leitão da Cunha lunched with Harriman and Gordon. Castello said that he favored sending Brazilian troops provided the OAS approved an "inter-American peace force," and he asked Harriman what the United States proposed to do if that approval were not forthcoming. Harriman said that even in that hypothesis the United States would not withdraw.[9] Therefore, after lunch, while Castello discussed the matter with Costa e Silva, Leitão told reporters that if the OAS did not approve the inter-American force, the United States troops should remain in the Dominican Republic. In defending the presence of those troops, numbering fourteen thousand, the Brazilian foreign minister spoke of the "imperious need to save lives, try to reestablish order, and prevent subversive forces from taking control."[10]

Before Harriman reached Montevideo, the Brazilian ambassador there, Manuel Pio Corrêa, heard Uruguay's acting foreign minister support the Soviet proposal to place the Dominican problem in the hands of the UN Security Council, bypassing the OAS. In reply to the Uruguayan's condemnation of the "unilateral action" by the United States, Pio Corrêa argued that the Latin American countries should cooperate

[7] *Jornal do Brasil*, May 4, 1965.

[8] Ibid.

[9] United States Embassy, Rio de Janeiro, cable to State Department, November 23, 1965, NSFB, LBJ Library.

[10] *Jornal do Brasil*, May 5, 1965; on May 6 *Jornal do Brasil* said that the United States troops in the Dominican Republic numbered 20,000; the figure 14,000 is given on p. 50 of Center for Strategic Studies, *Dominican Action—1965*, p. 50.

quickly to make the operation multilateral.[11] The ambassador's words were to no avail, and in Washington, on May 6, Uruguay joined four other OAS members in voting against the resolution to create the Inter-American Peace Force. Brazil's vote was among the fourteen that favored the resolution.[12]

While Castello prepared to consult the National Security Council and Congress, Leitão da Cunha and the United States were criticized. In Paris, Kubitschek declared that Washington "always arrogates to itself the right to tutor in the hemisphere" and "is inclined to see a leftist regime in every reformist movement." He explained that "in no Latin American country can the Communists reach power through free elections." Jânio Quadros, aboard the *Brazil Star* for an eye operation in England, said that "the United States never learns its lessons."[13]

Brazilian youth organizations issued manifestos to oppose the use of Brazilian troops to assist the United States in crushing "the liberation of a people exploited by the North American monopolies." A manifesto of intellectuals expressed "the most ardent repugnance for the attitude assumed by the Brazilian government in complicity with the malicious armed intervention of the United States." Its signers included Barbosa Lima Sobrinho, Antônio Calado, Hermano Alves, Jorge Amado, José Honório Rodrigues, Alceu Amoroso Lima, Di Cavalcanti, Carlos Heitor Coni, Márcio Moreira Alves, Nelson Werneck Sodré, Edmundo Moniz, Mário Pedrosa, and Joel and Paulo Silveira.[14]

Castello was not surprised at the attacks of PTB legislators against Itamarati, but he was worried about the opposition of Chamber of Deputies President Bilac Pinto to sending Brazilian troops. As in the case of agrarian reform, Castello debated with Bilac. At the president's request, Luís Viana Filho and Leitão da Cunha also talked with him, and the foreign minister put at Bilac's disposal the confidential papers of Itamarati.[15] After a study of three days Bilac issued a note to the press

[11] CIA Information Cable, May 5, 1965, NSFB, LBJ Library.

[12] The resolution is mentioned in Center for Strategic Studies, *Dominican Action—1965*, p. 51, and in A. J. Thomas, Jr., and Ann Van Wynen Thomas, *The Dominican Republic Crisis 1965: Background Paper and Proceedings of The Ninth Hammarskjöld Forum*, p. 37.

[12] The resolution is mentioned in Center for Strategic Studies, *Dominican Action—*

[14] Ibid., May 4, 6, 7, 1965.

[15] Castello Branco, *Os Militares no Poder: 1. Castelo Branco*, pp. 239–242 (Columns of May 8, 11, 1965).

that "energetically" condemned the United States for sending troops without previous authorization from the OAS. But the note explained that since the "deplorable error" of the United States had already been consummated, the only thing remaining for Brazil was cooperation with the other American republics to reestablish peace in the Dominican Republic. This conclusion coincided with that expressed editorially by *Jornal do Brasil,* and it was close to the "dominant opinion" in Congress, as described by columnist Carlos Castello Branco: condemnation of the United States, criticism of Itamarati, and support of the Brazilian president if he decided to send troops at the request of the OAS for purposes expressed in inter-American treaties.[16]

On May 13, after the OAS called on Latin America for 2,000 men, about half of them from Brazil, 270 soldiers from Costa Rica and Honduras went to Santo Domingo. The National Security Council, meeting with Castello at Laranjeiras Palace on May 15, unanimously approved sending Brazilian troops. During the debate that followed in the Chamber of Deputies, PTB leader Doutel de Andrade opposed the government's request, but PSD leader Martins Rodrigues argued that Brazil should send troops because its vote at the OAS had committed it to do so. On May 19 this view was accepted in the Chamber in a 190–99 vote. It was confirmed in the Senate after Krieger described the world as divided between the Communist and democratic ideologies and stressed the democratic and legalist way in which Castello was handling the matter.[17]

On May 20, Castello met with the executive commission of the Bloco Parlamentar Renovador to advise it that Brazil expected to send twelve hundred soldiers and marines, most of them within a week. Then the president flew to Santa Catarina. At a lunch in Florianópolis he announced signing a decree which placed the Brazilian force under Colonel Meira Mattos, the fifty-one–year–old FEB veteran who had been interventor in Goiás.[18]

While the first contingent left Santos Dumont Airport on the twenty-second, Castello was in Blumenau, Santa Catarina, where the reception was so warm that he left his security guard to walk through the streets. He was back in Rio the next day when the newspapers

[16] Ibid., p. 242; *Jornal do Brasil,* May 4, 7, 11, 1965.

[17] *Jornal do Brasil,* May 20, 1965; Krieger, *Desde as Missões,* p. 194.

[18] *Jornal do Brasil,* May 21, 1965.

published headlines ("a last kiss" and "the final embraces") that might have been appropriate for his own farewells to his family before leaving for Italy in 1944.[19]

With the new arrivals in the Dominican Republic, the United States prepared to withdraw a few thousand marines and looked to the OAS to name a commander of the Inter-American Force, which contained units from the United States, Brazil, Costa Rica, Honduras, and Nicaragua. The selection went to Brazil, with the result that General Hugo Panasco Alvim, another FEB veteran, became commander. Ambassador Gordon, laying a wreath in Rio at the Monument to the Unknown Soldier, remarked that whereas twenty years earlier FEB Commander Mascarenhas de Morais had served under an American general, the situation was now the reverse.[20]

Castello decided that the coordinating unit of the Brazilian force should be the General Staff for the Armed Forces (EMFA), which was headed by Admiral Luís Teixeira Martini following the transfer of Peri Beviláqua to the Superior Military Tribunal. The appointment of Admiral Martini, the first nonarmy man to hold the post in twenty years, reflected Castello's belief in rotation.[21]

Admiral Rademaker, who was criticizing Castello for wanting to create a Ministry of the Armed Forces, told Navy Minister Bosísio and the press that negative results had followed the presidential decree giving the EMFA the coordination of the military operations in the Dominican Republic. After Bosísio issued a bulletin for navy officers saying that he would tolerate no criticism of the presidential decree assigning the operations role to the EMFA, Rademaker, speaking to *Jornal do Brasil*, confirmed his criticism.[22]

Rademaker, punished by Bosísio with two days of house arrest, received messages of support from approximately seventy navy officers. Castello, speaking in the meantime at a Navy Ministry lunch, said that

[19] Ibid., May 23, 1965; Viana Filho (*O Governo Castelo Branco*, pp. 308–309) writes that by May 27 Brazil had completed its contingent in Santo Domingo, having sent in infantry battalion of 1,200 men, a marine unit of 250, and members of the airforce and navy.

[20] *Jornal do Brasil*, May 27, June 1, 2, 1965.

[21] *O Estado de S. Paulo*, March 4, 6, 1965; Lavanère-Wanderley, interview, August 12, 1977.

[22] *Jornal do Brasil*, June 11, 1965.

personalism and opposition to change created military reactionaries. Rademaker, when his house arrest was completed, issued a manifesto in which he said that he did not consider his opinions "reactionary, indisciplinary, or responsible for an emotional climate." "But," he said, "I accept the classification when my reaction is in the interest of the navy and Brazil."[23]

6. Coffee, Vietnam, and the Inter-American Peace Force (January–October, 1965)

Castello Branco's letter of January 8 to President Johnson about coffee was written at a time when coffee shipments from Brazil were down, due in part to the heavy world buying that had followed the August, 1963, frost, and were fetching prices lower than those prevailing in the middle of 1964. Although Brazilian coffee production, still suffering from the effect of the 1963 frost, had been meager, plenty of coffee was in storage in Brazil.[1]

The plans of the government were to reduce the excess of production that normally occurred in Brazil and to push for vitalization of the five-year 1962 International Coffee Agreement. Production would be reduced by an ambitious program of eradicating coffee trees in areas subject to frost and replacing them with crops less harmed by frost.[2] As for the International Coffee Agreement, it was clear that it would not function without controls by importing nations for disciplining the many exporting nations. Although in July, 1964, the Senate of the most important importer, the United States, had voted to implement the agreement, the House of Representatives, with the consumer in mind, had rejected implementation in August, 1964.[3]

President Johnson, replying to Castello on January 26, 1965, said that he attached "very high importance to the early enactment by the United States Congress of legislation to facilitate fulfillment of United States responsibility under the International Coffee Agreement," and

[23] Ibid., June 12, 19, 1965.

[1] World Coffee Information Center (WCIC), "The Coffee Agreement and Coffee Prices: Questions and Answers," September 1964.

[2] Roberto Campos, interview, December 23, 1974.

[3] UPI release, July 31, 1964; *New York Times*, August 25, 1964.

he expressed interest in the Brazilian suggestion of adjusting export quotas in accordance with prices.[4] After this suggestion was adopted by the members of the International Coffee Agreement in March, Juraci Magalhães and Assistant Secretary of State Thomas C. Mann held discussions with legislators in Washington. In Rio, Castello told Brazilian and foreign journalists that the world was developing "an increasing understanding of the importance of orderly marketing of coffee."[5]

Castello reviewed the situation with Commerce Minister Daniel Faraco and Brazilian Coffee Institute (IBC) President Leônidas Bório. Noting that Brazilian coffee exports had reached a very low level and that the competition from Africa had greatly increased, the president concluded that no effective international agreement existed. After listing the options, he decided that Brazil, which had not been cutting prices, should face the reality of a free-market situation and withdraw from the International Coffee Agreement unless a favorable decision was reached in Washington.[6]

The need to resort to such an extreme measure became unnecessary. On May 12 the House of Representatives approved the Senate bill that would permit full U.S. participation in the International Coffee Agreement. The approval, by a 300–97 vote, followed a two-hour debate in which opponents of the measure described it as an "unwise agreement to rig world markets." On the next day the Senate again voted for the legislation, this time approving two amendments added by the House.[7] Johnson, signing the legislation on May 24, said that the hopes of the coffee-producing nations for economic and social progress were tied to coffee, "A weak and disorderly coffee market," he said, "is of deep concern to them and to us."[8]

[4] LBJ, letter to HACB, The White House, January 26, 1965, Papers of LBJ, EX CO 32, Box 16, LBJ Library.

[5] Brazilian Embassy, *Survey of the Brazilian Economy*, 1966, p. 59; Thomas C. Mann, interview, Austin, Texas, September 4, 1975; Viana Filho, *O Governo Castelo Branco*, p. 270; HACB, *Entrevistas, 1964–1965*, p. 46.

[6] *Análise e Perspectiva Econômica* (APEC), September 13, 1965; Viana Filho, *O Governo Castelo Branco*, p. 270.

[7] Congressional Record (89th Congress), House of Representatives, Vol. 111, No. 85 (May 12, 1965), pp. 9887–9908 (see esp. pp. 9902 and 9905); WCIC release, May 14, 1965; *Congressional Record* (89th Congress), Senate, Vol. 111, No. 86 (May 13, 1965), pp. 10083–10084.

[8] WCIC release, May 24, 1965.

At this time Otávio Bulhões and other Brazilian government experts made their annual prediction about the size of the forthcoming Brazilian crop in order to establish the minimum price to serve as the basis for purchases by the IBC and loans by the Bank of Brazil. Foreseeing a 1965–1966 crop of thirty-two million bags, far in excess of the previous one, they drastically reduced the guaranteed price for producers.[9]

The United States legislation became effective on July 1, 1965, and was followed by a slight decline in the international price for Brazilian coffee. On the other hand, Brazilian exports increased considerably in the second half of 1965, when 8.6 million bags were shipped, compared with 5.0 million in the first half of 1965 and 7.5 million in the second half of 1964. *Conjuntura Econômica,* explaining the small amount shipped in the first half of 1965, said that Brazil tried "to defend the price even at the cost of losing markets" and that the buyers abroad lacked confidence in Brazil's ability to maintain prices "practically alone." "In the second half," *Conjuntura Econômica* wrote, "the situation improved because the operation of the International Coffee Agreement gained in efficiency."[10]

During 1965, Castello wrote to President Johnson about one other matter requiring U.S. legislation. As far back as 1962 Brazil had believed that it would receive, under legislation for loans and sales to friendly countries, four destroyers of the Fletcher class that the United States wanted to be standard in the major South American navies, and, in anticipation of their receipt, Brazil had scrapped three old destroyers and one destroyer escort. The loan to Brazil would enable its navy to improve its participation in anti-submarine warfare and merchant convoy missions, recognized by the U.S. joint chief of staff as key tasks of the Brazilian navy.[11]

Castello asked Leitão da Cunha and Juraci Magalhães to push the matter in Washington, and he discussed it several times with Gordon. Gordon explained to Washington that the receipt of the destroyers

[9] Dênio Nogueira, interview, December 20, 1977; Viana Filho, *O Governo Castelo Branco*, p. 268; Syvrud, *Foundations of Brazilian Economic Growth*, p. 247. A bag of coffee weighs 60 kilograms.

[10] *Conjuntura Econômica*, February 1966, p. 22, and February 1967, p. 63.

[11] Memorandum, William G. Bowdler to McGeorge Bundy, Washington, D.C., August 11, 1965, and Department of State, Briefing book for Fulbright trip to Brazil, August 1965, NSFB, LBJ Library.

would help Castello maintain "support from the Brazilian Congress of strongly pro-U.S. foreign policy" and help him "neutralize Navy resentment" against his naval aviation decision. "I need not reiterate," the ambassador added, "importance to us of maintaining pro-American orientation of officer corps, which would be seriously endangered if ship loans refused."[12] After Brazil supported the United States in the Dominican crisis, State Department officials reminded Senator Fulbright and others that Brazil considered "cooperation a two-way street." A White House staff member, reviewing the ship loan situation in August, 1965, described it as "one of those cases of incautious commitments on which we now have to make good."[13]

Castello's letter to Johnson was written on September 20, 1965, after the House of Representatives had acted favorably but before the Senate acted. Castello mentioned the importance of the legislation for Western Hemisphere defense and received a reply in which Johnson expressed his hope that the destroyers would be made available to Brazil.[14] Meanwhile, in New York, Leitão da Cunha learned from Secretary of State Rusk that the Senate Armed Services Committee had decided to cut from four to three the destroyers for Brazil (and from three to two the destroyers for Argentina). U.S. military authorities, the secretary of state said, were concerned lest the situation in Southeast Asia call for more U.S. naval strength.[15] Apparently the Senate shared this thinking, because the necessary legislation remained in abeyance.

President Johnson hoped that Brazil would participate on the side of the United States in Southeast Asia. But Gordon, who had heard Castello tell Harriman that Brazil would not become involved in the

[12] Department of State, Briefing book, August 1965; Lincoln Gordon, cable to Secretary of State, August 30, 1965, NSFB, LBJ Library.

[13] Department of State, Briefing book, August 1965; handwritten note (signed Bob K) on typewritten memorandum, William G. Bowdler to McGeorge Bundy, August 11, 1965.

[14] Cable, Secretary of State to Lincoln Gordon, September 1, 1965, NSFB, LBJ Library; HACB, letter to LBJ, September 20, 1965, Papers of LBJ, President's Staff File, Head of State Correspondence, Vol. 1, Presidential Correspondence, LBJ Library; LBJ, letter to HACB, The White House, September 29, 1965, File O1, PVCB.

[15] Memorandum of conversation (present: Rusk, J. M. Cates, Leitão, and Castro Alves), Secretary's Delegation to the 30th UN General Assembly, September 28, 1965, Document 133, NSFB, LBJ Library.

Dominican Republic without the legitimization of that action by a two-thirds vote of the OAS, appreciated that Brazilian participation in Vietnam without international political coverage would be impossible; and the ambassador opposed tying requests for such participation to financial assistance for Brazil. In May, 1965, Gordon told Washington that unless he were explicitly instructed otherwise, he would not speak to the Brazilian administration about sending troops to Vietnam. He said that he might raise the matter of symbolic cooperation, and he was asked to do so.[16] In June, 1965, the Brazilian government contributed four hundred kilograms of medicines to the government of South Vietnam, via the International Red Cross.[17]

Johnson, writing to Castello on July 26, 1965, said that the eighty thousand men of the U.S. forces already in Vietnam needed to be reinforced by an equal or greater number, and he said that he would welcome Castello's view about the additional steps that the free world might take to support South Vietnam.[18] Gordon, taking this letter to Leitão da Cunha for delivery to Castello, suggested that Brazil might reduce the pressure on U.S. military manpower by increasing its troops in the Dominican Republic. Leitão reacted favorably and said that this idea fitted in with Castello's "general stance." Leitão also explored the possibility of further nonmilitary aid from Brazil to Vietnam.[19] But Brazil throughout the rest of 1965 did not add to its four hundred kilograms of medicines. And the question of Brazilian troops or other assistance in Vietnam remained dormant until December, 1965, when Johnson was more eager than ever to escalate the internationalization of the effort there.[20]

Following Gordon's talk with Leitão da Cunha, Castello learned from his foreign minister, and also from his war minister, that the United States wanted an additional Brazilian military contingent sent to the Dominican Republic. Calling in Gordon on September 22, Cas-

[16] Gordon, interview, June 11, 1975.

[17] Background paper for the visit of Costa e Silva to Washington, January 25–27, 1967, "Brazil and Viet Nam," NSFB, LBJ Library.

[18] LBJ, letter to HACB, July 26, 1965, unofficial translation, File O1 (pp. 26, 26v), PVCB.

[19] Gordon, telegram, Rio de Janeiro to Washington, July 27, 1965, NSFB, LBJ Library.

[20] Gordon, interview, June 11, 1975.

tello explained that he had to bear three factors in mind: hemispheric security, Brazil's economic situation, and domestic pressure for an early withdrawal. He said that while he would like to reconcile all three, hemispheric security was paramount in his mind. The ambassador also gathered that Castello wished to free United States personnel for participation in "Vietnam and other western causes" supported by Brazil.[21]

Castello said he understood that the United States wanted two Brazilian battalions to remain in the Dominican Republic for a "substantial period," perhaps through the election and inauguration of a successor to Hector García Godoy, who had been installed by the negotiators as provisional president. For economic reasons, Castello pointed out, he would prefer to maintain one battalion, but he said that if continental security required it, he would add a second, probably sending marines instead of army men. He noted that the logistical cost, to be paid by the United States, was but a small portion of the total. He asked Gordon if the OAS might contribute and, after receiving a discouraging reply, said that he was considering reducing the high allowances for troops serving outside Brazil.[22].

Following this discussion, a policy was adopted for reducing the size of the Inter-American Peace Force in the Dominican Republic, and, therefore, when Brazil sent a second contingent early in November, it was merely to relieve men who had been serving since May.[23] In keeping with the new policy, the United States replaced the commander of its contingent with a general of lower rank. Castello decided that a major general should replace Army General Panasco Alvim.[24]

Panasco Alvim had started complaining in June when he said that U.S. negotiator Ellsworth Bunker was "exasperatingly and incomprehensibly slow." Later, Panasco Alvim described the Provisional Government as principally supported by Communists and their allies. Leitão da Cunha, after receiving "alarming reports," told the U.S. Embassy

[21] Gordon, cable from Rio de Janeiro to Washington, September 22, 1965, NSFB, LBJ Library.

[22] Ibid.

[23] United States Embassy, Rio de Janeiro, cable to Department of State, November 23, 1965, NSFB, LBJ Library; Coronel Carlos de Meira Mattos and officers of FAIBRÁS, *A Experiência do FAIBRÁS na República Dominicana*, pp. 52–53.

[24] Gordon, cable, September 22, 1965; United States Embassy, Rio de Janeiro, cable to Department of State, November 23, 1965.

that Brazil could well "find itself fighting for the installation of a Communist regime, which would be intolerable." Leitão also spoke of the differences in views between the Inter-American Peace Force commander and the negotiating committee that represented the OAS foreign ministers and added that the Peace Force should not be subject to the personal orders of nations contributing forces.[25]

Despite these problems, the Brazilian government saw advantages for the hemisphere in a permanent Inter-American Peace Force. Each country would set aside a unit for mobilization whenever collective action was sought by a two-thirds vote of the OAS. Castello felt that Brazil was opposed to unilateral decisions about continental security, and he considered it absurd to want collective protection but fail to create the appropriate mechanism.[26]

To avoid a clash with Latin American nations strongly opposed to a permanent force, Leitão da Cunha hesitated to seek a decision at the Second Special Inter-American Conference for reforming the OAS charter, which had been postponed until November, 1965. Speaking with Gordon in Rio in July and with Dean Rusk in New York in September, the Brazilian foreign minister suggested getting countries to sign a protocol, beginning with the countries that had supplied troops in the Dominican Republic. Leitão and Rusk, agreeing that it would be unrealistic to seek adoption of the permanent force at the Second Special Conference, agreed also that it would be worthwhile to encourage discussion of the idea by the foreign ministers who were to attend the conference.[27]

As the United States did not press for the idea as long as Brazil did, Argentines observed that the United States left Brazil "holding the baby."[28]

[25] United States Embassy, Rio de Janeiro, telegram to Washington, July 24, 1965; W. G. Bowdler, memorandum, Washington, October 27, 1965; Philip Raine, cable from Rio de Janeiro to Washington, October 26, 1965 (all in NSFB, LBJ Library).

[26] Leitão da Cunha, interview, November 23, 1974; Juraci Magalhães, interview, Rio de Janeiro, December 3, 1974; HACB quoted in Viana Filho, *O Governo Castelo Branco*, p. 435.

[27] Memorandum of conversation, Secretary's Delegation to the 30th UN General Assembly, September 28, 1965; United States Embassy, Rio de Janeiro, cable to Washington, July 11, 1965, NSFB, LBJ Library.

[28] United States Embassy, cable to Washington, July 11, 1965.

7. The Central Bank and Rural Credit

When Sir Otto Niemeyer, the British "father" of the central banks of Chile and Argentina, visited Brazil in 1931, he stressed that Brazil, too, needed a true central bank to establish and carry out monetary policy in a nonpolitical manner.[1] But Brazilian presidents and the powerful Bank of Brazil resisted the idea, and thus the Bank of Brazil remained what was often called "the last mixed bank in the world which acted as a commercial bank as well as a central bank." To pave the way for an independent central bank, the Brazilian government in 1947 followed a suggestion of Professor Otávio Bulhões and established the Superintendency of Money and Credit (SUMOC) with the finance minister as its chairman. But SUMOC was dominated by the Bank of Brazil, which remained in control of rediscount and foreign exchange operations. During the fifteen years before the fall of Goulart, legislative proposals for creating a central bank made no progress in Congress.[2]

After SUMOC Director Bulhões became finance minister in April, 1964, he consulted the financial community about banking reform. And he asked Dênio Nogueira, whom he planned to make director of the SUMOC, to go to Brasília to prevent passage of banking reform legislation which had been submitted earlier by the Bank of Brazil and which, in his opinion, was not a reform but simply a measure to preserve the privileges of the Bank of Brazil.[3] Dênio Nogueira told interested congressmen about the long-standing need of a reform that would create a central bank and a monetary council.

During a plane trip, Nogueira spoke with Congressman Herbert Levy, who had banking and agricultural interests in São Paulo. Levy agreed to vote for the new government's reform project, but in return he asked for support of one of his favorite ideas: the establishment of a Rural Bank to provide credits to the agricultural sector.[4] Neither

[1] Dênio Nogueira, interview, December 20, 1977.

[2] Paul Vanorden Shaw, "Central Bank Starts Activities," *Brazil Herald*, April 14, 1965; Syvrud, *Foundations of Brazilian Economic Growth*, p. 62; Gonzaga do Nascimento Silva, interview, October 25, 1975; Sant'Anna e Silva, memorandum, July 1979.

[3] J. O. Melo Flores, interview, Rio de Janeiro, December 20, 1977; Dênio Nogueira, interview, December 20, 1977.

[4] Dênio Nogueira, interview, December 20, 1977; Severo Gomes, interview, Rio de Janeiro, July 25, 1977.

Castello nor his financial advisers favored such a bank, which would duplicate extensive work done by the Bank of Brazil's agricultural credit department (headed by Severo Gomes). Nogueira suggested to Levy that further credit assistance be furnished the rural sector by legislation requiring all Brazilian banks to set up agricultural credit departments. Levy, who liked this proposal, agreed to support the banking reform after Nogueira promised that it would include an article saying that the president would soon submit a project for institutionalizing rural credit in all banks.[5]

At the suggestion of Bulhões, Senator Mem de Sá (Partido Libertador, Rio Grande do Sul) became *relator* of the government's banking reform project. Throughout the last half of 1964 the senator attended numerous discussions at which Bank of Brazil President Luís Morais Barros, of São Paulo, defended the position of the Bank of Brazil. At one of them, held on a holiday at the Alvorada Palace library, Bulhões greeted Castello, who was at the head of a marble table, and then took a seat on the president's left. When it seemed that Morais Barros, after greeting Castello, might occupy the chair on Castello's right, the president said to Mem de Sá, "this chair is for you." The gesture, Viana Filho writes, illustrated Castello's "sense of protocolar hierarchy."[6]

Following long negotiations, Mem de Sá completed a substitute amendment that was approved by both legislative houses late in 1964. Much to his surprise, he was called to Laranjeiras Palace on December 30. There he found the president, as solicitous and cordial as ever, in the company of Bulhões and Roberto Campos. The president thanked the senator for the tenacity that had resulted in the legislation. He added that Campos had found a few small matters not to his liking and had therefore proposed that presidential partial vetoes be used in the case of two articles. Castello did not want to do this without giving Mem de Sá the opportunity to present arguments that he might have. Mem de Sá, deeply moved by this consideration, said that he was happy to accept any suggestions of the planning minister.[7]

[5] Dênio Nogueira, interview, December 20, 1977.

[6] Mem de Sá, "Castelo e os Parlamentares," pp. 1–2; idem, letter to Luís Viana Filho, Brasília, October 7, 1971, p. 3; Viana Filho, *O Governo Castelo Branco*, p. 504. The *relator* studies, reports on, and handles the project in Congress.

[7] Mem de Sá, "Castelo e os Parlamentares," p. 2; idem, letter to Viana Filho, October 7, 1971, pp. 3–4.

As a result of the banking reform (Law 4,595 of December 31, 1964), the Central Bank of the Republic of Brazil opened its doors on March 31, 1965, with Dênio Nogueira as president. The powerful eleven-man National Monetary Council, described as the supreme organ of the national financial system, was headed by Bulhões. In addition to the ministers of finance, industry and commerce, and planning (the last two without votes), its members were the president and three directors of the Central Bank, the presidents of the Bank of Brazil and the National Economic Development Bank (BNDE), and two professionals outside government.[8] Professor Eugênio Gudin, writing to Castello on April 6, 1965, to explain why he was declining an invitation to serve on the Monetary Council, said that his presence was unnecessary because his dear friend Otávio Bulhões was extremely competent.[9] Dênio Nogueira, in a letter to England, delighted Sir Otto Niemeyer with the news of the turn of events in Brazil.

In accordance with the central banking law, Dênio Nogueira drew up a proposal for institutionalizing agricultural credit that was approved by Castello and submitted to Congress. The many amendments made by Congress included three provisions that would require banks to employ at least 10 percent of their deposits in agricultural loans, charge interest on them at rates below those collected on nonagricultural loans, and prohibit charges for commissions.[10] When the amended bill reached the president, he consulted Bulhões and Dênio Nogueira and then used partial vetoes to strip the bill of the three provisions that his financial advisers disliked. Nogueira felt that the interest rates on loans to the agricultural sector ought not to be below the inflation rate; he feared that if they were so low, the large agricultural properties would secure all the loans, with the small properties receiving none of them.[11]

Senator Daniel Krieger told Castello that agricultural activities were unable to support loans without the three provisions that had been removed by the vetoes. Castello replied that he would consult Bulhões, and soon after that the finance minister telephoned Krieger and defended the vetoes. Bulhões, unable to convince the senator, did not in-

[8] Banco Central da República do Brasil, report for 1965.

[9] Eugênio Gudin, letter to HACB, April 6, 1965, File M, CPDOC.

[10] Krieger, *Desde as Missões*, pp. 202–203.

[11] Dênio Nogueira, interview, December 20, 1977.

sist on having his way, but he did ask the senator to listen to Central Bank President Dênio Nogueira, who was in his office. Krieger found Nogueira intransigent, and so he cut off the conversation with him.[12]

After Castello decided to support his leader in the Senate, Congress overrode the vetoes that affected the three provisions that interested Krieger. They were therefore included in the final version, Law 4,829, that was published on November 5, 1965.

8. Magalhães Pinto Seeks a Meeting of Revolutionary Leaders (August–September, 1965)

The reduction of the annual inflation rate from around 70 percent in the first quarter of 1965 to around 20 percent in the final quarter was achieved in the face of a considerable rise in public utility rates and the elimination of rent controls.[1] Contributing to the success were the severe measures taken to restrict wage increases and reduce the federal budget deficit.

Wages in the private sector, which had been increased by more than 80 percent in the latter part of 1964, came under the control of the federal government in July, 1965, when Congress, at the request of the administration, voted Law 4,725 extending to the private sector the legislation of 1964 under which the National Council on Wage Policy determined new wage rates according to the formula that considered the living cost increase of the previous two years, productivity increases, and one-half of the inflation rate expected for the year ahead. This formula kept wage increases in the private sector between 40 and 45 percent in 1965, which was a little less than the twelve-month cost-of-living increase that had followed the previous wage adjustments. By means of another piece of congressional legislation, Law 4,789 of August 12, 1965, the annual bonus (the "thirteenth-month salary" instituted by the Goulart regime) became payable in two installments instead of one lump sum at the end of the year.[2]

[12] Krieger, *Desde as Missões*, pp. 202–203.

[1] *Conjuntura Econômica*, February 1966 (p. 63), and February 1969 (p. 30).

[2] Arnaldo Sussekind, "A gestão do Ministro Arnaldo Sussekind no Ministério do Trabalho e Previdência Social (3/IV/64–3/XII/65)" (paper prepared for Luís Viana Filho).

If workers in the private sector had reason to be upset by the new wage austerity, workers in the public sector in 1965 had more reason, for they received no pay increase throughout the year. As the press had been predicting a 40 percent pay increase, they were shocked to learn from Bulhões on July 25 that they would receive no revisions "either now or in the forthcoming budget."[3] While the National Union of Public Servants (UNSP) planned a "monster rally" and encampment in the Laranjeiras Palace gardens, Roberto Campos said that "the government is not going to squander sacrifices already made by increasing expenditures at the cost of productive investments." But he did say that an increase in 1966 would be considered, and Castello set up an interministerial commission, headed by the planning minister, to decide what to do about 1966.[4]

The President of the UNSP attacked the Government Plan of Action (PAEG) for "imposing merciless sacrifices" and asserted that each soldier sent to the Dominican Republic cost one million cruzeiros. Government workers, instead of carrying out the encampment, followed the advice of the Brazilian Confederation of Public Workers (CSPB): in July they sent thousands of letters to Castello pointing out that their families were in hunger. After Raimundo de Brito opposed wage increases for government workers, the CSPB accused the minister of health of advocating the death by starvation of 10 percent of the public work force.[5]

Senator William Fulbright, heading a U.S. mission to Brazil in August, 1965, praised the country for "its efficient work to stabilize its economy and control the inflation." Jack Valenti, who accompanied the Fulbright mission, wrote a confidential report to President Johnson to say that Castello Branco "is the only man in Brazil today who is able to get the full respect of the people and thus the only man able to shove unpalatable but necessary measures down the throat of the populace." Valenti expressed the hope that Castello would reconsider his decision not to run for reelection to the presidency.[6]

[3] *Jornal do Brasil*, July 17, 21, 1965.

[4] Ibid., July 22, 23, August 3, 5, 1965.

[5] Ibid., July 23, 24, 31, August 1, 1965.

[6] Ibid., August 13, 1965; Jack Valenti, Report to the President: Fulbright Mission

Lacerda, described by Valenti as "a gifted, talented man with much charisma and demagogic charm, but unreliable and erratic," declared that Castello was "surrounded by grave diggers."[7] He sent the president a fifty-five–page study that called for abandoning the PAEG and its "calamitous deflation," revising taxes to foment production, and "returning" purchasing power to the workers and middle classes. When Roberto Campos visited the Soviet Union, Lacerda asserted that the planning minister was trying to use blackmail to get funds from the United States, which, he said, "is not sending and will not send funds."[8] *O Estado de S. Paulo,* more sympathetic to the administration's economic views than its political views, replied that Campos' trip had nothing to do with blackmail and that if foreign capital was not coming to Brazil to the extent desired, it was largely due to Lacerda's pronouncements on economic matters, based "more on passion than on cold reasoning."[9]

For the hard-hit industrial worker, Lacerda's criticisms seemed to make sense, for although agricultural production rose about 14 percent in 1965, industrial production fell by about 5 percent.[10] IBOPE, a respected conductor of polls, showed that the debate between Lacerda and the federal government was a great popular success for Lacerda in Guanabara, for which it reported the following results:[11]

---

to Brazil, August 10, 1965, Confidential File, CO 1-3 (1966), CO-37, Box 7, LBJ Library.

[7] Valenti, "Report to the President," August 10, 1965; *Jornal do Brasil*, July 3, 1965.

[8] Lacerda, 55-page analysis of the government's economic policy, attached to covering letter to HACB, May 17, 1965, File N4 (p. 16), CPDOC (see pp. 12, 42, 43, 52, of Lacerda's analysis); *O Estado de S. Paulo*, September 2, 1965.

Before Roberto Campos went to Moscow early in September 1965, a majority of the members of the National Security Council expressed their opposition to the trip. But Castello Branco, taking the position that the council was merely giving him advice, approved of the mission, which would demonstrate that Brazil had options. Roberto Campos made an excellent impression on the Russians. Following his discussions about possible Soviet loans for Brazilian hydroelectric works, the United States furnished the loans (Sant'Anna e Silva, interview, June 30, 1979).

[9] *O Estado de S. Paulo*, September 2, 1965.

[10] Syvrud, *Foundations of Brazilian Economic Growth*, p. 50; "Panorama do Ano," *Conjuntura Econômica*, February 1966.

[11] *Jornal do Brasil*, September 4, 1965 (Coluna do Castello by Carlos Castello Branco).

Who Wins the Debate, Castello or Lacerda?

Lacerda	46%
Castello	14%
Don't know	40%

Who Better Represents the Objectives of the March '64 Revolution, Castello or Lacerda?

Lacerda	44%
Castello	21%
Don't know	35%

About the Contest of Lacerda against Roberto Campos?

Pro-Lacerda	56%
Pro-Campos	8%

Who Has the Greatest Prestige in Guanabara?

Lacerda	45%
Kubitschek	32%
Goulart	5%
Castello	4%

Like Lacerda, Magalhães Pinto wrote letters to Castello calling for a revision of the cabinet and the economic policy, and he filled the press with attacks against the government. Its policy, he told *O Globo* in June and July, 1965, was bringing it "greater and greater unpopularity" and had already brought "development to a standstill."[12]

Although Magalhães Pinto frequently referred to the "serious crisis" afflicting Brazil, Costa e Silva declared that everything was calm, with the army backing the president. Castello simply went ahead with his business. After the National Security Council decided to reverse the expropriation that Goulart had decreed for the private petroleum refineries and to allow private enterprise to engage in the petrochemical industry, the president issued the appropriate decree, which said that the March, 1964, expropriation had been carried out "in a climate of emotional tension and under the pressure of demagogic forces."[13]

But the so-called crisis was not completely ignored by Castello. He referred to in a conversation with a television news reporter at a lunch

[12] Magalhães Pinto, letter to HACB, Belo Horizonte, May 13, 1965, File N3, CPDOC; *O Globo*, June 25, July 6, 1965; *Jornal do Brasil*, July 29, 1965.

[13] *Jornal do Brasil*, July 3, 8, 10, 1965.

given in Brasília by Luís Viana Filho for members of the press. "Sometimes," Castello said to the news reporter, "you use a cavernous and gloomy voice that frightens me. One day, after you read a news item, you lowered your eyes and affirmed that 'the situation is grave.' "[14]

In part, according to Magalhães Pinto and Lacerda, the gravity of the situation was caused by Castello's failure to support the infuriated military hard-liners. Magalhães Pinto, in one of his letters to Castello, complained about the laxness that the government had shown in decreeing punishments under the Institutional Act.[15]

Colonel Osnelli Martinelli spoke to *Jornal do Brasil* and *Tribuna da Imprensa* about his disappointment in the government's failure to punish corrupt and subversive people, and then, in June, 1965, he and Colonel Gérson de Pina resigned from the IPM positions. After Martinelli gave another statement that cited "the case of Arraes, of sad memory," the Liga Democratica Radical (LIDER), in which Martinelli was influential, issued a manifesto which classified Castello as "nothing more than a delegate of the Supreme Command of the Revolution" who could not act "contrary to the revolutionary ideas, which are above those of the constitution itself."[16]

Castello declared that he could "admit no further excesses by the hard-liners" and was even ready to fight them because his personal determination was to reestablish democratic normalcy.[17] Martinelli was given a thirty-day prison term and placed in Fort Capacabana.

Magalhães Pinto told the press that the arrest of Colonel Martinelli, like that of Admiral Rademaker, was an example of the mistakes that stemmed from Castello's obstinacy.[18] Lacerda, accompanied by state Security Secretary Gustavo Borges and Colonel Gérson de Pina, called on Martinelli at Fort Copacabana in July. The governor reminded reporters of Martinelli's help with the defense of Guanabara Palace on April 1, 1964, and called attention to a case that he considered less valorous: that of Luís Viana Filho, who, he said, had been buying dollars before the revolution in order to flee from Communism by going abroad.[19]

[14] Ibid., July 10, 1965 (Coluna do Castello by Carlos Castello Branco).
[15] Magalhães Pinto, letter to HACB, May 13, 1965, File N3, CPDOC.
[16] *Jornal do Brasil*, June 21, 1965.
[17] Ibid.
[18] *O Globo*, June 28, 1965.
[19] *Jornal do Brasil*, July 3, 1965.

Air force Lieutenant Colonel Júlio Valente, in charge of an IPM in São Paulo, then accused Castello of protecting Ademar de Barros, "the corrupt governor of São Paulo," by having Air Minister Eduardo Gomes end investigations. Gomes sentenced Valente to thirty days of imprisonment.[20]

Castello Branco, in a letter to Costa e Silva, complained that officers connected with the IPM's were not acting in a way to give credit to the president or the war minister. They wanted, he wrote, to close down a theatrical production in Rio, *Liberdade*, and thus "terrorize" freedom of opinion. "Besides, some officers have ordered the seizures of books. That only serves to lower the intellectual level of the Revolution because . . . it constitutes a governmental act used only in Communist or Nazi countries. . . . The 'autonomous force' must . . . be properly enlightened, restrained, and, if necessary, repressed."[21]

When Magalhães Pinto spoke to reporters on August 24 about the "national crisis," he said that Castello should call a meeting of all the revolutionary leaders, civilian and military, so that they could voice self-criticisms, noting their responsibilities for the "crisis." The governor of Minas said that his idea was a last effort to "save the Revolution," which had been transformed into a simple coup because all power of decision had fallen into the hands of one man.[22]

Lacerda described the suggestion as an excellent one that would force Castello to change his cabinet and revise his methods of administration. On September 2 the Guanabara governor released to the press a long letter that he sent to Magalhães Pinto to support his idea. Lacerda wrote that the administration, by sending Roberto Campos to the USSR, was trying to show that Goulart had been right, and he accused Castello of trying to shove the governors of Minas and Guanabara aside. "All this and much more," Lacerda wrote, "can be discussed constructively around a table, under the presidency of the head of the government himself." Lacerda added that if Castello considered "representatives of the situation that the Revolution overthrew" to be members of

[20] Ibid., July 6, 8, 13, 1965.

[21] HACB, letter to Costa e Silva, July 5, 1965, PVCB. The complete letter is given in the Appendix.

[22] *Jornal do Brasil*, August 26, 31, 1965.

the "Bloco Revolucionário," there was no reason for him to object "to calling together the men who made the Revolution for them."[23]

Magalhães Pinto, called to Laranjeiras Palace to discuss his idea with Castello, found the president agreeable and in a good mood. Castello asked Magalhães Pinto to prepare the agenda and list those to be invited, and the governor, unwilling to break the cordial atmosphere, accepted the impractical task. Later, however, after Magalhães Pinto reviewed the matter with Lacerda, he told the press that he was surprised Castello had assigned him a task that belonged to the president himself.[24]

Costa e Silva, asked by a reporter if he would attend the meeting, said he did not know if he was on Magalhães Pinto's list. Mourão Filho told the press that he would not attend because he did not want to assume any responsibility for the errors of the Castello Branco government.[25]

Political commentators correctly predicted that Magalhães Pinto would never make the selection of those to be invited. They observed that his idea—which Castello had disliked but preferred not to veto—was dead.[26]

Despite the attacks of the two most prestigious governors, Magalhães Pinto and Lacerda, and despite the recession that gave them popular ammunition, President Castello Branco was scoring surprisingly well in Congress. The formation of the Bloco Parlamentar Renovador and the defeat of Mazzilli by Bilac Pinto were followed by a series of administration legislative victories, including the extension of wage controls and the decision to send troops to the Dominican Republic.

The administration's authority to punish arbitrarily had long since expired, and with the decision of the president and Congress to hold popular gubernatorial elections, the nation appeared to be returning to the practice of constitutional democracy.

[23] Ibid., August 29, September 3, 1965.
[24] Ibid., September 9, 10, 1965.
[25] Ibid., September 10, 11, 1965.
[26] Ibid., September 10, 1965.

Magalhães Pinto, critical of the government for scheduling the elections and critical of the president for his "laxness" in decreeing punishments, was well aware that the president's relations with the hard-liners had become worse than ever. In the release of Arraes, the arrest of Martinelli, and in other incidents, such as the *Liberdade* affair, the forces favoring legality were victorious. But another important test lay ahead: the carrying out of the elections scheduled for October.

The Hard Line Provokes a Crisis
(October–November, 1965)

Inclusion of the clause making me ineligible for reelection is a matter of my personal conscience, and I shall never sign the Ato without it.

1. Negrão de Lima and Israel Pinheiro Oppose the UDN (September, 1965)

MAGALHÃES PINTO, unable to prevent or postpone the direct gubernatorial elections of October 3, presided over the work to select a UDN candidate in Minas. The contest might have been limited to two state cabinet secretaries and the mayor of Belo Horizonte except that Oscar Correia, the most voted-for UDN congressman in Minas in 1962, decided to campaign, against the governor's wishes. After the mayor and one state secretary stepped aside, the balloting at the UDN convention pitted Correia against Health Secretary Roberto Rezende (who had married a niece of Magalhães Pinto). Rezende won.[1]

In Guanabara, Lacerda supported his transport secretary, Enaldo Cravo Peixoto, for the UDN gubernatorial nomination. The governor assailed the candidacies of Adauto Cardoso, most favored by Castello, and of popular congressman and radio commentator Amaral Neto. When a movement favoring Raimundo de Brito, well regarded by Castello, gained ground in May, Lacerdistas accused the health minister of using his federal office by offering posts in return for support. Vice-governor Rafael de Almeida Magalhães asked Castello to curtail this alleged activity, but the president merely showed displeasure with the request.[2]

After UDN opposition to the Cravo Peixoto candidacy forced Lacerda to look elsewhere, it appeared possible to unite the UDN behind

[1] Oscar Dias Correia, interview, September 24, 1975.

[2] Lacerda Paiva, interview, December 16, 1977.

Carlos Flexa Ribeiro, whose work as Guanabara education secretary was highly regarded. Flexa Ribeiro, the father-in-law of a son of Lacerda, was praised by Castello when Sandra Cavalcanti discussed the Guanabara political situation with the president. Adauto Cardoso, Bilac Pinto, and Raimundo de Brito sent Lacerda a message saying that Flexa Ribeiro alone could bring the Guanabara UDN together. Lacerda saw a maneuver unfavorable to himself in this message, but by the end of May the Flexa Ribeiro candidacy had become a certainty for the UDN.[3]

Early in June, Congress complicated the tasks of the opposition by enacting Constitutional Amendment 14 to rid the electoral process of corruption and subversion. The amendment itself stipulated that gubernatorial candidates were to have at least four years of voting residence in the states where they sought office, a requirement that threw doubt on the Guanabara candidacy of Marshal Henrique Lott and the Minas candidacy of PSD Congressman Sebastião Paes de Almeida, a former Kubitschek finance minister. Further uncertainty stemmed from the administration's proposed law of ineligibilities, which was sent to Congress on June 21 and was intended to complement the amendment.

The law project ruled against those who had "contributed to the formation of trusts" and "had carried out acts contrary to administrative probity"[4] and thus seemed to be aimed at Paes de Almeida, who was being accused of operating a plate glass trust and who was believed to have spent vast sums to secure his congressional seat. Another clause hit Hélio de Almeida, candidate of Goulart and the PTB in Guanabara, because it denied eligibility in 1965 to anyone who, not having been a legislator, had served in a nonmilitary federal cabinet post between January 23, 1963, and March 31, 1964. Congressman Nelson Carneiro (PSD, Guanabara) ridiculed the administration's project by suggesting a substitute bill to decree the ineligibility of "all Almeidas, or Sebastiões, or sons of Sebastiões."[5]

To the annoyance of the hard-liners, congressional leaders chose, as *relator* of the project, Congressman Oliveira Brito (PSD, Bahia), who had been a Goulart cabinet minister in 1963. After Brito said that no

[3] Ibid.; Cavalcanti, interview, November 18, 1975; Lacerda, *Depoimento*, p. 347; Castello Branco, *Os Militares no Poder*, p. 256.

[4] *Jornal do Brasil*, June 21, 1965.

[5] Ibid., June 23, 1965.

candidate should be declared ineligible just because he had not been a military man or legislator, Colonel Gérson de Pina announced that he would ask Congress to imprison Oliveira Brito.[6]

The proposed *lei das ineligibilidades* reached the Chamber plenary on July 6, accompanied by so many suggested changes presented by the PSD and PTB that passage of anything resembling the administration's wishes seemed in doubt. But hard-liners showed such determination to cancel the elections entirely that the administration's version came to be considered an instrument for allowing Castello to deal with the "crisis."[7] The administration got the law it wanted on July 10. Consequently, Hélio de Almeida withdrew from the race in Guanabara.

Paes de Almeida would not withdraw. He was nominated for governor of Minas on July 20, leading Magalhães Pinto to assert that the PSD state convention, with speeches by Auro de Moura Andrade and Tancredo Neves, had transformed itself into an "anti-Revolutionary campaign."[8] Nor did Marshal Lott withdraw in Guanabara, despite a "veto" by military leaders. Helped by unruly mobs in the galleries of Tiradentes Palace late in July and early in August, Lott won the PTB nomination in a close vote over Francisco Negrão de Lima, a former Kubitschek foreign minister. Lott proclaimed that the *cassados* should have their political rights returned.[9]

Castello met with the military ministers in Brasília on August 5 and then declared that the electoral tribunals should rule against the legality of candidates who were anti-Revolutionary, corrupt, or subversive. On the same day, he delivered a speech at the Superior Electoral Tribunal in which he said that "the national security can never be at the mercy of the same insignificant and audacious minority which on March 31 was at the service of subversion and corruption."[10]

In Washington, Juraci Magalhães was so worried to see the "adversaries of the Revolution take the offensive" that he wrote to Castello on August 10 to remind him that he had warned him, after the revolution, that "once again we might see a government fall due to its inability to use its power in a timely way." The selection of Negrão de Lima, Juraci

[6] Ibid., June 23, July 3, 1965.
[7] Ibid., July 6, 7, 9, 1965.
[8] Ibid., July 21, 1965.
[9] Ibid., August 1, 3, 4, 19, 1965.
[10] Ibid., August 6, 1965.

wrote, would not be a challenge to the Revolution, and therefore the Communists had taken advantage of the "senility of Lott, who for a long time has been their useful instrument. . . . We must face them with energy."[11]

In mid-August the Guanabara PSD convention issued a statement praising PTB candidate Lott, but its delegates were so certain that Lott's candidacy was illegal that they nominated Negrão de Lima. Lacerda's pleasure at having the opposition thus split was short-lived, for on September 6 the Superior Electoral Tribunal declared Lott ineligible because his voting residence was in the state of Rio de Janeiro. The PTB lost little time in nominating Negrão de Lima.

The Superior Electoral Tribunal also forced Paes de Almeida out of the Minas race on the grounds that, while not even living in Minas, he had secured his election to Congress from that state solely by the influence of gifts made during his campaign.[12] In Belo Horizonte the PSD then chose Israel Pinheiro, who had worked with Kubitschek to build Brasília and more recently presided at the convention that had nominated Paes de Almeida. The election in Minas received the blessing of the judiciary a week later when the Federal Supreme Court ruled unanimously that the extension of Magalhães Pinto's term by the state assembly had been illegal.[13]

Opposition candidates, such as Israel Pinheiro and Negrão de Lima, were assisted by the federal government's austere economic measures. The wages of bureaucrats, besides being frozen at levels reached in 1964, were often tardy in being paid.[14] Furthermore, Lacerdistas thought that they saw the clever hand of General Golberi do Couto e Silva working against Flexa Ribeiro in the developments that reduced the dispersion of the opposition to the UDN, practically indispensable for a UDN victory in Guanabara.[15] After the PSD and PTB both supported Negrão, the Lacerdistas sought to launch the candidacies of two popular radio broadcasters who could be expected to take votes away from Negrão. One of them, Alziro Zarur, seemed likely to capture one

[11] Magalhães, letter to HACB, Washington, D.C., August 10, 1965, File O2 (pp. 14v, 15), PVCB.

[12] *Jornal do Brasil*, September 7, 8, 1965.

[13] Ibid., September 23, 1965.

[14] Lacerda Paiva, interview, December 16, 1977.

[15] Almeida Magalhães, interview, August 8, 1977; Sandra Cavalcanti, interview, November 18, 1975.

hundred thousand votes, and the other thirty thousand. Attorneys, said to have been close to Planalto Palace, handled the cases of the eligibilities of the two candidacies at the Regional Electoral Tribunal, which found reason to deny both of them. Lacerda declared that "if we win it will be in spite of the president, and if we lose it will be because of him," and he predicted that Negrão de Lima, if elected, would reach an understanding with Castello for the elimination of Lacerda's presidential candidacy by establishing indirect elections in 1966.[16]

Three minor candidates remained in the Guanabara race, and they included Amaral Neto, who described Lacerda as "a mixture of Hitler, Pérez Jiménez, Mussolini, and Louis XV."[17] For a while it appeared possible that these minor candidates would prevent anyone from obtaining the absolute majority required by the new legislation, in which case the election was to be made by the state assembly, where, Lacerda declared caustically, he would buy enough votes to secure Flexa Ribeiro's victory. But in Guanabara the campaigning in the last week became almost completely polarized between the two leading candidates.[18]

Castello, faced with the threats of hard-liners to prevent the inauguration of men like Negrão de Lima and Israel Pinheiro in case they won, announced on September 23 that he had an agreement with the leaderships of the armed forces and the UDN to assure the inauguration of the eleven governors to be elected on October 3. Then Kubitschek, in Europe, angered hard-liners by letting it be known that he planned to return to Brazil shortly after the elections to renew his political activities and "consolidate democracy." The elections, Kubitschek said, would completely change the situation in Brazil.[19]

Following a meeting of Costa e Silva with the Army High Command, which included the commanders of the four armies, the press reported that the army would guarantee the inaugurations of the governors who were elected. But *O Estado de S. Paulo* condemned "the low demagoguery" practiced by "supporters of the counterrevolution" and

[16] *Jornal do Brasil*, September 23, 1965.

[17] Ibid., September 19, 1965. Besides Amaral Neto (Partido Libertador), the minor candidates in Guanabara were Aurélio Viana (Christian Democratic and Socialist Parties) and Hélio Damasceno (Partido Trabalhista Nacional).

[18] Newspaper clipping, File N5 (Anexo 9), CPDOC; Almeida Magalhães, interview, August 8, 1977; Castello Branco, *Os Militares no Poder*, p. 321.

[19] *Jornal do Brasil*, September 24, 1965; *O Estado de S. Paulo*, September 29, 1965.

concluded that Castello had "committed a bad mistake in listening to those who told him that the hour had come for the establishment of 'legal democracy.' "[20]

In Rio on September 30 the last day of campaigning was carried out during a heavy rain. Lacerda, who collapsed from exhaustion while inaugurating a building in the Bangu district that morning, was unable to be present at the final Flexa Ribeira rally. Negrão de Lima concluded his speechmaking by warning against what he called "the wave of rumors and intrigues at the end of the campaign, principally one concerning an alliance with the Communist party."[21]

Negrão's reference was to the investigative work of Colonel Ferdinando de Carvalho. The colonel, convinced that Negrão had purchased Communist electoral support, planned to make a last-minute television revelation of the details. But before the colonel could do so, high authorities in the Castello government stepped in to prevent Ferdinando's IPM study of the Communist party from involving itself in current politics.[22]

CAMDE, the women's organization that demonstrated for Flexa Ribeiro, warned against Communism. Castello, addressing the nation, admitted that subversive and corrupt elements had united around some of the gubernatorial candidates. He declared that he was assuring the inaugurations of the victors, but he was also careful to emphasize that "the Revolution will not be put off the track, because it is strong enough to repress any who try, by any method, to alter paths being followed by the nation."[23]

2. Planning a Postelection Role for Juraci (August–September, 1965)

Juarci Magalhães' letter of August 10, inspired by the "offensive" of "adversaries," drew a reply that was carefully prepared by Castello (it underwent three drafts). "I think," the president wrote, "that the

[20] *O Estado de S. Paulo*, September 30, 1965.
[21] Ibid., October 1, 1965.
[22] Carvalho, interview, November 10, 1967.
[23] *O Estado de S. Paulo*, October 1, 1965.

hour has come for you to play the principal role in my act of dealing with very serious problems." The president suggested that the ambassador become either foreign minister or justice minister, but he made it clear that if Juraci accepted the Itamarati post he should serve at the same time as the president's coordinator of top-level politics. Expressing the opinion that national politics was entering a period that would be a culminating one for the Revolution, Castello pointed to the need to complete the principal reforms and reorganize the nation's political structure, "so that the Revolution can be extended through the next four-year presidential term and become fully consolidated." In conclusion Castello wrote: "I am convinced that you can be the politician capable of helping the government in this work that is decisive for the destiny of the Revolution and the nation."[1]

Shortly after the Superior Electoral Tribunal voided the candidacies of Lott and Paes de Almeida, Juraci Magalhães reached Brazil for a one-week visit during which he conferred twice with Castello at Laranjeiras Palace and spoke with hundreds of people (including Magalhães Pinto, Lacerda, and Ernani Sátiro). Juraci learned that, for political reasons, the president planned, after the October 3 elections, to make changes in some of the nonmilitary cabinet posts that were not concerned with economic-financial policy. And while Itamarati was one of the ministries to be affected, Castello hoped that at least for a while Juraci would serve as justice minister, for Milton Campos was not regarded as the right man to deal with what Aliomar Baleeiro and Luís Viana Filho called "the urgent necessities of the moment." But Aliomar, speaking with Juraci after the ambassador had conferred with Castello, found him unenthusiastic about becoming justice minister and contemplating suggesting the name of a friend for the president's consideration.[2]

That Juraci would replace Milton Campos was reported in Carlos Castello Branco's column on September 16, together with the news that Juraci favored the indirect election of Castello's successor by the Congress that was to be elected in 1966. Lacerdistas were disturbed by this report and by the headlines that proclaimed Juraci to be Castello's candidate for the presidency. Juraci himself, well known for his benevolent

[1] HACB, letter to Juraci Magalhães, n.d., File M (p. 14), CPDOC.

[2] Baleeiro, "Recordações do Presidente H. Castelo Branco," pp. 27–28.

smile and advocacy of harmony, became furious at what he called the irresponsible distortions of the press.[3]

On September 18, Juraci returned to Washington, and on the twenty-fourth Castello cabled him that his resignation had been accepted and that his brilliant work had been an example for Brazilian diplomacy. "You leave your post at a time when your prestige in the United States is at its peak and when the internal politics of my government is in great need of your services," Castello said.[4]

On the same day, Castello wrote to Leitão da Cunha, who had gone to the United States, to ask him to take the place of Juraci in Washington. Health Minister Raimundo de Brito, traveling to the United States for meetings, delivered the letter in New York, where Leitão was at the United Nations. Writing longhand to Castello on September 28, Leitão reminded him of work that he wished to complete before leaving his cabinet position: "November 17 has just been set as the date for the start of the Second Special Inter-American Conference, a project on which we have been working for more than a year." Mentioning also a foreign ministers' conference to be held in Montevideo just before the Rio conference, Leitão wrote that he would be quite agreeable to carry on with work he had initiated, provided that the president would delay, until after the meetings, the announcement of his change of positions.[5]

Whereas the announcement about Leitão was delayed, the news of Juraci's resignation became known at once, leading to renewed speculation that he would become the "national unity" candidate for president and that he would replace Milton Campos, coordinating the work to bring about much-discussed changes such as the indirect presidential election and an increase in the number of Supreme Court justices. Milton Campos was reported to have disagreed with Castello's decision to add to the number of justices.[6]

On October 1, Milton Campos addressed a letter of resignation to Castello in which he said that he planned to return to the Senate and

[3] Castello Branco, *Os Militares no Poder*, p. 317; *Jornal do Brasil*, September 12, 14, 16, 1965.

[4] HACB, handwritten notes for cable to Juraci Magalhães, File M (p. 18), CPDOC.

[5] Vasco Leitão da Cunha, letter to HACB, New York, September 28, 1965, File O2 (p. 26), PVCB.

[6] Castello Branco, *Os Militares no Poder*, p. 322 (column of September 25, 1965).

felt than an opportune time to resign from the Justice Ministry was on the eve of the elections of October 3. "Your government, faithful to the revolutionary commitments of the Institutional Act, will have accomplished a phase of great significance, and I can feel that I have fulfilled, at least in part, my mission of assisting Your Excellency," Milton Campos wrote.[7]

Castello asked Milton Campos to keep the news of his letter from the public until after the elections. In the meantime, Juraci took his time about returning to Brazil. On boarding the *Argentina* in New York, he told reporters that he had no political ambition and would not even run for alderman.[8]

3. Kubitschek Returns while Ballots Are Counted (October 4, 1965)

Kubitschek, in a greater hurry than Juraci to reach Brazil, planned to arrive by plane early on Monday morning, October 4, when the counting of Sunday's votes was to begin. But before he made his trip, he was advised that it would be a mistake. Friends of Negrão de Lima and Israel Pinheiro feared that if these "Kubitschek men" won at the polls, the hard-liner reaction against their inaugurations would be worse than ever with the return of the former president.[1]

Sobral Pinto, Kubitschek's lawyer, was approached by a politician who claimed to represent Kubitschek's enemies and who said that Castello would find it difficult to prevent the military from humiliating and possibly jailing Kubitschek. The lawyer, after being asked to telephone this information to Kubitschek, guessed that the politician represented Castello and not the enemies of the former president (who were eager to humiliate and jail him). He agreed to phone Kubitschek if he could tell him that the message came from Castello. Receiving permission, he made the phone call, but Kubitschek refused to believe that Castello was behind the message. Anyway, he was very eager to return to Brazil.[2]

[7] Milton Campos, letter to HACB, Rio de Janeiro, October 1, 1965, File M (p. 9), CPDOC.

[8] *O Estado de S. Paulo*, October 8, 1965; *Jornal do Brasil*, October 9, 1965.

[1] Wilson Frade, "Notas de um repórter," *Estado de Minas*, February 22, 1976.

[2] Sobral Pinto, interview, December 9, 1975.

At Galeão Airport on the morning of the fourth, Kubitschek and his wife were greeted by a large crowd that included Negrão de Lima and the two Kubitschek daughters. When the smiling former president reached the airport building, he was hoisted onto admirers' shoulders. He told the press that he did not intend to return to Europe and would go to Belo Horizonte as soon as allowed by those conducting IPM's at which he was to be questioned. He was driven to his apartment in Ipanema and, at 2:30 P.M., reported to the barracks of the Army Police, where the IPM investigating the ISEB was installed. Assisted by Sobral Pinto, he answered questions for two and one-half hours and then was told to return in two days.[3]

That evening, when it became clear that Negrão de Lima and Israel Pinheiro enjoyed comfortable leads in the Guanabara and Minas balloting, Congressman Herbert Levy blamed "Lacerda's defeat" on "the errors and omissions of the Revolution." "We should," Levy said the next day, "give Roberto Campos credit for the defeats." Abreu Sodré said that "the government of Guanabara, thanks to its administrative work, obtained 43 percent of the Carioca electorate despite the opposition of the PTB, the PSD, the Communists, Ademar de Barros, Jânio Quadros, João Goulart, Leonel Brizola, Juscelino Kubitschek, and, why not say it, President Castello Branco himself, who joined those who were deposed by the revolution that he led. To give one single example: during the week of the election the federal government raised by 70 percent the fares on the suburban trains that transport almost one-third of the Guanabara electorate."[4]

O Estado de S. Paulo wrote that Castello Branco had every reason to be satisfied because "the repercussions abroad must have been most favorable. . . . His excellency, always so susceptible to the opinions of those gentlemen who know nothing about Brazilian reality, could not be insensitive to the stamp of approval of those foreign critics."[5]

Kubitschek received little respite from questioning, because on October 5 he had to testify for six hours before Colonel Ferdinando de Carvalho's IPM studying communism. The colonel heading the IPM about ISEB said at the War Ministry that Kubitschek would testify, as

[3] *Jornal do Brasil*, October 5, 1965.

[4] *O Estado de S. Paulo*, October 5, 6, 1965.

[5] Ibid., October 5, 1965.

an indicted person, for ten days and might be jailed by orders of First Army Commander Otacílio Ururaí if it was found that he had been influential in the "communization" of the ISEB.[6] In reply, Military Tribunal Justice Mourão Filho affirmed that only the Federal Supreme Court could arrest a former president, and thirty-seven Guanabara assemblymen sent a telegram of support for Kubitschek that cited his record of democratic conduct.[7]

The most serious problem for the administration was that created by officers of the armed forces in the Rio area, particularly those below the generalship rank who felt that control of their movement had fallen into the hands of top officers who had neither participated early in the anti-Goulart conspiracy nor shown sufficient revolutionary zeal after Goulart's fall.[8] On the evening of October 4, pro-Lacerda air force officers threatened to destroy the ballots that were being counted by six thousand fiscal agents in Maracanã stadium; at the same time, a preponderance of naval officers, also admirers of Lacerda, demanded intervention against the inauguration of Negrão.[9] Commanders of all the units at Vila Militar met with General Otacílio Ururaí on the evening of October 4 to explain that young army officers were so upset that disturbances might well occur.[10]

Copies of a manifesto, "The Revolution Is Irreversible," had just appeared in the barracks in Guanabara. It read, in part:

> Negrão de Lima represents the counterrevolution. As his campaign was inspired by revenge and backed by the Communists, it is certain that, with his election, the corrupt and subversives will soon be in positions allowing them to direct the destinies of the nation. His inauguration would be a premeditated, malevolent act, a defiance of the Revolution, which would then cease to be irreversible.
>
> Was it for this that you, without fearing sacrifices, cooperated with the movement of March 31?[11]

[6] *Jornal do Brasil*, October 6, 1965.

[7] Ibid., October 6, 7, 1965.

[8] Rui Mesquita, interview, November 6, 1965.

[9] Lacerda Paiva, interview, December 16, 1977; João Carlos Palhares dos Santos, interview, Rio de Janeiro, November 22, 1975.

[10] *O Estado de S. Paulo*, October 5, 1965.

[11] Ibid.

At Laranjeiras Palace on the morning of October 5, Castello discussed the situation with his military ministers, who then issued recommendations to their subordinates about discipline and respect for the hierarchy.[12] More important, Costa e Silva resolved to go to Vila Militar on October 6 to attend ceremonies to be held by the First Infantry Regiment (the Sampaio Regiment) to observe the twenty-first anniversary of its arrival in Italy. In an unusual request, the war minister asked that all officers at Vila Militar, about 250, be present when he spoke to the regiment.[13]

4. Pitaluga and Costa e Silva Disappoint Hard-Liners (October 5 and 6, 1965)

Lacerda was in the infirmary of a Bangu textile plant on the afternoon of October 5 when he received a visit from Colonel Plínio Pitaluga, commander of the tank regiment at Vila Militar. The colonel expressed his sympathy for the reverses suffered by Lacerda.

After the colonel left, Lacerda asked Rafael de Almeida Magalhães and Congressmen Godinho and Curi to go to the colonel's barracks to convey the governor's thanks for the visit. When the three envoys reached Vila Militar, Godinho recalls, "the place seemed ready for war." Pitaluga's officers, in uniform, "filled the casino" at his regiment and had the tanks "all set to move."[1] As Pitaluga was not present, Lacerda's representatives talked to the officers, who complained of Castello's "dealings with undesirable congressional groups." Arguing that the Revolution must be saved at once, the officers asked the vice-governor to remove the protection given to the Maracanã vote counters. When Rafael de Almeida Magalhães refused, saying that in the future he would not be proud of such behavior, the officers suggested the arrest of Negrão, and again the vice-governor objected. The third idea was to march on Rio to make demands and ask the chiefs, "What happened to the Revolution?" Ths idea, Rafael said, was the least inde-

[12] Ibid.

[13] Álcio Barbosa da Costa e Silva, interview, Rio de Janeiro, July 15, 1977.

[1] Antônio Godinho, interview, São Paulo, November 7, 1975.

fensible, but he suggested that the men speak first with Pitaluga, whom they trusted.[2]

When Pitaluga came to the barracks, the vice-governor advised him to have a frank talk with his officers, who, he said, were "nervous." Pitaluga did this, persuading them to desist from precipitous action. The colonel also sought to avoid misunderstandings by explaining to Costa e Silva the purpose of the visit of the Lacerdistas to the regiment, but the Lacerdistas nevertheless came to feel that Castello believed they went there to promote an uprising to overthrow the president. According to the impression that Lacerda received, Pitaluga and his officers were all set to move on Rio, but then Pitaluga changed his mind due to "interventions from above."[3]

Lacerda lost his patience while speaking with another officer who visited him in Bangu. The governor exclaimed: "And you people, with all those tanks, are going to turn them into tanks for washing clothes, because you are going to swallow all of this and become responsible for a military dictatorship in Brazil."[4]

Although nothing happened on the night of October 5–6, beyond the army being put on the alert, Rio was full of rumors about the burning of the ballot boxes, a coup, and a new institutional act. With most of the Vila Militar officers opposed to the inauguration of Negrão de Lima and Israel Pinheiro, many civilians felt that Costa e Silva, popular with the hard line, would take over from Castello, who was described as "too theoretical." Aliomar Baleeiro has written of "panic in the banks" and "people stockpiling foodstuffs."[5]

Coste e Silva, accompanied by Colonel Mário David Andreazza, chatted with Castello on the morning of October 6 before attending the Sampaio Regiment ceremonies. The colonel reports that the president and his war minister could not have been calmer or more sure of themselves. Castello, speaking with wit and vivacity, said that Costa e Silva was leaving for the "front line" and, as always had happened at deci-

[2] Almeida Magalhães, interview, November 19, 1975.

[3] Ibid.; Godinho, interview, November 7, 1975; Lacerda, interviews, February 17, 18, 1976; Lacerda, *Depoimento*, p. 350.

[4] Lacerda, *Depoimento*, p. 350.

[5] Peri Constant Bevilàqua, interview, Rio de Janeiro, December 21, 1977; Costa e Silva, interview, July 15, 1977; Baleeiro, "Recordações do Presidente H. Castelo Branco," p. 29.

sive moments in his military life, would come out well. The two leaders went over the main points to be made in the war minister's speech: Brazil would not return to pre-Revolutionary ways, and Castello would not continue as president beyond his term. During the drive to Vila Militar, Costa e Silva told Colonel Andreazza that he would leave his listeners with no doubt about his loyalty to Castello.[6]

Upon reaching Vila Militar the war minister was greeted by journalists. Denying reports that he was resigning, he warned against rumors: "The situation is perfectly calm; they said that the Vila was going to descend, which did not happen, as you gentlemen can see." Rumors, Costa e Silva said, "belong to the technique of the Communists, who want to spread turmoil." He added that the decision about the inauguration of the governors was in the hands of the president and Congress, not in the hands of the armed forces, which were nonpolitical.[7]

When the war minister gave his address, his audience of army officers was so large that many had to stand.[8] He was heartily applauded at the outset, when he praised the World War II veterans of the Sampaio Regiment, but as he continued with his improvised speech, the applause, Andreazza recalls, "progressively diminished."[9] Costa e Silva said: "While we do not fear counterrevolutions, we are worried about the enthusiasm, the ardor of youth eager for more revolution. But I guarantee, my young subordinates, that we know where we are going. The present chiefs, as I said yesterday and repeat today, are as revolutionary as the young revolutionaries. I guarantee that we are not returning to the past. The president has just authorized me to tell you that we are not returning to the past."

Declaring that military unity made it unreasonable to worry about the anti-Revolutionary "dwarfs," Costa e Silva warned against intrigue designed to undermine that unity. He demolished the rumor "that circulated here in Vila Militar yesterday, that the president is working to continue in office beyond his term." Giving his audience the president's word that this was a lie, the war minister praised Castello as "deserving our credence and respect." Then he defended the inauguration of the winners of an election that had been agreed upon, "so that

[6] Mário David Andreazza, letter to Luís Viana Filho, n.d., pp. 5, 6, 7, 10, 11.
[7] Costa e Silva, press interview, October 6, 1965, File P2 (p. 2), CPDOC.
[8] Costa e Silva, interview, July 15, 1977.
[9] Andreazza, letter to Viana Filho, p. 7.

we can demonstrate that men do not modify the regime and men are unable to undermine a Revolution."[10]

5. Law Projects to Strengthen Revolutionary Action (October 6–15, 1965)

By October 7, when Costa e Silva ended the army alert as "no longer necessary," more election returns had become known. Despite the dissatisfaction of hard-liners with the outcomes in Guanabara, Minas Gerais, and one or two other states, the overall results pleased the administration. Particularly welcome to the men in Planalto Palace were the results in Pará and Paraná (where the candidates favored by Governors Jarbas Passarinho and Nei Braga were successful), in Paraíba (where João Agripino was elected), and in Goiás.

Lacerda, in a radio-television broadcast on the evening of October 7, read a letter that he had just written to UDN President Ernani Sátiro "returning" his presidential candidacy to the UDN and adding, "I think that I have the right to appear at a national convention of the party to explain why I feel that my candidacy no longer makes sense." In the letter, he wrote about Castello's "obsession" with blocking direct presidential elections and the Lacerda candidacy. Addressing his radio-television audience, he spoke of the "just revulsions" of the workers, the "frustration" of the middle class, and the "diatribes" that Castello had authorized the government to write in reply to his criticism of the economic-financial policy.[1]

On the next day, Lacerda announced: "I did not resign anything." It was, he said, up to the party to decide about his candidacy. Speaking of his plan to enter private life on December 5, he added: "If they need me I shall never fail the call. . . . I cannot desist from something that was proposed by the UDN and not by me." *O Estado de S. Paulo* wrote that Lacerda, a fighter who could not be annihilated "by a small reverse," had simply invited the party to reexamine "the candidacy with which he distinguished it." The São Paulo daily attacked Castello Branco for efforts to "legalize" the regime, for "scandalous" dialogue

[10] Transcript of tape of speech of Costa e Silva at the First Infantry Regiment, Vila Militar, October 6, 1965 (tape made available by Álcio Costa e Silva, July 1977).

[1] *O Estado de S. Paulo*, October 8, 1965.

with the parties of Vargas, and for a "passive attitude in the face of the unacceptable decisions of a judiciary in which card-carrying Communists continue to pontificate."[2]

A few days later Lacerda made his break with Castello irreparable. He asserted irritably that he had "already vomited" Castello Branco and added: "If the president is ugly on the outside, he is, on the inside, a cause of horror."[3]

Castello, following the war minister's speech at Vila Militar, worked with advisers on legislative proposals to strengthen the government and calm the hard-liners. The proposals considered on the afternoon of October 6 would reform the national security law and the judiciary, curtail the activities of the *cassados,* facilitate federal intervention in the states, and authorize the federal government to name the state security secretaries.[4] A note to reporters, distributed by Presidential Press Secretary José Wamberto, advised that "it was decided to adopt rapidly various steps, including legislative ones, to strengthen revolutionary action."

Bilac Pinto, meeting with Milton Campos and government congressional leaders at Adauto Cardoso's home, advocated a "renewal of the revolutionary process." Milton Campos, uncomfortable with this prospect, said that it was time to make his resignation letter public. It appeared in the press the next day, October 8. Luís Viana Filho, who took over the Justice Ministry pending the arrival of Juraci Magalhães, asked Milton Campos if he had anything helpful to pass on. "I leave you only aspirins for headaches," the outgoing minister replied.[5]

Castello was ridiculed by *O Estado de S. Paulo* for expecting PSD leaders, such as Alkmin, Moura Andrade, and Filinto Müller, to support "a series of laws of exception."[6] But at Laranjeiras Palace the president persevered with his work on the two fronts, congressional and military. After meeting with many congressional leaders on October 8, he presided on the ninth over a meeting of military leaders and re-

[2] Ibid., October 9, 1965.

[3] *Última Hora,* October 12, 1965 (newspaper clipping, File N5, Anexo 10, CPDOC).

[4] *O Estado de S. Paulo,* October 7, 1965; Viana Filho, *O Governo Castelo Branco,* p. 340.

[5] Viana Filho, *O Governo Castelo Branco,* pp. 336, 338.

[6] *Jornal do Brasil,* October 12, 1965; *O Estado de S. Paulo,* October 10, 1965.

ceived their support. Then, while emissaries of Costa e Silva and Eduardo Gomes went to São Paulo to consult constitutional lawyer Vicente Ráo, Castello flew to Rio Grande do Sul, despite the advice of Sarasate that his trip during the crisis was inadvisable.[7]

Addressing a mayors' congress in Porto Alegre, Castello said that the revolution had been made "to consecrate the survival of democratic institutions." Adding that democracy needed to be protected as well as practiced, he said that his government had never failed to be mindful of the suggestions of all who had helped make the revolution. But he warned that the government would not yield to "those who, under the pretext of defending the Revolution, crave to crush liberty, hoping to be the beneficiaries of its disappearance."[8]

Arriving at the Brasília airport on October 12, Castello was received and applauded by an unusually large number of congressmen. With the help of Viana, he submitted to Congress on the next day a law project to regulate the activities of the *cassados* and proposals that would alter the constitution in order to (1) facilitate federal intervention in the states, (2) extend the authority of the military courts to civilians in cases of subversion, and (3) exclude acts carried out under the Institutional Act from judicial review.[9] When one congressman sought signatures for an amendment to make the election of the president and vice-president indirect in 1966, Castello let it be known that he personally opposed the idea. He said that while it was important to settle this matter, it was far more urgent to adopt the proposals that he had submitted.[10]

But the PSD, under Amaral Peixoto, started offering suggestions for making the proposals less drastic. Magalhães Pinto, on the other hand, declared that Castello's proposals were innocuous and would accomplish nothing. The Minas governor promised to take sixty-seven votes to the next UDN national convention to give support to Lacerda's position against Castello.[11]

On Friday, October 15, the president went to Rio. While awaiting

[7] *Jornal do Brasil*, October 9, 11, 1965; Viana Filho, *O Governo Castelo Branco*, pp. 337–338.

[8] HACB, *Discursos, 1965*, p. 30.

[9] *O Estado de S. Paulo*, October 13, 14, 1965.

[10] Ibid., October 15, 1965; *Jornal do Brasil*, October 13, 14, 1965.

[11] *Jornal do Brasil*, October 14, 16, 1965.

the arrival of Juraci, due to land on the eighteenth, he had a long discussion with Aliomar Baleeiro, who found him preoccupied with the need to impose military discipline. "I am distressed," Castello said, "at the idea of being overthrown by General X, who would be overthrown by General Y, and he in turn removed by General Z." "Or by Sergeant Batista," Baleeiro suggested.

Suddenly Castello asked: "And what if Congress does not vote the projects I sent it?" Baleeiro replied that he did not underestimate the consequences and would vote for the projects. Although he said that he would not vote for "full powers" for the executive, which were not being sought, he added that he did not fear abuse of such powers by Castello. Furthermore, Baleeiro said, if such powers were indispensable, a head of state should take the responsibility of assuming them, without asking Congress, which would not vote for them. Castello was quick to agree and said that he would not shun any responsibility. Baleeiro felt that the president, while determined to act forcefully if necessary, suffered from the conflict between his loyalty to the military and his loyalty to Congress. Speaking of the congressmen, Castello said that when he had worked to get their votes, not one of them had asked a favor in return.

Turning to the presidential succession, Castello asked Baleeiro how he felt about an indirect election. The congressman was agreeable provided it be by newly elected congressmen. Castello then placed his possible successors in three categories. He mentioned active military figures, naming Costa e Silva and Mamede; civilians, naming Bilac and Krieger; and the "amphibians" (half civilian and half military), naming Juraci, Cordeiro, and Nei Braga. He praised Bilac for the unique quality of never repeating what was said in conversations with the president, but Castello admitted that crises were apt to frighten Bilac and that Krieger, although lacking some of Bilac's fine qualities, might be a better leader. Castello criticized Lacerda and Magalhães Pinto severely.

"Perhaps," Baleeiro said, "when I am old, I'll write about the events and men I have known."

"What do you want to do," Castello asked, "scare us all?"[12]

[12] Baleeiro, "Recordações do Presidente H. Castelo Branco," pp. 31, 32.

Occasionally the president had spoken about leaving office on January 31, 1966, and he did so again one evening when he chatted with Lieutenant Colonel Jarbas Passarinho, not long after his talk with Baleeiro. The governor of Pará cited the one-year extension of Castello's mandate. "I didn't promise," Castello replied, "to respect the extension, but only the Ato Institucional." The problem being one of succession, Castello asked Passarinho who he thought should be the next president.

"Can he be a civilian?" Passarinho asked.

"Unfortunately, no. We must have another man from the barracks to consolidate the Revolution."

As Passarinho had no names to offer, Castello wrote the names of four army men on a sheet of presidential paper: (1) Juraci, (2) Cordeiro, (3) Mamede, (4) Costa e Silva.

"Please, Mr. President," Passarinho said, "the first two are not acceptable."

Castello, irked and deadly serious, asked: "Why?"

"One reason. I'll call, in support of my opinion, Humberto de Alencar Castello Branco."

"I don't appreciate the joke."

"It is not a joke," Passarinho said. "Let me explain."

After the president nodded, Passarinho, twice Castello's student in military schools, pointed out that Castello had always insisted that army officers keep out of politics.

Castello, less annoyed, asked: "How about Dr. Bizarria?"—his way of referring to intellectual General Jurandir de Bizarria Mamede, who was in Belém, Pará, commanding the troops of the Eighth Military Region and Amazônia.

"Mr. President, if I were choosing the best friend of the General Staff College, I would give you his name. But as you are looking for a president in a term that we know will be very difficult, I consider that the last name on your list is better."

Castello, who had once told Viana Filho that Mamede "would be a great president," let Passarinho know that the conversation was ended.[13]

[13] Jarbas Passarinho, interview, Brasília, November 11, 1975; Viana Filho, quoted in *Jornal do Brasil*, July 16, 1972.

6. The Supreme Court Defies the Military (October 20–25, 1965)

Before Juraci Magalhães reached Rio, Castello lunched with Krieger and discussed the reaction of the Revolutionaries to the composition of the Supreme Court. "I cannot shirk my Revolutionary duty," the president said, "but I have scruples about taking any step against the highest court of my country."

"Mr. President," Krieger said, "in order to end the possibility of partial decisions against the Revolution, you have an opportunity that will not hurt your susceptibilities: increase the number of justices."

"Coincidentally," Castello told the senator, "that has been the alternative that I have preferred. I am going to choose it."[1]

On October 19, during the Laranjeiras Palace ceremony at which Juraci became justice minister, Castello referred to studies that the ministry had already carried out about possible reforms.[2] On the same day, Chief Justice Álvaro Ribeiro da Costa, familiar with some of the studies, gave a statement about them to *Correio da Manhã* and *Folha de S. Paulo*. Published on October 20, the statement maintained that the plans to increase the number of justices from eleven to sixteen and create three sections of the court would have serious repercussions on the uniformity of jurisprudence and were "absurd" and improper to carry out unless requested by the court.

Ribeiro da Costa said that the armed forces had no right to express their opinion on the subject, "although, unfortunately, this has been happening, something never seen in truly civilized nations." He added that "the time has come for the armed forces to understand that in democratic regimes they do not exercise the role of mentors of the nation—as was practiced not long ago, with a dismaying rupture of sacred duties, by sergeants instigated by the Jangos and Brizolas."[3]

The words of Ribeiro da Costa, who had been a public servant for fifty years, forty of them a judge, provoked heated debates in Congress and the press. The oppositionist *Correio da Manhã* wrote that the chief justice had fulfilled a duty that needed to be fulfilled in other branches of the government. *O Estado de S. Paulo,* on the other hand,

[1] Krieger, *Desde as Missões*, pp. 195–196.

[2] HACB, *Discursos, 1965*, pp. 31–32.

[3] *Jornal do Brasil*, October 20, 1965; Trigueiro do Vale, *O Supremo Tribunal Federal*, pp. 102–105.

described Ribeiro da Costa as foolish and ungrateful when he "directed gibes" against the military, which, throughout the nation's history, had been "the only guarantee" of the political institutions.[4]

Costa e Silva, at the Second Army maneuvers in Itapeva, São Paulo, on October 22, defended the armed forces. In the presence of Castello, Amauri Kruel, and top army leaders, he gave a speech that was wildly acclaimed by officers and soldiers. Cries of "*manda brasa,* general!" (get the fire going, general) were mingled with shouts against the chief justice.[5]

Calling Ribeiro da Costa's statement "without doubt the greatest injustice ever practiced against the Brazilian soldier," the war minister said that the reference to sergeants, instigated by the Jangos and Brizolas, "places us on the same level as those we fought yesterday, when we returned the nation to tranquility, peace, and integrity. . . . We left the barracks at the call of the people. . . . And we shall only return to the barracks when the people so determine. I don't want to get excited, but, offended, attacked in my class, I cannot fail to strike back at this affront, regardless of the result. In some places they say that the president is politically weak, but it doesn't matter if he is politically weak, for he is strong militarily." Before closing his speech, Costa e Silva addressed Castello to ask the president's pardon if his words lacked the proper respect for the head of state and to explain that they were inspired by an old soldier's right to be offended by the declarations of the chief justice.[6]

Castello, in the final address, said that "General Costa e Silva, in the vehemence of his speech, mentioned me. . . . In a gesture of high esteem for his chief, he asked me to forgive him in case he went too far in his remarks. I must tell His Excellency that I was not disrespected. Why? Because I am the chief of one of the powers of the Republic and, in carrying out my duties, I defend the dignity of my post and the respect for the other two powers, the armed forces and the civilian sectors of Brazil."[7]

[4] Trigueiro do Vale, *O Supremo Tribunal Federal*, pp. 112–113; *O Estado de S. Paulo*, October 24, 1965.

[5] Palhares dos Santos, interview, November 22, 1975.

[6] Transcript of tape of speech of Costa e Silva, Itapeva, S.P., October 22, 1965 (made available by Álcio Costa e Silva, July 1977).

[7] HACB, *Discursos, 1965*, pp. 275–276.

The air force members of the presidential Gabinete Militar, exultant about the war minister's speech, declared that "now, for a change, things are going ahead."[8] But most of the members of the Gabinete Militar, and particularly João Carlos Palhares dos Santos (of the navy) and Major Murilo Santos (aide to and pilot for the president), felt otherwise. Discussing the Itapeva scene on the flight back to Rio, they recalled the emotional meetings conducted by supporters of Goulart and Brizola in March, 1964. Feeling that it was not up to the war minister to attack the chief justice, they wondered whether Castello would dismiss Costa e Silva. After all, Castello, in his closing remarks in Itapeva, had not answered the question of whether he believed that the war minister had gone too far. Palhares, on reaching Rio, spoke with Geisel and Golberi in the Laranjeiras Palace office shared by the two generals. In a reference to the strong movement in the army to make the war minister Castello's successor, Palhares asked: "What are we going to do when Costa e Silva assumes the presidency?" Geisel and Golberi replied with fervor that much water had yet to flow under the bridge.[9] When Geisel spoke with Castello, the head of the Gabinete Militar said that the "only solution" was to dismiss Costa e Silva for his emotional attack against the chief justice.[10]

On October 23, local army commanders met at the War Ministry, without Costa e Silva, to express their disgust at the reluctance of Congress to vote for the projects submitted by the executive on October 13. The commanders were reported to feel that the military should undertake "a solution of force, the only one capable of reinvigorating and consolidating the ideals of the Revolution." Meanwhile, Costa e Silva, in a speech at the Aviation School, declared that "without any doubt there is the need to toughen the Revolutionary action."[11]

While Third Army Commander Justino Alves Bastos said that Costa e Silva's words at Itapeva and the Aviation School expressed the sentiment of all the Brazilian military, Rio's *O Globo* lamented that with the fate of the Revolution at stake, only the executive power acted

[8] Palhares dos Santos, "Depoimento sôbre a Minha Convivência com o Presidente Humberto Castello Branco, prestado ao Seu Historiador Dr. Luiz Vianna Filho.

[9] Ibid., Palhares dos Santos, interview, November 22, 1975.

[10] Peri Beviláqua, interview, December 21, 1977.

[11] *O Estado de S. Paulo* and *Jornal do Brasil*, October 24, 1965.

in a pro-Revolutionary way.[12] But despite much acclaim for the war minister, Ribeiro da Costa prepared to reply. This led Juraci Magalhães to appeal to the judiciary to end its "bitter dispute with the armed forces." "If one side practiced excesses," he said in a radio-television broadcast, "those excesses were caused by foolish action by the other side."[13]

To show their support for Ribeiro da Costa, the Supreme Court justices voted to make him the presiding justice until his retirement in 1967, thus interrupting, for the first time in Brazilian history, the custom of rotating the headship of the court.[14] The justices also considered the habeas corpus petition, submitted by Sobral Pinto on behalf of Kubitschek, to "bring an end to the violence against, or restriction of, his liberty, resulting from the IPM's and the way they are conducted." A provisional ruling called for additional information from the IPM colonels.[15]

While Kubitschek awaited a final decision, he gained a respite because his doctors reported that he had suffered from a "circulatory disturbance." After a military medical commission of the First Army examined him on October 26, the colonel heading the IPM about the ISEB granted him a fifteen-day rest.[16]

7. Lack of an Absolute Majority in Congress (October 20–26, 1965)

Juraci Magalhães, bravely wearing a hearty smile, tried to persuade congressmen to vote for the administration's proposals "without altering a single line." Like Cordeiro de Farias, who assisted him valiantly, he explained that the administration, with an alternative in mind, was working on drafts of a second institutional act.

One of the drafts was drawn up by Gama e Silva, who had been

[12] Trigueiro do Vale, *O Supremo Tribunal Federal*, pp. 127–129.

[13] *O Estado de S. Paulo*, October 26, 1965; *Jornal do Brasil*, October 24, 25, 1965.

[14] *Jornal do Brasil*, October 26, 1965.

[15] Ibid., October 23, 27, 1965.

[16] Ibid.; according to Sobral Pinto (interview, December 9, 1975), Kubitschek had at this time three doctors, who "found him all right but who may have invented poor health to help him out."

justice minister in the Mazzilli cabinet. Upon being consulted by his friend Costa e Silva, he prepared a measure for giving Brazil "a real cleansing" and "a complete Revolution." It would close Congress and the local legislatures and install federal intervention in all the states.[1] Castello received this draft from the war minister, but he set it aside and did not show it to Juraci, who had asked law professor Nehemias Gueiros to work on a draft. Cordeiro told congressmen that while one project, "alien to the national interests," was being prepared under the inspiration of the armed forces, another project, "consulting exclusively the interests of the government," was being prepared by the executive.[2]

Juraci and Cordeiro kept repeating that they were not bluffing. "I don't know how to bluff," Juraci said, "and have therefore never been a poker player." The threat of a second institutional act helped Juraci in some areas where the administration was not popular. Amauri Kruel, influential in the PTB, pleaded that congressmen not "turn the president over to the hard line"; and Tancredo Neves, urging that the PSD support the administration, argued that while things might be bad under Castello, they would be worse without him.[3]

But Senator Mem de Sá, supporter of the administration, concluded that the PSD leadership this time was willing to "pay to see" the administration's cards.[4] Although it was known that Castello wished to avoid a second institutional act, the "pay to see" attitude of Amaral Peixoto and other PSD leaders was based not so much on the possibility that a "bluffing" administration would accept a PSD compromise as it was based on other considerations. "Imagine," one PSD source said, "the precarious position of the Minas PSD if it votes to abolish the special immunities of Kubitschek and automatically intern him." A part of the PSD agreed with Wilson Martins (UDN, Mato Grosso) when he stated that "this could be the last opportunity to demonstrate a worthy attitude in opposition to those who humiliate us."[5] Many con-

[1] Luís Antônio da Gama e Silva, interview, São Paulo, November 5, 1975; Viana Filho, *O Governo Castelo Branco*, p. 351.

[2] *Jornal do Brasil*, October 21, 1965.

[3] Ibid., October 22, 24 (Coluna do Castello), 26, 27, 1965.

[4] Mem de Sá, interview, October 31, 1975.

[5] *Jornal do Brasil*, October 21, 27, 1965; on October 25, 1965, *Jornal do Brasil* quoted Amaral Peixoto as saying that any agreement with the government would have to be based on the PSD alternative and not on the project elaborated by the executive,

gressmen felt that the prestige of the legislative branch would be best upheld if the administration's proposals were decreed by the executive rather than voted by Congress.

These politicians who considered the legislative proposals too radical to be accepted by Congress were joined by others who considered them not radical enough. Although Costa e Silva argued for a favorable congressional vote, some backers of his presidential ambitions preferred the more drastic solution that seemed certain to follow a defeat of the proposals in Congress.[6]

If the supporters of Lacerda's candidacy found themselves in a dilemma, they did not show it. At the moment when the UDN directorship decided to accept Lacerda's request for a new national convention,[7] the Lacerdistas followed a course that favored an institutional act that would reportedly do away with political parties and the direct 1966 presidential election that they wanted Lacerda to win.[8] Thus *O Estado de S. Paulo* declared that Juraci Magalhães was wasting his diplomatic talents by working for the administration's "nauseating little amendments."[9] Roberto Abreu Sodré defied the government "to issue a new institutional act for making the Revolution," and Lacerdistas in Congress dismissed as "professional politicians" all UDN legislators who favored the administration's proposals. Lacerda spokesman Jorge Curi (UDN, Paraná) announced that thirty UDN congressmen would oppose the administration.[10]

Despite the pledge of Ademar de Barros that allowed the government to count on twenty-one of the twenty-four PRP congressmen, the disagreements within the government's eight-month-old Bloco Parlamentar Renovador became so great that the bloc's leadership declared it "officially dissolved."[11] The administration could expect no difficulty in

according to which Kubitschek would lose his special immunity "guaranteed by the constitution."

[6] Bosísio, interview, November 8, 1975; Almeida Magalhães, interview, November 19, 1975; Castello Branco, *Os Militares no Poder*, p. 342; Luís Alberto Bahia, interview, Rio de Janeiro, December 8, 1975; Beviláqua, interview, December 21, 1977.

[7] *Jornal do Brasil*, October 22, 24, 1977.

[8] Ibid., October 27, 1965.

[9] *O Estado de S. Paulo*, October 26, 27, 1965.

[10] *Correio da Manhã*, October 16, 1965; *Jornal do Brasil*, October 21, 1965.

[11] *Jornal do Brasil*, October 21, 26, 27, 1965.

the Senate, where the bloc had not existed, but the impossibility of the administration's gathering the necessary 205 votes in the lower house was clear. Rui Santos, whose prediction was more favorable to the administration than the other estimates made at this time, gave the administration only 199 votes in the Chamber of Deputies.[12]

8. Deciding on a New Institutional Act (late October, 1965)

Professor Nehemias Gueiros, specialist in commercial law, received suggestions for the new institutional act from Francisco Campos, Carlos Medeiros Silva, Luís Viana Filho, Golberi, Geisel, Adauto Cardoso, and João Agripino.[1] The ideas of Carlos Medeiros Silva, author of much of the Ato of April, 1964, reached Gueiros through Luís Viana Filho, who spent hours at Medeiros Silva's home discussing ways of dealing with the October, 1965, crisis. Daniel Krieger and Pedro Aleixo, the government leaders in Congress, refused to participate in the elaboration of the new Ato lest such collaboration weaken their position in favor of action by Congress.[2]

Paulo Bosísio, persuaded to remain in the Navy Ministry on account of the crisis, participated in two days of special meetings held by Castello for a study of the Gueiros draft by the military ministers, the justice minister, and Geisel. After one such meeting, Costa e Silva advised Castello that when Magalhães Pinto had last visited him, the Minas governor had told the war minister to take over the government "because Castello cannot continue."[3]

Without the constitutional changes sought by the military, the continuation of Castello in office was considered unlikely by such veteran observers as Milton Campos and columnist Carlos Castello Branco. Furthermore, pressure for closing Congress was strong, especially if it re-

[12] Ibid., October 27, 1965.

[1] Juraci Magalhães, "Respostas do General Juracy Magalhães ao Professor John W. F. Dulles," Rio de Janeiro (typewritten), December 3, 1974, p. 4.

[2] Carlos Medeiros Silva, interview, Rio de Janeiro, November 12, 1975; Krieger, *Desde as Missões*, p. 198.

[3] Bosísio, interview, November 8, 1975; Viana Filho, *O Governo Castelo Branco*, p. 349.

jected the administration's proposals.[4] But Castello wanted the continuance of Congress along with the inauguration of governors recently elected, and he disliked the prospect of coups bringing a series of generals to the presidency. Therefore, he reluctantly decided to issue the Gueiros draft if Congress proved uncooperative.

The Gueiros draft, regarded by Medeiros Silva as a "collection of rulings, without any overall tie or philosophy," was far more radical than anything asked of Congress. Among other things, it would pave the way for a complete political party reform. Although some UDN leaders could be expected to oppose the dissolution of their organization, Juraci Magalhães writes that "the suggestion to end the existing political parties came from UDN companions who, like me, were convinced that it would be impossible to give the government a political base in Congress with the multiparty system then in effect."[5]

Other clauses would increase from eleven to sixteen the number of Supreme Court justices, renew the president's power to suspend political rights and cancel mandates, give the Military Justice system the competence to judge crimes against the national security, and make it easier for the president to declare a state of siege and intervene in the states. Further, the new act would suspend constitutional guarantees of tenure and end "special immunities" due to positions once held and would limit the activities and, "if necessary," the movements of the *cassados*. The judicial system was not to pass judgment on steps taken in accordance with the first institutional act or the new one.

Under the new Ato Institucional, which was to expire on March 15, 1967, the president would be able to issue "decree-laws about the national security," and "complementary acts" to the new Ato, including ones that would force legislatures into recess; during such a recess of Congress the president could legislate by decree-law. Law projects initiated by the president were given forty-five days in each legislative house, but if they were considered urgent by the president, a joint session had to act within thirty days or else the projects would become law.

[4] Viana Filho, *O Governo Castelo Branco*, p. 353 (quoting Milton Campos in an interview given to *Visão*); Castello Branco, *Os Militares no Poder*, p. 677; Afonso Arinos de Melo Franco, interview, Rio de Janeiro, October 31, 1975 (quoting HACB).

[5] Medeiros Silva, interview, December 18, 1975; Magalhães, "Respostas do General Juracy Magalhães," p. 4.

Only the president could initiate legislation increasing federal expenditures.

The proposed new Ato also stipulated that the next president and vice-president were to be elected by Congress no later than October 3, 1966. In this connection, Castello wrote a sentence in longhand that made him ineligible for reelection. He insisted on its inclusion despite the objections of many advisers, among them Costa e Silva, Luís Viana Filho, Cordeiro de Farias, Otávio Bulhões, Roberto Campos, and Leitão da Cunha.

Roberto Campos, phoning Brasília from Rio, urged Castello not to disqualify himself openly regardless of his decision to refuse to serve beyond March, 1967. He was, Campos said, "foresaking bargaining power for influencing a suitable succession." The planning minister added that "both the fight against inflation and the revival of investment, foreign and national, were slow and painful processes requiring all the psychological confidence that could be mustered for the stability of the rules of the game." But, Campos found out, the president felt that he owed it to his conscience and the nation to have it known that the process of purge and other revolutionary acts had been carried out to save the institutions and not to pursue personal power. Besides, Castello told Campos, "since the example of Vargas, *continuismo* has been the cancer of Brazil's fledgling democracy." When Leitão da Cunha told Castello that the clause might become inconvenient later, the president replied that the matter was one of his "personal conscience" and that he would never sign the Ato unless the clause were included.[6]

Costa e Silva spoke frankly, saying that the "unnecessary clause" would open the problem of the succession ahead of time. "Candidates will enter the field, and that includes me," the war minister said. Governor Paulo Guerra told Castello that if he made himself ineligible, "the command will go to Costa e Silva." But the president explained to Guerra that Lacerda would try to interpret the Ato "as though it were a maneuver of mine to continue." "I don't want to continue," Castello added. "I want the Revolution to have a good image before the world."[7]

[6] Antônio Carlos Magalhães, interview, August 11, 1977; Roberto de Oliveira Campos, Foreword to JWFD, *Castello Branco: The Making of a Brazilian President*, pp. xvi–xvii; Leitão da Cunha, interview, November 23, 1974.

[7] Krieger, *Desde as Missões*, p. 200; Guerra, interview, November 11, 1977.

Castello was in Brasília on October 25 when the situation in Congress persuaded him that he would have to issue the new Ato. Needing the signatures of the military ministers, as well as the justice and foreign ministers, he called Krieger to Planalto Palace to ask him to speak with Brigadeiro Eduardo Gomes, who had said that he would sign no Ato that would dissolve the UDN. At the palace, where the Senate leader found Castello with Cordeiro, Krieger explained that he held Gomes in such esteem he hesitated to take the matter up with him unless called by him to do so. Castello emphasized the need of political party reform: "Crushed under the old parties, the Revolution will not achieve its objectives of reconstruction and political perfection."[8]

After the office chief of Cordeiro's ministry brought Krieger a request from the *brigadeiro* for a talk, Gomes asked Krieger for his opinion about ending the political parties. Krieger, carrying out what he says was his most difficult mission of the Revolution, explained that "our party is in no condition to grow. Its mission was completed when the nation returned to the democratic regime. That purpose was its reason for existence, its banner. This is the opinion of almost all our fellow members."

Although Krieger offered to bring regional UDN leaders to Gomes to confirm his assertion, Gomes said: "Your testimony is sufficient. I am convinced. I shall sign the Ato."[9] The *brigadeiro*, like Juraci, felt that the Ato was necessary to assure the gubernatorial inaugurations and prevent a worsening of the crisis, and he trusted the president "not to misuse it."[10]

Navy Minister Bosísio, who wanted Congress to vote the administration's proposals and felt that Costa e Silva supporters made that impossible, reluctantly agreed to sign. Golberi, seeking the support of business leaders, phoned his friend Rio financier Melo Flores. Golberi also phoned Rio journalist Luís Alberto Bahia to explain the situation in Brasília: "We have been trying to resist issuing a new Ato, but the wall is caving in on us."[11]

At Planalto Palace on October 26, Castello told Krieger and Pedro

[8] Krieger, *Desde as Missões*, p. 200.

[9] Ibid.

[10] Beviláqua, interview, December 21, 1977; Juraci Magalhães, interview, December 3, 1974.

[11] Bosísio, interview, November 8, 1975; Melo Flores, interview, December 20, 1977; Bahia, interview, December 8, 1975.

Aleixo that he found himself forced to sign the new institutional act because of "the lack of understanding" of some congressmen. Pedro Aleixo asked for three more days to work on congressmen, and Castello agreed that the Chamber leader could have the additional time. Later that day Castello called Krieger back to the palace to ask a favor: "Before any voting begins, let me have your forecast. Don't worry about the time of night."[12]

That night Krieger phoned after midnight to advise that the amendments would be approved by the Senate and rejected by the Chamber. Castello then asked for one more favor: "Take the senators out of the plenary so that no vote will occur. I do not wish to decree tomorrow measures that Congress rejects." Both Krieger and Pedro Aleixo withdrew legislators. Therefore, on October 27, newspapers reported that the government had adopted obstructionist tactics to avoid a defeat, for it had only 190 votes in the lower house.[13]

9. Press Reactions to the Second Institutional Act (late October, 1965)

Castello, after less than four hours' sleep, phoned Juraci Magalhães at 6:30 A.M. on October 27 to ask that he meet with him at once at Planalto Palace. There he told the justice minister: "I have spent a night of civic vigil. I concluded that it is my duty to sign the Ato conditioned on my ineligibility." When Juraci remonstrated against the ineligibility clause, Castello said, "I can only sign an Ato if I make it clear that it does not benefit me."[1] The clause was discussed again at Castello's 8:30 A.M. meeting with the military ministers, and this time Costa e Silva asked about the eligibility of cabinet ministers, "such as Juraci," who were to sign the Ato along with the president. Castello said that none of the ministers should be ineligible.[2]

[12] Krieger, *Desde as Missões*, p. 199.

[13] Ibid.; Baleeiro, "Recordações do Presidente H. Castelo Branco," p. 33; *O Estado de S. Paulo*, October 27, 1965.

[1] Viana Filho, *O Governo Castelo Branco*, p. 354; close associates of Castello Branco advise that during the presidency he enjoyed full nights of sleep on all but two occasions: the night before the arrival of Perón and the night before the promulgation of Ato Institucional No. 2 (PVCB, memorandum, June 1979).

[2] Viana Filho, *O Governo Castelo Branco*, p. 354.

Authorities in Brasília were invited to attend the signing ceremony in the cabinet room beginning at 11:00 A.M., and those outside of Brasília were notified of the development. Juraci telephoned Magalhães Pinto but not Lacerda. However, Costa e Silva, in phone calls to the army commanders, asked them to notify the governors.[3]

At 11:00 A.M., while air force planes circled over Planalto Palace, Castello entered the cabinet room and was applauded by legislators, government officials, and military officers. Seating himself in front of two microphones at the head of the table, the president spoke to the nation in a forceful tone. Explaining that the Brazilian Revolution, like any national movement, was subject to contingencies, he asserted that it was up to the government, which had emanated from the Revolution, to guarantee the conquest of its objectives, above all because they coincided with those of the nation. He said:

> The Revolution is alive and is not receding. It has fostered reforms and will continue to carry out reforms, adhering patriotically to its goals for the economic, financial, political, and moral recuperation of Brazil. For this, tranquility is necessary. However, agitators of various sorts, and participants in the state of affairs that was put behind us, insist on taking advantage of constitutional guarantees and of the fact that the Revolution limited to a short duration its period of acting restrictively; and now they threaten the very revolutionary order just when that order, attentive to administrative problems, seeks to give the people the practice and discipline of exercising democracy. Democracy supposes liberty but it does not exclude responsibility or amount to a licence to oppose the very political vocation of the nation.[4]

Following Castello's introduction, Luís Viana Filho read Ato Institucional Number Two. Then it was signed by the president, the justice and foreign ministers, and the three military ministers. In addition, Castello and Juraci signed Ato Complementar No. 1 of the new Ato Institucional. It called for a three- to twelve-month detention of any *cassado* who participated in political activities or pronounced on political matters, and it stipulated equal punishment for anyone who helped

[3] Ibid.; *Jornal do Brasil*, October 28, 1965; Artur da Costa e Silva, interview as recorded by Rádio Gazeta SP, Rio de Janeiro, October 28, 1965 (transcript of tape supplied by Álcio Costa e Silva).

[4] HACB, *Discursos, 1965*, pp. 33–35.

the *cassados* to do so. Press or broadcasting organs that issued political declarations of the *cassados* were to be fined.

After the ceremony, the government announced that it would use its new powers only in cases of extreme necessity.[5] Congress, Baleeiro found that afternoon, acted "as though nothing serious or dramatic had occurred," and the U.S. Embassy cabled Washington that the issuance of the new Ato "has had almost no visible impact on the country." The lone show of protest occurred in Guanabara: students associated with the radical lefist Ação Popular led a parade featuring a banner that proclaimed the opposition of "students and workers" to the new measure.[6]

Castello, arriving in Rio on the afternoon of October 28, was surprised and pleased to find that over one hundred army officers had come to the military airport to greet him in a show of support for the step he had taken. But that night he experienced a different emotion. Standing alone at Laranjeiras Palace, after seeing Senator Sarasate off in his car, he heard the shout of "dictator" coming from one of the nearby buildings. He phoned his son immediately to express his sadness and disturbance.[7]

Correio da Manhã described the second institucional act as a "dry and arrogant" document implanting a dictatorship, for which Castello was responsible. It cited leading newspapers in New York and Europe that supported its oppositionist view, and it quoted "Democratic Senator Wayne Morse, prestigious Kennedian," as saying that unless the United States suspended all aid to Brazil, it would transform the Alliance for Progress into an alliance for progressive militarism. Rio's *O Jornal*, on the other hand, wrote that Senator Morse did not understand "the Brazilian political situation, the causes determining the adoption of Ato Institucional No. 2, and the superior objectives that inspired it. . . . The government of Brazil continues under the leadership of Marshal Castello Branco, and no civilian would direct it with

[5] *Jornal do Brasil*, October 28, 1965.

[6] Baleeiro, "Recordações do Presidente H. Castelo Branco," p. 33; United States Embassy, Rio de Janeiro, cable to Washington, October 27, 1965, NSFB, LBJ Library; *Jornal do Brasil*, October 28, 1965.

[7] PVCB, memorandum, June 1979.

the same democratic spirit and with equal respect for the liberties of the Brazilian people."[8]

Jornal do Brasil hoped that the new powers would be used to usher in an age of economic development and social well-being and soon be abandoned. While it felt that Castello probably would not act "arbitrarily or excessively," it expressed surprise that he should "be prisoner of principles that are contrary to his and our democratic formation."[9] *Jornal do Brasil*'s columnist Carlos Castello Branco wrote:

> What the governors of Minas and Guanabara preached was carried out in large part by Ato Institucional No. 2. Both accused the government of not wanting to assume the responsibility of practicing revolutionary acts. This responsibility has been assumed. Both alleged that the corrupt and subversives, under the shadow of temporizations, were returning. Against these two classes there have been dictated steps of containment insisted on by the most radical groups. Sr. Magalhães Pinto preached the extinction of the parties, as a step inherent to the revolutionary process. The parties have been extinguished. And, finally, Sr. Lacerda became noteworthy in a certain stage of his life by advocating a regime of emergency of limited duration. We are now in it.[10]

Writing in *O Globo*, former Finance Minister Eugênio Gudin said that the defect of Ato Institucional No. 2 was its short duration. "It is not possible to eradicate in two or three years a structure that Getúlio Vargas spent 15 years constructing and consolidating, using dictatorial power." Gudin wrote that no one in his right sense could believe that it would be possible to institute a normal constitutional regime in March, 1967, without "falling into the claws" of those who had "taken possession" of Brazil almost continuously from 1930 to 1964. He recommended adopting immediately the Mexican single-party system "that has given and is giving such good results." Explaining that "we must abandon the obstinate and absurd illusion that Brazil, or Mexico, or Argentina, etc., can practice the democratic representative regime with-

[8] *Correio da Manhã*, October 28, 30, 1965; *O Jornal*, October 31, 1965.
[9] *Jornal do Brasil*, October 28, 29, 1965.
[10] Ibid., October 28, 1965 (also Castello Branco, *Os Militares no Poder*, p. 352).

out restrictions," Gudin chided the United States for ridiculously wanting to apply its "uniform model of representative democracy to the Tsombes, the Lumumbas, the Salassies, to the countries of Apartheid, and to the semiprimitive populations of Paraguay and Bolivia."[11]

Whereas Vicente Ráo declared that it was absurd to speak about illegality or legality during a revolution, author Tristão de Athayde described himself as "horrified" by the "anti-Brazilian character" of the new measure. Magalhães Pinto admitted that the Ato would allow the government to free the nation from the "grave situation," but he made it clear that he would continue to oppose the economic-financial policy of the administration.[12]

O Estado de S. Paulo pointed out that it had been predicting "with an almost mathematical precision" the impasse which, due to Castello's mistakes, forced him to choose between "the Revolution's survival" and "the pure and simple return to the past." Writing that the government had failed in its job (except in the economic and financial sectors), *O Estado de S. Paulo* warned that new powers were not necessarily a good thing in the hands of those who had not known how to use the powers given them in the first place. The daily of the Mesquita family found the suppression of the political parties "profoundly disagreeable" and it objected to the indirect election of presidents. The Revolution, it said, should repair, cleanse, and discipline the national political life without altering the tradition of "the direct selection of the president by the people."[13]

10. Lincoln Gordon's Reactions (October 27–November 14, 1965)

Ambassador Gordon was in Washington from October 11 to October 26 for discussions about USAID to Brazil. Supplementing the program loan of $150 million for the fiscal year ending June 30, 1966, project loans were expected to provide $80 million, technical loans $14 million, and military assistance $15 million, with perhaps an additional $75 million available in the form of Export-Import Bank loans and wheat (to be furnished under Public Law 480). The Washington dis-

[11] Eugênio Gudin, "Ato Institucional No. 2," *O Globo*, October 29, 1965.
[12] *Jornal do Brasil*, November 7, 18, 1965.
[13] *O Estado de S. Paulo*, October 28, 29, 1965.

cussions also included a preliminary look at the fiscal year ending in June, 1967.[1]

While the ambassador flew back to Rio on October 26, officials in Washington learned that the Brazilian government, anticipating a defeat in Congress, might declare a state of siege or institutional act "to counter anticipated coup action by 'hard-liners.' " Specialists in the State Department and White House recommended "a position of complete neutrality in word and deed on this one."[2]

On the other hand, Gordon, when he learned in Rio about Ato 2, wanted the United States to express its regret in a formal declaration. His cable of October 27 expressed the belief that the Ato made too many concessions to the hard line, "engendered by unfortunate concomitance of Lacerda intemperance, Kubitschek return, provocative statements of Supreme Court president, and other adventitious factors generating emotional military reactions." "It is," Gordon cabled, "the price paid by Castello Branco for failure to start months ago the systematic building of a political base and his reluctance to develop a strong domestic program of propaganda and public relations." Gordon explained that the new Ato reflected a polarization of forces, "which it is in the U.S. interest to seek to depolarize in any way we can." A formal U.S. expression of concern, Gordon argued, would help Castello by strengthening his hand in resisting hard-line pressure.[3]

William G. Bowdler, of the White House staff, thought that it would be best if the U.S. expressions of concern were limited to private talks such as those the ambassador might have with Castello and Juraci. Any advantages of a public statement, he felt, might be outweighed by the charge of "intervention" and by such annoyance on the part of Brazil's "right wing military" that it would call for a withdrawal of the Brazilian forces in the Dominican Republic. McGeorge Bundy concurred.[4]

[1] Lincoln Gordon, AID presentation on Brazil, rev. draft, Rio de Janeiro, November 4, 1965, pp. 23–24, and McGeorge Bundy, memorandum to Gordon, Document 161, NSFB, LBJ Library.

[2] W. G. Bowdler, memorandum for McGeorge Bundy, October 26, 1965 (subject: Storm Clouds in Brazil), NSFB, LBJ Library.

[3] Gordon, cable to Secretary of State, Rio de Janeiro, October 27, 1965, NSFB, LBJ Library.

[4] Bowdler, memorandum to Bundy, October 27, 1965, Document 159, NSFB, LBJ Library.

The White House decision was resisted by Gordon, who cabled on October 29, citing the United States position about democracy in Latin America and arguing that an expression of regret would help get the country back eventually on the constitutional track and strengthen the desires of Castello and Juraci to use the new powers moderately. Juraci, Gordon said, had told him that, while he naturally preferred silence to condemnation, he saw no harm and some real merit in a high-level U.S. indication of regret that the Brazilian government had felt it necessary to adopt exceptional measures and of "understanding" that the objective was economic recovery, social progress, and the early reestablishment of full constitutional normalcy. Gordon concluded by telling Washington that he would have preferred an earlier statement to one that appeared to be made in response to pressure from the U.S. press or proddings from other Latin American countries. But he said that "since neither President Johnson nor Secretary [Rusk] nor Vaughn have so far said anything, I believe statement by one of them on above lines could be made without undue inconsistency and to overall benefit."[5]

Washington, however, preferred the use of private talks. Gordon, eager to express his concern to Castello, did not have to wait long, because Castello, disturbed by the reaction abroad, invited Gordon to Laranjeiras Palace on November 2, a holiday in Brazil. During the two-hour interview (Gordon's longest with Castello), the president said that his desire for constitutional normalcy had been mistaken as a willingness to return to the status quo before 1964. When Gordon expressed concern that Brazil might slide into outright military dictatorship, Castello replied that Gordon was too pessimistic and that Brazil would avoid a traditional Latin American or Nasserist dictatorship. A new political base, Castello said, would be built to support the goals of the Revolution.[6] He expressed his desire to have a long talk with Dean Rusk during the Second Special Inter-American Conference. Gordon found Castello "somewhat tired and still reflecting some of the extreme tension to which he had been subjected, but basically well composed and apparently conscious of heavy responsibilities he still faces and prepared to come to grips with them."[7]

[5] Gordon, cable to Secretary of State and Assistant Secretary Jack Vaughn, Rio de Janeiro, October 29, 1965, NSFB, LBJ Library.

[6] Gordon, "Recollections of President Castello Branco," pp. 19–20.

[7] Gordon, cable to Secretary of State, Rio de Janeiro, November 3, 1965 (Document 113a), NSFB, LBJ Library.

Two days later Gordon received an urgent request from McGeorge Bundy for a "redraft" of considerations and recommendations about USAID to Brazil during fiscal 1967. Together with the "redraft," Gordon sent a note to Bundy: "As you already know, I found last week's developments disappointing and disheartening. Nor am I yet persuaded that our official reaction was correct."[8]

Gordon's "redraft" listed four alternatives. The first, complete suspension of aid, with the offer of restitution upon the full reestablishment of constitutional democracy, would, Gordon wrote, "put us on record throughout the hemisphere in favor of democratic processes." But the ambassador concluded that this alternative might lead to the resignation of the team headed by Roberto Campos and would reverse a healthy foreign investment trend, encourage "all the negative nationalistic forces in Brazil," and weaken Castello's capacity to resist hardline demands.[9]

The second alternative, the reduction of aid to the minimum level required to avoid a renewed balance of payments crisis, would be the "worst" course of action in Gordon's opinion: it would provide most of the disadvantages of the first alternative without presenting "a clear-cut posture in favor of Latin American democracy." Gordon wrote that it would "critically reduce our leverage to influence either economic polices or political developments" and rule out effective assistance to the northeast and to education, agriculture, and health.

The third alternative, continuation of support at the current levels, was recommended by Gordon, for he saw it as a way to "help influence the course of political events" and to give the Castello Branco government "the benefit of the doubt concerning its goals." The fourth alternative, a substantial increase in aid, was rejected by the ambassador with the statement that the current levels were "close to the limit of what Brazil can effectively use."

Gordon conversed with Juraci late at night on November 6. The justice minister, having learned from Castello that Gordon "was obviously deeply worried but excessively pessimistic," emphasized that he and Castello had accepted the new Ato in order to save Brazilian de-

[8] Gordon, memorandum to Bundy, November 4, 1965, (Document 163), NSFB, LBJ Library.

[9] Gordon, AID presentation on Brazil, rev. draft, Rio de Janeiro, November 4, 1965.

mocracy, not destroy it. Juraci spoke of the improved Brazilian image that would result from the gubernatorial inaugurations, new party structures (he preferred two parties to three), direct elections in 1966 for more governors and for Congress, and moderate use of Ato 2. He also said that the government was moving to reduce the hard-liners' aggressiveness.

Juraci saw little difficulty in inaugurating Israel Pinheiro, whose offer of full cooperation to Castello and Juraci included the federal government's right to veto his nominations for state cabinet posts. Whereas the inauguration day of Pinheiro and most of the newly elected governors was January 31, the inauguration of Negrão de Lima was scheduled for December 5. This inauguration, Juraci told Gordon, would be the toughest battle, but he pointed out that it should be won because the military ministers were "now fully in line on supporting Castello Branco" on the issue.

When Gordon mentioned the need of "positive public relations," Juraci agreed and said that this was "one criterion" in the selection of new cabinet ministers. Explaining that Education Minister Suplici de Lacerda had submitted his resignation, Juraci expressed the hope for a replacement "with some political sense, who could conduct a dialogue with professors and students." "Positive public relations" would also be advanced, he said, when Roberto Campos, following Castello's suggestion, issued a statement to be used to attract congressmen to the government bloc and to establish the program of a new progovernment party. Juraci pointed out that vigorous editorial criticism of the government by *Correio da Manhã*, *Última Hora*, and *Tribuna da Imprensa* was not being restrained in any way, but he added that Ênio Silveira's "recently opened Communist-line weekly" had "transgressed tolerable limits" and required that "action be taken against him."[10]

Gordon cabled Washington that he found "the tone and substance" of Juraci's remarks "extremely encouraging." Again, on November 12, Gordon was cheerful because Castello, in a speech to the Rio de Janeiro state assembly, stressed the "economic achievements" of the administration and said that "our economy is beginning to be reactivated on a truly sound basis." Castello, Gordon cabled Washington, "was some-

[10] Gordon, cable to Secretary of State, Rio de Janeiro, November 7, 1965, NSFB, LBJ Library.

what overdue in demonstrating that the government is not only concerned with stabilization but also is dedicated to economic development and social welfare."[11]

On November 14, Gordon cabled that the "depressing and dangerous" situation had "brightened notably over the past several days" as the result of the Brazilian government's "campaign to expound positive aspects and purposes of Revolution." Nevertheless, the ambassador warned Washington that full confidence was impossible because Ato 2, regardless of how its powers were used, stood as a "symbol of authoritarianism to the outside world" and "could tempt extremist political and military leaders to seize control of this ready made dictatorial mechanism."[12]

Therefore, Gordon further advised, he would speak frankly to the Brazilian political leaders whenever opportunities arose, explaining the "serious danger of slippage into undisguised military dictatorship" unless some way were found to reassert unequivocally the "hierarchical authority of the President, military ministers, and major troop commanders over the radical elements among the middle rank officers." Gordon also told Washington that he had authorized Vernon Walters to convey, under the ambassador's "close direction," similar thoughts to selected senior- and middle-level military commanders. Walters, Gordon pointed out, "enjoys the respect and brotherly affection of almost every top figure in the Brazilian Army."[13]

11. The Inauguration of Negrão de Lima (December 5, 1965)

Juraci Magalhães, following an urgent call from General Ururaí, went to the First Army barracks on November 2. He found the First Army commander in the company of his full staff, which was headed by General Afonso de Albuquerque Lima.[1] Albuquerque Lima, an old friend of Juraci from the northeast, had recently served in Uruguaiana,

[11] Gordon, cable to Secretary of State, Rio de Janeiro, November 12, 1965, NSFB, LBJ Library.

[12] Gordon, cable to Secretary of State, Rio de Janeiro, November 14, 1965, NSFB, LBJ Library.

[13] Ibid.

[1] Magalhães, "Respostas do General Juracy Magalhães," pp. 1–2.

Rio Grande do Sul, following a ruling of Castello Branco which Albuquerque Lima disliked and which limited the amount of time that officers could be out of active army service. Upon succeeding Edson de Figueiredo as head of the First Army staff in September, 1965, Albuquerque Lima had been active in forcing Ato 2 on the government and had pressed for Costa e Silva to become Castello's successor. The hard-line movement, led by Albuquerque Lima, had the support of Ururaí and the overwhelming majority of the local army officers. "Our group had all the power in its hands," Albuquerque Lima recalls.[2]

Ururaí told the justice minister that he had called him to the barracks in order to work out an arrangement to prevent the inaugurations of Negrão de Lima, Israel Pinheiro, and Pedro Pedrossian (Mato Grosso). When Juraci said that the inclusion of Pedrossian's name was "news" to him, Ururaí said that Pedrossian was also corrupt and should not serve as governor under a Revolutionary regime.

Colonel Ferdinando de Carvalho showed Juraci an enormous volume, a result of his investigations, which contained evidence that the colonel thought should be the basis of the arrest and *cassação* of Negrão de Lima. Juraci, given photographs of Negrão campaigning for governor at the side of well-known Communists, mentioned similar pictures taken during past campaigns undertaken by himself, Otávio Mangabeira, and other "illustrious democrats" who could hardly be called Communists.[3] Juraci proposed that the inaugurations take place and that thereafter the governors be closely watched and accusations made if they violated the principles of the Revolutionary government. But, Juraci said, the use of force against the popular will, expressed at the polls, would have serious internal and foreign repercussions for the government. After Ururaí and his men strenuously disagreed with Juraci's proposal, the minister departed from what he has called an "icy" atmosphere.

At Laranjeiras Palace, Juraci reported at once to Castello and offered his resignation in case the president felt that it would strengthen the government. Castello, rejecting the offer, praised Juraci's handling of the First Army officers and immediately phoned the war minister about the need of an army *dispositivo* that would assure the inaugura-

[2] Afonso de Albuquerque Lima, interview, Rio de Janeiro, November 16, 1974.
[3] Magalhães, "Respostas do General Juracy Magalhães," pp. 1–2.

tions.[4] This would require command changes and perhaps more drastic steps in the Rio area.

The president, who flew to Brasília on November 3, received an evening visit at Alvorada Palace from Lieutenant Colonel Jarbas Passarinho, the successful outgoing governor of Pará. Passarinho told Castello that he had the painful task of bringing a message from his army colleagues in Rio: they were ready to act with troops against the inaugurations of Negrão and Israel Pinheiro and wanted Castello to know that if he would rule against those two inaugurations, troops from Vila Militar would descend on Rio and rally around the president, acclaiming him once again the leader whom they felt they had lost.

Castello smiled and said: "Governor, tell your companions that our Revolution does not have as a permanent objective the punishment of Brazilans. It differs from what is generally done in Latin America because it aims essentially to perfect the institutions. . . . What can be preserved in the name of democracy will be preserved. The chief work of a Revolution should not be evaluated on the basis of what it was able to wipe out but on the basis of what it managed to preserve." The president also told Passarinho that he had no vocation for being a dictator. But Castello added, "Go ahead with your mission. Go and see Daniel Krieger, my leader in the Senate; tell him the nature of your mission, and be sure to tell him of my decision."[5]

Passarinho, after thus coming to know Krieger, told his army colleagues in Rio that Castello and Krieger opposed their proposal. The officers, he found, were especially annoyed at the government's apparent lack of interest in the evidence that Colonel Ferdinando de Carvalho claimed to have found about Negrão de Lima's recent campaign. According to the colonel, Negrão, using Valério Konder and Roland Corbisier as intermediaries, had agreed to pay one hundred million cruzeiros to the Communist party and to supply it with small trucks. Ferdinando stated that the first installments on the payment, ten million cruzeiros, had been furnished by "Lima dos Hoteis" (who owned a chain of third-class hotels) and had been paid by Negrão to the Communists.[6]

[4] Ibid.

[5] Viana Filho, *O Governo Castelo Branco*, p. 366; *Jornal do Brasil*, July 18, 1977; Krieger, *Desde as Missões*, p. 193, quoting Jarbas Passarinho.

[6] Carvalho, interview, November 27, 1974.

Castello became so upset when Juraci showed him Ferdinando's written account of this matter that he phoned the colonel and asked: "Do you people want to depose me?" Ferdinando told the president that he wanted him to continue to be the leader. Nevertheless, the colonel persisted with his campaign against Negrão's inauguration. He submitted a long report to Costa e Silva, and when this produced no action, he turned to the Military Justice system. There he was frustrated because the government prosecutor had an automobile accident that kept him out of the picture for weeks.[7]

In the meantime, First Army officers dealt with Kubitschek. After they threatened to jail him for "dishonest handling of his income taxes and other grave matters," Sobral Pinto told him that he had better leave Brazil.[8] Castello authorized an arrangement that allowed him to depart secretly with his wife, using the military area of Galeão Airport, on November 9. In New Haven, Kubitschek said: "For the time being I do not intend to return to Brazil."[9]

On November 6 it was announced that General Ururaí was being transferred from the First Army to the Superior Military Tribunal, and later in the month other army command changes became known. Adalberto Pereira dos Santos, who had cooperated well in the south with Castello and Costa e Silva in March, 1964, was promoted to *general de exército* and shifted from Vila Militar (the First Infantry Division) to the position being vacated by Ururaí. Mamede was transferred from Belém to Vila Militar, and Albuquerque Lima, who did not like Adalberto Pereira dos Santos, was moved from the First Army staff to the directorship of Army Transport.[10] Rafael de Sousa Aguiar, the new commander of the First Military Region, learned from Castello: "I want you in command in order to end military pronouncements interfering with political matters." "The military," Castello admonished, "should be concerned with the profession and not with politics." Sousa Aguiar received plenty of complaints from his officers; he discussed

[7] Viana Filho, *O Governo Castelo Branco*, p. 366; Carvalho, interview, November 27, 1974.

[8] Sobral Pinto, interview, December 9, 1975; *Jornal do Brasil*, November 7, 1965. 7, 1965.

[9] *O Globo*, November 10, 1965; *Jornal do Brasil*, December 10, 1965.

[10] *Jornal do Brasil*, November 7, December 1, 1965; Albuquerque Lima, interview, November 20, 1974.

them with patience and reported some of them to the war minister.[11]

From Paris, Castello received a hard-line plea in a letter sent by Colonel Luís Gonzaga Andrada Serpa, who had headed an IPM before being appointed military attaché in France. The colonel wrote that he could not understand why the new Ato had not been applied against "three Supreme Court justices and the congressmen of the old group that now seeks revenge." He told Castello that he lamented the president's unfavorable references, made when the attaché was recently in Brazil, to those who wanted a more radical Revolution.[12]

On November 23, according to the CIA, Magalhães Pinto and others from Minas met with Sílvio Heck in the admiral's Rio residence to discuss a plan to overthrow the Castello Branco administration early in December following the OAS conference in Rio and just before the Guanabara gubernatorial inauguration date.[13] "The first move," CIA agents cabled Washington, would be "made by the colonels in charge of the IPM's." Their resignation of their IPM posts, accompanied by a manifesto severely critical of Castello, was to be the signal for armed civilian groups "to launch armed action." The report went on to say that

> Magalhães Pinto told Heck he would support the movement with his military police, but that he would not commit himself until after the armed groups had entered into action. In response to a question by Heck, a member of the Minas group present said that his group had enough men, but needed arms and ammunition.
>
> Magalhães also told Heck that he could not count on any help from the Brazilian Army units stationed in Minas Gerais because General Souto Malan, commander of the Fourth Military Region, is a firm supporter of Castello Branco.
>
> Magalhães plans to have another meeting with Heck and other conspirators in Petrópolis.

On the next day, November 24, Castello declared in a speech in

[11] Rafael de Sousa Aguiar, interview, Rio de Janeiro, August 8, 1977.

[12] Luís Gonzaga Andrada Serpa, letter to HACB, Paris, November 24, 1965, File N1, CPDOC.

[13] CIA, Intelligence Information Cable, Brazil, November 26, 1965 (date of information: early November, and November 23, 1965), NSFB, LBJ Library.

Alagoinhas, Bahia: "There are some who announce an insurrection. We prefer to face it directly rather than go around it. We do not recognize any autonomous force in the military circles of the country. If any exists, let it . . . pass from dilatory plotting to open action."[14]

On November 27, after Castello declined to meet with the colonels of Vila Militar, Lieutenant Colonel Francisco Boaventura Cavalcanti Júnior, chief of staff of the paratroopers, dispatched an open letter to the president in the name of the hard-liners.[15] Opening with a reference to Castello's speech in Alagoinhas, Boaventura wrote that "Your Excellency, in a gesture that has its inspiration in the nobility of the feudal knights, challenges the conspirators to an immediate struggle, frank and loyal, in an open field." The president, Boaventura said, had thus given the hard line the "imperious necessity" of sending him an open letter so that good Brazilians would know that while no conspiracy existed in the military area, the armed forces were "united, vigilant, dynamic, and resolute" in their determination to prevent the return of anarchy, corruption, and subversion.

Boaventura wrote that "sincere revolutionaries" found it impossible to understand the president's intransigent position in defense of the inauguration of those who "continue the work of corruption and subversion." Boaventura pointed out that "the laws for protecting the objectives of the Revolution are at the disposal of Your Excellency, and the hard line awaits, with impatience, a decision." Experts at military matters cited Boaventura's use of irony and "choice of expression that the marshal habitually used when he gave classes to the present colonels."[16]

Boaventura was placed under arrest at the barracks of the paratroop unit he served, and there he received visits from Colonels Martinelli and Gérson de Pina and some women "dissidents of the UDN and CAMDE." Colonel Hélio Lemos declared his support of Boaventura's position and therefore received a prison sentence from the new First Army commander.[17]

Lest Negrão de Lima be kidnapped, the Federal Department of Public Safety (DFSP) placed forty-eight agents at the disposition of

[14] *Jornal do Brasil*, November 25, 1965.

[15] Ibid., November 26, 28, 1965.

[16] Ibid., December 1, 1965 (Coluna do Castello); Castello Branco, *Os Militares no Poder*, p. 374.

[17] *Jornal do Brasil*, December 2, 4, 1965.

Juraci, who ordered them to protect the governor-elect. Army men received the unwelcome assignment of guarding Negrão's home, but Negrão did not spend his nights there because Juraci, recalling the hiding methods of conspirators in the 1920's, suggested that Negrão spend each night in the home of a different person.[18]

To the press, which had fun tracking down Negrão and photographing him, the governor-elect declared that he had had no agreements with Communist leader Valério Konder, but only disagreements, and that Roland Corbisier's so-called role of intermediary was pure fabrication. Nevertheless, on the eve of Negrão's inauguration, a judge ordered the imprisonment of Konder and Corbisier. Ferdinando de Carvalho, annoyed that Negrão had not been included with them, submitted a fifteen-page argument.[19] The Superior Tribunal prepared to settle the matter, but only after Negrão took office.

On Sunday, December 5, nearly two thousand security agents, many of them furnished by DFSP Chief Riograndino Kruel, were on hand to assure a peaceful inauguration. Juraci, representing Castello, was warmly applauded by the multitude in front of the state legislature, where the ceremony took place. Negrão received the governorship from the presiding officer of the local justice tribunal because no one connected with Lacerda or his administration wished to serve as the acting governor responsible for turning Guanabara over to Negrão.[20]

Two days after the inauguration, the government prosecutor for Military Justice (who had recovered from his automobile accident) declared that he opposed the imprisonment of Negrão because the material submitted by Ferdinando de Carvalho lacked documented proof. The Superior Military Tribunal gave a unanimous verdict in favor of the new governor.[21]

Columnist Carlos Castello Branco has pictured an "idealistic" and "obstinate" president spending a "Hamletian" moment when faced with the choice of "probable overthrow" or the issuance of Institu-

[18] Ibid., December 1, 1965; Magalhães, interview, December 3, 1974.

[19] *Jornal do Brasil*, December 1, 1965; Carvalho (interview, November 27, 1974) said that Konder and Corbisier were arrested but that the Military Justice, pressured by the government, did not arrest Negrão de Lima.

[20] *Jornal do Brasil*, November 25, 27, December 1, 3, 4, 1965.

[21] Ibid., December 8, 1965; Beviláqua, interview, December 21, 1977.

tional Act Number Two.[22] Neither choice was as serious as the fact of being forced to face such a choice. That Castello felt he had to do so spoke ominously about the future, for it revealed that even the toughest "legalist" in the presidency was at a disadvantage in dealing with a tendency which had been proclaimed virtuous by the mighty and which events—recent and not so recent—had encouraged: that of ignoring or modifying the rules of the game when it appeared important and useful to do so.

Despite the setback, Castello was determined that his successor would take over a nation that had returned to legalism. And in the meantime he expected to use Ato 2 as an instrument useful for his plans to modernize Brazilian institutions and to place the nation on a firm economic-financial foundation.

The discontented groups that had grown in power since April, 1964, were weakened as a result of the events of October, 1965. The hard line itself, now with less to complain about, could only admit that the president, supported by his loyal war minister, was clearly on top. While it submitted to orders that it attributed to Castello and his inner circle, it looked forward to the day when Costa e Silva would be free to do justice to hard-line views. The newly instituted indirect presidential election and Castello's self-elimination from the forthcoming contest seemed to open the way for the war minister who had so recently delighted hard-liners with his vehement attack on the chief justice.

[22] Castello Branco, *Os Militares no Poder*, pp. 676–677.

A Cabinet Reform and a Review of Relations Abroad

(November, 1965–February, 1966)

I must, step by step, but starting at once, reorganize part of my cabinet . . . in order to bring about a necessary and undeferrable strengthening of political support.

1. Castello Opens the OAS Conference (November, 1965)

AT 5:30 P.M. on November 17, Castello Branco reached Rio's Glória Hotel to open the Second Special Inter-American Conference, where all the OAS members except Venezuela were represented. Just outside the entrance Castello was confronted by nine intellectuals who raised placards and shouted, "Down with the dictatorship; we want liberty." The lively protest had been planned by a group that recognized the ineffectiveness of published manifestos and wanted to make a dramatic impact, especially on the U.S. delegation. After the careful Communist party leadership had refused to cooperate, plans for a mass demonstration had been abandoned by the eight organizing intellectuals, who were journalists Antônio Calado, Carlos Heitor Coni, and Márcio Moreira Alves; actors Gláuber Rocha, Joaquim Pedro de Andrade, and Mário Carneiro; theater director Flávio Rangel; and former diplomat (*cassado*) Jaime de Azevedo Rodrigues. During their demonstration within a meter or so of Castello, the eight were arrested, together with another intellectual who had joined them. They were frisked and sent to the Military Police barracks for detention.[1]

Castello's thirty-minute address at the Inter-American Conference advanced suggestions about economic matters made by Roberto Campos.[2] Thus Castello, while recognizing the virtues of the inter-American juridical institutions for peace and common defense, observed that the initiatives about economic cooperation had been less impressive, occur-

[1] Carlos Heitor Coni, interview, Rio de Janeiro, December 15, 1977.

[2] *Jornal do Brasil*, November 18, 1965.

ring "largely as a response to occasional crises."[3] He spoke of new "opportunities of commerce, reduced by the excessive protectionism of some industrialized countries," fair prices for raw materials, expanded markets for regional integration, and compensatory financing arrangements to allow the continuity of programs of economic development. In the case of coffee, Castello noted that Brazil had made sacrifices, despite the complaints of its exporters, in order to turn the International Agreement into an effective instrument. "We hope," he said, "that a similar system can be applied to other articles."

Castello argued for the unpopular idea of a permanent Inter-American Peace Force. He explained that Brazil was willing to participate in joint action "so that it not be said that the inaction of many justifies the isolated initiative of others," and he pointed out that the OAS system, conceived when the principal dangers had been border wars and armed aggression from outside the continent, was now faced with more subtle forms of aggression, through infiltration, subversion, guerrillas, and psychological warfare.

Democracy, Castello said, should not be "a mere game of appearances, in which liberty is confused with indiscipline, and social justice is perpetuated, disguised by the easy promise of demagogues. It should consist of the democratization of opportunities of access to land, housing, and education, consist of the promotion of development through austerity, savings, and continuity of effort, and consist of vigilance against the enemies of open society who make use of democratic freedoms to destroy it."

"We do not need lessons in democracy," Castello said. "We managed to save it, without asking help from anyone, from almost being destroyed in the hands of totalitarianism, and we are engaged in the great task of democratic renovation."[4]

Jornal do Brasil wrote that Castello's speech had advanced substantial criticisms of the OAS "in frank and clear language." Mexico and Chile issued statements condemning the creation of an inter-American force.[5]

After Juraci Magalhães announced that he opposed the immediate release of the nine intellectuals who had been seized, more than four

[3] HACB, *Discursos, 1965*, pp. 225–231.

[4] Ibid.

[5] *Jornal do Brasil*, November 18, 19, 23, 1965.

hundred writers, artists, and professors signed a manifesto describing them as the victims of aggression for having peacefully expressed their love of democracy, liberty, and the fundamental rights of man.[6] Sobral Pinto drew up habeas corpus petitions while Colonel José Maria Andrada Serpa, appointed to investigate, heard the testimonies of the prisoners. Juraci was particularly upset by the participation of Coni, who had written an unflattering article about the revolution as early as April, 1964, and former diplomat Azevedo Rodrigues. Castello was inclined to be less severe on the intellectuals than Juraci was, but for the time being the president left the matter in the hands of the Justice Ministry.[7]

On November 20, Castello had the discussion with Secretary of State Rusk that he had requested of Gordon. It took place in the company of Leitão da Cunha and Gordon. Rusk, who described the situation and prospects in Vietnam, was pleased to hear Castello say that the Brazilian government regarded the U.S. struggle there as one for the defense of the United States, the free world, the Western Hemisphere, and, therefore, Brazil.[8] At Castello's request, Rusk spoke also of the situation in Cuba and the Dominican Republic.

In no part of the world, Castello said, had there been a more systematic propagation of anti-American feeling than in Latin America. Noting that this was especially true among students, workers, journalists, and the cultural community, Castello recommended that the United States engage in active, cordial diplomacy and redouble its efforts under the Alliance for Progress. Recommending also the strengthening of the OAS, he observed that when the intervention in the Dominican Republic had become a multilateral affair, the major Brazilian opposition to the move and to Brazil's role had rapidly diminished.

Asked to comment on recent Brazilian developments, Castello told Rusk that the purpose of Ato 2 was to fortify democratic institutions. Digressing to make a point, Castello referred to his conversation during Harriman's visit in May when the roving ambassador had asserted that even if the OAS refused to support action in the Dominican Republic, the United States would not withdraw. Castello compared that dubious legal position, taken at a critical moment, to the case of Ato

[6] Ibid., November 20, 1965.

[7] Ibid., November 23, 1965; Coni, interview, December 15, 1977.

[8] United States Embassy, Rio de Janeiro, cable to the Department of State, November 23, 1965, NSFB, LBJ Library.

2, and he gave Rusk assurances about the gubernatorial inaugurations, the elections of 1966, and the reestablishment of political party life. "As time passes," he said, "public opinion will come increasingly to recognize that the government is moving to full democratic institutions."[9]

As Leitão da Cunha was chosen presiding officer of the OAS conference, Castello named Luís Viana Filho to head the Brazilian delegation. Working closely with Roberto Campos, Viana was happy when the conference accepted the principle that "economic development is the best guarantee for the political security of the continent."[10] When the planning minister's handling of an economic problem led the Chileans to describe him as having provided "new light" for the conference, Castello, fascinated by the talent of Roberto Campos, picked up the phone to congratulate him. He poured out praise on the phone, not realizing that he was talking to Otávio Bulhões, who had been trying to get a line through to the president. Bulhões was quite taken aback to receive so unexpectedly a wildly enthusiastic expression from the president.[11]

At the Military Police barracks the arrested intellectuals signed a letter saying that they had wanted to bring the dictatorial aspects of the regime to the attention of international opinion. The final judgment, reflecting Castello's wishes, found the intellectuals guilty of merely interfering with traffic at the time and place of an international meeting. Hard-line Colonel José Maria Andrada Serpa released a note to the press saying that their plans had not included violence against the regime. They were released on December 1.[12]

2. Robert Kennedy Visits Brazil (November, 1965)

On November 20, Senator Robert Kennedy and his party reached São Paulo, coming from Buenos Aires. A crowd, immense and admir-

[9] Ibid.

[10] Viana Filho, *O Governo Castelo Branco*, p. 437.

[11] Asdrubal Pinto de Ulyssea, letter to Luís Viana Filho, Rio de Janeiro, July 15, 1972.

[12] Coni, interview, December 15, 1977.

ing, received him at the airport, and when he spoke at the metalworkers' union in São Paulo, he was enthusiastically acclaimed. Especially hearty applause greeted his words: "The suffocation of liberties, including that of protesting, is the simplest method of destroying societies and institutions."[1]

That the Kennedy party would have nothing to do officially with the U.S. Embassy had already been decided by the advance team (including Richard Goodwin) that had planned the visit.[2] Embassy personnel, however, participated in Kennedy's meetings with top Brazilian authorities. Gordon and an embassy translator accompanied the senator when, after a trip to the northeast, he called on Castello in Rio on November 24, and it was at the embassy residence later that day that Kennedy, in Gordon's company, met with Juraci Magalhães. On the evening of the twenty-fifth Kennedy was the guest at a Thanksgiving dinner at the embassy residence.

During his conversation with Castello, Kennedy asked about the Brazilian northeast and about civil liberties. He asked the president why the minimum wage was not being paid to the sugar workers in the northeast. And Kennedy spoke about land reform. He attacked the destruction of democracy and the *cassações* and spoke about the situation of trade unions and students. The conversation went slowly due to the intervals of translating.[3]

After forty-five minutes Castello inquired whether he might ask a question, and the senator replied: "Of course." "You have," the president said, "been asking me questions for quite a while. And you have been traveling in Brazil and in much of South America. What is the object of this?"[4]

The visitor, nonplussed, hesitated and then spoke about the reasons that he said had not brought him to Brazil: "There are stories that I'm running for the presidency in 1968. But I've just been reelected senator. Johnson, recently overwhelmingly elected, will run for another term in 1968. My senate term lasts until 1970, and I'm not here to get media coverage"—a remark that Gordon doubted. Kennedy went

[1] *Jornal do Brasil*, November 21, December 3, 1965.
[2] Gordon, interview, June 11, 1975.
[3] Ibid.
[4] Ibid.; Viana Filho, *O Governo Castelo Branco*, p. 515.

on to say that he had not had much opportunity to get to know Latin America. "Jack was interested in Latin America. I am, too."

Castello did not press the matter. The interview ended, and Kennedy and Gordon were driven to the American Embassy residence. Kennedy, getting out of the car, asked Gordon: "Why did the President ask me what I had in mind?"[5]

Kennedy then met with Juraci Magalhães, who has reported that "Senator Robert Kennedy, during his entire visit to Brazil, harshly attacked the Brazilian government and the Revolution. He established contacts with members of the *esquerda festiva* [festive Left] and the *tout court* Left, and in the meeting that I had with him at the United States Embassy, in the presence of Ambassador Lincoln Gordon, we had a very rough conversation. Senator Kennedy committed the error, very common with certain American politicians, of speaking ex cathedra about the problems and the life of other people. It was his understanding that the Brazilian Revolution did not have the right to adopt measures of exception." Kennedy said that he did not believe that a purpose of Ato 2 was to assure the inaugurations of governors, and he called it a dictatorial act that submitted all the people to the mercy of the rulers.[6]

If, as Juraci recalls, his conversation with Kennedy was "very rough," the conversation that Kennedy had with Roberto Campos at the Gordons' Thansksgiving dinner was even more so.[7] Mrs. Gordon, with Kennedy on one side and Campos on the other, found herself in the midst of a heated quarrel.

More satisfactory were Kennedy's conversations with those described by Juraci as members of the "Left." One of them was publisher Ênio Silveira, a *cassado* who had testified at IPM's and had been imprisoned for nine days in 1964 and nine days in 1965, accused of "subversion." In *Revista Civilização Brasileira* he had recently published two open letters to Castello decrying conditions that had followed the 1964 revolution. Looking for a definition of "subversion—the magic word used to justify all the crimes and violences," Ênio Silveira had written:

[5] Gordon, interview, June 11, 1975.
[6] Magalhães, "Respostas do General Juracy Magalhães."
[7] Gordon, interview, June 11, 1975.

Subversive is the person who desires the peaceful modification of the socio-economic structure; *subversive* is the one who defended a legitimately constituted government that *nonsubversives* overthrew; *subversive* is the one who opposes the series of errors and outrages practiced daily by the direct collaborators of the present government: the purchase of the public utility concessions, the extravagant permission of a port for the Hanna Corporation, the modification of the law governing the remission of profits, the total submission of our foreign policy to the American interests, the opportunistic cynicism of the law about ineligible candidacies, the blows against Petrobrás represented by the recent arrangements about the petrochemical industry and the revocation of the act that expropriated the private refineries; *subversive* is the one who opposes the acts of violence committed by the United States in Vietnam and the Dominican Republic; *subversive* is every socialist; *subversive* is every materialist. *Subversive,* in short, is every one of those Brazilians who do not agree in gender, number, and degree with what is thought, said, or done by men of the so-called "revolution."[8]

Robert Kennedy's one-hour meeting with Ênio Silveira, arranged at the request of the senator, took place at the home of Sérgio Bernardes, a well-known architect. Kennedy not only wanted Silveira's views about the fall of Goulart and the main actors in the episode, but was also eager to hear his ideas about a continuing informal program of contacts between Brazilian and American intellectuals which Silveira had suggested at a meeting in Puerto Rico in 1963.[9] Richard Goodwin, who had been a panel member at the Puerto Rico meeting and had told Robert Kennedy about it, was at the discussion at Sérgio Bernardes' house. Several times he jokingly told Kennedy that Silveira was his "favorite Communist!" to which Silveira replied that Goodwin was his "favorite CIA agent!" Kennedy told Silveira that if he were elected president of the United States, he would give decided support to the program of contacts between Brazilian and American intellectuals.[10]

Kennedy, who was reported in the Brazilian press as wanting "a new policy for the continent," was obviously not in Brazil to please

[8] Ênio Silveira, "Epístolas ao Marechal," *Revista Civilização Brasileira*, Vol. I, No. 3.

[9] Ênio Silveira, letter to JWFD, Rio de Janeiro, December 10, 1975.

[10] Ibid.

U.S. Embassy officials. They found him rather arrogant and not very considerate.[11] Nor did he make a good impression on Amazonas Governor Artur César Ferreira Reis in Manaus. The demands on the senator's time allowed him and his party to accept only a fraction of the invitations received, but the failure of the group to show up when expected at a dinner carefully prepared by a religious group in Manaus was considered unfortunate by the governor. The senator, explaining that his chief interest was to "see the Īndios," learned from Reis of a camp of Indians civilized by missionaries. However, the river trip to the camp was described as requiring several days, and so the senator did not "see the Īndios."[12]

Governor Reis, an intellectual with a vast knowledge of the Amazon region, felt that the senator behaved stupidly and that the members of his party, with the exception of Mrs. Kennedy, had all the appearances of "a bunch of gangsters." They made off with so many "souvenirs" from the Manaus hotel that the authorities insisted on looking through their suitcases when they were about to depart at the Manaus airport. This demand led to a heated argument that was in full swing when Governor Reis reached the airport to greet the minister of transport and public works, Juarez Távora. The governor persuaded the authorities not to open the baggage of the Kennedy party. Later Reis received a letter from Kennedy apologizing for unfortunate incidents.[13] But Vernon Walters, his car damaged in Rio when it was borrowed by the Kennedy party, received no letter.

Juraci Magalhães wrote to Under Secretary of State Thomas C. Mann on November 30. "It was my impression," the justice minister said, "that Senator Kennedy came to obtain his information concerning the situation in Brazil from our opponents and debate with us in a manner that was generally not well received." Juraci wrote that he was particularly annoyed when Kennedy told him that the imprisonment of the "leftists," responsible for the incident at the Glória Hotel, was going to affect U.S. relations with Brazil. Juraci assured Mann that "all the equivocal statements of Senator Kennedy" would not affect Brazil's willingness to work for cooperation between the two

[11] Gordon, interview, June 11, 1975; Walters, interview, December 19, 1966.
[12] Artur César Ferreira Reis, interview, Rio de Janeiro, September 29, 1975.
[13] Ibid.

republics and, in a reference to Ato 2, he added that at a later date accusers might have a better understanding of "the imperious action we had to take." Mentioning the discussions he had had with Rusk and others at the OAS Conference, Juraci concluded: "All of them seemed to understand our problem and, as good friends, threw no stones at us, a task that remained for the regrettable action of Senator Kennedy."[14]

Juraci sent Mann an article from *O Globo* that said:

> If the senator's statements were politically inspired to appeal to an electorate, and such an excuse insults the senator's intelligence, such statements should be made in the United States, not in Brazil.
>
> We do not permit the Russians or the Chinese to interfere in Brazilian affairs, nor will we permit the North Americans to do so. Friendship does not permit the abuse of sovereignty.
>
> Brazil warmly received Senator Kennedy because of the memory of his brother. A change in this memory to the point of destruction depends on the sense of responsibility of Senator Bob Kennedy.

3. The Resignation of the Education Minister (November, 1965)

Education Minister Flávio Suplici de Lacerda succeeded in advancing the primary education of workers' children by means of the Salário-Educação. But he was unpopular among university students, whose leaders, with assistance from the Goulart administration, had played a role in agitating the country before April, 1964. These leaders condemned the education minister's Law 4,464, which was designed to alter the structure and practices of student organizations and which was passed by Congress in November, 1964. Known as the Suplici Law, it sought to provide a more legitimate student representation than had previously existed by requiring all students to vote in elections for "student directorships" to be formed at institutions of learning; and

[14] Juraci Magalhães, letter to Thomas C. Mann, Rio de Janeiro, November 30, 1965, NSFB, LBJ Library; Arthur M. Schlesinger, Jr., writes (*Robert Kennedy and His Times*, pp. 697–698) that the Kennedy party "reached Brazil in a state of exhaustion" and that "fatigue showed when he encountered the establishment. He lectured business leaders, argued sharply with Roberto Campos at the American embassy, and harassed Castello Branco, the military President, about the minimum wage."

it also looked to the formation of "state directorships" and a "national directorship." University administrators, state education secretaryships, and the federal Education Ministry were to have the authority to make sure that elections and financial transactions of the directorships were handled properly.[1]

Those who most strenuously opposed these provisions were associated with the student unions, such as the overall National Union of Students (UNE), that had come under the influence of the Communist party and the radical leftist Ação Popular (AP), offshoot of Juventude Universitária Católica (JUC). They resolved not to cooperate with the new legislation and to keep their organizations alive by holding meetings that the police presently tried to prevent. After delegates to the UNE's twenty-seventh annual congress avoided a conflict with the São Paulo DOPS in July, 1965, by meeting in secret, Suplici declared that the meeting places had been known only to the commanders of the Communist party and Ação Popular.[2]

Occasionally students demonstrated against the government and issued manifestos protesting the sending of Brazilian troops to the Dominican Republic. Some of them booed Castello when he appeared at the opening exercises of the Federal University of Rio de Janeiro in March, 1965. Rachel de Queiroz recalls the arrival of the president for a lunch at Editora José Olympio after this incident: "He entered with his eyes full of tears and his countenance shaken. 'Today,' he commented, 'I received my first boos.' "[3]

Suplici's ministry also had troubles with faculties, particularly at the University of Brasília. The *reitor* (university president) who took over the administration of the University of Brasília after the 1964 revolution found it strongly oriented to the far Left, and he dismissed thirteen professors and instructors considered sympathetic to the ideas of Marx. His successor, Reitor Laerte Ramos de Carvalho, grappled in 1965 with the problems provoked by a series of investigations of the university undertaken by the military. Castello, in the meantime, met

[1] Raimundo Moniz de Aragão, interview, December 16, 1975.

[2] *Jornal do Brasil*, July 25, August 3, 1965.

[3] Viana Filho, *O Governo Castelo Branco*, p. 122; Schneider, *The Political System of Brazil*, p. 230; Rachel de Queiroz in *Jornal do Brasil*, July 17, 1972 (an excerpt from a previously published article, see File HP5, CPDOC).

with professors, pleading that they give more attention to the problems of the students.[4]

After University of Brasília students went on strike in September, 1965, demanding the release of students held for military investigations, Castello met twice at Planalto Palace with the strikers' representative, a student who had been jailed by the police of Minas in April, 1964, and then had become director of the University of Brasília Federation of Students (officially considered extinct because of failure to adhere to the Suplici law).[5] Castello told him that the students could help by listing in writing the problems they felt could be solved immediately by the government. At the second meeting the president advised that he had ordered the release of one of the arrested students and that a favorable habeas corpus decision by the Supreme Court assured the release of another.

Speaking later to the press, the students' representative voiced a principal complaint of student leaders when he defended "the participation of the students in the great national decisions." Declaring that the chief mistake of Castello was the maintenance of Education Minister Suplici de Lacerda, he went on to say that the students of the University of Brasília were unanimous in their determination to struggle for democracy and against the dismissal of professors and the imprisonment of students involved in IPM's.[6]

Castello's dialogues with professors and students accomplished little. So bitter was the feeling that followed an order transferring a young sociologist from the University of Brasília to his former Education Ministry post that Laerte Carvalho, fearful of demonstrations, suspended classes early in October, 1965. Attacking "ideological sectarianism" as harmful to the university, he said that "sectarian professors do not offer options to the student, but mold his mentality according to their own points of view."[7]

On October 18, after course coordinators asked collectively to be relieved of their duties, Laerte Carvalho announced that he was dis-

[4] Viana Filho, *O Governo Castelo Branco*, pp. 124–125.

[5] *Jornal do Brasil*, September 2, 1965.

[6] Ibid.

[7] Viana Filho, *O Governo Castelo Branco*, p. 125; Schneider, *The Political System of Brazil*, p. 231; *Jornal do Brasil*, October 12, 1965.

missing 15 professors.[8] With this, 210 faculty members resigned, and students went on strike, adding a new crisis to the one that had followed the October 3 gubernatorial elections. Education Minister Suplici then closed down the University of Brasília.

Castello wrote to Suplici on November 4 to say that "this morning I reached the conclusion that I must, step by step, but starting at once, reorganize part of my cabinet . . . in order to bring about a necessary and undeferrable strengthening of political support." "Only compelling reasons," Castello added, "lead me to interrupt your inestimable collaboration." Suplici's reply, written on November 4, thanked Castello for presidential backing that had allowed him to leave the ministry in perfect order, with some reforms achieved and others in progress, and with no danger of a return "to the calamitous situation to which a state of anarchy, corruption, and crimes had led the nation."[9]

The announcement of Suplici's offer to resign inspired *Jornal do Brasil* to write that he had revealed himself "totally incapable all during his unfortunate term of office." "There is no way," *Jornal do Brasil* said, "to speak of social justice and equality of opportunities in a country that permits the marginalization, through ignorance, of half of its school-age population. . . . The number passing from the primary to secondary level suffers a drastic reduction, correctly described as a second discrimination, this time of an economic nature. . . . The preoccupation of offering university instruction practically free, in a country of insufficient resources, represents a luxury that is the equivalent of a true privilege for those who manage to pass beyond the secondary cycle."[10]

Juraci Magalhães was authorized by Castello to invite Magalhães Pinto to become education minister, but the outgoing governor of Minas declined. The president then considered other Mineiros, among them Professor Aureliano Chaves, a friend of Magalhães Pinto, and Roberto Rezende, who had lost the governorship race.[11]

Suplici, still in his post, asked the attorney general of the Republic

[8] Viana Filho, *O Governo Castelo Branco*, p. 125.

[9] HACB, letter to Flávio Suplici de Lacerda, November 3, 1965, File M, CPDOC; Flávio Suplici de Lacerda, letter to HACB, File M (p. 22), CPDOC.

[10] *Jornal do Brasil*, November 6, 1965.

[11] Viana Filho, *O Governo Castelo Branco*, pp. 361–362.

to annul the registration of the UNE. The UNE, he affirmed, "continues to be a den of political and social subversion, highly dangerous for the national security."[12] The cancellation of its legal status in December, 1965, a step that some educational administrators felt should have been taken in April, 1964,[13] only stimulated the student leaders associated with the UNE to defy the government more vigorously.

In January, 1966, Castello named congressional leader Pedro Aleixo, a Mineiro who had opposed Ato 2, to be minister of education. At the installation ceremony Castello described Pedro Aleixo as a professor who continued to have a "vocation for debate." He hoped that the new minister would spend a lot of time with students, convincing them that "the government was not a dictatorship." Suplici read a seventeen-page farewell speech in which he said that the Revolution had committed an error in allowing slanders to go unpunished. Juventude Universitária Católica, the Communist party, and Ação Popular, he said, thought that they had accomplished a great deal "just because I am leaving the ministry unpopular in the eyes of many young people." He attributed his unpopularity to the fulfillment of his duty.[14]

4. Other Administrative Changes (October, 1965–January, 1966)

Castello, in addition to altering the cabinet, named five new Supreme Court justices in accordance with Ato 2. After Milton Campos and Adauto Cardoso declined invitations to serve on the court, the final selections were Carlos Medeiros Silva, José Eduardo do Prado Kelly, Adalício Nogueira, Aliomar Baleeiro, and Osvaldo Trigueiro (who had been serving as attorney general of the Republic). Castello, receiving Baleeiro at Laranjeiras Palace on October 30 to tell him of his nomination, met the congressman on the ground floor and took him by the arm as they went to the second floor for a chat. The presi-

[12] *Jornal do Brasil*, November 26, 1965.

[13] Moniz de Aragão, interview, October 29, 1975.

[14] HACB, speech at the installation of Education Minister Pedro Aleixo (handwritten), File M, CPDOC; Viana Filho, *O Governo Castelo Branco*, p. 362; *Jornal do Brasil*, January 11, 1966.

dent spoke of cases that he said had been awaiting Supreme Court decisions for years.[1]

Krieger was upset to learn that Professor Rui Cirne Lima, candidate from Rio Grande do Sul, had been left aside because his appointment to the Supreme Court would displease Governor Ildo Meneghetti. Castello reexamined the matter and asked Krieger to invite Cirne Lima to serve on the Federal Court of Appeals, whose membership had also been increased by Ato 2, but Krieger made it clear that he felt Cirne Lima should serve on the highest court. After Juraci Magalhães tried unsuccessfully to soothe Krieger, Castello agreed that Cirne Lima would be invited to the Supreme Court when another vacancy occurred.[2]

Cabinet appointments made in December, 1965, brought Paraná Governor Nei Braga to the Agriculture Ministry (in place of technician Hugo Leme), Gaúcho federal Congressman Walter Peracchi Barcelos to the Labor Ministry (in place of Arnaldo Sussekind, another technician), and Admiral Araripe Macedo to the Navy Ministry (in place of Paulo Bosísio, who was eager to retire).

Daniel Faraco, of Rio Grande do Sul, surprised Castello by resigning the Industry and Commerce post in order to run for reelection to Congress.[3] The reaction of the Paulistas to this news was exemplified by a petition, signed by 85 of São Paulo's 115 state legislators, urging Castello to name a Paulista.[4] Roberto Campos and the president concurred that it would be useful to have a Paulista associated with the administration's economic policy. Campos therefore submitted four names to *O Estado de S. Paulo*'s Frederico Heller and other Paulistas with ties to São Paulo business, and Castello, as a result of these soundings, named Paulo Egídio Martins.[5]

Governor Ademar de Barros was upset because his own list of three names, submitted to Castello, had not included that of the thirty-six–year–old businessman who had unsuccessfully sought the mayorship in March, 1965, at the suggestion of opponents of the governor. Congressman Herbert Levy spoke for these opponents when, after a conversation with Castello, he told the press that the appointment of

[1] Baleeiro, "Recordações do Presidente H. Castelo Branco," p. 34.

[2] Krieger, *Desde as Missões*, pp. 196–197.

[3] Viana Filho, *O Governo Castelo Branco*, p. 363.

[4] *Jornal do Brasil*, January 1, 1966.

[5] Frederico Heller, interview, São Paulo, November 10, 1975.

Paulo Egídio should be considered a reconciliation between the federal administration and São Paulo. Castello, at Paulo Egídio's installation, spoke of the "milestone" achieved by "the ascension of the new generation of revolutionaries," who would supply youth and vigor as well as new ideas and methods.[6]

One of the most surprised politicians was Mem de Sá when he learned that he was to become justice minister following Juraci Magalhães' switch to the Foreign Ministry. As a senator belonging to the small Partido Libertador (PL) of Rio Grande do Sul, he had made bold declarations in the pre-1964 days condemning severe restrictions on foreign capital, and since then he had defended the economic program of the Castello regime, but, unlike Krieger, Pedro Aleixo, and others, he had not been close to Castello. Upon receiving the invitation, Mem de Sá consulted his doctor, for he had suffered a heart attack six months earlier. Learning that he was physically able to assume the Justice post, he called on Castello at Laranjeiras Palace to give his acceptance on condition that the president explain his choice.[7]

The president pointed out that he required a justice minister who would organize the progovernment political party and help select the gubernatorial candidates of 1966. In both of these "delicate tasks," Castello said, "the conflict of party interests between the ex-PSD members and ex-UDN members will be acute, if not explosive, requiring great tact and ability. Now, Congressman Pedro Aleixo, a friend whom I much admire, has the disadvantage of being, or of having been, an extreme Udenista. Therefore everything that he might do or propose for these missions will be received with no confidence by the PSD people, probably aggravating things." While the PL, Mem de Sá's party had long been allied with the UDN, Castello felt that its directors were all considered "independent men, free from factiousness." Besides, Castello added, he had learned that the Gáucho senator was warmly regarded by members of both the PSD and UDN.[8]

Not a few politicians saw something else in the choice of the new justice minister. Mem de Sá, a graduate of the Military Academy, had known the poker-playing Costa e Silva in the barracks of Rio Grande

[6] Anthony Vereker, report, January 19, 1966; *Jornal do Brasil*, January 12, 1966; HACB, *Discursos, 1966*, pp. 309–310.

[7] See Mem de Sá, *O Problema da Remessa de Lucros*; idem, letter to Viana Filho, October 7, 1971, p. 6.

[8] Mem de Sá, letter to Viana Filho, October 7, 1971, p. 6.

do Sul and did not consider him prepared to be president.[9] On the other hand, Krieger, a possible justice minister, was a friend of Costa e Silva. Pedro Aleixo told Krieger that probably the real mission of the Justice Ministry was to "torpedo the candidacy of the war minister" and that while Castello had good reason to say that the withdrawal of Krieger from the legislature would be a mistake, the principal reason for not inviting Krieger to be justice minister was related to the torpedoing mission. In any event, Krieger was happy to remain leader in the Senate.[10]

Some administrative changes made below the cabinet rank just before the promulgation of Ato 2 were of considerable interest to Roberto Campos and Otávio Bulhões. Housing Bank President Sandra Cavalcanti, having become as disenchanted with the top presidential advisers as they had become of her capabilities of running the bank, resigned on October 11 following Negrão's election. Roberto Campos and Otávio Bulhões, whom she attacked, settled on lawyer Luís Gonzaga do Nascimento Silva as her successor.[11]

Another who resigned in October, 1965, was Professor José Maria Arantes, director of the Administrative Department of Public Service (DASP), an organ whose long-time role in elaborating the federal budget was altered by the development of the Planning Ministry. Arantes, appointed by Castello to head DASP in 1964, disagreed with Roberto Campos about bureaucratic wage policy and other matters, and he resolved to leave office after learning that the president had named Campos, not Arantes, to head a commission for planning bureaucratic wage revisions.[12] The outgoing DASP director was visibly upset when his

[9] Mem de Sá, interview, October 31, 1975.

[10] Krieger, *Desde as Missões*, p. 222.

[11] Cavalcanti, interview, November 18, 1975; Melo Flores, interview, December 20, 1977; Nascimento Silva, interview, October 25, 1975; Viana Filho, *O Governo Castelo Branco*, pp. 143–144.

[12] Arantes, interview, November 22, 1974. Sant'Anna e Silva (memorandum, July 1979) points out that budget deficits had been the principal causes of the pre-Castello Branco inflation and that the DASP had lacked the authority to restrict the expenditures of ministries. With the Castello Branco government's decision to place budget policy in the hands of the Planning Ministry, Sant'Anna adds, the first DASP director in that government, Wagner Stelita Campos, cooperated fully with Roberto Campos, whereas the second, José Maria Arantes, was less cooperative, especially when the Planning Ministry sought to restrict the wage increases of government employees, civilian and military.

resignation became final during an interview with the president in October, 1965, and therefore Castello set up another appointment to see him. As things turned out, the new appointment coincided with so tense a moment in the October crisis that Arantes, making his way through military figures and politicians at Laranjeiras Palace, hardly expected the president to keep the appointment. But Castello received him on the dot. Smiling paternally, the president spoke in a kindly way to express regret that Arantes had been upset at their last meeting and to assure him of his appreciation of his work and of his hope that they would continue friends. Arantes was greatly moved.[13]

5. True and False Nationalism (December, 1965)

In another administrative change made before the promulgation of Ato 2, Navy Captain Euclides Quandt de Oliveira, an electronics and telecommunications expert, was transferred from the Gabinete Militar to the presidency of the government's National Communications Council (CONTEL). Among the tasks that Castello asked Quandt to undertake were the nationalization of important foreign-owned telephone companies and the settlement of the case created when TV Globo entered into a joint venture and technical assistance arrangement with Time-Life.[1] The TV Globo contract with the American firm, signed before Castello became president, was frequently described by Lacerda as illegal. Castello, replying to one of Lacerda's letters of late 1964, had promised an investigation. "I see by the newspapers," Castello had written, "that you are proclaiming a great scandal."[2]

Typical of the "bankrupt body" that the Castello Branco regime found itself administering in 1964 was Brazil's telephone service, victim of many years of inadequate rates. In the Rio de Janeiro–São Paulo area the shortage of instruments had reached eight hundred thousand,[3] and the interval between the request for an instrument and its installation had reached about ten years. This area was served by the Com-

[13] Arantes, interview, November 22, 1974.

[1] Quandt de Oliveira, interview, October 21, 1975.

[2] HACB, letter to Carlos Lacerda, December 3, 1964, File N4, CPDOC.

[3] *Jornal do Brasil*, December 23, 1965.

panhia Telefônica Brasileira (CTB), owned by the Canada-based Brazilian Traction, Light, and Power Company. Although the Castello administration took the unpopular step of raising telephone rates, the past experience of Brazilian Traction made it reluctant to invest the vast amounts needed for rehabilitation and modernization of telephone equipment.

Castello hoped that Brazilian private capital would purchase the CTB, along with the telephone property of IT&T in Rio Grande do Sul. Although Otávio Bulhões and Roberto Campos made every effort to interest suitable national private groups, these groups demanded excessive financial support from the Brazilian government (and the owners of the properties seemed inclined to regard the government as the most reliable payer). As the negotiations between the foreign companies and three Brazilian private groups dragged on, Castello set a deadline, and when it was reached without any agreement, he authorized CONTEL to try to arrange the purchase of the foreign telephone properties by the Brazilian government. To work out the details, he named a study group of four: Roberto Campos, Otávio Bulhões, Euclides Quandt, and Colonel Dirceu Coutinho.[4]

Bulhões maintained that the negotiations should be concluded in a manner that would not require the Brazilian Treasury to furnish any money to the sellers.[5] Thus, the final agreement reached with Brazilian Traction, which had the largest foreign investment in Brazilian telephones, stipulated that the payments for the properties would be made from future profits. The nationalized company, operating with the improved rate structure established earlier for Brazilian Traction, would pay a purchase price of $26,315,737 over twenty years and assume the indebtedness of $70 million owed by CTB to Brazilian Traction. The public was informed of the details early in the week beginning December 19, 1965, and was further advised that, as in the case of the AMFORP nationalization, the seller had "the obligation to invest in Brazil a part of the value of the transaction."[6]

At the same time that CONTEL released this news, Castello gave a graduation address at the National War College that defended ar-

[4] Ibid., December 21, 1965; Sant'Anna e Silva, memorandum, July 1979; Quandt de Oliveira, interview, October 21, 1975.

[5] Quandt de Oliveira, interview, October 21, 1975.

[6] *Jornal do Brasil*, December 21, 23, 1965.

rangements made by his government with foreign companies.[7] In reply to those who "repeated, with a singular intellectual dishonesty, that we purchase scrap iron," Castello explained that the value established for the purchase of the AMFORP electrical properties was substantially inferior to the true value as calculated by a well-known Swedish technical company. At least 70 percent of those properties, he said, had been constructed after World War II. The payments to AMFORP, to be made over forty years, were not to begin for three years, so the initial payment of ten million dollars would not be made before the U.S. government extended a twenty-four-million-dollar loan for six badly needed generators to be installed by Eletrobrás on the Rio–São Paulo border. Concluding that the payments to AMFORP would be considerably smaller than the interest and dividends that the company would have had the right to remit, had it not sold its properties, Castello declared that it was time to "put an end to malicious and unpatriotic accusations that benefit only the orators of national disintegration."

Because Lacerda, *Tribuna da Imprensa*, and others also frequently attacked the administration's iron ore export policy, Castello explained to the ESG graduating class some of the policy's provisions that affected foreign companies, such as the obligation to offer at least 40 percent of the company ownership to Brazilians and the reinvestment requirement that would allow no profit remittance for the first five years and no more than 12 percent thereafter. Furthermore, Castello was able to announce that Hanna's iron ore subsidiary in Brazil had just become a minority shareholder in a new company which would be controlled by Brazilians.

In the third place, Castello discussed the agreement of investment guarantees, worked out with the United States, for, as he remarked, "efforts at falsification" still persisted despite the exhaustive debate that had preceded the approval by Congress. Pointing out that "Brazil guarantees nothing," Castello explained that the U.S. government guaranteed its own investors against noncommercial risks abroad—with an innovating clause in the case of Brazil that required the U.S. government to consult Brazil before issuing any insurance policy, thus giving Brazil the power of veto in cases where it deemed foreign investments

[7] HACB, *Discursos, 1965*, pp. 109–123.

inconvenient. Castello blamed "an earlier period of demagogic xenophobia" for the interest of foreign investors in the guarantees, and he revealed that upon enactment of the guarantee accord with the United States, requests for guarantees had been received from U.S. firms wishing to invest $250 million in industries that were "essential for the renewal of development and the creation of productive jobs—unpostponable in a country whose population increases at a rate above our capacity to generate jobs exclusively with our internal savings." Also from West Germany, Castello said, new private investments were to be expected, for the West German unilateral decision to insure overseas investments had resulted in requests covering four hundred million marks for Brazil.

Castello asked his audience whether the term *nationalist* was the proper one to apply to "a behavior that condemns us to misery and consequent subversion, and that, in the name of our development and our economic emancipation, asphyxiates our capacity to save and make use of internal and external resources."

6. Vietnam and Other International Matters (December, 1965–February, 1966)

In December, 1965, Gordon received a cable authorizing him to advise the Brazilian government that President Johnson had approved the recommended $150 million program loan for the fiscal year ending in June, 1966. The cable, apparently labored over, also asked Gordon to raise with Castello Branco, as a separate matter, the question of Brazil's participation in the fighting in Vietnam.[1] The ambassador was to express appreciation for Brazil's participation in the Peace Force sent to the Dominican Republic and explain how the situation looked in Vietnam.

Gordon met with Castello on December 15. After a brief discussion about the replacements of generals in the Dominican Republic,

[1] Gordon, interview, June 11, 1975; for details about the final approval of the program loan, see Gordon, memorandum to Secretary of State, December 6, 1965, and Mann, message to White House ("relayed to the ranch for transmission to the President"), Washington, D.C., December 8, 1965, both documents in NSFB, LBJ Library.

Castello told the ambassador that the agenda was in his hands. Gordon said that he had two matters to bring up, the second being especially grave. He disposed of the first by explaining, in about ten minutes, problems involved in the authorization of the $150 million program loan, such as U.S. balance of payments and inflationary pressures and the economic impact of Vietnam. The ambassador pointed out that while the U.S. government admired Brazil's self-help steps and reform measures, some Washington technicians doubted the wisdom of transferring the full $150 million. Despite "divided counsels," Gordon said, President Johnson had decided on the full amount for Brazil.[2]

Then Gordon turned to Vietnam and pointed out that in 1966 it would be necessary to increase to four hundred thousand the number of troops sent there to help defend South Vietnam. Gordon said that Johnson was interested in having Brazil play a more active role, sending fighters (such as ground troops, ships, or planes), doctors, or even nurses. Castello listened carefully and said that he would take the matter under advisement.[3]

On December 31, Johnson sent Castello a letter saying that as he wished to leave no "stone unturned in the search for peace," he had ordered, on Christmas Eve, the suspension of the bombing of North Vietnam "for some days" while Ambassador Arthur Goldberg, exploring peace possibilities, visited the Pope and de Gaulle and while Ambassador Harriman visited Warsaw, Belgrade, and New Delhi. Johnson asked Castello for this thoughts and advice.[4]

Castello, writing a long memorandum for Juraci Magalhães on January 17, 1966, opened by saying that "the case of Vietnam is reverberating in full force on the government of Brazil." For his incoming foreign minister, the president reported the "suggestions" made by Gordon, and he asked Juraci to review correspondence in which Brazil had offered—in a letter that Castello described as "weak"—to cooperate in peace negotiations. Seven days after Castello wrote this

[2] Gordon, cable to Washington, December 17, 1965, NSFB, LBJ Library.

[3] HACB, handwritten memorandum for Juraci Magalhães, Rio de Janeiro, January 17, 1966, File O2 (pp. 1–6), PVCB; Gordon, interview, June 11, 1975.

[4] LBJ, letter to HACB, The White House, December 31, 1965, File O1 (pp. 29v, 30), PVCB.

memorandum, President Johnson received a warmly worded response to his year-end letter about peace efforts.[5]

A few days later, on the last day of January, 1966, Johnson wrote again to Castello, this time to advise that it had "become necessary . . . to end the suspension of bombing attacks against North Vietnam." Johnson reported that North Vietnam simply demanded conditions that would amount to the achievement of its objectives and had used the period of bombing suspension to send military forces and equipment into South Vietnam. He added that the United States remained determined that South Vietnam resolve "its own future without external interference."[6]

Castello and Juraci reacted quickly. Castello on February 2 wrote Johnson that the U.S. government had no alternative other than to resume bombing military objectives and that the Brazilian government supported this action and recognized that Johnson's objective was the freedom and integrity of Vietnam. On the same day, Juraci stated, in a press conference, that Brazil concurred in Johnson's decision to resume bombing North Vietnam since the United States had made the greatest possible effort to achieve peace.[7]

The matter of possible Brazilian participation in Vietnam remained dormant for almost another year. Ambassador Gordon never heard anything from Castello about the subject after Castello spoke of taking it "under advisement" on December 15.[8] But Gordon's opportunities were limited, because in February he left Rio to replace Jack Vaughn as assistant secretary of state for Latin American affairs. When the news of Gordon's transfer to Washington became known in mid-January, Castello told Walters that he would miss Gordon very much. Academy of Letters President Austregésilo de Ataíde wrote in a news-

[5] HACB, handwritten memorandum for Juraci Magalhães, January 17, 1966; Bundy, memorandum to LBJ (subject: Letter from Brazilian President), January 24, 1966, Papers of LBJ, President's Staff File, Brazil, Vol. 1, Presidential Correspondence, LBJ Library.

[6] LBJ, letter to HACB, The White House, January 31, 1966, File O1 (pp. 31, 32, 32v), PVCB.

[7] Benjamin H. Read (Executive Secretary, The Department of State), memorandum to McGeorge Bundy, February 4, 1966, Papers of LBJ, President's Staff File, Brazil, Vol. 1, Presidential Correspondence, LBJ Library; Bundy, memorandum for LBJ, February 4, 1966, Brazilian Memorandums, Vol. VI, NSFB, Box 3, LBJ Library.

[8] Gordon, interview, June 11, 1975.

paper column that Gordon had been an ideal ambassador at a time when painful transformations were taking place. "One never heard from him a word of boasting or haughtiness born of the consciousness of the power of the country he represented," Austregésilo affirmed.[9]

At the time that Gordon's new appointment became known, Rio de Janeiro suffered from its worst torrents of rain in approximately eighty years. Floods and collapsing buildings killed about 190 people, left an estimated 20,000 homeless, and caused material damage reported at fifty billion cruzeiros. Castello quickly authorized a credit to the Caixa Econômica so that it could loan up to five billion cruzeiros to flood victims.[10]

Lacerda released to the press a letter to Castello in which he said he would have written earlier but did not want it said that he was drawing conclusions favorable to his thesis about the Brazilian crisis, "more evident than ever with the tragedy of these days." The former governor referred to acts of gallantry of the Cariocas during decisive days—acts that he said Castello had been quick to forget. Arguing that Castello's administration had not paid, while Lacerda was governor, the debt owed the Cariocas by the nation and armed forces, he wrote that the time had come to pay it. "If you can give political help to the present state government, now you should give material help to this people," Lacerda wrote.[11]

Another letter to Castello, this one full of sympathy, was received from President Johnson. Soon after it was sent, the U.S. Embassy donated three billion cruzeiros each to the states of Guanabara and Rio de Janeiro in the name of the Alliance for Progress.[12]

Castello, reviewing Brazil's relations abroad in his memorandum of January 17 to Juraci, expressed the belief that "an atmosphere without irritation" would prevail in the Peace Force in the Dominican Republic after General Álvaro Alves da Silva Braga replaced General Hugo Panasco Alvim. Turning to other hemispheric matters, Castello asked Juraci to try to solve the long-standing problem of bringing gas

[9] United States Embassy, Rio de Janeiro, cable to Secretary of State, January 21, 1966, NSFB, LBJ Library.

[10] *Jornal do Brasil*, January 14, 12, 16, 1966.

[11] Lacerda, letter to HACB, January 13, 1966, File N4 (p. 20), CPDOC.

[12] See Bundy, memorandum to LBJ, January 24, 1966, LBJ Library; *Jornal do Brasil*, January 22, 1966.

by pipeline to Brazil from an old Brazilian concession in Bolivia, and he urged Juraci to give careful attention to Chile, where, he said, "the Christian Democratic Party and the Communists work with success against Brazil." Mexican foreign policy, Castello wrote, had a mania for upsetting mutual understanding in the continent but lacked the authority to do so, since Mexican leaders were "fascists of a single party who dedicate themselves to speaking about self-determination and nonintervention." In a brief notation about Venezuela, Castello wrote that "after my speech at the OAS, Venezuela entered into a deep underbrush; I don't think we should drive it into a corner." Castello praised the service rendered in Uruguay by Ambassador Pio Corrêa, who was advanced to the high post of secretary general of Itamarati.

Turning to Europe, Castello advised Juraci that the Brazilian ambassador to France was being transferred and that his successor should have the disposition to act against the "Communist central" in Paris and the enemies of the Brazilian Revolution who were there (Kubitschek, Samuel Wainer, and others). After Paris, Castello told Juraci, the most important embassies in Europe were those in Bonn and Rome, which "need to be seriously stimulated." Writing of the need for a new ambassador in Lisbon, Castello said: "Let's keep our distance from colonialism, for we favor methodical decolonialization."

Besides calling for a "less routine" type of representation at the UN, Castello asked Juraci to study the situation created by the so-called diplomatic tourists, some of whom served abroad as representatives of ministries other than Itamarati: "No one has been sent on my recommendation; I have the right to ask for a cleansing operation." Castello also argued that cultural attachés should not "grow old" at their posts (and "the culture with them"); they should be replaced every two or three years so that foreign nations would receive the most recent cultural information from Brazil. In conclusion Castello said that the Rio Branco Institute (the diplomatic academy) was completely in need of new life and expression. "It is," he wrote, "a sort of military academy without any renovating spirit."[13]

In the final paragraphs written to Juraci Magalhães, one can see the hand of the young army captain who shattered tradition at the

[13] HACB, handwritten memorandum for Juraci Magalhães, January 17, 1966.

Fifteenth Infantry Battalion to revitalize a moribund unit and the hand of the middle-aged supervisor of instruction who preferred the difficult task of devising and installing new systems to the simpler path of conformity with what he considered outmoded.

If Brazil as a whole was to receive "new life and expression" as an enduring result of the March, 1964, movement and the three-year Castello administration, much remained to be done in 1966. Having made some changes in his team with the purpose of promoting accomplishments that he had in mind, the president gave particular attention to political matters, for the nation's political system had been thoroughly disrupted by the events of October, 1965. What sort of political parties and elections would the Castello administration bequeath to the future, both by practice and by legislation?

VII

The Presidential Succession

(November, 1965–May, 1966)

Enthusiasts of the Costa e Silva candidacy push for its untimely adoption. . . . [They] ignore the existence of those who are responsible for national policy, including the president of the Republic. They turn to the opposition in search of supporters [and] agitate in military circles.

1. The Two New Political Parties (November, 1965–March, 1966)

LINCOLN GORDON has written that Brazil's pre-1965 political structure had become obsolete and the "main political parties basically irrevelant to Brazilian needs and conditions."[1] Juraci Magalhães found UDN members with a similar opinion. But UDN Secretary Oscar Correia, who felt otherwise, resolved to join no new party, and in order to prevent the office and property of the UDN from falling into the hands of the government, he created a study institute to hold the property as its principal asset. Partido Libertador (PL) President Raul Pila was so upset with the political party changes being instituted by the government that he considered terminating his long political career.[2]

Juarez Távora, unhappy at the prospect of the extinction of the Christian Democratic Party (PDC), urged Castello and Justice Minister Juraci Magalhães not to limit to two the number of new parties in Brazil. In a long letter to Juraci, he wrote that the world struggle was between capitalism and socialism but that many people, like himself, opted for neither because they believed that the solution lay in adopting the synthesizing ideas of the PDC. Thus, in addition to a party favoring "old ways" and another favoring "state socialism," Brazil needed, he said, one or more additional parties.[3]

Some politicians, among them former São Paulo Governor Carvalho Pinto, disliked the idea of Castello and Juraci to limit the new parties

[1] Gordon, "Recollections of President Castello Branco," p. 15.

[2] Oscar Correia, interview, September 24, 1975; Viana Filho, *O Governo Castelo Branco*, p. 370.

[3] Juarez Távora, letter to Juraci Magalhães, n.d., File N1, Part 1 (p. 9), CPDOC.

to two—one supporting and another opposing the Revolution. But Juarez Távora's nephew, Ceará Governor Virgílio Távora, wrote Castello to say that it would be disastrous to have more than these two. A third Party, Virgílio said, would assure the party of the Revolution of two foes, not one, during critical moments.[4]

To help induce politicians with divergent views to join forces in a single party of the Revolution, the formation of party *sub-legendas* (subdivisions) was advanced. This solution, sometimes attributed to Daniel Krieger and favored by him,[5] was explored at a meeting held by Castello in Planalto Palace in November, 1965. As the approximately thirty federal legislators discussed heatedly the difficulties of bringing long-time adversaries together, the *sub-legenda* formula emerged as the favorite device of the majority. Senator Mem de Sá argued that it had been used to advantage in Uruguay and had been included in the program of the PL. Castello, closing the meeting, named a commission to draw up legislative proposals. Among its members were Pedro Aleixo, who had spoken against *sub-legendas,* and Mem de Sá.[6]

During the following days the president received advice from Juraci, Cordeiro, Krieger, Pedro Aleixo, Bilac Pinto, Sarasate, Rui Santos, Antônio Carlos Magalhães, Adauto Cardoso, and Electoral Tribunal Minister Colombo de Sousa. Final touches were put on an appropriate Ato Complementar during a plane ride from Brasília to Rio on November 20, when Castello was accompanied by some of these men. The group spent part of the plane trip considering possible names for the progovernment political entity and finally settled on the suggestion of Sarasate: Aliança Renovadora Nacional (ARENA).[7]

Ato Complementar No. 4, issued on November 20, required the formation, within forty-five days, of provisional parties, each with no fewer than 120 federal congressmen and 20 senators. These minimums, while theoretically allowing the formation of three parties, eliminated

[4] *Jornal do Brasil*, December 18, 1965; Virgílio Távora, letter to HACB, Fortaleza, Ceará, November 1, 1965, File N1, Part 2 (p. 1), CPDOC.

[5] Teódulo de Albuquerque, interview, October 24, 1975; Almeida Magalhães, interview, August 8, 1977.

[6] Mem de Sá, letter to Viana Filho, October 7, 1971, p. 4.

[7] Viana Filho, *O Governo Castelo Branco*, p. 370; Antônio Carlos Magalhães, interview, August 11, 1977.

that possibility for all practical purposes. It was soon found difficult, in fact, for a single opposition party to meet the requirement. Oppositionists, principally from the old PTB, were quick to make the effort, calling themselves the Movimento Democrático Brasileiro (MDB). But by December 7, when the ARENA reported the adherence of 31 senators and 227 congressmen, the MDB could muster only 21 senators and 112 congressmen. Krieger writes that had it not been for the regional political conflicts and some help from the government, "the oppositionist group would certainly not have been able to comply with the conditions."[8]

Krieger also writes that Castello called him to Planalto Palace to tell him: "You are going to be national president of the ARENA and, as such, I want to submit to you the names we have in mind for the Executive Commission. You have the right to reject any and replace them, if you have candidates, because the responsibility of running the party will be yours." Krieger was pleased with the list. Noting that Castello had indicated two possibilities for secretary general of the Executive Commission, Krieger chose Rondon Pacheco (UDN, Minas Gerais), who was the government's vice-leader in the Chamber of Deputies. Other Executive Commission officers were Filinto Müller (PSD), Teódulo de Albuquerque (PTB), Wilson Gonçalves (PSD), and Antônio Feliciano (PSD); members serving without executive posts were Raimundo Padilha (UDN), Paulo Sarasate (UDN), Miguel Couto Filho (PSP), Leopoldo Perez (PSD), and Jarbas Passarinho.[9] Organization of the ARENA's National Directorship, a much larger body that included men of letters and elder statesmen as well as active politicians, continued into March, 1966, because the deadline for forming provisional parties was extended to March 15 by Ato Complementar No. 6, of January 3.

Largely responsible for this extension were the bitter local conflicts.[10] Although Castello finally persuaded Senator Vitorino Freire (PSD) to join the ARENA with his followers, it was soon evident that the long-time strongman of Maranhão felt that he could not re-

[8] *Jornal do Brasil*, November 27, December 8, 1965; Krieger, *Desde as Missões*, p. 204.

[9] Krieger, *Desde as Missões*, p. 204.

[10] Teódulo de Albuquerque, interview, October 24, 1975.

main in the same fold with incoming Governor José Sarney (UDN). Freire, in a bitter letter to Castello about press reports, asked permission "to withdraw at once from the ARENA."[11]

In São Paulo, Arnaldo Cerdeira and other followers of Governor Ademar de Barros in the PSP began to organize a local ARENA. The governor, seeking to bring the different São Paulo currents into the new organization, invited his political opponents, such as Abreu Sodré and Carvalho Pinto, to meet with him in the governor's palace, but the opponents failed to show up.[12] Lacerda's supporters in the São Paulo UDN, which had been under the presidency of Abreu Sodré, did not wish to join an organization that seemed to be in the hands of the Ademaristas; besides, Lacerda was attacking the ARENA.[13]

After Castello discussed the São Paulo ARENA with Minister Paulo Egídio Martins and Congressman Ernesto Pereira Lopes (UDN) late in January, a commission of five Paulista federal congressmen recommended that eleven state politicians set up the local ARENA executive commission. Castello let the executive commission end up under the presidency of Cerdeira, thereby recognizing the large popular backing of the PSP in the state.[14] Besides, this step widened the breach between Cerdeira and Ademar de Barros, who had decided that "all this business about the ARENA and MDB is not worth anyone's attention because everything is going to change in a little while."[15] But with the PSP domination of the São Paulo ARENA, the local UDN people ignored the pleas of Congressmen Pereira Lopes that they join up. Finally, three months after the initial discussions, a letter from Castello to Abreu Sodré convinced the UDN leaders in São Paulo that they should change their minds. They were moved by Castello's references to the responsibilities that they should feel for giving a political structure to the Revolution and by his appeal for help in the formation of the national ARENA.[16]

[11] Vitorino Freire, letter to HACB, Brasília, December 8, 1965, File N1, Part 2, CPDOC, and attached clippings from *Correio Braziliense*, December 8, 1965, *Correio da Manhã*, December 8, 1965, and *O Globo* of the same, or approximately the same, date; idem, interview, December 10, 1975.

[12] *Jornal do Brasil*, December 8, 1965.

[13] Roberto de Abreu Sodré, memorandum to JWFD, August 1977, p. 1, and letter to Luís Viana Filho, São Paulo, September 28, 1971, p. 16.

[14] *Jornal do Brasil*, February 11, 1966; Abreu Sodré, memorandum to JWFD, p. 2.

[15] *Jornal do Brasil*, January 29, February 1, 1966.

[16] Abreu Sodré, letter to Luís Viana Filho, September 28, 1971, p. 17.

Abreu Sodré and the former head of the São Paulo city UDN were delegated to advise Lacerda of the decision. During their somewhat stormy eight-hour talk in Rio, Lacerda asked them to join a third political party, the Partido Renovador Democrático (PAREDE), that was being organized by Rafael de Almeida Magalhães to advance Lacerda's presidential candidacy.[17] The UDN representatives from São Paulo, not wishing to be associated with a party led by Rafael de Almeida Magalhães, told Lacerda that he would be rendering a disservice to the Revolution by trying to form a third party and that it would certainly be unsuccessful. They argued that Lacerda should join the ARENA to strengthen the position of Castello, who had always shown himself willing to help them "get rid of corrupt people." Although Abreu Sodré suggested that Lacerda's chances of being a presidential candidate might revive if he joined the ARENA, the Paulista failed in his mission to Rio. It was followed by an angry exchange of letters.[18]

Flexa Ribeiro, the UDN's unsuccessful gubernatorial candidate in Guanabara, was quick to join the ARENA, which was being organized locally by Adauto Cardoso. Other Lacerdistas in Guanabara, including Assemblymen Mauro Magalhães and Célio Borja, issued a manifesto on behalf of the PAREDE. But the proposed third party floundered, so Rafael de Almeida Magalhães and others who had been connected with the Lacerda administration followed Flexa Ribeiro into the ARENA. Lacerdista state assemblymen and politicians in Guanabara generally turned to the MDB, which Lacerda preferred (at least for a while).[19]

When Minas Governor Magalhães Pinto complained to Bilac Pinto that he had not been invited to join the "government party," Bilac told him that invitations had not been issued and that Bilac himself had received none. Despite this explanation, Magalhães Pinto was reported to be considering invitations of opposition congressmen that he join the MDB.[20]

Castello was inclined to agree in part with a thought sent to him in November by Andrada Serpa, military attaché in Paris: "Re-

[17] Ibid., pp. 17–18, and memorandum to JWFD, pp. 1–2.

[18] Ibid.; Lacerda has recalled (*Depoimento*, p. 362) that Abreu Sodré came to Rio to appeal that he continue in public life, prompting Lacerda to reply, "No, I consider this an error, for I was beaten in Guanabara."

[19] *Jornal do Brasil*, December 22, 25, 26, 1965; January 27, 1966; Almeida Magalhães, interview, August 8, 1977.

[20] *Jornal do Brasil*, December 7, 1965 (Coluna do Castello).

gardless of all the resentment you might have for the governors of Minas and Guanabara as a result of their disastrous conduct during these nineteen months, it is necessary to preserve for the Revolution the part of the electorate that voted for their candidacies."[21] The president, in Minas on December 16 to speak at the inauguration of the Argentina Vianna Castello Branco School, had a good talk with Magalhães Pinto. But the outgoing governor, although announcing that he would remain in public life "to struggle for the people," continued to postpone deciding about his new party affiliation.

Magalhães Pinto and other former UDN leaders in Minas vetoed having the state ARENA presidency go to Israel Pinheiro, who had joined the ARENA and was to become governor on January 31. Castello discussed the problem with Magalhães Pinto and Israel Pinheiro in Três Marias on January 15. But it remained unresolved until late in February, when Israel Pinheiro and the UDN leaders in Minas agreed to place the selection of the state party presidency in the hands of Castello.[22] Castello decided that although a majority of the directors of the state ARENA were to be from the PSD, its president was to be the strongly pro-UDN Guilherme Machado, former state finance secretary to Magalhães Pinto.[23]

Late in February, Magalhães Pinto said that he would probably join the ARENA but would defend direct elections and keep on attacking the government's economic-financial policies. When he made his adherence official early in March he declared that he was accepting "a personal invitation of President Castello Branco" to enter the ARENA in order to become a member of the new party's National Directorship. *Correio da Manhã* observed that Magalhães Pinto was supported by forty of the eighty-four state assemblymen but that if he did not join the ARENA, his leadership would crumble, with Israel Pinheiro gaining complete control of the politics of the state.[24]

In the meantime, the MDB elected Senator Oscar Passos, a former PTB leader from Acre, to be its national president. It issued a mani-

[21] Gonzaga Andrada Serpa, letter to HACB, November 24, 1965, File N1, Part 1, CPDOC.

[22] *Jornal do Brasil*, December 17, 23, 1965, January 8, 12, 16, February 19, 1966.

[23] Viana Filho, *O Governo Castelo Branco*, p. 374.

[24] *Jornal do Brasil*, February 25, March 8, 1966; *Correio da Manhã*, March 8, 1966.

festo that condemned the government's economic-financial policies and deplored the "attitude of those who, supported only by force, merely seek to perpetuate themselves in power by processes that are ethically and juridically untenable."[25]

Adherence to the MDB and the ARENA by federal legislators belonging to the five most important political parties (of which there had been thirteen) is given in the table below.[26]

MDB	*Senators*	*Congressmen*
From the PTB	13	73
From the PSD	5	40
From the UDN	1	6
From the PDC	0	6
ARENA	*Senators*	*Congressmen*
From the UDN	16	83
From the PSD	15	67
From the PTB	4	38
From the PSP	0	22
From the PDC	0	12

2. Costa e Silva Throws His Cap in the Ring (December, 1965–January, 1966)

Castello Branco released a brief year-end message in Fortaleza, Ceará, that stressed how much determination was needed to fight the inflation and called attention to the international current account, favorable "for the first time in many years." As a result of the accumulation of foreign reserves of about five hundred million dollars, the president said, "we do not need to beg for loans and can instead negotiate for credits under normal conditions."[1]

Ademar de Barros, in a pessimistic mood, told a television audience

[25] Manifesto approved unanimously at the first plenary meeting of the national executive group and directive commission of the Movimento Democrático Brasileiro, Chamber of Deputies, Brasília, February 10, 1966, File P2 (p. 9), CPDOC.

[26] Hernani D'Aguiar, *A Revolução por Dentro*, p. 319.

[1] HACB, *Discursos, 1965*, pp. 125–127.

that the cost of living would "increase horrendously" in 1966. But Costa e Silva was full of hope for 1966 and full of praise for the accomplishments of 1965. Never before, he said, had so much been done "for the progress and well-being of the nation."[2]

Of greater interest were Costa e Silva's statements revealing his reaction to the pressure, exerted by hard-liners and others in the army, that he become a presidential candidate. After former War Minister Odílio Denys, resentful of the little attention he was receiving from Castello, conducted a survey that showed the army officers very favorable to the Costa e Silva candidacy, a group of officers in Rio decided that the time had come for Costa e Silva to speak out. They argued that while the war minister was abroad for thirty-five days, on a trip scheduled to begin on January 6, Generals Golberi and Geisel "and their clique" might precipitate some event to eliminate his candidacy, but that this would be more difficult if the candidacy, with its strong military backing, were to become definite before he left Brazil.[3]

Costa e Silva agreed. In his office on December 30 he told Costa Cavalcanti that he had decided to be a candidate to succeed Castello. When the congressman-colonel started to ask, "Are you saying this for me or . . . ," Costa e Silva said: "You can handle my statement in any way you choose." Indicating the door he wanted Costa Cavalcanti to use when he left, the war minister explained that Congressman Anísio Rocha, from Goiás, was coming in by another door.[4]

Anísio Rocha, who had belonged to the PSD and was now a member of the oppositionist MDB, told the war minister that former President Dutra was worried about reports that the war minister would refuse to be a presidential candidate. As the war minister wanted it known that the reports were untrue, the press on December 31 advised that Anísio Rocha had been authorized by Costa e Silva to say that he was willing to run for president, "like any citizen," and would do so "with humility, but also with the tenacity of one who has that right."[5]

[2] *Jornal do Brasil*, December 31, 1965, January 1, 1966.

[3] Vereker, report, January 19, 1966.

[4] Viana Filho, *O Governo Castelo Branco*, p. 380.

[5] Costa e Silva quoted in *Jornal do Brasil*, January 5, 1966; *Jornal do Brasil*, December 31, 1965.

Oath-of-office ceremony of President Humberto Castello Branco (left) and Vice-president José Maria Alkmin (right), Chamber of Deputies, Brasília, April 15, 1964. Senator Auro de Moura Andrade, president of the Congress, is between them. (Courtesy, *Manchete*)

Castello Branco speaks at Planalto Palace, Brasília, April 15, 1964, after receiving the presidential sash from Interim President Paschoal Ranieri Mazzilli. Mazzilli appears under the flag, with Luís Viana Filho beside him (arms folded on the chest) and Ernesto Geisel (in uniform, with glasses) just behind him. (Courtesy, *Manchete*)

In Belo Horizonte, Minas Gerais, the president visits the 12th Infantry Regiment, where he began his army career as a second lieutenant in 1921.

A cabinet meeting at Planalto Palace, Brasília. (Courtesy *O Globo*)

Left: Castello Branco with Roberto de Oliveira Campos. (Courtesy, *O Globo*)
Right: *O Globo* publisher Roberto Marinho (left) with Finance Minister Otávio Gouveia de Bulhões. (Courtesy *O Globo*)

Signing the strike law of May, 1964, at Laranjeiras Palace. Labor Minister Arnaldo Sussekind appears behind the microphones; the president of the Superior Labor Tribunal is on the other side of Castello Branco. (Courtesy, *O Globo*)

Conde de Boa Vista Avenue, Recife, early in June, 1964, during Castello Branco's first visit as president to the northeast. (Courtesy, *O Globo*)

Realengo Military Academy classmates (who graduated in January, 1921). *Left to right*: João de Almeida Freitas, Olímpio Mourão Filho, Humberto Castello Branco, Ademar de Queiroz, and José de Figueiredo Lôbo. Salvador, Bahia, August 7, 1964.

Left: UDN political party leaders Adauto Lúcio Cardoso and Carlos Lacerda. (Courtesy, *O Globo*) *Right*: Castello Branco with José de Magalhães Pinto, governor of Minas Gerais. (Courtesy, *O Cruzeiro*)

Left to right: Guanabara Governor Carlos Lacerda, President Castello Branco, Presidential Press Secretary José Wamberto, and Presidential Gabinete Militar Chief Ernesto Geisel. (Courtesy, *O Globo*)

Castello Branco with Guanabara Vice-governor Rafael de Almeida Magalhães (left) and Guanabara Education Secretary Carlos Flexa Ribeiro. Flexa Ribeiro became the unsuccessful UDN candidate for governor of Guanabara in the election of October 3, 1965. (Courtesy, *O Globo*)

Castello Branco with Charles de Gaulle during the French president's visit to Brazil in October, 1964. (Courtesy, *Jornal do Brasil*)

First Army Commander Otacílio Terra Ururaí, Federal Police Chief Riograndino Kruel (center), and Castello Branco, November, 1964. (Courtesy *O Globo*)

At Campos Elísios Palace on November 1, 1964, Castello Branco listens to São Paulo Governor Ademar de Barros (who is using his hands) while Second Army Commander Amauri Kruel (in uniform) lowers his head. (Courtesy, *O Globo*)

The president poses in Brasília on Christmas Day, 1964, with his daughter, Antonietta Diniz, and four of his grandchildren. (Courtesy, *O Globo*)

Admiral Paulo Bosísio (far left) takes over the Navy Ministry from outgoing Minister Ernesto Melo Batista (reading speech), January 18, 1965. Between them are War Minister Costa e Silva (wearing dark glasses) and Aviation Minister Eduardo Gomes (in dark suit and in full view). (Courtesy, *O Globo*)

General Carlos de Meira Mattos about to leave Brazil for the Dominican Republic in May, 1965. Among those bidding him farewell is Marshal João Batista Mascarenhas de Morais (wearing glasses), who commanded the Brazilian troops in Italy during World War II. (Courtesy, *O Globo*)

Left: Chamber of Deputies President Olavo Bilac Pinto, on the left, with Academy of Letters President Austregésilo de Ataíde. (Courtesy, *O Globo*) *Right*: Francisco Negrão de Lima, elected governor of Guanabara on October 3, 1965. (Courtesy, *Jornal do Brasil*)

Left to right (foreground): Senator Mem de Sá of Rio Grande do Sul (holding drink), Senator Milton Campos of Minas Gerais, and Congressman Raul Pila of Rio Grande do Sul. (Courtesy, *O Globo*)

Former President Juscelino Kubitschek at Galeão Airport, Rio de Janeiro, upon his return to Brazil, October 4, 1965. (Courtesy, *O Globo*)

At the maneuvers of the Second Army in Itapeva, São Paulo, on October 22, 1965, when War Minister Artur da Costa e Silva criticized the chief justice of the Supreme Court. *Left to right (foreground)*: Governor Ademar de Barros (with dark glasses), Castello Branco, Costa e Silva (with arm raised), First Army Commander Otacílio Terra Ururaí, and Gabinete Civil Chief Ernesto Geisel. Second Army Commander Amauri Kruel (looking upward) and General Mário Poppe de Figueiredo, both partly hidden, are between Castello Branco and Costa e Silva. (Courtesy, *O Globo*)

Luís Viana Filho reads Institutional Act Number Two in Planalto Palace on October 27, 1965. *Seated, left to right*: Aviation Minister Eduardo Gomes, War Minister Costa e Silva, and Justice Minister Juraci Magalhães. Standing between Viana Filho and Castello Branco are Minister for Coordination of Regional Agencies Osvaldo Cordeiro de Farias (with glasses) and Presidential Press Secretary José Wamberto. Education Minister Flávio Suplici de Lacerda is standing directly behind Castello Branco. (Courtesy, *O Globo*)

The five new justices of the Supreme Court pose in November, 1965. *Left to right*: Aliomar Baleeiro, José Eduardo do Prado Kelly, Adalício Nogueira, Osvaldo Trigueiro, and Carlos Medeiros Silva. (Courtesy, *O Globo*)

At the home of Roberto Campos, Castello Branco chats with Ambassador Lincoln Gordon (with pipe), Walt W. Rostow (adviser to President Johnson), and Roberto Campos (right). (Courtesy, *O Globo*)

Castello Branco with Senator Robert Kennedy and Ambassador Lincoln Gordon at Laranjeiras Palace, November 24, 1965. (Courtesy, *O Globo*)

Housing Bank President Luís Gonzaga do Nascimento Silva, who became labor minister, with Senator Mem de Sá (right), who became justice minister. Between them, in the background, is Foreign Minister Vasco Leitão da Cunha. (Courtesy, *O Globo*)

Left: Nilo Coelho, first secretary of the Chamber of Deputies, who was elected governor of Pernambuco in 1966. (Courtesy, *O Globo*) *Right*: General Golberi do Couto e Silva, who headed the National Information Service (SNI) during the presidency of Castello Branco. (Courtesy, *O Globo*)

Castello Branco trying to control his emotions during the ceremony at which Osvaldo Cordeiro de Farias left the Ministry for Coordination of Regional Agencies, June 16, 1966. (Courtesy, *O Globo*)

Left: Pedro Aleixo, Chamber of Deputies leader and education minister, who was elected vice-president of Brazil in 1966 as runningmate of Artur da Costa e Silva. (Courtesy, *O Globo*) *Right*: The president in Brasília in 1966. His son, Paulo V. Castello Branco, is at his side.

Castello Branco and Justice Minister Carlos Medeiros Silva (center) receive the draft of a new constitution from Levi Carneiro (far left), Temistocles Cavalcanti, and Orozimbo Nonato (far right) at Laranjeiras Palace on August 19, 1966. (Courtesy, *O Globo*)

Left to right: Dom Fernando Gomes (archbishop of Goiânia), Dom Hélder Câmara (archbishop of Olinda and Recife), Castello Branco, and Dom Eugênio Sales (archbishop of Bahia). (Courtesy, *O Globo*)

Raimundo Augusto de Castro Moniz de Aragão becomes education minister at the end of June, 1966. (Courtesy, *O Globo*)

Left: Raimundo Padilha, government leader in the Chamber of Deputies during the last year of Castello Branco's administration. (Courtesy, *O Globo*)
Right: Carlos Lacerda with former President Juscelino Kubitschek in Lisbon, Portugal, November 19, 1966. (Courtesy *O Globo*)

Senator Daniel Krieger of Rio Grande do Sul (left). His companions include Sérgio Correia da Costa, a member of the Brazilian diplomatic corps. (Courtesy, *O Globo*)

President-elect Costa e Silva and President Castello Branco receive a visit from Argentine President Juan Carlos Onganía in 1967.

Afonso Arinos de Melo Franco, speaking at the Law College of the Federal University of Rio de Janeiro. Pedro Calmon, former head of the university, is at the right. (Courtesy, *O Globo*)

Left: Former Finance Minister Eugênio Gudin (right) with Antônio Delfim Neto, who became secretary of finance of São Paulo State in June, 1966, and was named finance minister by President-elect Costa e Silva. (Courtesy, *O Globo*) *Right*: Senator Paulo Sarasate inscribes a copy of his book about the 1967 Constitution for Antonietta Diniz. (Courtesy, *O Globo*)

President Castello Branco with War Minister Ademar de Queiroz. (Courtesy, *Agência Nacional*)

Castello Branco about to depart from Alvorada Palace, Brasília, on March 11, 1967.

Castello Branco with his last cabinet. *First row, left to right*: Ademar de Queiroz (War), Carlos Medeiros Silva (Justice), President Castello Branco, Zilmar Campos de Araripe Macedo (Navy), and Juraci Montenegro Magalhães (Foreign Relations). *Second row*: Raimundo Moniz de Aragão (Education and Culture), Juarez do Nascimento Távora (Transport and Public Works), Otávio Gouveia de Bulhões (Finance), Severo Fagundes Gomes (Agriculture), Luís Gonzaga do Nascimento Silva (Labor), and Eduardo Gomes (Air). *Top row*: Ernesto Geisel (Gabinete Militar), Roberto de Oliveira Campos (Planning and Economic Coordination), Mauro Thibau (Mines and Energy), Raimundo de Moura Brito (Health), Paulo Egídio Martins (Industry and Commerce), João Gonçalves de Sousa (Coordination of Regional Agencies), and Luís Fraga Navarro de Brito (Gabinete Civil).

Head table at the farewell dinner given for Castello Branco by the foreign diplomats on March 12, 1967, at the Copacabana Palace Hotel in Rio de Janeiro. Apostolic Nuncio Dom Sebastião Baggio speaks. Among the listeners are Foreign Minister Juraci Magalhães (at the left of the picture) and Governor Negrão de Lima (at the right). (Courtesy, *O Globo*)

In making his farewells at the palace, the president speaks to Romana, former maid of Humberto and Argentina Castello Branco.

At Galeão Airport, July 13, 1967, awaiting the plane for the trip to Ceará. Former Health Minister Raimundo de Brito (far right) has come to bid farewell to the former president and his brother, Cândido Castello Branco (far left), and their sisters, Nina Castello Branco Santos Dias and Beatriz Castello Branco Gonçalves. (Courtesy, *Jornal do Brasil*)

The last photograph of the former president, taken at the Casa de Repouso São José in the Serra do Estêvão, Ceará, on the morning of July 18, 1967. Cândido Castello Branco is at the far right. (Courtesy, *Manchete*)

The crashed Piper Aztec outside Fortaleza, Ceará, July 18, 1967. (Courtesy, *O Globo*)

Juarez Távora and his wife at Castello Branco's coffin at the Military Club, Rio de Janeiro, July 19, 1967. (Courtesy, *O Globo*)

Jornal do Brasil explained that the war minister had decided to announce his willingness after being informed that General Cordeiro de Farias, a rival for the presidency, had told military leaders that the war minister would not be a candidate.

On January 3, Anísio Rocha had a second visit with Costa e Silva, after which he confirmed the war minister's candidacy—although he added that he was not doing this at the request of the minister, "a man too frank to use spokesmen." Major Alacid Nunes, governor-elect of Pará, praised the Costa e Silva candidacy, and Senator Benedito Valadares, launcher of Dutra's candidacy in 1945, was described as starting to work for Costa e Silva in Minas. Columnist Carlos Castello Branco noted the strength that the general's position had attained during his term as war minister but added that the president "would feel better if he could transfer the power . . . to someone of his own intellectual temperament."[6]

On January 3 and 4, Costa e Silva called on Castello and Justice Minister Juraci Magalhães, both of whom felt that Costa e Silva had been precipitous. Costa e Silva's purpose, to contradict reports that he would refuse to run, may have surprised the president, who said: "In Ceará they asked me if you would agree to participate in the contest for the presidency and I replied that 'whoever knows Costa e Silva knows that he is not going to refuse.' "[7]

After the call on Juraci, whose irritation at the "early" opening of the contest had been revealed in a public statement, Costa e Silva answered reporters' questions by saying: "I smashed the gossip that they were stirring up about me, and I declared that I would agree to contend." Together with this remark, *Jornal do Brasil* published a report that the war minister's name was backed by 85 percent of the army. Governors Paulo Guerra (Pernambuco), Virgílio Távora (Ceará), and Petrônio Portela (Piauí) praised the candidacy but added that they would back it only if this were indicated by Castello.[8]

Castello left Costa e Silva's backers uneasy and observers perplexed

[6] *Jornal do Brasil*, January 4, 1966.

[7] Krieger, interviews, October 21, 22, 1975; Costa e Silva, quoting HACB, in *Jornal do Brasil*, January 5, 1966.

[8] D'Aguiar, *A Revolução por Dentro*, p. 268; *Jornal do Brasil*, January 5, 6, 1966.

when he spoke at the ceremonies at which Costa e Silva, about to leave Brazil, transferred the War Ministry provisionally to Chief of Staff Décio Palmeiro de Escobar. In the past, the president said, the replacement of a military minister constituted a grave problem, whereas under the system implanted by the new administration, the president "can make this change peacefully, without bringing on a crisis."[9]

Costa e Silva, scheduled to depart on the evening of January 6, had a well-publicized lunch that day at the Museum of Modern Art with Marshals Dutra, Odílio Denys, and Mascarenhas de Morais. The press reported that Costa e Silva told the distinguished marshals that his candidacy had been launched in order to "establish a position" and "leave to others the responsibility of breaking military unity."[10]

When Costa e Silva, his wife, and the members of his traveling party reached Galeão Airport, all the generals of the Rio area were on hand, together with an estimated three thousand officers and many legislators. Costa e Silva, surrounded by reporters, was asked whether he was making his trip as a presidential candidate. He replied that he was leaving as minister and would return as minister.[11] The remark, interpreted by some as a denial of the suggestion given in the question, was interpreted by others as prompted by Castello's recent declaration about the ease with which military ministers could now be changed. Many felt that Costa e Silva was defying the president by implying that the president lacked the power to dismiss him.[12]

Immediately Justice Minister Juraci Magalhães went to Laranjeiras Palace to discuss the incident with Castello. "If you don't dismiss Costa e Silva at once," Juraci said, "you won't be able to do it later," and he added that he had in mind a good general to take over the War Ministry. Castello replied that Costa e Silva's words had not been a happy choice; he would reprimand Costa e Silva on his return, the president said.[13]

[9] *Jornal do Brasil*, January 5, 1966; D'Aguiar, *A Revolução por Dentro*, p. 268.

[10] *Jornal do Brasil*, January 7, 1966.

[11] Ibid.; D'Aguiar, *A Revolução por Dentro*, p. 268.

[12] D'Aguiar, *A Revolução por Dentro*, p. 268; Juraci Magalhães, interview, December 3, 1974; Eugênio Gudin described Costa e Silva's remark as "indisciplinary" (see Coluna do Castello in *Jornal do Brasil*, July 13, 1976).

[13] Magalhães, interview, December 3, 1974.

3. Castello's Memorandum about the Succession (January 27, 1966)

Following Costa e Silva's departure, Juraci Magalhães declared that there was no truth to the remark of Congressman Nelson Carneiro (MDB, Guanabara) that the war minister's candidacy had "bewildered" the government. But João Agripino, governor-elect of Paraíba, said that the candidacy, being of a military nature, had created problems for the government. Army officers, asked by Castello to learn the sentiment of officers in the barracks, reported enthusiasm for the candidacy. An EMFA officer, after sounding out opinion in the northeast, told Castello of a particularly strong Costa e Silva boom in the Fourth Army.[1]

Castello believed that the pro–Costa e Silva activities of some members of the War Ministry indicated they felt that an open presidential campaign was already under way. Therefore, on January 10, he called in Acting War Minister Décio Escobar, First Army Commander Adalberto Pereira dos Santos, and General Clóvis Bandeira Brasil, of the war minister's office, to warn that he would not permit a repetition of the situation of 1958–1959 when, according to Castello, War Minister Lott, a presidential candidate, had turned the War Ministry into a campaign center.[2]

General Jaime Portela, working on behalf of Costa e Silva, brought Daniel Krieger the war minister's request that the senator, chosen to head the ARENA, become the coordinator of the war minister's candidacy. Krieger, who knew that Castello felt the candidacy had been launched unsuitably and prematurely, told Portela: "If the minister wants to use force, he can become dictator, but he'll be president only with the backing of Marshal Castello Branco, who has absolute control of the ARENA. In case of divergency I'll stick with the president, notwithstanding my friendship for General Costa e Silva."[3] Portela replied that the war minister had no intention of becoming dictator but wanted to reach the presidency by means of the electoral college. Because of this, and because Krieger felt that no other candidate had the full backing of the armed forces, Krieger accepted the mission. But he laid

[1] *Jornal do Brasil*, January 9, 12, 18, 1966.

[2] Viana Filho, *O Governo Castelo Branco*, p. 380.

[3] Krieger, *Desde as Missões*, pp. 226–227.

down a condition that he felt was essential for securing Castello's official blessing: Costa e Silva, Krieger said, should make no political declarations abroad or upon his return to Brazil.

Costa e Silva was in Lisbon, where he conferred with Salazar on January 12, when an emissary of Portela gave him Krieger's message. Replying to reporters' questions in London on January 16 and in Paris on January 18, he said that he was not a candidate but would become one if nominated.[4] If there was any trouble, it was provoked in Lebanon by Jorge Curi, Lacerda's recent spokesman in Congress. Curi, one of the many Lacerdistas who hoped to see the war minister elected, told the Lebanese press that he had come to Beirut, as a member of the organizing commission of the ARENA, to persuade Costa e Silva to be the ARENA's standard-bearer and that the war minister appeared to react favorably. In Brazil, Mem de Sá, the new justice minister, asserted that Curi was not on the ARENA organizing commission and had no credentials for speaking in the name of the ARENA.[5]

On January 27, when Curi made his call on Costa e Silva in Beirut, Castello completed a memorandum, for presentation to the military ministers and others, to eliminate what *O Estado de S. Paulo* called intrigues and misunderstandings.[6] The president opened by writing that his views had already been made known verbally to Generals Décio Escobar, Adalberto Pereira dos Santos, and Clóvis Brasil, but not to Jaime Portela because of his absence from Rio. Castello said that he had also discussed his views with politicians supporting Costa e Silva's candidacy but had not done so with Costa Cavalcanti, who was in Recife, or with Filinto Müller, who felt the discussion should await the organization of the ARENA. Nor had Castello spoken with Anísio Rocha, "because he is a counterrevolutionary who has even insulted me."[7]

Castello defended his interest in the subject by writing that the government should provide guidance. And he explained that he, a declared noncandidate, had no wish to dominate the selection of his suc-

[4] *Jornal do Brasil*, January 14, 16, 25, 1966.

[5] Ibid., January 28, 29, 1966.

[6] *O Estado de S. Paulo*, February 3, 1966.

[7] HACB, "Aspectos da Sucessão Presidencial" (January 27, 1966), File P2 (pp. 2–4), CPDOC.

cessor. The president said that he would hinder no candidacy, "much less" that of the war minister, whose name he himself would present, "in the fulfillment of a political and military duty, if no one should remember it at the time of the selection."

Castello noted that dissensions within the Revolutionary ranks had developed because his government had resolved (1) to follow legal framework, (2) not to adopt the Lacerda candidacy two years ahead of time, and (3) not to relinquish political coordination, as desired by Magalhães Pinto. The first of these dissensions, "and perhaps one of the two others, or even both," Castello said, had been used, together with the opposition of the MDB and the counter-Revolutionaries, to combat and try to overthrow the government. "Therefore," he concluded, "no candidacy can come from these groups or be developed with their participation."

After stressing that the succession should not disturb governmental action in 1966, because the purpose of that action was to create the best conditions for 1967–1971, Castello attacked radical elements in the army. Explaining that some "call themselves hard-liners, others favor dictatorship, while still others are connected with dissident political sectors," he accused them of seeking to precipitate the work of the succession and even divide the armed forces. He wrote:

> With this spirit, enthusiasts of the Costa e Silva candidacy push for its untimely adoption. Thus we see it launched prior to the formation of, and outside, the ARENA. These enthusiasts ignore the existence of those who are responsible for national policy, including the president of the Republic. They turn to the opposition in search of supporters, agitate in military circles, and try to develop the incredible possibility of the war minister remaining at his post while assuming activities, a position, and a purpose in opposition to the president.

Castello said that it was deplorable that officers connected with the precipitous Costa e Silva propaganda had spread lies about the president being placed in a humiliating position by a strong and dominating attitude of the war minister and had "disfigured" Costa e Silva's loyalty to make it appear as a favor to the president. They had, he maintained, disparaged the courageous and loyal acts of Juraci Magalhães, building up enmity against him in the army, had reduced army confidence in

Cordeiro de Farais, had attributed malicious intrigues "to the correct and irreproachable work of the SNI," and had "spread untrue stories" about the presidential Gabinete Militar. "It is reprehensible," Castello wrote, "that dissidents in the military seek to tie the precipitous candidacy to the promise of revoking the decree about aircraft carrier aviation and to the prevention of the formation of a Ministry of the Armed Forces."

Castello recalled "the sad and childish scene" in the war minister's office when Lott, a presidential candidate, had made it a campaign headquarters, issuing propaganda and threatening recalcitrants. Stating that Lott's attitude had even brought about "military corruption," Castello wrote that "this greatly contributed to creating the spirit of the Revolution of March 31."

Having listed these considerations, Castello concluded that (1) precipitation in launching any candidacy was a disturbance to government work and a disservice to the candidate himself; (2) candidacies should be launched only in the ARENA; (3) military pressure, besides being highly disturbing, was harmful to the candidate it sought to favor; (4) the president would not submit to the impositions of any minister; and (5) the chosen candidate should continue with the Revolution and not invalidate the governmental activities of 1966.

Acting War Minister Décio Escobar, following Castello's instructions, distributed copies of the memorandum to army leaders, and so it was only a matter of days before it found its way to the press. It was not warmly received by Costa e Silva's supporters, but, one of them writes, it prevented some gross errors. For example, when an MDB congressman spoke of seeking Kubitschek's support for Costa e Silva, he was promptly persuaded to forget the idea.[8]

On February 1, Décio Escobar gave Castello a written reply that said the armed forces, being responsible for the regime, would not agree "to be left out in this emergency, even though under normal circumstances this attitude would be absolutely reprehensible." Because times were not normal, Escobar wrote, many Revolutionaries wished no hasty return to a normal, legal regime, under which it would be difficult to reformulate obsolete laws and exterminate vices. While he expressed the belief that these Revolutionaries preferred "an authoritarian

[8] D'Aguiar, *A Revolução por Dentro*, p. 271.

democracy, or disguised dictatorship, over a pure declared dictatorship," he himself had become convinced that "a frank dictatorship would have been better than the regime that was adopted." Without the legislatures and gubernatorial elections, he wrote, the regime could have carried out more rapidly the reforms and the "necessary cleansing in the political, administrative, economic, social, and educational areas." "I know," he admitted, "that it would have been necessary to handle repercussions abroad . . . , but I think we could have run that risk."

Escobar did not feel that oppositionists could provoke an armed movement, and he pointed out that the threat by antilegalist Revolutionaries was reduced because they included supporters of Costa e Silva, who was loyal to the president. He wrote that "overexcited, uncontrolled elements have always existed. Thoughtless acts and manifestations of indiscipline might very well occur. But neither Costa e Silva nor any leader will stimulate them. . . . Does the fact that overexcited people back Costa e Silva's candidacy invalidate it? An affirmative reply would be unjust." Escobar also suggested that the military who wanted to precipitate the presidential campaign lacked the importance attributed to them and that the large pro–Costa e Silva current in the army was simply hoping that the ARENA would nominate the war minister.

Escobar denied having any knowledge about lies humiliating to the president that were said by Castello to have been spread by officers supporting Costa e Silva. He admitted to having "heard it said" that officers did not want Juraci Magalhães to push aside Costa e Silva's candidacy but wrote that he had "never heard any reservations against Cordeiro de Farias." "Really," he said, "some do feel that General Golberi, the SNI, and the personnel of the office of the presidency that opposes the war minister are poisoning, voluntarily or not, the mind of the president against his helper. My purpose is to struggle against that climate of suspicions." While Escobar reported knowing nothing about promises made to revoke the aircraft carrier ruling or block the creation of a Ministry of the Armed Forces, he admitted that "some leaders, men of good faith," opposed the proposed new ministry. In conclusion Escobar wrote: "There is no way to prevent the supporters of a candidate from expressing their preference. . . . I feel that one should not confuse a demonstration of support, affection, appreciation, and admiration with electoral promotion. . . . I believe, sincerely, that exaggerations reach you about the activities of the supporters of the candidacy of Minister Costa e Silva, and that false intentions are attributed to these activities. I believe that you receive erroneous interpretations about attitudes, and that they are judged, perhaps involuntarily, as being against Your Excellency."[9]

Castello Branco did not reply to Escobar's memorandum, but in one of his conversations with the acting war minister about the Costa e Silva candidacy he said that Escobar's memorandum was not altogether coherent. Castello often told Escobar that it was too soon to take up the matter of the succession, and sometimes the president was not flattering about the family of the war minister. But the point that the president emphasized with the greatest regularity in these conversations was that the war minister was "an impulsive person."[10]

Escobar wrote a second, and shorter, paper for the president in which he argued that Costa e Silva had the best credentials for continuing to achieve the aims of the Revolution and that it was largely due to the war minister's frank and forceful activity as head of the army, and his loyalty to the president, that the country remained in peace, "resigned to the sufferings imposed by the regime of austerity."[11]

4. Institutional Act Number Three (February 5, 1966)

When legislators met in Brasília early in February for a special session to choose the officers of the two chambers, some of them felt that they might be called on to consider a constitutional amendment to make the 1966 gubernatorial elections indirect, a change recommended by many military leaders. But, although Senator Afonso Arinos de Melo Franco argued that such a change required a constitutional amendment, Justice Minister Mem de Sá announced that the government would promulgate "an instrument" that had been made necessary by the "omissions" of Ato 2. The executive branch was reported to feel that a long parliamentary debate about gubernatorial elections, ineligi-

[9] Décio Escobar, memorandum to HACB, Rio de Janeiro, February 1, 1966, File P2 (p. 5), CPDOC.

[10] Décio Escobar, interview, Rio de Janeiro, July 25, 1977.

[11] Décio Escobar, paper for HACB, "Meu Pensamento a Respeito do Quadro Sucessório," n.d.

bilities, electoral domicile, and election dates might take a toll among the forces that backed the government.[1]

Questions about eligibilities interested presidential and gubernatorial candidates. Costa e Silva's supporters maintained that the requirement that he leave his War Ministry post six months before the presidential election was a requirement applicable only to direct elections and that he could continue in the ministry throughout the period of his candidacy.[2] As for the gubernatorial races, Second and Third Army Commanders Amauri Kruel and Joaquim Justino Alves Bastos saw possibilities of being elected in São Paulo and Rio Grande do Sul, where they exercised their commands, provided a change were made in the article of Constitutional Amendment 14 (of June, 1965) that required a candidate for governorship of a state to have at least four years of voting residence in that state. But Military Club President Augusto César Moniz de Aragão, who was in Rio Grande do Sul keeping an eye on Alves Bastos, wrote to Castello to suggest that retention of the four-year requirement would be "beneficial to Rio Grande and to all of us military men who serve in this state."[3]

To settle these delicate electoral questions, Castello in Rio conferred with the military ministers and Mem de Sá about a new institutional act. Obviously it was possible for a new act to establish the presidential election date and the period of *desincompatibilização* (when candidates for elective office were not to hold government positions) in a way to bar the candidacy of the absent Costa e Silva.[4] But this was not the intent revealed in the draft of the new act which the National Security Council considered at Laranjeiras Palace on February 4. Following the council's discussion, which lasted for two and one-half hours, the act was signed by Castello, Mem de Sá, Juraci Magalhães, and the military ministers: Décio Escobar, Eduardo Gomes, and Araripe Macedo. Issued on February 5, it opened by stating that the constitutionalizing power of the Revolution was inherent in the Revolution itself and was to be used to institutionalize the Revolution and assure the continuation of

[1] *Jornal do Brasil*, February 1, 13, 1966.

[2] Ibid., January 6, 1966.

[3] Augusto César Moniz de Aragão, letter to HACB, Porto Alegre, February 4, 1966, File N1, Part 1 (p. 15), CPDOC.

[4] Viana Filho, *O Governo Castelo Branco*, p. 384.

the work mentioned in Ato 2. It also spoke of need to preserve political and social harmony.[5]

Besides providing for the indirect elections of governors (by absolute majorities of the state assemblies), the new Ato eliminated the gubernatorial candidacies of Generals Kruel and Alves Bastos, for it required two years of *domicílio eleitoral.* Mayors of the state capitals were to be named by the governors and confirmed by the state assemblies. The electoral calendar for 1966 was set up: gubernatorial elections on September 3, presidential election on October 3, and state and federal legislative elections on November 15. And, as the supporters of Costa e Silva's presidential ambitions noted, the new Ato stipulated a three-month period of *desincompatibilização.* Thus, the war minister could remain in his powerful post during most, or all, of the contest for the nomination by the ARENA and still be eligible for election.

O Estado de S. Paulo described the new institutional act as "nothing more than a complete farce." It did admit one positive aspect, the naming of the mayors of the state capitals by the governors, but it regretted the lack of retroactivity of that arrangement. "Marshal Castello Branco," it wrote, "cannot free himself from once again revealing the little liking he has for the Paulistas." It could find no other explanation for the proviso that would allow Mayor Faria Lima to continue in office.[6]

In Porto Alegre, General Alves Bastos raised his voice to complain that he was left "without any recognized domicile and almost without any home. The Revolution, which I helped to bring about, recently issued an impulsive act that has denied me my fundamental rights and seeks to transform me into an alien within the nation that I have always defended."[7]

Amauri Kruel hoped that the *domicílio eleitoral* requirement might yet be modified by a new constitutional amendment. But Castello Branco, answering a question about the requirement at a press conference at Laranjeiras Palace on March 22, was not encouraging. "I have," the president said, "obtained the opinions of various sectors of the ARENA and the government, and I have given much thought to the

[5] *O Estado de S. Paulo*, February 6, 1966.

[6] Ibid., February 8, 1966.

[7] *Jornal do Brasil*, March 9, 1966.

fact that the matter is regulated by a constitutional amendment and modified by Ato Institutional Number Three. We reached the conclusion that it would be inadvisable to present the measure to Congress and, above all, to issue a new Ato." Asked whether he thought it normal that an army commander be a candidate for governor of a state where he exercised his post, the president answered that he considered it normal "as long as the post is not used for propaganda or pressure, or as a political base." Castello went on to condemn *O Estado de S. Paulo* for appealing to the military to impose Costa e Silva's candidacy when the war minister went to Europe: "The newspaper considered the candidacy a military fact and the head of the nation already stripped of his authority. The editorials expressed the desirability of presidential elections being carried out practically in the barracks."[8]

Kruel kept in touch with congressmen. Early in April, two of them, MDB leaders Ulisses Guimarães and Doutel de Andrade, prepared to propose a constitutional amendment that would make the *domicílio eleitoral* requirement inapplicable to military officers, legislators, and bureaucrats who were subject to frequent transfers.[9] The subject came up when Kruel and Castello were together at an inauguration ceremony at Ilha Solteira, on the Mato Grosso–São Paulo border. Kruel, mentioning his possible candidacy for the São Paulo governorship, received the impression that the president favored the alteration of the *domicílio* requirement but preferred to have the proposed amendment introduced in Congress by the ARENA. Kruel, who had many friends in the MDB, told Ulisses Guimarães about his conversation. The general also worked to have an amendment proposed by the ARENA.[10]

5. The Election of Câmara Officers (February–March, 1966)

On January 31, two days before the special session of Congress, Castello Branco phoned Congressman Raimundo Padilha, of Rio de Janeiro state, to ask him for lunch the next day at Laranjeiras Palace. Although the president hardly knew the former UDN member who had

[8] HACB, *Discursos, 1966*, p. 370; D'Aguiar, *A Revolução por Dentro*, p. 273.
[9] *Jornal do Brasil*, April 8, 1966.
[10] Amauri Kruel, interview, Rio de Janeiro, July 22, 1977.

built up the prestige of the congressional foreign relations commission, he was aware that Padilha had won considerable respect (and the ill will of Paulistas) as *relator* of the tax reform legislation of 1965.[1] After the lunch Castello informed Padilha that he was to take the place of Pedro Aleixo, now the education minister, as government leader in the Chamber of Deputies. Castello, who had consulted Pedro Aleixo and other congressmen, told Padilha that his selection was "the decision of your own chamber." He asked Padilha to get the opinions of the ARENA congressmen about a new Chamber of Deputies president to succeed Bilac Pinto, whom Castello was about to appoint ambassador to France.

O Estado de S. Paulo reported that the choice of Padilha as government leader would help the campaign that Adauto Cardoso was carrying on within the ARENA against Nilo Coelho, of Pernambuco, for the Câmara presidency.[2] But Cardoso, writing to Castello on the night of February 1, was not optimistic. After mentioning press reports that Castello favored Nilo Coelho, a former PSD member who had always cooperated with the Castello administration, the Guanabara ARENA leader told the president that Nilo Coelho supporters promised that the election of the Pernambucano would bring a relaxation of the discipline and austerity imposed on the Chamber by Bilac. Adauto suggested that the poll being undertaken by Padilha would not reveal the "free and spontaneous will of our ARENA companions" and might force Adauto to deny the correctness of the result. A week later, in Brasília, Castello called Adauto to Planalto Palace to tell him that as the ARENA should present only one candidate for the Chamber presidency, he should submit his candidacy to the decision of the party and abide by that decision.[3]

Padilha, having completed his polling, called on Castello with Krieger and other leaders on February 14. He brought a sheet of paper showing 120 ARENA votes for Adauto Cardoso, 91 for Nilo Coelho, 11 abstentions, and 6 absences.[4] Castello, noting that Nilo Coelho was

[1] Padilha, interview, August 3, 1977.

[2] *O Estado de S. Paulo*, February 2, 1966.

[3] Adauto Lúcio Cardoso, letter to HACB, Brasília, February 1, 1966, File N1 (p. 16), CPDOC; *O Estado de S. Paulo*, February 9, 1966.

[4] Raimundo Padilha, note to HACB, Brasília, February 14, 1966, File N1, CPDOC.

the loser even if he should receive the votes of all those absent and abstaining, decided that Adauto Cardoso should be the ARENA candidate (which appeared to assure him of election, as the MDB could be expected to muster not many more than 130 votes). "This was," Padilha recalls, "the only case in my eighteen years in the Câmara in which its president was selected in this manner—that is, on the basis of the word of the government leader."[5]

Ademar de Barros explained the unexpected outcome by saying that "Nilo Coelho is paying for the evil that he did to Ranieri Mazzilli, for traitors are used only when it is interesting to use them, and then are thrown aside."[6] The outcome, reportedly pleasing to the military, upset a wing of the ARENA. Teódulo de Albuquerque, after declaring that Nilo Coelho had been "torpedoed by Padilha," received a phone call from Castello, who wanted to know whether the Chamber was upset.[7]

Teódulo: "Things are calm, Mr. President."
Castello: "What about your list of those who were not consulted?"
Teódulo reads list.
Castello: "In any event, this does not cover the difference."
Teódulo: "No, but the question is to know if Adauto Cardoso actually has 120 votes."

Castello told Teódulo that Nilo Coelho deserved to be praised and that this new devlopment confirmed once again Nilo Coelho's friendship. Teódulo remarked: "He certainly must be a very good friend to accept that result."

Preparing for the election of Câmara officers, Padilha suggested to Tarcilo Vieira de Melo (MDB, Bahia) that the MDB might be allowed to have the second vice-presidency and fourth secretaryship. Vieira de Melo indignantly rejected the suggestion, and the MDB resolved to obstruct the election and any future legislative wish of the government by walking out in a bloc. Nelson Carneiro said: "We have been the victims of a dirty game of the government majority. We'll force the government to maintain 205 congressmen permanently in Brasília if it wants to have any vote."[8]

[5] Padilha, interview, August 3, 1977.
[6] *Jornal do Brasil*, February 26, 1966.
[7] Ibid., February 16, 17, 1966.
[8] Ibid., February 26, 1966.

Teódulo de Albuquerque declared that he and about twenty other ARENA members, unhappy with Padilha's figures, would join the MDB in walking out. These ARENA "rebels" accused Nilo Coelho of going back on a promise to persevere to the end, heading a dissident slate.[9]

Castello, furious, met with Padilha and six former PSD congressmen who had become ARENA rebels. The president, whom they had never seen so vehement and irritated, asserted that the matter was no simple internal party conflict but the threat of a scission that would kill the ARENA. He could not, he said, understand how a government group could seek backing from the opposition, whose ultimate objective was the conquest of power. "If," he added, "you are getting involved in the rumored clash between the president of the Republic and General Costa e Silva, if you are getting involved in the downfall of the government, then you are very much mistaken, for nothing like this is going to happen." The president then walked out of the room, leaving the congressmen to continue the discussion among themselves.[10]

After Bilac Pinto, Adauto Cardoso, and Padilha asked Castello to help arrange the transport of congressmen to Brasília, Teódulo de Albuquerque said that if he and his companions joined the MDB walkout, "there will be no air shuttle capable of electing Bilac Pinto's successor." ARENA leaders then renewed efforts to persuade the MDB to name candidates for two of the seven officerships. But although they predicted an "extremely difficult" parliamentary year if the ARENA filled all seven posts, and although others explained the trouble as a consequence of creating "artificial parties," Castello showed no sympathy for these observations. He wanted the problem solved by a strong, united ARENA that did not negotiate with the opposition. The press and some ARENA leaders suggested that the president might decree a recess of Congress if the obstruction prevented the election of officers.[11]

On February 28 the Senate had a peaceful election in which Moura Andrade was reelected presiding officer. And on March 2 the Chamber of Deputies voted on an all-ARENA slate that was headed by Adauto Cardoso and included Nilo Coelho and one of the former PSD con-

[9] Ibid., February 26, 27, 1966.
[10] Ibid., February 26, 1966.
[11] Ibid., February 27, 1966, March 1, 1966.

gressmen who had threatened to walk out. After the failure of an MDB motion to postpone the election, all the MDB congressmen, with one exception, left the chamber, but no ARENA congressman followed this example.[12] Of the 162 congressmen who were not on the floor during the election, 136 belonged to the MDB and 26 were absent from Brasília (some being out of the country). In the balloting for presiding officer, carried out by 245 congressmen, Adauto Cardoso received 205 votes. The victorious slate consisted of:

President Adauto Lúcio Cardoso
1st Vice-president João Batista Ramos
2nd Vice-president José Bonifácio de Andrada
1st Secretary Nilo Coelho
2nd Secretary Henrique La Rocque
3rd Secretary Aniz Badra
4th Secretary Ari Alcântara

Following the balloting, the MDB's Vieira de Melo pointed out that never before, since the constitution was promulgated in 1946, had the minority been without representation among the Câmara officers.

6. Costa e Silva, "Candidate to be Candidate" (February–March, 1966)

In Paris, Costa e Silva caught a cold and tried without success to see de Gaulle. Meanwhile, back in Brazil, Sobral Pinto scolded Congressman Anísio Rocha for making what the lawyer called "the scandalously false" statement that the people wanted Costa e Silva. Lacerda said that a "simple change in generals" was of no interest and that his sole concern was to warn of the approaching "earthquake," or "national revolt against the revolution." On the other hand, Ademar de Barros, long a presidential hopeful, called Costa e Silva an "authentic revolutionary leader" and sent an emissary abroad to see him.[1]

With some dismay Justice Minister Mem de Sá observed that the appearance of Costa e Silva as "a solitary candidate" was "a poor symptom of democratic reality." Asserting that "at this stage we should

[12] Ibid., March 3, 1966.

[1] Mendes Vianna, letters to HACB, Paris, January 10, 13, 24, 1966, File O2, PVCB; *Jornal do Brasil*, January 7, 8, 21, 29, 1966.

already have five or six candidates," he listed eight possibilities: Costa e Silva, Eduardo Gomes, Roberto Campos, Otávio Bulhões, Nei Braga, Juarez Távora, Paulo Egídio Martins, and Milton Campos. Teódulo de Albuquerque told the press that the ARENA had three candidates: Costa e Silva, Amauri Kruel, and Bilac Pinto. But Amaral Neto, of the Guanabara ARENA, declared that the future would reveal Costa e Silva to be the only outstanding candidate. "I know him personally; he is human," Amaral Neto said.[2]

On February 17 a crowd of thirty-five hundred, mostly military officers, greeted the returning war minister. To combat the heat at Galeão Airport, fans were passed out, each picturing Costa e Silva with a map of Brazil over his heart and bearing the slogan: "A Heart That Beats for the People, the Nation, and Democracy." The general, suffering from the grippe ("a souvenir from Paris"), was asked if he remained a candidate. Whereas he sometimes referred to himself as "a candidate to be a candidate," this time he dodged the question entirely by speaking with enthusiasm about his trip and then kissing his granddaughter.[3]

After phoning Castello to say that he would "do everything in accordance with Planalto Palace," Costa e Silva went to Petrópolis to confer with confidants, who listed Generals Juraci Magalhães, Golberi, and Geisel as trying to "liquidate" his candidacy.[4] In Brasília on February 24, Costa e Silva and his wife, Yolanda, attended an Alvorada Palace lunch honoring the daughter of Spanish dictator Franco. Costa e Silva gave the president a present, a small television set. During the ninety minutes Costa e Silva spoke alone with Castello (who offered him pineapple ice cream), the president appeared to be understanding while the war minister explained the "early launching" of his candidacy. Costa e Silva complained about the hostility to him in Planalto Palace but expressed his full support for the administration's economic-financial policy. To the press, which found him tired by the heat and wearing a handkerchief on his forehead, Costa e Silva said that he would

[2] *O Estado de S. Paulo*, February 11, 15, 1966; *Jornal do Brasil*, February 17, 1966.

[3] Palhares dos Santos, interview, November 22, 1975; *Jornal do Brasil*, February 18, 1966.

[4] *Jornal do Brasil*, February 18, 19, 1966.

accept all the government's conditions about the election and, if elected, would govern Brazil in a "strictly democratic" regime.[5] Castello, speaking to Luís Viana Filho, said that his talk with the war minister had been good. "Psychologically," Castello added, "I found him more cautious than conciliatory."[6]

Lacerda, who called Costa e Silva "the next victim of the maneuvers of Sr. Castello Branco," continued to be popular in Rio. When the *Boletim Cambial* asked 678 members of the private enterprise managerial class whom they would choose for president (from a list already prepared), the results were as follows:[7]

	Votes	Percentage
Carlos Lacerda	216	31.7
Costa e Silva	117	17.3
Roberto Campos	95	14.0
Nei Braga	60	8.9
Juraci Magalhães	54	8.0
Carvalho Pinto	29	4.3
Castello Branco	26	3.8
Magalhães Pinto	26	3.8
Jurandir Mamede	13	1.9
Ademar de Barros	10	1.5
Cordeiro de Farias	8	1.2
Blank votes	24	3.6
	678	100.0

Besides Costa e Silva, the only general in active military service on this list was Jurandir Mamede. He had qualities, such as calmness and a respect for legality, that appealed to some civilian politicians, among them Adauto Cardoso and João Agripino, who were not so sure about the "strictly democratic" regime offered by Costa e Silva, favorite of the hard-liners. While it was known that Castello had a high regard for Mamede, it was also appreciated that the president

[5] D'Aguiar, *A Revolução por Dentro*, p. 272; *Jornal do Brasil*, February 25, 1966.

[6] Viana Filho, *O Governo Castelo Branco*, p. 386.

[7] *Jornal do Brasil*, February 26, 1966; *Boletim Cambial* poll reported in *Jornal do Brasil*, March 24, 1966.

could hardly push his candidacy without being considered responsible for stimulating a division in the military. But the launching of Mamede's candidacy by civilians seemed appealing, not only because a military candidacy proposed by civilians might be preferable to a military candidacy proposed by the military, but also because it could be considered as a means to promote the unity of all the forces that had made the 1964 revolution.[8]

João Agripino and Adauto Cardoso, who felt that a Mamede candidacy might be welcomed by men in high places, asked Rafael de Almeida Magalhães to sound out Mamede. But Mamede, citing the importance of unity in the army, rejected the idea. Then Rafael de Almeida Magalhães wrote Mamede a letter stating that sometimes the matter of unity in the army is less important than the health of the country.[9]

Meanwhile in Belém, Pará, Jarbas Passarinho received a visit from Colonel João Alberto Franco, who explained that he had been working in the war minister's office and was authorized by Costa e Silva to inquire about Passarinho's position. Passarinho, who headed the ARENA of Pará and had taken no position, was upset to learn from Colonel Franco that War Ministry rumors connected Passarinho's name with the candidacy of Cordeiro de Farias.[10] In a letter dated March 18 that Franco took to Costa e Silva, Passarinho said that he considered no civilian candidacy viable and therefore preferred the candidacy of the war minister.

Passarinho, writing to Castello on March 24, told of his letter to Costa e Silva and the circumstances that had led to it, and he said that he had never heard the president place any restrictions on Costa e Silva's candidacy. Passarinho praised the energy shown by the war minister in the past struggle to defeat Communism, "against which, as I see it, we are going soon to battle." He offered to resign his ARENA posts if the president backed another military candidate and added that it was a shame that neither Mamede nor Geisel was a candidate.[11]

[8] Almeida Magalhães, interview, August 8, 1977.

[9] Ibid.

[10] Passarinho, interview, November 11, 1975.

[11] Jarbas G. Passarinho, letter to HACB, Belém, March 24, 1966, copy supplied by Senator Passarinho in 1975; a copy is included in a letter, dated June 1, 1966, from Passarinho to the superintendent of Diários e Emissoras Associados that was published in *A Província do Pará*, June 2, 1966.

Passarinho's letter to the president was sent to Lieutenant Colonel Gustavo Morais Rego Reis, of the presidential Gabinete Militar, with a covering note asking Morais Rego to pass it on to the president. Subsequent communications between the president's office and Passarinho reflected the poor relations that had long existed between Morais Rego and Passarinho. Members of the president's office maintained that Passarinho was playing a double game in the case of Castello and the Costa e Silva candidacy, and as some versions in the press were unfavorable to Passarinho, Passarinho answered accusations in a press communication that included his letter to Castello. The tone of messages from Passarinho to the president's office did nothing to reduce the animosity felt there toward Passarinho.[12]

Castello disliked Passarinho's reaction to the visit of Colonel Franco, and he particularly disliked Costa e Silva's apparent use of the War Ministry to help his presidential campaign. In a heated conversation with Costa e Silva, the president accused him of having sent Colonel Franco to Pará. "So, you are in full campaign for president," Castello told his war minister. Costa e Silva denied having sent Franco to Pará and said that he had been sent by Colonel Mário David Andreazza, who was in the war minister's office and knew Franco to be a friend of Passarinho.[13]

On another occasion the president and his war minister had an angry exchange after Castello received a report that a general in Paraná had brought pressure on Governor Paulo Pimentel to support the war minister's candidacy.[14] One prominent figure, hoping to keep on the best of terms with Castello and Costa e Silva, addressed a flowery letter to each but got the envelopes mixed up. A worse situation almost developed when an envelope addressed to the presidency brought a letter to the war minister describing Castello as a terrible person. Even before the letter was found to be a forgery, assistants of the president persuaded him to drop his idea of forwarding it to the war minister with the remark, "See what your friends are saying about me."[15]

[12] Ibid.; Moscardo de Souza, interview, October 27, 1975; Passarinho, interview, November 11, 1975.

[13] Passarinho, interview, November 11, 1975.

[14] D'Aguiar, *A Revolução por Dentro*, p. 275 (quoting from *BC* of October 3, 1966).

[15] Moscardo de Souza, interview, October 23, 1975.

What was being said about the war minister by his detractors was more serious. After Orville L. Freeman, the U.S. secretary of agriculture, visited Brazil, he wrote President Johnson that Costa e Silva "is reportedly short tempered, sensitive, power conscious, and prone to alcohol. This is hearsay but is repeated widely."[16]

A barrage was aimed particularly at Yolanda Costa e Silva, who was described as unfit to be the First Lady. As for her husband, the stories went beyond his impetuousness, emotion, and poor health that made him tire easily. He was said not to have read a book in years and to enjoy the company, during hours spent in gambling at poker, of a class of people that was by no means the best. His advancement in the army was pictured as having been accomplished without any significant show of virtue. He was called a "croupier," a "bon vivant," and "that Mexican general."

Castello himself, speaking of Costa e Silva's wish to be simultaneously a popular "humanizer" and a hard-line revolutionary, called Costa e Silva a man who "wants to go out in the rain and not get wet."[17] More than once, Viana Filho recalls, the president, in a tone of affection for his schoolmate, said that "Costa e Silva does not have the health to be president." Flexa Ribeiro told Viana Filho that when he went to get the president's "instructions" about a list of candidates, the president entered into a discourse about the qualities the candidate should have. "The picture," Flexa Ribeiro said, "was utterly different from the figure of Costa e Silva. And yet, from time to time Castello interrupted his dissertation to say that he was not opposing his candidacy."[18]

In the company of Krieger and João Agripino, Castello spoke of his desire to see Krieger in the presidency. Although Agripino then expressed eagerness to work for Krieger's candidacy in the north, Krieger objected and pointed out to the president that, with his permission, he was already working for Costa e Silva.[19]

When Carlos Castello Branco analyzed the situation, he speculated that the presidential group, "notoriously hostile to the war minister,

[16] Orville L. Freeman, memorandum to LBJ, Washington, D.C., April 27, 1966, LBJ Library.

[17] PVCB, interview, November 23, 1974.

[18] Viana Filho, *O Governo Castelo Branco*, p. 390.

[19] Krieger, *Desde as Missões*, p. 228.

without being notoriously favorable to Marshal Cordeiro de Farias," hoped for a deadlock between the two in order to bring in Bilac Pinto, who, as ambassador to France, was strategically situated on the sidelines, as Juraci Magalhães had once been in Washington.[20]

Cordeiro was felt to have the support of some congressmen, especially from the northeast, where Nilo Coelho favored him.[21] But many congressmen prudently awaited developments, and Cordeiro held off launching his candidacy, thus satisfying Castello's wish for a delay of the formal debate about names that were being mentioned. Cordeiro was not particularly strong in the army, where many officers considered him too much of a politician. Hard-liners who admired his past role as an anti-Goulart conspirator felt that he had become a part of the Castello circle they disliked.[22]

Costa e Silva did well at keeping dry in the rain. São Paulo businessmen, unhappy with the administration's economic policies, supported the war minister because he promised to "humanize" the Revolution.[23] Magalhães Pinto, too, decided to support Costa e Silva, his reason being that the war minister was handling his candidacy as an "authentic revolutionary." On March 14, one week after Magalhães Pinto made this declaration, Castello phoned Costa e Silva to tell him that Magalhães Pinto was eager to coordinate the war minister's candidacy but that this was not something with which the president would agree. Costa e Silva replied that he had refused, three days earlier, to grant an audience requested by Magalhães Pinto.[24]

7. Cordeiro Withdaws from the Race (April 16, 1966)

At Laranjeiras Palace on Saturday afternoon, March 26, Castello discussed the presidential succession with Juraci Magalhães, Cordeiro

[20] Castello Branco, *Os Militares no Poder*, pp. 441, 449 (items for March 10 and 20, 1966).

[21] Ibid., p. 448; Vereker, memorandum, March 31, 1966.

[22] Vereker, memorandum, March 31, 1966; Castello Branco, *Os Militares no Poder*, p. 438; Viana Filho, *O Governo Castelo Branco*, p. 338; Boaventura Cavalcanti, interview, November 20, 1974.

[23] Paulo Egídio Martins, interview, November 10, 1975.

[24] *Correio da Manhã*, March 8, 1966; Viana Filho, *O Governo Castelo Branco*, p. 387.

de Farias, Mem de Sá, Luís Viana Filho, Ernesto Geisel, and Golberi do Couto e Silva. Plans were made for the nominating convention of the ARENA and for a possible consultation with its state directorships before the convention.[1]

The men who met with Castello gave their opinions about the Costa e Silva candidacy, leading Viana Filho to conclude that while that candidacy might preserve the unity of the armed forces, it certainly divided the government. Cordeiro de Farias said that it would be disastrous to have Costa e Silva succeed Castello. Mem de Sá expressed the same thought with vehemence. But Juraci Magalhães, who had failed in January to persuade Castello to dismiss the war minister, argued that his candidacy was inevitable and would preserve unity in the armed forces. Although Castello spent most of the time listening, he left the impression that he favored consultation with the state directorships of the ARENA. Cordeiro, feeling that such consultation would result in the nominating convention receiving only the name of the war minister, preferred a formula that would delay the selection until the nominating convention had considered the ideas to be presented to it by several candidates.

During the last days of March, Cordeiro's candidacy was launched by Congressman Geraldo Guedes, who had served under Cordeiro in the government of Pernambuco. But at the same time, the public learned that Paulo Sarasate and Juraci Magalhães had decided to support the war minister. When Sarasate phoned Costa e Silva to advise him of the position he had taken, the war minister told the Ceará politician: "You are my thermometer."[2]

Mem de Sá, speaking to Castello, said that with Costa e Silva in the presidency, "we might as well throw the Revolution and all its fruits out the window." The justice minister suggested that Ademar de Queiroz, a long-time prerevolutionary conspirator with qualities "far superior" to those of Costa e Silva, should be acceptable to the military. But Castello, remarking that he considered Ademar de Queiroz "like a brother," said that circumstances did not allow the decision that the justice minister was proposing.[3]

[1] Mem de Sá, letter to Viana Filho, October 7, 1971, pp. 13–14; Viana Filho, *O Governo Castelo Branco*, p. 391.

[2] *Jornal do Brasil*, March 27 (Coluna do Castello), 30, 1966.

[3] Mem de Sá, letter to Viana Filho, October 7, 1971, p. 14.

On the eve of the installation meeting of the ARENA, Adauto Cardoso released a list of names that he said would be presented to ARENA President Krieger. The withdrawals of Mamede and Milton Campos reduced Cardoso's list to five: Cordeiro, Ademar de Queiroz, Amauri Kruel, Bilac Pinto, and Costa e Silva.[4]

The installation meeting, for making the ARENA a provisional party, was held in the Chamber of Deputies on March 31 and attracted only about half the ARENA congressmen. Costa e Silva, seated in the front row between Magalhães Pinto and Governor Israel Pinheiro, listened to a speech by Krieger and then answered reporters' questions. Although the general expressed support for the government's economic program, his partisans soon pointed out that this support did not imply any admiration for Roberto Campos or Bulhões. Costa e Silva, they said, would fight inflation in a manner that would stimulate development. The candidate himself simply declared that "medicinal doses should be applied in accordance with the state of health of the patient."[5]

When Ademar de Barros and Magalhães Pinto made proposals to Costa e Silva about his candidacy, the war minister discussed them with Castello. He told the president that he was rejecting Magalhães Pinto's advice that his candidacy be backed by a "national union" which would include opponents of the regime.[6] He advised Castello of Ademar de Barros' proposal to back his candidacy in return for Costa e Silva's support until the end of Ademar de Barros' gubernatorial term, whereupon Castello told the war minister: "I do not plan to intervene in São Paulo, but, if Ademar attempts any movement, I shall do so; and then what will you do?" As for the Kruel presidential candidacy, which Costa e Silva feared might cause a split in the military, Castello had the word of Kruel, received during the Ilha Solteira talk, that the interest of the Second Army commander was in the São Paulo governorship, not the presidency.[7]

While Cordeiro's backers worked to get signatures on expressions of support for their candidate, Costa e Silva gained more ground. João Agripino, after consulting political leaders in the northeast, told the press that no one in the army wanted to cause a division by contesting

[4] *Jornal do Brasil*, March 31, 1966.

[5] Ibid., April 1, 2, 7, 14, 1966.

[6] Ibid., April 7, 1966; Viana Filho, *O Governo Castelo Branco*, p. 388.

[7] Viana Filho, *O Governo Castelo Branco*, p. 387; *Jornal do Brasil*, April 2, 1966.

Costa e Silva and that this attitude should be considered important by the president.[8]

For the April 15 issue of *Visão,* Juraci Magalhães prepared an interview supporting Costa e Silva's candidacy. As it would be the first expression of support by a member of the cabinet, the foreign minister showed Castello what he planned to have published. He told Castello that although Castello had mentioned various names other than that of the war minister, none of them had caught on. Juraci added that Costa e Silva was not a good choice but that it was better to put up with him than have the split in the military that might result if the administration backed another candidate.[9]

Castello accepted Juraci's reasoning, but at a later date he told Aliomar Baleeiro that Costa e Silva's selection was the responsibility of two people, Juraci and Krieger, and that he might have succeeded in having the thinking of civilian leaders prevail except that "Krieger remained obstinate and was supported by Juraci, whose interview made the situation past mending." From this conversation with the Supreme Court justice it is clear that Castello would have preferred a civilian, for he said: "In first place Bilac, but also Krieger and others who were mentioned, including Juraci. The worst Brazilian politician was not Carlos, but Magalhães Pinto."[10]

Juraci, in his *Visão* interview, declared that only the Costa e Silva candidacy had a "real and durable political repercussion." The candidacy, Juraci warned, offered two possible dangers: (1) the appearance of a militarist imposition and (2) a form of campaign in opposition to the Castello administration. But, Juraci concluded, these dangers had been eliminated by the wisdom shown by Castello and Costa e Silva. With the appearance of the interview, Costa e Silva telephoned the Foreign Minister to say "thank you so much." Juraci replied: "I did this not for you but for the Revolution."[11]

In Brasília on April 14 the eleven-man Executive Commission of the ARENA resolved to determine the presidential race preferences by

[8] Viana Filho, *O Governo Castelo Branco*, p. 392.

[9] Magalhães, interview, December 3, 1974.

[10] HACB quoted in Baleeiro, "Recordações do Presidente H. Castelo Branco," p. 38.

[11] Juraci Magalhães in *Visão*, April 15, 1966, quoted in Viana Filho, *O Governo Castelo Branco*, p. 393; Magalhães, interview, December 3, 1974.

submitting written inquiries to the state directorships and the state governors prior to April 25 and by hearing also from the ARENA blocs of federal legislators. The date of the national convention for choosing the ARENA's presidential candidate was set for May 26.[12] Paulo Sarasate, a member of the Executive Commission, explained to the press that "in accordance with the criterion established by the Executive Commission and President Castello Branco, only one candidate will be indicated to the party's national convention, although the consultations are being made on the basis of a list of six names."[13]

The six names, written by Castello on a copy of the April 14 resolutions, were Ademar de Queiroz, Costa e Silva, Bilac Pinto, Cordeiro de Farias, Etelvino Lins, and Nei Braga.[14] To keep the number at six after Milton Campos continued to refuse to be included, Krieger phoned former Pernambuco Governor Etelvino Lins, a minister of the federal Tribunal de Contas, on April 14 to tell him that Castello had suggested his name. Etelvino Lins said that he had committed himself to support Costa e Silva but had no objection to the inclusion of his name if it was simply to give the appearance of a democratic decision for the sake of the effects abroad.[15] Petrobrás President Ademar de Queiroz, his name reportedly written by Castello without consultation, was said to be unlikely to create difficulties by requesting a withdrawal. But Nei Braga was described as uncomfortable to be included in a list that was "merely to give coverage to the single candidacy of Costa e Silva."[16]

Cordeiro de Farias objected to the decision to send, after consultations, only one name to the ARENA nominating convention, and therefore he requested that his name be removed from the list. In his letter of April 16, withdrawing his name, he expressed his disagreement with "the methods, dates, and procedures established." He wrote that under those procedures it would be impossible for each candidate to disclose "his ideas and intentions to the organ of the party or to the specialized commissions established by it for this purpose."[17]

[12] Aliança Renovadora Nacional, resolutions, Brasília, April 14, 1966, File P2 (p. 13), CPDOC.

[13] *Jornal do Brasil*, April 16, 1966.

[14] Aliança Renovadora Nacional resolutions, April 14, 1966, File P2, CPDOC.

[15] Etelvino Lins, *Um Depoimento Político: Episódios e Observações*, p. 107.

[16] *Jornal do Brasil* (Coluna do Castello), April 16, 1966.

[17] Ibid., April 17, 1966.

Krieger and Castello were disappointed at Cordeiro's decision. On April 18, Krieger announced the possibility of more than one name being presented at the nominating convention on May 26, but on the next day Castello let it be known that he wanted only one name.[18]

8. The Costa e Silva–Pedro Aleixo Ticket (April–May, 1966)

In the last part of April, Castello gave the impression he considered that his role in guiding the presidential succession had ended. He turned his attention to persuading Cordeiro de Farias and Mem de Sá not to leave the cabinet. Cordeiro, who received similar pleas from Krieger, Sarasate, and Rondon Pacheco, agreed to remain until Costa e Silva became officially the candidate of the government party.[1]

Mem de Sá told Castello that he radically opposed the way in which the government had settled the question of the presidential succession and therefore could no longer head the ministry that handled political matters. "But," Castello said, "you are not, and will not be, minister of General Costa e Silva or of his candidacy. You are my minister and have my full confidence, and so I don't understand why you should resign." Mem de Sá pointed out that his position was untenable because he could hardly adopt measures favorable to a candidacy he was combatting and yet to refuse to do so would be disloyal to the president. Explaining that his decision to resign was irrevocable, he promised to delay announcing it and give Castello time to choose a successor.[2]

Opponents of the Costa e Silva candidacy expressed assurances that the war minister would have a contender at the ARENA nominating convention. After Sarasate said that in the north and northeast the most frequently mentioned contenders were Ambassador Bilac Pinto and Agriculture Minister Nei Braga, a drive to "coordinate" the candidacy of Bilac was reportedly initiated by João Agripino, Adauto Cardoso, Cordeiro de Farias, and São Paulo Mayor Faria Lima. But Krieger, hav-

[18] Ibid., April 19, 20, 1966.

[1] *Jornal do Brasil*, April 19 (Coluna do Castello), 23, 1966; Viana Filho, *O Governo Castelo Branco*, p. 394.

[2] Mem de Sá, letter to Viana Filho, October 7, 1971, pp. 14–15.

ing obtained the written expressions of over 150 federal legislators, announced that Costa e Silva was the preferred candidate of more than 90 percent and the only choice of more than 50 percent.[3]

Reports late in April from the ARENA state executive commissions also favored the war minister. The ARENA of Guanabara told the national Executive Commission that the Carioca directorship had given the general thirty-eight votes to twenty-two for Adauto and twenty for Bilac. Costa e Silva, with some help from Moura Andrade, was the unanimous choice of the São Paulo ARENA. In Mato Grosso he was far ahead of favorite son Filinto Müller, but, in Paraná, Nei Braga received forty-one votes to thirty-four for the war minister. Rio Grande do Sul gave Costa e Silva thirty-two votes to twelve for Nei Braga and one for Adauto. Espírito Santo went for Costa e Silva by acclamation. Ceará gave twenty-one votes to the war minister, fifteen to Bilac, eleven to Ademar de Queiroz, and nine to Nei Braga. In Goiás, Costa e Silva was ahead of Bilac and Nei Braga.[4]

Magalhães Pinto declared that the candidacy of Costa e Silva was "absolutely definitive." *Jornal do Brasil,* in agreement, expressed the hope that "from this moment on, General Costa e Silva will leave off being the candidate of accomodation, of systematic and pusillanimous adherence, and of contradictions and hesitations."[5] When Castello, on a visit to Belo Horizonte to observe the eighty-ninth birthday of his father-in-law, said that the ARENA presidential and vice-presidential candidates should travel all over Brazil promising an administration better than his own, the only question about the ticket concerned the name of Costa e Silva's running mate.[6]

Costa e Silva wanted to campaign at the side of his Paulista friend Auro de Moura Andrade, and therefore the Senate president's name appeared in first place on a list, attributed to the war minister, that also included Nei Braga, Magalhães Pinto, and Congressmen Gustavo Capanema and João Calmon.[7] But Costa e Silva was not disposed to get into an acrimonious dispute with Castello, who ruled against Moura

[3] *Jornal do Brasil,* April 20, 22, 1966.
[4] Ibid., April 23, 24, 1966.
[5] Ibid., April 27, May 1, 1966.
[6] Ibid., April 24, 26, 1966.
[7] Ibid., April 28, 1966.

Andrade, citing military opposition. After Castello told Krieger that Costa e Silva's running mate should be a "revolutionary politician" from Minas or the northeast, the names of Bilac Pinto and João Agripino came to the fore, followed by that of Pedro Aleixo (all former members of the UDN).[8] As Geisel told Agripino in Natal, Castello favored Agripino. But Costa e Silva opposed Agripino, and the military felt that his selection would create a problem because the vice-governor of Paraíba, in line to succeed Agripino, was under an IPM investigation. Castello, in Paraíba to give a May Day speech, found Agripino entirely happy to remain in the governorship.[9]

In Minas, Education Minister Pedro Aleixo had the backing of Governor Israel Pinheiro, who wanted a Mineiro in the vice-presidency. But he did not have the backing of Magalhães Pinto, whose supporters telegraphed Krieger on behalf of the recently retired governor. Furthermore, Pedro Aleixo, once an advocate of the movement of civilians favorable to Mamede, was regarded with reserve by Costa e Silva, who remarked that Pedro Aleixo was "very political and might create problems."[10]

Castello and Krieger, settling on Pedro Aleixo, received help from Rondon Pacheco, the government's congressional vice-leader. Pacheco persuaded Costa e Silva that his worries about Pedro Aleixo were unfounded. Soon Costa e Silva was citing the successes that Castello had had in Congress when Pedro Aleixo was his leader there.[11]

The last hurdle for the Pedro Aleixo candidacy developed on May 6, when Krieger and six other members of the ARENA's Executive Commission met to settle on the name it would present four days later to the larger National Directorship. On the first ballot Sarasate received three votes to two for Amazonas Governor Artur César Ferreira Reis and two for Pedro Aleixo. A second ballot gave the victory to Sarasate

[8] Auro de Moura Andrade stated (interview, São Paulo, November 10, 1975) that Castello Branco felt that Moura Andrade, who favored "an independent legislature," might be "inconvenient;" see also Viana Filho, *O Governo Castelo Branco*, p. 396; *Jornal do Brasil*, April 24, 28, 1966.

[9] *Jornal do Brasil*, April 24, May 3, 1966; Viana Filho, *O Governo Castelo Branco*, p. 395.

[10] Viana Filho, *O Governo Castelo Branco*, p. 396; *Jornal do Brasil*, May 7, 1966; Almeida Magalhães, interview, August 8, 1977.

[11] *Jornal do Brasil*, May 6, 8, 1966; Viana Filho, *O Governo Castelo Branco*, p. 396.

over Pedro Aleixo by four votes to two (with Sarasate voting in blank). Then with emotion Sarasate read a letter to Krieger in which he revealed his decision to withdraw, placing his loyalty to Castello above his candidacy.[12]

Thus, in Brasília, when fifty members of the National Directorship of the ARENA met on May 10, the Executive Commission recommended that the Costa e Silva–Pedro Aleixo ticket be submitted to the convention on the twenty-sixth.[13] After the recommendation was approved by acclamation, ARENA leaders brought official news of the result to Castello at Planalto Palace on May 11. The president, in a short speech, said that his participation in the presidential succession had been carried out to provide a selection process and "eliminate distortions, turn pressures aside, annul the effects of precipitous actions, and distinguish between the government program and maneuvers to demolish the government." He had, he said, helped dispel "imagined threats" to the unity of the armed forces and had warned against evilly planned reveries about "national union." He expressed his full support for the ARENA ticket.[14]

When Costa e Silva let it be known at an early date that he was a candidate for the presidency, he was quickly supported by most of the active military officers. They expressed dread at the thought of a break in military unity. But the war minister's nomination depended on the favorable voices of civilian politicians belonging to the ARENA. In view of the influence of Krieger and Castello Branco in the ARENA, the path of the Costa e Silva candidacy can be said to have been made rather smooth by the decisions of Krieger to support the candidacy and of Castello to assume a neutral position.

It was the role of President Castello Branco that was analyzed by Carlos Castello Branco late in April, 1966, after Costa e Silva's nomination was assured. The columnist made the assumption that the president sincerely hoped that the ARENA would act as a "free political body," and then he went on to write that this was an impossible ex-

[12] *Jornal do Brasil*, May 7, 8, 1966.

[13] Ibid., May 11, 1966.

[14] HACB, *Discursos, 1966*, pp. 43–45.

pectation. Carlos Castello Branco explained that politicians, who may have been aware of opposition to Costa e Silva's candidacy in Planalto Palace, waited patiently for indications of what path to follow. But a vacuum developed, a horror to politicians, with Castello Branco, "the dominant reference point in terms of power," standing aside so that the ARENA politicians could be free to make their selection. "What did they do with this liberty?" the columnist asked. They turned to the other power center, the war minister, "mindful of the basic reality of this Brazilian world following the March Revolution, that is, mindful that the power emanates from the armed forces and is exercised in their name. Thus, the politicians themselves, or politics itself, in an essentially realistic step, rejected the liberty that was offered."[15]

[15] Castello Branco, *Os Militares no Poder*, pp. 471–473.

VIII

Antigovernment Protests and Demonstrations

(March–October, 1966)

The duty of each and every one . . . is not simply to proclaim the suffering that we all recognize, but to point out remedies and co-operate with public and private entities in order that we can overcome, in the shortest possible time, the ills arising from underdevelopment.

1. Protests against the Government (March–April, 1966)

THE large monetary expansion of 1965, caused in part by the huge coffee crop, kindled inflationary forces in 1966. They were particularly evident during the first part of 1966, when the cost of living increased at an annual rate of about 50 percent, which exceeded the rate of increase in the last part of 1965.[1]

Steps taken in 1966 to reduce the inflationary pressures gave promise of showing results in the future. Monetary expansion, 76 percent in 1965, was only 13 percent in 1966.[2] The federal deficit was practically eliminated, and the deficits of the government-run enterprises were sharply reduced.

The minimum wage for the Rio de Janeiro and São Paulo municipal areas, set at sixty-six thousand cruzeiros per month in February, 1965, was increased 27 percent (to eighty-four thousand cruzeiros) by Castello's decree of March 2, 1966, hardly a consolation for the workers, whose living costs (in São Paulo city) increased 61 percent in 1965 and 47 percent in 1966.[3] Also during 1966 the legislation about wage revisions was handled austerely; the annual increases in the private sector ran between 30 and 35 percent.[4] They would have been higher had not the authorities, when establishing one of the factors in the wage revision formula, estimated the "inflationary residual" for the

[1] Variações percentuais trimestrais," *Conjuntura Econômica*, February 1969, p. 30.

[2] Syvrud, *Foundations of Brazilian Economic Growth*, p. 79.

[3] *Jornal do Brasil*, March 2, 3, 1966; *Anuário Estatístico do Brasil*, 1972, p. 350.

[4] Syvrud, *Foundations of Brazilian Economic Growth*, p. 157. (Wage revision legislation included Decree-Laws 15 and 17 of 1966 in addition to Law 4,725 of 1965).

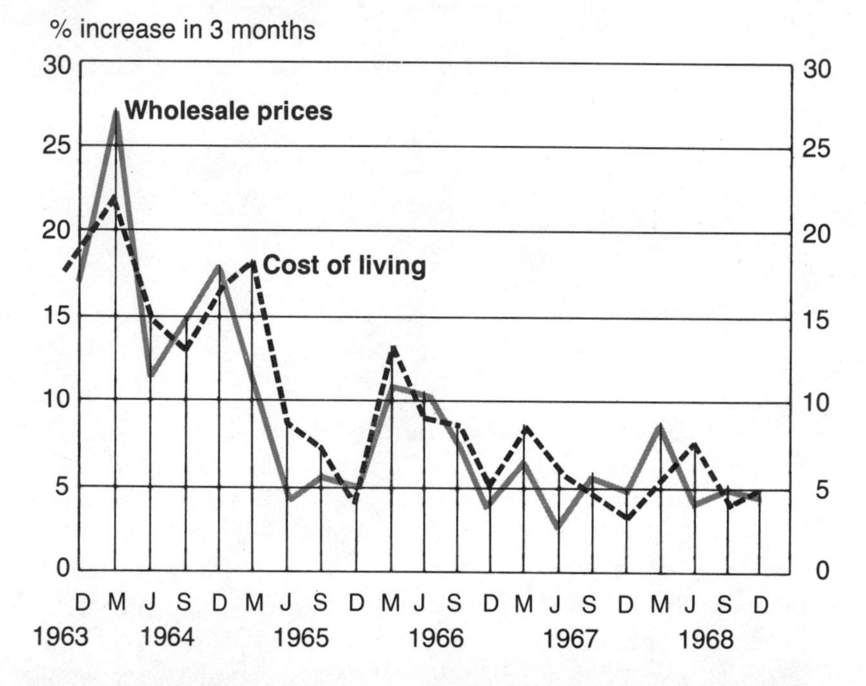

Percentage increases per quarters, between the quarter ending December 1963, and the quarter ending December 1968.
(Based on material published in *Conjuntura Econômica*, February 1968, p. 173, and February 1969, p. 30.)

succeeding twelve months at only 10 percent.[5] This overly optimistic view about the immediate trend of the inflation was reflected in the speeches of the president and other officials.

While Brazilians were afflicted by a combination of inflation and the painful measures taken to reduce it, popular politicians, such as Magalhães Pinto, Ademar de Barros, Herbert Levy, and Lacerda, issued a steady stream of stinging attacks on the government's economic policy. Workers, businessmen, and housewives made their unhappiness known.

Students, who had their own complaints, protested from time to time against the difficult situation of the workers, and so did the pro-

[5] "Panorama do Ano," *Conjuntura Econômica*, February 1967, pp. 9ff.

gressive wing of the Catholic church, whose Workers' Catholic Action, Rural Catholic Action, and Catholic Agrarian Youth issued a manifesto in March to condemn what they called the injustices suffered by laborers.[6] Workers themselves occasionally raised their voices. At a meeting of metalworkers in São Paulo in March, 1966, the speeches against the government's economic and social policies were violent. In Rio Grande do Sul, during the same month, the state Military Brigade uncovered a plot involving discontented workers in postal and telegraph offices and in rail transport who planned to start a rebellion with the help of a few officers of the brigade.[7]

On the whole, however, the workers were rather quiet except when the government appeared to threaten the thirty-year-old *estabilidade* arrangement that made it impossible for companies to dismiss workers who had been employed by them for over ten years. The failure of the workers to make more noise was attributed by *Jornal do Brasil* to a lack of authentic labor leaders. "The new rulers of the nation," it wrote, "have not had eyes to see that the class of union intermediaries is removed further than ever from the aspirations of the workers." It also declared that "two years after the democratic revolution of March 31, the May Day preparation has revealed in the working class the same feeling of separation that is experienced by an individual who knows that the celebration does not belong to him."[8]

The discontent of businessmen with the early 1966 tightening of credit was particularly evident in São Paulo. Ademar de Barros, proclaiming that the administration's economic-financial policy "asphyxiates the people with hunger," said that Castello Branco should resign "in a gesture of greatness and patriotism," turning the presidency over to Marshal Dutra, "who should carry out general, direct elections within 30 or 60 days."[9]

Sálvio de Almeida Prado (of the Sociedade Rural Brasileira) and other members of São Paulo's "producing" class complained about the government's restrictive credit policy and lack of assistance to coffee growers. Proud of the anti-Goulart March of the Family with God for

[6] Schneider, *The Political System of Brasil*, p. 235.
[7] *Jornal do Brasil*, March 9, 20, 1966.
[8] Ibid., May 1, 1966.
[9] Vereker, report, March 31, 1966; *Jornal do Brasil*, March 12, 1966.

Liberty held on March 19, 1964, they decided to hold a great March of Silence on Saturday, March 19, 1966. Commenting on the name of the new march, one of its sponsors observed that "today it is impossible to carry out any manifestation . . . for the entrepreneurial classes are dominated by agony" in the face of an administration "that seeks to bring an end to national industry and production."[10]

Members of "the producing classes of Minas" announced that they would participate in São Paulo's Marcha do Silêncio because, they said, the march was "the only form of protest against the economic-financial steps of the government."[11]

On March 18, the day before the Marcha do Silêncio, two thousand São Paulo students paraded with signs attacking the federal government and its failure to "open the polls." They were welcomed by applause and torn paper thrown from windows.[12]

But the Marcha do Silêncio was a failure and was received by the Paulistas with indifference. The participants, numbering about one hundred, attended Mass and then paraded with the flag used two years earlier to the Historical and Geographical Institute of São Paulo "so that our sons may have inspiration." *O Estado de S. Paulo* wrote that the only object of the 1966 march was to place the flag in the institute and that some Paulistas sought to take political advantage of the occasion. Sálvio de Almeida Prado attributed the lack of interest in the 1966 march to "a boycott of the press, which received pressures from political groups interested in discouraging the movement."[13]

As in São Paulo, students in Rio de Janeiro demonstrated in March. On the twenty-fourth, about three thousand gathered in front of the School of Philosophy of the University of Brazil (later called the Federal University of Rio de Janeiro), and from there they marched to the Guanabara Legislative Assembly building on Avenida Rio Branco, where they displayed signs and shouted, "Down with the Dictatorship" and "Power to the People."[14]

After the demonstration, the authorities accused Francisco Mangabeira of having used his professorship to subvert the ideology of stu-

[10] *Jornal do Brasil*, March 16, 1966.
[11] Ibid., March 17, 1966.
[12] Ibid., March 19, 1966.
[13] Ibid., March 20, 1966; *O Estado de S. Paulo*, March 20, 1966.
[14] *Jornal do Brasil*, March 25, 1966.

dents. Raimundo Moniz de Aragão, the director of university education, felt that while some agitating students were inspired by ideology, others were eager to become leaders, while still others went along with the demonstrations simply because they were followers or because they felt they should support those who had complaints. He points out that student leaders prior to April, 1964, had been used by the government, which had invested them with privileges and power. They resented the Suplici law, which regulated student elections and the financial affairs of student directorships, and they reacted to the government's closing of the UNE and failure to recognize student organizations that kept independent of the Suplici law.[15] An official note issued by the *diretório acadêmico* of the University of Brazil's School of Philosophy early in April, 1966, condemned "the constant acts of hostility carried out against Brazilian university students."[16]

One "act of hostility" was the decision of the University of Brazil's governing council to charge two hundred cruzeiros (about nine cents U.S.) for each meal served at the university student restaurants. Reitor Pedro Calmon, appearing personally at a restaurant on April 12 in order to try to reopen it, explained to students that the university needed the two-hundred-cruzeiro charge because it had an appropriation of one billion cruzeiros for the meals and was spending two billion. Later he was told by the president of the *diretório acadêmico* of the Engineering School: "We are not in favor of paying the 200 cruzeiros because we understand that, if we do not react, we shall soon have to make monthly tuition payments to our schools." The *reitor*, disappointed, replied that the restaurants would remain closed until all agreed to pay the charge.[17]

While some student leaders suggested a "general strike," others led an invasion of a restaurant. The invasion was followed by a general assembly, held at the Medical School, where it was resolved that the partial university strikes, then in effect, should become a general strike if the government commission, looking into who were responsible for the restaurant invasion, should decree any punishments. Crying "Down with the Dictatorship," the students burned two thousand brochures

[15] Moniz de Aragão, interview, August 2, 1977.
[16] *Jornal do Brasil*, April 5, 1966.
[17] Ibid., April 13, 1966.

that had been sent by the War Ministry to give the students "an idea of what the army seeks to do for the Brazilian people."[18]

Rio housewives, although not as well organized as students, demonstrated against the government's economic policy. Filling the auditorium of the Clube Sírio e Libanês to overflowing on April 12, they listened to the reading of a passionate manifesto that listed the price increases of staples. "Let us pray together," the manifesto said, "not just for the fall of a government or president, but for the overthrow of the malign Plan of Economic Action of the government." The housewives challenged Roberto Campos to a debate and made preparations for a March of the Family with God against the High Cost of Living to take place on April 29. At a meeting held on April 19 to organize the march, the movement was described as opposing "the affliction of the Brazilian people, who endured two years of sacrifices" only to discover that costs in the meantime had risen by "384 percent." Ademar de Barros was invited to attend a further organization meeting on April 26.[19]

The march of April 29 was a disappointment to the organizers, who had expected a turnout of thirty thousand. About fifteen hundred gathered at the Largo do Russel and started for Laranjeiras Palace forty five minutes behind schedule. Singing hymns as they went, they attracted another thirty-five hundred, but for the most part the spectators appeared cold and uninterested. At the palace the marchers left a mild memorandum for Castello Branco that expressed the hope that effective steps would be taken to contain living cost increases.[20]

2. Dialogue

When Castello Branco arrived at the fifth anniversary celebration of the erection of the statue of José de Alencar in Rio, few people clapped. But Academy of Letters President Austregésilo de Ataíde received an effusive applause when he reached the scene to give the oration. "You know," Austregésilo said to the president, "here I am be-

[18] Ibid., April 21, 1966.
[19] Ibid., April 13, 20, 1966.
[20] *O Estado de S. Paulo*, April 30, 1966.

loved and you are not." "You might think," Castello said, "that I seek the adulation of the people. But I do not. I put my duty first."[1]

Amazonas Governor Artur César Ferreira Reis, chatting one afternoon with Castello, said: "Mr. President, do you know that you are the most disliked man in the nation?" "I know," Castello replied quickly. "But that is of no importance. I am fulfilling my duty."[2]

The duty of his government, as Castello explained it at a press conference in Rio March 22, 1966, was to create the best possible conditions for the succeeding administration. This, he said, required the containment of inflation, the renewal of development, the reestablishment of credit abroad, the maintenance of public order, the breaking up of the Communist apparatus, and the conduct of the administration in a serious manner.[3] The renewal of development came slowly. The 5.1 percent increase in the gross national product reported for 1966 was achieved largely in the first half of the year in the industrial sector, where production had declined in 1965. It merely represented, *Conjuntura Econômica* wrote, a renewal of levels reached in 1964.[4]

Dr. Donald E. Syvrud, the U.S. Treasury attaché in Rio at the time, writes that "the causes of the business recession, which were not unique to the 1966 case but cover the entire period since 1962," lay in the lack of investment demand, which, he points out, resurged early in 1967. He also explains that delays characteristic of infrastructure loans from the international institutions "precluded any significant impact on the level of investments for the first few years after 1964."[5] Roberto Campos attributed the disappointingly small flow of investments from the large foreign companies to the time it took them to recover from fears built up in the pre-1964 period. Severo Gomes would add that the opportunities for investment in the industrialized countries remained good until 1967, but that beginning in 1967 they declined, with the result that companies in those countries then showed more interest in placing capital abroad.[6]

[1] Ataíde, interview, August 5, 1977.
[2] Artur César Ferreira Reis, paper for Luís Viana Filho, p. 8.
[3] HACB, *Discursos, 1966*, p. 369.
[4] "Panorama do Ano," *Conjuntura Econômica*, February 1967, pp. 9ff.
[5] Syvrud, *Foundations of Brazilian Economic Growth*, pp. 80, 48.
[6] Severo Gomes, interview, July 25, 1977.

Castello did not limit himself to expressions about doing his duty. He was eager to discuss, with anyone or any group that he felt might be open-minded, the government's position and possible revisions of its policies. However, he was inalterably opposed to setting up a bureau of progovernment propaganda even though he was criticized for not doing so. Osvaldo Trigueiro writes that Castello "respected liberty to criticize, and his austerity would not tolerate that the personal image of the head of the government be converted into a theme of publicity production."[7]

This matter came up one evening in 1966 when Castello was showing Vernon Walters and U.S. Colonel Arthur S. Moura through Alvorada Palace. Walters, noticing a copy of *Tribuna da Imprensa* in the president's bedroom, asked whether its attacks worried the president. Castello said that he slept peacefully, and, in a reference to *Tribuna*'s headline, he asked with a smile whether he was not "a terrible person." Turning to Moura, he asked whether "in the United States also" he was considered terrible. Moura replied that the people in his country were not well informed about what Castello was doing, and he suggested that Castello permit more to be written for the public about his accomplishments. With emphasis the president declared that he had gone to war to fight all that Goebbels stood for and was not going to allow government funds to be used for such publicity as Moura was suggesting.[8]

This position did not mean that he and his cabinet were not to defend the administration in frequent speeches and at gatherings with those who were in disagreement. Roberto Campos was often on the airwaves, quick to reply to attacks. Castello took his message all over Brazil. Speaking near Santos, São Paulo, on March 31, 1966, at the inauguration of the Paulista Steel Company (COSIPA), he stressed the role being given to private enterprise, which was placing large new investments in petrochemicals, and he defended unpopular decisions that had increased electricity and transport charges and the prices of petroleum and wheat. "We could," he explained, "have shown a much faster reduction of the inflation if we had transferred these problems to the future."[9]

[7] Trigueiro, "Humberto Castelo Branco," p. 5.
[8] Moura, interview, December 11, 1974.
[9] HACB, *Discursos, 1966*, pp. 21–22.

Castello engaged in dialogue. For over an hour at Laranjeiras Palace he listened while Paulista Assemblywoman Conceição da Costa Neves told him how badly things were going outside the palace walls, which she said, cut the president off from hearing the people in the streets. Castello said that he thought she was pessimistic, but he agreed to receive an official commission of São Paulo assemblymen, each reporting on the economic conditions in a particular realm of state activity. At the round-table meeting that took place four months after Castello agreed with Conceição to hold it, eleven assemblymen spoke. Following the last report, Castello replied to each assemblyman in order, assessing the contribution of each. As he had made no notes, the visitors were impressed with his memory.[10]

Meeting in Belo Horizonte on April 25, 1966, with university student leaders, Castello said that the government wanted a dialogue but warned that it would be possible only if the students adjusted to the Suplici law and the arrangements established by his Education Ministry. After the meeting the student leaders participated in a student assembly, where they concluded that "there was, in fact, no dialogue" with Castello. They distributed a note stating that the president "did not reply satisfactorily to our questions and, furthermore, demonstrated his intention to divide the university student movement, not recognizing the State Union of Students" (which remained outside the Suplici law).[11] Castello, in a speech in Paraíba on May 2, said that he had no idea of preventing free expression by students but felt that they should oppose "false movements" observable throughout the world and notably in Latin America. He added that "when it is asserted that movements are designed to free Brazil from dictatorship or from the game of a foreign country, we begin to see that, instead of blending with the idealism and purity of youth, they reveal objectives that have nothing to do with Brazil or with students."[12]

In a press interview in Brasília later in the year, Castello said that he had become surprised by the dishonest use of the word *dialogue*. "It is often invoked to cover up a determination not to exchange ideas," he said. Defending his government against the accusation of not having

[10] Conceição da Costa Neves, interview, São Paulo, August 1, 1977; idem, letter to JWFD, São Paulo, September 16, 1977.

[11] *Jornal do Brasil*, April 26, 1966.

[12] HACB, *Discursos, 1966*, pp. 163–167.

used dialogue, he spoke of all the interested groups that had been consulted before decisions had been reached about major pieces of legislation. He noted that as president he had visited ninety-seven Brazilian cities, exchanging impressions. "Dialogue," he said, "requires, above all, an honest revelation of purposes. The government has used it with the spirit of finding the right answers and serving Brazil."[13]

3. Varied Responses of Castello to Attacks (1966)

Among the specific charges with which Castello dealt were those leveled against the ethical conduct of his younger brother and himself and Lacerda's assertion that "the gentleman's agreement' between Castello and Roberto Marinho, of the proadministration *O Globo*, was a "disgrace" for the president.[1]

Humberto's younger brother, Lauro, a long-time Finance Ministry employee, was promoted in 1965 to be head of the tax collection department, made up of eighty-five hundred employees. About a year later, in February, 1966, a government decree increased the salaries of the tax collectors, and therefore early in March the tax collectors in the important São Paulo district received a circular from their local director urging them to attend a lunch to honor Lauro on March 12. The contributions collected from those invited far exceeded the cost of the lunch. When 638 São Paulo tax collectors gathered at the Fasano Restaurant, Lauro received a gift of a new automobile. Deeply moved by this expression of friendship, he accepted the car keys at the lunch.

The press carried the story and advised that the Rio tax collectors would follow the example of their São Paulo colleagues.[2] After Eduardo Lopes Rodrigues, director-general of finance, read about the gift in Rio's *O Jornal* on March 28, he issued a notice stating that Article 195 of the Statute of Public Employees, prohibiting such gifts or the circulation of lists seeking donations for them, would be rigorously upheld.

Much publicity followed a denouncement of Lauro made in the São Paulo state legislature on March 31 by MDB Assemblywoman Conceição da Costa Neves. Speaking dramatically on the revolution's second an-

[13] Ibid., p. 384.

[1] Lacerda, letter to presiding officer of investigating commission of the Justice Ministry, February 24, 1966, File N5 (Anexo 12), CPDOC.

[2] Costa Neves, interview, August 1, 1977; idem, letter to JWFD, September 16, 1977.

niversary, she quoted from the Statute of Public Employees and said that she was sending documents to the president together with a demand that he set up an IPM to investigate. After she declared in the assembly that "this is not the revolution of my dreams," other state legislators said that the leaders of the 1964 movement sought only to maintain their privileges and that corruption was widespread.[3]

The president, following a busy schedule that kept him flying between Santos, Vitória, Brasília, and Rio, was surprised when Geisel told him about Conceição's denouncement, for he had already phoned Lauro and received assurances of no wrongdoing on his part.[4] Following Castello's instructions, Luís Viana Filho ordered an immediate investigation by the director-general of finance, Eduardo Lopes Rodrigues. By this time Lauro had decided that the gift should be refused by him and his family; he persuaded a friend to move the new car from his garage and asked his São Paulo colleagues to come and fetch it.

By late Saturday, April 2, the president had enough information to conclude tearfully that he had to sign a decree dismissing Lauro from his post as director of tax collection. But before the decree of April 2 was published in the *Diário Oficial* on April 4, he spoke with his older brother, Cândido, and his sister, Beatriz. Beatriz, who liked to keep in close touch with the presidency, went to Laranjeiras Palace late at night and found Humberto surprised at what he had learned.[5]

Osvaldo Trigueiro points to this difficult decision by Castello as an example of his refusal to let his position benefit any member of his family. But Conceição renewed her attacks after she learned that Lauro, dismissed from the directorship of tax collections, remained a public servant.[6]

It was not Castello's custom to reply to personal attacks. He made an exception to this rule in August, 1966, after *Tribuna da Imprensa* charged that he was illegally receiving rent in dollars. According to *Tribuna*, Castello was being paid $350 a month for his Rio "house"

[3] *Diário da Noite* [São Paulo], *A Gazeta*, and *Diário Popular*, April 1, 1966; *Diário Oficial* [São Paulo], April 2, 1966.

[4] Júlio Pessoa, interview, November 21, 1975; Moscardo de Souza, interview, October 27, 1975.

[5] *Diário da Noite* [São Paulo], April 5, 1966; Pessoa, interview, November 21, 1975.

[6] Trigueiro, "Humberto Castelo Branco," p. 15; *Diário Oficial* [São Paulo], June 22, 1966, reporting on ordinary session, June 20, 1966.

while it was being occupied by a director of the USAID mission. A note was issued by Presidential Press Secretary José Wamberto explaining that the president owned no house but only Apartment 202 at Rua Nascimento Silva 518, for which he received 450,000 cruzeiros a month in accordance with a contract that would expire on January 31, 1967.[7]

Lacerda's charge that Castello had made a disgraceful gentleman's agreement with Roberto Marinho was the result of the TV Globo contract with Time-Life, which was signed in 1961 after *O Globo* President Marinho had received assurances from lawyers and government officials that it was legal and had notified the president of Brazil of his plans.[8] The joint-venture arrangement included a technical assistance contract and a large loan, which allowed Time-Life a 45 percent participation in the profits and was set up in a form that was legal in the strict sense.[9] But the arrangement seemed to contradict the spirit of Article 160 of the 1964 Constitution, which prohibited newspapers or broadcasters from issuing bearer shares or shares to foreigners and which ruled that Brazilians alone were to have the principal responsibility of giving intellectual and administrative management to newspaper and broadcasting companies. The contract with Time-Life, technically and financially useful in building TV Globo into a powerful broadcaster, was attacked by Congressman João Calmon of the Chateaubriand newspaper chain, which, according to Marinho, had tried and failed to make a deal with another U.S. group.[10]

Lacerda, replying in February, 1966, to an inquiry from the Justice Ministry, said that Castello had promised to investigate the Roberto Marinho–Time-Life deal a year earlier but had failed to keep his word, and Lacerda added that Marinho continued to hold the rank of chancellor of the National Order of Merit. Three months later Marinho wrote Castello that a chancellor of the Order of Merit should not be a person subject to slanderous accusations, and therefore he was resigning from that honorable post.[11]

[7] *Jornal do Brasil*, August 19, 1966.

[8] Marinho, interview, August 11, 1977.

[9] Quandt de Oliveira, interview, October 21, 1975; idem, quoted in *Jornal do Brasil*, May 25, 1966.

[10] Marinho, interview, August 11, 1977; idem, quoted in *Jornal do Brasil*, March 13, 1966.

[11] Lacerda, letter to presiding officer of investigating commission of the Justice

While a congressional inquiry commission examined the TV Globo–Time-Life arrangements, that contract was also studied by a group set up by CONTEL President Euclides Quandt de Oliveira, as recommended by Castello in 1965. Quandt's group reported in May, 1966, that "a whole range of economic and administrative arrangements prevents the affirmation that Time-Life is not participating, perhaps indirectly, in the orientation and administration of TV Globo." The Quandt group gave TV Globo ninety days to adjust the contract to the letter and spirit of the constitution. The report of the congressional commission, issued in August, 1966, called the contract contrary to the constitution and asked the executive branch of the government to punish TV Globo.[12]

Castello's response was to ask Justice Minister Mem de Sá to set up a commission. The three men thus chosen to reach a final decision were the prosecuting attorney of the republic, a lieutenant colonel representing the National Security Council, and a representative of the Central Bank. After Mem de Sá had been succeeded by Carlos Medeiros Silva, the commission, by a two-to-one vote, decided that the TV Globo–Time-Life contract was legal. Medeiros Silva reached the same conclusion after examining all the written agreements, but he acknowledged that he was in no position to say whether unwritten agreements existed.[13] Castello took steps to provide Brazil with tighter legislation that would allow no repetition of the case. Marinho, after enjoying for four more years the exclusive arrangement made possible by the lack of retroactivity of the new legislation, reached an agreement with Time-Life for terminating the much attacked contract.[14]

4. A Workers' Tenure Fund to Stimulate Housing (September, 1966)

When Castello Branco appeared before the Minas state legislature on February 28, 1966, he denied that the burden of the fight against

Ministry, February 24, 1966; Roberto Marinho, letter to HACB, May 24, 1966, File M, CPDOC.

[12] *Jornal do Brasil*, May 25, August 23, 1966.

[13] Medeiros Silva, interview, August 9, 1977.

[14] Marinho, interview, August 11, 1977.

inflation fell almost exclusively on the shoulders of the workers. In his speech, largely written by Roberto Campos,[1] he mentioned steps taken to assure that the rich would pay their income taxes and that companies would no longer withhold contributions payable to the pension institutes. He spoke of the elimination of "speculative credit," with which quick fortunes had been built in the past, and "subsidized credit," which allowed entrepreneurs to become unconcerned with austerity and careful planning.[2]

Castello attacked the "false friends" of labor who promised more than the economy could support and who favored the creation of "artificial" jobs such as those that had loaded the railroads with deficits and made port operations prohibitively costly. These false friends, he said, wanted unrealistically low prices for petroleum, wheat, and electric energy, more of a blessing to the middle and upper classes than to the poor, who had paid for the subsidies in the form of the inflationary issuances of currency. Going on to condemn "false leaders" who in the past had wrecked the finances of the pension institutes and fomented class struggle, Castello declared that "our old political vocabulary and administrative practice abused the expression 'acquired rights.' It is time for us to think a little more about 'unfulfilled duties.' Because a nation whose citizens insist only on the enjoyment of rights, forgetting the discipline of duties, is relegated to economic underdevelopment, the unjust perpetuation of privileges, and moral decomposition."[3]

A part of Castello's speech was devoted to criticizing the thirty-year-old Vargas-instituted arrangement of *estabilidade*, whereby companies could not dismiss workers who had been with them ten years or more. The arrangement, Castello said, was hard on the workers because companies customarily dismissed them before the ten-year deadline was reached, and, he added, it was hard also on the companies, for they found themselves faced with the choice of dismissing workers who had gained experience or of being encumbered with a large number enjoying *estabilidade*, with its "reduction of productivity and slackening of discipline." The rigidity of the system and the accompanying financial burdens, he said, made reorganizations difficult in times of recession, leading to bankruptcies that benefited no one. Fur-

[1] See HACB's notes for the preparation of this speech, File P1 (p. 13), CPDOC.
[2] HACB, *Discursos, 1966*, pp. 9–10.
[3] Ibid., pp. 5–8.

thermore, he pointed out, Brazil should make greater use of automation, which would require mobility in the work force.

Recommending an improved, socially and economically viable system that would provide true guarantees for workers, Castello suggested "a fund of social stability and housing" to be combined with "a system of security" for cases of unemployment. Explaining that the idea was still under study and that the final decision would be made by Congress, he invited labor unions, workers, and employers to submit suggestions.[4]

Organized workers, distrustful of the regime that had followed the fall of Goulart, resolved to inform the president of "the unrest reigning in all the nation in the face of the possible abolition of the *estabilidade* arrangement." Carioca, Paulista, and Minas labor leaders declared themselves totally opposed to replacing the existing system with the proposed fund and described such a step as contrary to the rights of the workers guaranteed by constitutional Article 157 (which mentioned *estabilidade*).[5]

In the meantime a group of technicians, charged with recommending alternatives to the *estabilidade* system, submitted proposals to Roberto Campos and Labor Minister Peracchi Barcelos. On March 10 the government announced that the recommendations were to allow workers the option of abiding by the old system or affiliating with a "Fund of Stability and Housing." The fund, the press reported, would have its value corrected for inflation and would be a charge against the employer—a sort of fourteenth-month salary per year that could be used by workers for the partial financing of residences. Roberto Campos, in an article published in April in support of the proposal, wrote that "man does not live by myths alone." The old system, he contended, promoted *instabilidade* for workers; he said that the new one, with its transferable savings fund, would allow them to switch from a stagnating company. Castello, speaking in Paraíba on May 1, reported that only 1 or 2 percent of the labor force had been on the job between nine and ten years because *estabilidade* encouraged dismissals shortly before the ninth year.[6]

[4] Ibid., pp. 12–13.

[5] *Jornal do Brasil*, March 11, 12, 1966.

[6] Ibid., March 11, 1966; Viana Filho, *O Governo Castelo Branco*, p. 490; HACB, *Discursos, 1966*, p. 40.

But the leaders of the largest labor confederations, those of workers in industry and commerce, continued to oppose the government's ideas despite figures drawn up by the National Housing Bank to confirm Campos' statement that under no conditions would the new system provide smaller indemnification payments than the old one. The labor leaders asked for a plan that would retain *estabilidade* together with the provisions of the new system. The administration rejected the suggestion.[7]

In June, Nascimento Silva and Mário Trindade, of the Housing Bank, delivered their final draft to Campos and Peracchi Barcelos. Early in August, on the occasion of the transfer of the Labor Ministry from Peracchi to Nascimento Silva, Castello's speech was almost entirely devoted to the new law project. He quoted from the "brilliant Exposição de Motivos," which had been written by Campos and Peracchi and which alluded to the doubts raised and the need to present justifications to support the government's ideas.[8]

Castello discussed with Krieger the administration's forthcoming message to Congress about what was now called the "Fundo de Garantia de Tempo e Serviço" (FGTS—Workers' Tenure Guarantee Fund). The senator studied the proposal and then told the president that *estabilidade*, while constantly evaded by large companies, was a mystical matter whose abolition would provoke "unrest and revolt" among the workers. "I have," Castello told him, "a formula for avoiding that reaction." He spoke of the option to be given to all workers, including those who would enter the work force in the future. They could choose to continue with the old system "without a line being changed." Krieger was satisfied.[9]

On August 19, when a commission of senators and congressmen met to give its verdict, the enormous National Confederation of Workers in Industry and the Federation of Workers in Spinning and Weaving condemned alteration of the institution of *estabilidade*. "The option," the confederation declared, "will submit the worker to coercion by the employer."[10]

MDB members of the joint congressional commission refused to

[7] Viana Filho, *O Governo Castelo Branco*, p. 491.

[8] HACB, *Discursos, 1966*, p. 340. Exposição de Motivos: Explanation of Reasons.

[9] Krieger, *Desde as Missões*, p. 210; HACB, *Discursos, 1966*, p. 340.

[10] *Jornal do Brasil*, August 20, 1966.

participate in its decision, but the ARENA had enough votes to send the proposal to the plenary with commission approval. However, in the plenary the obstruction of the MDB was effective, and the government was unable to muster a quorum. After a failure to produce a vote on the night of September 5, the government announced that the law would be promulgated by the executive in accordance with Ato 2 because Congress had not acted within thirty days.[11] Castello promulgated the bill (Law 5,170) on September 13, and on the fourteenth he gave it some refining touches by issuing Decree-Law 20.

The new legislation was the administration's most important step in the field of social legislation. Its advantages for the workers were such that in the following years they opted overwhelmingly to enroll in the new system.[12] At the same time, it provided, for the first time, ample funds for the Housing Bank, which, Syvrud writes, "came to influence about 2 percent of Brazil's national production."[13]

Already the companies and their employees were each contributing 8 percent of wages to the pension institutes. The numerous additional benefits being paid by companies included a few items, adding up to 5.2 percent of wages, that were now consolidated into, or replaced by, the new 8 percent for the Workers' Tenure Guarantee Fund (FGTS) under the administration of the Housing Bank. Mário Trindade, who succeeded Nascimento Silva as Housing Bank president, felt that the consolidation (coming to 8 percent in place of 5.2 percent of wages) represented no loss for the companies since certain dismissal payments actually amounted to more than those previously included in the 5.2 percent.[14]

With the new legislation, separate FGTS accounts for about 7.5 million workers were set up in the private banking network as a trust

[11] Ibid., August 20, September 6, 1966.

[12] Nascimento Silva, interview, October 25, 1975; Arnaldo Sussekind and Júlio César do Prado Leite, interview, Rio de Janeiro, December 20, 1974. As of July 1974, about 92 percent of workers who had the choice were enrolled in the FGTS system (9,698,853 out of 10,556,000) (Departamento de Receita, DRC, July 1974).

[13] Syvrud, *Foundations of Brazilian Economic Growth*, p. 47; Mário Henrique Simonsen, quoted in Viana Filho, *O Governo Castelo Branco*, p. 492, said that the Castello Branco government, in creating the FGTS, accomplished two objectives: "the elimination of the distortions of the old system of worker indemnizations and *estabilidade*," and the production of "the funds necessary for undertaking a housing program on a large scale."

[14] Mário Trindade, interview, Rio de Janeiro, November 28, 1966.

fund managed by the Housing Bank. The accounts, in addition to being subject to the monetary correction for inflation, were to receive 3 to 6 percent interest, depending on the length of their existence. Workers could use the accounts for down payments on housing and could draw on them for other purposes if they could prove exceptional necessity.[15]

5. Friction between the Army and Hélder Câmara (July–August, 1966)

Back in 1960, General Castello Branco had told Catholic intellectual Alceu Amorosa Lima: "I know that you are enthusiastic about the social action of the Church. I, however, consider that the Church is abandoning its religious function too much and intervening excessively in matters belonging to the State. That's what I said, a few days ago in Natal, to Archbishop Dom Eugênio Sales."[1]

In May, 1965, after Dom Hélder Câmara, archbishop of Olinda and Recife, organized a regional seminar of the northeast to focus attention on the misery in that area, Castello wrote a note to Luís Viana Filho: "Dom Hélder speaks at length about development, but he fails to say who should carry it out, not to say promote it. He repeats and repeats that the Church should take care of development and holds a seminar for that. . . . If the Church is separate from the State, material development belongs to the latter, while spiritual development belongs to the Church." Castello added that the Church could help the State by providing explanations, assisting the poor, and even building up a conscience about development.[2]

During the following month the bishop of Santo André, S.P., issued a manifesto blaming Castello and his government for the sufferings in Brazil,[3] and Dom Hélder made declarations in France that were

[15] Ibid.; articles about the FGTS by Délio Maranhão and Arnaldo Sussekind may be found on pp. 457–466 and 493–495 in *Instituições de Direito do Trabalho* by Arnaldo Sussekind, Délio Maranhão, and Segadas Vianna.

[1] Viana Filho, *O Governo Castelo Branco*, pp. 530–531.

[2] Ibid., p. 531.

[3] Orlando Chaves (archbishop of Cuiabá, Mato Grosso), letter to HACB, Cuiabá, June 12, 1965, and to Jorge de Oliveira (bishop of Santo André), Cuiabá, June 11, 1965, File S (pp. 2v, 3), PVCB.

regarded as censuring the Brazilian government. The Brazilian ambassador to the Vatican then had an audience with Pope Paul VI, who praised Cardinal Agnelo Rossi of São Paulo and Archbishop Eugênio Sales of Salvador in contrast to some other Church leaders, who, the pope said, "chose the wrong path." These words encouraged the ambassador to express concern about Dom Hélder's declarations in France, whereupon the pope was quick to say that Dom Hélder's inaugural speech at the regional seminar of the northeast had been unfortunate and that he had so informed Dom Hélder.[4]

Dom Hélder, who had responsibility for the Church's Northeast II area (Pernambuco, Paraíba, Rio Grande do Norte, and Alagoas), called the bishops of that area together in July, 1966, to issue a bishops' declaration that supported the recent manifesto of Workers' Catholic Action, Rural Catholic Action, and Catholic Agrarian Youth denouncing unjust structures of government and society and lamenting police persecutions, violations of labor laws, and the injustices suffered by labor.[5] As a result of the Bishops' Declaration, the army's Tenth Military Region, with headquarters in Fortaleza, distributed on July 22 copies of a "secret circular" describing Dom Hélder as an agitator who took pleasure in "histrionic excesses and show-off attitudes on TV" and who had so disorganized the Church in Pernambuco that it was ripe for Communist infiltration.[6]

Dom José Delgado, head of Northeast I and archbishop of Fortaleza, wrote to Tenth Region Commander Itiberê Gouveia do Amaral, saying that the Brazilian army should not be identified with soldiers who attacked Dom Hélder, "acclaimed in Europe and the Americas as one of the greatest Brazilians of the historic moment in which we live." In a letter to Castello, José Delgado said that the army circular had been distributed to priests and religious groups, bypassing the bishops. "In the history of the Brazilian army," he wrote, "never has there been so absurd an occurrence and one deserving of greater repulsion." He

[4] Henrique Sousa Gomes, letter to HACB, File O2 (p. 38), PVCB.

[5] *Le Monde* (Paris), August 31, 1966, quoted in *Jornal do Brasil*, September 1, 1966; José de Broucker, *Dom Hélder Câmara: The Violence of a Peacemaker*, p. 43; Schneider, *The Political System of Brazil*, p. 235.

[6] Schneider, *The Political System of Brazil*, p. 235; Remo Rocha (chief of staff of the 10th RM), *Ofício* to José de Medeiros Delgado, Fortaleza, July 22, 1966, File S (p. 11), PVCB.

condemned also methods used in Recife, including distribution there of the same circular, to combat Dom Hélder.[7]

In Recife, General Antônio Carlos da Silva Murici, commander of the Seventh Military Region, had been trying to comply with Castello's instructions to avoid a clash between the Church and the government, but he had found Dom Hélder "rather vain."[8] As a result of arrangements made by Murici, Castello had a long conversation with Dom Hélder at the governor's palace on August 14, when the president visited the northeast. After Dom Hélder defended his position, Castello urged him to make denials when the press misquoted him sensationally. The talk went well, and each left with the impression that the other sincerely wanted to contribute to relaxing the strain.[9] A contribution by Castello was the immediate transfer of General Itiberê Gouveia do Amaral from his command of the Tenth Military Region.[10] Cardinal Agnelo Rossi of São Paulo, the president of the Central Commission of the National Conference of Bishops of Brazil, wrote to Castello to congratulate him on his "intelligent, opportune, and efficacious initiative of conversing with D. Hélder Câmara, thus dissipating an unpleasant atmosphere of conflict between the Church and State that some want to build up in order to exploit popular discontent and nourish a sensationalist press."[11]

But when Castello addressed the Federal University of Pernambuco on August 15, he upset Dom Hélder. The president told his audience that what was unjust and incomprehensible was that responsible people still sought to use the suffering of the northeasterners as a motive for propaganda and agitation. He said that such attitudes, if not harmful, would in no way reduce or shorten "the anguish of those who suffer, not as a result of the errors or injustices of today, but thanks to the injustices and errors accumulated over many decades and which we

[7] José de Medeiros Delgado, letter to Itiberê Gouveia do Amaral, August 6, 1966, File S (pp. 14v, 15), PVCB, and to HACB, Fortaleza, August 6, 1966, File S (pp. 13v, 14), PVCB.

[8] Antônio Carlos da Silva Murici, interview, Rio de Janeiro, November 18, 1975.

[9] *Jornal do Brasil*, August 16, 1966; HACB, letter to Hélder Câmara, Rio de Janeiro, August 28, 1966, File S (p. 18), PVCB; Hélder Câmara, letter to HACB, Recife, August 18, 1966, File S (p. 17), PVCB.

[10] De Broucker, *Dom Hélder Câmara*, p. 44.

[11] Agnelo Rossi, letter to HACB, São Paulo, August 20, 1966, File S (p. 16), PVCB.

are seeking to repress with energy and determination. The duty of each and every one, a duty that is the greater the higher one is in the hierarchy, is not simply to proclaim the suffering that we all recognize, but to point out remedies and cooperate with public and private entities" seeking to overcome underdevelopment.[12]

As Castello said in his speech, it would take time to remedy the situation in the northeast, and, as he also said, effective work was being done especially by SUDENE (the Superintendency for the Development of the Northeast). João Gonçalves de Sousa, a technician who became head of SUDENE in mid-1964, had eliminated prejudices in the organization against private enterprise and the United States and had defeated threats by congressmen and others to end the legislation that provided income tax deductions for all who would invest in the northeast. New private investments (stimulated by this legislation), together with contributions by USAID and the funds for investment on hand earlier in the Bank of the Northeast, were being used to start enough new projects in the region to give the appearance of the beginning of an industrial boom there.[13]

Dom Hélder Câmara wrote to Castello on August 18, 1966, to say that on the fourteenth he had found him eager to end mistakes that had caused trouble, and therefore those responsible for Northeast I (José Delgado) and Northeast III (Eugênio Sales) had been on the point of joining Dom Hélder in drawing up a tranquilizing note. However, Dom Hélder continued, the president's speech on August 15 in Recife, as reported by the press, was unfriendly and contained "undisguised and unfair references to the Declaration of the Bishops."[14]

Castello, replying to Dom Hélder on August 28, said that he had sought to repel the unjust accusations of those who denied the zealous and persistent effort of the government to revive the northeast. In a reference to Dom Hélder's expressed hope that the presidential press secretary would dispel intrigues, perhaps caused by the way in which the press reported Castello's speech, Castello wrote that no denials had ever been issued when evangelical priests had given Dom Hélder their

[12] HACB, *Discursos, 1966*, p. 222.

[13] João Gonçalves de Sousa, interviews, Rio de Janeiro, November 28, 1966, and Washington, D.C., June 11, 1975; idem, "Luta contínua pelo manutenção do mecanismo do 34/18 e o Presidente" (paper prepared for Luís Viana Filho), n.d.

[14] Câmara, letter to HACB, August 18, 1966.

support in the "struggle against oppression and in favor of justice for the oppressed and persecuted," despite the attack against the government contained in those words.[15]

Before Castello wrote this letter, two developments occurred: sociologist Gilberto Freire became engaged in a public controversy with Dom Hélder, and Castello changed the command of the Fourth Army, whose headquarters were in Recife. Freire, in letters to Dom Hélder that appeared in the press, accused the archbishop of serving the "leftist cause" and referred to "a dangerous politicizing that could make Brazilian Catholicism an auxiliary line of Communism." Freire wrote that Dom Hélder enjoyed political struggle and was opposing a government which was freeing Brazil from the chaos of 1964.[16]

Castello's choice of General Rafael de Sousa Aguiar to head the Fourth Army was a good one, because Sousa Aguiar had become very friendly with Dom Hélder in Rio in the 1950's, especially when the general had helped put out a fire in a slum.[17] Sousa Aguiar, head of the First Military Region since Castello's trouble with the hard line there, was invited with his wife to lunch at Laranjeiras Palace. During the meal the president informed his guest of his new mission, which meant advancing him in rank. Asking him to take over the Recife post in two days, Castello said, "The Fourth Army is in conflict with the federal government, the state government, and the clergy. I want you to end all of these." Castello explained that Fourth Army Commander Francisco Damasceno Ferreira Portugal had asked to be retired to the reserve following the discovery of a bomb at the front door of his residence.[18]

Sousa Aguiar, parting from the First Military Region on August 22, promised to "maintain a dialogue of peace with Father Hélder Câmara." But when he reached Recife the next day, Dom Hélder, as the press noted, was not on hand for his arrival or his takeover of the command.[19]

Although Dom Hélder and Sousa Aguiar tried to see each other on the twenty-fourth, they missed at first and did not meet until later in

[15] HACB, letter to Câmara, August 28, 1966.

[16] *Jornal do Brasil*, August 24, 1966.

[17] Sousa Aguiar, interview, August 8, 1977.

[18] Ibid.

[19] *Jornal do Brasil*, August 23, 24, 1966; Sousa Aguiar, interview, August 8, 1977.

the day, by which time the new commander's chief of staff issued an Army Week proclamation praising the ideas of Professor Gilberto Freire and warning against "the slavery of Moscow and Peking." When at length Dom Hélder met with his old friend, he said, "General, I did not go to your command takeover because I was afraid that I would be mistreated by your officers." Sousa Aguiar replied: "You forget that as commander, I command, and that in my area and in my house God is always present. In my area, and in my house, you will never be mistreated."[20]

The appointment of Sousa Aguiar solved the immediate crisis that had arisen between Fourth Army officers and Dom Hélder. Late in 1966 *Jornal do Brasil* wrote that the general "obtained the best results in the northeast, adopting persuasive procedures to establish normalcy in the relations between the Church fathers and the army officers."[21]

But the conflict of July and August had stirred up much comment, and throughout the latter part of August and early September voices continued to be raised in favor of Dom Hélder. The archbishop of Vitória denounced the "semidictatorial state" and said that the word of Hélder Câmara, although "often irksome," was "opportune and just." The archbishop of Teresina praised Dom Hélder's "unusual and significant qualities" and described him as "a man who lives, with passion, the drama of the third world." The archbishop of Aracajú stated that capitalism was cruel and inhuman. Speaking for Protestants, the president of the Latin American Church and Society Council suggested that the "conservative" position of Gilberto Freire might be due to his advanced age, and he joined the president of the Council of Methodist Bishops in declaring that "the Protestants condemn the exploitation of man by man."[22]

In Minas, Father José de Sousa Nobre, an MDB congressman, warned Castello that "the Church does not relinquish, under any circumstances, its right to express its opinion about social justice." The MDB of Minas, giving a unanimous vote of support for Dom Hélder, approved a statement that spoke of "the rightist dictatorship that suffocates us, turning our people over to international and national mono-

[20] Sousa Aguiar, interview, August 8, 1977; *Jornal do Brasil*, August 25, 1966.

[21] Schneider, *The Political System of Brazil*, p. 235; *Jornal do Brasil*, November 26, 1966.

[22] *Jornal do Brasil*, August 26, 28, September 2, 6, 7, 1966.

polistic groups." The statement praised the "lucid and courageous manifesto of the bishops of the northeast."[23]

In Paris, *Le Monde* wrote that "Dom Hélder was once again accused of being a Communist, which provoked a movement in his defense by a part of the Catholic organizations and Protestant groups. The movement became so great that the government was forced to abandon its plan to push the clergy aside."[24]

Castello conferred with Cardinals Augusto Silva (Bahia), Agnelo Rossi (São Paulo), and Jaime de Barros Câmara (Guanabara). On August 25, Papal Nuncio Sebastião Baggio, leaving Laranjeiras Palace after seeing Castello, told the press that he considered the religious-military conflict in the northeast "the result of mistakes in understanding that we are trying to eradicate."[25]

Writing to Archbishop Eugênio Sales on September 9, Castello said: "Your Most Reverend Person knows of my respect for the prelates, your companions, here in Brazil. My attitude as a citizen, Catholic, and president cannot be otherwise. And therefore I am filled with perplexity and heartbreak when I see accusations against me and members of my government due to the want of respect of archbishops, bishops, and priests. Believe me that it has been even with humility that I have read the declarations of solidarity with the Archbishop of Olinda and Recife."[26]

6. An Attempt to Kill Costa e Silva (July 25, 1966)

At the national convention of the ARENA, held in Brasília on May 26, Costa e Silva and Pedro Aleixo were nominated for the presidency and vice-presidency of the republic, each receiving 329 out of 361 votes.[1] During June, Castello accepted the resignations of Coordination of Regional Agencies Minister Cordeiro de Farias and Justice Minister Mem de Sá. Both opposed the Costa e Silva candidacy, and Mem de Sá was further disturbed by the manner in which Castello

[23] Ibid., August 30, 1966.

[24] *Le Monde*, August 31, 1966, quoted in *Jornal do Brasil*, September 1, 1966.

[25] *Jornal do Brasil*, August 26, 28, 1966; HACB, letter to Agnelo Rossi, Rio de Janeiro, September 9, 1966, File S (p. 23v), PVCB.

[26] HACB, letter to Eugênio de Araújo Sales, Rio de Janeiro, September 9, 1966, File S (p. 24), PVCB.

[1] *Jornal do Brasil*, May 27, 1966.

handled the gubernatorial succession in Rio Grande do Sul. Late in June, Castello also had to accept the resignations of Costa e Silva and Pedro Aleixo.

The education post went to Professor Raimundo Moniz de Aragão, director of university education, and the justice ministry post was again filled provisionally by Luís Viana Filho. In the case of the Coordination of Regional Agencies, Castello accepted Cordeiro's suggestion that SUDENE head João Gonçalves de Sousa be his successor. At the transfer-of-office ceremony in Brasília on June 15, João Gonçalves de Sousa had the awkward experience of finding himself standing between Castello and Cordeiro when they were both so filled with emotion that they seemed to be about to fall into each other's arms.[2] Castello read notes that he had jotted down about his feeling for Cordeiro, his "old companion of war, peace, and revolution," the army general who during difficult days in Italy in 1944 had revealed himself "more than a brother-in-arms—a friend."[3]

As the press reported, Castello kept the country guessing about his choice of a new war minister. He rather enjoyed keeping Vernon Walters guessing. During a chat with Walters, with whom he occasionally enjoyed a dish of ice cream, he suddenly switched the conversation to ask: "Who do you think I am going to appoint minister of war? Just tell me your guess; I won't tell you even if you guess right." Walters said that Castello probably would not name Lyra Tavares, "as you feel he would make a good minister for Costa e Silva," or Geisel, "as you want to save him for the future. I think you will want a man in whom you have complete confidence, and who knows your thinking, to see Brazil through the difficult electoral period." Walters guessed Petrobrás President Ademar de Queiroz, and although Castello had already asked Ademar de Queiroz, not a muscle on the president's face moved as he simply said: "Well, you will find out in a day or so." After the appointment became known the following afternoon, Castello phoned Walters to say: "That was a good guess. Do you have any tips on the horses, Walters?"[4]

[2] Gonçalves de Sousa, interview, June 11, 1975.

[3] HACB, "Discurso na Saída de Osvaldo Cordeiro de Farias," Brasília, June 15, 1966, File M (p. 52), CPDOC.

[4] Walters, interview, June 12, 1975; idem, "Humberto de Alencar Castello Branco," p. 3.

Castello's choice of the retired marshal, his closest friend, surprised those who had been thinking of an active four-star general, such as Décio Escobar, Lyra Tavares, Adalberto Pereira dos Santos, or Orlando Geisel.[5] The selection was followed by a transfer-of-office ceremony at which the president aimed his fire at those who, he said, would listen to his words and study his gestures in order to twist the truth and even produce shameless lies about his relations with Costa e Silva.[6]

Castello, visiting Bahia with his new war minister on July 25, was in an expansive and happy mood, laughing at the commentaries of Ademar de Queiroz. At a recently discovered oil field the president delivered a short improvised speech in which he said that Petrobrás was better off for having abandoned the old "nationalistic" dogma of being "untouchable" and that the government preferred that "the company be untouchable in the fulfillment of its programs and projects."[7]

On that morning Costa e Silva was campaigning in the northeast. Scheduled to fly from Fortaleza to Recife, he learned that his plane had engine trouble and set out, instead, by car. Therefore he was not at the Recife airport when a bomb went off amidst the large crowd gathered to receive him. It killed two local officials and a member of the Guarda Civil and injured nine people. At the same time, two other bombs exploded in downtown Recife, causing property damage at the student union headquarters and the U.S. Information Service movie theater.[8]

Costa e Silva, after his late arrival, visited the wounded and declared that the criminal assault would not alter his pacific strategy. The federal government said that Castello would not "depart from normality." Juraci Magalhães spoke of the threats of Fidel Castro to wage revolutionary war in Brazil, and John dos Passos, in Brazil to write a book, declared that the attempt to kill Costa e Silva "is good evidence of the power of the Communists in Pernambuco."[9]

Pernambuco police, checking personal indentifications and arresting known Communists, turned three suspects, all young Peruvians,

[5] *Jornal do Brasil*, June 21, 1966.

[6] Ibid., July 22, 1966; HACB, *Discursos, 1966*, pp. 327–330.

[7] *Jornal do Brasil*, July 26, 1966.

[8] *Brazil Herald*, July 26, 1966.

[9] *Jornal do Brasil*, July 26, 27, 1966; *Brazil Herald*, July 26, 1966.

over to the Fourth Army barracks on July 26. One was Ciro Coronado, charged with stealing the key to a room in which Costa e Silva was to meet with SUDENE technicians, and another was his sister, Dora, a SUDENE employee. Although a third, a Peruvian student, was released on July 28, another Peruvian was locked up in his place.[10]

Castello had recommended "a rapid and austere inquiry,'[11] but the inquiry did nothing to solve the case. With the suspects still under arrest late in August, a secretary of the Peruvian Embassy went to Recife. Declaring that the innocence of his countrymen had been "thoroughly proved," he called on Archbishop Hélder Câmara for support. The archbishop assured the diplomat that it would be a pleasure to fulfill his Christian duty by providing moral and spiritual help to the arrested Peruvians. Following their release on September 2, the mother of Ciro and Dora Coronado came from Peru to take her children back to their native land. But they were unwilling to leave Recife.[12]

Elsewhere in Brazil late in August, authorities arrested others who they believed were responsible for trying to kill Castello and Costa e Silva. The individual accused of plotting against Castello's life escaped from an army hospital in Rio, where he was being held for a mental examination, and found asylum in the Embassy of Uruguay. The alleged new attempt against Costa e Silva was blamed on a twenty-year-old student who was found with a .22-caliber automatic in a hotel in Manaus when the presidential candidate was campaigning there.[13]

7. Student Demonstrations (July–September, 1966)

While Raimundo Moniz de Aragão, the new education minister, worked on the restructuring of university education, he was faced with student unrest. It began after Castello Branco signed the decree of July 25 that closed the State Union of University Students (UEE) of Minas Gerais, an important component of the already outlawed UNE.

The UEE of Minas, according to Golberi and the SNI, was promot-

[10] *Brazil Herald*, July 27, 1966; *Jornal do Brasil*, July 27, 29, September 4, 1966.
[11] *Jornal do Brasil*, July 27, 1966.
[12] Ibid., September 4, 1966.
[13] Ibid., August 25, 1966.

ing meetings "of unmistakable Communist inspiration."[1] But this description did not mean that all was well between the Brazilian Communist Party (PCB) and Ação Popular (AP), the offshoot of Catholic University Action (JUC). AP, which was dislodging the PCB in the now nonlegal university student organizations, condemned the PCB's reluctance to advocate violence. "Texts for Militants," "Revolutionary Strategy," and other bulky mimeographed documents of AP sought to prepare for the violent overthrow of Brazil's social and political structure and preached the need of "pure socialism" to replace what AP called United States–supported capitalism and imperialism. Although keen rivals, AP and the PCB agreed on the need to campaign against the Suplici law, the "Brazilian dictatorship," and the government's attempt to collect annual tuitions of about thirteen U.S. dollars (twenty-eight thousand cruzeiros) per student for university education.[2]

When student leaders convened in Belo Horizonte on July 28 to participate in the UNE's twenty-eighth National Congress, the military police sought to prevent the congress from taking place, leading Congressman Simão da Cunha (MDB, Minas) to accuse the government of wanting "to massacre the students."[3] The police, apparently successful, made eight arrests, bringing the total of arrested students in Belo Horizonte to twenty-seven. But the remaining UNE delegates were given asylum by religious orders, which the authorities did not wish to invade. On the night of July 28, the 152 UNE delegates (including 53 from Minas, 37 from São Paulo, and 23 from Paraná) moved from the Dominican convent to the Franciscan convent, where they held their congress on July 29.[4]

The lack of government support among the university students was revealed in August, when, in accordance with the Suplici law, elections for *diretórios acadêmicos* were held at ten university-level schools or colleges in Guanabara, about 25 percent of the total in the area. All but one of those ten chose slates of officers who opposed the government and the Suplici law. For example, the Federal University law students, voting for the directorship of CACO (Centro Acadêmico Cândido de Oliveira), elected a slate that declared the UNE to be the

[1] *Jornal do Brasil*, July 28, 1966.
[2] Ibid., September 14, 1966.
[3] Ibid., July 28, 1966.
[4] Ibid., July 30, 1966.

only authentic representative of the students.[5] Vladimir Palmeira, who won the CACO presidency by 871 votes to 500, campaigned against the payment of tuition for higher education (a provision of the 1946 Constitution that was only made effective when the Castello Branco administration called for symbolic payments).

At the School of Architecture on September 8, Vladimir Palmeira gave a rousing speech to students of architecture, engineering, law, philosophy, and chemistry during a meeting that had been forbidden by the director of the School of Architecture. "For several years," Palmeira said, "we have been required to ask permission of USAID before saying or doing anything. The epoch in which we accept punishments in silence has ended. The fight against tuitions is the fight against dictatorship." The students resolved to hold a march on September 15.[6]

The *conselho* (directive council) of the Federal University of Rio de Janeiro decided to dissolve the *diretório acadêmico* of the School of Architecture, whereupon the *diretório acadêmico* promoted a strike that was joined by engineering, law, and medical students. The university *conselho* then closed the venerable CACO with the aid of the police. Law students, yelling "UNE, UNE, UNE," and "Down with the dictatorship," held a protest meeting.[7]

In São Paulo, forty-eight hundred students of the School of Philosophy were already on strike because one student, seized on September 7 when the police prevented a São Paulo UEE congress, remained under arrest. In Belo Horizonte university students scheduled a parade to protest the São Paulo imprisonment, the closing of the CACO, and the federal government's "general arbitrariness" and "inability to conduct a dialogue."[8]

Castello had never hesitated to express his views to students. Luís Antônio da Gama e Silva recalls an incident that occurred during an earlier São Paulo student strike when Castello, being driven from a formal university affair in a car with Gama e Silva, Ademar de Barros, and Geisel, was booed by about two hundred students. The president

[5] Ibid., August 21, 1966; a short history of the CACO is in the September 11, 1966, issue.

[6] Ibid., September 9, 1966.

[7] Ibid., September 10, 13, 1966.

[8] Ibid., September 13, 1966.

ordered the car stopped and got out. Looking rather small as he faced the students (with their placards that disparaged the government), he gave an improvised speech about the role of the educator, the university, and the students. The president, Gama e Silva says, was in excellent form and was applauded when he finished.[9]

At Laranjeiras Palace on September 13, 1966, Castello expressed his views during a ceremony in which he delivered twenty billion cruzeiros to the University Foundation for Economic and Social Development. The creation of the foundation, he said, offered young people "the opportunity to transfer the empty protest and the shouting of slogans into effective action for correcting injustices, reducing sufferings, and perfecting the productive capacity of the community."

> I speak to you with the authority of one who is prepared to resolve problems instead of postpone them, of one who renounces being agreeable in order to be useful, of one who believes that this nation needs austere and rational administrators and not charismatic personalities who sometimes dangerously confuse their own personal glorification with the destinies of the nation.
>
> Our youth has been stimulated only to contemplate and condemn the injustices that still persist in our social system. This condemnation is necessary and, when it comes from young people, is authentic. But I am worried about the lack of connection between this protest and a constructive and renovative perception of the Brazilian reality.
>
> The government understands that it has become urgent to have an alliance between those who condemn what exists and those who construct what is necessary.[10]

On the next day Education Minister Moniz de Aragão used a radio-television network to appeal to parents not to let students participate in the parade planned to be held in Rio on the fifteenth, for, he said, the police would have to prevent it in the absence of the fulfillment of the legal steps for holding it. "The objective of the parade, he said, "may be to bring about a conflict, creating a victim, and we

[9] Gama e Silva, interview, November 5, 1975.

[10] *Jornal do Brasil*, September 14, 1966.

cannot allow anyone to be sacrificed to spurious ideas and to serve the instigators of disorder."[11]

Despite the plea, about one thousand students tried to march in downtown Rio and clashed with the police; during the melee a bomb exploded at the Municipal Theater, and the use of tear gas sent crowds scurrying from Rio Branco Avenue. The police suffered five injuries and the students none, but about fifty students were arrested. Governor Negrão de Lima pointed out that if the students had requested legal permission for their parade, it would have been granted and the repression avoided. Lacerda said that the outbreak had been "inevitable because youth wants a revolution that was not carried out."[12]

8. The "Day of Protest against the Dictatorship" (September 22, 1966)

Following the disturbance in Rio on September 15 and a similar one in Porto Alegre on the sixteenth, Raimundo Moniz de Aragão declared that many who had been arrested were not students but individuals with police records who had infiltrated the students. The students, he said, had the mission of purging the agitators and, if they wished, could open a dialogue with the authorities, provided that they did not first impose demands.[1]

Student leaders replied by proclaiming that September 22 was to be observed all over Brazil as the "National Day of Protest against the Dictatorship." While in many cities students prepared to start demonstrating late on the twenty-first, Castello issued orders to have the police avoid excesses "in order to prevent the agitators from achieving their objective: the beating of students for protesting against the government." Speaking in Planalto Palace with Raimundo Moniz de Aragão, whom he had called to Brasília, the president recommended "the maximum of moderation, without, however, hurting the maintenance of public order."[2]

[11] Ibid., September 15, 1966.
[12] Ibid. and *Brazil Herald*, September 16, 1966.
[1] *Jornal do Brasil*, September 17, 1966.
[2] Ibid., September 22, 1966.

The education minister, leaving Castello's office, told the press that the student movement had become exclusively political in character and was following the lead of professional agitators. In the Chamber of Deputies, Raimundo Padilha stated that "the instructions of international Communism are being rigorously fulfilled by the leaders of the Brazilian student movement."[3]

Late on September 21 and on September 22, students and police clashed in São Paulo, Rio de Janeiro, Brasília, Goiânia, Fortaleza, Curitiba, and Salvador, and student strikes were announced in Natal, João Pessoa, and elsewhere. Students in Belo Horizonte held a "public mass meeting" or "trial" for judging the Castello Branco administration, and, after the administration was condemned "unanimously" at the meeting, the students celebrated by singing the national anthem.[4]

The demonstration in São Paulo, undertaken by three thousand students on the twenty-first, was only partially suppressed by the police. In Brasília students sought to confuse the police by holding a series of "lightning meetings," and some of them, shouting "Down with Imperialism," used steel bars to smash the glass front of the Thomas Jefferson Library of the U.S. Information Service. In Salvador, after the police made one hundred arrests, author Jorge Amado called the repression "a repetition of the times of Hitler" and described the students as "the victims of the most bestial violence."[5]

In Rio, about five hundred students barricaded themselves in the School of Medicine building. Governor Negrão de Lima wanted to use the police, but kindhearted Reitor Pedro Calmon objected.[6] Calmon, however, failed to persuade the students to leave, and therefore the education minister authorized the police to act. Although it was 3:00 A.M., by which time many students were exhausted, the invasion of the school was not peaceful. The police, met by a hail of stones and other missiles, used tear gas before they forced an entry, and then they allowed the students to depart in small groups. Thirty-two people, among them ten policemen, were admitted to hospitals, but only one,

[3] Ibid.

[4] Ibid., September 23, 1966.

[5] Ibid. and *Brazil Herald*, September 23, 1966.

[6] Moniz de Aragão, interview, August 2, 1977.

a policeman, needed more than one day of treatment. The school's installations were damaged.[7]

The "National Day of Protest" resulted in one fatality. In Goiânia a Military Police corporal was killed during an intense exchange of shots while the police sought to guarantee that classes could be held. Castello, in a telegram to the governor, lamented the death and observed that "the fulfillment of duty does not exclude risk, especially when the folly of some is directed by the confection of objectives contrary to Brazil. It is well known that the goal of such guides is coldly to bring about 'the sacrifice of a student.' "[8]

Despite skirmishes in Goiânia and Recife in the following days, students in most of the states returned quickly to their classrooms. Moniz de Aragão, meeting with Castello at Laranjeiras Palace on September 26, proposed dialogues between representatives of the government and the *diretórios acadêmicos,* and he reviewed the final draft of his plan to restructure the federal universities.

The law project, which Castello sent to Congress on September 27, divided university teaching into two steps (the first to handle preprofessional basics and the second to handle professional knowledge); it prohibited a university from having two or more organs devoted to the same purpose (whereby, for example, chemistry was taught in each of a number of schools or colleges); and it ended the separation of teaching and research (stipulating that each department should have both). The law project, it was hoped, would provide better utilization of available resources and more unity to the university concept.[9]

Pedro Calmon, *reitor* of the Federal University of Rio de Janeiro for eighteen years, was surrounded by unfriendly students in a room of the Law School. They shouted "assassin, assassin" and demanded an explanation of the recent police invasion of the School of Medicine. The *reitor* maintained that the circumstances were not suitable for holding a dialogue, but finally he said that he had not ordered the invasion. Only with difficulty was he able to break through the students and

[7] *Brazil Herald*, September 24, 1966.

[8] *Jornal do Brasil*, September 23, 1966; HACB, notes for telegram to Otávio Lajé, File P1 (p. 15), CPDOC.

[9] Moniz de Aragão, interview, October 29, 1975; *Jornal do Brasil*, September 28, 1966.

take an elevator to another floor, and he did not leave the building until most of the students had left.[10]

While authorities of the university carried out an investigation to look into the disrespect shown to the *reitor,* the thirty-eight–member *conselho* of the university selected Moniz de Aragão for a three-year term to succeed Calmon as *reitor* (a post which Moniz de Aragão could occupy only briefly as long as Castello, who wanted him in the Education Ministry, was president). Later the *conselho* ratified the expulsions of some students and extended the date by which tuitions were to be paid. Despite pressure, many students paid their tuitions. The Law School director, whose expulsion list included the name of Vladimir Palmeira, declared that all law students had paid their tuitions and that a new strike, planned by "the extinct CACO," was a complete failure. "We are," he said, "faced with a grave dilemma: either we expel the agitators of this establishment or we shall have to close it down. They even supply bombs to be thrown in the school."[11]

On October 3, when Costa e Silva became president-elect by the vote of 295 federal legislators, law students in São Paulo set up a voting booth to get the opinions of passers-by. They reported that the approximately five thousand ballots gave the lead to Kubitschek and Lacerda. Students in Belo Horizonte sponsored a march of protest against the election of Costa e Silva. It attracted about five hundred demonstrators and resulted in the arrest of fifteen students, eight of whom were released quickly. When the Minas students of medicine, engineering, and law cast their votes for officers of the *diretórios acadêmicos* later in October, the balloting was won by the candidates affiliated with the UNE.[12]

Castello's concern about the student movement has been mentioned by Aliomar Baleeiro, who, late in September, attended a lunch in Brasília at which Castello was present. The president was in a particularly good mood, joking about some of the press attacks against him. But during the lunch Geisel informed Castello about the violence of students during and following the attack on the Thomas Jefferson Library. Castello became somber.[13]

[10] *Jornal do Brasil*, September 28, 1966.

[11] Ibid., October 13, 1966.

[12] Ibid., October 4, 6, 20, 1966.

[13] Baleeiro, "Recordações do Presidente H. Castelo Branco," p. 36.

The president, at a press conference in Brasília on October 1, replied to a question about "the recent demonstrations by students." Explaining that the essential thing was to give university students the knowledge necessary to carry out a profession, and that the Education Ministry was being equipped to do this, he added that the university student should also be permitted to gain experience for engaging in public life. "However," he said, "the guarantee of student liberty must not be confused with agitation carried out for purposes that are neither civic nor political. The attack on the library, crowned with the name of Thomas Jefferson, cannot be included among the items listed as student demands." Castello praised an *O Globo* editorial which pointed out that the sacrifice of a soldier in Goiás might, instead, have turned out to be the sacrifice of a student and which said that the students, due to inexperience, were serving those who wanted to reap political dividends from a climate of national disturbance.[14]

There was no great movement of national disturbance during the Castello Branco presidency. But the small minority of activists among the university students, including those who favored the violent overthrow of the social and political structure, was successful in provoking clashes. The activists might be said to have gained some practice which they could use later. About a year after Castello left office, they found themselves with a martyr when a youth was killed during a demonstration. Subsequently, the student movement became so violent that it made the occurrences before 1968 seem mild.[15]

The progressive wing of the Church did not create a serious problem for the Castello Branco government, which handled the trouble in the northeast effectively. Here again, developments became much worse after Castello left office. Ronald M. Schneider has written that "whereas Castelo had managed to avoid significant clashes with the

[14] HACB, *Discursos, 1966*, pp. 382–383.

[15] See Georges-André Fiechter, *Brazil since 1964*, pp. 138–140, for an account of student unrest, 1966–1968, and for a distribution of univeristy students, based on *O Cruzeiro* (December 9, 1967), in categories of active or passive, and in categories of conservatives, moderate reformers, or revolutionaries; the survey, made in 1964, shows 15 percent as active and 85 percent as passive; Fiechter writes that "the active stream represented 3 per cent conservatives, 7 percent more-or-less moderate reformers and 5 per cent revolutionaries."

Church (although the hard line took verbal pot shots at the progressive clergy), the Costa e Silva regime quickly found itself embroiled in a series of conflicts with reform minded sectors of the clergy."[16]

Most surprising was the failure of the protest movement by those who suffered deeply from the effects of the Castello Branco government's fight against the inflation. Even those who sponsored the São Paulo March of Silence and the Rio March of the Family with God against the High Cost of Living had to admit that the numbers participating were extremely disappointing. The economic pain was widespread, but perhaps many felt that the circumstances were no longer such that the size of the marches might influence events and policies.

Organized labor followed an old historical pattern by remaining rather quiet when the economy was poor. Contributing factors may have been the Revolution's removal of some of Brazil's most effective labor leaders and the enactment and application of the strike legislation of the new regime. When organized labor did choose a cause, the defeat of the Workers' Tenure Guarantee Fund (FGTS), it hardly made a good selection.

[16] Schneider, *The Political System of Brazil*, p. 233.

IX

Electoral Contests and The Frente Ampla

(May-December, 1966)

At the elections of November 15 the people will render their decision not about me but about the whole policy of the Revolution that we have carried out, as well as its future.

1. The Sao Paulo ARENA Chooses a Gubernatorial Candidate (May, 1966)

THE ARENA of São Paulo, a collection of old political rivals, revealed its disunity in March, 1966, when the officers of the state legislature were chosen. Although eighty-nine assemblymen were considered to be associated with the ARENA, giving it a large majority, forty of the eighty-nine rejected the "official candidate" and joined with twenty-four MDB assemblymen to elect an assembly president supported by the opposition.[1]

This outcome in the assembly, which had the responsibility of choosing a new governor later in the year, was explained in a memorandum sent to Castello Branco by state ARENA President Arnaldo Cerdeira and other local party officers. They called the opposition victory a victory for the forces of Governor Ademar de Barros, former Governors Quadros and Carvalho Pinto, and Mayor Faria Lima and mentioned the excellent climate for demagoguery created by the federal government's economic-financial and labor policies. These analysts also mentioned corruption ("proposals of payments in the plenary") and the role of Quadros in giving the opposition much more discipline than was evident in the ARENA.[2]

In memorandums written to Castello a little later, Cerdeira com-

[1] *Jornal do Brasil*, March 13, 1966; Arnaldo Cerdeira, Batista Ramos, Antônio Feliciano, Hamilton Prado, and Pereira Lopes, "Conclusões a serem tiradas dos resultados da eleição da mesa e de fatos que concorreram para os mesmos," Câmara dos Deputados (Brasília), n.d. File N1, Part 2, CPDOC.

[2] Ibid.

plained of a lack of support from the federal authorities, who, he said, had not consulted the São Paulo ARENA in planning Castello's March 31 visit to São Paulo. Cerdeira wrote that "cabinet ministers come to São Paulo without advising the ARENA . . . , and, what is worse, maintain close contacts with state and municipal authorities who act against the government."[3]

On the morning of May 4, Castello advised Cerdeira that he wished to meet at Laranjeiras Palace that afternoon with the executive commission of the Paulista ARENA to discuss the gubernatorial succession. Some of the ten commission members felt that the president would impose a candidate, and one member suggested that it would be Industry and Commerce Minister Paulo Egídio Martins, but others, familiar with Castello's recent discussion with Congressman Guilherme Machado about possible formulas for picking gubernatorial candidates, believed that the president had democratic ideas in mind.[4]

Castello, with his soldierly bearing and ceremonial gestures, entered the Laranjeiras Palace room where the Paulista politicians were waiting. He was in an agreeable mood and greeted each with an appropriate remark. After asking them to be seated, he spoke of his admiration of the people of São Paulo and went on to say that he had no desire to select a candidate, or even lay down rules for making the selection, because outside interference should be avoided and because he felt that the state's ARENA leaders could work out an arrangement with him that would satisfy, in a democratic manner, the interests of the Revolution, São Paulo, and the party.

During a long discussion it was decided, thanks to some suggestions of Abreu Sodré, that the name to be presented to the ARENA state convention and state legislature would be determined by the votes of São Paulo ARENA members who belonged to the party's state directorship or to the federal or state legislatures; each of these electors would vote for three names.[5]

During the next week the São Paulo ARENA received new adherents, bringing the number of electors up to 137. But Carvalho Pinto

[3] Arnaldo Cerdeira, letter to HACB, Câmara dos Deputados (Brasília), n.d., File N1, Part 2, CPDOC; idem and secretary of São Paulo ARENA Executive Commission, memorandum to HACB, São Paulo, April 5, 1966, File N1, Part 2, CPDOC.

[4] Abreu Sodré, letter to Viana Filho, September 28, 1971.

[5] Ibid.; idem, memorandum to JWFD, August 5, 1977.

said that he would not join the ARENA in order to seek the governorship. By May 13, when the voting by the electors was to start, nine candidates had been inscribed: Paulo Egídio Martins, Herbert Levy, Vice-governor Laudo Natel, São Paulo University Reitor Gama e Silva, Auro de Moura Andrade, Abreu Sodré, businessman Gastão Vidigal, Arnaldo Cerdeira, and Santos Mayor Sílvio Fernandes Lopes.[6]

Costa e Silva's advisers supported Gama e Silva, while *O Estado de S. Paulo* supported wealthy Gastão Vidigal and Ademar de Barros supported Sílvio Fernandes Lopes. Ademar de Barros' adversaries, who were apt to underestimate the break between Cerdeira and the governor, expressed the fear that the governor would select his successor because the non-PSP currents were split among many candidates. Castello appealed to the ARENA on May 11 to work for greater union, and Cerdeira, after leaving Castello's office that day, said that the president was concerned lest divisions "pulverize the strength of the ARENA in São Paulo."[7]

On May 12 some self-styled "revolutionaries of São Paulo" who disliked Cerdeira sent an appeal to Castello for "firm federal action" lest "the second most important post in the country" be "auctioned off" to the advantage of Ademar de Barros. Castello, who was receiving a mountain of correspondence from half the states about the gubernatorial races, learned from this appeal that São Paulo's "authentic revolutionaries" liked Paulo Egídio Martins, General Meira Mattos, Herbert Levy, Gastão Vidigal, and Abreu Sodré (who had connections in the assembly, where he had once been presiding officer). The appeal described the assembly as a political riffraff, avid to sell votes, and lamented that that state's revolutionaries lacked leadership.[8]

As the week of voting began, Cerdeira and the press gave the impression that the balloting was to determine a list of three names to be submitted to Castello and the ARENA state executive commission for a final decision. Ademar de Barros suggested that Amauri Kruel's name be included among the three. Moura Andrade, explaining that

[6] *Jornal do Brasil*, May 7, 12, 17, 19, 1966; Abreu Sodré, memorandum, August 5, 1977.

[7] Abreu Sodré, memorandum, August 5, 1977; *Jornal do Brasil*, May 12, 18; unsigned memorandum, "Situação política em São Paulo," May 12, 1966, File N1, Part 2, CPDOC.

[8] Unsigned memorandum, "Situação política em São Paulo."

he disliked the selection method, withdrew during the contest. After it was over, the count was as follows:[9]

Roberto de Abreu Sodré	73
Laudo Natel	64
Sílvio Fernandes Lopes	62
Paulo Egídio Martins	62
Gastão Vidigal	39
Herbert Levy	38
Arnaldo Cerdeira	36
Gama e Silva	29

The thesis that the voting was to determine a list of three (becoming four on account of the third-place tie) received the support of Paulo Egídio's backers. After Paulo Egídio sought Costa e Silva's support for the idea, the war minister and Paulo Egídio turned to Castello for a decision. Castello, who would have liked to have seen Paulo Egídio the ARENA candidate, explained: "I adopted a criterion together with the executive commission of the regional directorship of the ARENA and even though I have a personal preference for one of the names on the so-called list of three, I am not a man to break agreements. My decision is in favor of the one who received the most votes."[10]

Abreu Sodré issued a statement to say that his decision to enter the ARENA had sprung from his conviction that the Revolution, having created an instrument of political action, was going to work to reach the perfect restoration of democracy. His step, he added, had brought him into conflict with Lacerda.[11]

2. Alves Bastos Loses Command of the Third Army (May 19, 1966)

In April, 1966, before the São Paulo ARENA decided how to pick its candidate for governor, Second Army Commander Amauri Kruel

[9] *Jornal do Brasil*, May 12, 17, 1966; Abreu Sodré memorandum, August 5, 1977.

[10] Abreu Sodré, memorandum, August 5, 1977; Abreu Sodré (interview, July 28, 1977) recalls that Costa e Silva was one of those who favored the "list of three" thesis.

[11] *Jornal do Brasil*, May 27, 1966.

discussed the electoral domicile requirement with Costa e Silva. The war minister then spoke to Tarso Dutra, ARENA congressman from Rio Grande do Sul, about the possibility of having the ARENA propose a constitutional amendment to favor military officers who wanted to be gubernatorial candidates. Castello, hearing about Costa e Silva's talk with Tarso Dutra, asked Daniel Krieger to work against the proposed amendment.[1]

Amauri Kruel, in Rio Grande do Sul in mid-May, attended a barbecue with Third Army Commander Alves Bastos. To those around him at the barbecue, Alves Bastos said that "the electoral domicile requirement is a monstrosity that separates me and General Amauri Kruel from political life." Analyzing the economic situation, Alves Bastos attacked the plans of Roberto Campos and said that since their "invention," the poor "have never been so poor." Kruel spoke of the need to "follow paths that are not those trodden up to now" and added that "the president told me that he absolutely would not interfere in the domicile question and I hope that he fulfills his word."[2] After the barbecue, Alves Bastos gave a statement to *Revista do Globo* describing the electoral domicile requirement as "absurd and almost monstrous" because it was contrary to democratic fundamentals.[3]

Without the two generals knowing it, a reporter had recorded their informal remarks at the barbecue. When the reporter took his tape to the governor's palace to have a transcript typed, secret service agents seized it.[4] Nevertheless, parts of the conversation at the barbecue found their way to the press.

War Minister Costa e Silva called Alves Bastos to Rio. General Augusto César Moniz de Aragão, brother of Raimundo and commander of the Fourth Infantry Division in Rio Grande do Sul, reached Rio before the Third Army commander and reported at once to the war minister. When journalists accosted him, Moniz de Aragão limited his comments to the Military Club election, in which he was the candidate of the "single slate" to be reelected president. Alves Bastos' arrival in

[1] Kruel, interview, July 22, 1977; *Jornal do Brasil*, April 8, May 1, 3, 1966. According to the press, Kruel told Costa e Silva that he would not consider an MDB offer of the presidential nomination provided the *domicílio eleitoral* matter was resolved in a satisfactory manner.

[2] *Jornal do Brasil*, May 19, 1966.

[3] Ibid., May 20, 1966.

[4] Ibid., May 21, 1966.

Rio was also preceded by the publication in the Carioca press of the Third Army commander's accusation that Castello had failed to comply with his promise to have the ARENA work for the modification of the electoral domicile requirement.[5]

A nervous Alves Bastos, wearing civilian clothes, reached Rio's Santos Dumont Airport on May 19. "This atmosphere in Rio," he told reporters, "amazes me because everything is calm in the south." He confirmed the statement he had given to *Revista do Globo* but said he was surprised that his earlier observations, given to close military friends at a barbecue, had become public. They were, he said, strictly private and had been made "in confidence."[6]

Castello signed decrees on May 19 retiring Alves Bastos and naming Ernesto Geisel's brother Orlando commander of the Third Army. While Moniz de Aragão, reelected president of the Military Club, took over the Third Army command provisionally, Rio newspapers published unflattering stories about Alves Bastos, including the declaration of a Porto Alegre alderman who said that Alves Bastos had sent an emissary to Montevideo to seek Goulart's support for his gubernatorial ambitions.[7]

General Panasco Alvim, back from the Dominican Republic, was rumored to be about to take over the Second Army from Kruel. But after Kruel denied authorship of a declaration attributed to him in support of Alves Bastos, the government revealed that it had reviewed the case of Kruel and that he would remain at his São Paulo post. Panasco Alvim became director-general of Army Personnel in the place of Orlando Geisel.[8]

3. Ademar de Barros, Cassado (June 6, 1966)

Ademar de Barros, who had tried to advise Alves Bastos to defy the War Ministry by not reporting to it on May 19,[1] made plans late in May to discuss with oppositionist Congressman Doutel de Andrade

[5] Ibid., May 19, 1966.
[6] Ibid., May 20, 1966.
[7] Ibid., May 20, 21, 1966.
[8] Ibid., May 21, 1966.
[1] *Jornal do Brasil*, May 21, 1966.

the staging of a great popular rally in São Paulo on behalf of reestablishing direct elections. After Juraci Magalhães described the governor's plan as part of a subversive maneuver, General Olímpio Mourão Filho said that "if preaching the reestablishment of direct elections is subversive, then I am also subversive because I am working for that. Brazilian democracy exists only in the Dominican Republic."[2]

What seriously concerned the administration were the reports about Ademar de Barros's "vast plan . . . to conquer a majority of the state assembly."[3] The governor, who had reverted to his prerevolutionary custom of charging a personal commission of 10 percent on the business transactions of private firms with the state, was said to be offering thirty-five million cruzeiros (about sixteen thousand dollars) for each vote that assemblymen would cast as he wanted for the next governor.[4] Equally serious were the steps being taken by Ademar de Barros that would wreck the financial policy of the Castello Branco administration, not to mention the state's finances. While the *Diário Oficial* of the state revealed an orgy of new appointments, Ademar de Barros prepared a huge program of loans by the official state bank and massive emissions of state bonds, whose attractive interest rates would leave the national treasury obligations without buyers.[5]

Armed with copies of the state *Diário Oficial*, Abreu Sodré went to Rio on Friday, June 3, to discuss these alarming steps with Otávio Bulhões, Mem de Sá, and the president's staff. He agreed with Luís Viana Filho that Ademar de Barros, a man of courage, was not to be underestimated, but he suggested that the support given to the governor's anti-Castello manifestos by many Paulista businessmen was due more to dislike for the government's economic policy than to love for the governor. Viana took Abreu Sodré to speak with Castello, and the president asked him to leave the copies of the *Diário Oficial* with him.[6]

Abreu Sodré, back in São Paulo, told his supporters to be patient, because a settlement of the São Paulo crisis would probably take a month. But Castello decided to act quickly on a drastic step that he had long avoided: the suspension of the political rights of Ademar de

[2] Ibid., June 1, 2, 1966.

[3] Viana Filho, *O Governo Castelo Branco*, p. 413.

[4] Vereker, memorandum, June 8, 1966.

[5] Mem de Sá, letter to Viana Filho, October 7, 1971, p. 9.

[6] Abreu Sodré, letter to Viana Filho, September 28, 1971, pp. 20–21.

Barros and the cancellation of his mandate. Unable to discuss the matter first with Justice Minister Mem de Sá, because he could not reach him after Abreu Sodré left the palace, the president spoke with Costa e Silva. The war minister assured Castello that Kruel would cooperate despite his close connections with Ademar de Barros.[7]

The justice minister, reaching Laranjeiras Palace late that Friday afternoon, opened the conversation with Castello by recommending that the press receive unofficial reports that the justice minister, aware of the plan to buy the votes of São Paulo assemblymen, was ready to cancel the mandates of those assemblymen, whose names he knew. Mem de Sá, telling Castello of his talk with Bulhões, said that quick action was needed "to annul the corrosive work of the São Paulo governor."[8]

Castello listened attentively to his justice minister and then said with a slight smile: "I approve your steps and applaud the rapidity of your action. But, Mr. Minister, since I, too, have been thinking about the Paulista situation, I want to ask you if you do not consider that a radical measure, which I am prepared to adopt, would be more efficient: the *cassação* or the overthrow of Governor Ademar de Barros."

In a kindly manner Castello asked to be excused for discussing the matter first with the war minister, who was about to leave Rio. Then Castello asked Mem de Sá whether he agreed that other people should be heard, still "in this phase of absolute secrecy," before a final decision was reached the next day. Mem de Sá suggested consulting Otávio Bulhões and Roberto Campos; they might, he felt, prefer a postponement of the proposed action lest it adversely affect negotiations about new credits being carried out with representatives of the World Bank or IMF, who were in Brazil.

Castello, agreeing to call them in the morning, took the justice minister by the arm and led him to the office door. Thinking of the heart attack that Mem de Sá had suffered a year earlier, Castello said affectionately: "Look here, Mr. Minister, don't worry yourself about this, because everything will be all right and everything has been well planned. Go to your home, take your tea, watch television, and go to sleep early and peacefully."

"No, Mr. President, you don't know me well. I am not at all wor-

[7] Viana Filho, *O Governo Castelo Branco*, p. 415.

[8] Mem de Sá, letter to Viana Filho, October 7, 1971, p. 9.

ried and I even feel good, because my participation in politics has always been a fighting one. Tonight I shall be up late because I am going to dine with Professor Eugênio Gudin, who always offers excellent wines."

"So much the better," Castello said.[9]

Roberto Campos was in São Paulo to give a reply on television to attacks made by Ademar de Barros. Receiving a message from the president late Friday night at his hotel, he flew to Rio early the next morning. At Laranjeiras Palace, Campos told Castello that the Paulista businessmen would welcome a change, due to the economic and administrative disorder caused by the governor, and he said that negative international repercussions, following the federal government's authoritarian step in the most important state, would be short-lived, with business groups and diplomatic representatives explaining why the step had been inevitable. When Castello asked about a possible "popular reaction" in São Paulo, the planning minister said that "Ademar is a *político clientelesco*, not *ideológico*." The latter, "men like Brizola," Campos added, were the dangerous ones because they "could inspire fanatic loyalty." He predicted that the "clients" of Ademar de Barros would seek a new *patrão* right away.[10]

When Castello saw Mem de Sá on Saturday morning, he told him that Bulhões and Campos felt that the step against Ademar de Barros would have excellent repercussions in international financial circles. It should, Castello said, be carried out on Monday right after the publication of the decree in the federal *Diário Oficial.* Castello also advised that he had asked Vice-governor Laudo Natel to come to Rio and speak with him, for he wanted the succession to conform to constitutional precepts.[11]

Mem de Sá offered to go to São Paulo to arrange to have the decree carried out, but Castello laughed and said: "Send my minister of justice for such a mission? That would give too much importance to the governor! It is proper to give the job to the general commanding the Second Army. Therefore I have called him here."

Mem de Sá was astonished. He ventured: "But Mr. President, did

[9] Ibid., pp. 9–12.
[10] Viana Filho, *O Governo Castelo Branco*, p. 414.
[11] Mem de Sá, letter to Viana Filho, October 7, 1971, p. 10.

not General Amauri Kruel recently make a public manifestation at a festivity, intentionally scheduled in Porto Alegre by the commander of the Third Army, that was clearly discordant, if not hostile, to the policy of the federal government? I believe that, under some pretext, he should be kept apart from the events, and, if possible, kept away from São Paulo."

"No, Mr. Minister," Castello said, "General Kruel is, above everything else, a good soldier. He will accept and fulfill an order of the commander-in-chief of the armed forces."

"But Marshall, does this not incur a serious risk?"

"I think not, but if that should be the case, it will be a very well calculated risk." The president's smile, Mem de Sá noted, was slightly malicious.[12]

The final decision to suspend the political rights of the São Paulo governor was reached at a meeting that Saturday attended by Castello, Generals Geisel and Golberi, and Ministers Mem de Sá, Otávio Bulhões, and Pedro Aleixo. Following the meeting, Mem de Sá and his chief administrative assistant, Professor João Leitão de Abreu, worked on an appropriate decree. They surmounted a problem stemming from the fact that the reference made in Ato 2 to the cancellation of mandates was to legislative mandates.[13]

Early on Sunday, June 5, Castello received Amauri Kruel. The general accepted the order of the commander-in-chief to depose Ademar de Barros, but he did not agree with it. He rejected Castello's argument that the São Paulo governor was taking steps against the administration, and he told Castello that the *cassação* was a demonstration of ingratitude toward a man who had helped make the revolution. Kruel believed that Ademar was popular in the state legislature and with the Paulistas and was justified in wanting to name his successor. "You are taking away Ademar's rights," Kruel said, "because you want to elect your own candidate."[14]

The president sent Luís Viana Filho to speak with Vice-governor Laudo Natel, who had arrived in Rio. Viana brought Castello's sugges-

[12] Ibid., p. 11.

[13] Viana Filho, *O Governo Castelo Branco*, p. 412; Mem de Sá, letter to Viana Filho, October 7, 1971, p. 12.

[14] A. Kruel, interviews, December 11, 1975, July 22, 1977.

tions that Army Colonel João Batista Figueiredo be named commander of the state police and that Antônio Delfim Neto, highly regarded by Roberto Campos, be named state finance secretary.[15]

Mem de Sá, working on the decree in Laranjeiras Palace, was interrupted by Castello, who said that Kruel, "being the good soldier that he is," had agreed to fulfill his mission. Castello asked Mem de Sá if he knew "an economist named Delfim Neto." The justice minister described Delfim Neto as a "man of great talent and knowledge." He added:

> I can tell you this because I have a son, with a Ph.D. from the Massachusetts Institute of Technology, who works . . . with a group that Minister Roberto Campos organized, made up of a dozen North American professors and an equal number of Brazilians, to prepare programs of government action and the future planning of our economy. Such is the esteem of Roberto Campos for Delfim Neto that he asked for his collaboration in this work. Therefore every Monday, Delfim comes early in the morning from São Paulo and remains . . . until 8:00 in the evening. . . . And my son assures me that he is one of the most gifted men that he has ever known.

"Ah," Castello said, "that is why Campos suggested to me that he be finance secretary of the Laudo Natel government, to bring order to the chaos that resulted from the earthquake of Ademar."[16]

At 9:30 on Sunday evening Ademar de Barros, already advised of the presidential decision, arrived at Campos Elíseos Palace in São Paulo to spend some last moments. Troubled by a hernia, he had had a fever for three days, and he reached the palace with a two-day growth of beard. He received a shave and then posed for photographs with members of his staff. Leaving before midnight, he spoke of making a trip to Beirut, via Madrid. On Monday the governorship was assumed by Laudo Natel, a calm, forty-five–year–old banker who had achieved popularity as president of the São Paulo Football Club.[17]

After Natel became governor, Castello made a brief trip to São Paulo and returned to Rio with the determination to take more steps

[15] Viana Filho, *O Governo Castelo Branco*, p. 416.
[16] Mem de Sá, letter to Viana Filho, October 7, 1971, pp. 12–13.
[17] *Jornal do Brasil*, June 7, 1966.

to hold back corruption in the states and punish the guilty. Mem de Sá, warning the public that new *cassações* could be expected, sat down with Golberi to examine charges of political corruption in the legislative assemblies of the twelve states where indirect elections for governors were scheduled for September 3.[18]

The MDB condemned the *cassação* of Ademar de Barros and announced that it would not participate in the indirect elections for governors and for the president of the Republic.[19]

4. The Gubernatorial Candidacy in Pernambuco (May, 1966)

As in São Paulo, the election of officers of the Pernambuco state assembly in March disappointed Castello. The contest reflected the struggle between Governor Paulo Guerra, who had belonged to the PSD, and Congressman Cid Sampaio, a former UDN governor. Victory went to the slate backed by Cid Sampaio after he made a deal that gave the MDB three officerships of the assembly. According to the SNI, the victory of Cid Sampaio's slate was assisted also by timely decisions about loans from the Institute of Sugar and Alcohol. After Castello received a telegram from Cid Sampaio explaining the compromise with the MDB as "a normal fact of legislative life," the president wired back to say that he disagreed with this remark and was "disappointed and sorrowful" at the arrangement worked out between ARENA dissidents and the "counterrevolutionaries."[1]

A few days later Seventh Region Commander Antônio Carlos Murici wrote the president to advise that his name had been launched for the Pernambuco governorship by civilians who believed that his candidacy, unconnected with political groups, was the only one that would "permit unity" in the Pernambuco ARENA. General Murici wrote that Colonels Antônio Bandeira and Costa Cavalcanti were felt to be asso-

[18] Ibid., June 7, 8, 10, 1966.

[19] Ibid., June 8, 9, 1966.

[1] Antônio Carlos da Silva Murici, letter to HACB, Recife, March 25, 1966, File N1, Part 3, CPDOC; Pernambuco governor's office, "Eleição da Mesa da Assembléia Legislativa," File N1, Part 3; Cid Sampaio, telegram to HACB, Recife, March 15, 1966, File N1, Part 3; HACB, telegram to Cid Sampaio, File N1, Part 3; see also Sampaio, letter to HACB, Rio de Janeiro, March 21, 1966, File N1, Part 3.

ciated with Paulo Guerra or Cid Sampaio, and he added that Governor Guerra had told him that it appeared impossible "to put in a civilian if we want the Revolution to continue."[2]

When Murici and his wife, Virgínia, lunched with Castello at Laranjeiras Palace, the president asked the general, who knew the northeast well, whether he was certain that he could unite the people around the Revolution. Murici replied that he knew of no one else who could do it. The president said that he was not planning to make a decision about the selection of a candidate. "So," he told Murici, "the problem is yours."[3]

Castello soon received a letter from Fourteenth Infantry Region Commander Antônio Bandeira, who wrote that Paulo Guerra and other politicians found the Murici and Costa Cavalcanti candidacies "ineffective" and therefore urged him to run for governor. Castello replied that the selection would be made by the state ARENA and that he was "absolutely against agitation by military people in connection with military candidates."[4]

"Bandeira," Murici wrote Castello, "is considered to be connected with Paulo Guerra and the ex-PSD and has troubles with the ex-UDN. Costa Cavalcanti has achieved no bases in Pernambuco." In letters that were a bit gossipy, Murici told the president that Costa Cavalcanti "is quietly remarking that he has your backing and that of Costa e Silva," and that Congressman "Nilo Coelho of the PSD does not have goodwill in the ex-UDN or the backing of Paulo Guerra, who does not intend to divide the leadership." Murici advised Castello of reports that "the governor created five hundred teaching posts and two hundred posts in other sectors, making no nominations, to use them for bargaining." Later, Recife's *Diário da Noite* made the charge public.[5]

Castello, after his discussion about selection criteria with the São Paulo ARENA, sent for Paulo Guerra and other Pernambuco ARENA leaders such as Costa Cavalcanti and Monsenhor Alfredo Arruda Câmara, federal congressman and president of the state party. At Laran-

[2] Murici, letter to HACB, March 25, 1966.

[3] Murici, interview, November 18, 1975.

[4] Antônio Bandeira, letter to HACB, Socorro, April 23, 1966, File N1, Part 3 (p. 88); HACB, telegram to Bandeira, File N1, Part 3, CPDOC.

[5] Murici, letters to HACB, April 25, May 4, 1966, File N1, Part 3, CPDOC; *Diário da Noite* [Recife], May 5, 1966.

jeiras Palace on May 6 these leaders agreed on a selection procedure similar to the one established two days earlier for São Paulo. In this case, as Paulo Guerra described it to the Carioca press, the purpose of the voting, in which each elector would mark three names, was to provide a final list of the strongest candidates that would be reviewed by Castello and the ARENA leaders in order to choose the candidate "most closely identified with the Revolution." Of the seventy-five electors, Paulo Guerra believed that Cid Sampaio controlled about twenty-seven and he himself most of the others[6]

While in Rio, Paulo Guerra gave the press a list of three names which he put "in order of importance": Antônio Bandeira, Nilo Coelho, and Costa Cavalcanti.[7] Bandeira, like Murici and Costa Cavalcanti, was an "authentic revolutionary" who had worked early for the movement of 1964, and the appearance of his candidacy, with strong political backing, divided the Fourth Army. It weakened the position of Murici, whom Castello described to Guerra as "a revolutionary of the first hour, my friend, and a person of the highest category." The president, hoping that the selection formula would provide a fair settlement, told Guerra that the Revolution had not been made "to put" military people in power. He asked Guerra how many supporters he thought that Murici had among the seventy-five electors. When the governor replied, "Between seven and nine," Castello said: " I would like to see Murici's face when he gets seven votes!"[8]

Guerra, on his return to Recife, called Murici to his home and spent two hours trying to convince him to desist. But the general, having received satisfactory responses when he called individually on members of the ARENA state directorship, told the governor that he did not need his approval to become his successor. Guerra asked him if he felt he needed Cid Sampaio's approval, and Murici said that he did not. After Murici left, Guerra spoke with Cid Sampaio, who said that he would not back Murici.[9]

Guerra let it be known in Pernambuco political and military circles that Castello and Costa e Silva opposed the candidacies of Murici and

[6] *Jornal do Brasil*, May 7, 1966; Guerra, interview, November 11, 1975.

[7] *Jornal do Brasil*, May 12, 1966.

[8] HACB, handwritten memorandum, n.d., File N1, Part 3, CPDOC; Guerra, interview, November 11, 1975.

[9] Guerra, interview, November 11, 1975.

other military figures, whereupon Bandeira withdrew from the race and Costa Cavalcanti declared that he was a "civilian" candidate.[10] But the war minister and the president reacted to Guerra's step. The War Ministry announced that Costa e Silva was not involved in the selection.[11] Castello dispatched a telegram to Fourth Army Commander Portugal: "I have been informed of a version that exists there that I am opposed to the candidacies of military men. I want to make it clear that I am only against any candidacy that is functionally military and am against agitation in military circles in favor of this or that name. I ask you to make this information known but without using newspaper publication. Also I ask you to show this message to Governor Paulo Guerra."[12]

The press stated that Castello's message to General Portugal was a denial of Paulo Guerra's "news" of a presidential veto of Murici's candidacy. Such a denial, according to offers recently made by Guerra to Murici, was supposed to be followed by the advancement of Murici to first place on Guerra's list.[13] But Guerra decided to support no military man, and thus his list of three was reduced to one name, that of Chamber of Deputies First Secretary Nilo Coelho, who was in Europe.

On the eve of the May 16 voting, Guerra gave each elector a ballot with votes marked for three names that were different from the combinations on the other ballots. Even though an elector's name was not put on his ballot, each vote for a certain combination would give the information necessary for Guerra to know whether his "friends" had stayed in line and thus were to continue in the governor's favor.[14]

The results, officially recorded by Arruda Câmara and three others, were received by the press with expressions of surprise at the poor showing of Murici and the strong showing of Eraldo Gueiros, prosecuting attorney of the Military Justice System.[15] They were:

[10] *Jornal do Brasil*, May 12, 1966; Murici, letter to HACB, May 7, 1966, File N1, Part 3, CPDOC (this is a continuation of the letter started on May 4).

[11] *Jornal do Brasil*, May 12, 1966.

[12] HACB, telegram to Francisco Damasceno Ferreira Portugal, File N1, Part 3, CPDOC.

[13] *Jornal do Brasil*, May 12, 1966; HACB, handwritten memorandum, n.d., File N1, Part 3, CPDOC.

[14] Guerra, interview, November 11, 1975; Murici, interview, November 18, 1975.

[15] *Jornal do Brasil*, May 17, 1966; Arruda Câmara and three others, "Resultado geral da apuração devidamente rubricado pela mesa apuradora," File N1, Part 3, CPDOC.

Nilo Coelho	46
Eraldo Gueiros	41
Arruda Câmara	36
Costa Cavalcanti	29
Leal Sampaio	23
João Cleofas	22
José Neves	15
Antônio Carlos Murici	6
Apolônio Sales	1

Murici told General Portugal that he was convinced the voting had been carried out improperly and was considering a legal appeal. Portugal sent this information to Castello and advised also that he had authorized Murici to go to Rio to see the president.[16]

Castello, reviewing the situation in a longhand memorandum, wrote that as a "consequence of the military agitation," army officers in Recife had held an evening meeting to discuss "the need of federal intervention in Pernambuco." He noted that the army officers had mentioned "the corruption in Pernambuco, the free access of Communists to the palace, . . . trafficking of influence, . . . threats in handling municipalities represented by the assemblymen, and the use of marked ballots." Castello wrote that Colonel Bandeira and the state secretary of security were "especially hot-tempered" and that the latter threatened to resign, following the example of the colonel in charge of port administration, who had already resigned. The president added that the army officers, claiming that the local air force personnel shared their indignation, planned to reach a final decision at a larger meeting.[17]

Virgínia Murici, writing to Castello on May 18, explained that her husband had restrained the officers who wanted to depose Guerra. But she also said that "public opinion in Pernambuco is completely disgusted with the outrage publicly committed against a general of the Brazilian army." Advising that "everyone awaits the attitude that you will take," she condemned the "gang, linked to venal business, that dominated Pernambuco" and the "four chiefs, Paulo Guerra, Cid Sam-

[16] Francisco Damasceno Ferreira Portugal, telegram to HACB, File N1, Part 3, CPDOC.

[17] HACB, handwritten memorandum, n.d., File N1, Part 3, CPDOC.

paio, Cleofas, and Arruda Câmara," who had "forgotten their squabbles" to unite against a man who wanted to "change the face of politics in Pernambuco by decent means." "Ask," she wrote, "for the envelope in which the votes are contained and see with your own eyes the extent of the vileness of the debauched Paulo Guerra."[18]

Murici, seeking an annulment of the recent vote, called on Costa e Silva and Castello. He made no declarations and was praised in government circles for having behaved better than Alves Bastos or Amauri Kruel and for having "restrained the impetuosity of his subordinates."[19] Following Murici's departure from Laranjeiras Palace, Castello held a long meeting with Guerra, Cid Sampaio, and Congressman João Cleofas. Guerra insisted that Eraldo Gueiros, alone among the top vote-getters, had the virtue of never having been a politician. But after Castello met again on May 19 with Guerra, Sampaio, and Cleofas, a decision was reached in favor of Nilo Coelho. In Recife the state security secretary and the commander of the state police, supporters of Murici, submitted their resignations to Governor Guerra.[20]

Castello was described by the press as the "agent of conciliation." In his presence at Planalto Palace on May 26, an agreement was signed by Guerra, Arruda Câmara, Cleofas, and Cid Sampaio. It provided that Nilo Coelho's running mate would be Salviano Machado, of the UDN wing, and that Cleofas, another former UDN member, would be the ARENA's candidate to fill a senate seat that was about to become vacant.[21]

5. Rio Grande do Sul and the Act of Party Loyalty (June–July, 1966)

Castello hoped that Justice Minister Mem de Sá, long prominent in the Partido Libertador (PL) of Rio Grande do Sul, could help with the problems that the ARENA was having in that state. The assembly

[18] Virgínia Murici, letter to HACB, Recife, May 18, 1966, File N1, Part 3, CPDOC.

[19] *Jornal do Brasil*, May 19, 1966.

[20] Ibid., May 19, 20, 24, 1966.

[21] Ibid., May 24, 27, 1966.

was closely divided between the ARENA and the MDB (practically synonymous with the old Gaúcho PTB, which had close ties to Brizola and Goulart in Uruguay.) The balance was in the hands of a few ARENA assemblymen from the PL, who voted sometimes with the MDB.

Before the Rio Grande do Sul assembly chose its officers, Castello told Mem de Sá, Krieger, and Labor Minister Peracchi Barcelos, all Gaúchos, that he was going to suspend the political rights of several Gaúcho assemblymen whose dossiers had recently been studied by investigators. Mem de Sá said that *cassações*, on the eve of the assembly election, would appear to be politically inspired. Castello, after hearing Krieger, agreed to postpone the *cassações* and to send Peracchi Barcelos to Porto Alegre to see what he could do about the election. Colonel Peracchi was successful because Alfredo Hoffmeister was chosen assembly president.[1]

The state ARENA, planning a gubernatorial nominating convention in July, was split between the supporters of Peracchi Barcelos and Congressman Tarso Dutra. The president explained to Krieger and Mem de Sá that an open clash would be a disaster for the ARENA, the state, and the Revolution, and then, turning to the justice minister, he said that only Krieger could solve the problem. Krieger, on excellent terms with Tarso Dutra and Peracchi, would be the perfect ARENA gubernatorial candidate—"the ideal formula," Castello said.[2]

Krieger, ill at ease, begged the president not to consider him as a possible governor and then left. Castello asked Mem de Sá to try to persuade the senator to accept. Mem de Sá, however, was not optimistic. He told Castello that he could not picture Krieger accepting "an executive post that requires patience, concentration, and long hours and days in a room, putting up with bores. . . . He is a born leader who is completely happy in the activity, at times feverish and exhausting, of conferences, of bringing people together, or regimenting companions for a cause, and in the strategy and combat against adversaries."

By the time Mem de Sá spoke to Krieger, Tarso Dutra and Peracchi had offered the senator their full support. But Krieger, demonstrating

[1] Krieger, *Desde as Missões*, p. 211.

[2] Mem de Sá, letter to Viana Filho, October 7, 1971, p. 7.

his customary straightforwardness, exclaimed to the justice minister: "Mem, you know that I don't have the temperament to fill such a post, because I am nervous, restless, a man . . . born for political and legislative action. Please ask the president not to insist, because I don't know how to decline anything that he might suggest. But I know that, as governor, I would be a disappointment to him."[3]

So the contest between Peracchi and Tarso Dutra continued. However, whether either would become governor remained in doubt, for several ARENA assemblymen switched to the MDB, giving the opposition party a majority of three.[4] Moreover, at the suggestion of Assemblyman Paulo Brossard de Sousa Pinto, the MDB presented a highly regarded gubernatorial candidate in Rui Cirne Lima, whom Krieger had wanted Castello to appoint to the Supreme Court. Cirne Lima, a law professor, had served as a PL member of the cabinet of Governor Ildo Meneghetti but had resigned when the PL had turned against Meneghetti, calling his administration corrupt. Now Paulo Brossard and another PL veteran left the ARENA to support Cirne Lima, thus giving the opposition a majority of five in the assembly. Mem de Sá telephoned Brossard, his former student and friend, and broke with him, calling him a person "without character."[5]

"Mr. Minister," Castello told Mem de Sá, "Rio Grande is important not just because it is the third Brazilian state politically and economically, but also because it is geographically adjacent to Argentina and Uruguay, where the Brazilian exiles are." The president said that without a state government with the confidence of the federal government, much impetus would be given to the work of Brizola and the guerrillas and Cubans who were in touch with Brizola. Mem de Sá predicted that within two months after Cirne Lima's election, Brossard and Cirne Lima would be attacking each other as energetically as they had done before their recent alliance. But Castello was not disposed to wait for them to have their falling out.[6]

At Laranjeiras Palace on June 26, Castello met with Governor Meneghetti (president of the state ARENA), Krieger, Tarso Dutra,

[3] Ibid., p. 8.

[4] Mem de Sá, interview, October 31, 1975.

[5] Ibid.

[6] Ibid.

Mem de Sá, and Peracchi Barcelos. In a clear reference to Mem de Sá and Krieger he said: "I was badly advised and did not carry out the *cassações* when I should have. But it does not matter, for I am assuming before history the responsibility of not turning Rio Grande do Sul over to the adversaries of the Revolution. Let the ARENA convention choose its candidate. Of the candidates, and they are here now, I insist that the loser give his support to the winner and I also insist that the president of the party produce an enthusiastic convention."[7]

Castello vigorously rejected the request of Mem de Sá and Krieger that *cassações* be postponed until after the gubernatorial election.[8] Therefore, that afternoon Mem de Sá made a last call, as justice minister, on the president. He told Castello that of the six assemblymen who were to have their political rights suspended, at most two were corrupt. "The others are good democrats. One is a democratic socialist, just as I am. If you suspend his political rights you must suspend mine also." Mem de Sá added: "You say that you must save the country from danger. But I am not president. . . . I am a minister whose resignation has already been submitted. I respect your decision, even applaud and approve it. But my resignation must be effective at once."[9]

In his letter of resignation of June 26, Mem de Sá said that he prayed fervently that he would be able to give President Costa e Silva "the praise and assurance of support that I do not grant now." Discussing the election system, he wrote that "I learned . . . , with Joaquim Francisco de Assis Brasil, during my earliest days in political life, that the system of indirect election is not only perfectly democratic, but also presents the advantage of permitting the selection of the best executive, and not just the best candidate, as necessarily occurs in the process of direct suffrage."[10]

In Rio Grande do Sul on June 27 the candidacy of Cirne Lima was launched in a statement signed by twenty-seven MDB assemblymen and four ARENA assemblymen, enough to assure his victory over the candidate to be chosen by the ARENA.[11] In Brasília the next day, Gaúcho Congressman Raul Pila, the grand old man of the PL, wrote Castello to say that "the revolutionary objectives cannot be entrusted to

[7] Krieger, *Desde as Missões*, p. 212.

[8] Viana Filho, *O Governo Castelo Branco*, p. 417.

[9] Mem de Sá, interview, October 31, 1975.

[10] Mem de Sá, letter to HACB, June 26, 1966, File M (p. 43), CPDOC.

[11] *Jornal do Brasil*, June 28, July 2, 1966.

better or safer hands than those of Professor Cirne Lima." Similar thoughts were expressed by Gaúcho professional groups.[12]

Luís Viana Filho, who became acting justice minister, writes that Krieger and Governor Meneghetti provided "equilibrium and peace" at the Gaúcho ARENA convention in Porto Alegre on July 2. At the time that the nation learned of Peracchi Barcelos' narrow victory over Tarso Dutra, Castello, at Laranjeiras Palace, signed decrees suspending the political rights of forty-six individuals. Four Gaúcho assemblymen and two alternates were affected. The list, made up principally of assemblymen of other states, included former Governors Mauro Borges (Goiás) and Seixas Dória (Sergipe).[13]

With only one dissenting vote, the Gaúcho assembly passed a motion deploring the latest cancellation of mandates. Amauri Kruel wrote a letter of protest to Castello, and Cirne Lima declared that "in the electoral field the cancellation of mandates cannot be justified." But Costa e Silva, campaigning in his home state of Rio Grande do Sul, denied that the *cassações* of Gaúcho assemblymen had the object of assisting Peracchi in his contest with Cirne Lima, "because if this had been the purpose, the number of *cassações* would have been greater."[14]

With the press reporting that Viana would study the possibility of canceling more mandates, Congressman José Bonifácio de Andrada stated that the punitive measures being contemplated were "very soft" considering that "the revolutions in other countries customarily punish their enemies with shootings and mass deportations." A fear that the government might suspend mandates of federal congressmen led both José Bonifácio and Viana to announce that Castello was not planning to carry out *cassações* in the federal Congress. Câmara President Adauto Cardoso, who had been giving similar assurances for three months, was reported to be relying on "a commitment assumed by the president of the Republic himself."[15]

On July 18, Castello canceled the mandates of more local political figures, including four more Gaúcho assemblymen. At the same time, the president and his acting justice minister issued Ato Complementar No. 16 to make it impossible for any legislator to vote, in an indirect

[12] Raul Pila, letter to HACB, Brasília, June 28, 1966, File N1, Part 2, CPDOC; *Jornal do Brasil*, July 2, 1966.

[13] Viana Filho, *O Governo Castelo Branco*, p. 148; *Jornal do Brasil*, July 5, 1966.

[14] *Jornal do Brasil*, July 5, 6, 8, 1966; A. Kruel, interview, December 11, 1975.

[15] *Jornal do Brasil*, July 8, 9, 12, 1966.

election, against the candidate of his party. The new Ato Complementar, called the Act of Party Loyalty (Ato de Fidelidade Partidária), spoke of the need to strengthen the political parties and the need of the parties, "as organized forces of democracy," to "bind their members to the duties of discipline and of respect for programmed principles." According to the new ruling, which applied to elections by federal and state legislators, votes would be voided if cast by legislators for candidates belonging to parties other than their own.

Cirne Lima described the new rule as "inconceivable" and the *cassações* as "iniquitous."[16] Mem de Sá issued a lengthy pronouncement objecting to the *cassação* of Gaúcho assemblyman Cândido Norberto, who, he maintained, was never subversive or corrupt. "On one's fingertips," he said, "one can count those who had the courage to face and struggle against Leonel Brizola in the manner of Cândido Norberto."[17]

Army officers reaching Rio from the far south expressed concern about the new *cassações*, especially that of Cândido Norberto. General Moniz de Aragão, they said, had submitted a report to Castello warning against the new *cassações*, which, coming at a moment of "tremendous economic crisis" for Rio Grande do Sul, could stimulate "the penetration of unhealthy ideas" against which the Third Army had been struggling. On July 23, three days after the officers from the south expressed this concern, nine guerrilla fighters, caught in the Brazilian interior, were reported to have mentioned Brizola as the instigator or supporter of their ineffective movement.[18]

Late in July, MDB members of the Gaúcho assembly resolved to resign their mandates and to ask the national directorship of their party to dissolve the MDB completely. In August, Cirne Lima withdrew from the Rio Grande do Sul gubernatorial contest. The government, he said, could alter the electoral rules in its favor as many times as it wanted.[19]

6. Medeiros Silva Becomes Justice Minister (July, 1966)

During June it became clear that Luís Viana Filho, head of the

[16] Ibid., July 21, 1966.
[17] Ibid., July 23, 1966.
[18] Ibid., July 21, 23, 1966.
[19] Ibid., July 21, August 18, 1966.

presidential Gabinete Civil, would be elected governor of Bahia. His handling of the duties of justice minister, when Mem de Sá left the office on June 29, was to be brief. And even before he assumed the duties, he undertook to help Castello find someone who might serve until the end of the administration. The search was complicated by the desire of many political figures to compete in the congressional elections in November.

In Brasília on June 19, Viana called on Supreme Court Justice Carlos Medeiros Silva to wish him a happy birthday. Viana found that the constitutional lawyer, who had written most of the First Institutional Act, was unhappy with the isolation of Brasília and the separation from his family and wanted to leave the court. Viana gave this information to Castello, who authorized him to offer the Justice Ministry to Medeiros. When Viana did this, he explained to Medeiros that the President was worried about the disagreements plaguing a commission that was drafting a new constitution for Brazil. Medeiros, willing to become justice minister in order to work on a new constitution, received a formal invitation later when he lunched with Castello at Alvorada Palace.[1]

At the ceremony of the transfer of office from Viana, held in Planalto Palace on July 19, Castello spoke at length about the need to reform the constitution, the national security law, the press law, the federal administration, educational legislation, the state police forces, and the arrangements governing the responsibilities of companies, political parties, and federal and state executives. During the following two weeks, Castello, Medeiros Silva, and others worked on a pile of presidential messages to present to Congress when it renewed its labors early in August. Also, late in July, the president and his justice minister issued Atos Complementares 17 and 18 to regulate the registration of congressional candidates and to limit the rights of Congress to alter the federal budget submitted by the executive. Congress, already prohibited from increasing the total budget, was now prohibited from transferring proposed expenditures from one category to another.[2]

Although the opposition in Congress failed in its effort to call a special session late in July to interrogate the new justice minister, both

[1] Viana Filho, *O Governo Castelo Branco,* p. 403; Medeiros Silva, interview, November 12, 1975.

[2] HACB, *Discursos, 1966,* pp. 331–338; *Jornal do Brasil,* August 2, 1966.

Medeiros Silva and Viana were called on to answer questions after Congress convened on August 1 in the session scheduled to last until November 30. Viana, asked to explain the *cassações* of Gaúcho assemblymen, said that they were not based on corruption but had been made "necessary" on account of "subversion, a political reason." Amaral Neto accused Viana of protecting a congressman from Bahia whom he called corrupt, whereupon Antônio Carlos Magalhães, also from Bahia, lunged at Amaral Neto while Franco Montoro screamed that Castello was a dictator. Teódulo de Albuquerque threatened to punch Franco Montoro.[3]

Several questions that MDB congressmen were preparing to ask Medeiros appeared in the press late in July, and therefore Castello set down replies in longhand to guide Medeiros in August. Castello wrote that *cassações* were authorized by the Institutional Act, a constitutional measure, and that the president, in carrying them out with the approval of the National Security Council, exercised an imperative of the Revolution. The proposals to suspend the political rights of the Rio Grande do Sul assemblymen, he wrote, had been received as far back as 1964.

Castello took exception to the wording of a question which suggested that the "climate of constant threats and violence" by the government might invalidate elections where the government was "fervently interested in the results." Commenting on a description of Congress as "mutilated," he asked whether the departure of the *cassados* had deformed the moral and civic condition of the two chambers and pointed to the volume of modern legislation produced in 1964, 1965, and 1966.

Castello's notes advised that while the government had no intention of abandoning any punitive clause of Ato 2 before the expiration date, it would close down all the old IPM's. But in a reference to the bomb aimed at Costa e Silva, he asked whether an IPM should not be "set up to investigate the terrorism that occurred yesterday in Recife." And he also asked about looking into "the obstinate and subversive provocation of elements of the extinct UNE."[4]

The justice minister, answering questions concisely in Congress on

[3] *Jornal do Brasil*, August 4, 1966.

[4] HACB, "Os sete quesitos da interpelação: Algumas observações," July 26, 1966, File P1 (p. 8), CPDOC, and accompanying newspaper clipping, "Quesitos da Oposição."

August 9, declared that the authority to suspend political rights would not be renounced as long as the institutional acts were in effect. Asked whether "the phase of the IPM's, with all their pressures, threats, and terror," was definitely closed, he replied affirmatively and pointed out that the inquiries had been based on legislation.[5]

Later in the month Medeiros Silva was asked what the government would do about Lacerda, who gave an interview to *Visão* in which he said that Castello was a confused, incapable, personalistic usurper. The minister replied that he had no interest in punishing Lacerda.[6]

7. The Indirect Elections of September and October, 1966

In the case of Ceará, Governor Virgílio Távora found his role in the gubernatorial succession reduced by individuals close to the president, particularly former Governor Paulo Sarasate.

Virgílio Távora's differences with these men were not recent, and he sometimes felt that but for Castello, whom he had known for twenty years, he might have been deposed during the postrevolutionary uncertainties. He had never hidden his gratitude to President Goulart for having provided funds for making the electrical connection between Paulo Afonso and Ceará. When the electrical line was inaugurated in Ceará in February, 1965, Virgílio Távora noted that Castello's speech included no word of thanks to Goulart or himself "for years of struggle," and so Virgílio, in his speech, corrected the omission as far as Goulart was concerned. During a discussion with Castello, Virgílio said, "If I was not *cassado,* it was in homage to the Távora family." The remark infuriated the president.[1]

When a list of five candidates for the Ceará succession emerged from confabulations, it was shown, as a *fait accompli*, by Castello to Virgílio Távora. The governor was upset at the exclusion of the name of Colonel Adauto Bezerra, and he blamed the omission on Sarasate. If Sandra Cavalcanti felt that the weakness of Castello Branco was Roberto Campos, Virgílio Távora felt that the president's weakness was Sarasate.

[5] *Jornal do Brasil*, August 10, 1966.

[6] Ibid., September 1, 1966.

[1] V. Távora, interviews, October 22, 25, 1975.

The president, aware that Sarasate was suffering from an advanced stage of cancer, did nothing to help Sarasate fulfill his ambition of returning to the governorship.[2] Castello wrote the ailing congressman an affectionate letter, praising his idealism, thanking him for his constant backing, and explaining how difficult it was to "dominate impulses of the heart in order to speak to you more in my position of head of state than as your friend."[3]

The executive commission of the Ceará ARENA, meeting with Castello Branco to consider the list of five, picked Congressman Plácido Aderaldo Castelo, who had been the state agriculture secretary in the early 1950's when Castello had been stationed in Fortaleza. To advise of the outcome, Castello Branco sent a telegram to one of the candidates on the list of five, Fortaleza Mayor Murilo Borges, a long-time friend:

> I did not ask anyone to vote for anyone, and much less did I impose a candidate. My role does not permit me to invade the areas of the executive commissions or state directorships. In the selection of Plácido Castelo, mutually complimentary circumstances prevailed, following the withdrawal of Sarasate, who besides being a capable public man, united the most diverse sectors of the Ceará ARENA. Even if I had wanted to impose the selection of your name, the votes would not have supported my proposal. Up to now, in the states and in the case of the presidential succession, the ones indicated have been only those who received the most votes.[4]

In the state of Rio de Janeiro, Krieger says, Castello hoped to see his Chamber of Deputies leader Raimundo Padilha succeed Governor Paulo Torres. But Marshal Paulo Torres, a World War II associate of the president who had not been in politics before 1964, bitterly opposed Padilha. He described Padilha as a fascist because Padilha had belonged to the Green Shirt movement in the 1930's.[5]

Paulo Torres at first supported a nephew.[6] But when the ARENA

[2] Ibid.

[3] HACB, letter to Paulo Sarasate, Rio de Janeiro, May 7, 1966, File N1, Part 2, CPDOC.

[4] HACB, telegram to Murilo Borges, n.d., File P1 (p. 16), CPDOC.

[5] Krieger, *Desde as Missões*, p. 218; Torres, interview, December 19, 1977; *Jornal do Brasil*, July 1, 1966.

[6] Schneider, *The Political System of Brazil*, p. 181.

state executive commission gathered to consider eleven names, in order to forward recommendations to a state convention, it gave the most votes to Padilha. Padilha therefore insisted that his name alone should be examined by the convention. However, Paulo Torres reached an understanding with Castello that would allow the convention to settle the conflict, when it met on July 15, by considering also the name of Paulo Mendes, leader of the Torres administration in the state assembly. After this decision was ratified at one of the stormy meetings of the strife-torn executive commission, thirty-eight of the fifty-six members of the state assembly sent a message to Castello to express their satisfaction that two names would be presented to the convention.[7]

While Padilhistas were accused of not cooperating with plans for reaching an amicable solution, Padilha withdrew his candidacy. This step inspired *Jornal do Brasil* to proclaim on page one, "The State of Rio Is Free of Padilha," and it seemed to leave the way clear for Paulo Mendes, the candidate of Torres. But Castello, concluding that the divergencies between Torres and Padilha were insurmountable, was determined to help preserve party unity by means of a "conciliatory formula." The president therefore held a series of meetings with Jeremias Fontes, head of the state executive commission, and with its other members, to urge the selection of a name capable of pacifying the state politically.[8]

When the convention met on July 15, it decided that the best choice for pacifying the two wings of the party was Jeremias Fontes himself, and it nominated him for governor. Raimundo Padilha considered resigning as Castello's leader in the Chamber of Deputies, but Krieger convinced him that if he resigned he would be unfair to Castello, who, Krieger maintained, had not opposed Padilha and could hardly have acted differently than he did.[9]

Although the MDB said early in July that it would participate in no indirect election, it continued to support Cirne Lima in Rio Grande do Sul until he withdrew in mid-August. And for a while in São Paulo the MDB had a gubernatorial candidate in General Dalísio Mena Barreto, who had uncovered corruption in the São Paulo state govern-

[7] *Jornal do Brasil*, July 1, 3, 5, 10, 15, 1966; Torres, interview, December 19, 1977.

[8] *Jornal do Brasil*, July 12, 14, 15, 1966.

[9] Ibid., July 16, 1966; Krieger, *Desde as Missões*, p. 219.

ment before he was replaced as IPM investigator. As a gubernatorial candidate, Mena Barreto declared himself deeply moved by expressions of support from Eurico Gaspar Dutra, Odílio Denys, and Sílvio Heck, but a faction of the São Paulo MDB expressed dissatisfaction with him and resolved to enter into "true combat" against the government. Mena Barreto's first campaign pronouncement, recognizing his small chance of victory, was followed by the government's issuance of the Act of Party Loyalty. The new act, which prompted *Jornal do Brasil* to ask, "What Parties?" resulted in the withdrawal of Mena Barreto's candidacy.[10]

Cassações of assemblymen in Acre, including the MDB's probable candidate, assured an ARENA victory there.[11] Thus, early in September the public was not surprised to learn that the ARENA had won all of the twelve gubernatorial elections.

The public showed interest in the popular elections for seats in the federal Congress and state assemblies scheduled for November 15. It had no reason to be interested in the indirect presidential election of October 3 but plenty of reason to assess Costa e Silva, who was traveling around the country with his wife, Yolanda. Georges-André Fiechter describes the marshal's "campaign": "Always affable and smiling, talking a lot but never giving away his future policy, playing with his enormous dark glasses, he did a public relations job which paid off all the better because it contrasted strongly with the 'clinical' style of Castello Branco. . . . Politically he promised to 'humanize' the regime, to hasten re-democratization, to concern himself with social problems and to champion a kind of economic nationalism." He offered to improve relations between employers and employees and to initiate a dialogue with the students after his election.[12]

While Costa e Silva campaigned, Brasília appeared to have been abandoned by cabinet ministers and legislators. With administration proposals becoming laws because no quorums could be mustered, Adauto Cardoso complained that the MDB's "indiscriminate obstruc-

[10] *Jornal do Brasil*, July 17, 21, 1966; Schneider, *The Political System of Brazil*, p. 181.

[11] Schneider, *The Political System of Brazil*, p. 182; *Jornal do Brasil*, July 20, 1966.

[12] Fiechter, *Brazil since 1964*, p. 108; *Jornal do Brasil*, September 28, 29, 30, 1966.

tion" was causing the disparagement of Congress. Finally, on September 20, MDB congressmen voted, forty-seven to twenty-nine, to suspend "total obstruction," a victory for the MDB "moderates." However, opposition leader Vieira de Melo announced that the MDB would expel any congressman or senator who appeared in Congress for the October 3 presidential election.[13]

Senator Afonso Arinos de Melo Franco, who had joined the ARENA, said that he felt inclined not to show up at the election, which he described as a proof of the "submission" of Congress; and he added that "Congress cannot express the immediate popular view about preferences between candidates, which makes its representation unauthentic, besides being antidemocratic." But the government's legislative leaders were assisted by telegrams from Castello to the governors urging that they join with the local ARENA directorships in making sure that congressmen came to Brasília. Two hundred fifty-five congressmen and 40 senators voted for Costa e Silva on October 3. They included MDB Congressman Anísio Rocha, the initiator of the war minister's candidacy in December, 1965, and he was expelled from the MDB immediately after the vote.[14]

8. The Resignations of the Kruels (August, 1966)

Second Army Commander Amauri Kruel maintained that the purpose of the 1964 revolution had been to "end the Brizola business, end the *república sindicalista* idea, and redemocratize Brazil." He was known to dislike Ato 2, and after he delivered a speech in Paraná supporting Ademar de Barros' call for direct elections, he believed that Castello regarded both him and Ademar de Barros as men who "did not take orders."[1] Amauri objected to the *cassações* of Ademar de Barros and the Gaúcho assemblymen and believed that Castello had gone back on his word about modifying the "discriminatory" electoral domicile requirement.

[13] *Jornal do Brasil*, August 21, September 5, 6, 17, 21, 30, 1966.

[14] Ibid., September 29, 30, October 4, 1966.

[1] A. Kruel, interviews, December 11, 1975, July 22, 1977. *República sindicalista*: a republic run by labor unions.

Costa e Silva, shortly before leaving the War Ministry, spoke with Riograndino Kruel, head of the Federal Department of Public Safety (DFSP) and asked him to persuade his brother to accept a transfer to Rio to become head of the Army General Staff (EME). Riograndino asked Costa e Silva to let Amauri stay in São Paulo, and then he called on Castello in Brasília and argued that Amauri had the right to remain in São Paulo because the revolution had been successful due to him.[2]

Following Castello's suggestion, Riograndino spoke in Rio with the new war minister, Ademar de Queiroz, who explained in a friendly way that the president was eager to resolve the matter about Amauri. Castello, when he made his next trip to Rio, also discussed the case with Ademar de Queiroz, with the result that Amauri received a letter from the war minister asking him to head the EME. Castello, back in Brasília, told Riograndino that the decision to transfer Amauri to Rio was definite.[3]

Amauri Kruel refused to accept the transfer.[4] On August 9 he retired to the army reserve, with the rank of marshal, and announced that he would issue a manifesto the following day.

Kruel's manifesto, released a few hours before he left São Paulo for Rio, condemned presidential acts that were ushering in "the darkness of absolutism."[5] It blamed these acts, "manipulated with hypocrisy," for the national "intranquility," and it ascribed the lack of foreign capital to "governmental blundering, revealed in the repeated measures of exception, promulgated in defense of personal power."

Amauri Kruel compared his own role in 1964, when he set friendships aside, buried past differences, and, despite risk, led the "fearless troops of the Second Army," with the role of those who now considered themselves the only authentic revolutionaries—"as though, in order to be a revolutionary, it is enough to criticize a government in private, drink whiskey in the comfort of apartments, hang on to telephones for conspiratorial whispers, and await the hour of the victory of the forces engaged in the struggle, in order to go into the streets and take over quickly the key posts that have been abandoned." He ex-

[2] Riograndino Kruel, interview, Rio de Janeiro, September 21, 1975.

[3] Ibid.

[4] A. Kruel, interview, December 11, 1975.

[5] *Jornal do Brasil*, August 11, 1966.

plained that he had not opposed the suspension of the political rights of those who were "incompatible with democratic, moralizing, and regenerating practices," but that he could hardly applaud "the use of those expedients as a simple instrument for electing the candidate who is personally pleasing to the chief of the executive power."

On August 11, when Amauri's manifesto appeared in the press, Riograndino and Castello were both in Brasília. Riograndino addressed a long letter to the president asking to be relieved of his position as head of the DFSP.[6] Amauri, he said, had remained loyal despite differences about "fundamental political problems of the Revolution" and despite being thwarted in his legitimate aspiration to be governor of São Paulo. Riograndino cited the frustration of his own effort to bring about harmony and the failure of his appeals, made without Amauri's knowledge, that Amauri be allowed to remain in São Paulo for the few final months of his active army service.

When Riograndino entered Castello's Planalto office to present his resignation letter, the two old friends, who together with Amauri had been classmates as boys in Porto Alegre, were full of emotion. Castello said that he was in no condition to read the letter but would do so later at Alvorada Palace.[7]

Castello replied in longhand on August 12. Dismissing as "vulgar and vile" the press reports that he had handled the case of Amauri for "the cold purpose of eliminating a possible adversary," the president praised the feelings that had led Riograndino to bring about the renewal of relations between Amauri and Castello early in 1964 and said that he himself had cooperated not only to help the revolution "but also because it touched my best sentiments to have a return to an affection that began in the big house of Várzea of Porto Alegre."[8]

This is not the time for me to justify myself, nor for us to judge the final conduct of the former commander of the Second Army. I am here, above all, face to face with your person. And now I recall the time when you came to the front of my house, before March, 1964, to tell me that you were joining the ranks of the Revolution, speaking to me resolutely. . . .

[6] Riograndino Kruel, letter to HACB, August 11, 1966, File M, CPDOC.

[7] R. Kruel, interview, September 21, 1975.

[8] HACB, letter to R. Kruel, August 12, 1966, copy in File M, CPDOC, original in possession of R. Kruel.

You ask to resign. You are going to leave, not because of you or me, but because of unavoidable circumstances. I am going to take the matter up with the justice minister. That is painful for me.

Amauri Kruel, along with Lott, Taurino de Rezende, and Oscar Passos, was invited to be present at the MDB headquarters in Rio on the evening of August 19 for a "Liberty Rally" organized by the Group of Students, Intellectuals, and Workers (GEIT). He replied that he was completely in favor of the rally but could not attend because of a commitment to appear on television in São Paulo. At the São Paulo MDB headquarters he asserted that "Brazil is under a dictatorship" and added that although he did not know the details of an impeachment action being brought against Castello by two Paraná congressmen, "there are more than enough reasons for it."[9]

While Amauri went on to become a candidate of the Guanabara MDB for federal congressman, Riograndino kept insisting with Ernesto Geisel that his resignation be accepted. Castello discussed the replacement of Riograndino with Justice Minister Carlos Medeiros Silva, who was poorly impressed with Riograndino Kruel and the way he had run the DFSP. On August 22, Castello submitted to the Senate his selection for replacing Riograndino Kruel: Lieutenant Colonel Newton Cipriano de Castro Leitão, the head of the economic section of the SNI.[10]

9. The Manifesto of the Frente Ampla (October 27, 1966)

Late in August, 1966, Lacerda started working on a prodemocracy, antigovernment manifesto with the thought that it might be signed by himself, Kubitschek, Goulart, and perhaps Quadros. That Lacerda might run into difficulties caused by his past denunciations of these now-silenced leaders seemed likely.

Renato Archer, president of the MDB of Maranhão, was surprised when Lacerda informed him that he had a message from Kubitschek authorizing Archer to act for the former president in connection with the formation of an antidictatorial Frente Ampla (Broad Front). For

[9] *Jornal do Brasil*, August 19, 20, 1966.

[10] Medeiros Silva, interview, August 13, 1977; *Jornal do Brasil*, August 23, 1966.

one thing, Archer, who had assisted San Tiago Dantas in running the Foreign Ministry when Goulart was president, had been associated with the PSD opponents of Lacerda. For another thing, Archer was puzzled by the objectives of Lacerda. At any rate, while Archer could not see how Goulart could profit from joining a *frente* with Lacerda, he felt that such an alliance might be helpful to Kubitschek, long accused by Lacerda of corruption.[1]

Early in September, Archer and writer Edmundo Moniz paid calls on Kubitschek in Lisbon, and Congressman Doutel de Andrade went south to consult with Goulart about the Frente Ampla. Lacerdistas announced that the "unification of the oppositions" was practically complete. But Amaral Peixoto came closer to the truth when he spoke of the difficulties of forming a Frente Ampla. Kubitschek did not wish to enter into any alliance with Goulart or sign anything that might get his associates in Brazil into trouble. Within the MDB, opinions about the Frente Ampla differed, as was apparent in Minas, where the state MDB president, Senator Camillo Nogueira da Gama, expressed enthusiasm while Congressman Tancredo Neves objected to the inclusion of Lacerda.[2]

Lacerda argued forcefully that past "resentments" should be set aside in order to "win the war against misery, backwardness, and ignorance." In articles published late in September, Lacerda spoke of the understandings that he had with men who were "blessed with popular leadership," and he wrote that the first person who would "take the initiative of reviewing the *cassações* is named Costa e Silva." Lacerda told Abreu Sodré that he believed the Frente Ampla would be the only instrument capable of giving Costa e Silva a popular base.[3]

Castello, speaking in the territory of Roraima late in September, described the Frente Ampla as a reconciliation, "which one should call spurious," of frustrated ambitions, vanished privileges, or political concepts that were threatened by the national recuperation. He said that "people who have lost their memories or who are blinded by ambitions and interests, elements of the most diverse and antagonistic origins, are

[1] Renato Archer, interview, Rio de Janeiro, September 30, 1975.

[2] *Jornal do Brasil*, September 7, 9, 10, 13, 14, 1966; Castello Branco, *Os Militares no Poder*, pp. 562–567; Lacerda, *Depoimento*, p. 382.

[3] *Jornal do Brasil*, September 17, 23, 1966; newspaper clipping in Anexo 52, File N6, CPDOC; Castello Branco, *Os Militares no Poder*, p. 576.

certainly forgetful that the people have the habit of keeping their eyes open and minds informed. And so no one is fooled when individuals change disguises or renounce ideas, judgments, and sentiments." Answering a question at the press conference at Planalto Palace on October 1, the president said that the articulators of the so-called Frente Ampla sought to deceive each other.[4] When Castello lunched with Austregésilo de Ataíde at Laranjeiras Palace and the subject of Lacerda came up, the president broke his habit of not speaking critically about people to Austregésilo. Lacerda, Castello said, had sought funds for a personal purpose from the presidency because in April, 1964, he had asked for a post abroad with the explanation that he lacked the money to go abroad but wanted to do so to arrange for an ear operation for his wife.[5]

During most of October the public was kept in suspense by conflicting reports about whether Kubitschek, or perhaps Kubitschek and Goulart, would join Lacerda in signing the Frente Ampla manifesto and about how it would be made public. At first Raul Brunini, a Lacerdista in the Guanabara state assembly, was expected to read it in Tiradentes Palace while simultaneous readings occurred in local and federal legislative houses. Then it was announced that MDB leader Vieira de Melo, an oppositionist without past Lacerdista connections, would read it "to demonstrate that the opposition was a monolithic bloc." After Kubitschek, touring the United States, decided to consult further before signing, Vieira de Melo apologized to the press for canceling the reading of a manifesto that was to be signed by Lacerda and Kubitschek and left Rio for the congressional campaign in Bahia.[6]

The manifesto was read to representatives of the press by Lacerda, with Hélio Fernandes at his side, in the office of *Tribuna da Imprensa* on October 27. Lacerda, in his introductory remarks, attributed the absence of the signatures of Kubitschek and Goulart to "threats unleashed at the last moment by the government," which, he said, "is characterized by neofascism and the philosophy of the semiliterate Sorbonne

[4] *Jornal do Brasil*, September 21, October 2, 1966.

[5] Austregésilo de Ataíde, interview, August 5, 1977.

[6] *Jornal do Brasil*, October 8, 27, 1966; Castello Branco, *Os Militares no Poder*, p. 579; "Brunini vai ler na AL manifesto da Frente Ampla," newspaper clipping in Anexo 64, File N6, CPDOC; Hélio Fernandes, "JK não assina mas dá adesão," *Tribuna da Imprensa*, October 28, 1966.

Group that prepares to make Brazil a satellite of the Department of State."[7] Hélio Fernandes, in a *Tribuna da Imprensa* account of "these 64 days of negotiations," wrote that Kubitschek had made suggestions about the wording (some of them "very valid") and had actually signed the manifesto but had been forced to withdraw when friends had been threatened by "the cops of the government." Goulart was quoted by Fernandes as being perfectly willing to sign with Lacerda, who had never betrayed or deceived him, in contrast to "certain figures who backed the present government after having participated in my government."[8]

The lengthy manifesto described the Castello Branco government as "subservient to decisions made abroad, hostile to the people and fearful of their judgment, using abusively the arms of national security to coerce and immobilize the people, implanting insecurity, unbelief, and anguish in all the homes." After addressing itself in turn to the workers ("expelled from the community as though they were pariahs"), students, women, middle classes, and entrepreneurs, it called for direct elections, to be held quickly, and for "juridical guarantees and individual rights."

The manifesto asserted that economic policy "ought to be clearly dictated only by the national interest." Emphasizing the need to return to "creative optimism" and economic development, it condemned "rigid formulas, conceived by rich nations." The policy "imposed by the IMF," it said, had resulted in unemployment, decadence, disorder, and despair. "The economic policy must bring about the expansion of the internal market, higher wages to increase the capacity to consume, and the incorporation of the rural sectors that have been left out of the economic process."[9]

Jornal do Brasil explained the Frente Ampla as caused by "the interruption of the democratic process" and suggested that the Castello Branco government devote less attention to repression and more attention to "a debate that could oxygenize the heavy Brazilian atmosphere of this hour." While *O Estado de S. Paulo* agreed on the need for di-

[7] *Jornal do Brasil*, October 28, 1966. Sorbonne Group: term applied to an influential group of instructors at Brazil's National War College (ESG).

[8] Fernandes, "JK não assina mas dá adesão."

[9] *Tribuna da Imprensa*, October 28, 1966.

rect elections and a new political party reform, it opposed the manifesto's stand about economic-financial matters and an "independent foreign policy." Above all, *O Estado de S. Paulo* disliked Lacerda's approach to Kubitschek and Goulart and wrote that in making that approach, Lacerda was probably guilty of the error that Castello had committed. Castello, *O Estado de S. Paulo* wrote, "allied himself with some of the most typical representatives of the past whom the Revolution should have rooted out. . . . And that is why everything still remains to be done in the area of the country's political reorganization."[10]

10. A Forced Recess of Congress (October, 1966)

During the negotiations that led to the issuance of the manifesto of the Frente Ampla, rumors circulated that Castello would cancel the mandates of some congressmen who were handling the matter with Goulart and Kubitschek. Câmara President Adauto Cardoso denied the rumors. As far back as March 4, 1966, Cardoso had maintained that *cassações* of federal congressmen were a thing of the past, Congress having already paid "a heavy price" in 1964; in July he had renewed his assurances to congressmen, letting it be known that he had a commitment from Castello.[1]

In the first days of October, Cardoso and Senate President Moura Andrade, speaking with Castello about the role of Congress in the work on a new constitution, sought the revocation of the articles of Ato 2 that permitted the chief executive to suspend political rights. Castello, in a speech in Campinas on October 5, said that "the acts will remain in effect until they end on the dates established in them." But it was known that the president had resolved that no federal legislator would lose his mandate "as a result of his behavior regarding the government's project" of a constitution.[2]

On October 11 the reports about possible new *cassações* appeared serious, with specific mention of Congressmen Ranieri Mazzilli, Doutel

[10] *Jornal do Brasil* and *O Estado de S. Paulo*, October 28, 1966.

[1] Castello Branco, *Os Militares no Poder*, p. 438; *Jornal do Brasil*, July 12, 1966.

[2] Castello Branco, *Os Militares no Poder*, p. 575; HACB, *Discursos, 1966*, pp 63–66; *Jornal do Brasil*, October 7, 1966.

de Andrade, and César Prieto in view of the "apprehension of the correspondence of these lawmakers with former Presidents Juscelino Kubitschek and João Goulart." Adauto Cardoso declared: "I repeat that there will be no cancellations of mandates in the Chamber of Deputies."[3]

But on the morning of October 12, Philip Raine, chargé at the American Embassy in the absence of Ambassador Tuthill, was advised by Acting Foreign Minister Pio Corrêa that Castello intended to suspend the political rights of about ten politicians, including six federal congressmen, within the next few days. Pio Corrêa, apparently hoping that the advance information would keep adverse reactions to a minimum in the United States, said that five of the congressmen would be *cassados* for "extreme leftism" and one for "corruption." The purpose, Pio Corrêa explained, was to keep the undesirables from being returned to their legislative seats in November.

Raine concluded his report to Washington by saying that the decision "raises questions as to the President's freedom of action since all indications are that he did give Adauto Cardoso assurances no more federal deputados would be cassated. It should be noted that this action follows closely on heels October 6 meeting all military commanders."[4]

The news of the *cassações* became public on the evening of October 12, when Castello signed orders punishing ten politicians. The six congressmen included MDB vice-leader Doutel de Andrade, César Prieto, and Sebastião Paes de Almeida, but not Mazzilli. A spokesman for the president declared that the *cassações* were based on papers handled some time earlier by the National Security Council.[5]

Adauto Cardoso was shocked. He let it be known that during a half-hour conversation with Castello at Laranjeiras Palace on the afternoon of the twelfth he had become convinced that no *cassações* would affect federal lawmakers, and then, later at home, he had been surprised by the news. Resolving to interrupt his campaigning, he resumed his post in Brasília with the hope that his example would be followed by

[3] Castello Branco, *Os Militares no Poder*, pp. 578–579.

[4] Philip Raine, cable to Washington, October 12, 1966, NSFB, Vol. VI, Box 3, Document 55, LBJ Library; according to Sátiro (interview, December 17, 1975), Castello had earlier told Adauto Cardoso that he did not plan to ("*não pretendo*") carry out more *cassações* of federal congressmen, but this was not a promise.

[5] *Jornal do Brasil*, October 13, 1966.

at least forty more congressmen, the minimum necessary for holding a Câmara session.[6]

Despite the efforts of MDB Acting President Franco Montoro and MDB congressional leader Vieira de Melo, no quorum of forty-one materialized by October 15, the end of the week. Unable to deliver his pronouncement to a session of Congress, Adauto released a note declaring that the decision about canceling mandates belonged exclusively to the Chamber, leaving it clear that the six congressmen were considered to be unaffected by the action of Castello.[7]

Doutel de Andrade was arrested, with Justice Minister Medeiros Silva explaining that he had lost his parliamentary immunities and had to testify at an inquiry about corruption in Santa Catarina. But Vieira de Melo won Doutel de Andrade's release with a habeas corpus petition based on the note of the Câmara president, and so Doutel joined four of the other new *cassados* in the congressional building, where Adauto assured them of the full exercise of their mandates.[8] They lived in the building, made statements against the government, and met with the press, which carried stories about how beds and food had been arranged for them.

Adauto issued a terse official note to Castello to advise that the question of the mandates, after study by the appropriate congressional commissions, would be discussed and voted in the plenary. Senate President Moura Andrade announced that Adauto was handling the matter perfectly.[9]

Despite the open rebellion, Castello was reluctant to decree a congressional recess in accordance with powers granted by Ato 2.[10] One alternative was to obtain a progovernment decision by Congress, and another was to persuade Adauto to adopt a different course. Thought was given to having the *mesa*, or board of Câmara officers, rule against Adauto's position. But after one of the officers of the Câmara unexpectedly supported Adauto, it seemed dubious that the *mesa* would desert its president; and it was not clear whether the *mesa* had the power to reverse his decision. Mazzilli, Ulisses Guimarães, and Nelson

[6] Ibid.

[7] Ibid., October 16, 1966; Castello Branco, *Os Militares no Poder*, pp. 580–581.

[8] *Jornal do Brasil*, October 17, 18, 1966.

[9] Ibid., October 16, 18, 1966.

[10] Antônio Carlos Magalhães, interview, August 11, 1977.

Carneiro issued opinions to show that Adauto did not need the *mesa*'s approval.[11] As for a decision by the plenary, this appeared impossible because almost all the congressmen were intent on campaigning.

Castello phoned Supreme Court Justice Aliomar Baleeiro in Brasília and asked him to talk with Adauto. Castello, Baleeiro learned, was upset at Adauto's protection of Doutel de Andrade, who was calling Castello a liar. When the name of Sobral Pinto came up, Castello told Baleeiro that "he is a diabolic creature who, together with Sandra, dominates Adauto." Castello admitted that developments might result in Adauto's resignation, but he told Baleeiro that the alternative was his own resignation from the presidency.[12]

Baleeiro lunched with Adauto and found him furious because during his half-hour talk with Castello at Laranjeiras Palace on the twelfth nothing had been said about the *cassações*. Others who spoke with Adauto on behalf of Castello were Raimundo Padilha and Pedro Aleixo. In particular Castello relied on Pedro Aleixo, whom he phoned with instructions to stay close to Adauto and prevent him from joining "the radicals."[13]

Adauto remained intransigent despite the fact that the rebellion had gained all the earmarks of a revolt against the Revolution. *O Estado de S. Paulo* wrote that what had begun as one more crisis, "provoked by Marshal Castello Branco's lack of political feeling," had turned into "open defiance of . . . the regime installed after the victory of March 31. The counter-Revolution unmasked itself and attacked at the opportune moment" taking advantage of "the unspeakable cowardice of the ARENA."[14]

Congressman Luís Viana Filho, who arrived in Rio on October 19 at the request of Castello, was brought up to date by Geisel, Golberi, and Congressman Antônio Carlos Magalhães. Medeiros Silva and Castello showed Viana the draft of a new *ato complementar* that would decree a recess of Congress. The president, Viana found, wanted to have everything ready and felt that the presidential authority ought not to be allowed to erode any further.

At 6:00 P.M. on the nineteenth, news from Brasília made it clear

[11] *Jornal do Brasil* and *O Estado de S. Paulo*, October 20, 1966.

[12] Baleeiro, "Recordações do Presidente H. Castelo Branco," p. 36.

[13] Antônio Carlos Magalhães, interview, August 11, 1977.

[14] *O Estado de S. Paulo*, October 20, 1966.

that no negotiated solution could be reached. The president instructed Medeiros Silva, Cordeiro de Farias, Antônio Carlos Magalhães, and the war and navy ministers to join him at 9:00 P.M. War Minister Ademar de Queiroz phoned General José Nogueira Paes, commander of Brasília and the Eleventh Military Region, to summon him urgently to Rio. And the war minister made final arrangements for the closing of Congress by phoning Colonel Carlos de Meira Mattos, who had become head of the Polícia do Exército (Army Police) after serving in the Dominican Republic.[15]

At 3:25 A.M. on October 20, General Nogueira Paes returned to Brasília after his brief visit to Rio. He brought Ato Complementar No. 23, signed by Castello, Medeiros Silva, Pio Corrêa, and the three military ministers. It declared Congress in recess until November 22 and authorized the president to issue decree-laws during the recess. In its introductory clauses it said that the procedure proposed by the Câmara president about the *cassações*, besides being improper, had been taken at a time when the Câmara could not count on the presence of enough members to deliberate, because of the election campaign.

At 5:00 A.M., after General Nogueira Paes presented a copy of the Ato Complementar to Nilo Coelho at his residence in Brasília, troops of the marines, air force, and Polícia do Exército surrounded Congress. Meira Mattos, who had a recommendation from Castello to avoid the use of force against individuals, decided to cut off the electric power, phone service, and water in the congressional buildings.[16]

While military trucks with sirens and red lights circled the buildings, the seventy-eight congressmen (including the five *cassados*) who were inside suddenly found themselves in darkness. Some of them yelled: "To the plenary! They must find us in the plenary!" When Meira Mattos, leading the invasion by the Polícia do Exército, entered the plenary, he ordered everyone to leave. Legislators demanded that the new decree be shown them by one of their members. After Nilo Coelho presented the decree, the congressmen decided to leave. The operation against Congress had taken about five minutes.[17]

[15] Viana Filho, *O Governo Castelo Branco*, p. 466.

[16] *Jornal do Brasil*, October 20, 1966; Meira Mattos, interview, January 5, 1976.

[17] Luís Barbosa (of JB Brasília office), "Sem Água e sem Luz, o Congresso Cedeu," and José Leão Filho (of JB Brasília office), "Uma Operação de 5 Minutos," *Jornal do Brasil*, October 21, 1966.

Adauto Cardoso said to Colonel Meira Mattos: "General, it is a surprise for me to see you, whom I considered a democrat, heading the forces that surround the national Congress." Meira Mattos replied: "Deputado, it is a surprise for me to see you, whom I considered a Revolutionary, leading a rebellion by the anti-Revolutionary and Communist forces." Adauto explained: "General, I represent the civil power." The colonel said: "Deputado, I represent the Revolutionary power."[18]

While it was still dark, naval officers entered the offices of *Correio Brazilense*, Brasília's only newspaper. The chief of staff of the naval district ordered the newspaper to print no news about the forced recess of Congress. But this censorship ended within twenty-four hours after it had been announced that it had not been authorized by the presidency.[19]

MDB President Oscar Passos was so upset by the forced recess that he suffered a heart disturbance. Senator Milton Campos, speaking in Belo Horizonte, said that he had disagreed with Ato 2 and therefore could not approve of its consequences, such as the decreed congressional recess. "I speak," he said, "as a democrat who longs for constitutional normality."[20]

Castello, who was kept informed about developments in Brasília by phone calls from Meira Mattos, received many telegrams of support. The Executive Commission of the ARENA came to Laranjeiras Palace on October 21 to deliver a motion backing the president. After it was read by Krieger, Castello told his visitors that the recess of Congress "is nothing more than the defense of the elections."[21]

In São Paulo, Franco Montoro accused Castello of violating a law that prohibited the executive from exerting pressure to influence the elections.[22] But *O Estado de S. Paulo* defended the forced recess of Congress, which it blamed on Adauto Cardoso's "wounded vanity and electoral interests" and Castello's "obstinacy and political inexperience." Observing that the culmination of the crisis had been received with complete indifference in Brazil, *O Estado de S. Paulo* warned that

[18] Meira Mattos, interview, January 5, 1976.

[19] *Jornal do Brasil*, October 21, 22, 1966.

[20] Ibid., October 21, 1966.

[21] Meira Mattos, interview, January 5, 1976; *Jornal do Brasil*, October 23, 1966.

[22] Ibid.

the foreign press, knowing nothing about Brazil, would take a hostile attitude.[23] *O Estado de S. Paulo* described most of the members of Congress as "the dregs of the nation" and Castello as overly interested in the views of the foreign press.[24]

Castello received Hal Hendrix, of the Scripps-Howard newspapers, on October 21. The president, cordial and relaxed, said that "what is happening in Brasília is an episode and it will be no more than that. It is an attempt by counter-Revolutionaries who are desperate. Furthermore, they do not have the support of public opinion. Their shouts are falling into a void. We will not cede." The president also told the American journalist that the aim of his government for almost three years had been to establish the best conditions possible for the installation again of a normal government on March 15, 1967. "Insofar as the economic situation is concerned we have established the basis for the beginning of development again on a realistic basis." The year 1970, Castello predicted, would be a great one for Brazil.[25]

On October 23, Castello went to Brasília for a National Security Council meeting at which he explained recent events. "I assure you that the president of the Republic never made any commitment to anyone not to make further use of Articles 14 and 15 of Ato Institucional Number Two." Castello next denied "another improper accusation": that he had hidden from Adauto Cardoso the *cassações* decrees on the very day of their issuance. When he saw Adauto, he said, he had not completed the task of collecting the opinions of the National Security Council members.

Castello argued that while the effort of "the counter-Revolutionaries" had attracted no national support, a prolongation of the situation "might have disturbed the life of the national Congress and, above all, served as a motive for the opposition to act against holding the elections of November 15." Denying that his latest move was inconsistent with his past record of defending the existence of Congress, he said that "after the advent of the Revolution, I always participated in

[23] *O Estado de S. Paulo*, October 21, 1966.

[24] Ibid., October 16, 23, 25, 27, 1966.

[25] U.S. Embassy, Rio de Janeiro, cable to Washington, October 21, 1966, NSFB, Vol. VI, Box 3, Document 57, LBJ Library.

the decisions to guarantee the Câmara and the Senate, and now I have sought to protect them and assure, as best I can, their survival.'[26]

In Washington, Assistant Secretary of State Gordon and Ambassador Tuthill took note of the "setback" of their political hopes for Brazil when they drew up recommendations to President Johnson for a program loan to Brazil of up to one hundred million dollars in calendar year 1967 and project loans of up to ninety million dollars in fiscal year 1967. "On the political side," the report to Johnson said, "the Castello Branco Government has caused us some concern recently." Mention was made of *cassações* decreed in July "with obvious purpose of influencing indirect governorship elections" and the more recent *cassações* of six federal congressmen followed by the decreed recess of Congress. Gordon and Tuthill were, however, optimistic about the future. The report to Johnson said that "Castello Branco seems determined to assume personally all of the criticism being levelled against the Brazilian Government for anti-democratic actions so as to permit Costa e Silva to assume the Presidency March 15, 1967, with a relatively cleansed governmental structure and one free of authoritarian overtones.'[27]

11. Hélio Fernandes, Cassado during Electioneering (November 10, 1966)

Lacerdistas in Guanabara, eager to compete as oppositionists in the November elections, suspected that the Tribunal Regional Eleitoral (TRE) would not accept the registration of the PAREDE. When they turned to the Guanabara MDB, made up largely of old PTB foes of Lacerda, they were refused admittance. They therefore appealed to the MDB's national directorship in Brasília, which handed them a favorable ruling.[1] But their squabbles with the Guanabara MDB continued.

[26] *Jornal do Brasil*, November 8, 1966. (Castello Branco's statement to the National Security Council was released to the press by the presidential press secretary on November 7, 1966.)

[27] William S. Gaud, memorandum ("Economic Assistance Program for Brazil") for LBJ, Office of the Administrator, AID, Washington, D.C., n.d., NSFB, Document 102a, LBJ Library.

[1] Almeida Magalhães, interview, August 8, 1977.

The Guanabara MDB, told by the TRE to reduce the number of its candidates for the state assembly, included four Lacerdistas in its cut of twenty-three, whereupon irritated Lacerdistas asked the TRE to reject all the MDB candidacies because of "irregularities in the party regional convention."[2]

Next the TRE told the Guanabara MDB that some of its ninety-nine candidates for state and federal legislative seats were subversive. The head of the local MDB discussed the matter with the TRE's attorney and then agreed to drop twelve of the ninety-nine, among them federal congressional candidates Paulo Silveira, José Frejat, Mário Pedroso, Hermano Alves, and Márcio Moreira Alves. However, on October 25 the TRE ruled against this deal by a 3–2 vote that was loudly celebrated by the twelve who would have been removed from the list.[3]

The TRE met again on October 27 to study the claim of the government that some of the registration applications of would-be MDB candidates were technically defective in their wording. While Hélio Fernandes, owner of *Tribuna da Imprensa,* participated with Lacerda in unveiling the manifesto of the Frente Ampla, the TRE decided that registration flaws invalidated his federal congressional candidacy along with those of Marshal Taurino de Rezende and Hugo Bloise. The three appealed to the Federal Supreme Court.[4]

At the end of the first week in November, while the Supreme Court decision was awaited, electoral tribunals ruled in favor of the four Lacerdistas whom the MDB had agreed to eliminate from the Guanabara assembly race. But Lacerda, disappointed by a local tribunal decision against the PAREDE, declared that the MDB and the ARENA were both worthless and that he would organize "a true Partido Popular Brasileiro." He promised to do this after the elections, which, he said, he was not taking "very seriously." That some people were taking the elections seriously appeared evident in Goiás, where the head of the MDB of the city of Ananás was assassinated by the revolver shots of ARENA supporters.[5]

[2] *Jornal do Brasil*, October 12, 13, 1966.

[3] Ibid., October 15, 18, 26, 1966.

[4] Ibid., October 28, 30, 1966; Hélio Fernandes, interview, Rio de Janeiro, July 6, 1977.

[5] *Jornal do Brasil*, November 4, 8, 9, 1966; *Diário de Notícias*, November 8, 1966.

In Brasília, MDB President Oscar Passos, recently released from a hospital, expressed profound concern about the decision reached by student leaders and other oppositionists to protest against the regime by voting in blank or invalidating their ballots by writing, "Down with the Dictatorship" on them. Such behavior, he said, would hurt the MDB. Meanwhile, in Minas, Magalhães Pinto campaigned for a congressional seat on the ARENA ticket by making speeches that belittled the ARENA and assailed the Castello Branco administration. He stated that the existing parties lacked any popular base and should be replaced, and he accused Castello of having "established a personalist government, setting the people aside, very different from what we wanted to implant when we made the revolution of March 31."[6]

At 1:30 P.M. on November 10, a Supreme Court justice issued a preliminary ruling that would assure the registration of the candidacies of Hélio Fernandes and Marshal Taurino de Rezende. But at 1:55 P.M. the political rights of Hélio Fernandes and seventeen others were suspended by a decree signed by Castello.[7]

Hélio Fernandes announced that he would not recognize the decree and would continue writing in *Tribuna da Imprensa,* "where I shall be if they want to arrest me." Lacerda, leaving that evening for Europe, told a multitude at Galeão Airport that Hélio Fernandes had lost his political rights because his independent position was becoming disturbing to the American groups that had taken charge of Brazil.[8]

On November 11, Fernandes published a defiant article in which he spoke of his determination to continue denouncing treasonable and arbitrary acts, which, he wrote, were "based only on the personal will of an insane and crazy dictator, who uses the entire nation as an arena to satisfy his self-worship and his autocratic and frenzied egocentrism." He asserted that he had been "*cassado* by the great tribunal of the international trusts, whose representatives in Brazil are Castello Branco, Roberto Campos, Walter Moreira Salles, and others."[9]

[6] *Jornal do Brasil*, November 1, 1966.

[7] Ibid., November 11, 1966; Hélio Fernandes, *Recordações de um Desterrado em Fernando de Noronha*, p. 13.

[8] *Jornal do Brasil*, November 11, 1966; see also newspaper clipping, File N6 (Anexo 70), CPDOC.

[9] Fernandes article reproduced in *Recordações de um Desterrado em Fernando de Noronha*, pp. 132–136.

Also on November 11, Colonel Newton Leitão, head of the DFSP, warned Hélio Fernandes that he would be punished if he continued to sign articles of a political nature.[10] Therefore Fernandes' articles began appearing under the pseudonym João da Silva.

12. The Congressional Elections of November 15, 1966

Castello Branco was on a trip to Paraná and Santa Catarina on November 11 and 12. He delivered speeches, inaugurated popular dwellings, and sometimes mingled with the local citizens, whom he praised for their hard work, spirit of order, and "exuberant joy of living." While accepting an honorary citizenship of Lajes, Santa Catarina, he said that on November 15 the people of Brazil would render their decision not about himself but about "the whole policy of the Revolution that we have carried out, as well as its future."[1]

Meanwhile, in Brasília the Tribunal Superior Eleitoral, denying government appeals, upheld the MDB candidacies of Paulo Silveira, Hermano Alves, Márcio Moreira Alves, and Mário Pedroso for the federal Congress. Also during the final days the press carried the recommendations of Carlos Lacerda: Mário Martins for the federal Senate, Raul Brunini for the federal Chamber of Deputies, and Mauro Magalhães for the Guanabara state assembly. All three belonged to the MDB. Mário Martins, a journalist running against senatorial candidates of both parties, complained that his microphones went dead when he was proclaiming that the struggle of the people was against the government. This may have been due to a government regulation, difficult to enforce, that candidates were not to defame individuals or the government while campaigning.[2]

The voting went calmly throughout Brazil. In the states of Guana-

[10] *Jornal do Brasil*, November 12, 1966.

[1] HACB, *Discursos, 1966*, pp. 121–126; *Jornal do Brasil*, November 12, 13, 1966.

[2] *Jornal do Brasil*, November 13, 1966; Fiechter, *Brazil since 1964*, p. 110; Fiechter also writes that during the campaigning "there were to be no calls to violent action likely to disturb the peace: nor was public opinion to be inflamed or 'urban property negatively affected' "; this last remark, he explains (p. 243), "avoided the traditional avalanche of electoral stickers, posters stuck all over the place, slogans hastily sketched and banners stretched across the streets."

bara, São Paulo, and Rio de Janeiro the campaign of the small, radical Ação Popular for null and blank votes may have had some effect, for such votes cast in those areas came to 25.4, 35.4, and 25.9 percent, respectively, compared with the national average of 21 percent.[3] The Brazilian Communist Party, at odds with Ação Popular, had been urging its followers to vote for opposition candidates.

As the count began to appear in the press several days after the elections, it was clear that the ARENA was victorious in almost all of Brazil and the MDB victorious by large margins in the states of Guanabara and Rio de Janeiro and narrowly in Rio Grande do Sul. The final national results gave the ARENA an edge of 8,731,635 votes to the MDB's 4,195,470 in the races for federal congressmen. The ARENA elected 277 federal congressmen, and the opposition party 132. The ARENA won 731 state assembly seats, compared with 345 won by the MDB.[4] Castello Branco, in Belo Horizonte on November 19, told the press that the election results represented "an overwhelming victory of the Brazilian Revolution of March 31, 1964, by means of the mighty ARENA, and the rest is of secondary importance."[5]

In Minas, Magalhães Pinto was the state's most voted for candidate for federal congressman. There the senate race was won by Milton Campos (ARENA). Senators elected elsewhere included Jarbas Passarinho (ARENA, Pará); Paulo Sarasate (ARENA, Ceará); João Cleofas (ARENA, Pernambuco); Vieira de Melo (MDB, Bahia); Paulo Torres (ARENA, Rio state); Carvalho Pinto (ARENA, São Paulo); Nei Braga (ARENA, Paraná); and Siegfried Heuser (MDB, Rio Grande do Sul). The MDB elected only four senators.

Among the congressmen elected were Virgílio Távora (ARENA) and Martins Rodrigues (MDB) in Ceará; Raimundo Padilha (ARENA) and Amaral Peixoto (MDB) in Rio state; Aluísio Alves (ARENA) in Rio Grande do Norte; Cid Sampaio and Costa Cavalcanti (both of the ARENA) in Pernambuco; Franco Montoro (MDB), Cunha Bueno (ARENA), and Herbert Levy (ARENA) in São Paulo;

[3] Figures from Schneider, *The Political System of Brazil*, p. 190.
[4] Ibid., pp. 190–191; Fiechter, *Brazil since 1964*, pp. 110–111.
[5] *Jornal no Brasil*, November 20, 1966.

and in Minas (in addition to Magalhães Pinto) João Herculino, Tancredo Neves, and Renato Azeredo (all three of the MDB).

In Guanabara the federal senate seat was won by Lacerda's choice, Mário Martins of the MDB. Successful MDB contestants for federal congressional seats from Guanabara included Chagas Freitas (in first place), Raul Brunini, Rubem Medina, Gonzaga da Gama, Amaral Neto, Márcio Moreira Alves, and Hermano Alves (in fifteenth place). Successful ARENA contestants for federal seats from Guanabara included Rafael de Almeida Magalhães (in first place), Veiga Brito, Flexa Ribeiro, Lopo Coelho, and Ângelo Mendes de Morais.[6]

Amauri Kruel, MDB candidate for Congress, was edged out in Guanabara by journalist Hermano Alves and thus became a first alternate instead of an elected congressman. Asking the Tribunal Regional Eleitoral (TRE) for a recount, the marshal accused the counting commission of having shifted some of his votes to Hermano Alves. But when Kruel sought the backing of a lawyer who served as an MDB delegate to the TRE, the lawyer said that Kruel had no basis for his claim.[7]

O Estado de S. Paulo attributed the triumph of the MDB in Guanabara not to MDB prestige but to the influence of Lacerda and other popular politicians. Similarly, it called Carvalho Pinto's overwhelming senate victory in São Paulo a personal achievement and not an ARENA victory. It tended to view the overall results as a defeat for the government, taking into consideration the blank and invalidated votes and the "climate of force and fear" instituted by the federal administration. *Jornal da Tarde,* the Mesquitas' afternoon newspaper, called the elections the latest act in the "political farce" of the Castello government.[8]

Lacerda, speaking early in December to reporters of *O Cruzeiro* magazine, denied that the ARENA victory was an expression of support of the Castello government. Asking "how many candidates of the ARENA were elected by campaigning against the government?" Lacerda said that Carvalho Pinto's victory had nothing to do with the

[6] Ibid., November 20, 1966.

[7] Ibid., November 29, 1966.

[8] *O Estado de S. Paulo*, November 17, 18, 19, 1966; *Jornal da Tarde*, December 1, 1966.

Revolution or Castello Branco. Milton Campos, he said, had won "precisely with his manifesto against the government." Lacerda mentioned also the victories of Aluísio Alves ("vetoed by Castello"), Cid Sampaio and João Cleofas ("passed over by Nilo Coelho"), and Magalhães Pinto. "In Guanabara," Lacerda added, "the victory of our candidates was independent of the labels of the ARENA and MDB and was the victory of the government that we administered."[9]

13. The "Declaration of Lisbon" (November 19, 1966)

When the Tribunal Regional Eleitoral rejected the registration of the PAREDE, Lacerda began to speak of his inclination to visit with Kubitschek in Lisbon. He sought the opinion of Rafael de Almeida Magalhães, whose campaign as an ARENA congressional candidate was going well. Rafael had suggested a Lacerda-Kubitschek alliance soon after Negrão de Lima's gubernatorial election in October, 1965, in order to increase the likelihood of Lacerda's popular election to the presidency and thus counter the arguments of military figures who used the possible defeat of Lacerda as a reason for issuing Ato 2. In November, 1966, however, Rafael doubted that an alliance with Kubitschek would be to Lacerda's advantage.[1]

Despite this opinion, the press on November 9 advised that Lacerda was considering speaking with Kubitschek about founding a "truly popular Brazilian party" that might be a vehicle for a Lacerda presidential candidacy in 1970. And when Lacerda left for Europe on November 10, he told the crowd at Galeão Airport that he would see Kubitschek "in order to seek a union of the people against what is going on here."[2]

As Lacerda explained later to *O Cruzeiro* reporters, he felt that military intervention had been made necessary because "old resentments" had divided political forces, "leaving civilian leadership des-

[9] Carlos Lacerda, "Os 10 Pecados da Revolução São 11," *O Cruzeiro*, December 10, 1966.

[1] Almeida Magalhães, interview, August 8, 1977.

[2] *Jornal do Brasil*, November 8, 9, 1966; newspaper clipping, File N6 (Anexo 70), CPDOC.

titute." He therefore sought understandings with Kubitschek and Goulart and believed it appropriate to meet first with Kubitschek because Kubitschek had provided free elections and tried to promote development through optimism.[3]

Speaking further to the *O Cruzeiro* reporters, Lacerda said that in Lisbon on Saturday, November 12, "I dialed Juscelino Kubitschek and expressed my desire to meet with him. He replied that he had to go to the United States to carry on with his lectures, . . . but would postpone his trip and be waiting for me the following Saturday. Already this meeting had been in the making for much time. Since the time when Rafael de Almeida Magalhães, Roberto de Abreu Sodré, Sandra Cavalcanti, and Padre Godinho—to cite only politicians—went to converse with the former president following the 'revolution.' "

Lacerda, after attending to business affairs on the continent, returned to Lisbon on November 18, and on the next day he went to the large, sparsely furnished, modern apartment of Kubitschek. He gave the former president a Chico Buarque de Holanda recording of "Bandinha," which Lacerda considered "the only happy thing to have happened in Brazil since March 31, 1964."[4] According to one reporter's version of the meeting, Sra. Sarah Kubitschek, "the angel of the home," played the "Bandinha" record while "the thundering voice of Lacerda and the soft voice of Kubitschek" could be heard from another room. The reporter saw the two men "smiling, embracing, their faces like those of schoolboys. . . . The two leaders were up in the heavens together."[5]

Toward evening, after a two-hour discussion, the two former leaders spoke to reporters. Kubitschek read the "Declaration of Lisbon" that he and Lacerda had just signed, and then they alternated in answering questions.

The Declaration of Lisbon affirmed that a policy of peace and liberty was necessary for the renewal and acceleration of development. It described the directives of the manifesto of the Frente Ampla as indispensable and recommended that urgent steps be taken to form a popular political party so that the people could be mobilized to achieve

[3] Lacerda, "Os 10 Pecados da Revolução São 11."

[4] Ibid.

[5] Section in ibid. about a *Diário de Notícias* reporter in Lisbon.

the objectives defined in that document. All Brazilians, especially the young, were asked to organize in order to be able to work "without tutelage, without fear, and without discouragement."[6]

Kubitschek told reporters: "After two and one-half years of exile, I think of nothing else but to see Brazil pacified so that it might carry on with its march, and this is also the thought of Governor Carlos Lacerda, and this has been the constant theme of our conversation." Lacerda said that he did not let himself become frightened by threats to suspend his political rights, for he owed nothing to anyone and feared nothing.[7] In a note that Lacerda distributed that night, he declared that his meeting with Kubitschek had been public because not for a single moment did he behave "in a secret manner" as Castello had done in April, 1964, when (according to Lacerda) the general had sought out Kubitschek to get his support to reach the presidency.[8]

The press in Brazil assailed Lacerda's latest move. *Jornal do Brasil* wrote that while the nation clamored for new leaderships, nothing could be more paradoxical than the "fraternization in Lisbon of the representatives of old leaderships, two politicians moved by the same craving for power and always eager to conquer the power at any price." *O Estado de S. Paulo* called the Declaration of Lisbon an "unfortunate document" but promised to support Lacerda whenever he repudiated the steps taken by Castello for superimposing his personal interests on the objectives of the Revolution.[9]

Lacerda has written that when he returned to Brazil on November 23 he found that most of his political friends, most of the UDN, and most of the electorate could not understand what he had done, and that, not unexpectedly, *O Globo* "poisoned everything." Noting that "from the first moment of the Frente Ampla I lost almost all my friends and political backing," he concluded that his action may have been premature and that he "bet a little too much on the political intelligence of Brazilians."[10]

Late in November, 1966, however, Lacerda told reporters that he

[6] Newspaper clipping, File N6 (Anexo 72), CPDOC.

[7] *Diário de Notícias,* November 20, 1966.

[8] Ibid., and newspaper clipping, File N6 (Anexo 76A), CPDOC.

[9] Lacerda, *Depoimento*, p. 381; *Jornal do Brasil* and *O Estado de S. Paulo*, November 22, 1966.

[10] Lacerda, *Depoimento*, pp. 381, 391, 392.

could count on enough federal congressmen to found a party and expected to obtain signatures of the necessary thirty thousand voters, 2 percent of those voting in the recent election. He spoke of the interest of Magalhães Pinto, who was reported to have urged Lacerda to go to Montevideo to see Goulart. But Lacerda continued to respect the opinion of Kubitschek, who said that the inclusion of Goulart would be "too much."[11]

Lacerda asked reporters: "If Dr. Kubitschek and I understand each other, why can't we both have understandings with Costa e Silva?"[12] In articles published around the end of 1966, Lacerda kept the door open for Costa e Silva to "legitimize his mandate." But Lacerda expressed fear that his own efforts to secure peace and a constructive future were being distorted by the "bosses" of Golberi and Roberto Marinho and presented as a plan to create an "inferno" for Costa e Silva. Referring again to the meeting of April, 1964, between Kubitschek and Castello (called "Papa Doc Castello Branco" in one of Lacerda's articles), Lacerda wrote that if his own understanding with Kubitschek was a crime, "Castello should punish himself."[13]

In Lisbon on January 12, 1967, Kubitschek and Lacerda resumed discussions about the new political party, to be called the Partido Popular de Reforma Democrática. Upon returning to Brazil, Lacerda announced that the Frente Ampla hoped to establish a "modus vivendi" with the MDB. He added that "the third political party" would support Costa e Silva, provided that his government would revive economic development, guarantee democratic liberties, promote pacification by revising the *cassações*, and undertake "an eminently nationalist policy."[14]

As in the case of the presidential nomination, Castello Branco did not dominate the selections of gubernatorial candidates made by the

[11] *O Jornal* and *Jornal do Brasil*, November 25, 1966; Lacerda, *Depoimento*, p. 382.

[12] *Jornal do Brasil*, November 25, 1966.

[13] Newspaper clipping (December 2, 1966), File N6 (Anexo 78A), CPDOC; Lacerda, interview in *O Cruzeiro*, December 10, 1966; *Tribuna da Imprensa*, January 6, 1967.

[14] *Correio da Manhã*, January 13, 1967; newspaper clippings, File N6, (Anexos 85, 87), CPDOC.

ARENA. But he did favor the observance of a few restrictions. One of them reflected the president's long-standing conviction that it was a mistake for active military officers to devote attention to personal political opportunities. When Castello published articles over the signature of "Colonel Y" in 1933, he wrote that "as a rule the officer who dedicates himself to other activities is a mediocre professional."[15]

In handling the state and congressional elections of 1966, Castello bore in mind the need to smooth the path for a new regime that would no longer enjoy "laws of exception" (institutional acts). He hoped for a new constitution that would give the executive the power to deal with serious political crises without deviating from the constitution, and he hoped to eliminate the trouble spots that gave promise of bringing on the worst of such crises.

The language of Ato 2 was stretched in order to eliminate the influence of Ademar de Barros in São Paulo. And the term *subversive* was given a broad interpretation when *cassações* were used to prevent the Rio Grande do Sul state government from becoming associated with oppositionists linked to exiled "counter-Revolutionaries" and to prevent a handful of "undesirables," mostly would-be crisis makers, from gaining or regaining federal legislative seats. Well aware of the problems that would confront a constitutional regime, Castello was determined, as Gordon and Tuthill reported, "to assume personally all of the criticism being levelled against the Brazilian Government for anti-democratic actions."[16]

But there was much more democratic action than anti-democratic action. Fiechter writes that "even if the elections of 15 November 1966 were slightly manipulated at the stage of candidate selection, they went off peacefully and formally at least as freely as under the preceding regime if not more so. The invigilation system and the power of dissuasion which the electoral officials had was sufficient to prevent certain time-honored faults from being perpetrated."[17] Schneider calls

[15] HACB ["Coronel Y"], "A Defesa Nacional na Constituinte," *Gazeta do Rio*, December 8, 1933.

[16] As will have been noted, the Castello Branco administration failed in its effort to persuade the Tribunal Superior Eleitoral to void some of the MDB candidacies in Guanabara, including that of Márcio Moreira Alves. As things worked out, an anti-military speech by Moreira Alves in Congress in September 1968 led to the political-military crisis that ushered in Ato Institucional No. 5, thus ending the regime of government without "laws of exception" that Castello Branco set up in March 1967.

[17] Feichter, *Brazil since 1964*, p. 110.

attention to the "very substantial freedom of press and speech."[18] The Brazilian electorate, concerned more about individuals than party labels, made its selections on November 15 from long lists in which the opposition to the government was well represented.

[18] Schneider, *The Political System of Brazil*, p. 186.

The Reform Movement of Late 1966

(July-December, 1966)

On March 15, 1967, the Revolution is going to complete its basic institutionalization in order that, in the following phase, it can strengthen Brazilian democracy and economic development.

1. Inflation and Taxes (July–August, 1966)

DECREES issued late in July, 1966, called for closer executive supervision of wages and the federal budget. Ato Complementar 18, which ended the right of Congress to transfer budget allocations from one account to another, was resented by congressmen who had been in the habit of presenting amendments to favor projects in their states. Finding their budget role limited to approving or rejecting the entire budget, some of them complained after Congress opened its session on August 1. Josafá Marinho (MDB, Bahia) said that Ato Complementar 18 completed Castello's "strangulation and usurpation of the legislative power," and Nelson Carneiro (MDB, Guanabara) declared bitterly that the "ideal would be for the Castello Branco government to repeat what Getúlio Vargas had had the courage to do: close down Congress." After Krieger told the lawmakers that Castello was really very good about heeding criticism, a new Ato Complementar, Number 21, was issued to allow congressional amendments to specify the use of expenditures in cases where the budget authorized expenditures unassigned to specific projects and provided that the amendments did not modify "the amount, nature, or objective of the expenditure." The 1967 budget that Castello Branco submitted was in balance: receipts and expenditures were both set at 6,614 billion cruzeiros.[1]

As for wages, it was noted that in the twelve months ending in July, 1966, the upward adjustments in the private sector had been about 40 percent, whereas in companies controlled by the National

[1] *Jornal do Brasil*, August 2, 5, 1966.

Council on Wage Policy they had been about 30 percent. Thus it was apparent that despite previous legislation, unions had retained some bargaining power and labor tribunals some independence.[2]

The government attributed the disparity in wage increases, sometimes occurring "even within the same professional category," to a lack of "necessary uniformity in the establishment and application of indices for reconstructing the real average wage in the preceding 24 months, the basis of the wage policy followed by the government as an instrument for fighting inflation."[3] To rectify this situation, Decree-Law 15, signed by Castello on July 29, 1966, stipulated that the executive branch would publish monthly the indices to be used. On August 3 the press carried the first set of these coefficients to reflect the inflation for the previous twenty-four months, together with a calculation showing that wage increases for labor contracts up for renewal in August, 1966, would be 27.875 percent. To this figure, which already included 5 percent representing half of the year-ahead "inflation residual," there would be added whatever the government determined the productivity increase to be. (The productivity increase was later set at 2 percent.)[4]

The head of the National Confederation of Workers in Credit Establishments said that "if the working class has already suffered from the containment of its wages, now the situation becomes even more crushing." Lawyers of the National Confederation of Workers in Industry described the new law as "offensive to social peace."[5]

Roberto Campos, speaking on August 4 to the Armed Forces General Staff, said that the twenty-four–month formula established in July, 1965, avoided having wage increases guided by the peak statistics for inflation. He reported that the June-to-June inflation had been 68 percent for 1962–1963, 97 percent for 1963–1964, 70 percent for 1964–1965, and 40 percent for 1965–1966 and he quoted German Professor Hermann Abs as saying that while the German inflation had been only an abscess, relatively easy to lance, the Brazilian inflation was a blood poisoning that had invaded all the organs. Campos rejected "the utopian option" suggested by those who imagined that inflation could be

[2] Departamento Intersindical de Estatística e Estudos Sócio-Econômicos, "10 Anos de Política Salarial" (São Paulo, 1975), p. 14.

[3] Introductory remarks of Decree-Law 15 of July 29, 1966.

[4] *Jornal do Brasil*, August 3, October 12, 1966.

[5] Ibid., August 4, 6, 1966.

fought by increasing production without containing the excess of the money supply.[6]

The nomination of Walter Peracchi Barcelos for the governorship of Rio Grande do Sul required a search for a new labor minister. Although Castello, Otávio Bulhões, and Roberto Campos favored Housing Bank President Nascimento Silva, Nascimento Silva told all three that he preferred to stay with the bank, which was about to move into a more dynamic phase with the receipt of income from the Workers' Tenure Guarantee Fund. However, when Nascimento Silva was in Washington late in July, 1966, arranging a twenty-million-dollar loan from the Inter-American Development Bank, he received a cable saying that it was the president's decision that he should become labor minister at once and that Mário Trindade, highly regarded by Nascimento Silva, should head the Housing Bank. Nascimento Silva, canceling an appointment with Hubert Humphrey, flew to Brazil to become labor minister.[7]

After the installation ceremony at Planalto Palace on August 1, Nascimento Silva went to Castello's office. The president indicated no policy to be followed by his new minister but simply said: "You know the law and are free to make the decisions." Castello added that he expected to return to Brasília in two weeks and that if Nascimento Silva had any matters with which the president could help, he should see the president. When he did see the president in the months that followed, it was sometimes due to his disagreements with Roberto Campos and Bulhões. Nascimento Silva would argue that the working class should not be called on to make the greatest sacrifice in the fight against inflation.[8]

The fight against inflation was carried on spectacularly by the Income Tax Department, headed by Orlando Travancas. Especially after the enactment of laws in 1965 that drastically increased penalties and allowed jail sentences for tax evasion, the days of easy evasion ended. Some observers remarked that the Revolution's greatest victory was in getting Mineiros to pay their income taxes. Fiechter writes that "taxes, which nobody had talked about before, became overnight the hot drawing-room topic. The walls of São Paulo were covered with giant posters

[6] Ibid., August 5, 1966.

[7] Ibid., July 23, 1966; Nascimento Silva, interview, October 25, 1975.

[8] Nascimento Silva, interview, October 25, 1975.

representing an eye with a computer for its iris, and bearing the warning 'Look out, the computer is watching you!' The result was electrifying."[9] New fiscal agents were appointed on the basis of competitive tests instead of political reasons and received training from the U.S. Internal Revenue Service. They investigated the sources of income of people who lived in comparative luxury. Income taxes, reported as equivalent to $250 million U.S. in 1963, rose to the equivalent of $990 million in 1966. The zeal of Travancas and his agents was helpful to the northeast: of the $990 million figure for 1966, about $182 million was forgiven in return for investments made in projects approved by SUDENE.[10]

The collection of income taxes from wage earners by the companies paying the wages, a concept introduced in Brazil in 1954, was made effective during Castello's presidency, and the forwarding of the funds to the government by the companies was stimulated by Bulhões' introduction in 1964 of the monetary correction for tax collection purposes. An efficient and cost-saving innovation, in the case of federal tax collections, was the use of the private banking system; this led to the elimination of the obsolete system of government collection agencies with their thousands of bureaucrats. Furthermore, the Finance Ministry set up a computer system (Empresa de Processamento de Dados—SERPRO), first used for paying employees and later for income tax collections.[11]

Income taxes remained, however, greatly inferior to indirect, or consumption, taxes. To modernize the latter, Roberto Campos and Otávio Bulhões introduced sweeping changes that were enacted in 1965. After being upgraded, the changes were made part of a national tax code that was sent to Congress in September, 1966. ARENA congressmen, in Brasília for the presidential election of October 3, resolved to act on the code. They overruled a decision made earlier by Moura Andrade to file the project of the code and thus have it become law due

[9] Fiechter, *Brazil since 1964*, p. 100.

[10] Orlando Travancas, interview, Rio de Janeiro, November 25, 1966; idem, quoted in *Jornal do Brasil*, December 27, 1966.

[11] Eduardo Lopes Rodrigues, interview, Rio de Janeiro, August 10, 1979; Sant'-Anna e Silva, interview, August 4, 1979; Sant'Anna e Silva, memorandum, July 1979.

to the failure of Congress to act within thirty days. The project was approved by Congress on October 4.[12]

The new code would leave Brazil with three main taxes: the income tax and a tax on manufactured products (Impôsto de Produtos Industrializados—IPI) both collected by the federal government, and a value-added tax, called a tax on the circulation of goods (Impôsto de Circulação de Mercadorias—ICM), collected by the state governments. The ICM, or value-added tax, replaced a sales tax arrangement that had provided what Roberto Campos called "a cascading effect." And, as described by Syvrud, the new ICM became "a potent weapon against tax evasion, since it is to the advantage of each business to ensure compliance by previous businesses in the productive process." Other advantages seen in the new code were a clearer allocation of taxing power between the federal and state governments, a prohibition against the raising of new and disguised forms of taxation, and the unification of tax rates applicable to interstate transactions.[13]

Early in 1967, when the tax reforms were put into practice, objections to the ICM were voiced in some states, particularly by Guanabara Finance Secretary Márcio Alves (father of the recently elected congressman). But the finance secretary of Rio de Janeiro state praised the reform for "eliminating double taxation." Bulhões admitted that in Guanabara and São Paulo, where the old sales taxes had been lower than in other states, the introduction of the ICM might cause an immediate increase in some prices. He calculated that in no cases would these increases exceed 2 or 3 percent.[14]

A few reductions were made in the import tariffs, but on the whole those tariffs were high, as they had been since 1957. The truly revolutionary (and refreshing) change was made in the customs laws. Before the Castello Branco government, they had consisted of a mountain of regulations calling for heavy fines (often in connection with documentary details), and these, together with the steep storage charges incurred during any discussion of fines, had severely added to the cost and pain

[12] *Jornal do Brasil*, October 4, 5, 1966.

[13] Syvrud, *Foundations of Brazilian Economic Growth*, p. 124; Campos, interview, December 23, 1974.

[14] *Jornal do Brasil*, January 12, 24, 1967.

of importing. Technicians of the Finance Ministry and of the Getúlio Vargas Foundation, working together, abolished almost 70 percent of the fines and reduced all the others. Professor Eduardo Lopes Rodrigues, who was director-general of finance, feels that "the customs law was the best example of great achievement by the Castello Branco administration—a better example even than the income tax matter."[15]

2. Military Matters (August–November, 1966)

Discussion about the creation of a Ministry of the Armed Forces was most evident in August and September, 1966. To advance the discussion within the top military organs, Castello drew up a memorandum. Explaining that the idea "does not have to do with fusion," he pointed out that "the forces should have their organizations, logistics, and activities coordinated" and that "their own planning should spring from a general planning." According to Castello's proposal, the president would command the military through the minister of the armed forces, who in turn would exercise his command through three assistant ministers, each in charge of a branch of the military. The minister of the armed forces would be assisted by the EMFA (Armed Forces General Staff) and by Departments of Administration and Logistics. While the new ministry would handle military research, the teaching in each force would be under the control of the staff of that force. Castello's memorandum also proposed having a "High Command of the Armed Forces" to be made up of the president, the three assistant ministers, all the chiefs of staff, and the head of the presidential Gabinete Militar. "The president," Castello added, "would be able to delegate the chairmanship of the meetings to the executive of the supreme command (minister of the armed forces)."[1]

Based on these ideas, the EMFA elaborated a project that was largely the work of Brigadier General Reinaldo Melo de Almeida. Former Air Force Minister Lavanère-Wanderley, who became head of the EMFA in April, 1966, found most of the air force officers opposed

[15] Lopes Rodrigues, interview, August 10, 1979.

[1] HACB, "Ministério das Fôrças Armadas," File RI (p. 1), CPDOC.

to establishing the ministry. But their feeling was mild compared with that of the navy, whose opposition took the form of distributing thousands of copies of a book condemning the idea. The navy was said to consider its "survival" at stake.[2]

Lavanère-Wanderley felt that if the army was keen on a Ministry of the Armed Forces, it would be created. But Castello, as he explained to journalist Prudente de Morais Neto one day at lunch, wanted a more general understanding and acceptance of the idea and hoped that the diplomatic Ademar de Queiroz could arrange its adoption without stirring up problems.[3] However, even in the army the response was largely negative. Lavanère-Wanderley found that army officers feared the armed forces minister might be a civilian or be chosen by rotation from among the three branches. Medeiros Silva, preparing the new constitution and administrative reform, concluded that the army considered the proposed change a threat to its predominance.[4]

By mid-September, 1966, the army leadership concluded that implementation of the idea should be postponed. Army Chief of Staff Décio Escobar, while personally supporting the proposed ministry, declared that studies for indoctrinating the military were necessary. Ademar de Queiroz told Castello that the Army High Command found the new ministry a good idea but one that ought not to be put into practice during the Castello administration due to the controversial aspects, the lack of air force enthusiasm, and the violent reactions in the navy. The Army High Command even felt that the reform might "provoke a military crisis, considering the agitated electoral politics."[5]

According to Luís Viana Filho, "inertia and the sea of problems that involved Castello" prevented achievement of the Armed Forces Ministry. Time being too short for the necessary persuasion, Castello decided to promote the coordination that he deemed essential by using administrative reform to increase the importance of the EMFA and to

[2] Reinaldo Melo de Almeida, interview, Rio de Janeiro, October 17, 1975; *Jornal do Brasil*, September 17, 1966; Lavanère-Wanderley, interviews, December 10, 1974, August 12, 1977.

[3] Prudente de Morais Neto, interview, Rio de Janeiro, October 8, 1975.

[4] Lavanère-Wanderley, interview, December 10, 1974; Medeiros Silva, interview, July 22, 1977.

[5] *Jornal do Brasil*, September 17, 1966.

establish a High Command of the Armed Forces, which would report to the presidency.[6]

Castello also felt that the study of strategy, as conducted by the separate staffs of the military branches, was not broad enough. Therefore, on the morning of Saturday, October 22, 1966, he called EMFA Chief Lavanère-Wanderley and National War College (ESG) Commander Lyra Tavares to his private quarters in Laranjeiras Palace for a long discussion. He recommended that at the end of each year the EMFA give instructions to the ESG about a high-level study of strategy to be carried out in the following year at the school. And he remarked to Lavanère-Wanderley and Lyra Tavares that, upon leaving the presidency in 1967, he planned to do some writing about strategy.[7]

Décio Escobar, who some felt should have succeeded War Minister Costa e Silva, retired from active service, and his army chief of staff post was assigned provisionally to General de Divisão Álvaro Tavares Carmo. Escobar retired just in time to become a marshal. For, according to Castello's decree of December 16, 1965, the promotion of military officers upon retirement came to an end on October 9, 1966.

A particularly disappointed general was General de Divisão Carlos Luís Guedes, who had commanded the Second Military Region in São Paulo when Amauri Kruel had lost his command of the Second Army. Guedes, popular with *O Estado de S. Paulo*, hoped to replace Kruel, but, instead, Mamede was named head of the Second Army and Guedes was transferred to the Army Department of Personnel. Guedes, some felt, had hardly been discreet when making political pronouncements. He had described Lacerda as the great uniter of the 1964 revolution and had told the press that Costa e Silva had appeared as a revolutionary only on April 2, 1964, when he became war minister due to seniority. Guedes had spoken out in favor of direct gubernatorial elections.[8]

With the promotions to the four-star rank (*generais de exército*), announced late in November, 1966, comment was widespread about the advancement of Ernesto Geisel and the bypassing of Guedes and Sizeno Sarmento, both considered to be connected with Lacerda. In the list

[6] Viana Filho, *O Governo Castelo Branco*, p. 482; Vereker, report, August 25, 1966; Lavanère-Wanderley, interview, December 10, 1974.

[7] Lavanère-Wanderley, interview, December 10, 1974.

[8] *O Estado de S. Paulo*, February 9, August 10, 1966.

below, showing dates when generals became *generais de divisão*, an asterisk indicates promotion to *general de exército* late in November, 1966:[9]

*Alberto Ribeiro Paz	November 25, 1963
*Augusto Fragoso	March 25, 1964
*Rafael de Sousa Aguiar	July 25, 1964
*Álvaro Alves da Silva Braga	July 25, 1964
Carlos Luís Guedes	July 25, 1964
*Jurandir de Bizarria Mamede	July 25, 1964
*Antônio Carlos da Silva Murici	July 25, 1964
Sizeno Sarmento	July 25, 1964
Alfredo Souto Malan	July 25, 1964
Álvaro Tavares Carmo	November 25, 1964
*Ernesto Geisel	November 25, 1964

Lacerdistas and hard-liners suffered also in the promotions in the lower ranks.[10]

Jornal do Brasil reported that the bypassing of Guedes and Sarmento caused unfavorable repercussions in the War Ministry and resulted from the vetoes of Castello, who favored Geisel's promotion. *O Estado de S. Paulo* called the latest decisions about army promotions "one more arbitrary act that Marshal Castello Branco and his direct collaborators put into practice so that the Revolution be totally excluded from the government." *Jornal da Tarde* reminded its readers that Guedes had initiated the movement of March 31, 1964, and that Sarmento had been a "historic revolutionary," whose struggle against the enemies of democracy "did not begin simply on the eve of March 31."[11]

3. Plans for a New Constitution (July–October, 1966)

In April, 1966, at the suggestion of Mem de Sá, Castello appointed Levi Carneiro, Seabra Fagundes, Orozimbro Nonato, and Temístocles

[9] *Almanaque do Exército*, 1966.

[10] Schneider, *The Political System of Brazil*, p. 211; *Jornal do Brasil*, November 26, 1966.

[11] *Jornal do Brasil*, November 26, 1966; *O Estado de S. Paulo*, December 2, 1966; *Jornal da Tarde*, December 1, 1966.

Cavalcanti to draft a revision of the 1946 Constitution. Soon Levi Carneiro, the octogenarian chairman, had difficulties with Seabra Fagundes, who had been justice minister under President Café Filho. Fagundes believed that the commission should offer only "four or five consolidative amendments" because Congress lacked the authority to enact a new constitution. After his colleagues set out to draft a completely new text, Seabra Fagundes found that their ideas showed "little innovation," and he proposed changes, one after the other, that ran counter to the ideas of Levi Carneiro. Levi Carneiro, handling the meetings in an authoritarian way and habitually rejecting the suggestions of Seabra Fagundes, maintained that there was no reason to prolong debates when the views of members were already well known. Seabra Fagundes, supporting popular presidential elections, submitted a paper for the purpose of altering his colleagues' preference for the use of a large electoral college, but his arguments seemed to make no impression.[1]

At the ceremony installing Medeiros Silva as justice minister on July 19, Castello explained that the government was awaiting the draft of the "eminent jurists" in order to give it some final touches, and he argued for a strong presidential system that would "reinforce" the chief executive's authority "in the face of threats of subversion and attacks on lives, liberty, and the property of citizens."[2]

When Castello met with the "eminent jurists" in Rio on August 6, he accepted the resignation of Seabra Fagundes, who had stopped attending commission meetings late in July. A week later, in Maceió, Alagoas, Castello asserted that "the present national Congress received from the Revolution the task of being a constitution-making organ," and he reminded his listeners of how Congress had incorporated itself long before March 31, 1964, in the movement against the "illegal and senseless" government of that time. Castello attacked those who opposed "the inevitable and unpostponable constitutional evolution of Brazil." "They forget," he said, "that the Revolution is going to complete, on March 15, 1967, its basic institutionalization in order that, in

[1] Seabra Fagundes quoted in *Jornal do Brasil,* August 31, 1966; Levi Carneiro, quoted in *Jornal do Brasil*, September 10, 1966; Temístocles Cavalcanti, interview, Rio de Janeiro, September 22, 1975.

[2] HACB, *Discursos*, *1966*, pp. 331–338.

the following phase, it can strengthen Brazilian democracy and economic development."[3]

At Laranjeiras Palace on August 19, Castello, accompanied by Medeiros Silva and others, received the constitutional draft from the three remaining commission members. Levi Carneiro explained that it maintained the Brazilian tradition of federalism, juridical administration, and presidentialism. He gave a résumé of the draft, which, as finally written, called for direct presidential elections but stipulated that in the case of no absolute majority the Congress would choose between the two candidates having the most votes.[4]

Senator Antônio Carlos Konder Reis, who was present, sensed that Castello was disappointed in Levi Carneiro's remarks and résumé. Luís Viana Filho writes that the first impression of the draft revealed a "conservative orientation" and "little innovation from the constitutions of 1934 and 1946. Incomplete with respect to the reformist aspiration of the president, it was a far cry from the concepts of Justice Minister Carlos Medeiros, for whom liberalism, harmony of the powers, and other constitutional precepts, in their classic expressions, were outdated, and would not avoid the political and social crises of the nation."[5]

In Brasília on August 30, Castello told the National Security Council that the 1946 Constitution was "a factor of crises" and that the best opportunity for "a distinct constitutional evolution" lay in the pre–March 15, 1967, institutionalizing phase of the Revolution. "After March 15, 1967," he said, "it appears that what will be suitable is only what can be done by normal processes."[6] Examining alternatives like an army staff officer performing an exercise, he read from his notes: "1. Before November 15 (this Congress); 2. After November 15, from December to the end of January (this Congress); 3. In January and February and early March 1967 (new Congress); 4. After March 15; 5. Decree" (by the executive, without action by Congress). Most of the National Security Council members favored action by the Congress then in session, with the president calling it to meet in December. But Cas-

[3] Ibid., pp. 59–61.

[4] *Jornal do Brasil,* August 20, 1966; T. Cavalcanti, interview, September 22, 1975.

[5] Viana Filho, *O Governo Castelo Branco*, p. 452.

[6] HACB, "Reunião Constitucional, 30 VIII-66" (handwritten notes), File Q (Section 2), CPDOC.

tello, who had yet to make arrangements with the legislative leaders, kept his options open, including simple promulgation by the executive. Education Minister Moniz de Aragão said that it was well known that constitutions so promulgated were short-lived. "Who said that?" Medeiros Silva asked.[7]

Medeiros Silva told the National Security Council that the Levi Carneiro commission draft was "conservative, not revolutionary." It was decided that the draft would be studied by the cabinet ministers and the ARENA and their suggestions considered by the justice minister when he revised the draft.[8]

Early in September, Medeiros Silva announced that a new Ato Institucional would have to be issued to define the role of Congress in creating a new constitution. Câmara President Adauto Cardoso replied that Congress should establish the rules without outside interference. Eurico Rezende, vice-leader of the government in the Senate, said that the existing Congress, made up of men who had become "*cassados* by the people," lacked the necessary authority and that Castello should transform the future Congress into a constitutional assembly and present his project to it ten days before leaving office.[9]

By early October, Medeiros Silva had received many opinions and was well along with the revision of the original draft. In the case of presidential elections he included an idea that had occurred to him while he was on the Supreme Court. It called for an electoral college made up of the houses of Congress, representatives of the state assemblies, and representatives of cultural and class organizations (such as workers and employers). A purpose was to have a balancing one-third of the college uncommitted, in contrast to two-thirds that would be committed by the Act of Party Loyalty.[10]

Castello favored indirect presidential elections and a government with instruments strong enough to prevent constitutional violations and dictatorship in times of trouble. Nobody, Castello told Sarasate, could predict to what point the country might go if the government lacked

[7] Severo Gomes, interview, July 25, 1977.

[8] Ibid., Viana Filho, *O Governo Castelo Branco*, p. 454; Paulo Sarasate, *A Constituição do Brasil ao alcance de todos*, p. 53; Medeiros Silva, interview, July 22, 1977.

[9] *Jornal do Brasil*, September 7, October 12, 1966.

[10] Sarasate, *A Constituição do Brasil ao alcance de todos*, p. 53; Medeiros Silva, interview, July 22, 1977.

security arrangements that could be used promptly at the appropriate moment. For this reason Castello, inspired by an article of the French Constitution, asked Medeiros Silva to provide the executive with the power to declare a state of emergency when the institutions were gravely threatened. According to one formula, the president would be able to do this after hearing the National Security Council and the presidents of the Supreme Court and two houses of Congress. Another proposal would require the president first to receive authorization from a "Council of Emergency" (the heads of the three powers, the vice-president, the leaders of the Senate and Câmara, the military ministers, and the justice minister).[11]

After Medeiros Silva took his draft of the new constitution to the president on October 14, Castello drew up a list of nearly one hundred points to be considered. Many of Castello's suggestions were for changes in wording (in several places he changed "the federal government" to read "the Union"), and more than once he wrote that "we might hear the ministers of finance and planning."[12] In a note about the formulation of the budget, Castello wrote:

> The people of the DASP combat the existence of the Ministry of Planning, and seek to spread the idea that this organ "manipulates" the president, and is headed by a "prime minister," that the ministries do not repel the domination, etc. I receive all this with humility. There is no leader of the ministries, the minister of planning does not make incursions into the other ministries. He carries out, it is true, the planning of the government and the budget. Did not the DASP make a budget (and what a budget!)? Why, then, cannot a ministry, also directly connected with the president, make a budget? The DASP is going to deserve in the constitution the emaciation of its tasks, some of which have already been withdrawn by evolution: budget, personnel, materials, buildings, and documentation. I ask you that we discuss the matter.[13]

Castello sought clarification about the ability of the executive to issue decree-laws and about the function of the National Security Coun-

[11] Viana Filho, *O Governo Castelo Branco*, pp. 455–456.

[12] HACB, "Observações," File Q (Section 3), CPDOC, see Note 31.

[13] Ibid., see Note 48.

cil (to which he proposed adding the head of the SNI and the vice-president of the Republic). Castello wrote that the National Security Council (CSN) "advises the president, who makes the decisions, enlightened by it, but who can decide against the opinion of all its members. This arrangement is very arbitrary and could be an authoritarian and personalist arm. We must discuss this."[14] (In the end, the CSN was left largely as an entity for studying problems related to the national security, but its prior approval was to be obtained for certain acts, such as the concession of land, the building of international bridges and roads, and the establishment of industries affecting the national security.)[15]

Arguing that voluntary retirement should be available to the military after thirty years compared with thirty-five years for civilians, Castello wrote: "I believe that there is a very big difference, from the point of view of physical capacity, between the civilian and the military. The former is commonly located in one place and almost always leads a sedentary life. The latter goes to many places and needs to have good physical condition and health or, better, resistance for carrying out his functions. There is a difference in wear and tear."[16]

4. Finalizing the Draft for Congress (November–December, 1966)

Late in October, while Congress was on its forced recess, Castello spoke with Senator Krieger about the need of a new constitution and mentioned the timetable possibilities that he had suggested to the National Security Council. Krieger stated that Congress maintained, permanently, constitution-making powers but could not abolish the Republic or the Federation. He felt that the new constitution "should be voted by the present Congress, because we can count on a solid majority there, devoted to the Revolution and appreciative of the desired reforms." Kriger recommended doing this during December and January.[1]

On November 6, with congressional electioneering in full swing,

[14] Ibid., see Notes 15, 37, 50, 51.

[15] Article 91 of the 1967 Constitution.

[16] HACB, "Observações," see Note 59.

[1] Krieger, *Desde as Missões*, pp. 241–242.

Krieger was in Porto Alegre. There, General Golberi, also a Gaúcho, brought him a letter and a box of cigars from Castello, together with a copy of Medeiros Silva's draft of a constitution. The letter suggested use of the cigars at the preelection barbecues and expressed hope for "complete success on the fifteenth." It requested that Krieger make notes about, and "even write amendments" to, the draft. By November 8, Castello wrote, "I shall have distributed copies to Costa e Silva, Pedro Aleixo, and some cabinet ministers." The president wrote of plans to collect "impressions and suggestions" soon after the elections, in order to have a document to present to the top directors of the ARENA.[2]

Jornal do Brasil reported on November 7 that while the Medeiros draft excluded "the much-discussed 'state of emergency,' " this question had yet to be resolved by the ARENA. The draft, the newspaper said, called for indirect presidential elections. Senator Afonso Arinos de Melo Franco declared that "politicians, like all the people, do not accept indirect elections." He said that the Medeiros project had no chance of being approved by the outgoing Congress and that Castello would therefore have to decree the new constitution, which might last unaltered for three years, while a period of political "prohibition" continued in effect. This view differed from that of Castello, who had spoken, when installing Justice Minister Medeiros, of "an instrument of peace and order, destined to last for several decades."[3]

Following the congressional elections, Krieger flew to Rio, but at Laranjeiras Palace on November 17 he did not have time for a full discussion of the draft and merely mentioned some reservations and suggested some additions. Castello flew on the nineteenth to Belo Horizonte, where he expressed pleasure at the election results and announced that he had in mind promising soon to refrain from issuing *cassações* during the period that Congress worked on the constitution.[4]

With Congress about to reopen after its recess, the president signed decree-laws in Brasília on November 22. At Planalto Palace on the twenty-fourth, he and Medeiros met with Auro de Moura Andrade, Adauto Cardoso, Filinto Müller, Raimundo Padilha, and Pedro Aleixo to discuss issuing an Ato Complementar or Ato Institucional for ar-

[2] Ibid., p. 242.
[3] *Jornal do Brasil*, November 11, 1966; HACB, *Discursos, 1966*, p. 333.
[4] Krieger, *Desde as Missões*, p. 242; *Jornal do Brasil*, November 20, 1966.

ranging to have Congress study and vote on the new constitution in December or January. "Let's concentrate on listening," Castello suggested to Medeiros before the meeting. Moura Andrade attacked the government's plans and suggested having Congress file away the "Medeiros draft" and draw up its own version of a constitution.[5] After the meeting, Castello announced that he had decided to call Congress on December 12, at which time he would submit the project of a constitution. The government leaders in Congress, Castello said, were to reach understandings with Moura Andrade and Adauto Cardoso about an appropriate calendar.[6]

Adauto Cardoso had been reelected to Congress, but he was in a difficult position because a majority of the Câmara's board of officers (*mesa*) refused to back his opposition to the *cassações* of the six congressmen in October. Adauto admitted to Krieger that under the circumstances his resignation from the Câmara presidency would be a logical step but said that before he took it he wanted a letter from Castello, already promised, "about not canceling mandates during the elaboration of the constitutional reform." Krieger spoke with Castello, who at first objected to issuing a letter earlier than he had planned but then agreed to do so.[7]

Castello's letter, dated November 25, was addressed to Krieger. In it the president reviewed suggestions made to him earlier in the year by Krieger and others for suspending Articles 14 and 15 of Ato 2. He advised that after meditation and consultation he had become convinced that Ato 2 was "untouchable" but that a solution would be "simply the agreement not to apply Articles 14 and 15 in the case of congressmen and senators." Subsequently, Castello wrote, he had consulted the National Security Council about some *cassações* indispensable for "freeing Congress from the presence and influence of elements incompatible with the principles of the Revolution." On October 13, he wrote, he had acted on those cases, which had been pending for a long time. Under those conditions, and with Congress scheduled to start considering the constitution in December, Castello advised Krieger that "I am today in

[5] *Jornal do Brasil*, November 25, 1966; Medeiros Silva, interview, July 22, 1977; Pedro Aleixo, letter to Luís Viana Filho, Belo Horizonte, September 21, 1971, p. 1.

[6] *Jornal do Brasil*, November 26, 1966.

[7] Krieger, *Desde as Missões*, p. 239.

a position to assure the top directorship of the ARENA, through Your Excellency, that the present congress will not" be affected by further applications of Articles 14 and 15. In conclusion Castello wrote that the agreement was not a political transaction but was "based on the types and number of *cassações* already carried out in Congress and on the recommendation that the ARENA expressed initially through Your Excellency."[8]

On November 28 the *mesa* of the Chamber of Deputies declared that the six congressmen *cassados* in October had lost their mandates. A few minutes later Cardoso resigned as president of the Chamber with the explanation that he was not in a position to carry out that decision. He was replaced provisionally by João Batista Ramos, the Paulista who had been vice-president of the Chamber.[9]

By this time Moura Andrade was reported to be unwilling to preside over Congress because the Medeiros draft would return the presidency of the Senate and the combined federal legislative houses to the vice-president of the Republic, thus depriving Moura Andrade of posts he had been holding. On the more positive side, Senator Filinto Müller revised his "pessimistic position" and admitted that approval of the new constitution could be obtained peacefully before January 20. Müller's optimism resulted from a "formula of conciliation" to improve the acceptance of the project by Congress and yet retain the indirect election of the president: governors and mayors would be elected by direct vote.[10]

In Rio late in November, Castello held discussions to consider the suggestions of Roberto Campos, the ARENA, and Costa e Silva's study group. Campos gained acceptance of his idea for guaranteeing permanence of principles enacted about taxation. But Castello's "state of emergency" proposal, which had stirred up more opposition than the administration's preference for indirect elections, ran into trouble. Vicente Ráo, consulted by Costa e Silva, favored its omission. Ailing Francisco Campos, who received a visit from Castello, argued that the "state of emergency," as regulated in the project, was basically only a repetition of the state of siege. Afonso Arinos de Melo Franco, also

[8] Ibid., pp. 240–241.
[9] *Jornal do Brasil*, November 29, 1966.
[10] Ibid., November 27, 29, 1966.

consulted by the president, felt that the "state of emergency" was simply "a limitless aggravation of the state of siege." Congressman Gustavo Capanema, whom Castello respected, told the president that the "state of emergency" proposal would not be passed by Congress.[11]

Castello was in Brasília on November 30 when the end of the regular session of Congress was observed by the reading of a message from Moura Andrade that criticized the Castello administration for what Moura Andrade called its "little interest in collaborating with the legislature," its failure to explain vetoes, and its effort to have legislation elaborated at too fast a pace. At the customary presidential reception for congressmen and senators, tradition was broken because champagne and snacks were not served. About sixty legislators filed past Castello, who exchanged a few words with each.[12]

Castello was about to fly to Amazônia, but before he left, he participated in a final discussion with Costa e Silva, Pedro Aleixo, Medeiros, Roberto Campos, Padilha, Krieger, and Müller about the draft of the new constitution. Krieger caused some surprise by supporting Moura Andrade's wish that the constitution not designate the vice-president of the republic to preside over the Senate. More surprising was the acquiescence of Vice-president-elect Pedro Aleixo.[13] The decision to drop the "state of emergency" was also reached amicably. And after Müller and Krieger argued for the direct election of governors, this principle was adopted. To appease the ARENA leaders, Medeiros' idea of having the president and vice-president chosen by a large electoral college was modified by excluding the "noncommitted" one-third that was to have been made up of representatives of cultural and class organizations.[14]

Krieger, recalling that Carvalho Pinto had joined the ARENA upon being assured that the party was not committed to indirect elections, said that he wished to preserve for ARENA members the right to modify the provision about indirect presidential elections. However, Krieger himself was coming to the conclusion that indirect presidential

[11] Ibid., November 29, 1966; Viana Filho, *O Governo Castelo Branco*, pp. 456–457; Melo Franco, interview, October 31, 1975.

[12] *O Estado de S. Paulo*, December 2, 1966.

[13] Krieger, *Desde as Missões*, pp. 243–244.

[14] Medeiros Silva, interview, July 22, 1977; *O Estado de S. Paulo*, December 3, 1966.

elections might be best "considering the vast territory of the nation and the stage of education of its people." When Costa e Silva suggested direct elections with a transitory provision making the next election indirect, Krieger told him: "That would diminish the authority of your investiture; we should have indirect election in the body of the constitution."[15]

5. Operação Amazônia (December 3, 1966)

Castello left Brasília on a trip that took him on December 2 to Porto Velho, Rondônia, and on December 3 to Manaus, Amazonas, where Operação Amazônia was launched in the presence of a large and distinguished group.

Speaking in Porto Velho, the president mentioned the recent discoveries of cassiterite (tin ore) in Rondônia by prospectors. But he added that discovery in a haphazard manner was being replaced by "meticulous study undertaken by technicians" who specialized in new processes and were guided by the government's "Ten-Year Master Plan for the Appraisal of the Mineral Resources of Brazil." In this way, he said, aerial photographic studies and initial geologic mapping revealed vast extensions of the mineralized areas worked by the local prospectors and provided optimistic "perspectives of finding large reserves, not only of cassiterite but also of gold and copper."

Castello stressed that the administration's mineral policy, announced in July, 1964, gave the government the "pioneer function of building up basic knowledge and clearing the wild growth" but offered to private companies the task of "transforming the discovered natural resources into effective riches." He said that "only organized mining, based on specific legislation and under the control of the competent authorities, can make the nation self-sufficient."

After reviewing recent mineral discoveries in Brazil, the president spoke of the competition stemming from the world-wide abundance of Brazil's "major mineral reserves, particularly iron and manganese ore." Here, he said, the government's policy of coordinating its own efforts with those of private initiative had been successful. The president

[15] Krieger, *Desde as Missões*, pp. 243–244, 254.

called particular attention to the great strides made by the government's iron ore company, Companhia Vale do Rio Doce (CVRD): "the construction of the port of Tubarão in record time, the modernization of the mines and the railroad, and the extension of the latter to the iron quadrilateral of Minas Gerais." "The government," he said "is now helping the company to assure itself of independent sea transport through its subsidiary, DOCENAVE, a preponderant factor in the conquest of new markets."[1]

O Estado de S. Paulo liked the president's speech about mining. It praised the government's policy of making use of its own forces and those of private inititative, and it agreed that the advances by CVRD were "magnificent." It concluded that "as to the manner in which Brazil faces its great problems, it is indisputable that the Nation is frankly entering what we might call a positive phase of evolution."[2]

The impressive gathering of representatives of private enterprise in Manaus on December 3 had been arranged by the government and the National Confederation of Industries. The latter had invited top businessmen and bankers, high government officials, and all the state governors to join in a seven-day, one-thousand-mile boat trip down the Amazon from Manaus to Belém. The government was armed with a development plan and new legislation about incentives that was even more liberal than the legislation enacted for developing the northeast.[3]

The purpose of the boat trip, in the words of a participant from the private sector, "was not simply to show the never-tiring spectacle of the unfolding Amazon, with its impenetrable forest, thousands of islands and inlets, canals and tributaries," but also to give the participants "a feeling of the Amazon reality and encourage them to hear opinions and enter into discussions"; careful attention would be given when projects received "criticisms from experienced businessmen and industrialists from the advanced south."[4]

The meeting, scheduled to end soon after the *Rosa da Fonseca* reached Belém on December 11, was called the First Meeting of Incentive for Developing Amazônia. It began with a banquet held on

[1] HACB, *Discursos, 1966*, pp. 347–352.

[2] *O Estado de S. Paulo*, December 4, 1966.

[3] Anthony Vereker, "Operação Amazônia," February 15, 1967.

[4] Ibid.

December 3 in the historic Teatro Amazonas in Manaus. Among those present were Paulo Egídio Martins, Eduardo Gomes, the commanders of the military regions of Amazônia, technicians, and the governors of São Paulo, Amazonas, Goiás, Acre, Maranhão, Pará, Mato Grosso, Amapá, Rondônia, and Roraima.[5]

Castello told the audience that previous administrations had "lacked a definite policy, a plan of action, and the indispensable mechanisms to give reality to good intentions." Speaking of the new laws, especially those creating the Superintendency of Amazônia Development (SUDAM) and the Bank of Amazônia, he said that what was needed now was the initiative of his audience, men of business. While they descended "the Great River," he said, they would receive plans and projects from federal and state government specialists. He mentioned projects for fertilizers, fibers, vegetable oils, shipyards, metals, construction materials, animal slaughtering, meat canning, cold storage facilities, and the raising of rice, fruits, and buffaloes.

Castello admitted that entrepreneurs, like the workers, had been called on to make sacrifices: "We have insisted on greater faithfulness in the payment of taxes, greater effort at productivity, greater discipline in the access to credit, and greater acceptance of competition." He argued that the former "unrealistic rates for energy and transport, which apparently reduced the cost of production," ended up in scarcities, rationing, and deteriorization as a result of the lack of investments in the public service companies.

"In listing their complaints," Castello said, "some entrepreneurs lose sight of the innumerable steps taken for strengthening companies." Modernization of the fiscal system, he pointed out, eliminated taxation on fictitious gains and on the maintenance of working capital, permitted realistic depreciation, facilitated the sale of shares, replaced the obsolete stamp tax, and ended the cascading effect of state and municipal taxes. Castello added that the Brazilian entrepreneur was no longer threatened by expropriation, could at long last borrow abroad on reasonable conditions, could calculate his wage costs, and no longer faced the perspective of continuous strikes, politically inspired.

Castello condemned "false nationalists . . . who rail against foreign capital but offer no recipe for increasing national savings." He was

[5] *O Estado de S. Paulo*, December 4, 1966.

critical of those who carried on "irresponsible discussion of the denationalization of companies, citing examples that are not very numerous and are sometimes totally false. They forget that in fundamental sectors, such as electric energy, telecommunications, and mining, property worth half a trillion cruzeiros has been brought under national control in these last two years, and that foreign companies are continually opening themselves to national participation, spurred by tax legislation that discriminates in favor of companies with open capital."

Turning to "examples of true nationalism," Castello cited austere planning of government expenditures that had allowed government infrastructure investments to assume in two years a much higher percentage of the total budget. He said: "An example of true nationalism is the restoration of the various government-owned companies, which have become efficiently run and are no longer the offspring of corruption and political perturbation, and simple entities for making employment. . . . An example of true nationalism is the effort to integrate economically underdeveloped areas, such as the northeast, today revitalized through SUDENE, and this immense north, through Operação Amazônia, for which we bring together all the devotion of the public sector and all the vital energy of the private sector."[6]

6. The First Plenary Vote on the Constitution (December 21, 1966)

On December 6, when Castello was again in Rio, copies of the government's draft of a constitution were made public together with the text of Institutional Act Number Four. Auro de Moura Andrade criticized the government for having waited so long to release "material that has already been studied for eight months." He said that the delay made it appear to him that the executive had no interest in having the constitution discussed "in all of its angles."[1]

Institutional Act Number Four declared that "the present national Congress, which made the ordinary legislation of the Revolution," should elaborate the constitution of the movement of March 31, 1964, and should therefore meet between December 12 and January 24. It

[6] HACB, *Discursos, 1966*, pp. 241–250.
[1] *O Estado de S. Paulo*, December 7, 1966.

called for a preliminary vote on the draft by a joint session, following a report by a mixed legislative commission; if the vote was favorable, the commission was to devote twelve days to a study of all proposed amendments that received the approval of at least one-quarter of the membership of either chamber. The commission's report on the proposed changes would be followed by discussions in the plenary during a second twelve-day period, after which the proposals would be put to vote, with an absolute majority required in each chamber for incorporation in the new constitution; officers of the two chambers were to promulgate the final document on January 24.

Krieger, handing MDB President Oscar Passos a copy of the draft of the constitution at Monroe Palace on December 6, said that he would be "pleased if the opposition, before December 10, would offer suggestions that could be used in the final product."[2] The ARENA president admitted to oppositionists Amaral Peixoto, Tancredo Neves, and Antônio Balbino that the draft could be improved. Although on December 7 Balbino was the only oppositionist to state that the MDB should cooperate, other "moderates" in the MDB felt that same way. Like Tancredo Neves, they believed that the alternative to a new constitution was a military regime, and they recognized that the 1946 Constitution had obsolete features, such as those which had seriously delayed the enactment of legislation.[3]

Oscar Passos and MDB Senate leader Josafá Marinho denounced the "authoritarian project," and *O Estado de S. Paulo* wrote that it corresponded "in no way to the traditions of national juridical culture." Former UDN Secretary Oscar Dias Correia, who now belonged to no party, said that the government's proposal was so bad that he would submit a substitute project of his own. Krieger, finding that most of the congressmen had reservations about the government's proposal, sought to play the role of conciliator, and therefore his relations with Carlos Medeiros Silva deteriorated. Krieger turned to Afonso Arinos de Melo Franco, expert in constitutional law, and received from him two memorandums with suggested changes.[4]

[2] Ibid.

[3] Ibid., December 6, 8, 1966; Tancredo Neves, interview, Brasília, October 22, 1975.

[4] *O Estado de S. Paulo*, December 6, 8, 1966; Krieger, *Desde as Missões*, pp. 244–245.

Castello met with Krieger and Padilha to discuss the selection, which was in the hands of these two leaders, of the eleven senators and eleven congressmen making up the mixed Grande Comissão. The decision to put four opposition senators and four opposition congressmen on the commission resulted in Oscar Passos becoming a member. Padilha urged the inclusion of Adauto Cardoso. When Castello asked, "My leader, do you have confidence in Adauto?" Padilha replied that Adauto was well trained in the law. Adauto was included.[5]

Pedro Aleixo, long known for his anti-authoritarian views, was chosen by the commission members to be their presiding officer. He agreed that the commission's *relator* should be Antônio Carlos Konder Reis, the young, liberal senator from Santa Catarina who had lost a close race for the state's governorship in October, 1965. Konder Reis was neither a well-known constitutional lawyer nor a distinguished orator. But he was a hard worker who could be expected to carry out the tremendous amount of required reading (although he had only one good eye). More important, he respected adversaries, was not combative, and made a point of correct procedure.[6]

Congress, inaugurating its historic session on December 12, received a message from Castello and Medeiros Silva that spoke of the need to replace the 1946 Constitution. Then, while the commission members spent three days studying the draft, speakers in the plenary delivered opinions that were generally unfavorable to the administration's views, and sometimes they declared that the executive lacked the authority to turn Congress into a constitution-making body. Most of the speeches were by MDB members, but partyless Oscar Correia and ARENA Senator Afonso Arinos de Melo Franco attracted particular attention.

Afonso Arinos, speaking in the Senate on December 15, said that a basic contradiction, the contradiction between hope and fear, between civilian and military power, made it impossible to elaborate a democratic constitution, and he added that "it is very easy for the military to conquer the power, but their perpetuation in the power is impractical." He declared that the draft, reflecting "total pauperism and outrageous incompetence," was a conglomeration, essentially contradic-

[5] *O Estado de S. Paulo*, December 10, 1966; Padilha, interview, August 3, 1977.
[6] Padilha, interview, August 3, 1977.

tory, without any doctrine. The wording, he said, was so bad that he had to admit that never in his life had he seen such a text. Speaking of studies, "capricious and errant," that had lasted for months and months, he asserted that the amount of time alloted thereafter for an examination by Congress was "absolutely insufficient."[7]

Castello, after discussing inter-American affairs at lunch on December 15 with Gordon, Tuthill, Roberto Campos, and Otávio Bulhões, joined Krieger, Padilha, Roberto Campos, and Konder Reis at a meeting where it was agreed that all amendments proposed for incorporation in the constitution would be studied by the executive and its parliamentary leadership.[8] On the next day the president flew to Rio to participate in the closing sessions of military schools.

In his speech at the National War College on December 17, Castello said:

> in this century, until recently, democratic regimes disintegrated due to the insistence of preserving archaic formulas, alien to national and world reality. And they gave accomodation to economic stagnation and the perversion of fundamental liberties. . . .
>
> The imperative need of Brazil is to possess a constitution that is democratic, with liberty and responsibility, and in which there are secure means of defending the institutions. . . .
>
> With the constitution vulnerable to various types of crisis, the Nation has long been agitated between the inevitable alternatives of anarchy and dictatorship. The Revolution eliminated one and avoided the other. Why not complete now the institutionalization of the Revolution?

In a reference to one of Afonso Arinos' criticisms, Castello told the graduating class that the project of the constitution did not "presuppose the coexistence, on the same level, of the civilian and military power, nor a contradiction between those powers. The national political power, alone and sovereign, and the juridical power, the guarantee of the former, have been structured objectively. Which shows that the future constitution does not include the intention of dictatorship, while at the same time it does not vulgarize itself by the formulation of empty and

[7] *O Estado de S. Paulo*, December 16, 1966.

[8] Ibid.

innocuous propositions, impractical or destitute of objectivity in the preservation of democracy."[9]

In Brasília on December 17 the joint commission presented two reports to Congress. The fifty-six-page report of Konder Reis, approved by a majority of the commission members, analyzed the main points of the draft and quoted past statements by Barbosa Lima Sobrinho and Otávio Mangabeira to defend the rigid time periods set up in Ato 4. The report concluded that the draft respected democratic postulates and satisfied, in a general way, the requirements of a modern state. A *global* approval by Congress, Konder Reis wrote, would "open sufficient opportunities for offering amendments that reflect the most advanced thinking and the perfecting of the democratic regime."[10]

The MDB members of the commission maintained that Ato 4 allowed insufficient time and that, in any case, Congress was not empowered to approve a new constitution. They complained that the draft, expressing the thinking of a dominating group, limited the rights of Congress and was antidemocratic (calling for indirect elections of presidents). The minority report, signed by all eight MDB members, also objected to the fact that while the draft was "rigid" and "arbitrary" in its political and institutional concepts, it was liberal and "concessionary" in its "arrangements about the economic life and the exploitation of the Nation's wealth, notably when it emphasizes that 'the economic activities will be organized and exploited by private companies with the stimulus and backing of the State.' "[11]

Outside Congress, Levi Carneiro observed that the arduous work he and others had put into their draft during four months had been "ridiculously futile." But the old lawyer found two reasons to praise the government's project. One was its "relative conciseness (it has 180 articles)." The other was "the christening of the country 'Brazil' only, instead of 'United States of Brazil.' The new name is better adjusted to the historic truth and eliminates possible confusion with our good friends of North America and some others of South America."[12]

Castello, back in Brasília on December 19, was told by Krieger, Padilha, and Rui Santos that when Congress voted on December 21,

[9] HACB, *Discursos, 1966*, pp. 79–80.

[10] Sarasate, *A Constituição do Brasil,* pp. 59–60 (quoting the report of the *relator*).

[11] Ibid., pp. 61–62.

[12] *O Estado de S. Paulo*, December 18, 1966.

the administration's draft would receive more than the necessary affirmative votes of 202 congressmen and 33 senators. The shocked *O Estado de S. Paulo* lamented that some MDB members seemed inclined to cooperate with Krieger, thus overlooking "a unique opportunity to give difficulties," and that Milton Campos, Mem de Sá, and Adauto Cardoso did not respond to the wishes of the nation by giving "a definite NO to the abuses of power of Sr. Castello Branco."[13]

The speeches in Congress hardly indicated a vote favorable to the administration. Amaral Neto, in an impassioned speech, said that vice-president-elect Pedro Aleixo should not preside over making an "authoritarian constitution" that might one day give him dictatorial powers, and he criticized the presence of former Goulart cabinet minister Oliveira Brito on the mixed commission. The future constitution, the orator declared, might properly be called the "Oliveira do Pombal Constitution."[14]

Afonso Arinos, in his fourth speech about the project, disagreed with Medeiros Silva's philosophy, which left it up to common law to delineate the specifics about individual rights. "This," the senator said, "is subversion of the democratic order." As the time for the vote approached, Afonso Arinos completed work on a project to give Brazil a parliamentary form of government starting in 1971, and Congressman Humberto Lucena (MDB, Paraíba) drew up a proposal to have the government's project submitted to a plebiscite, regardless of its approval by Congress.[15]

On the evening of December 21, with the voting about to take place, the project was defended by Krieger and two ARENA congressmen and was attacked by six MDB congressmen. The last speaker was Konder Reis, who argued that Congress should institutionalize the 1964 Revolution, giving it a juridical instrument. During the night, Congress gave its approval subject to the forthcoming consideration of the proposed amendments. In the lower house 223 voted in favor and 110 voted against; in the Senate the affirmative vote was 37 to 17.[16]

[13] Ibid., December 17, 20, 21, 1966.

[14] Ibid., December 20, 1966.

[15] Medeiros Silva, interview, November 12, 1975; *O Estado de S. Paulo*, December 20, 21, 1966.

[16] *O Estado de S. Paulo*, December 22, 1966.

Milton Campos explained his favorable vote as inspired by his desire to see a return to constitutional normalcy and by his knowledge that the project would be amended in the days ahead. According to *Jornal do Brasil,* the ARENA, "anticipating an understanding with the MDB," agreed to approve an amendment of Milton Campos for the guarantee of individual rights. Krieger, however, said that he had assumed "no formal commitment with the MDB about this or that amendment."[17]

7. Closing Out 1966

Afonso Arinos de Melo Franco made a profound impression when he argued in the Senate on December 19 that the new constitution should include a section guaranteeing individual rights. On the next day Pedro Aleixo asked him to draw up an appropriate chapter. Krieger made the same request later in the day, when he and Afonso Arinos were dining with Senators Dinarte Mariz and Milton Campos. Afonso Arinos asked the ARENA president whether he would give his support to such a chapter. Krieger replied in the affirmative, just as Pedro Aleixo had done. Besides, Krieger added that if the proposed chapter were defeated, the government would have to find a new Senate majority leader to handle the voting on the constitution.[1]

With this encouragement Afonso Arinos spent part of the night at the Hotel Nacional drawing up a proposal whose only substantial modification from similar chapters, enacted in past constitutional legislation, was the inclusion of the prohibition of racial discimination. Afonso Arinos' text, with a few slight word changes by Senate Vice-leader Eurico Rezende, was handed to Castello by Krieger during the plane trip from Brasília to Rio on December 22. "Mr. President," Krieger said, "we are strengthening the executive power, but democracy does not exist without individual rights and guarantees. I cannot agree to a constitution without that chapter." The president promised to examine the proposal with care.[2]

[17] Ibid. and *Jornal do Brasil*, December 22, 1966.

[1] Afonso Arinos de Melo Franco, *Planalto*, pp. 279–280.

[2] Ibid.; Krieger, *Desde as Missões*, pp. 244–245; Krieger, interview, October 21, 1975; *Jornal do Brasil* (Coluna do Castello), December 22, 1966.

Before leaving Brasília on December 22, Castello submitted a press law project to Congress, thus assuring himself of a barrage of attacks by newspapers and lawmakers. And he reached an unpopular decision about wage increases of the military and the bureaucrats.

Otávio Bulhões and Roberto Campos had been arguing that the government would be in a better position to grant a 25 percent wage increase if it could decrease the income tax "incentives" for helping the north and northeast or if it could make temporary use of so-called idle funds that had accumulated, as a result of those incentives, in the Bank of the Northeast and Bank of Amazônia.[3] Upset by this prospect, João Gonçalves de Sousa, minister of the coordination of regional agencies, had handed Castello a letter with his views during the ceremony at the National War College in Rio on December 17. The president had crushed the letter in his hand and put it in his pocket in a manner discouraging to João Gonçalves, and, during subsequent discussions in Brasília, Castello, Bulhões, and Campos had spoken to João Gonçalves and representatives of the northeast about the possible need to cut back drastically on projects, such as road building, if the "idle funds" could not be used temporarily for purposes other than originally intended.[4] But Castello put off reaching a decision about tampering with the "incentives" arrangements and funds and thus disappointed Bulhões and Campos, at least for the time being.

Upon reaching Rio on December 22, Castello spoiled Christmas for many by announcing that the wage increases of the military and bureaucrats would be limited to 25 percent. Military officers wrote memorandums of protest for Ademar de Queiroz and Costa e Silva (who was in Europe on the first leg of a round-the-world tour). Navy Club President Saldanha da Gama described the restrictive wage increase as "a grave error."

Civil servants expressed the hope that Roberto Campos would be filled with remorse when he sat down before his "plentious" Christmas dinner. Their leaders, denouncing the government's capacity "for creating the gravest of social problems," looked to Costa e Silva to reverse the "outrageous injustice" by means of a 100 percent wage increase.

[3] João Gonçalves de Sousa, "V Round da Luta pela Manutenção dos Artigos 34/18" (typewritten), Rio de Janeiro, December 30, 1966, p. 1.

[4] Ibid., p. 4; Gonçalves de Sousa, interview, June 11, 1975.

During the outcry Castello issued Ato Complementar No. 30, which prevented the states, municipalities, government companies, and companies of mixed economy from increasing wages by more than 25 percent. Increases of 35 percent, recently granted in São Paulo, were affected by a clause voiding increases above 25 percent.[5]

Castello's own financial condition had recently been made public in accordance with an article of Constitutional Amendment 15 requiring the heads of the executive and legislative powers to issue declarations of assets ninety days before leaving office. The president's statement revealed that since taking office he had transferred his shares in Minas banks to his children and sold his Aero-Willys automobile and apartment on Rua Jangadeiros in Rio; with the proceeds from the sales and savings made while he was president he had purchased Apartment 202 at Rua Nascimento Silva 518 in Rio.[6]

Castello spent Christmas Eve and Christmas day with his family and close aides at Alvorada Palace and then flew to Ceará. Speaking at Crato, Ceará, on December 28, he argued that it was possible to have a government that was constitutional but at the same time ineffective due to a lack of authority. He reminded his audience that dictatorships could develop where constitutions were "inadequate for the epoch, progress, and national security" and that constitutional regimes, removed from the realities of the nation, brought about "the paralyzation of creative activities" and smothered actions by the state and productive forces. The new constitution, he said, would establish "responsible powers" with clearly defined means of action and limits on action. And for promoting development, it would provide modern fiscal, financial, and economic arrangements.[7]

Answering reporters in the governor's palace in Fortaleza on December 30, Castello said that his government would grant amnesty to no one, and, unfortunately, had no plans to reexamine the recent deci-

[5] *Jornal do Brasil*, December 23, 24, 1966.

[6] Ibid., December 17, 1966; the president received a monthly salary of 2,455,000 cruzeiros plus 1,000,000 cruzeiros for expenses, equivalent to $1,116 and $455, respectively (Mercadante, "Este É o Humberto").

[7] HACB, longhand notes, File P1 (p. 12), CPDOC; *Jornal do Brasil*, December 29, 1966.

sion about wage increases. Reacting to a question about his possible plans to seek a Senate seat from Ceará, Castello declared that "no one was authorized to deal with this personal political matter."[8]

In his year-end message, released in Rio, Castello admitted that 1966 had been "arduous" and that the inflation had not been "completely overcome." But he described himself as comforted "to be able to believe in a Brazil more prosperous, more sovereign, and conscious of its destiny, as I make this, my last, message of the new year as president of the Republic."[9]

Jornal do Brasil noted that 1966 had been a year of contradiction, with arbitrary *cassações* accompanied by a nationwide election and a turn toward institutional normalization, and it concluded from the government's interest in security and press laws that the regime could be characterized as one that did not represent "the national aspirations." Members of the National Confederation of Industries, also unhappy, released a statement objecting to "execssive legislation," whose "avalanche of alterations" left industralists unclear about what they should do. The industralists added that they were being choked by high taxes and high interest rates and afflicted by the drop in consumption, which they described as 35 percent in Guanabara, 26 percent in São Paulo, and 18 percent in the state of Rio de Janeiro.[10]

Among the year-end comments made abroad was the accusation of the Mexico City daily *Novedades* that Castello Branco was guilty of despotism and brutality.[11] The CIA, drawing up a report in Washington about Brazil, wrote that the Castello Branco regime had failed almost completely to establish "rapport with labor, students, and intellectuals." While the CIA credited the regime with maintaining a favorable trade balance and reducing budgetary deficits, it noted that the inflation rate in 1966 had been rather high: 41 percent (compared with 45 percent in 1965 and 87 percent in 1964). And it added that "as far as the public is concerned, austerity has introduced a new set of problems." Fears of a recession abounded, particularly in São Paulo.

[8] HACB, *Discursos, 1966*, pp. 395–399.

[9] Ibid., pp. 83–85.

[10] *Jornal do Brasil*, January 1, 1967; *Brazil Herald*, December 15, 1966.

[11] *Jornal do Brasil*, December 27, 1966 (quoting *Novedades*).

Coffee and sugar growers were furious about the government's pricing policies for their products.[12]

The American Embassy in Rio cabled Washington that "President Castello Branco's administration will probably end as one of the most unpopular in the country's recent history but paradoxically the man himself is just as likely to be remembered with nostalgia within two years. He has been a severe taskmaster, often called ruthless and dictatorial but few indeed credit him with other than the best of motives and objectives." According to this cable, Castello, although "often thought to be ill-advised by his technocrats on the economic side and sometimes forced to take extreme actions by military hardliners," managed to preserve something of a father image and was admired at least for his honesty and integrity.

Commenting on economic matters, the American Embassy found that future growth could be expected to result from a reduced inflation rate, tax reform, banking reform, budget reform, a heavy decrease in the subsidization of state-owned enterprises, signs of foreign interest in renewing investments, improved commodity price support programs, removal of price controls, a wider agricultural credit system, and greater freedom to export. However, the embassy concluded, the beneficial effects of the long-range program were unfortunately not felt by the "man on the street," who was suffering from the effects of "short-term dislocations."[13]

The political developments during the late 1960's and early 1970's would have disappointed Castello Branco, who considered March 15, 1967, as the date on which Brazil would relinquish its use of "measures of exception" and embark on a long period of "basic institutionalization," becoming strong democratically.[14] The crisis that began in September, 1968, and came to a head in December of that year (considered by Schneider as "broadly comparable" to the crisis of October,

[12] Central Intelligence Agency, Weekly Review, January 20, 1967, NSFB, Brazilian Memorandums, Vol. VI, Box 3, LBJ Library.

[13] American Embassy, Rio de Janeiro, cable to Secretary of State, January 24, 1967, NSFB, Cables, Vol. VI, LBJ Library.

[14] HACB, *Discursos, 1966*, p. 61.

1965)[15] gave Brazil its harshly dictatorial Institutional Act Number Five.

Daniel Krieger, writing about the constitution that was completed early in 1967, writes that he was one of those who, late in 1966, favored the deletion of the clause about the state of emergency, but he goes on to say that he now considers that he was wrong. "President Castello Branco was the one who was right: the state of emergency would have neutralized the pretext for issuing Institutional Act No. 5."[16] Others have maintained that Castello Branco's reservations about the selection of his successor proved to have been right.

One can speculate what the post–Castello Branco political era might have been like if Castello had had his way about such political matters. But even if he had had his way, could he have achieved the essential reform—a reform in the attitude of those who were in a position to scratch or injure constitutions? The events that preceded 1964 and the events that occurred in 1964 and the next two years contributed to an attitude which was difficult to extinguish overnight by legal documents, no matter how carefully prepared.

[15] Schneider, *The Political System of Brazil*, p. 273.
[16] Krieger, *Desde as Missões*, p. 243.

XI

The Last Months of the Administration

(January–March, 1967)

I never made use of the power for myself. I used it, yes, to save the institutions, defend the principle of authority, extinguish privileges, correct the vacillations of the past, and patiently plant the seeds that will make the greatness of the future.

1. The Constitution Commission Studies Amendments (December 26, 1966–January 9, 1967)

FOLLOWING the *global* approval given by Congress on December 21 to the administration's draft of the constitution, the members of the mixed commission spent a busy holiday season. Often they worked from 9:00 A.M. to 4:00 A.M. to complete reports on proposed amendments by January 3 so that they could begin voting on them on January 4. By December 26, the last day for proposed amendments to reach the commission, 884 proposals had received the necessary approval of one-quarter of the members of either chamber. However, Paulo Sarasate has written, some proposals concerned several subjects, and thus the number of proposed changes reached 1,504. According to subject matter, they were distributed to the commission's assistant *relatores* (Oliveira Brito, Vasconcelos Torres, Acióli Filho, Adauto Cardoso, Wilson Gonçalves, and Djalma Marinho).[1]

Relator Konder Reis told the press on December 26 that the original work of Justice Minister Medeiros Silva needed to be considerably altered, and he agreed with those who favored a revision of the section on individual guarantees. Soon it was common knowledge that Konder Reis was refusing to answer calls from the justice minister, who wanted Konder Reis to go over the amendments with him. The *relator* maintained that the justice minister did not have that authority and that the minister's debates with representatives of the commission should occur

[1] Padilha, interview, August 3, 1977; Sarasate, *A Constituição do Brasil ao alcance de todos*, p. 61.

only at the meetings that Castello had scheduled.[2] One such meeting, scheduled for January 2, would bring commission members Pedro Aleixo and Konder Reis together with Castello, Medeiros Silva, Roberto Campos, Krieger, and Padilha at Laranjeiras Palace.

Krieger, flown from the south to Rio in a presidential plane on January 2, was met by senators who told him that Konder Reis, unhappy at pressure exerted by Medeiros Silva, was talking about resigning his *relator*'s post. At the Laranjeiras Palace meeting Krieger participated in a discussion about the individual rights amendment of Afonso Arinos. Such was the disfavor with which Afonso Arinos was viewed by "the most orthodox circles of the government" that the amendment was presented as that of Eurico Rezende.[3]

"The amendment," Medeiros Silva said, "is very badly drawn up!" Krieger answered that "the one who drew it up knows much more about constitutional law than Your Excellency."

When Medeiros alleged that the amendment had been drafted by adversaries of the Revolution, Krieger said: "Your Excellency already collaborated in making the 1937 Constitution, and the nation paid a very heavy tribute. I was imprisoned several times. My capacity for compromising has reached its limit. I am unwilling to let go of a single provision of the chapter."

Castello spoke to Medeiros: "Mr. Minister, you have the glory of having elaborated the draft. Let us give heed to our leader."[4]

That night Krieger telephoned Castello to thank him for his support and apologize for his aggressive conduct. "You did not go too far," Castello said. "One who defends his convictions with ardor and sincerity does not go too far. I took a copy of the amendment that you gave me, and, during Christmas night, I sought the inspiration of Jesus and my wife. Upon waking up, I was convinced that you were right. No one would move me from the decision that I made."

Pedro Aleixo congratulated Krieger and told him that he could now approve the constitution with a peaceful conscience.[5]

[2] *Jornal do Brasil*, December 27, 1966, January 3, 1967.

[3] Krieger, *Desde as Missões*, p. 245; Castello Branco, "Coluna do Castello," *Jornal do Brasil*, January 4, 1967.

[4] Castello Branco, "Coluna do Castello," January 4, 1967; Krieger, *Desde as Missões*, p. 246.

[5] Krieger, *Desde as Missões*, p. 246; Melo Franco, *Planalto*, p. 280; Castello Branco, "Coluna do Castello," January 4, 1967.

Castello prepared notes about some of the proposed amendments for use at further sessions with those who had recently met with him. On the "question of petroleum" Castello wrote:

a) Amendment 883/14 is vague and opens the way to possible absurd steps. It even covers the gasoline pump.

b) The amendment previously studied (Teódulo-A. Arinos Filho) is less inconvenient. Here is its wording: "The search for and the production of petroleum in the national territory constitute a monopoly of the Union."

c) The best would be the manner of the Constitution of '46, which says nothing about the matter. If this should not be possible, and I leave the answer to this up to the leaderships, then make an effort for the approval of the Teódulo-A. Arinos amendment.[6]

Roberto Campos argued for handling the subject as had been done in the 1946 Constitution. Finding it difficult to convince Krieger, he said that "no one wants to suppress the monopoly; only we think that it should not be in the text of the constitution." Krieger replied: "If there is no wish to suppress the monopoly, why not have it expressed in the constitution?" Castello, who had been listening attentively, agreed with the adoption of the amendment proposed by Teódulo de Albuquerque and Afonso Arinos de Melo Franco Filho.[7]

Before the mixed commission met on January 3 to hear the reports of Konder Reis and the assistant *relatores*, Pedro Aleixo spoke to Castello about the commission members who he felt had worked most efficiently. When he praised the collaboration of Adauto Cardoso, Castello said that he had been considering appointing Adauto to fill the Supreme Court vacancy brought about by the retirement of Álvaro Ribeiro da Costa but was not certain that he should do so.[8]

Before Castello's troubles with Adauto in October, the president had told Adauto that he would appoint him to the court when a vacancy occurred. Now the president consulted some of the legislative leaders. In a phone call to Krieger, Castello mentioned his "old commitment to Adauto" and asked, "Do you think, after what happened, I can make the nomination without incurring deserved criticism?"

[6] HACB, handwritten notes, File Q4, CPDOC.

[7] Krieger, *Desde as Missões*, p. 247.

[8] Aleixo, letter to Viana Filho, September 21, 1971, p. 4.

Krieger said that he thought the president could, but Castello phoned him again later to ask if he had meditated about the matter. "I assure you," Krieger said, "that the party and the Congress will have no restrictions." Pedro Aleixo also advised Castello that he favored Adauto's appointment to the Supreme Court.[9]

When Castello told Ernani Sátiro that the question might be one "of honor" because of his past promise, Sátiro maintained that Castello was no longer bound by the promise in view of what had happened in October. But Castello said, "I have given my word of honor and so I'll keep it."[10] In a letter dated January 5, Castello extended the invitation to Adauto and added that he was doing so because of his "sentiments" and because the reasons that had led him to make the offer in the first place continued "without restriction."[11]

Adauto accepted at once, whereupon some members of the *mesa* of the Câmara expressed indignation at the "reward." They pointed out that they had supported the president during the October, 1966, crisis, despite possible unfavorable effects on their campaigns for Congress, and now found themselves uncertain about retaining their *mesa* posts. Moura Andrade complained that Adauto Cardoso, "who threw Congress into a hazardous adventure," was receiving a lofty appointment, whereas the government seemed to want to replace Moura Andrade in the Senate presidency. But Moura Andrade, supported by Krieger, seemed a good bet to retain his post. It was in the lower house, where Ernani Sátiro challenged Acting Chamber President Batista Ramos, that the outcome was in doubt.[12]

The mixed commission considering the constitution approved the Eurico Rezende individual rights amendment, and it supported the government's idea of having mayors of state capitals named by the governors. A clause allowing the Supreme Court to suspend from two to ten years the political rights of those found guilty of subversion or cor-

[9] Ibid.; Krieger, *Desde as Missões*, p. 241.

[10] Sátiro, interview, December 17, 1975.

[11] HACB, letter to Adauto Lúcio Cardoso, January 5, 1967, File M (p. 74v), CPDOC; Cardoso, letter to HACB, Brasília, January 5, 1967, File M (p. 75v), CPDOC. Cardoso modestly wrote that Castello was "undoubtedly inspired more by generous sentiments than by reality."

[12] Castello Branco, *Os Militares no Poder*, p. 635; *Jornal do Brasil*, January 6, 8, 1967.

ruption was amended to make this punishment of federal lawmakers dependent on the approval of their fellow legislators. The amenders, however, failed in their attempt to modify a clause in the government project that would have the military courts judge civilians accused of violating the national security.[13] Nor was anything done to restrict the president's power to issue decree-laws in case of "danger" to the national security; an amendment extended this decree-law power to the field of public finances.[14]

Paulo Sarasate, having been elected senator, gave a farewell speech in the Chamber of Deputies in which he defended his proposed amendment to require that 3 percent of the government receipts be devoted to the development of the north and northeast (as had been written into the 1946 Constitution). After he sent Castello a copy of his speech together with an appeal for support, the president wrote his old friend that he had a "mistaken conception about a modern constitution." "I want," Castello said, "to express my complete disagreement with your points of view about constitutional entailments to the budget. Their approval would be a disservice to the rational modernization of the constitution, and their rejection a benefit to financial truthfulness and the national reality. And the attitude of the government will never retard the development of the Brazilian northeast."[15]

2. Congress Acts on the Constitution (January 12–20, 1967)

Congress, scheduled to start voting on January 16 on amendments to the administration's draft of the constitution, commenced four days of discussion on January 12. "Curiously," Luís Viana Filho reports, the economic innovations, "probably more radical than the political ones, aroused little debate." The economic innovations included one that prohibited the increase of government expenditures by the initiative of Congress.[1]

[13] *Jornal do Brasil*, January 5, 6, 7, 1967; already Krieger had arranged that appeals to the Supreme Court could be made in the case of these military court decisions (Krieger, *Desde as Missões*, p. 247).

[14] *Jornal do Brasil*, January 10, 1967.

[15] Ibid., January 12, 1967; Viana Filho, *O Governo Castelo Branco*, p. 472.

[1] Viana Filho, *O Governo Castelo Branco*, p. 461.

At Planalto Palace, Castello, Roberto Campos, Pedro Aleixo, Konder Reis, Krieger, Müller, and Padilha decided that about 10 percent of the amendments approved by the mixed commission were objectionable, and therefore the government was unwilling that every amendment approved by the commission be included in a *global* vote. Pedro Aleixo showed concern lest Moura Andrade, presiding officer of the combined chambers, handle "obstructive questions of order" raised by the opposition in a manner that would prevent Congress from completing its task on schedule, but Krieger expressed faith in Moura Andrade.[2]

On January 16, Moura Andrade announced the voting program: (1) a *global* vote on material with favorable commission reports, except for special cases; (2) a *global* vote on material with unfavorable commission reports, except for special cases; (3) a *global* vote on special cases that both parties agreed to approve; (4) a *global* vote on special cases that both parties agreed to reject; (5) a vote on individual amendments considered important by the MDB (such as direct presidential elections, amnesty, and military tribunal judgments of civilians); and (6) a vote on the preferred items of the ARENA. The number of special cases to be considered exceeded five hundred, due more to the requests of individual lawmakers than the requests of the parties. So large was the number that Moura Andrade ruled that in the case of amendments not voted by January 21, those with favorable commission reports would be considered approved and those with unfavorable reports would be considered rejected. The ruling upset Pedro Aleixo and Paulo Sarasate, but it promoted an effort by the ARENA to negotiate with the MDB about amendments.[3]

Castello was so interested in the developments that he canceled his trip to Rio, planned for January 18, and thus missed, as he rarely did, the anniversary lunch of the Military Academy class of January, 1921. When the congressmen were working on clauses about the legislative power, Castello decided that he wanted to discuss the matter with Senator Josafá Marinho (MDB, Bahia), who had been attacking the government. Phoning the senator, he said: "This is President Castello Branco. Good morning. I would like to meet with you and exchange

[2] *Jornal do Brasil*, January 12, 13, 1967; Viana Filho, *O Governo Castelo Branco*, pp. 457–458, 470–471; Krieger, *Desde as Missões*, p. 247.

[3] *Jornal do Brasil*, January 17, 18, 1967.

ideas about constitutional reform." After Josafá Marinho agreed to the meeting, Castello turned to Asdrubal Ulysséa, his assistant for legislative matters, and said: "The senator seemed surprised." A few moments later Navarro de Brito, head of the Gabinete Civil, answered a phone call in which the senator asked whether the call he had just received had been authentic.[4]

Negotiations between Krieger, Pedro Aleixo, and MDB leader Humberto Lucena were carried out in the presence of Moura Andrade and resulted in a memorandum of understanding. The two ARENA representatives, having consulted Castello, agreed to the provision requiring legislative approval before the Supreme Court could suspend the political rights of federal legislators. They agreed also that workers would have the constitutional right to participate in company profits (an idea that appealed to Castello) and that the Petrobrás monopoly might be included in the constitution as long as it was limited to the search for, and production of, petroleum. The ARENA representatives also gave assurances that thirteen amendments, desired by the MDB, would be peacefully adopted. But the memorandum took a firm ARENA stance against some MDB proposals, such as a revision of "revolutionary punishments" and the elimination of the decree-law powers of the president.[5]

The government's position prevailed on January 18 when Congress determined the fate of amendments about the Petrobrás monopoly, the election of presidents, and possible amnesty. The so-called Petrobrás monoploy clause, or Adolfo de Oliveira amendment, giving the government a monopoly in the search, extraction, and industrialization of petroleum and atomic minerals, had received a favorable commission vote because of the absence of ARENA commission members.[6] The president of the Federation of Industries of São Paulo telegraphed a plea to Castello urging that private companies be allowed to participate in the industrialization of petroleum, and National Petroleum Council President Emílio Maurel Filho declared that rejection of the Adolfo de Oliveira amendment would assure Brazilian self-sufficiency in petrochemicals in five years. *O Jornal*, usually critical of the Castello admin-

[4] Ibid., January 19, 1967; Pinto de Ulysséa, letter to Viana Filho, July 15, 1972.

[5] Krieger, *Desde as Missões*, p. 248; *Jornal do Brasil*, January 20, 1967.

[6] *O Globo*, January 12, 1967.

istration, praised the government for showing a "belated" interest in the private sector by opposing the Adolfo de Oliveira amendment and by completing the sale of the government's money-losing Fábrica Nacional de Motores to an Italian firm.[7] The Adolfo de Oliveira amendment was attacked by Raimundo Padilha during a heated Câmara debate. It was defeated, 186 to 132 and therefore did not go to the Senate.

Padilha was active also in orating against the Josafá Marinho amendment to make presidential elections direct. Although Josafá Marinho supported his case by quoting former UDN leaders Eduardo Gomes and Prado Kelly, his amendment was rejected, 182 to 143. The amendment for allowing a revision of the "revolutionary punishments" was defeated, 183 to 111.

MDB congressmen, furious at the agreement that Humberto Lucena had reached with Pedro Aleixo and Krieger, arranged to hold a meeting on January 19, and there the MDB voted, 48 to 26, to reject the agreement and obstruct the remaining work by staying away from the plenary. Moura Andrade described himself as deeply hurt by this "unpatriotic and negative decision." Krieger said that he would nevertheless see to it that the ARENA upheld its part of the agreement by supporting the thirteen amendments favored by the MDB. Krieger's declaration was regarded by the MDB as a "gesture of superiority" and an effort to make it appear that the ARENA, even without the MDB, was seeking to improve the constitution.[8]

The fate of more than three hundred amendments was left for January 20. The session that night became the stormiest, despite the absence of the MDB. But it started out calmly enough, with decisions that left the voting of illiterates up to ordinary law and that rejected making labor union membership obligatory. Some discontent was evident with the defeat of seven proposals which would guarantee that specific geographical regions receive definite percentages of federal receipts. Then, with the session approaching its end, Moura Andrade arranged for the "liquidation" of about three hundred remaining amendments by *global* votes carried out three times in a row. During the violent protests against this procedure, one congressman said that it

[7] *Jornal do Brasil*, January 19, 1967; *O Jornal*, January 18, 1967.
[8] *Jornal do Brasil*, January 20, 1967.

affected six amendments that were supposed to be voted on separately in accordance with prior agreements.[9]

The greatest stir was caused by Herbert Levy. When the session was about to close, he read a declaration, signed by 106 ARENA congressmen, that condemned the new constitution for giving "excessive powers to the president of the Republic"—namely the authority to issue decree-laws and to enact a state of siege without hearing Congress. After reading the declaration, which warned of such powers in the hands of irresponsible presidents, Levy called the declaration "a cry of protest against the way in which the new constitution was elaborated and voted." He added that more than 106 congressmen might have signed the declaration except that it had just been drawn up the previous day.

Konder Reis, upset by the declaration, spoke of his own work to limit excessive presidential powers in the case of the two items mentioned in it. As general *relator*, he lamented profoundly that, "together with the criticisms of the two constitutional provisions, there was no praise for the work done to improve the constitution."[10] While the MDB denounced the declaration's signers for not having joined the opposition in an effort to correct errors "condemned by all nations," Raimundo Padilha described the signers as "romantic congressmen" eager to exude rhetoric.[11]

3. Promulgation of the Constitution (January 24, 1967)

With the lawmakers trying to complete the press law as well as the constitution, the officers of Congress decided to dispense with a final separate vote on each part of the constitution. A "symbolic vote" on the whole would take place on Saturday evening, January 21, lest failure to comply with the time schedule enable the executive branch to decree its original project.

Even with this change in the plan, the reading of the document took so long that it seemed out of the question to complete the "sym-

[9] Ibid., January 21, 1967.
[10] Ibid.
[11] Ibid.; Castello Branco, "Coluna do Castello," January 24, 1967.

bolic vote" before the midnight deadline. The congressional clocks were therefore set back—a step occasionally taken in past years when budgets, opposed by long-winded orators, had to be enacted by deadlines. Moura Andrade, ordering the disconnection of the congressional clocks at 11:40 P.M., reflected that it was really 10:40 except for daylight saving time and that daylight saving time had been instituted "to save energy, not to affect constitutional matters."[1]

With the constitution thus approved, *Jornal do Brasil* wrote that the "degrading predawn . . . outrage against the hands of the congressional clocks" reflected the "artificial manner" in which the government sought to "order national political life"—elaborating a constitution "in secrecy, far from national debate." Describing the new document as a "Constitution of Transition," completed under rigid rules "in a setting of popular indifference," the Rio daily expressed the hope that it would "help with the peaceful transition to a future stage of institutional normalcy." *Correio da Manhã* reported that Castello had obtained *his* constitution during a period of mad frenzy and would go down in history as the author of a hopeless, last-minute dictatorial document. *O Estado de S. Paulo* called the new constitution no "victory" for Castello and said that "never in the history of the Republic has a chief executive been so unanimously repudiated by all who are possessed of a grain of good sense."[2]

Mem de Sá wrote to Krieger and Filinto Müller to explain why he had abstained from voting for the constitution. "After ten days and nights of grievous, intimate debate," he wrote, he had come to see the moral impossibility of his voting to give the president vast powers or supporting other propositions that likewise contradicted his political thinking, built up in almost forty-five years of public life. He also expressed his dissatisfaction with Ato Institucional No. 4 and his regret that so "little consideration" had been given to the early project of "the illustrious lawyers" whom he had chosen.[3]

In accordance with Ato Institucional No. 4, the new constitution

[1] Medeiros Silva, interview, August 9, 1977; Moura Andrade, interview, November 10, 1975.

[2] *Jornal do Brasil*, January 22, 24, 1967; *Correio da Manhã*, January 22, 1967; *O Estado de S. Paulo*, January 24, 1967.

[3] Mem de Sá, quoted in Krieger, *Desde as Missões*, pp. 250–254.

was promulgated on January 24. During the one-hour ceremony in Congress, Konder Reis, Raimundo Padilha, and Moura Andrade spoke. Luís Viana Filho writes about Moura Andrade: "After having provoked so many worries, the hour arrived for him to congratulate himself on the victory."[4]

Castello, receiving legislators at Planalto Palace after the ceremony, said that "the constitution that Your Excellencies have just given Brazil is going to open the second and long phase of Brazilian renovation." He described it as a realistic document that provided for the "coexistence of liberty and authority," the concept of development as an objective, and "national security to guarantee national integrity and social peace."[5]

Krieger persuaded Castello to attend a barbecue given that evening by the ARENA at a restaurant close to the lake near Brasília. Following a welcome by Senator Rui Palmeira, Castello, in his usual formal attire, spoke in defense of politicians. On the next day Castello cabled Costa e Silva, who had reached the United States, to advise "his dear friend and president-elect" of the promulgation of the constitution on January 24, "a great historic day in the life of the Brazilian Republic."[6] Krieger, reaching Rio, declared that the movement that had been started for the revision of the new constitution had no chance of success. In São Paulo, Herbert Levy disagreed with him.[7]

Krieger has pointed out that the authority given in the new constitution to the executive power to issue decree-laws about national security and public finances did not reduce the authority of Congress, because "the final decision was left to it." The congressional lack of "financial initiative," he has explained, was "an imperative of the inflationary situation and of national development, which requires planning with appropriate application of public receipts."[8]

Although Krieger had given Moura Andrade some satisfaction by helping to preserve the Senate's right to choose its presiding officer

[4] Viana Filho, *O Governo Castelo Branco*, p. 475.

[5] Ibid., p. 476.

[6] Krieger, *Desde as Missões*, p. 254; Viana Filho, *O Governo Castelo Branco*, p. 476.

[7] *Jornal do Brasil*, January 25, 1967.

[8] Krieger, *Desde as Missões*, p. 254.

(which the original project had assigned to the vice-president of the Republic), the new constitution returned to the vice-president the prerogative of presiding over the combined national Congress. Moura Andrade, starting to wrangle with Pedro Aleixo over the interpretation of this provision, appealed to Krieger for additional help.[9]

4. The Press Law Project Provokes a Storm (December, 1966–January, 1967)

Castello Branco, speaking on July 19, 1966, at the ceremony at which Medeiros Silva became justice minister, had said that "liberty of the press is one of the conquests of Western civilization that our constitutional texts have assured as an expression of thought, each responding to the abuses he commits." He added that the government was elaborating a text "with the purpose of assuring, before everything, the liberty of thought, without giving room for abuses that place in risk the principal interests of the nation and the honor and dignity of its citizens."[1]

The existing Press Law, that of November 12, 1953, was generally regarded as innocuous. Roberto Campos and Mines Minister Mauro Thibau, pictured frequently as traitors in *Tribuna da Imprensa* articles that were filled with untruths, failed to receive any satisfaction when they undertook a libel suit late in 1964. Castello told Medeiros Silva that, while he wanted no censorship, he wanted him to draft a law to prohibit abuses. "Do you want it enacted as a decree-law or by Congress?" Medeiros asked. Castello, whom Medeiros regarded as liberal and idealistic, said, "By Congress." "All right," Medeiros replied, "then you are going to pay the price."[2]

In September, *Jornal do Brasil* wrote that it could not believe the government was really considering the enactment of a new Press Law, and it argued that ordinary legislation offered all necessary punitive measures, the only missing factor being the will to carry them out. Austregésilo de Ataíde published an article that scolded those who con-

[9] Castello Branco, "Coluna do Castello," January 27, 1967.

[1] HACB, *Discursos, 1966*, p. 335.

[2] Medeiros Silva, interviews, November 12, 1975, August 9, 1977.

templated legislation, "repugnant to the general conscience," that would reduce the freedom of the press. Like *Jornal do Brasil*, he noted that Castello's government had carried out its program without yet having harmed the freedom of the press in any way.[3]

Castello mentioned the matter in his "press conference" of October 1 in Brasília—one of those occasions that Theophilo de Andrade said were not really press interviews "in the true sense of the word because they lacked the conditions of spontaneous dialogue" and turned journalists into simple audiences "for the reading of replies" to a few questions previously selected.[4] This time Castello told his audience that his government did not contemplate a measure as harsh as that described by Austregésilo, and he denied *Jornal do Brasil*'s thesis that the current legislation provided the means for its own proper execution. He insisted that the government's objective was "simply to defend the truth" and assure a process in which the accuser and accused would receive equal treatment.[5]

Although not until December 12 was Medeiros reported by *Jornal da Tarde* to be on the verge of beginning to draft the law, that same newspaper described the law on December 9 as "a dictatorial Press Law that will practically transform the newspapers, radios, and televisions into official dailies."

Castello transmitted the government's project to Congress on December 22 and gave Congress thirty days to act on it. The accompanying message referred to the provisions of Institutional Act No. 2 which established that judges, instead of special Press Law juries, should decide Press Law cases and which forbade "propaganda of war, subversion of order, or bias of race or class."[6]

The project included these provisions. It also limited newspaper ownership to native Brazilians "in full possession of their civil and political rights" and listed crimes, such as slander and defamation, and established punishments for the crimes—detentions and fines, in most cases. A stiff punishment of from one to four years of "imprisonment"

[3] "Duplo Prejuízo," editorial, *Jornal do Brasil*, September 28, 1966, and a newspaper article by Austregésilo de Ataíde, both in File P1, CPDOC.

[4] Theophilo de Andrade, "Mea culpa, mea máxima culpa," *O Jornal*, January 18, 1967, citing an article of April 21, 1966, by the same writer.

[5] HACB, *Discursos, 1966*, pp. 381–392.

[6] *O Estado de S. Paulo*, December 23, 1966.

was set for those who divulged state secrets or "practiced any crimes defined in the law as against the national security or military institutions." Controversial Article 13 made it a crime "to publish or transmit false news or divulge true facts in a garbled or deformed way, capable of: (1) provoking the disturbance of public order or social alarm; (2) provoking distrust in the banking system or upsetting the credit of a financial institution; (3) harming the credit of the Union, a state, or municipality; (4) causing the rise or fall, in the market, of the value of merchandise or securities."

According to Article 23, unsigned articles were the responsibility of (1) the editor of the section, (2) the director or editor-in-chief, and (3) the manager or owner. Article 33, also controversial, ruled that if the author of a law-breaking piece of published writing was out of the country or was not competent to respond for the crime, the responsibility lay with the director or editor-in-chief. And if the director or editor-in-chief was out of Brazil or not competent to respond, then the responsibility lay with the manager or owner. Article 33 placed responsibility on the distributors or sellers of illicit or clandestine publications when the author, editor, and publishing company were not known.[7]

In São Paulo, *Jornal da Tarde* wrote that "if the Press Law were already in existence, all the newspapers of the nation would have their directors imprisoned" because "the ministers of the Castello government are specialists in lying, and the newspapers reported their declarations." Citing possible sources of inspiration for the law project, *Jornal da Tarde* listed the Germany of Hitler, the Italy of Mussolini, Communist Russia, and the People's Republic of China.[8]

In Rio, *Correio da Manhã* wrote that the law closed "the circle of repression against liberty," while *Última Hora*, also of the opposition, called it a "gag law." *Jornal do Brasil*, in editorials that it published almost daily against the law, repeated that no special law for the press should exist. It pointed out that the president had "bragged about" having respected fully the opinions of newspapers, even in the most dramatic moments of crisis, and therefore nothing was stranger than

[7] Ibid.

[8] *Jornal da Tarde*, December 23, 1966, January 4, 1967.

his switch, which appalled the nation and would destroy "the little that remains abroad concerning our democratic concepts."[9]

The International Press Institute, headquartered in Zurich, and the Inter-American Press Association, of which Júlio de Mesquita Filho was president, sent telegrams of protest to Castello Branco. In Brazil, where newspaper publishers issued joint manifestos of protest to the nation, the Brazilian Press Association (ABI) and the National Federation of Professional Journalists sent denouncements to the United Nations and international newspaper organizations.[10] A Commission for the Liberty of the Press, set up by Brazilian unions of journalists, proposed to newspaper publishers that newspapers never again mention the name of Castello Branco or of anyone who collaborated for the approval of the new law. After São Paulo journalists proposed that newspapers cease publishing news about the government, *Jornal da Tarde* remarked that the publication of such news would be restricted to the *Diário Oficial* ("which reaches São Paulo fifteen days late") and Rio's *O Globo* ("which approves of the dictatorship").[11]

A few days later *O Globo* wrote that while the proposed law contained some useful measures, it could not agree with all of them, and it objected to the failure of Article 13 to distinguish between errors made in good faith and bad faith. *O Globo*'s name was included among those of eighteen newspapers and magazines that issued a manifesto on January 6 warning of the threat against liberty of thought.[12]

Roberto Campos declared that he had to conclude, from a careful reading of the project and from discussions with journalists, that "very few people have read the project, and therefore the critics base their arguments largely on presuppositions." Surmising that the denouncements of *Le Monde* (Paris) and *Novedades* (Mexico City) were based also on presuppositions, he expressed himself as surprised by them, considering that "rather severe press laws" existed in France and Mexico. The planning minister cited "a whole list of liberties" spelled out in the new project and said that he saw no reason for the reaction, inasmuch as the project simply was more specific than the former one

[9] *Jornal do Brasil*, December 24, 1966.

[10] *Jornal da Tarde*, December 30, 1966; *Tribuna da Imprensa*, December 31, 1966.

[11] *Jornal da Tarde*, December 30, 1966, January 3, 1967.

"about cases of abuses of liberty." Besides, he said, criminologist Nelson Hungria had found the existing law an "absurdity" that "should never have left the inkwell." Perhaps, Campos concluded, "the project will protect the honor of public men, subject to a daily diet of slanders."[13]

Roberto Campos' defense of the project was followed by attacks against it by Mem de Sá and Military Tribunal Judges Peri Beviláqua and Mourão Filho. Beviláqua compared the project with "taking a lung from a human body," while Mourão asserted that the project assured that the Brazilian people would "live in a complete medieval night." Mem de Sá said: "I have not read, nor do I desire to read, the text that, according to information that reached me, is a shameful thing."[14]

The unfavorable opinions of forty prominent persons, given on January 8 by *Correio da Manhã*, included those of Magalhães Pinto, Rafael de Almeida Magalhães, cinema star Luís Carlos Barreto, and São Paulo state Deputada Conceição da Costa Neves. The *deputada* said that "the new law is the last shovel over the corpse of Brazilian democracy."[15]

From the United States, Castello received a protest made with "the greatest energy" by the Inter-American Press Society in the name of "more than 750 newspapers and magazines." The *New York Times* wrote that the only hope lay in Castello's recognizing the great harm his "iniquitous" bill was "doing to freedom in his own country and to Brazil's image abroad."[16]

5. The Press Law Is Completed (January–February, 1967)

Congressman Ivan Luz, tall, handsome professor of constitutional law from Paraná, was in New York in December, 1966, working with the United Nations when he received a telephone call from the Brazilian presidency summoning him to Brazil. Luz, who had long been associated with Raimundo Padilha in politics and who had been *relator* of

[13] *Jornal da Tarde*, January 7, 1967.

[14] *Correio da Manhã*, January 8, 1967.

[15] Ibid.

[16] Ibid.; *New York Times*, editorial, January 7, 1967.

the legislation about the Workers' Tenure Guarantee Fund, correctly assumed that Castello and Padilha wanted him to serve as *relator* of the Press Law project.[1] He returned to Brazil and accepted the new mission from Padilha.

After Luz studied the project, he was invited by Castello to discuss it at 10:00 P.M. at Alvorada Palace. Reaching the palace early, he awaited the president in the first-floor library, which reflected the silence of the night. Castello, entering the room at 10:00 P.M. on the dot, appeared fresh—just as though he were starting a workday, Luz thought.

Luz said that the project was defendable, in its general lines, but made observations about things he did not like about it. Castello wrote notes on the margin of his own copy of the project and said that he agreed with Luz's observations. Castello insisted on "liberty with responsibility" and added that he would never suggest more restrictive legislation. The government, the president said, did not want to gag the press. Luz, who had several more meetings with the president, found him firm, direct, and a bit disturbing in addressing people. Luz recalls that "Castello sought to penetrate the thinking of the speaker. He had a rapid mind, but used few words. He would look straight at the person he was with. He expressed himself well."[2]

After meetings with Castello at Planalto Palace on January 6 and 11, Luz told reporters that the president's objective was to increase the responsibility of journalists and the vigilance of newspapers. Luz said that Castello, with this in mind, wanted the project to be improved as much as possible and "was leaving the *relator* with complete liberty to examine the matter, without any pressure." Luz also told the reporters that the time schedule made it too late for the government to present a substitute project but that the schedule allowed time enough for the presentation of the necessary amendments. And he said that he would present amendments of his own if the amendments submitted to him did not provide all the modifications that he felt were desirable.[3]

Krieger, after meeting with Castello, announced that the president

[1] Ivan Luz, interview, Brasília, October 27, 1975.

[2] Ibid.

[3] *O Estado de S. Paulo*, January 7, 12, 1967.

did not want the Press Law to become effective automatically due to the failure of Congress to act but wanted Congress to amend the project as it saw fit. Moura Andrade stated that the officers of Congress agreed with this view, but he criticized the government for having submitted the Press Law project when Congress had to work on the constitution.[4]

Ivan Luz received 363 proposed amendments, 40 of them from Mem de Sá, a member of the congressional joint commission studying the Press Law project. When Luz reported on January 16 to the commission, which was to render its verdict on January 19, he delivered opinions favorable to 31 proposed amendments and otherwise favorable to the government's project.[5] Luz's report quoted authorities who had found the 1953 law defective, and it cited an unsuccessful effort made to correct the legislation in 1956. Noting that it was not abnormal to attack the new project on the basis of "suppositions," Luz wrote that the important thing was to know how to draw the line in a way to hold back disciplinary action and yet preserve rights that could be hurt if they were abused.[6]

Luz quoted international authorities, among them former Florida Governor LeRoy Collins, who had said that individuals were free to do many things that, due to their damaging effects on the rest of society, could "cause the loss of some of our greatest freedoms." Luz recalled that Léon Blum, at a time of difficulties for France, had said that "not to permit repressive intervention until after the disturbance of peace will be a true mockery of the law." Remarking that the government's project did not deserve the lively condemnation that it had received, Luz turned to Helenic legislation and French authority André Toulemon to defend the principle of "co-authorship"—responsibility of editors, publishers, and so on.[7]

The *relator* rejected proposals to reestablish the "jury of the press." But he accepted an amendment of Mem de Sá that made it illegal to compel the disclosure of sources of information. And he agreed with

[4] Ibid., January 5, 1967.

[5] Ibid., January 17, 1967.

[6] Congresso Nacional, Parecer No. 2, de 1967 (C.N.)—Da Comissão Mista, sôbre o Projeto de Lei No. 23, de 1966 (CN), que "regula a liberdade de manifestação do pensamento e de informação."

[7] Ibid.

the suggestion of João Calmon and Chagas Freitas for the fulfillment of the penalty of a journalist "in an establishment distinct from those holding criminals guilty of common crimes."[8]

On January 19 the commission rejected, by a 10–9 vote, Mem de Sá's proposal to reestablish the "popular jury," and it approved, by a 13–8 vote, an amendment of Luz to establish the principle of co-authorship even in the case of signed articles. Then Mem de Sá announced that he was leaving the commission because his presence was useless. Rejecting pleas of congressmen that he return, he changed his mind when newspaper reporters made similar pleas. "I cannot flee from the appeal of the press," he said.[9]

On January 21, Castello met at Alvorada Palace with Luz, Padilha, Krieger, and Müller to establish the government's position about the commission's alterations to the Press Law project. Padilha argued, as others had done, that it was "absurd" to consider the editor, director, or editor-in-chief responsible in the case of signed articles. Castello agreed, and this became one of three modifications to the commission's version that the government decided to support in the plenary. The other two would strike out the provision about "secrets of state" (to be handled by the forthcoming National Security Law) and the provision to prevent the distribution of national news in Brazil by foreign news agencies.[10]

Mem de Sá, pleased about the resolution to eliminate the principle of co-authorship of signed articles, occupied the tribune to praise Sarasate for the convincing arguments he had presented to Castello and to praise Castello for his willingness "to turn back on positions taken when he recognizes that they are not the best." He closed his oration by saying: "We should rejoice on account of the results that have been obtained, even though they are not the best possible." During the congressional vote on the Press Law on the evening of January 21, the three modifications to the commission's version were enacted. Then by a "symbolic" vote the law was approved just before Moura Andrade had the congressional clocks disconnected.[11]

[8] *O Estado de S. Paulo*, January 17, 1967.
[9] Ibid. and *Jornal do Brasil*, January 20, 1967.
[10] Padilha, interview, August 3, 1977; *O Estado de S. Paulo*, January 22, 1967.
[11] *O Estado de S. Paulo*, January 22, 1967; *Jornal do Brasil*, January 22, 24, 1967.

Although fears of what presidential vetoes could do to the final project were expressed by *O Estado de S. Paulo, Jornal da Tarde* could not help but feel elated. It wrote that even if Castello Branco "annuls all the improvements that Congress approved in the face of government pressure, it is undeniable that the Brazilian press won a great victory in its struggle against the dictatorial offensive."[12]

The fears of presidential vetoes were groundless. As became known when the Press Law was sanctioned by the president on February 10, Castello used his veto only in the case of two minor matters, making changes that were regarded by the press as either irrelevant or beneficial and that lawyers agreed were necessary.[13] *O Estado de S. Paulo* expressed relief that the president had not used his power to revive the original "spirit of a totalitarian doctrine, against which the nation arose in a body." The outcome, it wrote, was a "victory of national public opinion."[14]

Medeiros Silva also expressed satisfaction with the new law, which, he said, preserved the government's project "in a proportion of 98 percent, since the amendments of Congress were almost symbolic."[15]

6. The New Cruzeiro, Devaluation, and Other Financial Matters (January–February, 1967)

Otávio Bulhões, speaking on television late in January, 1967, admitted that the monetary expansion of 1965 had been a principal error but said that the results of the government's policy had been generally satisfactory "to an extent that one can foresee that prices in 1967 will increase less than in all the other years of the present five-year period."[1]

The inflation rate of about 38 percent in 1966 had led the monetary authorities late that year to recommend to Castello that the cruzeiro be devaluated to prevent Brazilian exports from becoming uncompetitive, but Castello had refused to agree without first consulting

[12] *Jornal da Tarde*, January 24, 1967.

[13] Ibid. and *O Estado de S. Paulo*, February 15, 1967.

[14] *O Estado de S. Paulo*, February 15, 1967.

[15] *Jornal do Brasil*, February 11, 1967.

[1] *Jornal do Brasil*, January 24, 1967.

the president-elect, who was touring the world. Costa e Silva, after returning on February 1, referred the matter to his financial advisers, Delfim Neto, Hélio Beltrão, and Nestor Jost, and they took the position that the question was one for the Castello administration to resolve.[2]

In an effort to make things difficult for speculators, who were guessing that a devaluation would take place on February 3, the Friday before Carnaval, the National Monetary Council waited until Ash Wednesday, February 8, before settling the issue. It decreed that a new unit of currency (the *cruzeiro novo*) would start to circulate on Monday, February 13, and that banks would be closed until then. At the same time, the Monetary Council devalued the currency in terms of the dollar. The dollar, quoted at 2,200 old cruzeiros ever since November 16, 1965, would now be equivalent to 2,700 old cruzeiros, or 2.7 new cruzeiros.[3]

The unpopular devaluation, undertaken to establish a realistic exchange rate two months before the end of Castello's administration, provoked a storm. Banker Maurício Chagas Bicalho, former Brazilian representative on the IMF, stressed the harmful effect that price increases, resulting from the devaluation, would have on the people. Businessmen echoed this fear and also complained about the shortage of time for adapting to the new monetary system.[4]

Professor Eugênio Gudin, interviewed in Petrópolis, condemned the establishment of the new cruzeiro when price instability was prevalent and said that the increase in living costs resulting from the devaluation would bring billions of cruzeiros of harm to the nation. Describing the new exchange reform as "one of the most disgraceful that Brazil has ever known," he said that it had provided incalculable profits to groups which suspected that the reform would be decreed when it was. Glycon de Paiva, a member of the National Economy Council, declared that the devaluation would increase gasoline prices 25 percent and living costs possibly 8 percent. He felt that the devaluation would please exporters and the manufacturers of automobiles

[2] Dênio Nogueira, interview with Byron Coelho, Rio de Janeiro, February 1979.

[3] Ibid.; *Jornal do Brasil*, February 9, 1967; see Syvrud, *Foundations of Brazilian Economic Growth*, p. 189.

[4] *Jornal do Brasil*, February 10, 11, 1967.

and other products for which foreign competition was feared, but he argued that the step would not turn Brazilian industrial managers into productive competitors. And he insisted that the step was not dictated by Brazil's credit standing abroad or by any shortage of dollars.[5]

Otávio Bulhões, returning to television on February 9, denied that the readjustment would provoke a general price increase, but he did estimate that it might raise costs of production by 2 percent and the cost of imports by 10 to 15 percent. Dênio Nogueira, president of the Central Bank, defended the issuance of the new cruzeiro and the devaluation by citing statistics to show that the inflation rate had recently fallen to about 1 percent a month. When Krieger learned that Costa e Silva supporters protested that the devaluation would substantially increase living costs after the inauguration of the president-elect, he brushed aside their objections. Castello, he told reporters, was "clearing the ground" for his successor or "preparing the circus ring" to facilitate Costa e Silva's action. On the next day, February 10, Castello sought to alleviate the situation a little by signing a decree reducing import duties 20 percent.[6]

While the MDB demanded a congressional investigation of the devaluation "scandal" and newspaper headlines called attention to food price increases, the National Council on Wage Policy met on February 14 to consider new minimum wages. Labor Minister Nascimento Silva told the press that Castello might prefer to postpone any decision until March 1. But Castello, showing no inclination to postpone, signed a decree on February 15 setting minimum wages at 105 new cruzeiros per month for Guanabara, São Paulo, and Rio state and at lower amounts elsewhere. The decree ruled that the minimum for children would be half that of adults. The new amounts for adults, which were to become effective on March 1 and prevail "for the next three years," were 25 percent above the previous amounts (established a year earlier). *Jornal do Brasil* wrote that the new minimum wage was equal to what a worker spent on rice and beans alone.[7]

Bankers sought more available credit by proposing that banks be

[5] Ibid.; *Correio da Manhã*, February 11, 1967.

[6] *Jornal do Brasil*, February 10, 11, 1967.

[7] *Correio da Manhã*, February 11, 1967; *Jornal do Brasil*, February 14, 15, 16, 17, 1967.

required to keep 15 percent of their deposits, instead of 25 percent, with the Central Bank. The Central Bank rejected the suggestion, which, it explained, was unnecessary and contrary to the government's monetary policy.[8]

Castello, "clearing the ground" for his successor, suspended the political rights of forty-four more individuals, including many old labor leaders with Communist connections who were in hiding or living abroad.[9] And he spent two hours each night late in February signing decree-laws after discussing them at Laranjeiras Palace with interested cabinet ministers.[10] Ato Institucional No. 4 stipulated that his authority to sign decree-laws about financial and administrative matters would end when the new Congress met on March 1.

One of the two-hundred-odd decree-laws signed late in February called for the government to donate to the Brazilian Academy of Letters the property in Rio that adjoined the Academy's Petit Trianon. Academy President Austregésilo de Ataíde, answering the phone at 7:00 A.M. on February 28, heard Castello say that "in Brazil one man is crazier than you." "Who?" Austregésilo asked. Castello explained: "I am crazier than you; I signed a decree transferring to the academy the property that you wanted for it."[11]

Castello decided that his law project to allow workers to participate in profits (implementing a provision of the new constitution) should be submitted to the incoming Congress. He felt that the level of education of the workers was not high enough to recommend worker participation in company management, but he did want to give workers a sense of co-responsibility in the economic results and believed it important gradually to implant arrangements for worker participation in profits.[12]

According to Medeiros Silva, "Castello Branco favored worker

[8] *Jornal do Brasil*, February 18, 19, 23, 1967.

[9] Ibid., February 28, 1967.

[10] Ibid., March 3, 1967; Mendes de Morais, interview, December 20, 1975.

[11] Ataíde, interview, August 5, 1977; see Decreto-Lei 232 of February 28, 1967 (signed by HACB, Otávio Bulhões, and Raimundo Moniz de Aragão), *República do Brasil, Coleção das Leis, 1967*, Vol. 1, p. 375.

[12] *Jornal do Brasil*, March 1, 1967; Roberto Campos, "O repouso do guerreiro," *O Globo*, July 15, 1969; Roberto Campos, "Govêrno de entressafra," *O Globo*, July 16, 1968.

participation in profits because he was generous and an idealist." According to Roberto Campos, Castello preferred such participation to the already accepted custom of payment of the "thirteenth month" of wages, which gave the impression that income was unconnected with work, and Castello hoped also to lessen the concentration of worker demands on the wage adjustment and to prevent the "increasing alienation of the working class, seduced by unscrupulous demagogues."[13]

Castello, like Medeiros and the ministers in the economic area, was well aware of the complications of regulating workers' participation in profits. But what led him to wait until the last minute before placing a proposal in the hands of Congress was the argument of the ministers in the economic area, who urged the president to consider the danger of implanting the principle "at a time when businessmen were still hesitant about investing" and before the economy had demonstrated that it was advancing strongly.[14]

Investments were not pouring into the stock markets despite the enactment in July, 1965, of the Capital Markets Law. This law, as described by Howard S. Ellis, gave the Monetary Council and the Central Bank "functions comparable to the Security Exchange Commission in the United States" and laid "the groundwork for protecting the security-buying public and minority stockholders." The "Democratization of Capital" was the aim of several of the law's provisions.[15]

7. João Gonçalves Opposes Bulhões and Campos (February, 1967)

Floods ravaged the Rio area late in January, 1967, as had happened in January, 1966. They killed about three hundred people in the states of Guanabara and Rio de Janeiro and left the city of Rio with power shortages. As the cave-ins of buildings were frequently close to the places where such damage had occurred in 1966, the Guanabara state

[13] Medeiros Silva, interview, August 9, 1977; Campos, "O repouso do guerreiro"; Campos, "Govêrno de entressafra."

[14] Campos, "Govêrno de entressafra."

[15] Howard S. Ellis, "Corrective Inflation in Brazil, 1964–1966," in *The Economy of Brazil*, see p. 209.

government was criticized for having taken no preventive steps.[1] By mid-February, 1967, the supply of electricity in Rio approached normal, and arrangements had been made to have six thousand displaced persons, dwelling temporarily in the Maracanãzinho stadium, transferred to a model farm.[2]

Castello and Governor Negrão de Lima inspected some of the destruction in the Laranjeiras district just after firemen and soldiers, working in the ruins there and in the Riachuelo district, had found forty-six bodies, leaving a reported two hundred still unrecovered. Residents of Laranjeiras received Negrão and Castello with indifference.[3]

João Gonçalves de Sousa, minister of the coordination of regional agencies, spent two weeks in the disaster area visiting thirty-seven municipalities. Preparing to go on a visit early in February, he invited Castello to accompany him, and the president accepted. When they were returning, João Gonçalves spoke of the tax incentive laws for bringing investments to the north and northeast.

"I understand," João Gonçalves said, "that you are willing to change the tax incentive laws. Is that true?" The president, his countenance serious, gave a response that João Gonçalves considered typical of Castello: "Who told you that?"

The minister simply repeated that he knew it. As Castello said nothing, João Gonçalves launched into arguments that he had used in December, 1966, saying that if the law of incentives were broken, regardless of good reasons, three years of work would be destroyed and so would the Amazônia plans; the interest of private enterprise in the projects would be destroyed, the minister said.[4]

Despite these thoughts, the views of Otávio Bulhões prevailed, because on February 10, Castello issued Decree-Law 157 to allow 20 percent of the funds, derived from tax incentives for projects in the north and northeast, to be used for urgent working capital needs of companies in industrialized regions, particularly São Paulo.[5]

[1] *Jornal do Brasil*, January 24, 25, February 24, 1967.

[2] Ibid., February 14, 23, 1967.

[3] Ibid., February 21, 1967.

[4] Gonçalves de Sousa, interview, June 11, 1975.

[5] Gonçalves de Sousa, letter to HACB, February 1967; *Jornal do Brasil*, February 17, 1967.

A women's democratic crusade in the northeast released a manifesto condemning Decree-Law 157. The Pernambuco state legislature and the federations of industry of nine northeastern states held meetings to decide on steps to take. Influential Congressman Ernani Sátiro of Paraíba promised to fight for the cancellation of the new decree-law, which he attributed to poor advise given to the president.[6]

Castello received first-hand impressions of the reaction during a visit to Rio Grande do Norte, where he inaugurated a housing project and spoke about agrarian reform on February 19. Back in Rio on the twenty-first, he phoned João Gonçalves de Sousa, who had just returned from an OAS meeting in Buenos Aires, and asked him to be at Laranjeiras Palace on the twenty-third for a conference to which Campos, Bulhões, and SUDENE Superintendent Rubens Costa were also invited.[7]

At the conference Castello asked for the comments of Bulhões, the first to have suggested changing the law on incentives. Bulhões made a point briefly and said that Campos could give a better explanation. Campos presented many arguments that were familiar to Gonçalves, who felt that the planning minister had little knowledge about Brazil's underdeveloped areas. Castello, who was listening intently, said, "Just a minute," not because he liked to interrupt but because he wanted to explore a point at depth. Then, while each side explained its position several times, Gonçalves and Campos became emotional. An angry Campos maintained that the Bank of the Northeast had an excess of 256 million new cruzeiros. "I do not understand," he said, "how the government, with limited funds, opens new industry in the northeast, which may or may not be good, if it means closing down industry in São Paulo."[8]

Castello, addressing Bulhões, referred to the part of the income tax of individuals that remained with the government after taxpayers, who made use of the incentive program, invested 50 percent of their tax bills in the north or northeast: "50 percent," Castello said, "be-

[6] *Jornal do Brasil*, February 17, 22, 1967.

[7] HACB, *Discursos, 1967*, pp. 11–12; Gonçalves de Sousa, typewritten notes, February 24, 1967, p. 2.

[8] Gonçalves de Sousa, interview, June 11, 1975.

longs to the government. Can we take a small percentage of that, say 5 or 10 percent, to do something for the industrialized area?"[9] Bulhões said this might be done. Castello asked the four men to return the next day after trying to agree on the text of a decree that would not interfere with the SUDENE and SUDAM arrangements in effect before Decree-Law 157.[10]

The four men, carrying on with their work in Bulhões' office, could reach no agreement and finally accepted Bulhões' suggestion to take alternative proposals to Castello and let him decide. That evening Campos appealed to Rubens Costa to accept the view favored by Bulhões and himself, and João Gonçalves spoke on the phone with Castello, explaining in detail the alternatives that would be presented to him the next day, February 24.[11]

At Laranjeiras Palace on the twenty-fourth, Castello chose the alternative favored by João Gonçalves and SUDENE. Roberto Campos, preparing to leave, took Gonçalves by the arm and said: "João, if you will allow me to say it, you have just rendered a disservice to our government and country."[12] Then Castello, addressing Campos and Bulhões, said: "In three months I'll phone you both, expecting to hear you say that the decision I have just made is the best." João Gonçalves, for whom Castello had no remark, told the president that he need not phone him because he would be in Washington, which was expensive to phone, and because he was certain that the president had made a wise decision.[13]

Returning to his office, João Gonçalves wrote to the president to thank him and to apologize if at any time he had been rude while arguing. He said that he had noted well "the obstacles that the president had to surmount in the search for the compromise solution that was finally reached, thanks to the patience and the method which Your

[9] Ibid

[10] Gonçalves de Sousa, typewritten notes, February 24, 1967, pp. 2–3.

[11] Ibid.

[12] Gonçalves de Sousa, interview, June 11, 1975.

[13] Gonçalves de Sousa, typewritten notes, February 24, 1967, p. 6; João Gonçalves de Sousa recalls (interview, June 11, 1975) that a year later, when he and Roberto Campos were in Washington, Campos told him that he had been right about the matter and that the decision of Castello had been a suitable one.

Excellency knew how to apply in handling a matter so affected by interests and emotion."[14]

On February 25 the press carried the news that Castello, Campos, Gonçalves de Sousa, and Rubens Costa had modified the provisions of Decree-Law 157 in order to maintain fully the resources for developing the north and northeast. Furthermore, in the words of Mário Henrique Simonsen, individuals would be permitted "to apply 10 percent and corporations 5 percent of their income tax to the purchase of new shares through financial institutions."[15]

Jornal do Brasil's editorial of March 3 praised the new arrangement and said that the earlier one would have impaired the liquidity of the Bank of the Northeast. *Jornal do Brasil* added that the long-term repercussions of the earlier arrangement would have been serious for the nation, which needed the new markets that could be expected when the more backward areas became incorporated into the capitalist economy.[16]

Among the many decree-laws issued by Castello at the end of February, 1967, were two others of considerable interest to the Ministry for Coordination of Regional Agencies. One provided the arrangements for the operation of the Free Trade Zone of Manaus, an area of ten thousand square kilometers, which foreign merchandise could enter without the payment of import duties. The other established SUDESUL (Superintendency of the Southern Region) to replace a former agency whose objective of assisting frontier municipalities in the states of the far south had become distorted by politics during past regimes. SUDESUL, which would operate without the benefit of tax incentives, was to coordinate programs designed to extend the economic moderni-

[14] Gonçalves de Sousa, letter to HACB, February 1967 (copy attached to typewritten notes of February 24, 1967).

[15] *Jornal do Brasil*, February 25, 1967; Gonçalves de Sousa, typewritten notes, February 24, 1967, p. 5; Mário Henrique Simonsen, "Inflation and the Money and Capital Markets of Brazil," in *The Economy of Brazil*, ed. Ellis, see p. 156; see also Decreto-Lei 157 on pp. 177–181 of República do Brasil, *Coleção das Leis, 1967*, Vol. 1. The impressive growth of "DL-157 funds" (shares of new investment funds in accordance with revised Decree-Law 157) from 1967 to 1969 is described in Syvrud, *Foundations of Brazilian Economic Growth*, pp. 264–266.

[16] *Jornal do Brasil*, March 3, 1967.

zation of the southern states to their somewhat stagnant border towns.[17]

8. Costa e Silva's Cabinet (February, 1967)

While Costa e Silva traveled around the world with his wife and a small group that included Colonels Mário Andreazza and Hernani D'Aguiar, he received reports from General Jaime Portela, head of the president-elect's political office in Rio. There "Costistas" described the trip, paid for by the Foreign Ministry, as a "temporary deportation" designed to preserve the authority of the "Castellistas." They were displeased with the appointment of retired Marshal Ademar de Queiroz to be war minister instead of General Lyra Tavares, and they criticized some of the army promotions and command changes. They had long been on guard lest a clever maneuver by "the Planalto team" thwart their hopes.[1]

Meanwhile, the name of the traveling president-elect was mentioned in connection with "new political movements" and "a third political party," said to have the backing of critics of Castello Branco such as Magalhães Pinto, Amauri Kruel, Justino Alves Bastos, and Mourão Filho. Kruel declared that Costa e Silva favored redemocratization but could achieve it only with "a party of deep roots, able to give him the necessary popular backing."[2]

Late in January the shadow of the absent Costa e Silva fell on the contest for the presidency of the Chamber of Deputies. Although acting Chamber President João Batista Ramos appeared to have the most supporters among the ARENA congressmen elected on November 15, he told Krieger that he hesitated to fight for the post against the

[17] João Gonçalves de Sousa, "Como e Porque Fui ao MECOR; Pontos Principais do Trabalho" (typewritten paper for Luís Viana Filho), p. 4; *Jornal do Brasil*, March 3, 1967; João Gonçalves de Sousa, "SUDESUL" (typewritten), pp. 1–3; see Decreto-Leis 288 and 301 (both dated February 28, 1967), regarding the Free Trade Zone of Manaus and the creation of SUDESUL, on pp. 492–497, 530–543 of República do Brasil, *Coleção das Leis*, 1967, Vol. 1.

[1] D'Aguiar, *A Revolução por Dentro*, pp. 278, 285; *BC Semanal*, October 3, 1966, quoted in ibid., p. 283.

[2] *Jornal do Brasil*, January 13, 14, 1967; *Correio da Manhã* February 17, 1967.

will of Costa e Silva, who was known to favor Ernani Sátiro. Krieger, who was in the vast throng that greeted Costa e Silva at Galeão Airport on February 1, suggested to Costa e Silva that he tell the press he had no preferred candidate for the Câmara presidency. Costa e Silva did this at the airport, where he said that all the candidates for the post "really deserve the honor."[3] Batista Ramos won the support of the ARENA congressmen, and then Portela and Congressman Rondon Pacheco gave Sátiro the invitation of Costa e Silva to be the leader of the new government in the Câmara.[4]

The chief interest was in the makeup of the cabinet of the new administration. Castello's interest, dating before Costa e Silva's departure early in December, 1966, lay in the reappointment of Finance Minister Otávio Bulhões, which he felt would be useful to the new government and the nation. At Castello's urging, Krieger had made the suggestion to Costa e Silva as coming from Krieger, because Castello had not wanted to appear to be interfering. But Roberto Campos, in an effort to assure the success of Costa e Silva in the United States, had advised Costa e Silva to make an early announcement of the retention of Bulhões, and the president-elect, considering Campos' advice as an imposition, had decided not to reappoint Bulhões.[5]

Costa e Silva's cabinet list, which appeared in the press on February 11, showed São Paulo Finance Secretary Delfim Neto as finance minister, Magalhães Pinto as foreign minister, Lyra Tavares as war minister, Rademaker as navy minister, Passarinho as mines and energy minister, Costa Cavalcanti as labor minister, Andreazza as transport minister, Gama e Silva, as education minister, Albuquerque Lima as regional agencies minister, and Hélio Beltrão as planning minister, with the Gabinetes Militar and Civil headed by Jaime Portela and Rondon Pacheco, respectively.[6]

Krieger, in Rio Grande do Sul, was unhappy because he had an agreement with Costa e Silva that the ARENA would have a voice in the formation of the new cabinet, Advised by Portela that Costa e Silva wanted to see him, Krieger came to Rio. In Costa e Silva's Copa-

[3] Krieger, *Desde as Missões*, p. 268; *Jornal do Brasil*, February 2, 1967.
[4] *Jornal do Brasil*, February 4, 1967.
[5] Krieger, *Desde as Missões*, pp. 265–266.
[6] *Jornal do Brasil*, February 11, 1967.

cabana Avenue office he was met by Colonel Andreazza, who said that the Third Army had vetoed Tarso Dutra for education minister because he had once supported Kubitschek's candidacy. Krieger replied that the charge was untrue besides being immaterial. Then Costa e Silva received him and furnished the names of the "probable ministers." Krieger, disappointed, took his leave.

That evening Andreazza phoned Krieger to ask him to see Costa e Silva again the next morning. Krieger said: "The president is elected and doesn't need me anymore. But also I won't need him. I feel as well in the opposition as in the government."

Nevertheless, Krieger agreed to another talk. Costa e Silva, assuming a conciliatory attitude, said that since Krieger refused to become justice minister, he would make Gama e Silva justice minister, allowing Tarso Dutra to become education minister. And he mentioned other changes.

"Mr. President," Krieger said, "my dissatisfaction resulted from the acceptance of a veto without foundation and in the manner in which the list of ministers was presented to me, already a consumated fact, when you, spontaneously, agreed to hear me. But in view of your new attitude, my inconformity has dissolved. I think you should not move Colonel Andreazza from the Ministry of Transport and not take the Interior Ministry from General Afonso de Albuquerque Lima, who, I am informed, has great knowledge about the problems of the north and northeast. Permit me, further, to make a suggestion: instead of having Passarinho in Mines and Energy and Costa Cavalcanti in Labor, turn these two around." The suggestions were accepted.[7]

Costa e Silva, explaining the Magalhães Pinto appointment to Krieger, spoke of the Mineiro's ability, service to the nation, and support of Costa e Silva's candidacy. He added that in view of Magalhães Pinto's "well-known political shrewdness in domestic affairs," he preferred to place him in the Foreign Ministry.[8]

Krieger felt that it would be a good idea to turn the ARENA presidency over to Castello after Castello left the presidency. The senator had observed in Castello "daily, during three years of intense work together, a sensitivity for, and pleasure in, politics," and he felt that

[7] Krieger, *Desde as Missões*, pp. 263–265.

[8] Ibid., p. 267.

Castello should direct the party he had founded and strengthened. "I did not want," Krieger writes, "to have his extraordinary personality separated from active and direct participation in events. I foresaw the fragility of the institutions and wanted to defend them. In command of the party, he would be a factor of security and a link between civilians and the military."

Costa e Silva appealed to Krieger not to carry out this idea. It would, Costa e Silva said, mean the existence of two conflicting powers, with the inevitable consequence of a break between the party and the government.

Krieger closes this matter by writing: "The request of Costa e Silva did not move me, but I was convinced by the refusal of Castello, who saw the possibilities of friction."[9]

9. Portents of Less Linkage to the United States

Costa e Silva's selection of Magalhães Pinto to be foreign minister seemed to confirm the feeling expressed in January, 1967, by the U.S. Embassy that the new Brazilian government's foreign policy would be less "clearly linked" to the United States. *Jornal do Brasil* wrote in February that Costa e Silva and Magalhães Pinto would seek to stamp an independent character to foreign policy, although "without the follies and exaggerations of the past." The incoming government was not about to agree with Juraci Magalhães' much-criticized statement that "what is good for the United States is good for Brazil."[1]

The choice of Magalhães Pinto was announced a few days before the start of an OAS meeting in Buenos Aires (the Third Extraordinary Inter-American Conference of Foreign Ministers) called to prepare the way for an Inter-American Summit Meeting of heads of state.

Plans for the summit meeting dated back to June, 1966, when President Johnson, in a message to Castello Branco, expressed the hope that it might occur before the end of 1966 and asked for suggestions.[2] Castello, who shared Johnson's hopes about the timing, relied heavily on

[9] Ibid., pp. 254–255.

[1] United States Embassy, Rio de Janeiro, cable to State Department, January 24, 1967, NSFB, LBJ Library; *Jornal do Brasil*, February 22, 1967.

[2] Raine, communication to Juraci Magalhães, Rio de Janeiro, June 13, 1966, File O1 (pp. 33v, 34), PVCB.

Roberto Campos for suggestions to send to Johnson. In the political area, Brazil suggested a protest against the "program of subversion coming from the Third Tricontinental Conference in Havana." The message to Johnson went on to urge the renouncement of unilateral government actions for hemispheric security without previous consultation, and it added that in view of the reluctance of some governments to establish a permanent Inter-American Peace Force, a compromise might allow the creation of a temporary "expeditionary force" when recommended by the appropriate inter-American consultive organ. Also, in accordance with Campos' ideas, Castello included economic proposals, such as a system of defensive trade preferences to counter the preference given Afro-Asiatic products by Europeans, a special Industrial Readaptation Fund to help with the readjustments resulting from implanting the regional common market, a program of "education for development," and the promotion of highway integration.[3]

These ideas were discussed in Brasília on December 15 when Gordon and Tuthill joined Castello and some of his ministers. Castello was disappointed that the timing of the summit would not allow him to speak for Brazil, but he observed that it would be advantageous to have Brazil represented by a recently installed president.[4]

In preparation for Costa e Silva's visit to Washington in January, 1967, U.S. officials examined the possibility of Brazil making a larger contribution to the action in Vietnam. They noted that outside of expressions of support, Brazil's contribution had been limited to the donations of medical supplies in 1965 and 1966 and a shipment of one thousand bags of coffee delivered to Saigon in a Brazilian Air Force plane in January, 1967. But they also noted that on December 31, 1966, Itamarati Secretary General Pio Corrêa had suggested to Ambassador Tuthill a formula for a United States contribution to the Brazilian Navy "which could ease the Brazilian government into a United Nations role," possibly to be demonstrated by a "shakedown cruise" with U.S. naval forces in Vietnamese waters.[5] The formula was studied at a time when reports showed that it was doomed. According to the

[3] Roberto Campos, "Sugestões para carta ao Presidente Johnson," File O1 (pp. 35–37), PVCB; Brazilian Foreign Ministry, communication to John Wills Tuthill, July 25, 1966, File O1 (p. 37v), PVCB.

[4] Gordon, "Recollections of Castello Branco," p. 10.

[5] "Brazil and Viet Nam," background paper for Costa e Silva visit to Washington, January 1967, NSFB, LBJ Library.

U.S. Embassy in Rio, the resentment of the U.S. role in Brazil and the world, intense among intellectuals and students, was now shared by businessmen who had felt that the competition of U.S. business enterprises. "The Castello Branco administration's all out public support for United States policies," the embassy added, "has served rather to increase anti-Americanism than to lessen it." In Washington the CIA reported that Costa e Silva, not having served with the Brazilian Expeditionary Force in World War II, lacked a feeling of camaraderie with the U.S. military. When Costa e Silva, tired from his travels, discussed the USAID program in Washington, he lectured Gordon on the excessive rigidity of the program and made unflattering remarks about the IMF. Gordon sought to lighten the discussion with a humorous remark that fell flat.[6]

Costa e Silva was already back in Brazil on February 15 when Juraci Magalhães and Roberto Campos attended the opening of the OAS meeting in Buenos Aires. The Brazilian suggestion of a limited Inter-American Peace Force, defended by Juraci Magalhães, was defeated, eleven votes to six. (With the United States abstaining, the support came from Argentina, Brazil, Honduras, Nicaragua, Paraguay, and Salvador). Two days before the vote was taken, Costa e Silva and Magalhães Pinto announced that they opposed the idea that Juraci Magalhães was defending.[7]

Early in March, Costa e Silva went to Buenos Aires for three days of talks with General Juan Carlos Onganía, president of Argentina. The Brazilian president-elect was accompanied by Magalhães Pinto, Jarbas Passarinho, Jaime Portela, Rondon Pacheco, and diplomats. Upon their return, Magalhães Pinto was asked by the press to compare the foreign policy of the Castello administration with that to be carried out after he became foreign minister. "I am," he replied, "being careful about the already known difficulties that I had with President Castello Branco and at this moment we are not going to aggravate the situation further."[8]

Lacerda, less careful, published articles saying that Castello, by sup-

[6] United States Embassy, Rio de Janeiro, cable to State Department, January 24, 1967; CIA, "Costa e Silva, Brazil's Next President," special report, January 20, 1967, NSFB, memorandums, Vol. VI, Box 3, LBJ Library; Gordon, interview, June 11, 1975.

[7] *Correio da Manhã*, February 22, 1967; *Jornal do Brasil*, February 22, 23, 1967.

[8] *Correio da Manhã*, March 3, 7, 8, 1967.

porting an inter-American force, "is transforming Brazil into a hoodlum of interventionism and wants to reduce the Brazilian Army to the instrument of interventions against governments that do not say amen to the United States." "The disastrous term of Sr. Juraci Magalhães," he wrote, "harmonizes very well with the stupidity of the Castello Branco government."[9]

10. The Administrative Reform Law (February 25, 1967)

In the case of the Administrative Reform Law, which Castello planned to decree, a close liaison between the incoming and outgoing administrations was Hélio Beltrão, chosen to be the next planning minister. The scholarly Beltrão, after playing a constructive role in Lacerda's Guanabara cabinet, had become a member of the Special Commission to Study Reform, headed by Roberto Campos.

After its creation in October, 1964, the special commission reviewed the work of commissions appointed by past administrations that had unsuccessfully sought to reform the structure of the federal administration. It completed a draft that was discussed at a meeting of federal administrators in January, 1966.[1] At this meeting Roberto Campos observed that Castello, addressing Congress, had said that the main objective of the administrative reform was to raise the productivity of the administrative machine in order to have "the government sector operate with the efficiency of a private company." According to Campos, past attempts at reform had erred in dealing excessively with administrative structure. He wanted a reform "destined to launch great principles that renew the traditional concept of public administration," leaving the executive the authority to work out structural details, and he emphasized the need of modern processes of management, training programs to provide a staff for good planning, and methods of control to measure the contribution of administrative units.

Beltrão, who had similar ideas, called for a courageous break from

[9] Carlos Lacerda, "A fôrça de intervenção armada," *Tribuna da Imprensa* (late January 1967), File N6 (Anexo 110), CPDOC; idem, "A recuperação do Itamarati," *Tribuna da Imprensa*, File N6 (Anexo 111), CPDOC.

[1] *O Estado de S. Paulo*, January 28, 1966. (The Special Commission to Study Reform was the Comissão Especial de Estudos de Reforma.)

"a series of habits, preconceptions, routine procedures, and consolidated vices" and said that "it is better to run risks of decentralization than risks of stagnation." He clashed with the special commission's executive secretary, Nazaré Teixeira Dias, who seemed inclined to try to perfect the Amaral Peixoto project, drawn up during the Goulart regime. For Beltrão, Viana Filho writes, the idea of drawing up a new organization chart "meant putting clothes on a sick person." Castello, who liked Beltrão's ideas, remarked during a debate about the reform: "Don't speak of organization charts; Dr. Beltrão doesn't like that."[2]

With the backing of Campos, Beltrão presented a new project in August, 1966. But the work then came to a standstill while the military debated and rejected the idea of establishing a Ministry of the Armed Forces. Only in January, 1967, were new meetings held, and they generally included Geisel and Golberi. During the first half of February, the president discussed the reform further with Nazaré Dias and Beltrão, who were the principal authors of the final product. Nazaré Dias took care of structure and details, whereas principles and concepts were furnished by Beltrão, with some help from Roberto Campos.[3]

Shortly before Castello signed the reform law, he and Beltrão, together with Colonel Andreazza and Rondon Pacheco, were the guests at a small dinner given by Costa e Silva at his Avenida Atlântica apartment. Castello was disturbed to receive the impression that Costa e Silva was not in good health. Although Castello noted what he considered some "petulance" on the part of Andreazza, the relations between the president and the president-elect could not have been warmer. On the balcony after dinner they reminisced about their days together as cadets and as participants in the revolution of 1964.[4]

The Administrative Reform Law, signed on February 25, became known as Decree-Law 200. It reorganized the cabinet ministries and provided for "planning, coordination, decentralization, delegation of authority, and control." The ministries found themselves with more organs to supervise because the number directly subordinated to the presidency was greatly reduced. Reporting to the presidency, which in-

[2] Viana Filho, *O Governo Castelo Branco*, pp. 480–483.

[3] Ibid.; *Correio da Manhã*, February 14, 1967.

[4] Viana Filho, *O Governo Castelo Branco*, p. 483 (including statements by Rondon Pacheco and Hélio Beltrão).

cluded the Gabinete Civil and Gabinete Militar, were the ministries, the National Security Council, the SNI, the EMFA, the Administrative Department of Civilian Personnel, the Legal Consultantship of the Republic, and the High Command of the Armed Forces.[5]

The number of ministries was increased to sixteen with the replacement of the former Ministry of Transport and Public Works by two ministries, one for Transport and the other for Communications, and with the inclusion, for the first time on a permanent basis, of the Ministry of Planning and General Coordination and the Ministry of the Interior (formerly the Ministry for Coordination of Regional Agencies). The Ministry of Justice and Internal Affairs became simply the Ministry of Justice, and the War Ministry was renamed the Ministry of the Army.

The government banks were placed "within the spheres" of some of the ministries. Thus, the sphere of the Finance Ministry included the Central Bank, the Bank of Brazil, and the *caixas econômicas*, while the sphere of the Interior Ministry included the Bank of Amazônia, the Bank of the Northeast, and the Housing Bank. The BNDE and the Bank of Cooperative Credit were placed in the spheres of the Planning and Agriculture Ministries, respectively.

A feature of Decree-Law 200 allowed the central direction of each organ to concentrate on planning, supervision, coordination, and control by freeing it from the routine of execution. Stressing decentralization and the need to stem the increase of the federal machinery, the new law encouraged federal organs to turn, for execution, to state and municipal organs and the private sector, but control and fiscalization would be exercised by the federal organs. Sectoral and regional programs were to have plurennial duration and were to be elaborated by the appropriate ministries and then reviewed and coordinated by the president with the assistance of the planning minister. The government's general programming was to be handled by the president and the planning minister.

The new law dealt with the abolishment of unnecessary posts and the verification of the existence of unnecessary, or idle, personnel in

[5] *O Estado de S. Paulo*, March 1, 1967. (Organs reporting to the president were the Conselho de Segurança Nacional, Serviço Nacional de Informações, Estado-Maior das Forças Armadas, Departamento Administrativo do Pessoal Civil, Consultoria Geral da República, and the Alto Comando das Forças Armadas.)

order to eliminate or redistribute them. While the law was to go into effect on March 15, 1967, it was felt that the full achievement of the fundamental principles (planning, coordination, decentralization, delegation of authority, and control) would take time, and therefore the reform, according to one of its clauses, was to be accomplished in steps. Castello established a fund of twenty million new cruzeiros for implementing the reform.

11. The National Security Law (March 13, 1967)

In the case of the National Security Law, which Castello also planned to decree, the link between the outgoing and incoming administrations was provided by General Jaime Portela. Before the president-elect traveled abroad, he instructed Portela to keep him posted on the elaboration of the new law. Portela did more than this. Calling frequently at the house of Justice Minister Medeiros Silva during and following Costa e Silva's trip, Portela submitted written suggestions in the name of Costa e Silva.[1]

The work to be done by Medeiros Silva was given impetus by Castello Branco on July 19, 1966, when the president, installing the new justice minister, said that the law of 1953 had proven "inefficacious." "Despite the legislation in effect," Castello said on this occasion, "the Revolution of March 31, using powers conferred by its Institutional Acts, had to face extremely serious cases in order to restore the morality of public affairs on the federal, state, and municipal levels." Castello, who had given much study to the concept of national security while serving in the army, said that a new law was needed to prevent a repetition of the "lamentable events" of the past. Calling for new definitions of crimes, he pointed out that "the so-called revolutionary war, whose multiple and insidious aspects are well known by those who study the new techniques of subversion, . . . still remains without a legal definition." He also favored "adequate regulation" to allow that cases be judged. "The peace and public safety," he said, "cannot be at the mercy of complicated and dilatory judicial customs that frequently

[1] *Correio da Manhã*, February 5, 1967; Medeiros Silva, interview, August 13, 1977.

bring impunity to those indicted, thus stimulating the repetition of the criminal acts."[2]

Paving the way for the new National Security Law, the 1967 Constitution stated that the state, or the Union, was to "plan for and guarantee the national security" and that "every person, natural or juridical, is responsible for the national security, within the limits defined by the law." This idea of the responsibility of every person differed from that of the 1946 Constitution, which considered the national security a matter for the armed forces.[3]

In December, 1966, and January, 1967, before work was completed on the new law, the press was full of forebodings. *Jornal da Tarde* predicted that the law would permit the president to cancel mandates, suspend political rights, and decree legislative recesses whenever it was his opinion that the legislature provoked social unrest, directly or indirectly. *Correio da Manhã* wrote that the EMFA had presented suggestions to Medeiros that amounted to the "pure and simple institution of a military dictatorship."[4]

Despite press reports, the EMFA had nothing to do with drafting the law. Ernesto Geisel, as secretary of the National Security Council, assisted Castello, while Portela presented the views of Costa e Silva to Medeiros. The final form of the law was the work of Castello and Medeiros.[5]

In the opinion of Medeiros, the heart of the law consisted of two articles, written by Castello at Laranjeiras Palace, that represented a view that became prevalent in various nations as a result of "Hitler's fifth-column activities in Austria and elsewhere."[6] The two articles, consisting of definitions, were the longest of the four articles making up Chapter I of the law.

"The national security," Castello wrote, was "the guarantee of the attainment of the national objectives against internal and external an-

[2] HACB, *Discursos, 1966*, pp. 334–335.

[3] 1967 Constitution, Articles 8 and 89; Medeiros Silva, interview, August 13, 1977.

[4] *Jornal da Tarde*, December 23, 28, 1966; *O Estado de S. Paulo*, December 31, 1966; *Correio da Manhã*, January 15, 1967.

[5] Lavanère-Wanderley, interview, August 12, 1977; Viana Filho, *O Governo Castelo Branco*, p. 484; Medeiros Silva, interview, August 13, 1977.

[6] Medeiros Silva, interview, August 13, 1977. (Use of the past tense in describing the law of March 1967 is appropriate because on September 29, 1969, it was replaced by a new law, Number 898.)

tagonisms" and consisted of "measures designed for the preservation of external and internal security, including the prevention and repression of adverse psychological warfare and revolutionary or subversive warfare." Internal security was concerned with "antagonistic threats or pressures, of whatever origin, form, or nature," within the nation. Adverse psychological warfare was defined as "the employment of propaganda, counterpropaganda, and actions in the political, economic, psychosocial, and military areas designed to influence or provoke opinions, emotions, attitudes, or behavior of foreign, enemy, neutral, or friendly groups against the attainment of the national objectives." Furthermore, Castello described "revolutionary war" as "internal conflict, generally inspired by an ideology, or assisted from abroad, which seeks subversive conquest of the power by means of progressive control of the Nation."

The law contained two additional chapters that were put together from old drafts and from suggestions submitted to Medeiros.[7] They listed crimes and punishments (Chapter II) and rules for handling cases (Chapter III). Chapter II decreed four to twelve years of imprisonment for those found guilty of promoting armed insurrection or trying to subvert the political-social structure "in order to establish a dictatorship of class, political party, group, or individual." Lesser penalties were listed for those who provoked revolutionary warfare, offended the honor or dignity of foreign heads of state or certain top Brazilian officials, or used strikes or lockouts to paralyze public services or essential activities "with the intent of coercing any of the powers of the Republic." Six months to two years of confinement was to be the penalty for issuing false or biased news that would endanger "the name, authority, credit, or prestige of Brazil." Chapter II called for a similar sentence of confinement for those guilty of subversive propaganda that threatened the national security, and it added that the judge could further suspend for thirty days the circulation of publications whose directors were responsible for that propaganda.

Chapter III said that the constitutional clause, allowing the use of the military justice system to judge civilians as well as the military, was applicable in the case of the crimes listed in the new law. It also established that those considered responsible for "flagrant crimes" against

[7] Ibid.

the national security were to be suspended from the exercise of their professions.

The decree-law was signed when Castello met with Medeiros at Laranjeiras Palace on March 11 and was published in the *Diário Oficial* on March 13, becoming known as Decree-Law 314.

It would be perfectly legitimate, *Jornal do Brasil* wrote, to blame the National Security Law on the "secret desire" of the Castello government to prevent the return to normality by its successor, in whom it lacked confidence. *O Estado de S. Paulo* complained of the "extreme broadness" of the definitions in Chapter I of the new law, and it noted that penalties for crimes, including those "practiced by means of the press," were much more severe than those in the law of 1953. *Jornal da Tarde* wrote:

> There were moments during the discussion by Congress of the projects of the new constitution and the new Press Law when we came to think that we had been unjust to Marshal Castello Branco. . . . No one could deny that some of the worst articles of both laws were abolished without objections from President Castello Branco.
>
> Today, however, we appreciate that not only were we not unjust in our criticism, but we were, indeed, excessively benevolent. In truth, never, not even in the worst moments of the political action of the government which is leaving, could we imagine to what point Marshal Castello Branco planned to go in his willingness to definitely liquidate a democratic regime in this nation.[8]

12. Approaching the End of the Administration (March 2–13, 1967)

As March 15 drew near, presidential aides released statistics that showed that in the "thousand days" of the regime, Castello had received 613 office visits by governors and 1,966 by federal legislators. He had met with the full cabinet sixteen times (eleven in 1964) and with the National Security Council seventeen times. Of the cabinet ministers, Roberto Campos had been most frequently in the president's

[8] *Jornal do Brasil*, March 17, 1967; *O Estado de S. Paulo*, March 14, 1967; *Jornal da Tarde*, March 15, 1967.

office. His 325 visits compared with 295 by Otávio Bulhões and just barely exceeded the total number of visits by the three justice ministers (Milton Campos, Mem de Sá, and Carlos Medeiros Silva).[1]

Roberto Campos spoke of his own role in the "thousand days" during an interview in São Paulo on March 2. Appearing downcast, he blamed his "bruises" on his "inability to communicate," but he also mentioned a considerable lack of "seriousness" in the press. He confessed to having underestimated the strength of the Brazilian inflation and the difficulty of the psychological transformation following "twenty-five years of inflationary concupiscence," and he attributed the excessive monetary expansion in 1965 to a coffee crop of thirty-eight million bags, price supports for agricultural products, and the government's decision to increase the reserve of dollars. Criticizing economists who said that the gross national product was decreasing, he said that they suffered from an "eclipse of memory, for we all know that the increase was 2% in 1963, 3.1% in 1964, and 4.7% in 1965." He quoted Bank of Brazil estimates that showed a 6 percent increase in São Paulo in 1966, and he added that some economists estimated that the increase in the northeast was 11 percent.[2]

Carlos Lacerda observed what he called Castello's best act (the decision to leave the government) by publishing an article in which he wrote that "the absolute lack of generosity, the sterility of imagination, the morbid distrust, the total disbelief in persons . . . all make up that twisted and forbidding figure . . . who filched the Brazilian revolution, transforming it into an inglorious and sterile military *golpe*, by which the nation is choked today."[3]

On March 4 and 5, Castello visited the northeast for the last time as president. Speaking in the presence of nine governors at the inauguration of the seventh generating unit of the Paulo Afonso hydroelectric works, he noted that the transmission lines from the falls, having been extended to over seventy-five hundred kilometers, brought energy to more than seven million Brazilians. Within a few months, he

[1] José Wamberto, *Castello Branco: Revolução e Democracia,* Appendixes 8 and 9 (compiled by Júlio Sérgio Vidal Pessoa); *Jornal do Brasil,* February 5, 1967.

[2] *Jornal do Brasil,* March 3, 1967; Syvrud shows (*Foundations of Brazilian Economic Growth,* p. 127) GNP increases of 1.5 percent in 1963, 2.9 percent in 1964, 2.7 percent in 1965, and 5.1 percent in 1966.

[3] Carlos Lacerda, "Como choram os pequeninos," File N5 (Anexo 33), CPDOC.

said, the eighth and ninth generating units would be installed, "giving the northeast double the installed potential that it had when I became president." He said that the necessary funds, coming from the Inter-American Development Bank and the earnings of the Paulo Afonso works, resulted from the policy that the Revolution had had the courage to implant. Rejecting demagoguery, the Revolution had attended "the needs of the nation" by establishing realistic electricity rates based on "true costs plus a controlled rate of return."[4]

In Brasília, Castello nominated Golberi to the national *tribunal de contas* and Press Secretary José Wamberto to the *tribunal de contas* of the federal district. ARENA Congressman Jorge Curi declared sarcastically that Castello was rewarding them for their attacks against *O Estado de S. Paulo* and for other such services to Castello. Another unhappy ARENA lawmaker was Filinto Müller, the political sponsor of Mato Grosso Governor Pedro Pedrossian. Pedrossian, recently dismissed by Castello from a railroad administrative position for what Juarez Távora called "criminal" behavior, appeared to be in danger of losing his mandate. But Krieger, after speaking with Castello, was able to assure Müller that Pedrossian would remain in the governorship.[5]

On March 8, while Castello was in Brasília, Roberto Campos appeared voluntarily before Congress to answer the MDB charges about the "scandalous" cruzeiro devaluation of February. Discussing the fight against inflation, Campos revealed that the monetary expansion, which had been 86 percent in 1964 and 75 percent in 1965, had been only 18 percent in 1966.[6] Turning to the charge that the government had been helpful to speculation by exchange operators, Campos declared that it would be slanderous to suggest that a few advisers of the president and president-elect, conversant with the plans, had broken secrecy. Speculation, he said, was an inevitable phenomenon in a capitalist economy, and not an altogether undesirable one. He pointed out that speculators in dollars in 1966 had been hurt when no devaluation had

[4] HACB, *Discursos, 1967*, pp. 27–29.

[5] *O Estado de S. Paulo*, March 8, 9, 1967; Krieger, *Desde as Missões*, p. 263.

[6] *O Estado de S. Paulo*, March 9, 1967; Syvrud shows (*Foundations of Brazilian Economic Growth*, p. 89) money supply increases of 84.5 percent in 1964, 76.5 percent in 1965, and 15.8 percent in 1966; he shows (p. 89) general price index increases of 37.9 percent in 1966 and 28.4 percent in 1967.

occurred then. No one, he added, had demanded congressional investigations to look into those losses of speculators.

Castello was unable to hide his irritation at the MDB's charge that the government had assisted speculators. He said that the opposition, "lame in its action and twisted in its thinking," was not carrying out its historic mission. *Correio da Manhã* replied that Castello had no right to criticize an opposition that he himself had destroyed by tyrannical acts.[7]

On the morning of March 10, Castello bade farewell to all who had served in Alvorada Palace, because, upon returning to Brasília for Costa e Silva's inauguration, he planned to use the Hotel Nacional. For almost two hours he went around the palace and its grounds, expressing thanks to gardeners, guards, cooks, servants, and telephone operators, many of whom showed deep emotion. Before departing for Rio he also thanked the presidential group of the air force that in less than three years had taken him on over 970 hours of flights, covering more than four hundred thousand kilometers to visit 123 towns and cities.[8]

In Rio, Castello attended a farewell lunch given him by the top military officers. In response to a speech by Ademar de Queiroz, Castello declared that he was at the end of his mission and proposed a toast to the unity of the navy, air force, and army. Later, in the patio of Laranjeiras Palace, Castello expressed his thanks and farewell to each member of the palace staff. Many wept.[9]

13. "Security and Development" (March 13, 1967)

A few hours before flying to Brasília on March 13, Castello spoke to the National War College (ESG) for the last time. Opening the school year of the ESG with an address on "security and development," Castello said that security presupposed development just as development presupposed "a minimum of security and stability of the institutions." Making it clear that he was referring to both social and economic development, he argued that "even a satisfactory economic development,

[7] *O Estado de S. Paulo*, March 10, 1967; *Correio da Manhã*, March 11, 1967.
[8] *O Estado de S. Paulo*, March 11, 1967.
[9] Ibid., March 12, 1967; Vidal Pessoa, interview, November 21, 1975.

if accompanied by excessive concentration of income and an increasing difference of social levels," fostered tensions that prevented good use of the institutions and ended in the compromise of economic development itself.[1]

Castello rejected accommodation to inflation and efforts to hide its effects through rationing and price controls. Advocating use of the federal budget as a stabilizing instrument, he informed the ESG that the federal deficit, about 4 percent of the gross national product in 1964, would be less than 1 percent in 1967 "if the budget program is adhered to." Likewise he rejected palliatives in the case of foreign exchange, such as exchange controls that retarded foreign commerce and unrealistic exchange rates that increased indebtedness "as was done during the so-called development period, when the problems were pushed into the future."

The importance of international relations for national security, he said, lay in the economic and social interdependence of the world, and also in the need to turn abroad to find associative schemes that would reduce defense costs and to find capital and technology that would contribute to economic development. Affirming that true independence could be exercised within the continental security arrangement, he declared that Brazil was not inhibited in disciplining foreign capital and in developing commerce freely. "My government," he said, "was the one that did the most to increase commerce with the socialist area." But he added that Brazil had not altered its convictions about the merits of an Inter-American Peace Force despite the "inflamed debate, often destitute of realism, at recent inter-American conferences."

Castello had praise for nationalism, "an engine of human history," when it contributed to the mobilization of the national effort, the acceptance of the sacrifices required of development, and the reduction of conflict between classes. But he opposed its manipulation by groups seeking to avoid competition, to raise barriers against the importation of foreign technology, and to maintain mineral resources locked up in the ground. The true nationalist, he said, carried out his nationalism as a duty, without displaying it as a privilege. "He seeks to adopt attitudes useful to the nation's development, stimulating savings, bettering his own education and technical training, . . . and he does not simply reject

[1] HACB, *Discursos, 1967*, pp. 53–69.

the foreign contribution and reject also the promotion of internal savings." But, Castello added, Brazil had recently witnessed a grotesque deformation of the concept of nationalisim, with the power of invective replacing the capacity for analysis and with the "pseudonationalist arrogating to himself the monopoly of patriotism, imputing hidden motives to all who disagree with him and not hesitating to apply insulting jargon against authentic patriots."

Analyzing political structure, Castello suggested that the well-known advantages of the federative organization (political and administrative decentralization) should not obscure drawbacks, such as separatist movements. To safeguard against them, he advocated the reduction of the economic disequilibrium between states and regions. But he warned that a difficult balance had to be achieved in order not to weaken the rhythm of capital accumulation in the more developed and productive regions, thus reducing their capacity to export capital and technology for the correction of regional disequilibrium. Citing the danger of encouraging investments inappropriate to regional conditions, he called for an end to deals in which states offered political fidelity to the federal government in exchange for the approval of projects, regardless of their merit.

Castello called attention to "an almost universal tendency" for modern constitutions to provide a strong role to "the Central Power" for handling economic planning and monetary policy. The more restrictive role of the legislature in budget formulation, he said, avoided "regionalist pulverization of the resources, the disintegration of programs of action, and the aggravation of inflationary pressures by excessive regional demands." Noting that in some industrialized nations, such as the United States, difficulties of a monetary nature had arisen, he said that growing countries, in need of promoting development and restraining inflation, had had "to strengthen the Central Power, despite doctrinary preferences, sometimes deep-rooted."

Finally, Castello warned that in developing nations, subject to great tensions of change, the democratic system was exposed to special dangers, for the motivation to resolve acute problems far exceeded the capacity to select and apply adequate solutions. This context of frustration, he pointed out, was propitious for two protagonists fatal to wise democratic government: the demagogue, who promised to resolve all problems at once, and the extremist, who renounced "the arduous efforts of solutions for improvement that in successive increments relieve social ills." He added that, "in search for a degree of consensus to make development on democratic bases viable, eyes must not be closed to real difficulties, principally when, as happened in Brazil in the recent past, and was again more recently tried, the demagogues join with the radicals, all eager to offer miraculous formulas of salvation and all fawning upon the people."

14. Farewell to the Nation (March 14, 1967)

Following his address at the ESG, Castello visited Guanabara Palace to bid farewell, as president, to Governor Negrão de Lima. The president devoted time and care to his farewells and to the inscriptions that he wrote on documents and photographs of himself that he presented at this time to his associates. One of many examples is an inscription, recalling prepresidential days, on a volume of his recent speeches that he gave in March, 1967, to Lieutenant Colonel Gustavo Morais Rego Reis, assistant to Ernesto Geisel: "We reach the end of a mission, yours and mine. For me it is the last of my phase of public life. You will continue, and will continue well, due to your character, intelligence, knowledge, and work. You helped me a great deal, as in Amazônia, in the Fourth Army, and in the Army General Staff, not to speak of the friend of the unforgettable and sad days of Recife. I am very, very grateful! May you be happy."[1]

Upon reaching Brasília on the afternoon of March 13, Castello visited the Senate and Chamber of Deputies and paid calls on presiding officers Moura Andrade and Batista Ramos. "Without the cooperation of Congress," he said, "the Revolution would not have been institutionalized." He told Krieger that he had earned a plaque on his office door reading "Leader with the courage to defend the government."[2]

At Planalto Palace on March 14 the members of the SNI and the Gabinetes Civil and Militar presented the outgoing president with a

[1] *O Estado de S. Paulo*, March 14, 1967; Gustavo Morais Rego Reis, interviews, Brasília, October 22, 23, 1975.

[2] *O Estado de S. Paulo*, March 14, 1967.

silver tray at a ceremony in which Navarro de Brito, head of the Gabinete Civil, spoke on behalf of those present. He stressed the enthusiasm and sense of unity that Castello's leadership had given them from the first day, and he referred to their awareness of the profound change that the administration had brought to Brazil. "Your example, personal honor, and devotion to duty," Navarro de Brito said, "do not allow the melancholy of the end of the administration to dominate this palace." The press, reporting on the ceremony, noted that in his three-year term the president had not missed a single day of work because of illness.[3]

Castello's farewell speech to the nation was broadcast from the cabinet room of Planalto Palace on March 14. In the presence of the cabinet, legislative leaders, and five governors, Castello said: "In calling you to this last meeting, I cannot forget that it allows us to turn our minds and hearts to a Brazil that is within our reach to construct, whose dimensions we can foresee, and in whose greatness we have confidence."[4]

Recalling the prerevolutionary chaos, with its government subsidies, unrealistic prices and public utility tariffs, rent ceilings, and runaway inflation, Castello said that the "sham of authority" had explained its own impotence, and had tried to justify or disguise the crises, by placing the blame on an alleged joint action of internal and external forces, said to be eager to impede Brazil's development, strangle its independence, and dishonor its democracy; wide publicity had therefore been given to the picture of Brazil despoiled from abroad and strangled from within. Castello described the "impasses" that had been set up and the manner in which his administration had handled them when dealing with fiscal matters, foreign exchange, housing, minerals, labor unions, students, the military, the infrastructure, and international policies.

Brazil's pre-1964 international policy, Castello said, was based on fear and the tactic of opportunism. "We were making the gesture of independence while we were begging for loans and rejecting the austere sacrifices that independence demands"; assistance from abroad had

[3] Speech of Luís Navarro de Brito, File M (p. 77v), CPDOC; *O Estado de S. Paulo*, March 15, 1967.

[4] HACB, *Discursos, 1967*, pp. 70–85.

been sought not on the basis of the merits of projects and administrative seriousness, but by trafficking Brazil's convictions in opportunistic maneuvers that compromised her security. Castello cited the postrevolutionary policy that had been guided by Brazil's affinity for nations of the Western world which favored free initiative and democracy, but he warned that Brazil's interests often differed from those of such nations and that it was necessary to reject anything that did not contribute to making Brazil great and strong. Thus, his administration rejected the proposal to denuclearize Latin America.

The solution of the impasses, Castello said, required modern instruments and institutions as well as changed attitudes, and therefore the Central Bank had been created, capital markets and the federal administration had been reformed, and the country had received a new constitution with its "rules for the elaboration and voting of the budget."

Castello felt that all the old impasses and winds of irresponsibility had had the purpose of weakening the political institutions. The numerous political parties of the past had lost their sense of commitment and turned instead to bartering, or deals, that had ruined the treasury and "threatened to convert the job of the government from a rational effort of persuasion into transactions of personal interests." The postrevolutionary political legislation, Castello explained, had the dual purpose of restoring morality and promoting efficiency.

Repeating what he had said when opening Congress a few days earlier, Castello emphasized that "Brazil has ceased being a nation of impossible problems, of political impasse, of social instability, of administrative immobility." The incoming administration, he said, would be able to act objectively, with numerous impasses behind it, and would also have the benefit of a Ten-Year Plan of Economic and Social Development. This recently completed plan, designed to reduce "deep-rooted vices" such as demogogic, procrastinating, and utopian solutions, was concerned with four priorities: increasing the economic infrastructure, modernizing agriculture, expanding the industrial sector, and advancing the social infrastructure by programs for education, health, and housing. To press forward with these priorities, Castello said, it was important to strengthen the national private companies and to replace "the exasperating inefficiency of the state machinery" by a rational mechanism with instruments of planning and economic coordination. He felt that the Ten-Year Plan would allow the incoming administration to start with "an adequate amount of information and elements for judgment."

"Our independence," Castello declared, "will depend, more and more, on our capacity for financing our investments internally. . . . No country, new or old, capitalist or socialist, develops by means of political irresponsibility, superfluous consumption, malevolent ostentation, or criminal disorderliness."

In closing, Castello said that as president he had accepted with humility, but with full firmness, the responsibility of displeasing "those who think only of the present or dwell only on the past," and he had understood the need of anyone in government to disconnect himself from myths and face reality. He added:

> I did not want and I did not use the power as an instrument of despotism. I did not want and did not use the power for personal glory or the vanity of easy applause. I never made use of the power for myself. I used it, yes, to save the institutions, defend the principle of authority, extinguish privileges, correct the vacillations of the past, and patiently plant the seeds that will make the greatness of the future. I used it to enrich the nation, preparing it to bring about the happiness of the generations of tomorrow.

Correio da Manhã wrote that Castello's emphatic pronouncement about not using the power "as an instrument for despotism" revealed his hypocrisy.[5]

O Estado de S. Paulo, in a review of Castello's administration, told its readers that the president had found his principal advisers from among the notoriously corrupt members of the prior regime and, "with a moral insensibility comparable only to that of the former chief of the Estado Novo, destroyed in the political field all that the Nation had constructed in twenty-odd years." *Jornal do Brasil,* although well impressed with Castello's speech to the ESG, was shocked by the National Security Law; while this law was in effect, it wrote, talk about a return to a constitutional regime made no sense.[6]

[5] *Correio da Manhã*, March 15, 1967.

[6] *O Estado de S. Paulo*, March 15, 1967; *Jornal do Brasil*, March 14, 17, 1967.

The Constitution of 1946, which had made it possible for Congress to increase expenditures without arranging for increased revenues to cover them, was in many ways a reaction to the immense executive powers enjoyed by Vargas between 1937 and 1945. Although Castello had some preferences that were not included in the Constitution of 1967 (such as a Ministry of the Armed Forces and a possible "state of emergency"), the new constitution went a long way in reestablishing the authority of the executive branch. *O Globo* wrote that Castello Branco "bequeathed a constitution that gives room for the administration of the State and confers on the Legislature a highly expressive political role. He strengthened the executive branch, but not to the point of releasing it from democratic controls."[7]

If Castello sometimes did not have his way about political matters, it was otherwise in the economic-financial sector. There, he and his team were in full command during the three-year term. It is true that the Ten-Year Plan of Economic and Social Development "was promptly consigned to oblivion," as Roberto Campos has written.[8] Nevertheless, one must look to the years that followed the Castello Branco government for any assessment of the economic-financial measures undertaken by that government.

"On its advent to power," Ellis writes, "this government inherited an inflation running at an annual rate of 140 percent; at the end of its term in March 1967 the annual rate had been reduced to 35 percent without any catastrophic wave of unemployment."[9] Syvrud gives a general price increase of 28.4 percent for all of 1967.[10] But even that is probably unfair to the work done by the government that went out of office in March, 1967, both because antiinflationary measures are slow to show results and because the cruzeiro devaluation of February, 1967, brought prices up quickly. By December, 1967, the cost of living increase was running at an annual rate below 20 percent.[11] The reduction since March, 1964, had been achieved while absorbing the cost of eliminating distortions that the pre–Castello Branco regime had created

[7] *O Globo*, July 18, 1967 (editorial).

[8] Roberto de Oliveira Campos, "A Retrospect over Brazilian Development Plans," in *The Economy of Brazil*, ed. Ellis, see p. 343.

[9] Ellis, "Corrective Inflation in Brazil, 1964–1966," see p. 211.

[10] Syvrud, *Foundations of Brazilian Economic Growth*, p. 89.

[11] *Conjuntura Econômica*, February 1969, p. 30.

by trying to fight inflation by using controls to hold down prices, rents, and utility rates. In addition to handing its successor an economy free of these distortions, the Castello Branco government bequeathed stocks of coffee and sugar that could be sold because overproduction had been eliminated. The inflationary impact of the stockpiling had already been absorbed.[12]

No doubt the most spectacular result of establishing a sound basis for the economy was the so-called Brazilian economic miracle. Syvrud writes that "the economic statistics for the five years 1968 to 1972 show an incredible, almost miraculous, rate of economic growth."[13]

During the dark days when the foundations were being laid, Director-General of Finance Lopes Rodrigues once remarked to Castello Branco: "I feel sorry for you. You must have a terrible life, and perhaps can't sleep nights." The president replied: "You are wrong. I have a system. My system is Campos and Bulhões. I rely on them."[14]

[12] Campos, interview, December 23, 1974; Campos estimated that the Costa e Silva administration had the benefit of 2 billion dollars in stored coffee and 800 million dollars in stored sugar.

[13] Syvrud, *Foundations of Brazilian Economic Growth*, p. 2.

[14] Lopes Rodrigues, interview, August 10, 1979.

XII

Out of Office

(March–July, 1967)

Henceforth music will be my great companion.

1. Castello Leaves the Presidency (March 15, 1967)

BEFORE Castello Branco left Planalto Palace on March 14, he suspended the political rights of a few military officers and one civilian. At the Hotel Nacional, where he and his children and their families spent the night, dignitaries and friends visited the presidential suite on the ninth floor. Vernon Walters, invited by Castello to dinner, said that his acceptance might be used against the outgoing president. But the American military attaché decided to accept after Castello said with a smile: "They have accused me of having you to the first lunch with me. Now all that they can say is that you also had the last supper with me."[1]

At Planalto Palace on the morning of March 15, Castello signed his message to Congress asking for worker participation in company profits, and he said farewell to each member of the cabinet. Late in the morning he descended the Planalto Palace ramp in the company of Geisel, Navarro de Brito, and Protocol Chief Paulo Paranaguá in order to greet Costa e Silva. The former war minister, who had come from Congress after making his pledge to uphold the constitution, was accompanied by Pedro Aleixo and Rondon Pacheco. A crowd of two thousand, pleased that the early morning rain had let up, watched the two marshals slowly ascend the ramp for the transfer-of-office ceremony. At the top of the ramp Costa e Silva smiled to the crowd; Castello appeared rigid and serious.[2]

[1] *Jornal do Brasil*, March 15, 1967; Walters, "Humberto de Alencar Castello Branco," p. 6.

[2] *O Estado de S. Paulo* and *Correio da Manhã*, March 16, 1967.

During the ceremony in the presidential office on the third floor, the incoming president, in the presence of his cabinet, received the presidential sash. Apparently bothered by the heat, he occasionally wiped his forehead with his handkerchief. Castello, in a rapidly delivered speech, said that democracy required that the power, emanating directly or indirectly from the people, always be temporary. Pointing out that all revolutions "have to perfect and transform," he defended "the period of revolutionary processes that ends today and whose value and importance posterity will judge." He attacked those who, in a subtle effort to involve Costa e Silva and himself "in a militarism," might describe their ceremony as a "surrender of the guard" rather than a transfer of government. And he called on God to inspire Costa e Silva "in providing days that keep getting better, in assuring the collective well-being, and in strengthening the position of Brazil in the concert of nations."[3]

Then Costa e Silva and Castello returned to the top of the ramp for another appearance before the people. After they embraced, the new president went inside the palace again, and Castello, a private citizen, descended the ramp while the spectators applauded politely. Looking upward, Castello remarked: "Thank God my duty has been completed."[4] Upon reaching the ground level, he was driven to the Hotel Nacional to lunch with his family and close friends.

At the Brasília airport, spirited applause and farewells were expressed by a crowd that included many officials, a few congressmen, and a large number of former assistants and their families. As Castello waved goodbye from the entrance of the presidential Viscount, women wept. Upon the arrival at Rio's Santos Dumont Airport, about one hundred people, including Cordeiro de Farias, Aliomar Baleeiro, and Eugênio Gudin, were on hand to greet Castello and his family.[5]

Castello was driven to São João Batista cemetery to spend fifteen minutes at his wife's grave, and then to the apartment he had purchased while president: No. 202 at Nascimento Silva 518, the same building in Ipanema where his son, Paulo, and his family occupied

[3] Ibid.; HACB, *Discursos, 1967*, pp. 89–90.

[4] PVCB, interview, December 15, 1974.

[5] *O Estado de S. Paulo*, March 16, 1967; Baleeiro, Recordações do Presidente H. Castelo Branco," p. 37.

Apartment 401. After Castello said goodbye to Geisel and Golberi, his grandchildren called his attention to flowers that residents of the building had left in the lobby "to welcome our new neighbor." Later some of Castello's grandchildren helped Paulo explain to reporters that Castello was too tired to give an interview.[6]

During the supper in Paulo's apartment, Colonel and Sra. Haroldo Mattos dropped in, and they were followed by Antônio Carlos Magalhães. Later, when Castello was showing his modest second-floor apartment to Antônio Carlos, he called attention to the arrangements he was setting up for providing music in the apartment. "Henceforth," Castello told the congressman from Bahia, "music will be my great companion."[7]

2. Life in Retirement in Rio (March–May, 1967)

On the morning of March 16, Castello had a light breakfast, chatted with Paulo's daughters, and read the newspapers. *Correio da Manhã* described scenes of "uncontained euphoria" in downtown Rio and in Ceará occasioned by Castello's departure from office, and it cited an editorial in *O Nordeste,* a Catholic newspaper in Ceará, entitled: "Good afternoon Ceará, thanks to God, Castello left." The press gave publicity to the fact that Hélio Fernandes had signed his own name to a front-page editorial in *Tribuna da Imprensa* on March 15 describing the end of Castello's mandate as the end of a catastrophe.[1]

When Aliomar Baleeiro phoned on the morning of March 16 to ask if he might drop in, Castello suggested that he come right over. During their two-hour talk, Castello expressed optimism about the future, explaining that Costa e Silva understood he would not be governing without politics or without the ARENA; but, Castello said, Costa e Silva would not be able to govern by relying on consultations with General Jaime Portela, whose influence, Castello felt, was not good.[2] Castello gave Baleeiro the impression that, but for Krieger and

[6] *O Estado de S. Paulo*, March 16, 1967.
[7] Magalhães, interview, August 11, 1977.
[1] *Correio da Manhã*, March 16, 1967.
[2] Baleeiro, "Recordações do Presidente H. Castelo Branco, pp. 37–38.

Juraci Magalhães, Brazil would have had a civilian president because Castello could have handled "the military question" despite "some passing tension."

"If it is not indiscreet," Baleeiro asked, "which candidacy did you prefer?" Castello put Bilac Pinto in first place but also added Krieger and Juraci. He praised the advice that Bilac had given and said that if Bilac had sometimes been emotional during the first moments of a crisis, he had often asked for a little time and then, on the next day, had given opinions that were clear and correct and always disinterested. Krieger, Castello said, had also been a good adviser. Perhaps, Castello told Baleeiro, he would write about his experiences as president.[3]

When Baleeiro left, Castello insisted on accompanying him in the elevator and out to his car. A little later, Castello, who had always been a poor driver and now lacked practice, drove his own car in order to leave roses at the grave of his wife, Argentina. He asked reporters not to photograph him in this "very intimate, very private act," and he promised an interview at a later date. Returning to the apartment, he spent much of the afternoon and evening receiving visitors. They included Chief Justice Luís Galotti, Juraci Magalhães, Luís Viana Filho, and the governor of Sergipe.[4]

When Ambassador Manuel Pio Corrêa and his wife came to the apartment late on the morning of March 17, Castello, wearing his pajamas and a dressing gown, opened the door. It was obvious to the Pio Corrêas that Castello was truly pleased to have left office. They found him "happy as a cricket," arranging his books with the aid of a stepladder. Along with books and papers that had been brought from the studio living room of Alvorada Palace was the painting of Argentina wearing a pink dress and carrying white gloves and a small white purse. Castello, who had one servant, a fat woman with the ability to cook, asked the Pio Corrêas to stay for an "extemporary lunch," and it was served in the kitchen. "The point is," Pio Corrêa says, "that I never saw him happier."[5]

When Castello went to dine at the Baleeiros' on the rainy evening of March 19, he was in an excellent humor. Reminiscing with the

[3] Ibid.

[4] *O Estado de S. Paulo*, March 17, 1967.

[5] Pio Corrêa, interviews, December 23, 1974, December 19, 1977.

Baleeiros, the Viana Filhos, the Prado Kellys, and one other guest, he stayed until 11:30 P.M. He said that in the middle of March, 1964, he had not believed that the revolution was so close at hand; he and Ademar de Queiroz had considered Baleeiro a "utopic dreamer" with "the delirium of a civilian." Castello also spoke of a moment during his presidency when War Minister Costa e Silva had said to him, "So that you can see how loyal and frank I am with you, let me mention what happened yesterday: Magalhães Pinto suggested that I overthrow you and assume the presidency."[6]

The activities of the former president were hardly conducive to keeping his weight down, especially considering the splendid meals served at many of the homes he visited. His appointments book soon showed a full schedule of lunches, dinners, and other get-togethers.[7] Among the many individuals mentioned in the book (sometimes more than once) were Paulo Sarasate, Armando Falcão, Roberto Campos, Raimundo de Brito, Mauro Thibau, César Montagna de Sousa, José Bonifácio, "the Paranaguá couple, lunch at our home," Assis Ribeiro, Américo Lacombe, Paulo Egídio Martins, Waltrudes and Justina Amarante, his older brother Cândido Castello Branco, Golberi do Couto e Silva, Luís Galotti, Jorge Amado, Eugênio Gudin, Adauto Lúcio Cardoso, Luís Gonzaga do Nascimento Silva, and José Olympio.

On April 17, Castello lunched with Costa e Silva at the Military Club, and he dined with Roberto Campos that evening. A few days later he attended the theater with Ernesto Geisel, Roberto Campos, and Otávio Bulhões. When General Reinaldo Melo de Almeida came to call, he brought his father, José Américo de Almeida, the writer and presidential candidate of the 1938 election that Vargas canceled. Vernon Walters, who writes that he saw Castello more frequently after he left the presidency, departed from Brazil in May. Castello attended a reception and dinner for the outgoing attaché, and, on the night that he sailed, Castello and Paulo went to the dock to see him off.[8]

So full was Castello's calendar that the organization of papers and books went slowly. But Iris Coelho, who had received his permission to keep his longhand notes while she served as presidential secretary,

[6] Baleeiro, "Recordações do Presidente H. Castelo Branco," p. 39.
[7] HACB, personal calendar, 1967, File EX3 (p. 1), CPDOC.
[8] Walters, "Humberto de Alencar Castello Branco," p. 6.

arranged the notes carefully without his knowledge. Calling on the former president with Gustavo Moraes Rego Reis not long after Castello had settled in his Rio apartment, she surprised him by bringing him all the papers.[9] Castello added to his notes by making a three-day visit to São Paulo early in May. Using the office of Paulo Egídio Martins, he spent his time reading the issues of *O Estado de S. Paulo* that corresponded to the last days in his presidency. He told Paulo Egídio that he had lost his own copies.[10]

Early in March, Castello had said that after leaving the presidency he would make a "sentimental trip" to Ceará, accompanied by his sisters Beatriz and Nina and his brother Cândido, who had retired from the Bank of Brazil. But in the latter part of March he decided first to visit Europe. He was encouraged by cables from the ambassadors to France and Belgium. The Bilac Pintos cabled that a "trip of rest abroad" was justified after Castello's three years of intense activity, and Ambassador Antônio Castello Branco, his cousin, advised that the embassy in Brussels "is attractive" and "now we are in springtime."[11]

Castello thought long about whether to accept an offer of the Ministry of Foreign Affairs which would provide him with an expense-paid official trip to Europe. He decided not to accept it. As he wrote later to Paulo and Nena (Paulo's wife): "I did well not to accept it. You will recall that shortly before the trip, the minister of foreign affairs attacked me in an arrogant and untruthful manner. But it cost me many dollars."[12] He bought a round trip to Lisbon from Transportes Aéreos Portugueses and made his reservation on the inaugural flight, leaving Rio on the afternoon of May 24.

At a farewell dinner in Rio, Castello told Paulo Egídio Martins: "After my visit to Europe I shall visit Ceará. And after that I shall spend a few days with you at Campos do Jordão."[13]

[9] Coelho, interview, December 15, 1977.

[10] Martins, interview, November 10, 1975.

[11] Olavo Bilac Pinto and Carminha Pinto, cable to HACB, File EX3, CPDOC; Antônio Castello Branco, cable to HACB, Brussels, March 29, 1967, File EX3 (p. 2), CPDOC.

[12] HACB, letter to Paulo and Nena Castello Branco, Hotel Ritz, Lisbon, May 27, 1967, File EX3 (p. 10), CPDOC. When HACB was an ex-president, no arrangement was in effect to provide a pension to former presidents, but he did receive his army retirement pay.

[13] Martins, interview, November 10, 1975.

3. The Visit to Portugal (May 25–June 1, 1967)

At the Lisbon airport on the morning of May 25, Castello explained to the press that he was traveling as a tourist, and later, at the Hotel Ritz, he became known for his obstinacy in refusing to give interviews or answer the questions of reporters. He also became known for his fondness for losing himself in museums and bookstores. When, as he liked, he left the embassy car to walk from bookstore to bookstore, he was often greeted by an admiring public. A Brazilian who recognized him and joined him in a bookstore took him for a refreshment in an old café frequented by Lisbon literary and newspaper people.[1]

The press wrote of his inclination to have meals alone at his hotel. But he was just as often at elaborate meals given in his honor, as at the Portuguese Foreign Ministry and the Brazilian Embassy. Writing to Paulo and Nena on May 27, he said:

> I have been very warmly received by the Portuguese government and by the Brazilians, including the members of the Embassy. It is well recognized that I am making a personal trip. . . .
>
> . . . I did not expect to be recognized on the streets, all this from newspaper pictures. And, from all this, the attention doubles, respectful acts of kindness develop, and everyone wants to be useful. I am greatly surprised: soldiers and sailors salute me. I am not, therefore, an unknown.
>
> I have no news from Brazil, not even from newspapers. I read the Portuguese and French press. This in order to adapt myself to the environment. Bilac Pinto has just phoned me, charming in his kindness.[2]

Castello made a trip north from Lisbon on May 28, 29, and 30. After being driven to Coimbra, where he saw the *reitor* of the university, he went to Santarém and placed flowers on the grave of Pedro Alvares Cabral, discoverer of Brazil. Then he visited the town of Castello Branco, where one of his ancestors had assumed the Castello Branco name after valiant feats in battle in the fourteenth century. Before reaching the town, he was met by the governor of the district,

[1] Santana Mota, "Mantém discrição," newspaper article, File EX3 (p. 13), CPDOC.
[2] HACB, letter to Paulo and Nena Castello Branco, May 27, 1967.

who accompanied him during the festive entry. He got out of the car and joined a procession, which was led by children and students, and was followed by a crowd waving Brazilian flags. From windows and balconies flowers and colored pieces of paper were thrown. In the town square he said: "Never have I had a reception that moved me so much."[3]

Castello spent the night of May 29 in Fátima and on the next morning visited the shrine there.[4] Back at the Hotel Ritz in Lisbon on the afternoon of May 30, he found messages from officials and friends as well as confirmations of appointments with top Portuguese leaders on May 31, his last full day in Portugal. He ate alone in the Hotel Ritz dining room on the evening of the thirtieth, and this gave rise to two letters that were delivered to him on the next day from a Brazilian couple who could not refrain from staring at him in the dining room. "In my opinion," one letter said, "you made only one mistake and that was not to remain in power another five years. In that way Brazil would have become fixed up once and for all." But the writer admitted that the rare example he had given of not remaining in office was a reason for Brazilians to respect him.[5] As for the Portuguese who spoke with Castello, the Salazaristas usually argued that he ought not to have left office after only three years, whereas members of the opposition in Portugal congratulated him for having retired at the end of his term.[6]

On May 31, following a lunch given him by the president of Portugal, Castello called on the foreign minister and the navy minister. From the latter he received books about Portuguese naval history. Late in the afternoon he was received by Prime Minister Antônio Oliveira Salazar at his residence. According to the press, this cordial visit was "so discreet" that no newspaper photographer was advised in time to allow posterity to have a picture of the "historic meeting."[7]

But the press was present at the airport the next morning when Castello departed for Paris. "Since I left the presidency on March 15,"

[3] Card in File EX3 (p. 7), CPDOC; Mota, "Mantém discrição."

[4] "Castelo Branco Visitou Fátima," newspaper clipping, File EX3 (p. 6), CPDOC.

[5] Celia Azusem Furtado and Roberto Azusem Furtado, letters to HACB, Hotel Ritz, Lisbon, May 31, 1967, File EX3 (pp. 11, 12), CPDOC.

[6] PVCB, memorandum, June 1979.

[7] "Salazar Recebe Castelo," newspaper clipping, File EX3 (p. 6), CPDOC.

he said, "these have been the best moments of relaxation that I have had." He thanked the Portuguese authorities and people and added that he expected to spend a week in Paris.[8]

4. The Visits to France and Belgium (June, 1967)

Castello spent most of June in France. Shortly after reaching Paris, where he was the guest of Bilac and Carminha Pinto, he visited the apartment at which he had resided with his family when taking the Ecole Supérieure de Guerre course in 1936–1938. During the next two weeks he made trips outside Paris. He visited Saclay, the French atomic center. In Normandy he stood where the Allies had landed in World War II. And he inspected the Maremotriz electrical production plant.[1]

Starting on June 15, Castello was the honored guest at a few dinners and many lunches in Paris. Paulo Paranaguá, secretary of the Brazilian Embassy, has written that "Ambassador Bilac Pinto, who is the perfect host, ably succeeded in prolonging the stay in Paris, organizing a number of lunches with different groups."[2] In a series of embassy lunches, held on June 16, 19, 20, and 23, Castello met directors of the French press, members of the theatrical world, leaders of the French legislature, and officers of the French foreign service.[3]

The second lunch of the series, Paranaguá says, brought Castello together with Maurice Chevalier, "whom the president was delighted to know personally"; Geneviève Page, "whom the president had applauded and come to know in the Rio Municipal Theater"; Pierre Barouh; and Anouk Aimée. Also present were Geneviève Page's industrialist husband, the director of Artistic Interchange of the French Foreign Office, the administrator of the Comédie Française, and Ambassador Carlos Chagas (of the Brazilian UNESCO delegation) and his wife. On the day after this lunch, Cristina Isabel Chagas sent a note to Castello: "I received your present today. How it delighted me! I knew

[8] "Castelo Vai Bem," newspaper clipping (France Press, Lisbon), File EX3 (p. 6), CPDOC.

[1] Paulo Henrique de Paranaguá, "Viagem à Europa: Maio e Junho 1967," File EX3 (p. 3), CPDOC.

[2] Ibid.

[3] Guest lists are in File EX3 (p. 17), CPDOC.

that you were aware that I am a great admirer of Maurice Chevalier, but I never thought I would have an autographed record. I don't know how to thank you for your gift."[4]

A high point of Castello's stay in Paris was the lunch given in his honor by the President of France and Madame de Gaulle at the Palais de l'Elysée on June 22. In preparation for the occasion, Castello met with Brazilian diplomats to receive their briefings about Franco-Brazilian relations. At the lunch, de Gaulle was seated at the center of one side of a long table. He faced Castello, who was seated on the other side.[5] Among the other guests were Bilac Pinto, French Minister Louis Joxe, and their wives.

De Gaulle appeared to Castello to be in good health at seventy-seven, and he displayed the charm, knowledge, and concern about international affairs that he had shown when visiting with Castello in Brazil in 1964. The conversation of the two men at the Palais de l'Elysée was continued after the meal, when they spoke in private. De Gaulle expressed great interest in the new Brazilian Constitution, and when he compared it with the French Constitution, he revealed that he was well informed about its essential points.[6]

The Communists, Castello suggested to de Gaulle, were convinced that they could not conquer any government of Western Europe "by means of revolutionary strategy" and would have to accept the "democratic rules of the game," seeking the support of public opinion and votes to reach power. De Gaulle and Castello agreed that Western Europe was hungry for peace and that the prosperity there, aided by the European Common Market, had "generated forces capable of supplanting ideologies that place tranquility in risk." Turning to Latin America, the French president and his visitor concluded that the situation there was completely different, with the "word of order" being revolution—"a whole gamut of subversive activities," not excluding

[4] Cristina Isabel Chagas, note to HACB, June 20, 1967, File EX3 (p. 23), CPDOC. Castello Branco, returning to Brazil from Europe in 1938, had brought Chevalier records.

[5] Newspaper clippings, File EX3 (p. 18), CPDOC; diagram for seating at the lunch given by President and Madame de Gaulle, June 22, 1967 (à 13 heures 15), File EX3 (p. 18), CPDOC.

[6] "A Última Palavra de Castelo" (interview given by HACB to Arnaldo Lacombe, Rio de Janeiro, July 4, 1967), *Visão*, July 28, 1967.

"the appeal to arms through the guerrillas." Care and energy would have to be used by Latin American governments to prevent a "repetition of the success of Fidel Castro."

De Gaulle and Castello concluded that a new world conflagration could be avoided and that the atomic arsenal was "more a factor of containment than of stimulus for a new war," which neither the Soviet Union nor the Western powers wanted. The China "of Mao or his successor" was pictured as being in no condition to launch a nuclear conflict due to internal struggle and the "simultaneous homicidal and suicidal" nature of the country.

The impression that Castello gained from his conversations with de Gaulle and others was that France would not align herself with the so-called Third Force or Neutralist Bloc. In Castello's opinion neutralism had become perverted, weak, and unattractive because of the work of those who wanted to transform it into a movement to support "theses of greatest interest to Communism." As Castello put it later, "France is herself, with her own position. Integrated into the West in her essential fundamentals. It may be that she is more France than Western, but the truth is that nothing connects her substantially or intimately with the Eastern Bloc."

Castello found time to browse in the Paris bookstores, where he bought six books about military strategy and two about philosophy.[7] Also he frequently attended the theater in accordance with plans, outlined in his letter from Lisbon to Paranaguá, that called for "not many dinners and quite a few theatrical performances." Paranaguá, who accompanied Castello twice to the theater, recalls that "during the intermissions we drank 'um ver de champagne' that the president so much enjoyed." Carlos and Cristina Isabel Chagas also attended the theater with Castello.[8]

On June 23, Castello went alone in the Paris-Brussels train to spend the weekend with Ambassador Antônio Castello Branco and his wife, Maria. Castello, Paranaguá writes, "was happy and in the best of spirits to be again with Maria, whom he enjoyed so much and always remembered. He promised to return when he had time for a longer

[7] "Livros que comprou em Paris para si mesmo," File EX3 (p. 26), CPDOC.
[8] Paranaguá, "Viagem à Europa, Maio e Junho 1967."

stay. He had a commitment, . . . arranged by his brother, for the fateful trip to Ceará."[9]

Already Castello had received a letter from Paulo, dated June 8, that said, "Candinho is asking about the date of your return in order to arrange the departure for the North." Paulo also wrote: "I can imagine your fond remembrances and even emotion to see once again the most important places of our stay of 1936–38."[10]

Castello, back in Paris on Monday, June 26, bought fourteen bottles of perfume to take to Brazil as gifts. He also made arrangements to fly directly from Paris to Brazil instead of returning via Lisbon.[11] He reached Galeão Airport early on the morning of June 28.

5. The Last Days in Rio (June 28–July 13, 1967)

At his apartment in Rio on June 29, Castello received a visit from U.S. Colonel Arthur S. Moura and his wife and daughter. They invited Castello to attend a U.S. Embassy cocktail party to be given that evening in honor of Colonel Moura, who was taking the place of General Vernon Walters. Castello was delighted to see the Mouras. He had met Second Lieutenant Moura at Fort Benning in October, 1945, and he and Argentina had seen the Mouras frequently between 1951 and 1955 when Moura was stationed in Brazil. Now Castello told the Mouras that he was so touched by their act of calling on him to invite him to the party that he would accept, making an exception to his policy, as a man out of government, not to attend functions of that nature. Castello was the first to arrive at the party and was among the last to leave. He was, Moura recalls, exuberant the whole time.[1]

Castello continued to enjoy excellent health. This was confirmed early in July when he saw his personal physician, Américo S. Mourão, and underwent physical examinations, carried out by several specialists.[2] After his last visit to his doctor, Castello lunched at the fine home

[9] Ibid.

[10] PVCB, letter to HACB, June 8, 1967, File EX3 (p. 14), CPDOC.

[11] Bill of 1,128 francs, Parfumerie Cambray Fréres, June 26, 1967, File EX3 (p. 19), CPDOC; newspaper clipping in File EX3 (p. 27), CPDOC.

[1] Moura, interview, December 11, 1974; HACB, personal calendar, 1967, notation for June 29, 1967.

[2] Viana Filho, *O Governo Castelo Branco*, p. 549; PVCB, interview, December 21, 1974; see results of physical examination, File EX3 (p. 31), CPDOC.

of Raimundo de Brito, who had served as his health minister. That evening he dined at another fine home, that of José Nabuco, and on the next day he lunched with José Olympio.[3]

Early in July, Castello and his older brother, Cândido, and their sisters Beatriz and Nina, settled on July 13 as the date for leaving for Ceará. Cândido, known affectionately as Candinho, had been irked by the postponement of the "sentimental trip" occasioned by Humberto's delay in returning from Europe. It was well understood that Cândido, a good organizer, was in charge of the trip. This was due not simply to the deference that Humberto always showed his older brother in family matters, but also to the intense interest that Cândido took in the family's Ceará origins and in the history of Ceará. During his thirty-three years with the Bank of Brazil, Cândido had made many business trips to Ceará and was acknowledged to be the expert on the family background.[4]

With the date of the trip settled, Humberto addressed a letter on July 6 to Fortaleza physician Otávio Pontes and his wife. Using his new stationery, bearing the Castello Branco coat of arms, Humberto apologized to his "good friends Dona Elza and Dr. Octavio" for being behind on his letter writing. He spoke of possible arrangements for getting a secretary, and he wrote that since he had left the presidency he had been touched by the attentions and affections shown him by Elza and Otávio. Castello told of the plan to leave Rio on a Cruzeiro do Sul flight on the thirteenth and added:

> I give up my place in your home to my two sisters, and to Candinho if there is room. But I shall always be at the table of the friendly house. . . .
>
> . . . In Europe I had an agreeable recreation. There the memories of Argentina (oh! how she enjoyed Europe) accompanied me.[5]

Visitors kept dropping in at Castello's apartment. On the day after he wrote to Elza and Otávio Pontes, Senator Krieger took the new labor minister, Jarbas Passarinho, to call. The relations between Passarinho and Castello had been regarded as poor as the result of the

[3] HACB, personal calendar, 1967, File EX3 (p. 1), CPDOC.

[4] Rachel de Queiroz and PVCB, interview, November 15, 1974.

[5] HACB, letter to Elza and Otávio Pontes, Rio de Janeiro, July 6, 1967, File EX3 (p. 32), CPDOC.

reactions in Planalto Palace to charges made in some of the letters that Passarinho had addressed to the presidency after his early indication of support for Costa e Silva's candidacy. The conversation of July 7, Passarinho felt, ended the differences that he had had with Castello.[6]

Speaking to some other visitors on July 11, Castello expressed disappointment in many of the individuals who had served in his administration. Referring principally, but not entirely, to men in the second and third echelons, Castello said that his principal problem had been caused by the fact that "less than 10 percent of the men I had confidence in, men who filled the jobs, did what I had hoped they would do."

On the morning of July 13, Castello reviewed the writeup of an interview that he had given at his apartment on July 4 to Arnaldo Lacombe, the director of Agência Nacional during the Castello Branco administration. Castello made a few changes in the text, which recorded his impressions of his trip to France and principally of his meeting with de Gaulle.

Then, early on the afternoon of July 13, Humberto, Cândido, Nina, and Beatriz went to Galeão Airport for the Rio-Salvador-Recife-Fortaleza flight. Raimundo de Brito, who was at the airport to see them off, had plenty of time for conversation, because the plane did not leave until 4:00 P.M., about one and one-half hours late.[7]

6. Fortaleza (July 13–16, 1967)

The Cruzeiro do Sul flight reached Fortaleza at 11:30 at night, more than two hours behind schedule. Cândido, Nina, and Beatriz went to the Otávio Pontes' house, and Humberto went directly to the São Pedro Hotel's presidential suite, which had been reserved for him by the state government.[1] While some of the local press reports, written before the plane's arrival, correctly attributed the marshal's trip to his fondness of being in Ceará, *O Nordeste* speculated that he might be considering a candidacy for a Senate seat from Ceará that would become vacant in 1970.[2]

[6] Passarinho, interview, November 11, 1975.

[7] Beatriz Castello Branco Gonçalves and Nina Castello Branco Santos Dias, interview, Rio de Janeiro, July 12, 1977; Brito, interview, December 22, 1974.

[1] *Jornal do Brasil*, July 19, 1967.

[2] Newspaper clippings, File EX3 (p. 34), CPDOC.

Telegrams, letters, and messages at the hotel contained invitations. A telegram from Maranhão Governor José Sarney expressed the hope that his state might soon have the opportunity to welcome the former president, and Colonel César Cals, in Recife, sent a telegram to invite Castello to visit the Boa Esperança hydroelectric works. A letter from Armando Falcão suggested that when Castello visited the ranch of Rachel de Queiroz, he allow Falcão to send a station wagon to bring him to the Falcão ranch, in the general neighborhood of that of Rachel.[3]

After breakfasting at the hotel on Friday, July 14, Castello called on former Governor Raul Barbosa, whose son had died of a brain hemorrhage on the previous evening.[4] Barbosa had governed Ceará when Castello had headed the Tenth Military Region, with headquarters in Fortaleza, from 1952 to 1954, a time of great happiness for Humberto and Argentina.

Along with his brother and sisters, Castello was the lunch guest of Otávio and Elza Pontes at their home. Late in the afternoon he went to the Palácio da Luz for a visit with Governor Plácido Aderaldo Castelo, who offered to put a small plane at the disposal of Castello on Monday morning for the 172-kilometer journey to the ranch of Rachel de Queiroz. But at dinner in the Pontes' home, when the trip was discussed, it was decided to use the narrow-gauge trolley from Fortaleza to get to the ranch. Another decision was to leave Nina and Beatriz in Fortaleza so as not to bring too large a party to Rachel's ranch.[5]

Saturday morning was a time for remembering things past. Candinho, Humberto, Nina, and Beatriz went to the town of Messejana, about twelve kilometers from Fortaleza, to visit places they had known as children. They loitered in the old market. After a look at a reservoir of water that Humberto had inaugurated when he was president, they called on the parish vicar, and then they went to the Messejana cemetery.[6] They put flowers on the graves of their parents, and they walked among the gravestones of many Alencars, including that of their great

[3] José Sarney, telegram to HACB, File EX3 (p. 36), CPDOC; César Cals, telegram to HACB, Recife, July 14, 1967, File EX3 (p. 35), CPDOC; Armando Falcão, letter to HACB, "Massapê-Grande," Quixerámobim, July 7, 1967, File EX3 (p. 37), CPDOC; Falcão, interview, October 10, 1975.

[4] *Jornal do Brasil*, July 19, 1967.

[5] Castello Branco Gonçalves and Castello Branco Santos Dias, interview, July 12, 1977.

[6] *Jornal do Brasil*, July 19, 1967.

grandfather, Tristão Antunes d'Alencar (1825–1907), at whose nearby country place they had spent pleasant days in their youth.

Castello lunched in Fortaleza with Virgílio Távora at the Náutico Atlético Cearense, an elegant club facing the ocean. After enjoying a *feijoada* (black beans boiled with bits of pork and sausage, served with rice and manioc meal), he wandered through the club, conversing happily with members.[7]

On Sunday, Castello went to the airport to see Virgílio Távora off, and later he called at the homes of Senators Paulo Sarasate and Francisco Meneses Pimentel. In the evening he attended a dinner at which one of the guests was Alba Frota, the well-known authoress.[8] As she was a long-time friend of Rachel de Queiroz, Castello invited her to go on the trip the next morning to Rachel's ranch, and she accepted. Alba Frota, fifty-nine years old, had attended school with Rachel de Queiroz and was one of the leading characters in Rachel's novel *As Três Marias*. Her work on behalf of children had resulted in the founding of Fortaleza's Cidade da Criança and she had directed it until she joined the faculty of the Universidade Federal do Ceará in 1955.[9]

7. Não Me Deixes (July 17, 1967)

Early on the morning of July 17, Humberto, Cândido, and Alba Frota got into the motor trolley together with Major Manuel Nepomuceno de Assis, of the Tenth Military Region, who was serving as Humberto's aide. The trip south took five hours and was uncomfortable for Humberto because of his bad spinal column.[1] When the trolley reached a road crossing near the Daniel de Queiroz station, the travelers were met by Oyama de Macedo, Rachel's husband. A car and a jeep took them over a dirt road for four kilometers to the ranch, Não Me Deixes. Humberto rode in the jeep, deferring to his brother, who occupied a good seat in the car.

Arriving at Não Me Deixes shortly after 11:00 A.M., Humberto

[7] Ibid.

[8] R. de Queiroz, interview, November 15, 1974.

[9] "Gritos de desespêro após o choque," newspaper clipping, File EX4 (p. 5), CPDOC.

[1] R. de Queiroz and PVCB, interview, November 15, 1974.

greeted Rachel with a happy cry that referred to Alba Frota: "I have brought you a surprise."[2]

During the stay at Não Me Deixes, which lasted until about 5:00 P.M., Humberto, Rachel found, was happier than at any time she had seen him since the death of Argentina in 1963. For one thing, as many had already noted, he was delighted to be out of office, and one cannot help recalling his reaction in Italy when World War II came to an end: "No more combats, no more operations orders! The relief is so great that I still cannot believe that I am awake."[3]

For another thing, Castello was pleased to be in Ceará and to be in good company at Não Me Deixes. The simple one-story white *fazenda* building, with its porch and blue window shutters and doors, was close to a small lake that was surrounded by *ipê* trees in full bloom. The other side of the cottage looked out onto cotton trees. Castello enjoyed the setting, particularly the view of the lake.[4]

He brought presents: whiskey for Oyama and perfume for Rachel. The other bottles of perfume which he had purchased in Paris had gone to members of his family (such as his daughter and daughter-in-law) and to the wives of some of his cabinet ministers.

Castello was wearing a sports shirt, which was unusual, and it was the first time he had done so since coming to Ceará.[5] Although he was not a demonstrative person, his good spirits were obvious. He joked frequently. Teasing Rachel's husband, he asked "Oyama, what on earth possessed you to raise goats!" He played with Rachel's nephews and nieces.

At lunch, where turkey, tenderloin, and *doce de leite* were served, Castello ate well. He denied that he was interested in seeking a Senate seat. Speaking of his trip to Europe, he repeated anecdotes that had circulated in France about de Gaulle. He also mentioned his discussion with the French president about the new Brazilian Constitution.[6]

Following the meal, Castello went to compliment the cook, and

[2] Ibid.

[3] HACB, letter to Argentina, May 5, 1945, File H2 (p. 30), PVCB.

[4] R. de Queiroz, interview, November 15, 1974.

[5] *O Estado de S. Paulo*, July 21, 1967. (On the rare occasions when HACB wore sports shirts, he wore them with long sleeves.)

[6] R. de Queiroz, quoted in *O Povo*, July 21, 1967; idem, interview, November 15, 1974.

then he adhered to his practice of taking a short after-lunch nap. Rachel thought that he should occupy the best room available, but again he showed his deference to his older brother and used another room.

Humberto napped for about forty minutes. When he rejoined the others, Oyama and Rachel tried to persuade their guests to spend the night, but only Alba Frota could do so. Humberto explained that he had an appointment at 6:00 P.M. with Armando Falcão. As for the return to Fortaleza in the morning, Humberto decided to avoid another five-hour trolley ride by accepting the use of the small airplane offered by the state government.

Rachel spoke of her promise to give a book by José de Alencar, bearing Alencar's signature, to the president of the Writers' Syndicate of Rio de Janeiro. Humberto agreed to deliver the book. This prompted some joking, with Rachel saying that she did not trust Humberto to deliver it. Cândido said that he would take it.[7]

At about 5:00 P.M. Cândido, Humberto, and Major Assis were driven to the Daniel de Queiroz station. There they took a trolley eighteen kilometers south to Quixadá, a town of about forty-five thousand close to scenic stone mountains and surrounded by farms. They expected to be met by Falcão and driven to Quixerámobin, forty-eight kilometers south of Quixadá. Falcão, however, understood that they were to meet on the following evening, and so Humberto, Cândido, and Major Assis found themselves stranded in Quixadá.

The mayor of Quixadá had no interest in greeting the former president of the Republic. But a Quixadá physician, surprised to discover Castello and his companions, put himself out to help them.[8] As the local hotel offered poor rooms and service, he felt it best to take the group in his car to the Casa de Repouso São José, in the Serra do Estêvão, to the west. The twenty-one-kilometer climb up the Serra was a bumpy one over a road that might have been impassable in the rainy season (January to May).

8. The Serra do Estêvão (July 17–18, 1967)

Early in the century the Casa de Repouso São José had been a Benedictine school, the Ginásio São José. In the 1920's an effort had been

[7] R. de Queiroz, interview, November 15, 1974.

[8] Ibid.; the physician was later elected mayor of Quixadá on the MDB ticket.

made to turn it into a sanatorium. After that had failed, due to a scarcity of doctors, the buildings were used as a *casa de repouso*, or vacation spot, run by nuns. The climate helped make it popular and it became a sort of Petrópolis for the middle class of Ceará. Guests enjoyed magnificent views when they looked down on the surroundings of Quixadá and on a large lake, formed by the Cerdo Dam. In July, when the scenery below was a lush green following the rainy season, the *casa de repouso* was rather full because students were on vacation.[1]

The unexpected arrival of the former president and his two companions caused much excitement. The nuns received them warmly. Castello told the sister superior, a German, that he looked forward to moments that would certainly be pleasant and to satisfying a curiosity: he wanted to see the panorama offered by the high altitude.[2]

The room assigned to Humberto and Cândido was, like the forty others, about three by four meters in size. The furnishings included two small beds, a small table, a candle, and a water pitcher of hardened clay.

Humberto, Cândido, and Major Manuel Assis were in time to have supper in the dining room. There, a schoolgirl about ten years old read a welcoming speech. Everything, she said, had become cheerful on account of the presence of "such an eminent citizen."[3] In his reply Castello declared that during his military life and his government, the exercise of his posts had brought him "various honors," but none touched his heart more than "this homage which is simple but which I know is sincere, expressed in the words of this girl." He added that he was hoping to see the sunrise.[4] After dinner Castello chatted happily with guests and then retired, going to sleep at 9:00 P.M.

The ringing of the chapel bell at six the next morning brought Castello out to admire the view, but as it was cloudy, he did not see

1 Manoel Oliveira Bandeira and others, interview, Serra do Estêvão, Ceará, December 27, 1975; R. de Queiroz and PVCB, interview, November 15, 1974.

2 "Últimos instantes de Castello Branco na Serra do Estêvão," *O Povo*, July 20, 1967.

3 Notes for expression of welcome, signed Disce, File EX3 (p. 38), CPDOC. (The girl, who had written the words, signed her first name on the sheet of paper and it was given to HACB.)

4 "Últimos instantes de Castello Branco na Serra do Estêvão." (The last two sentences of HACB's response have been placed in a frame that hangs in the room that he and his brother occupied at the Casa de Repouso São José.)

the sun rise. He and Cândido attended Mass and then breakfasted in the company of the priest. Preparing to leave, they were photographed with the priest, the sister superior, and others. They signed the guest book, Castello giving his occupation as "retired" and Cândido writing "banker."[5]

Meanwhile, in Fortaleza, Francisco Celso Tinoco Chagas and his son, Emílio Celso Moura Chagas, both pilots, prepared to fly a two-motor four-passenger Piper Aztec, property of the Superintendency of Economic Development of Ceará, to the Quixadá airfield. They had been asked to reach the airfield at 8:00 A.M., but rain in Fortaleza delayed their departure until 7:30, so they reached Quixadá ten minutes late.[6]

The light rain at Não Me Deixes prompted Rachel de Queiroz to suggest to Alba Frota that she take the trolley north, all the way to Fortaleza, instead of using it to go eighteen kilometers south to reach the Quixadá airfield. But Alba Frota pointed out that she had to be at her university administrative post at 11:00 A.M. and would therefore have to use the plane.[7]

At the airfield, ten or twelve people gathered to see the travelers off. The pilot, who had known Castello during previous flights in the area, presented his son Emílio to the former president. Then Emílio, who was serving as copilot, put the baggage in the Piper Aztec.[8]

The passengers belted themselves in. Castello took a left-hand seat directly behind the pilot, with Alba Frota on his right, behind the young co-pilot. The two rear seats were occupied by Major Assis, on the left, and Cândido, on the right. As the plane left the ground for its forty-minute flight, Cândido followed his custom of writing the exact takeoff time on a slip of paper. He wrote: "9:08" and "PP-ETT" (the plane's initials of designation).[9]

[5] Ibid.; notes from trip with Manoel Oliveira Bandeira, Ceará, December 27, 1975.

[6] Emílio Celso Moura Chagas, interview, Rio de Janeiro, December 10, 1975.

[7] R. de Queiroz, interview, November 15, 1974.

[8] *O Povo*, July 20–21, 1698 (Edição histórica), p. 2; Moura Chagas, interview, December 10, 1975.

[9] Moura Chagas, interview, December 10, 1975; slip of paper found in a pocket of Cândido Castello Branco, File EX4 (p. 5), CPDOC.

9. The Plane Crash (July 18, 1967)

Upon leaving Quixadá, the veteran pilot flew over Não Me Deixes to give the passengers a view of the *fazenda* where he believed they had spent the night. After heading for Fortaleza, he pointed out some mountains and other places to Castello, who was in a good mood. For the most part the passengers conversed cheerfully among themselves while the pilot and his son occasionally exchanged comments about flights made in recent days.[1]

About twenty minutes out of Quixadá the Piper Aztec was fifteen hundred meters over the town of Ararape. The pilot called to Castello to suggest he look below. "Here is where I was born, Marshal," the pilot said.[2]

Fifty kilometers separated Ararape from Fortaleza's Pinto Martins Airport, where Governor Plácido Castelo, Tenth Military Region Commander Dilermando Gomes Monteiro, and others had for some time been awaiting the arrival of Castello and his party. In the Piper Aztec, copilot Emílio Celso used the radio to advise the airport control tower of the plane's position (above Ararape) and to ask permission to descend. The tower gave permission, together with information about the wind and temperature.

"All of us civilian pilots," Emílio recalls, "felt some tension because of the military jets training in the area. More than once a collision almost occurred."[3] By switching the radio frequency, it was customary for civilian planes to listen to the tower's answers to the FAB's small training jets. But at the moment Emílio found no evidence of jets in the vicinity.

The lack of evidence was misleading. At 8:20 A.M. a squadron of four shiny single-seat training jets from nearby Aquiras had taken to the air. After the jets completed their maneuvers, the squadron leader asked the Fortaleza airport control tower for permission for the squadron to pass at an altitude of fifteen hundred feet (about 457 meters) above an airport runway that adjoined an area where traffic at the fif-

[1] *O Povo*, July 20–21, 1968; Moura Chagas, interview, December 10, 1975.

[2] Ibid.

[3] Moura Chagas, interview, December 10, 1975.

teen-hundred-foot altitude was reserved for the jet training. Permission was given because, according to an official report drawn up later, no traffic was known to exist that would interfere with the jets.[4] The four training jets, after passing over the runway, made the customary half-circle to their left, still at fifteen hundred feet, to get in a position of approach for landing. This half-circle took the four jets about ten kilometers from the Fortaleza airport.

In the meantime, the Piper Aztec had been descending. At 9:40 A.M., when it was ten kilometers from its destination, it was struck by the number two training jet piloted by FAB Officer-candidate Alfredo Malan d'Angrogne, whose father, General Alfredo Souto Malan, was serving as director of army engineering. Young Malan had not seen the Piper Aztec, nor had anyone in the Piper Aztec seen the jets. At the time of the collision, Malan noticed just enough to feel that his jet might have hit some object. Actually, the collision resulted in his jet losing its left ejectable wingtip tank. After that, the jet, which was at the extreme right of the four in a row, did not adhere exactly to the squadron's formation, but it made a normal landing.[5]

On the other hand, the two-motor Piper Aztec was seriously damaged, for it lost the upper part of its tail section, including the vertical stabilizer and the rudder. The plane went into a horizontal spin, characterized by the nose going around and down. The plunge was not as fast as if the plane had gone into a vertical spin, but the latter would have offered some possibility for the pilot to make a recovery.[6]

While passengers screamed and the pilot tried unsuccessfully to regain control by manipulating the flaps on the ends of the wings, the Piper Aztec crashed to the ground in the brush about one and one-half kilometers from Siguaú Lake between Messejana and Mondubim. The impact of the crash wiped out the lives of the passengers at once. Castello was killed by a blow to his lungs. The accident left his body bleeding and both legs broken.[7]

Electrical line workers, who had seen the fall of the Piper Aztec,

[4] Ministério da Aeronáutica, Inspetoria Geral da Aeronáutica, Serviço de Investigação e Prevenção de Acidentes Aeronáuticos, final report, November 2, 1967, File EX4 (p. 4), CPDOC.

[5] Ibid.

[6] Moura Chagas, interview, December 10, 1975.

[7] Ibid.; *O Povo*, July 20–21, 1968; *Jornal do Brasil*, July 19, 1967.

ran to the scene of the crash accompanied by farm workers. Arriving at the wreck in about fifteen minutes, they found that the pilot and his son were still alive. Lacking hammocks or stretchers, the workers used a seat of the plane to convey the bodies from the wreck.

"How is my son?" the dying pilot asked.[8]

The son, who had suffered a broken lower jawbone and had lost four teeth, regained consciousness when placed under a tree. He instructed the men to cut off the plane's electricity and fuel, for a fire had started on the wing to the right of the motor. And he asked about his father.[9]

The father died later in the day after being taken to the air force base hospital in Fortaleza. The son became unconscious for a second time before he was conveyed to the hospital, but his consciousness returned after twenty-four hours. He was the Piper Aztec's only survivor.

10. Reactions to Castello's Death

At Não Me Deixes, Rachel de Queiroz interrupted her knitting to turn on a radio to hear the reception ceremonies which the governor had planned for Castello at the Fortaleza airport. The news she heard was that an official plane, headed for Fortaleza, was lost. A later bulletin identified the plane as a Piper of the state government, and a still later one announced the death of Castello Branco, his brother, his aide, the pilot, and the copilot. Nothing was said about Alba Frota, who was like a sister to Rachel.[1]

In the wreckage of the plane the José de Alencar book was found, wrapped in paper bearing the name of Rachel de Queiroz. Therefore the radio soon told of the "irreparable loss" to Ceará: the deaths of the former president and of "our Rachel."[2]

When Rachel's brother Roberto, a judge in Fortaleza, received a phone call asking about his sister, he replied that he was certain she had not taken the plane. He went to the military hospital where the

[8] Moura Chagas, interview, December 10, 1975.

[9] Ibid.

[1] R. de Queiroz, interview, November 15, 1974; idem, quoted in *O Povo*, July 21, 1967.

[2] R. de Queiroz, interview, November 15, 1974.

bodies were being brought by jeep, and there he found the body of Alba Frota and straightened out the mistake that had been made. By the time Nina and Beatriz returned from a drive outside Fortaleza with Otávio and Elza Pontes, the news broadcasts had the correct story. Nina and Beatriz learned of the plane crash from a member of the Pontes family.[3]

In Rio, as in the north, the news given by radio broadcasts shocked the relatives and friends of the Castello Brancos. Members of the family, such as Cândido's widow and son and Humberto's daughter, Nieta, and her family, were flown from Rio to Fortaleza. It was announced that funeral services would be held for the former president in Fortaleza on the morning of July 19 and that the coffin would then be flown to Rio, where it would be placed in the Military Club before the burial, on July 20, at the São João Batista cemetery.

Navy Captain Paulo Castello Branco was in Fort Benning, Georgia, doing course work of the ESG when he learned of his father's death from the State Department; after being flown to New York by the U.S. Air Force, he took a VARIG night flight to Rio. In Belo Horizonte doctors recommended a delay in giving the news to Humberto's frail old father-in-law, Artur Vianna.[4]

Costa e Silva issued a statement deploring the loss of "a great friend and companion, besides the irremediable loss that the Nation suffers in its political and moral patrimony." He told the press that he would uphold the flag that he and Castello had "unfurled together" to save the nation. Lacerda, on a ranch in Rio Grande do Sul, said that, "while I differed with Castello's policies, I was really sorry and shocked by his death. Brazil lost one of the greatest men of these last generations." Jânio Quadros spoke of the "errors and mistakes committed" by Castello, but he spoke also of the "respect and honor that his spirit and patriotism always merited."[5]

Roberto Campos recalled Castello's passion for truth, absolute moral integrity, and courage in making decisions, and he recalled "the sacrifice of one who accepts the labor of planting without having the satisfaction of harvesting." Campos also said that in his work he had been

[3] Ibid.; Castello Branco Santos Dias and Castello Branco Gonçalves, interview, July 12, 1977.

[4] *Jornal do Brasil*, July 19, 20, 1967; Arídio Brasil, interview, Rio de Janeiro, November 21, 1974; *Correio da Manhã*, July 19, 1967.

[5] *Correio da Manhã* and *Jornal do Brasil*, July 19, 1967.

struck more and more by Castello's "serene courage of assuming responsibilities, constant concern about fulfilling duties without claiming rights, and capacity to analyze coldly and plan for the long term, always convinced that the function of government is to serve the people but not to flatter the people." In an article written for *O Estado de S. Paulo*, Campos declared that Castello had transformed Brazil into a "solvent Nation, serious and respected."[6]

O Estado de S. Paulo wrote that the nation had had the sensation of experiencing a "veritable miracle, such is the difference between the situation that we enjoy today and the one that tormented the nation" in March, 1964. "The great factor in the success," it added, "was the confidence that all placed in the unstained, fearless, and honest man whom the Revolution raised to the presidency." *O Globo* agreed that Brazil, under Castello Branco, had gone from an era of misgovernment, chaos, and insecurity to a creative one based on seriousness and equilibrium. Pointing to the "institutional modernization" and "consolidation of democracy" that Brazil had received, *O Globo* added that although no other president enjoyed so great a legacy of power, Castello had always rejected "the seductions of dictatorship." Reviewing his entire life, it concluded that "his dedication to the service of the nation has no parallel in our history."[7]

Jornal do Brasil said that Castello, from the start, had not hidden his intention of restoring the civilian power and that this preoccupation, associated with his moderating attitude, had given him difficult, and perhaps unexpected, moments. It continued:

> No one can deny that in those moments his choice was always made on behalf of the public interest, without personal considerations. On signing Ato Institucional No. 2 . . . , President Castello Branco invested himself with exceptional powers, but he did not lose the conviction that it was his duty to preserve and perfect the national institutions.[8]

The *New York Times* felt that "time brought forth the man who was needed in Brazil" but it also felt that

[6] Newspaper clipping (*O Povo*), File HP1 (p. 13), CPDOC; *O Estado de S. Paulo*, July 20, 1967.

[7] *O Estado de S. Paulo*, July 19, 1967; *O Globo*, July 18, 1967.

[8] *Jornal do Brasil*, editorial, "Vocação Democrática," July 20, 1967.

politics and statesmanship demand other and different virtues—or perhaps abilities—which Castello Branco lacked. This was especially true among the easy-going, warmly human, live-and-let-live Brazilians. Democracy was not a way of life the marshal understood or admired. . . . He was, if not anti-intellectual, certainly not intellectually inclined, and therefore his high-handed treatment of students, professors, writers and scientists outraged the academic world. He approved an economic austerity and orthodoxy that was generally successful, but not exactly popular.[9]

The *Washington Post* found that there was every reason to believe that "the disreputable Goulart regime" had been taking Brazil toward chaos and anarchy and that there would almost certainly have been "a great deal more to criticize" about the 'inevitable unheaval against Goulart, had Castello Branco not been persuaded to take over the presidency". It went on to say:

Where he failed, he did so by being too much the reformer and too little the practical, power-seeking politician, by being tough-minded instead of popularity-minded, by trying to do too much too fast. At times he seemed to be the heavy-handed military man, ruling by decree. But in almost every situation what he did was less than what his military associates would have done if he had not been there to exercise a restraining influence.

The *Washington Post* concluded that although Castello had retired from the presidency "in a hail of criticism," his loss could not be afforded because almost inevitably he would have been called on for help in an emergency.[10]

Undoubtedly the most savage obituary was that which was signed by Hélio Fernandes and published on the front page of *Tribuna da Imprensa* on July 19:

With the death of Castello Branco . . . , humanity lost little, or, rather, it did not lose anything. With the ex-president, there disappeared a man who was cold, merciless, vindictive, ruthless, inhuman, calculating, easily offended, cruel, frustrated, without greatness, without nobleness, dry inside and outside, with a heart that was a true Sahara Desert.

[9] *New York Times*, editorial, July 19, 1967.
[10] *Washington Post*, editorial, July 19, 1967.

. . . Castello in his long life never loved or was loved. How can one shed tears about such a man whose death only aroused indifference, whose life was a deliberate act of distrust and of ill will, without any unselfishness, without a gesture of courage, without a sign of emotion, without a moment of greatness, without an instant of self-communion, or of humility.

On the poor gravestone that must cover the sad mortal remains of Humberto de Alencar Castello Branco, and where he will sleep the eternal sleep of the unjust, there will not even be room for an epitaph. Unless in a marvel of sincerity it is possible to write on the cold marble: "Here lies one who scorned humanity so much and ended up scorned by it."

In an article on an inside page, Hélio Fernandes wrote that Roberto Campos should "be at the brink of despair and at the point of shooting a bullet into his head." Fernandes added:

Now alone, and with his connections with the Pentagon and State Department fully discovered, and unable to count on the protection of the personal honesty of Castello, Roberto Campos is liquidated and will have difficulty freeing himself from an ostracism that is the best thing that could happen to him.[11]

11. Burial (July 20, 1967)

Among the dignitaries who attended the funeral in Fortaleza on the morning of July 19 were Marshal Ademar de Queiroz, General Alfredo Souto Malan, São Paulo Governor Abreu Sodré, and five governors from the north and northeast. After the service the coffin was put aboard a plane with the help of some of the governors.[1]

At about 3:20 P.M. the plane reached Rio's Santos Dumont Airport, where an enormous throng awaited. Costa e Silva and members of his cabinet moved the coffin to a funeral car, but the car was not used to take the coffin to the Military Club, about three kilometers away, because civilians and officers of the armed forces decided spontaneously to carry it on foot. While they did so, periodic shots were heard from the bay, where the cruiser *Barroso* paid tribute to the late president.[2]

[11] *Tribuna da Imprensa*, July 19, 1967.
[1] Photographs, File HP1, CPDOC.
[2] *Jornal do Brasil* and *O Estado de S. Paulo*, July 20, 1967.

In the club's Marshal Floriano Room the casket was guarded by veterans of the Italian campaign and a detachment of cadets in which the three armed services were represented. Among those who came to pay their respects were many who were known to have worked with Castello, and they were sought out by reporters. General Adalberto Pereira dos Santos spoke to them about Castello's "extraordinary vision as a statesman." Ademar de Queiroz told reporters that he could only say that he had lost his best friend and old Military Academy companion. He added: "Brazil finds itself deprived of this great public man, a statesman of the highest rank, who did so much for the nation and who still could have done so much more, such were his exceptional merits and profound patriotism."[3]

Between 4:00 P.M. and 7:00 P.M., an estimated five thousand persons passed by the coffin, and during the night and a part of the next morning the figure grew to an estimated twenty thousand, of whom nine thousand signed sheets of paper to be put in a book of condolences. Paulo and Nieta remained by the coffin throughout the night.[4]

Colonel Ardovino Barbosa, a former Guanabara police chief, went all through the Military Club because he wanted to find and expel the *Tribuna da Imprensa* reporter.[5] Retired General José da Silva Matos leaned so heavily on the glass that protected the late president's body that he broke it, but a Military Club carpenter quickly replaced it. Replying to reporters' questions, General Matos said that Castello was a "saint" who "could not die." "He helped me when I was a bootblack in Realengo many years ago. He was a lieutenant and I was a poor boy."[6]

At 9:50 A.M. Paulo Castello Branco closed the coffin of his father. He and Costa e Silva were at the front of those who carried the coffin down the club's stairs; they were closely followed by Juarez Távora, Ernesto Geisel, and Paulo Egídio Martins and were accompanied by a

[3] *O Estado de S. Paulo*, July 20, 1967.

[4] Ibid., July 21, 1967; *Última Hora*, July 20, 1967; *Correio da Manhã*, July 21, 1967.

[5] *Correio da Manhã*, July 21, 1967; for his article in *Tribuna da Imprensa*, Hélio Fernandes was sentenced to two months of confinement on Fernando de Noronha Island (see Fernandes, *Recordações de um Desterrado em Fernando de Noronha*, pp. 74–76, and *O Globo*, July 21, 1967). With support from Roberto Campos and Luís Gonzaga do Nascimento Silva, PVCB sued Hélio Fernandes on account of his article.

[6] *Correio da Manhã*, July 20, 1967.

crowd. In front of the club the coffin was placed on a large army tank.

Ten thousand members of the armed forces lined the streets, and fourteen military planes flew overhead as the funeral procession of cars, led by the tank, made its way to the cemetery where Castello Branco was to be buried next to the grave of his wife. Along the way, flowers were thrown from the crowd. The only disturbance was caused by an onlooker who cried out that foreign groups were responsible for the death of Castello Branco. He was arrested by the Secret Service of the army.[7]

From the cemetery gate the coffin was carried to the burial place by President Costa e Silva, Governor Negrão de Lima, cabinet ministers, and former cabinet ministers. Graveside speeches were given by General Murici, Senators Sarasate and Krieger, and Governor Luís Viana Filho. Murici, speaking for the armed forces, stressed that Castello had struggled to prevent Brazil from adopting a military dictatorship and had maintained the armed forces united, disciplined, and devoted to the ideal of serving Brazil. Sarasate, speaking for the government of Ceará, pictured Castello as the defender of liberty and said that the Revolution would continue united in the memory of the statesman who had always preferred to serve the people than seek applause. Krieger, who spoke for the federal government and the ARENA, was firm but affectionate and often referred to Castello as "my president." He said that Castello had "never succumbed to discouragement" and was one of those men who continued to provide leadership even after dying.[8]

Luís Viana Filho addressed the departed statesman. "Save for the sunshine of glory, and the light of immortality," he said, "nothing more will touch you. The infamy of enemies, who are portrayed in their own denouncements, the praise of friends, whose admiration overflows, no longer will change the lines of your work and the foundations of the nation that you loved and served." "Even above your work," Viana also said, "stands your example. This will live with the nation and be passed on to future generations."[9]

[7] Ibid., July 21, 1967.

[8] *Última Hora*, July 20, 1967; *O Estado de S. Paulo*, July 21, 1967.

[9] *O Globo*, July 21, 1967.

Some Concluding Observations

A study of the Castello Branco presidency is a study in leadership. William F. Buckley, Jr., in a column about leadership, writes that "a leader would show a people anxious to travel the road from A to X—from high inflation and stagnation, to a stable dollar and full employment—what is the route. He would warn of the rigors of the journey. Between A and X are mountains and swamps and deserts, and the journey will require sweat and stamina. But once across the barriers, one comes upon the Promised Land." Buckley adds that "A politician who promises that you can travel from A to X without any strain, enjoying yourself all along the way, getting more and more services free from the taxpayers' pool, is not a leader. He is a demagogue, telling the people what they want to hear, and expressing his innate contempt for them by the very act of suggesting that the road from A to X can be negotiated by merely getting into a federally operated elevator and pushing the correct button."[1]

Castello Branco in 1964 fulfilled Buckley's precepts of crystallizing what the people desired, illuminating the rightness of that desire, and coordinating its achievement. In the case of the last step, he shared the opinion of *O Estado de S. Paulo* that banking reform and other complex problems were not to be decided by public opinion polls. The chief executive, once elected, was to turn for guidance to competent and disinterested experts, in and out of politics, and then have the

[1] William F. Buckley, Jr., column in *Austin American-Statesman*, September 22, 1979.

route explained to the people. Despite the roughness of the road, the route was to be adhered to. In this connection much has been said about Castello Branco's lack of interest in "immediate applause." But more should be said about Castello Branco's ability to instill such a disinterested attitude in others, politicians as well as technicians.

In the practice of leadership, Castello Branco had the advantage of a career during which, as instructor and commander, he sought to bring out the best in people. Typical of the recollections about the instructor is that of Luís Mendes da Silva, a cadet in 1927, who has written that "in this daily work of developing the maximum potential of each cadet, Castello Branco received, if not the affection of all, the respect of the entire class."[2]

To bring out the best in people, it is necessary to have principles for defining what is best, and in the case of Castello Branco, these were the principles of a God-fearing man. Nor can one bring out the best in people unless one is a good judge of character (a quality that Glycon de Paiva and others found highly developed in Castello Branco).

In his relationship with individuals, Castello Branco made them members of a team. Colonel José Lindenberg, analyzing General Castello Branco's manner of handling missions at the National War College in 1958, spoke of the general's custom of always giving "each person a part of the responsibility and effort."[3] When goals were set up by the presidency, Castello Branco wanted the participation of all team members, even if he had to probe to get ideas from the more reticent ones.

Members of the team, which included congressional leaders, knew that they enjoyed the confidence of the president and could count on his support. They were involved in a mission of achieving goals that were set high. The army maneuvers that had been planned in past years by Castello Branco and his army unit staffs had always been ambitious undertakings, far beyond what was routine. To belong to the team was a reason for pride.

One clue to Castello Branco's achivement of bringing out the best in people may be found in his statement that "authority cannot be im-

[2] Luís Mendes da Silva, "Testemunho," Part 1, "Castello Branco, Tenente Instrutor."

[3] José Lindenberg, typed pages, Rio de Janeiro, September 25, 1958, File G1, CPDOC.

posed; it is earned by our example in fulfilling our duty."[4] If the leader, in the decision-making process, sets an example of serving his own interest, of putting his personal popularity ahead of the national interest, he can hardly expect to instill the necessary disinterestedness in others.

Castello Branco offered more than example. He frequently brought out the best in men by making it clear that he felt that they, too, were disinterested when they persevered in their work or gave him their opinions. There was something infectious about the patriotic feeling that Castello gave to the discussions. The president was able to declare to Aliomar Baleeiro that in his work to get the votes of congressmen, not one of them had asked a favor in return for a vote. When Carlos Lacerda criticized Baleeiro, it was because the governor felt that the congressman was considering politics from a national perspective and not from a Carioca perspective.[5]

In this exercise of leadership Castello Branco was eminently successful. But he had disappointments. Some of the individuals who were particularly prominent in April, 1964, due to earlier events, and who therefore had presidential ambitions, lost influence with the administration. This was not because of their presidential ambitions but because the president rejected opinions when he detected that they were inspired by self-seeking interests.

Castello Branco did not reject opinions on the ground that they differed from his own. During the careful work of reaching decisions, he welcomed and sought out such opinions. They were to serve in the discussions, where logic, not the self-interest of individuals or groups, was to be the determining factor in the achievement of the greatness of Brazil.

Luís Viana Filho was right when he said that the example of Castello Branco stands even above his work. It is an example that might well be given study by would-be leaders and by those who have the responsibility of selecting leaders.

[4] Albuquerque, speech in Congress (typewritten manuscript, n.d., probably 1967), p. 3.

[5] Baleeiro, "Recordações do Presidente H. Castelo Branco," pp. 32, 20.

Appendix, Sources of Material, and Index

Appendix

Letter, Castello Branco to Costa e Silva, Brasília, June 2, 1965:

My dear Costa e Silva:

I wish to express clearly my thoughts about the behavior of certain military groups that consider themselves an "autonomous force."

No President of the Republic has deserved such loyalty from his Minister of War as I have received. Almost all Ministers of War have been involved in a circle of interests, susceptibilities, or important controversy. Not you. Always frank, clear, and coherent, you give me your opinions with an exemplary autonomy and conduct yourself with a model loyalty to the decisions of the Government.

Without doubt the same is true in the case of our old comrade Ururaí.

Some of the officers in charge of investigations and indeed other officers who, it is said, are not in agreement with the acts of the Government and want to react against them, seem not to understand the determination of the Minister of War and the Commander of the First Army to serve the Government well. I am advised that they believe there is a difference of opinion among us about the matter. On the other hand, various Commanders, who share our ideas, are absolutely in disagreement with those groups who wish to form an "autonomous force." But they are not decisive with their subordinates, alleging, almost always, that they must act with care or adroit tact in order not to offend those who are at fault. Now, nothing is better in these cases than to act persuasively. It is preferable to convince than to impose. But we know that there is a limit to the use of that method when it is a matter of the exercise of authority.

It is not necessary now to recall the failings of some of those who are in charge of investigations. However, as a general rule, when they take certain steps, an abrasion afflicts the Army Commander, you, and me.

It is openly announced that officers associated with those who direct the investigations want to close down the theater where "Liberdade" is being performed. I sought at once to learn the nature of the play. The DOPS of Guanabara examined it and decided that it is not a cause of disturbance of public order and is without subversive content. Furthermore, Riograndino sent his most intelligent and most revolutionary assistant to observe and hear the play. He agreed with Colonel Gustavo Borges. Nevertheless, the threats that officers are going to close it down are terrifying freedom of opinion.

Besides, some officers have ordered the seizure of books. That only serves to lower the intellectual level of the Revolution. In addition to accomplishing nothing, it constitutes a governmental act used only in communist or nazi countries.

Therefore I ask you to examine and do your best to take care of the matter that I have mentioned. The "autonomous force" urgently needs to be properly enlightened, restrained, and, if necessary, repressed.

I believe that the Army Commanders, you, and I should appear as a single block, with a single decision and a single manner of action. This necessarily to the benefit of the Army, the Armed Forces, the Government, and the Revolution.

I renew the expressions of my respect.

Humberto Castello Branco

Sources of Material

NOTE: When there is more than one item to list under one name, the order has been guided principally by chronological considerations, and the interviews with JWFD have been placed at the end. The references to CPDOC are to the Centro de Pesquisa e Documentação de História Contemporânea do Brasil in the Instituto de Direito Público e Ciência Política, Fundação Getúlio Vargas, Rio de Janeiro. References to HACB and PVCB are to Humberto de Alencar Castello Branco and his son, Paulo V. Castello Branco.

Agripino Filho, João. Testimony, February 12, 1965, at Parliamentary Investigating Commission examining Hanna. *Diário do Congresso Nacional,* Seção I, Suplemento ao No. 54. Brasília, May 13, 1967, pp. 24–31.

———. Letter to HACB, João Pessoa, September 21, 1966. File N1, CPDOC.

Aguiar, Rafael de Sousa. Interview, Rio de Janeiro, August 8, 1977.

Albuquerque, Theódulo de. Speeches in Congress, 1967 and 1974, honoring the memory of HACB. Typewritten. Copies in Possession of JWFD.

———. Interview, Brasília, October 24, 1975.

Aleixo, Pedro. Letters to Luís Viana Filho, Belo Horizonte, September 21, 1971; November 7, 1972. Copies in possession of PVCB.

Aliança Renovadora Nacional (ARENA). *Medidas e Propostas para o Desenvolvimento do Nordeste e sua Integração à Economia Nacional.* Brasília: Comissão Coordenadora de Estudos do Nordeste (COCENE), 1971.

———. Resolutions, Brasília, April 14, 1966. File P2, CPDOC.

———. Nota do Gabinete Executivo (supporting HACB following the forced recess of Congress), October 21, 1966. File P2, CPDOC.

———, Pernambuco. Reports to HACB, Recife, May 1966. File N1, CPDOC.

———, São Paulo. Letters to HACB, São Paulo, 1966. File N1, CPDOC.

Almeida, Reinaldo Melo de. Interview, Rio de Janeiro, October 17, 1975.

Alves, Aluizio. *Sem ódio e sem mêdo.* 2d ed. Rio de Janeiro: Editôra Nosso Tempo, Ltda., 1970.

———. *A verdade que não é secreta.* Rio de Janeiro: Nova Lima Artes Gráficas Ltda., [1976 or 1977].

———. Interview, Rio de Janeiro, December 16, 1977.

Amaral Neto, Fidelis. Interview, Brasília, October 23, 1975.

Análise e Perspectiva Econômica [APEC]. Fortnightly economic letter. Issue of September 13, 1965. Rio de Janeiro: APEC Editôra.

Anderson, Marvin Sydney. "The Planning and Development of Brazilian Agriculture: Some Quantitative Extensions." Ph.D. thesis, Latin American Studies Program Dissertation Series, Cornell University, 1972.

Andrade, Auro de Moura. Interviews, São Paulo, November 6, 10, 1975.

Andrade, Theophilo de. "Mea culpa, mea máxima culpa." *O Jornal,* January 18, 1967.

Andreazza, Mário David. Letter to Luís Viana Filho, n.d. Copy in possession of PVCB.

Aragão, Augusto César Moniz de. Letter to HACB, Porto Alegre, February 4, 1966. File N1, CPDOC.

Aragão, Raimundo Moniz de. Interviews, Rio de Janeiro, November 4, 1965; October 11, 1966; October 29, December 16, 1975; August 2, 1977.

Aranha, Osvaldo G. Interview, Rio de Janeiro, September 25, 1975.

Arantes, José Maria. Interviews, Rio de Janeiro, November 22, December 26, 1974.

Araripe, Luís de Alencar. Interview, Rio de Janeiro, November 20, 1974.

Archer, Renato. Interview, Rio de Janeiro, September 30, 1975.

Athayde, Austregésilo de. "Por que Perder êste Título?" Newspaper article, [September 1966.]. File P1, CPDOC.

———. Interview, Rio de Janeiro, August 5, 1977.

Athayde, Tristão de. "Um homen." *Jornal do Brasil,* November 5, 1965.

Aymoré, Artur. "A Devoção de uma Vida" [based on interview with Wilson Leal]. *Jornal do Brasil,* July 13, 1972 (Caderno B).

Bahia, Luís Alberto. Interview, Rio de Janeiro, December 8, 1975.

Baleeiro, Aliomar. *Direito Tributário Brasileiro.* 7th ed. Rio de Janeiro: Forense, 1975.

_______. "Recordações do Presidente H. Castelo Branco." Typewritten manuscript, n.d. Copy in possession of JWFD.

_______. Interviews, Rio de Janeiro, September 19, December 26, 1975; July 11, 1977.

Banco Central da República do Brasil. *Relatório de 1965.* Rio de Janeiro, n.d.

Banco Nacional da Habitação. *F.G.T.S.: Incidência sobre horas extraordinárias.* BNH, Coordenação geral do fundo de garantia do tempo de serviço, [1973 or 1974].

Bandeira, Antônio. Letter to HACB, Socorro, April 23, 1966. File N1, CPDOC.

Bandeira, Manoel Oliveira. Interview, Serra do Estêvão, Ceará, December 27, 1975.

Barbosa, Luís. "Sem Água e sem Luz, o Congresso Cedeu." *Jornal do Brasil,* October 21, 1966.

Barbosa, Raul. Interview, Washington, D.C., June 13, 1975.

Barros, Ademar de. Interview, São Paulo, December 1, 1965.

Basbaum, Leoncio. *História Sincera da República,* vol. IV, *De Jânio Quadros a Costa e Silva (1961–1967).* São Paulo: Editôra Fulgor, 1968.

Bastos, Joaquim Justino Alves. Interview, Rio de Janeiro, August 10, 1977.

Batista, Ernesto de Melo. Letter to HACB, Rio de Janeiro, January 14, 1965. File R2, CPDOC.

_______. *See* Reis, Levy Penna Aarão.

Bell, David E. Memorandums, Washington, D.C., 1964. Papers of Lyndon B. Johnson, LBJ Library, Austin, Texas.

Bevilacqua, Pery Constant. "Hanna É Altamente Lesiva ao Legítimo Interêsse Nacional." *Tribuna da Imprensa,* November 22, 1967.

_______. Interview, Rio de Janeiro, December 21, 1977.

Black, Jan Knippers. *United States Penetration of Brazil.* Philadelphia: University of Pennsylvania Press, 1977.

Books purchased in Paris by HACB, June 1967. List. File EX3, CPDOC.

Borges, Mauro. *O Golpe em Goiás: História de uma Grande Traição.* Rio de Janeiro: Editôra Civilização Brasileira S.A., 1965.

Borges, Murilo. Letters to HACB, Fortaleza, 1966, 1967. File N1, CPDOC.

Bório, Leônidas Lopes. Letter to Luís Viana Filho, Rio de Janeiro, July 20, 1972, with accompanying papers about coffee. Copies in possession of PVCB.

_______. Interview, Rio de Janeiro, December 22, 1977.

Bosísio, Paulo. Letter to HACB, Rio de Janeiro, March 10, 1966. File N1, CPDOC.

_______. Interview, São Paulo, November 8, 1975.

Boto, Carlos Pena. Interviews, Rio de Janeiro, October 3, 1966; December 10, 1967.

Bowdler, William G. Memorandums, Washington, D.C., 1965. National Security Files, LBJ Library, Austin, Texas.

Braga, Nei. Interview, Brasília,October 23, 1975.

Branco, Antônio Castello. Cable to HACB, Brussels, March 29, 1967. File EX3, CPDOC.

Branco, Carlos Castello. *Os Militares no Poder: 1. Castelo Branco.* Rio de Janeiro: Editora Nova Fronteira S.A., 1976.

———. "Coluna do Castello." Daily political columns in *Jornal do Brasil*, 1964–1967.

———. Interview, Brasília, October 24, 1975.

Branco, Humberto de Alencar Castello. *Discursos, 1964.* Secretaria de Imprensa, n.d.

———. *Entrevistas, 1964–1965.* Secretaria de Imprensa, 1966.

———. *Discursos, 1965.* Secretaria de Imprensa, n.d.

———. *Discursos, 1966.* Secretaria de Imprensa, n.d.

———. *Discursos, 1967.* Secretaria de Imprensa da Presidência da Republica, n.d.

———. Papers in the Castello Branco Collection, CPDOC, and in possession of PVCB.

———. Letters to Argentina Castello Branco, Italy, 1944, 1945. Files H1 and H2, PVCB.

———. "O Dever Militar em Face da Luta Ideológica: Palestra Proferida a 15 de Dezembro de 1961, na ECEME." Typewritten manuscript received by JWFD from PVCB.

———. Letters to Lyndon B. Johnson, 1964–1967. Papers of Lyndon B. Johnson, LBJ Library, Austin, Texas.

———. Letters to Carlos Lacerda, 1964–1965. File N4, CPDOC.

———. "Política Internacional." Typewritten memorandum sent to Ministry of Foreign Relations, mid-1964. Copy in possession of JWFD.

———. Letter to Paulo, Nena, Heloiza, Helena, and Cristina Castello Branco, Rio de Janeiro, July 30, 1964. Longhand. File P1, CPDOC.

———. Letters to Hélio Ibiapina, Brasília, June 25, 1964; Rio de Janeiro, September 10, 1964. File P1, CPDOC.

———. Letter to War Minister Artur da Costa e Silva, Brasília, June 2, 1965. PVCB.

———. Handwritten memorandum about foreign affairs for Juraci Magalhães, Rio de Janeiro, January 17, 1966. File O2, PVCB.

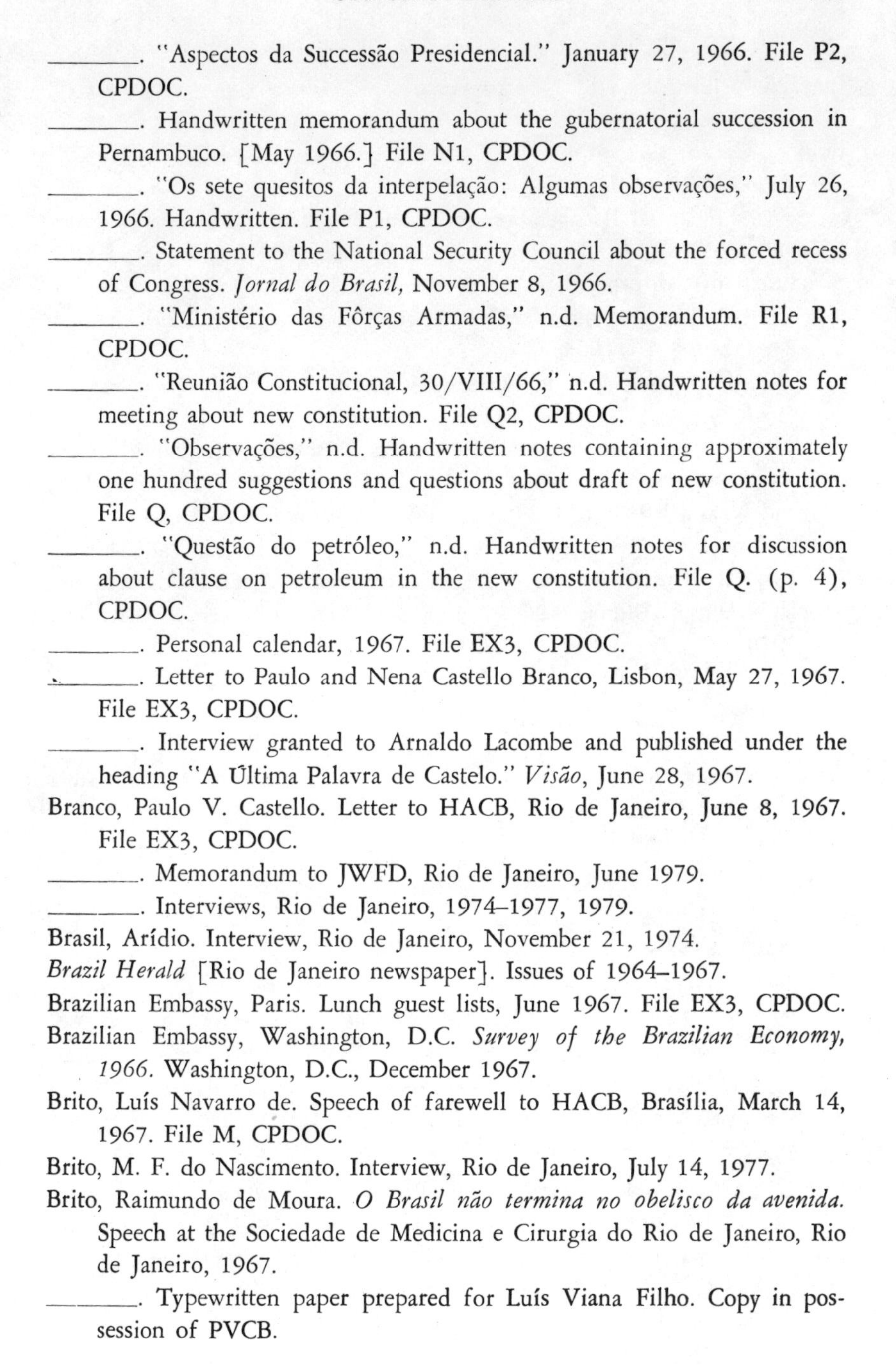

———. "Aspectos da Successão Presidencial." January 27, 1966. File P2, CPDOC.

———. Handwritten memorandum about the gubernatorial succession in Pernambuco. [May 1966.] File N1, CPDOC.

———. "Os sete quesitos da interpelação: Algumas observações," July 26, 1966. Handwritten. File P1, CPDOC.

———. Statement to the National Security Council about the forced recess of Congress. *Jornal do Brasil,* November 8, 1966.

———. "Ministério das Fôrças Armadas," n.d. Memorandum. File R1, CPDOC.

———. "Reunião Constitucional, 30/VIII/66," n.d. Handwritten notes for meeting about new constitution. File Q2, CPDOC.

———. "Observações," n.d. Handwritten notes containing approximately one hundred suggestions and questions about draft of new constitution. File Q, CPDOC.

———. "Questão do petróleo," n.d. Handwritten notes for discussion about clause on petroleum in the new constitution. File Q. (p. 4), CPDOC.

———. Personal calendar, 1967. File EX3, CPDOC.

———. Letter to Paulo and Nena Castello Branco, Lisbon, May 27, 1967. File EX3, CPDOC.

———. Interview granted to Arnaldo Lacombe and published under the heading "A Última Palavra de Castelo." *Visão*, June 28, 1967.

Branco, Paulo V. Castello. Letter to HACB, Rio de Janeiro, June 8, 1967. File EX3, CPDOC.

———. Memorandum to JWFD, Rio de Janeiro, June 1979.

———. Interviews, Rio de Janeiro, 1974–1977, 1979.

Brasil, Arídio. Interview, Rio de Janeiro, November 21, 1974.

Brazil Herald [Rio de Janeiro newspaper]. Issues of 1964–1967.

Brazilian Embassy, Paris. Lunch guest lists, June 1967. File EX3, CPDOC.

Brazilian Embassy, Washington, D.C. *Survey of the Brazilian Economy, 1966.* Washington, D.C., December 1967.

Brito, Luís Navarro de. Speech of farewell to HACB, Brasília, March 14, 1967. File M, CPDOC.

Brito, M. F. do Nascimento. Interview, Rio de Janeiro, July 14, 1977.

Brito, Raimundo de Moura. *O Brasil não termina no obelisco da avenida.* Speech at the Sociedade de Medicina e Cirurgia do Rio de Janeiro, Rio de Janeiro, 1967.

———. Typewritten paper prepared for Luís Viana Filho. Copy in possession of PVCB.

_______. Interview, Rio de Janeiro, December 22, 1974.

Buckley, William F., Jr., Newspaper column, *Austin American-Statesman,* September 22, 1979.

Bulhões, Octavio Gouvea de. *Dois Conceitos de Lucro.* 3d ed. Rio de Janeiro: APEC Editora S.A., 1969.

_______. "Financial Recuperation for Economic Expansion," in *The Economy of Brazil,* ed. Howard S. Ellis. Berkeley and Los Angeles: University of California Press, 1969.

_______. Declarations on television reported in *Jornal do Brasil,* January 24, February 10, 1967.

_______. Interviews, Rio de Janeiro, December 30, 1974; December 22, 1977.

Bundy, McGeorge. Memorandums to Lyndon B. Johnson and Lincoln Gordon, 1964–1966. Papers of Lyndon B. Johnson, President's Staff File, and National Security Files, LBJ Library, Austin, Texas.

Byars, Robert Stafford. "Small Group Theory and Political Leadership in Brazil: The Case of the Castelo Branco Regime." Ph.D. dissertation, University of Illinois, 1969. Ann Arbor: Xerox University Microfilms, 1976.

Café Filho, João. Letter to HACB, Guanabara, March 7, 1966. File N1, CPDOC.

Cals, César. Telegram to HACB, Recife, July 14, 1967. File EX3, CPDOC.

Cámara, Hélder, *Revolução dentro da Paz.* Rio de Janeiro: Editôra Sabia Ltda., 1968.

_______. Letter to HACB, Recife, August 18, 1966. File S, PVCB.

_______. Interview, Recife, October 15, 1968.

Câmara dos Deputados. *Commissão Parlamentar de Inquérito para estudar o problema do minério de ferro no Brasil, sua exploração, transporte e exportação, bem como as atividades do Grupo Hanna no Brasil, através suas subsidiárias.* 197-page report in *Diário do Congresso Nacional,* Seção I, Suplemento ao No. 54. Brasília, May 13, 1967.

_______. *Deputados Brasileiros: Repertório biográfico dos membros da Câmara dos Deputados, Sexta Legislatura (1967–1971).* Brasília: Biblioteca da Câmara dos Deputados, 1968.

_______, Diretoria de Documentação e Publicidade. *Endereços dos Senhores Deputados.* Issues of December 1963, November 1964, June 1967. Brasília: Departamento de Imprensa Nacional, 1964; Imprensa Universitária (Goiânia), 1964; Serviço Gráfico do IBGE, 1967.

Campos, Milton, *Testemunhos e Ensinamentos.* Rio de Janeiro: Livraria José Olympio Editora, 1972.

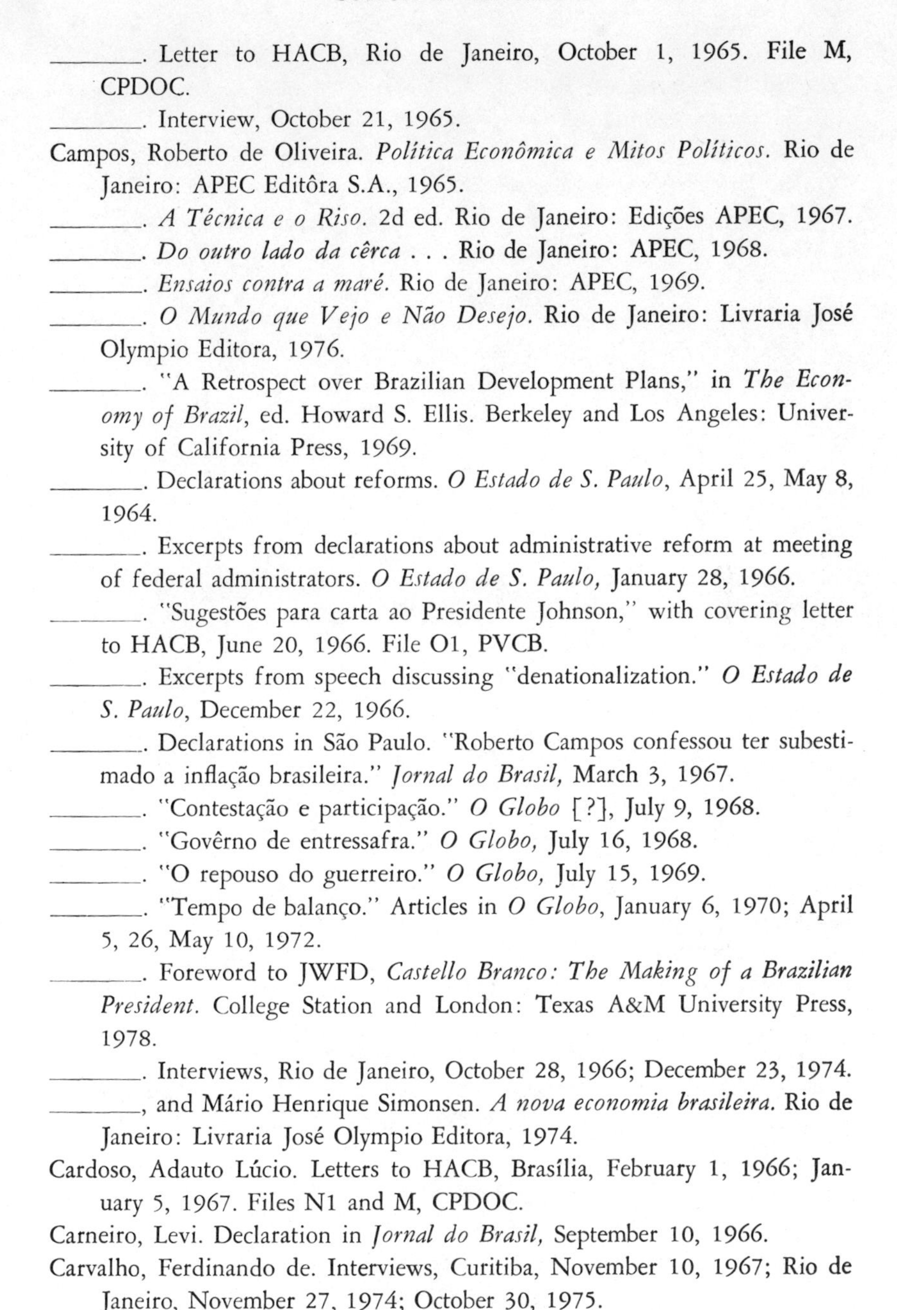

———. Letter to HACB, Rio de Janeiro, October 1, 1965. File M, CPDOC.

———. Interview, October 21, 1965.

Campos, Roberto de Oliveira. *Política Econômica e Mitos Políticos.* Rio de Janeiro: APEC Editôra S.A., 1965.

———. *A Técnica e o Riso.* 2d ed. Rio de Janeiro: Edições APEC, 1967.

———. *Do outro lado da cêrca . . .* Rio de Janeiro: APEC, 1968.

———. *Ensaios contra a maré.* Rio de Janeiro: APEC, 1969.

———. *O Mundo que Vejo e Não Desejo.* Rio de Janeiro: Livraria José Olympio Editora, 1976.

———. "A Retrospect over Brazilian Development Plans," in *The Economy of Brazil*, ed. Howard S. Ellis. Berkeley and Los Angeles: University of California Press, 1969.

———. Declarations about reforms. *O Estado de S. Paulo*, April 25, May 8, 1964.

———. Excerpts from declarations about administrative reform at meeting of federal administrators. *O Estado de S. Paulo,* January 28, 1966.

———. "Sugestões para carta ao Presidente Johnson," with covering letter to HACB, June 20, 1966. File O1, PVCB.

———. Excerpts from speech discussing "denationalization." *O Estado de S. Paulo*, December 22, 1966.

———. Declarations in São Paulo. "Roberto Campos confessou ter subestimado a inflação brasileira." *Jornal do Brasil,* March 3, 1967.

———. "Contestação e participação." *O Globo* [?], July 9, 1968.

———. "Govêrno de entressafra." *O Globo,* July 16, 1968.

———. "O repouso do guerreiro." *O Globo,* July 15, 1969.

———. "Tempo de balanço." Articles in *O Globo*, January 6, 1970; April 5, 26, May 10, 1972.

———. Foreword to JWFD, *Castello Branco: The Making of a Brazilian President.* College Station and London: Texas A&M University Press, 1978.

———. Interviews, Rio de Janeiro, October 28, 1966; December 23, 1974.

———, and Mário Henrique Simonsen. *A nova economia brasileira.* Rio de Janeiro: Livraria José Olympio Editora, 1974.

Cardoso, Adauto Lúcio. Letters to HACB, Brasília, February 1, 1966; January 5, 1967. Files N1 and M, CPDOC.

Carneiro, Levi. Declaration in *Jornal do Brasil,* September 10, 1966.

Carvalho, Ferdinando de. Interviews, Curitiba, November 10, 1967; Rio de Janeiro, November 27, 1974; October 30, 1975.

"Castello: Os Arquivos do Marechal Revelam um Militar Revolucionário e Liberal." *Veja,* April 5, 1972.

"Castello, uma vida em revisão há 10 anos." *Jornal do Brasil*, July 18, 1977.
"Castelo Branco chega a Paris iniciando visita de uma semana à França." Newspaper clipping from *Jornal do Brasil,* June 1967. File EX3, CPDOC.
"Castelo Branco Visitou Fátima." Newspaper story from Lisbon. *O Globo,* [approx. June 1, 1967]. File EX3, CPDOC.
"Castelo Vai Bem." Newspaper story from Lisbon. France Press, [approx. June 1, 1967]. File EX3, CPDOC.
"Castelo com de Gaulle." Newspaper clippings, June 1967. File EX3, CPDOC.
Cavalcanti, Sandra. Interviews, Rio de Janeiro, October 21, 1966; November 18, 1975.
Cavalcanti, Temístocles. Interview, Rio de Janeiro, September 22, 1975.
Cavalcanti Júnior, Francisco Boaventura. Open letter to HACB. *Jornal do Brasil,* November 28, 1965.
———. Interview, Rio de Janeiro, November 20, 1974.
Center for Strategic Studies, Georgetown University. *Dominican Action—1965: Intervention or Cooperation?* Washington, D.C.: The Center for Strategic Studies, 1966.
Cerdeira, Arnaldo. Letters and memorandums to HACB, 1966. File N1, CPDOC.
Chagas, Cristina Isabel. Note to HACB, Paris, June 20, 1967. File EX3, CPDOC.
Chagas, Emílio Celso Moura. Interview, Rio de Janeiro, December 10, 1975.
Chaves, Orlando. Letters to Jorge de Oliveira and HACB, Cuiabá, June 11, 12, 1965. File S, PVCB.
Cline, William F. *Economic Consequences of a Land Reform in Brazil.* Amsterdam and London: North-Holland Publishing Company, 1970.
Código Eleitoral e Legislação Complementar. Rio de Janeiro: Gráfica Auriverde, Ltda., 1965.
Coelho, Iris. Interview, Rio de Janeiro, December 15, 1977.
Coelho, Nilo. *Discurso de Posse . . . perante a Assembléia Legislativa do Estado, em 31 de Janeiro de 1967.* Recife: Imprensa Oficial de Pernambuco, 1967.
———. *Mensagem Desenvolvimentista do Novo Nordeste.* Recife, 1967.
———. *O Nordeste e a Cooperação Internacional.* Recife, 1967.
———. Telegrams to HACB, [1966]. File N1, CPDOC.
———. Interview, Recife, October 27, 1967.
Congressional Record, U.S. 89th Congress. Washington, D.C., 1965.

Coni, Heitor Carlos. Interview, Rio de Janeiro, December 15, 1977.

Conjuntura Econômica [Rio de Janeiro monthly published by the Fundação Getúlio Vargas]. Issues of 1964–1969.

Conselho Superior da Aeronáutica. "Uma Sugestão," n.d. Typewritten. File R2, CPDOC.

Constituição do Brasil promulgada em 24 de Janeiro de 1967. Departamento de Imprensa Nacional, 1967.

Corrêa, Manuel Pio. Interviews, Rio de Janeiro, December 23, 1974; December 19, 1977.

Corrêa, Marcos Sá. "A Constituição que Nasceu Morta." *Jornal do Brasil*, January 30, 1977.

Corrêa, Oscar Dias. *Porque Abandono a Vida Pública: Discurso proferido na Câmara dos Deputados, na sessão de 23 de março de 1966*. Brasília: Departamento de Imprensa Nacional, 1966.

———. *A Constituição de 1967: Contribuição Crítica*. Rio de Janeiro: Forense, 1969.

———. Interview, Rio de Janeiro, September 24, 1975.

Correio da Manhã [Rio de Janeiro newspaper]. Issues of 1964–1967.

Costa, César Távito Lopes. Interview, São Paulo, July 28, 1977.

Cruzeiro, O [Rio de Janeiro magazine]. Issue of December 10, 1966.

Cunha, Vasco Leitão da. Letter to HACB, New York, September 28, 1965. File O2, PVCB.

———. Interview, Rio de Janeiro, November 23, 1974.

———, Dean Rusk, and others. Memorandum of conversation, UN General Assembly, New York, September 28, 1965. National Security Files, LBJ Library, Austin, Texas.

D'Aguiar, Hernani. *A Revolução por Dentro*. Rio de Janeiro: Editora Artenova S.A., 1976.

———. Interview, Rio de Janeiro, July 29, 1976.

Dean, Robert W. Memorandum, São Paulo, August 13, 1964. National Security Files, LBJ Library, Austin, Texas.

———. Telegrams to secretary of state, Brasília, November 16, 27, 1964. National Security Files, LBJ Library, Austin, Texas.

De Broucker, José. *Dom Hélder Câmara: The Violence of a Peacemaker*. Maryknoll, N.Y.: Orbis Books, 1970.

"Decretada a reforma administrativa." *O Estado de S. Paulo,* March 1, 1967.

Delgado, José de Medeiros. Letters to Itaberê Gouveia do Amaral and HACB, Fortaleza, August 6, 1966. File S, PVCB.

"Demagogia em torno da exportação de minérios." *O Estado de S. Paulo*, December 18, 1964.

Departamento Intersindical de Estatística e Estudos Sócio-Econômicos [DIEESE]. "Política Salarial." São Paulo, n.d.

_______. "Nota sobre a Política Salarial." São Paulo, n.d.

_______. "10 Anos de Política Salarial." São Paulo, 1975.

Diário da Noite [Recife newspaper]. Issue of May 5, 1966.

Diário da Noite [São Paulo newspaper]. Issues of April 1, 5, 1966.

Diário de Notícias [Rio de Janeiro newspaper]. Issues of 1966–1967.

Diário do Congresso National [Brasília]. Issues of June 27, 1964; May 13, 1967.

Diário do Executivo [Belo Horizonte, Minas Gerais]. Issue of June 27, 1964.

Diário Oficial [Brasília]. Issues of 1964–1967.

Diário Oficial [São Paulo]. Issues of April 2, June 22, 1966.

Diário Popular [São Paulo]. Issue of April 1, 1966.

Dias, Nina Castello Branco Santos. Interview, Rio de Janeiro, July 12, 1977.

Diniz, Antonietta Castello Branco. Interview, Rio de Janeiro, December 13, 1975.

Duarte Filho, João. Letter to HACB, Rio de Janeiro, April 20, 1965. File N1, CPDOC.

Ellis, Howard S. (ed.). *The Economy of Brazil.* Berkeley and Los Angeles: University of California Press, 1969.

Encarnação, Antônio. Interview, Rio de Janeiro, December 14, 1966.

Escobar, Décio Palmeiro de. *Discursos, 1965–1966.* N.d.

_______. *Despedida do General Décio Palmeiro de Escobar.* Rio de Janeiro: Estado-Maior do Exército, Ministério da Guerra, 1966.

_______. Memorandum to HACB, Rio de Janeiro, February 1, 1966. File P2, CPDOC.

_______. "Meu Pensamento a Respeito do Quadro Sucessório." Memorandum for HACB, n.d. Copy in possession of JWFD.

_______. Interview, Rio de Janeiro, July 25, 1977.

Escola Interamericana de Administração Pública. *Aspectos da Reforma Tributária.* Monograph No. 4, Instrumentos Administrativos de Implementação Econômica. Fundação Getúlio Vargas. Rio de Janeiro, 1967.

_______. *Instrumentos da Política Cafeeira.* 2 vols. Monograph No. 9, Instrumentos Administrativos de Implementação Econômica. Fundação Getúlio Vargas. Rio de Janeiro, 1967.

Estado de S. Paulo, O [São Paulo newspaper]. Issues of 1964–1967.

Fagundes, Seabra. Declaration in *Jornal do Brasil,* August 31, 1966.

Falcão, Armando. Letters to HACB, Rio de Janeiro, October 5, 1965; Quixerámobim, July 7, 1967. Files N1 and EX3, CPDOC.

_______. Interview, Rio de Janeiro, October 10, 1975.

Farias, Osvaldo Cordeiro de. Interviews, Rio de Janeiro, December 16, 26, 1974.

Fernandes, Hélio. *Recordações de um Desterrado em Fernando de Noronha.* Rio de Janeiro: Editora Tribuna da Imprensa, 1967.

_______. "JK não assina mas dá adesão." *Tribuna da Imprensa,* October 28, 1966.

_______. Articles occasioned by the death of HACB. *Tribuna da Imprensa,* July 19, 1967.

_______. Interview, Rio de Janeiro, July 6, 1977.

Ferraz, Otávio Marcondes. Letter disassociating himself from UDN. *O Estado de S. Paulo,* September, 2, 1964.

_______. "Castello Branco." Paper prepared for Luís Viana Filho, n.d. Copy in possession of PVCB.

Fiechter, Georges-André. *Brazil since 1964: Modernization under a Military Régime.* New York and Toronto: John Wiley & Sons, 1975.

Flores, J. O. Melo. Interview, Rio de Janeiro, December 20, 1977.

Flynn, Peter. *Brazil: A Political Analysis.* London: Ernest Benn Limited, 1978.

Folha de S. Paulo. Special section, July 17, 1977, "Castelo Branco: O Homem e a Obra," with articles by Luiz Vianna Filho, Mem de Sá, Octávio Gouvea de Bulhões, Roberto de Oliveira Campos, Severo Gomes, Carlos Medeiros Silva, Roberto de Abreu Sodré, Cordeiro de Farias, Paulo Egídio Martins, Laudo Natel, Délio Jardim de Mattos, Guilherme Rebello Silva, Francisco Negrão de Lima, Paulo Castelo Branco, Ricardo Arnt, Plínio Catanhede, and Aliomar Baleeiro.

"Fórmula de Castello, A." *Jornal do Brasil,* February 3, 1976.

Frade, Wilson, "Notas de um repórter." *Estado de Minas,* February 22, 1976.

Franco, Afonso Arinos de Melo. *Planalto: Memórias.* Rio de Janeiro: Livraria José Olympio Editora, 1968.

_______. Excerpts from Senate speech arguing for "individual rights" chapter in new constitution. *O Estado de S. Paulo,* December 20, 1966.

_______. Interview, Rio de Janeiro, October 31, 1975.

Freeman, Orville L. Memorandum to President Lyndon B. Johnson, Department of Agriculture, Washington, D.C., April 27, 1966. Copy in LBJ Library, Austin, Texas.

Freire, Victorino. *Defesa do General Ernesto Geisel: Discurso proferido no Senado Federal, na sessão de 8 de novembro de 1967.* Brasília, 1967.

———. Letters to HACB, Rio de Janeiro, July 26, 1965; Brasília, December 8, 1965. File N1, CPDOC.

———. Interview, Rio de Janeiro, December 10, 1975.

Furtado, Celia Azusem and Roberto Azusem. Letters to HACB, Lisbon, May 31, 1967. File EX3, CPDOC.

Gama, José Santos de Saldanha da. Letter to HACB, Rio de Janeiro, August 19, 1964. File R2, CPDOC.

———. Interview, Rio de Janeiro, October 24, 1966.

Gaud, William S. "Brazil Program Loan." Memorandum for Walt Rostow, The White House, Washington, D.C., November 18, 1966. National Security Files, LBJ Library, Austin, Texas.

———. "Economic Assistance Program for Brazil." Memorandum for Lyndon B. Johnson, [1966], Office of the Administrator, AID, Washington, D.C. National Security Files, LBJ Library, Austin, Texas.

Gazeta, A [São Paulo]. Issue of April 1, 1966.

Globo, O [Rio de Janeiro newspaper]. Issues of 1964–1967, 1978.

Godinho, Antônio. Interview, São Paulo, November 7, 1975.

Gomes, Henrique Sousa. Letter to HACB [Rome, July 1965]. File O2, PVCB.

Gomes, Lúcia Maria Gaspar. "Cronologia do govêrno Castelo Branco." *Dados*, 1967.

Gomes, Severo. Interview, Rio de Janeiro, July 25, 1977.

Gonçalves, Beatriz Castello Branco. Interview, Rio de Janeiro, July 12, 1977.

Gordon, Lincoln. Telegrams and memorandums from the Embassy of the United States, Rio de Janeiro, to Department of State and others in Washington, D.C., 1964–1966. Copies in LBJ Library, Austin, Texas.

———. AID presentations on Brazil, 1964–1966. National Security Files, LBJ Library, Austin, Texas.

———. "Recollections of President Castello Branco." Typewritten manuscript prepared at the request of Luís Viana Filho, Washington, D.C., July 28, 1972. Copy in possession of JWFD.

———. "Castello perdeu a batalha." Interview. *Veja*, March 9, 1977.

———. Interview, Washington, D.C., June 11, 1975.

Gralla, A. R. Letter to HACB, at sea enroute to Salvador, Brazil, November 18, 1965. File R2, CPDOC.

Grau, Werner. Interview, Rio de Janeiro, December 27, 1974.

"Gritos de desespêro, após o choque." Newspaper clipping, July 1967. File EX4, CPDOC.

Gudin, Eugênio. Letter to HACB, April 6, 1965. File M, CPDOC.

———. "Ato Institucional No. 2." *O Globo*, October 29, 1965.

______. Declarations in Petrópolis about cruzeiro devaluation. *Correio da Manhã*, February 11, 1967.

______. "Para Presidente da República Humberto de Alencar Castello Branco." *O Globo*, January 2, 1978.

Guedes, Carlos Luís. *Tinha que Ser Minas*. Rio de Janeiro: Editora Nova Fronteira, 1979.

Guerra, Paulo. Letter and telegram to HACB, n.d. File N1, CPDOC.

______. Interview, Brasília, November 11, 1975.

Heller, Frederico. "Doutrina e ação econômicas de Castello Branco." *O Estado de S. Paulo*, May 19, 1976.

______. Interview, São Paulo, November 10, 1975.

"Inatividade dos Militares da Marinha, da Aeronáutica e do Exército." Law 4902 of December 16, 1965. *Diário Oficial*, December 20, 1965.

"Influential Brazilian: Humberto Alencar Castelo Branco." *New York Times*, April 6, 1964.

Institute for the Comparative Study of Political Systems. *Brazil: Election Factbook*. No. 2, September 1965. Washington, D.C., 1965.

Jaccoud, Vera. Interview, Rio de Janeiro, December 14, 1966.

Jobim, Danton Pinheiro. Interview, Brasília, October 22, 1975.

Johnson, Lyndon B. Letters to HACB, 1964–1967. File O1, PVCB, and Papers of Lyndon B. Johnson, LBJ Library, Austin, Texas.

Jornal da Tarde [São Paulo newspaper]. Issues of 1964–1967.

______. Articles about Press Law. January 1967.

______. "Castello Branco: Dez anos depois de sua trágica morte." Articles by Antônio Carbone, JWFD, and another [unsigned]. July 17, 1977.

Jornal do Brasil [Rio de Janeiro newspaper]. Issues of 1964–1967, 1972, 1976, 1977.

Jornal, O [Rio de Janeiro newspaper]. Issues of 1965–1967.

Krieger, Daniel. *Desde as Missões . . . : Saudades, Lutas, Esperanças*. Rio de Janeiro: Livraria José Olympio Editora, 1976.

______. Interviews, Brasília, October 21, 22, 1975.

Kruel, Amauri. Manifesto. *Jornal do Brasil*, August 11, 1966.

______. Interviews, Rio de Janeiro, December 11, 1975; July 22, 1977.

Kruel, Riograndino. Letter to HACB, August 11, 1966. File M, CPDOC.

______. Interview, Rio de Janeiro, September 21, 1975.

Kurzman, Dan. "Arrests Estimated at 10,000: Brazil Caught in Grip of Army Dictatorship." *Washington Post*, May 3, 1964.

Lacerda, Carlos. *Depoimento*. Rio de Janeiro: Editora Nova Fronteira S.A., 1978.

______. Letters to HACB, 1964–1966. File N4, CPDOC.

———. "Programa Econômico-Financiero." 55-page typewritten study sent to HACB with covering letter of May 17, 1965. File N4, CPDOC.
———. Letter to Gildo Corrêa Ferraz, Rio de Janeiro, February 24, 1966. File N5, CPDOC.
———. Interview about iron ore. *Manchete*, September 5, 1964.
———. "Em Defesa da Revolução." *Tribuna da Imprensa*, December 2, 1964.
———. "A Revolução ou a Hanna." *Tribuna da Imprensa*, December 3, 1964.
———. "O Golpe da inelegibilidade." *O Estado de S. Paulo*, March 2, 1966.
———. "O Paraguai e o silêncio." *O Estado de S. Paulo*, March 23, 1966.
———. "O Que Pensa e o Que Quer." *Correio da Manhã*, September 2, 1966 [reprint of a recent article in *Visão*].
———. "Os 10 Pecados da Revolução São 11." *O Cruzeiro*, December 10, 1966.
———. "A força de intervenção armada" and "A recuperação do Itamarati." *Tribuna da Imprensa* articles, n.d. File N6, CPDOC.
———. "Como choram os pequeninos." Newspaper article, n.d. File N5, CPDOC.
———. Interviews, Rio de Janeiro, September 23, 1975; Tucson, Arizona, February 17, 18, 1976.
Lacerda, Flávio Suplici de. Letter to HACB, November 4, 1965. File M, CPDOC.
———. Interview, Brasília, October 16, 1965.
Lacombe, Arnaldo. Letter to HACB, July 7, 1967. File EX3, CPDOC.
———. Interview with HACB [under the heading "A Última Palavra de Castello"]. *Visão*, July 28, 1967.
Lavanère-Wanderley, Nelson Freire. Written statement about HACB presidency prepared for Luís Viana Filho, n.d. Copy in possession of Nelson Freire Lavanère-Wanderley.
———. Interviews, Rio de Janeiro, December 10, 1974; August 12, 1977.
Leal, Wilson. *See* Aymoré, Artur.
Leão Filho, José. "Uma Operação de 5 Minutos." *Jornal do Brasil*, October 21, 1966.
Leite, Cleantho de Paiva. Interview, Rio de Janeiro, December 14, 1974.
Leite, Júlio César do Prado. Interview, Rio de Janeiro, December 20, 1974. Also papers about wages and wage legislation received at the interview and with his letter, Rio de Janeiro, December 9, 1975.

Leonardos, Thomas. Interview, Rio de Janeiro, September 19, 1975.

Lerner, Max. "Brazil's Paradoxical Regime." *Evening Star* [Washington, D.C.], April 30, 1966.

_______. "Brazil's Castelo Branco Shy and Introverted." *Evening Star* [Washington, D.C.], May 3, 1966.

Levy, Herbert V. *Revolução: Erros e Acertos*. Brasília: Senado Federal, n.d.

_______. Interview, São Paulo, November 7, 1975.

Lima, Afonso de Albuquerque. Interviews, Rio de Janeiro, November 16, 20, 1974.

Lima, Francisco Negrão de. Handwritten memorandums for Luís Viana Filho and JWFD, n.d.

_______. Interview, Rio de Janeiro, December 10, 1975.

Lindenberg, José. Remarks at ceremony marking HACB's promotion to *general de divisão*, Rio de Janeiro, September 25, 1958. Typewritten. File G1, Castello Branco Collection, CPDOC.

Lins, Etelvino. *Um Depoimento Político: Episódios e Observações*. Rio de Janeiro: Livraria José Olympio Editora, 1977.

Lopes, Lucas. Testimony, March 17, 1965, at Parliamentary Investigating Commission examining Hanna. *Diário do Congresso Nacional*, Seção I, Suplemento ao No. 54. Brasília, May 13, 1967, pp. 78–87.

Lott, Henrique Batista Duffles Teixeira. Interview, Rio de Janeiro, October 13, 1975.

Ludwig, Armin K., and Harry W. Taylor. *Brazil's New Agrarian Reform: An Evaluation of Its Property Classification and Tax Systems*. New York, Washington, and London: Frederick A. Praeger, 1969.

Luz, Ivan. "Parecer da Comissão Mista, sôbre o Projeto de Lei No. 23 de 1966," with amendments submitted by members of the commission studying the Press Law, n.d. Copy in possession of JWFD.

_______. Interview, Brasília, October 27, 1975.

Macedo, Zilmar Campos de Araripe. Letter to João Carlos Palhares dos Santos, Rio de Janeiro, March 29, 1967. File R2, CPDOC.

_______. Interview, Rio de Janeiro, August 9, 1977.

Magalhães, Antônio Carlos. Interview, Rio de Janeiro, August 11, 1977.

Magalhães, Juracy. *Minha Experiência Diplomática*. Rio de Janeiro: Livraria José Olympio Editora, 1971.

_______. Letters to HACB, Washington, D.C., 1965. File 02, PVCB.

_______. Letter to Thomas C. Mann, Rio de Janeiro, November 30, 1965. National Security Files, LBJ Library, Austin, Texas.

_______. "Juraci acha que Lacerda é ciclotímico." Letter from Juraci Magalhães. *Jornal do Brasil*, November 23, 1966.

———. "Respostas do General Juracy Magalhães ao Professor John W. F. Dulles," Rio de Janeiro, December 3, 1974. Typewritten.

———. Interview, Rio de Janeiro, December 3, 1974.

Magalhães, Rafael de Almeida. Interviews, Rio de Janeiro, November 19, 1975; August 8, December 21, 1977.

Mann, Thomas C. Cables from Department of State (Washington, D.C.) to United States Embassy, Rio de Janeiro, 1964–1965. National Security Files, LBJ Library, Austin, Texas.

———. Message to The White House, Washington, D.C., December 8, 1965. National Security Files, LBJ Library, Austin, Texas.

———. Interview, Austin, Texas, September 4, 1975.

Maranhão, Délio. *See* Sussekind, Arnaldo.

Marinho, Roberto. Letter to HACB, May 24, 1966. File M, CPDOC.

———. Interview, Rio de Janeiro, August 11, 1977.

Martinelli, Osneli. Interview, Rio de Janeiro, October 12, 1966.

Martins, Paulo Egydio. *Revolução e Progresso: Discursos e Pronunciamentos.* Ministério da Indústria e do Comércio, 1966.

———. Interview, São Paulo, November 10, 1975.

Mattos, Carlos de Meira. Interviews, Washington, D.C., January 5, August 2, 1976; March 18, 1977.

———, and officers of FAIBRÁS. *A Experiência do FAIBRÁS na República Dominicana.* N.d.

Mattos, Haroldo. Interview, Rio de Janeiro, December 21, 1977.

Melo, Márcio de Sousa e. Letters to HACB, Rio de Janeiro, January 6, 1965. File R2, CPDOC.

———. Interview, Rio de Janeiro, December 17, 1965.

Mercadante, Luiz Fernando. "Este É o Humberto." *Realidade,* June 1966.

Mesquita, Rui. Interview, São Paulo, November 6, 1975.

———, and Gilles Lapouge. *31/3.* São Paulo: Editôra Anhambi S.A., 1964.

Ministério da Aeronáutica, Inspectoria Geral da Aeronáutica, Serviço de Investigação e Prevenção de Acidentes Aeronáuticos. Final report [on plane crash in which HACB was killed]. November 2, 1967. File EX4, CPDOC.

Ministério da Agricultura, Instituto Nacional do Desenvolvimento Agrário [INDA]. *The Land Statute: Law 4504 of November 30, 1964.* Rio de Janeiro: INDA's Assessoria de Informação Agrária, n.d.

———, ———. *Regulamento Geral: Decreto No. 55890 de 31 de março de 1965.* Departamento de Imprensa Nacional, 1965.

———, ———. *1st National Assembly of Mayors of Brazil's Model*

Municipalities, Promoted by INDA, Held in Rio de Janeiro, April 11–15, 1966: Basic Document. Rio de Janeiro: INDA's Assessoria de Informação Agrária, n.d.

_______, _______. *The Church, the State and the Agrarian Development in Brazil: INDA's Invitation to the Church for a New Role.* Rio de Janeiro: INDA's Assessoria de Informação Agrária, n.d.

Ministério da Guerra. *Almanaque do Exército, 1966.*

_______. *Lista de Endereções de Oficiais-Generais: Até 30 de Julho de 1965.* Rio de Janeiro: Imprensa do Exército, 1965.

Ministério da Indústria e do Comércio. *Seis Mêses de Ação.* Volta Redonda: SIDERGRÁFICA, [January–June 1966].

Ministério da Saúde. *Cartilha de Saúde.* Rio de Janeiro, 1967.

Ministério da Viação e Obras Públicas. *Programa de Ação Imediata: Triênio 1964–1966.* Documento CE No. 1. Rio de Janeiro: Serviço de Documentação, 1965.

_______. *O Nôvo Plano Nacional de Viação.* Documento CE No. 2. Rio de Janeiro: Serviço de Documentação, 1965.

Ministério do Interior. *Jurisdição e Competência.* Rio de Janeiro, 1967.

Ministério do Planejamento e Coordenação Econômica. *Programa de Ação Econômica do Govêrno, 1964–1966 (Síntese), Incluindo a Versão Revista do Programa de Investimentos para 1965.* 2d ed. Documentos EPEA (Escritório de Pesquisa Econômica Aplicada), May 1965.

_______. *O Programa de Ação e as Reformas de Base.* 2 vols. Documentos EPEA (Escritório de Pesquisa Econômica Aplicada), December 1965.

Ministério do Planejamento e Coordenação Geral. *Anuário Estatístico do Brasil, 1972.* Rio de Janeiro: Instituto Brasileiro de Estatística, 1972.

Ministério Extraordinário para a Coordenação dos Organismos Regionais. *Uma Nova Filosofia de Govêrno.* Serviço Gráfico do IBGE, [1966 or 1967].

Morais, Ângelo Mendes de. Letter to HACB, n.d. File N1, CPDOC.

Morais, Frederico Mendes de. Interview, Rio de Janeiro, December 20, 1975.

Morais Neto, Prudente de. Interviews, Rio de Janeiro, October 8, November 15, 1975.

Morel, Edmar. *O Golpe Começou em Washington.* Rio de Janeiro: Editôra Civilização Brasileira S.A., 1965.

Mota, Santana. "Mantém discrição." Newspaper article, dated Lisbon, May 30, 1967. File EX3, CPDOC.

Moura, Arthur S. Interviews, Rio de Janeiro, December 11, 1974; July 19, 1976.

Mourão, Américo Soverchi. Report about the health of HACB, Brasília,

April 2, 1975. Typewritten, 3 pages, no title. Copy in possession of JWFD.

Movimento Democrático Brasileiro [MDB]. Manifesto approved by national executive group and directive commission, Chamber of Deputies, Brasília, February 10, 1966. File P2, CPDOC.

Müller, Henrique G. Interview, Rio de Janeiro, July 25, 1977.

Murici, Antônio Carlos da Silva. Letter to Golberi do Couto e Silva, Itamaracá, December 3, 1965. File N1, CPDOC.

———. Letters to HACB, Recife, March, April, May 1966. File N1, CPDOC.

———. Interview, Rio de Janeiro, November 18, 1975.

Murici, Virgínia. Letter to HACB, Recife, May 18, 1966. File N1, CPDOC.

Nery, Sebastião. *Folclore Político: 350 Histórias da Política Brasileira.* 2d ed. Rio de Janeiro: Editora Tora Ltda., [1973].

———. *Folclore Político: Mais 350 Histórias.* Rio de Janeiro: Editora Record, n.d.

Neves, Conceição da Costa. Declarations reported in *O Jornal*, April 1, 1966; *A Gazeta*, April 1, 1966; *Diário da Noite* [São Paulo], April 1, 5, 1966; *Diário Oficial* [São Paulo], April 2, June 22, August 11, 1966; *Correio da Manhã*, April 2, 1966.

———. Letter to JWFD, São Paulo, September 16, 1977.

———. Interview, São Paulo, August 1, 1977.

Neves, Levy. Letter to HACB, Rio de Janeiro, August 9, 1965. File N1, CPDOC.

Neves, Tancredo. Interview, Brasília, October 22, 1975.

New York Times. Issues of 1964 and 1967.

Nogueira, Dênio. "A Desvalorização Cambial de 1967," Rio de Janeiro, February 14, 1979. Typewritten. In possession of JWFD.

———. Interview with Byron Coelho, Rio de Janeiro, February 1979.

———. Interview, Rio de Janeiro, December 20, 1977.

Nova Lei de Estabilidade: Fundo de Garantia do Tempo de Serviço. Rio de Janeiro: Gráfica Auriverde, Ltda., 1966.

Nôvo Regulamento do Impôsto de Renda. Rio de Janeiro: Gráfica Auriverde, Ltda., 1966.

Oliveira, Euclides Quandt de. Interview, Brasília, October 21, 1975.

Olympio, José. Letter to HACB, Rio de Janeiro, March 5, 1966. File N1, CPDOC.

———. Interview, Rio de Janeiro, December 22, 1977.

Padilha, Raimundo. *Popularidade e Estima Pública: Homenagem Póstuma da Câmara dos Deputados ao Presidente Humberto de A. Castello*

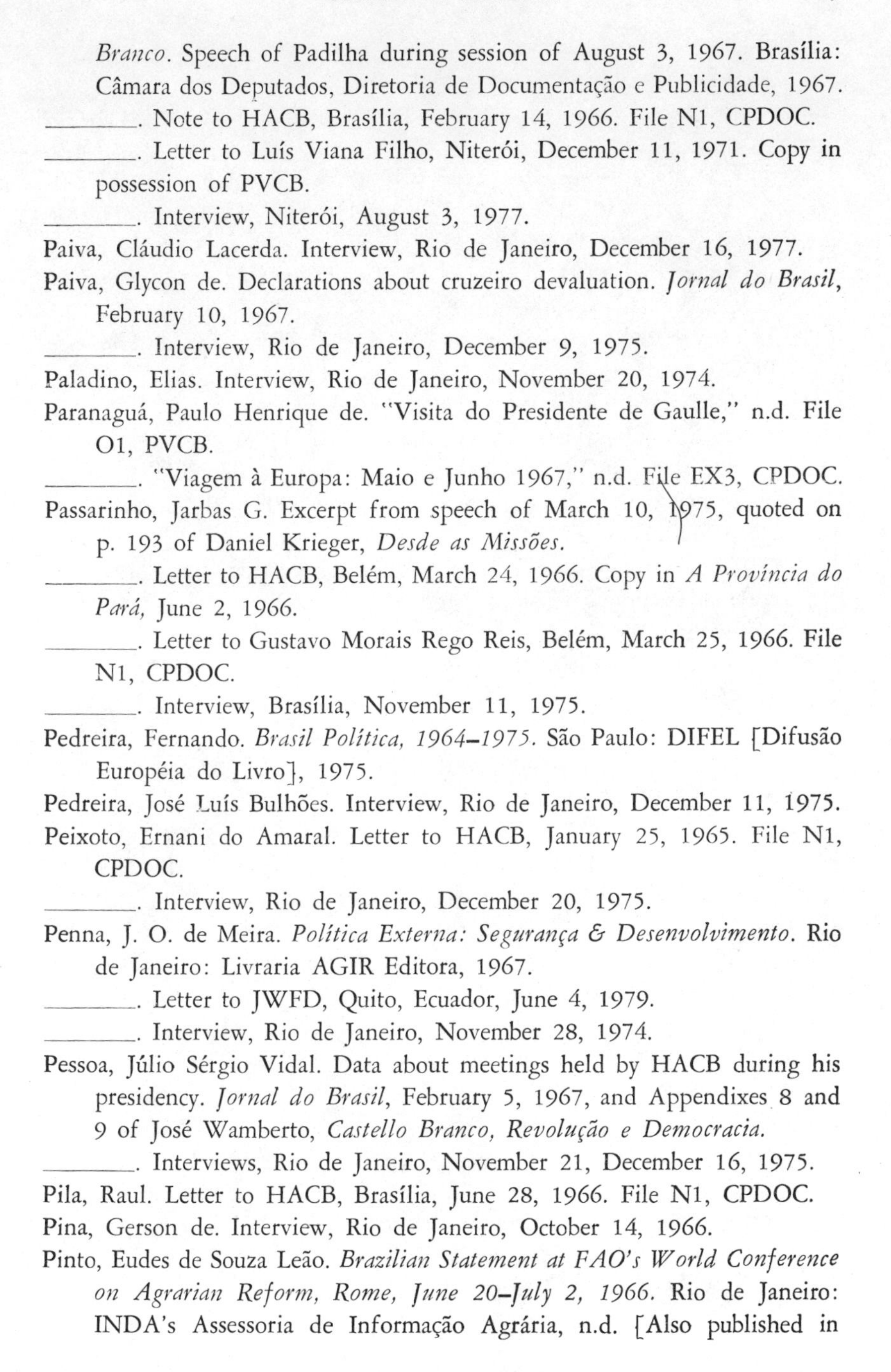

Branco. Speech of Padilha during session of August 3, 1967. Brasília: Câmara dos Deputados, Diretoria de Documentação e Publicidade, 1967.

_______. Note to HACB, Brasília, February 14, 1966. File N1, CPDOC.

_______. Letter to Luís Viana Filho, Niterói, December 11, 1971. Copy in possession of PVCB.

_______. Interview, Niterói, August 3, 1977.

Paiva, Cláudio Lacerda. Interview, Rio de Janeiro, December 16, 1977.

Paiva, Glycon de. Declarations about cruzeiro devaluation. *Jornal do Brasil*, February 10, 1967.

_______. Interview, Rio de Janeiro, December 9, 1975.

Paladino, Elias. Interview, Rio de Janeiro, November 20, 1974.

Paranaguá, Paulo Henrique de. "Visita do Presidente de Gaulle," n.d. File O1, PVCB.

_______. "Viagem à Europa: Maio e Junho 1967," n.d. File EX3, CPDOC.

Passarinho, Jarbas G. Excerpt from speech of March 10, 1975, quoted on p. 193 of Daniel Krieger, *Desde as Missões.*

_______. Letter to HACB, Belém, March 24, 1966. Copy in *A Província do Pará,* June 2, 1966.

_______. Letter to Gustavo Morais Rego Reis, Belém, March 25, 1966. File N1, CPDOC.

_______. Interview, Brasília, November 11, 1975.

Pedreira, Fernando. *Brasil Política, 1964–1975.* São Paulo: DIFEL [Difusão Européia do Livro], 1975.

Pedreira, José Luís Bulhões. Interview, Rio de Janeiro, December 11, 1975.

Peixoto, Ernani do Amaral. Letter to HACB, January 25, 1965. File N1, CPDOC.

_______. Interview, Rio de Janeiro, December 20, 1975.

Penna, J. O. de Meira. *Política Externa: Segurança & Desenvolvimento.* Rio de Janeiro: Livraria AGIR Editora, 1967.

_______. Letter to JWFD, Quito, Ecuador, June 4, 1979.

_______. Interview, Rio de Janeiro, November 28, 1974.

Pessoa, Júlio Sérgio Vidal. Data about meetings held by HACB during his presidency. *Jornal do Brasil*, February 5, 1967, and Appendixes 8 and 9 of José Wamberto, *Castello Branco, Revolução e Democracia.*

_______. Interviews, Rio de Janeiro, November 21, December 16, 1975.

Pila, Raul. Letter to HACB, Brasília, June 28, 1966. File N1, CPDOC.

Pina, Gerson de. Interview, Rio de Janeiro, October 14, 1966.

Pinto, Eudes de Souza Leão. *Brazilian Statement at FAO's World Conference on Agrarian Reform, Rome, June 20–July 2, 1966.* Rio de Janeiro: INDA's Assessoria de Informação Agrária, n.d. [Also published in

Portuguese with the title of *O Brasil em Face da Reforma Agrária.*]
———. Interview, Rio de Janeiro, December 2, 1966.
Pinto, Heráclito Fontoura Sobral. Interview, Rio de Janeiro, December 9, 1975.
Pinto, José de Magalhães. Letters to HACB, 1964, 1965. File N3, CPDOC.
———. Letter to HACB, October 16, 1964 [about Hanna]. *Correio da Manhã*, November 15, 1964.
———. Letter to HACB, December 15, 1964 [about Hanna]. *Jornal do Brasil*, December 17, 1964.
———. Declarations in newspapers, 1964–1967. Clippings in File N3, CPDOC.
———. Interview, Brasília, October 24, 1975.
Pinto, Olavo Bilac. Interview, Brasília, October 21, 1975.
———, and Carminha Pinto. Cable to HACB, [1967]. File EX3, CPDOC.
Portugal, Francisco Damasceno Ferreira. Telegram to HACB, [Recife, May 1966]. File N1, CPDOC.
Povo, O [Fortaleza newspaper]. Issues of 1967 and 1968.
Presidência da República, Gabinete Militar. *Lista de Endereços e Telefones, 2° semestre, 1966.*
———, Instituto Brasileiro de Reforma Agrária. *Estatuto da Terra: Lei No. 4504, de 30 de novembro de 1964.* Departamento de Imprensa Nacional, 1965.
———, ———. *Instrução Especial IBRA No. 1.* Departmento de Imprensa Nacional, 1965.
———, ———. *Nucleo Alexandre de Gusmão, Distrito Federal: Proyecto Ejecutivo para la Radicaciós de 1,000 Colonos: Sintesis.* IBRA, 1966.
Pupo Neto, Trajano. Interviews, São Paulo, November 15, 1975; July 27, 1977.
Queiroz, Ademar de. Letter to HACB, May 27, 1963. File L2, CPDOC.
Queiroz, Rachel de. Quoted in *O Povo* [Fortaleza newspaper], July 21, 1967, and in *Jornal do Brasil*, July 17, 1972.
———. Interviews, Rio de Janeiro, November 15, 1974; July 25, 1976; July 3, 1977.
Raine, Philip. *Brazil: Awakening Giant.* Washington, D.C.: Public Affairs Press, 1974.
———. Cables to Washington, D.C., from United States Embassy, Rio de Janeiro, 1965–1966. National Security Files, LBJ Library, Austin, Texas.
———. Interview, Rio de Janeiro, October 6, 1966.

Ramos, João Batista. Report on petition of Carlos Pena Boto, Brasília, n.d. File R2, CPDOC.

Read, Benjamin H. Memorandum to McGeorge Bundy, February 4, 1966. Papers of Lyndon B. Johnson, LBJ Library, Austin, Texas.

———. "Inflation in Brazil." Memorandum for Walt W. Rostow, Department of State, Washington, D.C., January 13, 1967. LBJ Library, Austin, Texas.

Reforma Administrativa: Legislação Completa e Atualizada. Rio de Janeiro: Gráfica Auriverde, Ltda., 1974.

Reis, Artur César Ferreira. Memorandum for Luís Viana Filho, n.d. Typewritten. Copy in the possession of PVCB.

———. Interview, Rio de Janeiro, September 29, 1975.

Reis, Gustavo Morais Rego. Interviews, Brasília, October 22, 23, 1975.

Reis, Levy Penna Aarão. Letter to HACB, Rio de Janeiro, January 15, 1965. File R2, CPDOC.

———. Interview, Rio de Janeiro, December 15, 1977.

———, Ernesto de Mello Baptista, Waldeck Lisboa Vampré, Mário Cavalcanti de Albuquerque, and Armando Zenha de Figueiredo. "O Segundo Revez Político na Aviação Naval (1964) ou O Escandalo da Aviação Embarcada," Rio de Janeiro, 1965. Typewritten (42 pp.). Copy in possession of JWFD.

República do Brasil. *Coleção das Leis, 1967. Vol. 1: Atos do Poder Legislativo; Atos Legislativos do Poder Executivo; Leis de Janeiro a Março.* Departmento da Imprensa Nacional, 1967.

Revista Brasileira de Política Internacional. Journal of the Instituto Brasileiro de Relações Internacionais, Rio de Janeiro. Ano VII, Nos. 26, 27 (June, September 1964), Ano VIII, Nos. 30, 31, 32 (June, September, December 1965).

Revista Civilização Brasileira. Vol. I, Nos, 3, 4. Rio de Janeiro, 1965.

Rocha, Remo. *Ofício* to José de Medeiros Delgado, Fortaleza, July 22, 1966. File S, PVCB.

Rodrigues, Eduardo Lopes. "Tributação dos Dividendos de Ações ao Portador" and "Arrecadação das Rendas Federais através dos Estabelecimentos Bancários," n.d. Typewritten. In possession of JWFD.

———. Interview, Rio de Janeiro, August 10, 1979.

Roett, Riordan. *Brazil: Politics in a Patrimonial Society.* Rev. ed. New York: Praeger Publishers, 1978.

——— (ed.). *Brazil in the Sixties.* Nashville: Vanderbilt University Press, 1972.

Rosenbaum, H. Ron, and William G. Tylor (eds.). *Contemporary Brazil: Issues in Economic and Political Development.* New York, Washington, and London: Praeger Publishers, 1972.

Rossi, Agnelo. Letter to HACB, São Paulo, August 20, 1966. File S, PVCB.

Rusk, Dean. Cables from Department of State (Washington, D.C.) to United States Embassy, Rio de Janeiro, 1964–1965. National Security Files, LBJ Library, Austin, Texas.

———. *See* Cunha, Vasco Leitão da.

Sá, Mem de. *O Problema da Remessa de Lucros.* [Rio de Janeiro]: Associação Comercial da Guanabara, 1962.

———. Typewritten papers about HACB: "Castelo e os Parlamentares" (2 pp.), "Processos e táticas do Presidente" (3 pp.), "Um Plano que Quase Deu Certo . . ." (1 p.), "A Ternura de Castelo Branco" (2 pp.), n.d. Copies in possession of JWFD.

———. Letters to Luís Viana Filho, Brasília, October 7, 1971, 18 pp. and 2 pp. Copies in possession of PVCB.

———. Interview, Rio de Janeiro, October 31, 1975.

"Salazar recebe Castelo." Newspaper clipping [June 1976]. File EX3, CPDOC.

Salles, José Bento Teixeira de. *Milton Campos: Uma vocação liberal.* Belo Horizonte: Editora Vega S.A., 1975.

Sampaio, Cid. Telegram and letter to HACB, Recife and Rio de Janeiro, March 1966. File N1, CPDOC.

Sandoval, Fernando (with some collaboration from Hugo Estenssoro and Paulo Sérgio Pinheiro). "E o Brasil quase foi à guerra: A história das frustradas negociações para o envio de tropas brasileiras ao Vietnã." *Istoé,* December 14, 1977.

Santos, João Carlos Palhares dos. "Depoimento sôbre a Minha Convivência com o Presidente Humberto Castello Branco, prestado ao Seu Historiador, Dr. Luiz Vianna Filho," São Paulo, December 1971. File R2, PVCB.

———. Interview, Rio de Janeiro, November 22, 1975.

Santos, Rui. Letter to HACB, Brasília, June 17, 1966. File N1, CPDOC.

———. Interview, Brasília, October 27, 1975.

Sarasate, Paulo. *A Constituição do Brasil ao alcance de todos.* Rio de Janeiro and São Paulo: Livraria Freitas Bastos, 1967.

———. Letters to HACB, Fortaleza and Brasília, 1966, 1967. File N1, CPDOC.

Sarney, José. Letters to HACB, São Luís, February 1966. Telegram to HACB, [July 1967]. Files N1 and EX3, CPDOC.

Sátiro, Ernani. Letter to JWFD, Rio de Janeiro, January 20, 1976.

_______. Interview, Rio de Janeiro, December 17, 1975.

Sayre, Robert M. Memorandums, The White House, Washington, D.C., 1964. National Security Files, LBJ Library, Austin, Texas.

Schilling, Paulo R. *Hélder Câmara.* Montevideo: Biblioteca de Marcha, 1969.

Schlesinger, Arthur M., Jr., *Robert Kennedy and His Times.* Boston: Houghton Mifflin Company, 1978.

Schmitter, Philippe C. *Interest Conflict and Political Change in Brazil.* Stanford: Stanford University Press, 1971.

Schneider, Ronald M. *The Political System of Brazil: Emergence of a "Modernizing" Authoritarian Regime, 1964–1970.* New York and London: Columbia University Press, 1971.

_______. *Brazil: Foreign Policy of a Future World Power.* Boulder: Westview Press, 1976.

"Segurança irá sufocar a imprensa." *O Estado de S. Paulo,* March 14, 1967.

Senado Federal. *Lista de Endereços dos Senhores Senadores.* Brasília, 1965.

_______, Directoria de Informação Legislativa. *Lei Orgânica dos Partidos Políticos: Histórico da Lei No. 4740, de 15 de Julho de 1965.* 2 vols. Brasília: Senado Federal, Serviço Gráfico, n.d.

_______, _______. *Reforma Agrária.* 2 vols. Brasília: Serviço Gráfico do Senado Federal, 1969.

_______, Divisão de Edições Técnicas. *Legislação Constitucional e Complementar.* Brasília, 1972.

Serpa, Luís Gonzaga Andrada. Letter to HACB, Paris, November 24, 1965. File N1, CPDOC.

Shaw, Paul Vanorden. "Central Bank Starts Activities." *Brazil Herald,* April 14, 1965.

Silva, Álcio Barbosa da Costa e. Interview, Rio de Janeiro, July 15, 1977.

Silva, Artur da Costa e. "Costa e Silva Relata Episódios da Revolução." Speech at ECEME, April 1, 1965. *O Estado de S. Paulo,* April 4, 1965.

_______. Speech at Escola de Aperfeiçoamento de Oficiais, Vila Militar, June 21, 1965. Transcript of tape recording loaned by Álcio da Costa e Silva.

_______. Speech at First Infantry Regiment, Vila Militar, October 6, 1965. Transcript of tape recording loaned by Álcio da Costa e Silva.

_______. Speech at closing of maneuvers at Itapeva, São Paulo, October 22, 1965. Transcript of tape recording loaned by Álcio da Costa e Silva.

_______. Interview given to Rádio Gazeta of São Paulo, at Rio de Janeiro residence of war minister, October 28, 1965. Transcript of tape recording loaned by Álcio da Costa e Silva.

Silva, Carlos Medeiros. Interviews, Rio de Janeiro, November 12, December 18, 1975; July 22, August 9, 13, 1977.

Silva, Luís Antônio da Gama e. Interviews, São Paulo, November 18, 1966; November 5, 1975.

Silva, Luís Gonzaga do Nascimento. Interview, Brasília, October 25, 1975.

Silva, Luís Mendes da. "Testemunho." Typewritten manuscript received from PVCB, 1974.

Silva, Sebastião de Sant'Anna e. Memorandums to JWFD, Rio de Janeiro, June, July 1979.

_______. Interviews, Rio de Janeiro, June 30, August 4, 1979.

Silva, Yolanda Costa e. Interview, Rio de Janeiro, July 15, 1977.

Silveira, Ênio. "Epístolas ao Marechal." *Revista Civilização Brasileira*, Vol. I, Nos. 3, 4. Rio de Janeiro, 1965.

_______. Letter to JWFD, Rio de Janeiro, December 10, 1975.

_______. Interview, Rio de Janeiro, November 26, 1975.

Simonsen, Mário Henrique. *Inflação: Gradualismo X Tratamente de Choque.* Rio de Janeiro: APEC Editôra S/A, 1970.

_______, and Roberto de Oliveira Campos. *A nova economia brasileira.* Rio de Janeiro: Livraria José Olympio Editora, 1974.

"Situação política em São Paulo." Unsigned memorandum to HACB, May 12, 1966. File N1, CPDOC.

Skidmore, Thomas E. "The Politics of Economic Stabilization in Latin America." Discussion Paper Series, Graduate Program in Economic History, University of Wisconsin. Madison, February 1975.

_______. "The Years between the Harvests: The Economics of the Castelo Branco Presidency, 1964–1967." *Luso-Brazilian Review*, Vol. 15, No. 2 (Winter 1978).

Slater, Jerome. *Intervention and Negotiation: The United States and the Dominican Revolution.* New York: Harper & Row, 1970.

Sodré, Roberto de Abreu. Letter to Luís Viana Filho, São Paulo, September 28, 1971. Copy in possession of PVCB.

_______. Memorandum of August 5, 1977, sent to JWFD with letter, São Paulo, August 10, 1977.

_______. Interview, São Paulo, July 28, 1977.

Sousa, João Gonçalves de. "Luta continua pelo manutenção do mecanismo do 34/18 e o Presidente," n.d. Typewritten paper. Copy in possession of PVCB.

_______. "V Round da Luta pela Manutenção dos Artigos 34/18," Rio de Janeiro, December 30, 1966. Typewritten paper. Copy in possession of PVCB.

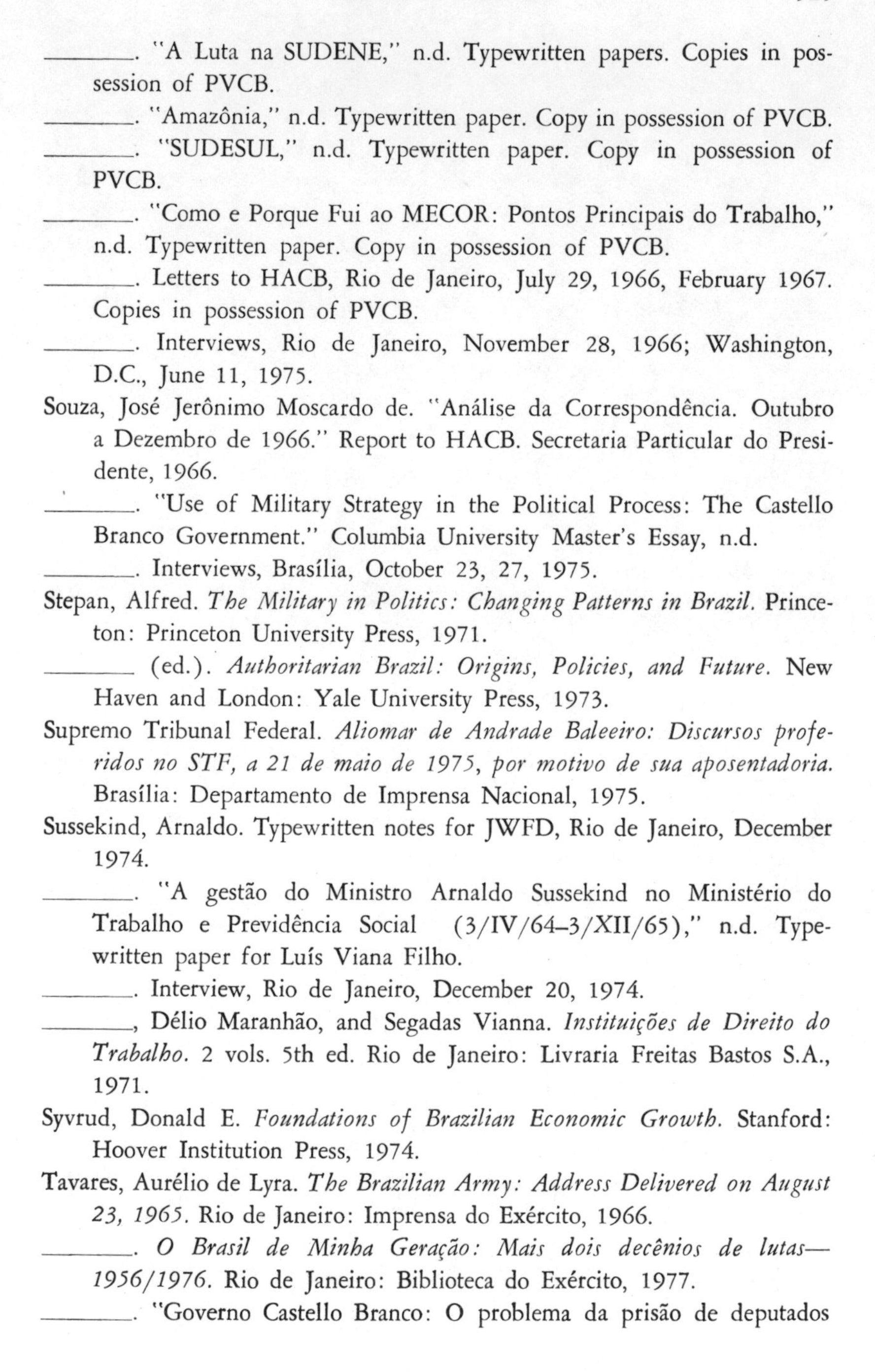

———. "A Luta na SUDENE," n.d. Typewritten papers. Copies in possession of PVCB.

———. "Amazônia," n.d. Typewritten paper. Copy in possession of PVCB.

———. "SUDESUL," n.d. Typewritten paper. Copy in possession of PVCB.

———. "Como e Porque Fui ao MECOR: Pontos Principais do Trabalho," n.d. Typewritten paper. Copy in possession of PVCB.

———. Letters to HACB, Rio de Janeiro, July 29, 1966, February 1967. Copies in possession of PVCB.

———. Interviews, Rio de Janeiro, November 28, 1966; Washington, D.C., June 11, 1975.

Souza, José Jerônimo Moscardo de. "Análise da Correspondência. Outubro a Dezembro de 1966." Report to HACB. Secretaria Particular do Presidente, 1966.

———. "Use of Military Strategy in the Political Process: The Castello Branco Government." Columbia University Master's Essay, n.d.

———. Interviews, Brasília, October 23, 27, 1975.

Stepan, Alfred. *The Military in Politics: Changing Patterns in Brazil.* Princeton: Princeton University Press, 1971.

——— (ed.). *Authoritarian Brazil: Origins, Policies, and Future.* New Haven and London: Yale University Press, 1973.

Supremo Tribunal Federal. *Aliomar de Andrade Baleeiro: Discursos proferidos no STF, a 21 de maio de 1975, por motivo de sua aposentadoria.* Brasília: Departamento de Imprensa Nacional, 1975.

Sussekind, Arnaldo. Typewritten notes for JWFD, Rio de Janeiro, December 1974.

———. "A gestão do Ministro Arnaldo Sussekind no Ministério do Trabalho e Previdência Social (3/IV/64–3/XII/65)," n.d. Typewritten paper for Luís Viana Filho.

———. Interview, Rio de Janeiro, December 20, 1974.

———, Délio Maranhão, and Segadas Vianna. *Instituições de Direito do Trabalho.* 2 vols. 5th ed. Rio de Janeiro: Livraria Freitas Bastos S.A., 1971.

Syvrud, Donald E. *Foundations of Brazilian Economic Growth.* Stanford: Hoover Institution Press, 1974.

Tavares, Aurélio de Lyra. *The Brazilian Army: Address Delivered on August 23, 1965.* Rio de Janeiro: Imprensa do Exército, 1966.

———. *O Brasil de Minha Geração: Mais dois decênios de lutas—1956/1976.* Rio de Janeiro: Biblioteca do Exército, 1977.

———. "Governo Castello Branco: O problema da prisão de deputados estaduais, Ceará, Outubro de 1964." Typewritten paper. Copy (dated Rio de Janeiro, July 24, 1977) in possession of JWFD.

_______. Interview, Rio de Janeiro, July 18, 1977.

Távora, Juarez, *Missão Cumprida: Relatório Sôbre Ativadades do extinto Ministério da Viação e Obras Públicas, no Triênio Abril, 1964–Marco, 1967*. Rio de Janeiro, 1969.

_______. *Uma Vida e Muitas Lutas: Memórias*, vol. 3, *Voltando à Planície*. Rio de Janeiro: Biblioteca do Exército, 1977.

_______. Declarations about iron ore. *Tribuna da Imprensa*, October 22, 1964.

_______. Letter to Juraci Magalhães, n.d. File N1, CPDOC.

_______. Letter to HACB, Rio de Janeiro, October 1966. File N1, CPDOC.

_______. Interview, Rio de Janeiro, October 5, 1966.

Távora, Virgílio. Letter to HACB, Fortaleza, Ceará, November 1, 1965. File N1, CPDOC.

_______. Interviews, Brasília, October 22, 25, 1975.

Taylor, Harry W. *See* Ludwig, Armin K.

Tendler, Judith. *Electric Power in Brazil: Entrepreneurship in the Public Sector*. Cambridge, Mass.: Harvard University Press, 1968.

Thibau, Mauro. Interview, Rio de Janeiro, June 6, 1972.

Thomas, A. J., Jr., and Ann Van Wynen. *The Dominican Republic Crisis 1965: Background Paper and Proceedings of the Ninth Hammarskjöld Forum*. Published for the Association of the Bar of the City of New York by Oceana Publications, 1967.

Torres, Paulo. Interview, Rio de Janeiro, December 19, 1977.

Travancas, Orlando. Interview, Rio de Janeiro, November 25, 1966.

Tribuna da Imprensa. [Rio de Janeiro newspaper]. Issues of 1964–1967.

Tribunal Regional Eleitoral da Guanabara, Centro de Estudos Políticos. *Ementário de Legislação Político-Eleitoral Brasileira (1821–1966)*. Rio de Janeiro: Livraria Brasiliana Editôra, 1966.

Trigueiro, Osvaldo. "Humberto Castelo Branco," n.d. Typewritten manuscript. Copy in possession of JWFD.

_______. Interviews, Brasília, October 23, 1975; Rio de Janeiro, July 11, 1977.

Trindade, Mário. Interview, Rio de Janeiro, November 28, 1966.

Tuthill, John W. Telegrams and memorandums to Washington, D.C., from United States Embassy, Rio de Janeiro, 1966–1967. National Security Files, LBJ Library, Austin, Texas.

Ũltima Hora [Rio de Janeiro newspaper]. Issues of 1965–1967.

"Últimos instantes de Castello Branco na Serra do Estêvão." *O Povo* [Fortaleza], July 20, 1967.

Ulyssea, Asdrubal Pinto de. Letter to Luís Viana Filho, Rio de Janeiro, July 15, 1972. Copy in possession of PVCB.

U.S., Central Intelligence Agency. Intelligence information cables from Brazil, 1964–1967. National Security Files, LBJ Library, Austin, Texas.

———, ———. "Political situation, Brazil: Meaning of Second Institutional Act." Special memorandum 29–65, November 29, 1965. National Security Files, LBJ Library, Austin, Texas.

———, ———. "Costa e Silva, Brazil's Next President." Directorate of Intelligence, Weekly Review, Special Report, Washington, D.C., January 20, 1967. LBJ Library, Austin, Texas.

———, Department of State (Washington, D.C.). Cables to United States Embassy, Rio de Janeiro, 1964–1967. National Security Files, LBJ Library, Austin, Texas.

———, ———. Briefing Book for Fulbright Mission to Brazil, August 1965. National Security Files, LBJ Library, Austin, Texas.

———, ———. Monthly Economic Summary, Brazil, October 1966. November 29, 1966. LBJ Library, Austin, Texas.

———, ———. Background paper, January 18, 1967, for Washington, D.C., visit of Costa e Silva, January 26–27, 1967. National Security Files, LBJ Library, Austin, Texas.

———, Treasury Department, Commission of Internal Revenue. "Material for the President's meeting with the President-elect of Brazil." Memorandum to Walt W. Rostow, Washington, D.C., January 18, 1967. LBJ Library, Austin, Texas.

Vale, Osvaldo Trigueiro do. *O Supremo Tribunal Federal e a Instabilidade Político-Institucional.* Rio de Janeiro: Editora Civilização Brasileira S.A., 1976.

Valenti, Jack. Report to the President: Fulbright Mission to Brazil. Washington, D.C., August 10, 1965. Papers of Lyndon B. Johnson, LBJ Library, Austin, Texas.

Valle, Hedyl Rodrigues. "Roberto Campos é sócio de dirigentes da Hanna." *Tribuna da Imprensa,* November 4, 1964.

Varejão, Ajuary. Laboratório de Análises Clínicas. Report on medical examination of HACB, Rio de Janeiro, July 1967. File EX3, CPDOC.

Vargas, Protásio D. Letter to Ivan Lins, Porto Alegre, December 13, 1965. File N1, CPDOC.

Vereker, Anthony. Typewritten reports to JWFD on political and economic situation in Brazil, Rio de Janeiro, January 19, March 22, May 10, June 8, July 12, July 20, August 25, September 6, September 15, 1966.

_______. "Operação Amazônia," Rio de Janeiro, February 15, 1967. Typewritten report. Copy in possession of JWFD.

Viana Filho, Luís. *O Governo Castelo Branco.* Rio de Janeiro: Livraria José Olympio Editôra, 1975.

Vianna, Antônio Mendes. Letters to HACB, Rome and Paris, 1964–1966. File O2, PVCB.

Victor, Mário. *Cinco Anos que Abalaram o Brasil (de Jânio Quadros ao Marechal Castelo Branco)*. Rio de Janeiro: Editôra Civilização Brasileira S.A., 1965.

Vidigal, Gastão Eduardo Bueno. Letter to HACB, São Paulo, May 27, 1966. File N1, CPDOC.

Vieira, Paulo José de Lima. Letter to HACB [about iron ore]. *Correio da Manhã,* November 15, 1964.

_______. Letter of resignation to HACB, December 28, 1964. File M, CPDOC.

Wahrlick, Beatriz. Interview, Rio de Janeiro, December 27, 1974.

Walters, Vernon. *Silent Missions.* Garden City: Doubleday & Company, Inc., 1978.

_______. "Humberto de Alencar Castello Branco: The Years of the Presidency," n.d. Typewritten manuscript. Copy in possession of JWFD.

_______. Interviews, Rio de Janeiro, December 19, 1966; McLean, Virginia, June 12, 1975; Arlington, Virginia, July 15, 1976.

Wamberto, José. *Castello Branco: Revolução e Democracia.* Rio de Janeiro, 1970.

_______. Interview, Brasília, October 24, 1975.

Washington Post. Editorial, July 19, 1967.

Werneck, Carlos. "Denúncia Apresentada contra o Sr. Presidente da República, Marechal Humberto de Alencar Castello Branco, pelo Almirante Penna Boto," *relator's* report, Brasília, May 9, 1966. File R2, CPDOC.

World Coffee Information Center. "The Coffee Agreement and Coffee Prices: Questions and Answers." Washington, D.C., September 1964.

_______. Release of May 24, 1965.

Index